Libido, Culture, and Consciousness

Libido, Culture, and Consciousness

Revisiting Freud's Totem and Taboo

Daniel S. Benveniste, PhD

International Psychoanalytic Books (IPBooks)
New York • IPBooks.net

Libido, Culture and Consciousness

Published by IPBooks, Queens, NY
Online at: www.IPBooks.net

Copyright © 2022 Daniel S. Benveniste, PhD

All rights reserved. This book may not be reproduced, transmitted, or stored, in whole or in part by any means, including graphic, electronic, or mechanical without the express permission of the author and/or publisher, except in the case of brief quotations embodied in critical articles and reviews.

ISBN: 978-1-949093-99-5

Portions of this book were first presented in:
Benveniste, D. (1983). The archetypal image of the mouth and its relation to autism. *Arts in Psychotherapy, 10*(2), 99–112.
Benveniste, D. (1988). Cosmogony, culture, and consciousness. *San Francisco Jung Institute Library Journal, 8*(1), 33–53.
Benveniste, D. (1990). Tantric art and the primal scene. *San Francisco Jung Institute Library Journal, 9*(4), 39–55.
Benveniste, D. (1998). Play and the metaphors of the body. *The Psychoanalytic Study of the Child*. Vol. 53.
Benveniste, D. (2005). Recognizing defenses in the drawings and play of children in therapy. *Psychoanalytic Psychology, 22*(3).
Benveniste, D. (2013). Sigmund Freud and the question of God—Parts I and II. *Forum: The Newsletter of the Northwest Alliance for Psychoanalytic Study*. January 2013 and May 2013.
Benveniste, D. (2020). Libido, culture, and consciousness: Revisiting "Totem and Taboo." *The American Psychoanalyst, 54*(1).
Benveniste, D. (2021). Mother-infant observations: A view into the wordless social instincts that form the foundation of human psychodynamics. *Journal of the American Psychoanalytic Association*, 69/1, pp. 33–50.

Other books by Daniel S. Benveniste

The Interwoven Lives of Sigmund, Anna, and W. Ernest Freud:
Three Generations of Psychoanalysis (2015)

Anna Freud in the Hampstead Clinic:
Letters to Humberto Nágera (2015)

The Venezuelan Revolution:
A Critique from the Left (2015)

Praise for

Libido, Culture, and Consciousness:
Revisiting Freud's Totem and Taboo

Daniel Benveniste's new book is a tour de force that emerges from his life-long study of psychoanalysis including his eleven years of living and working in Venezuela. He possesses a rare gift for understanding the workings of the mind individually and in groups of all sizes. I don't know of anyone in the field of psychoanalysis or anthropology to have written so beautifully and passionately about such a vast range of human experiences. In his new book, Benveniste proposes that when primate instincts are processed through human symbolic function, they give rise to metaphors that are co-created in the space between the individual and the culture. He proposes a new dimension of human development, the psychomythic, and a new way of looking at psychopathology, both of which are inseparable from the cultural and the mythic dimensions of human experience. This is a book not to be missed.

—Thomas H. Ogden, MD, author most recently of *Coming to Life in the Consulting Room: Toward a New Analytic Sensibility* and *Reclaiming Unlived Life.*

Daniel, having read your new book, *Libido, Culture, and Consciousness: Revisiting Freud's Totem and Taboo*, I couldn't help but remember the early years of your work with Rollo. He prophesied you would contribute fresh and fascinating ideas to the field. I know Rollo would have loved your book. You were always one of his favorite students. I wish you success with this book and the ones to follow. Fondly,

—Dr. Georgia L. May

The first impression I had in reading this piece of work is the wonder and admiration of the vast information and encyclopedic knowledge Dr. Benveniste has gathered. He brings together his knowledge of human evolution, prehistory and anthropology, ethology, autism, and psychosexual development with the work of Freud on monotheism, cannibalism, and more. It is a piece of work that looks at the evolution of man, from the caveman to today, and compares it to psychosexual development in psychoanalysis.

It is a monumental treatise that will be a mandatory text to read and study to learn more about the creation of the mind, language, and the soul in the evolution of human history and its relationship to the psychological development of the child. Dr. Benveniste's vast knowledge of anthropology, diverse cultures, and rituals, which he always relates to psychoanalytic thought, is astonishing and fascinating.

The author's curiosity is amazing whether he is looking at archaeological artifacts or is in search of the origins of autism. At the end of chapter 3 he recognizes a relationship between autism, early infancy, and the myth of death and rebirth which he sees as analogous to the child's psychological birth. His knowledge of the mechanisms of autism and his creation of the term "embodiment" is amazing. Frances Tustin comments on it as follows: "I found your notion of the importance of 'embodiment' relevant to these children—they've no notion of 'insides,' and it's a great progress when they begin to 'embody' and to 'internalize.'"

In short, this is a book written by a wise man who carries inside of him a curious boy and a teenager in love with his wife, to whom he expresses his love and gratitude in the acknowledgments of this book.

As a final synthesis, I can only say that Daniel Benveniste's work is a monumental revision of psychosexual development and human history.

—**David Rosenfeld, MD**, author of *The Soul, the Mind, and the Psychoanalyst*

Daniel Benveniste has written a book that Freud would relish as much as anything else that has been written about psychoanalysis since his passing. He provides the sequel to *Totem and Taboo*, which Freud considered along with *The Interpretation of Dreams* to be his most important written contribution towards the advancement of understanding human psychology. *Libido, Culture, and Consciousness: Revisiting Freud's Totem and Taboo* extends the anamnesis of humankind that Freud took as far as was possible in his time. Benveniste incorporates fascinating findings in anthropology, archaeology, primatology, cultural history and mythology that amplify many of Freud's theories and understandings while opening up new vistas that Freud couldn't have imagined but ones that he would have looked upon with great satisfaction and pride, especially because they are built upon the foundations of *Totem and Taboo*. Benveniste lays out convincingly the parallel developmental lines of culture evolution and individual human development and explains just how and why this is so. Clinicians after reading this magnum opus will have a much clearer understanding of humanity's psychological and cultural development plus a vastly enriched capacity to understand the clinical presentations and challenges encountered in their day to day clinical work.

—**Jeffrey L. Sandler, MD**, San Francisco Center for Psychoanalysis and the Psychoanalytic Institute of Northern California

PRAISE FOR LIBIDO, CULTURE, AND CONSCIOUSNESS:

In March 2021, Dr. Daniel Benveniste sent me the manuscript of *Libido, Culture, and Consciousness: Revisiting Freud's Totem and Taboo* and asked if I would write a brief comment for the book. I readily agreed but had to put it off for a while, as I was deeply involved in various psychological crisis intervention efforts throughout China.

It is really a gift from God that I have Dr. Daniel Benveniste and his wife, Adriana Prengler, teaching in our Psychotherapy Training Program in the Wuhan Mental Health Center in China. In his 2019 lecture, Daniel presented on <u>Crisis Intervention After Major Disasters</u>, based on his work following the Venezuelan flood of 1999. Since then Dr. Benveniste's paper (translated into Chinese) has repeatedly appeared on the We-media (social media platform) in the Mental Health field in China following the well-known outbreak of COVID-19 in Wuhan, the flood in Wuhan in the summer of that same year, and the great flood in Henan that is taking place as I write these words. His paper has played an important role in helping the Chinese people who have suffered and survived these terrible disasters.

Reading Dr. Benveniste's book, you will see his erudition stemming from his diligence and hard work, as well as from his luck in having opportunities to learn, discuss, and even debate with so many Freudian and Jungian scholars, exploring what a human being is from the ancient to the modern, from the west to the east.

Benveniste's new book is profound. Revisiting Freud's *Totem and Taboo* during the COVID-19 pandemic, has been of great significance to me. When I followed his lead and reread Freud's *Totem and Taboo* I was very impressed and it made me think about the themes of killing the enemy in war, calling it a sacrifice, and mourning the dead. Freud says, "We may be inclined to suppose that savage and half-savage races are guilty of uninhibited and ruthless cruelty towards their enemies. We shall be greatly interested to learn, then, that even in their case the killing of a man is governed by a number of observances which are included among the usages of taboo." Freud then cites Frazer's description of a rite of appeasement in Timor after the triumph of a warring expedition. The eulogy goes like this: "Be not angry because your head is here with us; had we been less lucky, our heads might now have been exposed in your village. We have offered the sacrifice to appease you. Your spirit may now rest and leave us in peace. Why were you our enemy? Would it not have been better that we should remain friends? Then your blood would not have been spilt and your head would not have been cut off" (*Totem and Taboo* pp. 36–37). Have we evolved or become more savage? There are a thousand Hamlets in a thousand people's eyes. At present, in the historical process, revisiting Freud's *Totem and Taboo* will undoubtedly enhance our reflection perhaps even torture our souls. But Daniel's thought in his new book will enrich our minds and let us keep thinking.

—**Prof. Dr. Jun Tong, MD, PhD**, President of IPA Study Group of China

Libido, Culture, and Consciousness is a masterpiece of synthesis, drawing extensively on clinical observation, paleoanthropological, archaeological and primatological data to make its case. Benveniste is among those rare theorists who continue Freud's "phylogenetic project" in the service of a systematic psychoanalytic theory of cultural evolution. He takes seriously Freud's question to Wilhelm Fliess in 1897: "Can you imagine what endopsychic myths are?" Freud called these projections "psychomythology" and Benveniste demonstrates that they are the very stuff of human consciousness. The clinical implication of Benveniste's accomplishment is that it attunes the clinician to the metaphors they and their analysands live by, those very "metaphors that enslave us and those that can open doors to new experience." Benveniste ventures beyond psychosexual and psychosocial theory into the "psychomythic" dimension of human experience. He demonstrates early cultural evolution to be the corollary of symbolically constituted self-consciousness—the *soul*—and its tragic dimension, the "anxiety of *being* in the face of non-being." He constructs a schematic description of the spiritual adaptations that evolved to protect the human psyche from the overwhelming consequences of this consciousness. The resulting "stratigraphy of religious ideas" is a brilliant extension of Freud's insights on the function of culture as a compromise solution to the conflicts between Id and Ego, between the pleasure principle and the exigencies of reality. Benveniste applies Freud's clinical principle "Where Id was, Ego shall be" to psychomythology and society: "Where chaos was, there cosmos shall be. Where wilderness was, there culture shall be." He follows Freud's examination in *Totem and Taboo* of "points of agreement" between ontogeny and phylogeny. From this emerge clusters of metaphors corresponding to the different stages of cultural evolution; these same metaphors show up in the analogous stages of human psychosexual development. Benveniste's fundamental assumption is that human cultural experience is rooted in primate ritualizations, which serve to neutralize aggression; in the course of human evolution these social instincts became symbolized, thus forming the basis of human psychodynamics. With an eloquence that characterizes the entirety of Benveniste's writing, he asserts that "from the profane and brutish to the sacred and sublime, we have taken our very human experience, created with it a world in our own image, and projected our deepest concerns onto the walls of the universe."

With *Libido, Culture, and Consciousness* a gauntlet has been thrown down on behalf of psychoanalysis and the importance of Freud's phylogenetic project. Along with its remarkable breadth and depth, Benveniste has also managed to pose this challenge with a "playful and humble attitude before the enormity of the task." His hope (and mine also) is that others will find inspiration and build upon this groundbreaking opus.

—**Michael J. Poff, MA, MSW**, author of *Totem and Taboo: Freud Was Right*
The Carter-Jenkins Center Psychoanalytic Institute website

PRAISE FOR LIBIDO, CULTURE, AND CONSCIOUSNESS:

Daniel Benveniste and I hit it off right away. It was like we were old friends at our first meeting. It was in the Sino-American Psychoanalysis Training Class in Wuhan, China. I was attracted by his "candid nature." We talked about our mentors in San Francisco, some of whom we shared in common. His "candid nature" was my distinct impression. The image for "candid nature" in Chinese characters (shuai xing) embodies the teaching of The Doctrine of the Mean: *"What Heaven confers is called "nature," "candid nature" is called the Way, Cultivating the Way is called "education."* Soon thereafter, I invited Daniel to give lectures to the China Society for Analytical Psychology, and the Oriental Academy for Analytical Psychology. He readily agreed, and naturally promoted the integration of Freudian psychoanalysis and Jungian analytical psychology in China. Daniel's erudition and wisdom are welcomed by Chinese candidates both for Psychoanalysis and Analytical Psychology. This erudition and wisdom are also present in his new book: *Libido, Culture, and Consciousness: Revisiting Freud's Totem and Taboo*. Daniel has a passion for appreciating the natural ways of the psyche, and a special gift from the heart to the world.
—**Heyong Shen, PhD**, Jungian analyst, President of China Society for Analytical Psychology

In a daring or even audacious project of comprehending what human life is all about Benveniste calls on archaeology, anthropology, philosophy, psychology, psychoanalytic theory, sociology, and religion to get a full picture of human development. He shows parallels between individual, group and cultural development and in the process corrects some of Freud's ideas about these disciplines as Freud wrote about them in *Totem and Taboo*. A monumental read.
—**Arlene Kramer Richards, EdD**, author of *Psychoanalysis: Listening to Understand: Selected Papers of Arlene Kramer Richards*

Libido, Culture, and Consciousness is a feast for any analyst who loves the theoretical part of psychoanalysis. The amount of research, thoughtfulness, and scholarship in this book is most impressive. The review of the theoretical literature is quite comprehensive. It's a fascinating book that has stimulated my own (speculative) thinking.
—**William M. Greenstadt, PhD**, Assistant Clinical Professor, Mount Sinai Hospital.

Beginning around 1908, inspired by the earlier work of Abraham and Rank, Freud and Jung began a rich correspondence concerning the possibility of a psychoanalytic approach to mythology and folklore. In a 1909 letter to Freud, Jung writes: "Archaeology or rather mythology has got me in its grip, it's a mine of marvelous material. Won't you cast a beam of light in that direction, at least a kind of spectrum analysis *par distance*?" Several days later, Freud responded enthusiastically: "I am glad you share my belief that we must conquer the whole field of mythology. Thus far we have only two pioneers: Abraham and Rank. We need men for more far-reaching campaigns. Such men are so rare."

In this compelling book, Benveniste joins the ranks of these pioneers in applied psychoanalysis. Audaciously reviving their long-abandoned project in psychomythology, he creatively merges Freud's evolutionary phylogenetic project with the developmental/ontogenetic approach to the symbolic function developed in later years by Róheim. Then, bringing these ideas to bear on data culled from the best contemporary work in primatology, archaeology, and ethnography, he presents us with a detailed and provocative analysis of the broad evolutionary sweeps of human prehistory interpreted through the lens of Freud's model of psychosexual development.

As a dual-trained anthropologist-psychoanalyst, I am perhaps excessively wary of psychoevolutionary accounts. Too often, they are constructed upon a house of cards, combining some of Freud's worst psychoevolutionary speculations with cherry-picked or outdated anthropological data. Benveniste deftly sidesteps these pitfalls. Throughout, his reading of Freud (and others, such as Rank, Abraham, Róheim, and Jung) is both deep and judicious, his mastery of the anthropological data is comprehensive and disciplined, and his interpretations are illuminating and provocative. Although some of his paleopsychological "musings" may seem bold—even startling—Benveniste is careful to hedge his claims with clear recognition of the limitations inherent in psychological reconstructions of deep history. But as any anthropologist will tell you, we too are in the business of interpretation. And inasmuch as the evolution of culture is a foundational concern of anthropology, we too must grapple with how best to put flesh on the bones of the past, to make mute stones speak. The striking psychological, cultural, and evolutionary parallelisms revealed by Benveniste's inspired presentation demand an accounting, and with his seminal book the psychomythological gauntlet has once again been thrown!

—**Kevin P. Groark, PhD**, Macquarie University (Sydney, Australia) and New Center for Psychoanalysis (Los Angeles, CA).

This work is truly amazing, not only for its evident cultural magnitude, the multidisciplinary breadth of its exploratory views, its powerful innovative vision, and the courage with which it proposes a thoughtful and documented revisiting of almost sacred conceptions in psychoanalytic literature; but also for the balance and harmony with which the cultural and exquisitely psychoanalytic concepts are used here and woven together in a clear, natural, and fruitful way.

Together with the enormous scientific and cultural value of this splendid research, what strikes us in this text is Benveniste's refined critical balance and his profoundly creative

PRAISE FOR LIBIDO, CULTURE, AND CONSCIOUSNESS:

elaboration, which goes far beyond mere erudition. There is an extraordinary passion in this book, and in the very first pages the author appropriately gives us some unforgettable images of how it was born and developed in his mind over a lifetime, from his childhood and youth; to the point that we could now say to him: "Mission accomplished!"

Quite frankly, I believe that this work should be considered one of the fundamental texts on the relationship between history, archaeology, biology, anthropology, philosophy of science and psychoanalysis, to be recommended to all experts in these areas, and certainly also to all those who already work in our field or are in analytical training.

Finally, I would like to point out how, from a strictly psychoanalytic point of view, this work proposes an innovative perspective that can extend from clinical work to the study of the development of individual and community minds, to their interconnections with cultural and social structures, and all the way to unexpected future extensions of psychoanalysis to the difficult and very delicate area of psycho-socio-politics.

–**Stefano Bolognini, MD**, Past-President of the International Psychoanalytical Association (2013–2017)

A marvelous conception!

–**John Weir Perry, MD**, author of *The Far Side of Madness*

This book is dedicated
with gratitude to my teachers,
with humility to my readers,
and with hope and best wishes
to the young people of today
and the generations yet to come.

Acknowledgments

This work began in my early childhood when the wonders of nature awakened my scientific curiosity, dazzled my aesthetic sensibility, and stirred within me a trembling awe. I collected bugs, butterflies, seashells, frogs, lizards, leaves, bird nests, and, by the age of 9, my first fossil—a mussel clamshell embedded in stone 70 miles from the seashore. As a teenager I was interested in geology and became an avid fossil hunter. In college I was fascinated with theories of human development and the curious relation between psychology and mythology. In 1975 I laid the foundation for the work before you and then spent the next 40-plus years researching and developing ideas concerning the relationship between psychological development and cultural evolution.

Many people along the way introduced me to material and supported my ongoing interests. Though there are too many to mention by name, allow me to say thanks to the following psychologists, psychiatrists, and other mental health professionals with whom I had the privilege of speaking on one or more occasions on subjects directly related to this work: Nathan Adler, Gene Alexander, Samuel Arbiser, Fernando Batoni, Frank Baudry, John Beebe, Bruno Bettelheim, Murray Bilmes, Harold P. Blum, Stefano Bolognini, Mary Burt, Doug Chavis, Michael Cornwall, Andy Curry, John and Nicole Dintenfass, Joseph Epstein, Anne Faught, Charles P. Fisher, W. Ernest Freud, Steven Friedlander, Javier Galvez, Ruth Goldman, Jeff Golland, Iden Goodman, William M. Greenstadt, Gary Grigg, Kevin Groark, Jules Grossman, Joseph L. Henderson, Yingchun Hou, Peggy Huntington, Robert G. Janes, Beth Kalish, Christopher J. Keats, Rhoda Kellogg, Mariam King, David Levine, Wolfgang Lederer, Norm Livson, Zvi Lothane, Philip Luloff, Farzin Malaki, Frances Marton, Georgia May, Rollo May, Pilar Montero, Humberto Nágera, Haskell Norman, Thomas H. Ogden, David O'Grady, Ann Paras, Andre Patsalides, John Weir Perry, Harvey Peskin, Michael Poff, Harry Prochaska, María Eugenia Rangel Domene, Leo Rangell, Arlene Kramer Richards, Arnold D. Richards, Michael D. Robbins, David Rosenfeld, Jeffrey L. Sandler, Heyong Shen, Claire Steinberger, Louis Stewart, Tina Stromsted, Bob Suczek, Hillel Swiller, Jun Tong, Wendy Perry Tucker, Frances Tustin, Robert S. Wallerstein, and Peter Zelles.

I trace my lineage to Sigmund Freud through my relationship to John Weir Perry, who studied with Carl Gustav Jung, who studied with Freud, and through my relationship to

Nathan Adler, who studied with Siegfried Bernfeld, who studied with Freud. John Weir Perry's beautiful prose and theoretical thinking inspired me into the heavens, and Nathan Adler's overwhelming teaching and clinical ability planted me on the earth and gave me a career. With Nathan Adler and John Weir Perry as my two primary mentors, I was able to witness my own Freud-Jung controversy between my own two temples and was fortunate to avoid a split. My other two most influential mentors, Rollo May, who studied with Alfred Adler, and Joseph L. Henderson, who studied with Carl Gustav Jung, gave me their friendship and aided me in the integration of my theoretical and clinical thinking. All of my mentors were big enough to welcome my challenging questions and never turned their backs on me, even when I disagreed with them. To all of them I offer my heartfelt thanks.

Harvey Peskin, Bob Suczek, Ruth Goldman, Jules Grossman, Louis Stewart, Robert S. Wallerstein, Joan Erikson, W. Ernest Freud, Humberto Nágera, and Arnold D. Richards blessed my life by opening doors for me. Warm thanks to them all.

I very much appreciate the opportunities I had to present various aspects of this work to a number of professional groups, including the Faculty Psychotherapy Conference in the Psychiatry Department of the Icahn School of Medicine at Mount Sinai Hospital in New York City; the Carter-Jenkins Center in Tampa, Florida; La Escuela Venezolana de Psicología Profunda in Caracas, Venezuela; the C. G. Jung Institute of San Francisco; the San Francisco Center for Psychoanalysis; and the 47th Congress of the International Psychoanalytical Association in Mexico City.

I had valuable conversations with Aranaga Epieyu and Hugo Lucitante regarding indigenous cultures in South America. I'm also grateful to Adrian Amaya, Adrian Fuentes, Goyo, Sarrago, Benito, Axel Kelemen, Hector Abreu, José Garcia, and Jesús Garcia, who served as outstanding guides for my three expeditions into the Venezuelan jungles of the Upper Orinoco to visit contemporary aboriginal communities. There are no words that can express the depth of my gratitude to the indigenous people I met along the Upper Orinoco who shared their lives with me, invited me into their homes, and allowed me to take photos and videos of their community life. They are the Yanomami, the Panare, the Yavarana, and the Hoti.

From Susanna Bonetti at the Erik Erikson Library in the San Francisco Center for Psychoanalysis, Stephen Damon and Fred Martin at Browser Books, Richard Hackney at Fields Book Store, and John Gach at John Gach Books, I received informed and intelligent assistance in locating the most important books for my research. The Archive for the Research of Archetypal Symbolism in San Francisco was a helpful treasure trove of symbolic representations, which I used especially in my exploration of the symbolism of the mouth. My lengthy conversations with Jeffrey L. Sandler, Mariam King, and John

ACKNOWLEDGMENTS

G. Cobley about evolution, consciousness, and related matters have sustained me over the decades. My countless conversations with my brother, Mark Benveniste, regarding his views of consciousness and spiritual matters have been formative and inspiring throughout my life. I had other valuable conversations regarding Eastern philosophy and Tantric art with Ramamurti Mishra, Brahmananda Sarasvati, Vishrumbardas, Ajit Mookerjee, Madhu Khanna, Jian Chong, Ram Dass, and Frederic Spiegelberg. Furthermore, hearing Joseph Campbell lecturing on mythology, on several occasions in San Francisco, was always inspiring.

I have also been deeply influenced by the kindness and unshakable confidence bestowed upon me by my fifth-grade teacher, the incomparable Mrs. Martha Garrett, and the formidable learning experiences I received under the inspired tutelage of my ninth-grade geology teacher, Bill Heinkel. Both of them granted blessings that give me strength to this day.

My contacts with archeologists and paleoanthropologists have been of profound significance to me. Those I have had the privilege of meeting personally, even if briefly, include Louis S. B. Leakey, Donald Johanson, William Kimble, Tim D. White, Sally Binford, Jean-Philippe Rigaud, Marija Gimbutas, Maria Magdalena Antczak, and Andrzej Antczak. And the archeological expeditions in search of stone tools in the deserts of Paleolithic Venezuela with Miklos Szabadics Roka; his wife, Eva; and his daughter, Jenny, were among the richest experiences of my life. While these archeologists would be unlikely to share my conclusions, I am nonetheless grateful for having met them and having the opportunity to study their work.

My ever so brief contacts with primatologists Jane Goodall, Penny Patterson, Bill Wallauer, and John Crocker were informative and inspiring.

Special thanks to archeologist Jenny Szabadics for permission to include in this volume photographs from *Archeology of the Prehistory of Venezuela*, written by her father, Miklos Szabadics Roka.

Wendy Perry Tucker kindly gave me her permission to publish large quotes from the works of her father, John Weir Perry, which I greatly appreciate.

I am very grateful to "Jimmy," a young boy with autism described in chapter 3, whose drawings and commentary launched this investigation more than 40 years ago. I am also grateful to his parents, who granted me full permission to write about my work with "Jimmy" and to reproduce his verbatim comments and photographs of his drawings.

Special thanks to my incomparable copyeditor, Jill R. Hughes (The Editor's Mark), who time and again helped me to get out of my way and say what I was trying to say. I am also grateful for the additional editorial advice and direction I received from Eve Golden, MD, who read the entire manuscript and helped me with suggestions for shaping it into a book. I am also grateful to the production team at IPBooks - Tamar and Larry Schwartz, Kathy Kovacic, Noel Morado, Leonard Rosenbaum, and Arnold D. Richards. They made it happen.

Finally, I am grateful for the love of my father and mother, Jack and Lucie Benveniste; my brothers, Mark and Rick; my father-in-law and mother-in-law, Pepe and Ofelia Prengler; my brothers-in-law, sisters-in-law, nephews and niece, and my stepson, Leonardo Levy. To my lovely wife and colleague, Adriana Prengler de Benveniste, I thank you for accompanying me up the Rio Orinoco to visit the Yanomami; out into the deserts of Venezuela in search of stone tools; around Glass Mountain in California to find pieces of worked obsidian; off to a Caribbean beach to conduct research on human ritualizations; over to Seattle's Pacific Science Center to view the bones of the famous Australopithecus afarensis, Lucy; and out to Ellensburg, Washington, to visit the chimpanzees who communicate in sign language. Who else would accompany me to these far-out ends of the earth? Only you. *Solo tu. Te quiero mucho.*

The comparison between the childhood of individual men and the early history of societies has already proved its fruitfulness in several directions, even though the study has scarcely more than begun.
—Sigmund Freud, *The Claims of Psycho-Analysis to Scientific Interest*

Contents

Praise for *Libido, Culture, and Consciousness*: vii

Acknowledgments xvii

Introduction xxix

Part 1 The Phylogenetic Project of Psychoanalysis

1 The Phylogenetic Fantasies of Charles Darwin and Sigmund Freud 1
    Charles Darwin: Natural Selection, Sexual Selection, and Cultural Evolution 1
    Ernst Haeckel: Ontogeny Recapitulates Phylogeny 7
    Sigmund Freud and the Phylogenetic Project of Psychoanalysis 8
        Totem and Taboo 13
        Freud and Anthropology 23
        Freud's Phylogenetic Fantasy 29
        Géza Róheim and the Shift to the Ontogenetic Explanation 30
    Basic Ideas upon Which to Advance the Phylogenetic Project of Psychoanalysis 33

2 Brief Psychotic Disorder and the Myth of Sacral Kingship 37
    Kingship in Ancient Egypt 47
    The Chiao: A Taoist Ritual in Ancient China 50
    Quetzalcoatl among the Toltecs 52
    The Festival of Sukkoth in Ancient Israel 52
    John Weir Perry, Sigmund Freud, and the Phylogenetic Project 53
    Schemas Based on Freud's and Perry's Work 59

3 Infantile Autism and the Myth of Death and Rebirth 61
   A Boy Named Jimmy 65
   Jimmy's Drawings 65
   Jimmy's Commentary 68
   The Mouth 70
   The Symbolism of Jimmy's Commentary 71
   The Mouth and Orality 73
   The Symbolism of the Mouth 75
   The Mouth as the Hero's Passageway to Death 77
   The Mouth as the Birth Canal of the Reborn Hero 78
   The Mouth as the Passageway for the Soul's Embodiment 79
   The Mouth as the Passageway for the Soul's Disembodiment 80
   The Mouth as Integral Consciousness 80
   The Autistic Child as a Soul Unable or Unwilling to Embody 85
   The Ritual of Opening the Mouth 87
   The Role of the Mouth in the Funerary Ritual 91
   Autism and Embodiment 92
   Funerary Rituals, the Mouth, and the Soul 95
   Death and Rebirth and the Phylogenetic Project of Psychoanalysis 100

4 Human Evolution: How We Got to Be the Way We Are 107
   Primate Ritualizations and Social Instincts 108
      Greeting Behavior and Mother-Infant Bonding: Orality 113
      Dominance and Submission: Anality 114
      Copulation Interference: The Oedipus Complex 115
      Sexual Inhibitions and Incest Taboos: The Latency Phase 117
      Displaying, Battling, Courtships, and Mating: Adolescent Genital Stage 117
   Konrad Lorenz and Aggression 119
   From Higher Primate Ritualizations to Human Psychodynamics 120
      The Human Symbolic Function 121
      Chimpanzees, Humans, and the Symbolic Function 122
      Evolution of the Symbolic Function 124
      Hominin Evolution 127
   The Lower Paleolithic 131
   The Middle Paleolithic 133

PART 2 From Infancy to Adolescence, From the Paleolithic to the Urban Revolution

5 The Upper Paleolithic Period and the Oral Stage of Libido Development 143
- The Paleolithic Funeral and the Awareness of Death 147
- Paleolithic Cannibalism and the Internalization of the Other 154
- Amulets: Homes for the Souls of the Ancestors 157
- Stone Tools and Technological Evolution 160
- Painting and Sculpture: Projections into the World 163
- A Kind of Garden of Eden 175

6 The Neolithic Period and the Anal Stage of Libido Development 195
- The Wall and Personal Boundaries 197
- The House and the Self 199
- The Stone and the Psychic Center 202
- Sacrifice and the Renunciation of Instinct 205
- Money, Trade, and Toilet Training 209
- Agriculture and Culture 217
- Clay and Feces 223
- Weaving and the Fabric of Reality 224
- The Fall from Grace 225

7 The High Neolithic Period and the Phallic Stage of Libido Development 245
- Oedipus as a Metaphor 246
- Large Earthworks and Ambition 249
- The Stone Phallus 251
- Metallurgy and the Fires of Passion 256
- Imagining Our Way into the High Neolithic 258
- The High Neolithic, Hero Mythology, and Fertility Rites 261
- The Hero Looks to the Sky 265

8 The Urban Revolution and the Genital Stage of Libido Development 281
- Mircea Eliade and the Ancient New Year Festivals 283
- The Ancient Mesopotamian New Year Festival 288
- The Psychomythic Schema of Development 292

Part 3 Libido, Culture, and Consciousness

9 Cosmogony and Cosmology, Anamnesis and Psychic Structure 307
    Hero Mythology and the Structure of the Psyche 308
    Cosmogonic Mythology and Narrative Structure...........................309
    From Cosmogony to Cosmology...321
    Psychomythic Pyramid 323
        The Seven Heavens..323
        The Significance of Seven..327

10 Psychomythology: Projections onto the Walls of the Universe 331
    The Psychomythic in Religion 331
    The Psychomythic in Politics 343
    The Psychomythic in Philosophy 344

Concluding Thoughts 351

Appendix 1..357
Chapter 1 Elaborations 357
    Carl Gustav Jung and the Collective Unconscious 357
    Sándor Ferenczi's *Thalassa* 360
    Theodore Reik and the Cannibalizing of the Father 361

Appendix 2..362
Chapter 2 Elaborations 362
    Anton T. Boisen and His Exploration of the Inner World................362
    Chronic Schizophrenia 362
    Richard Bucke and Cosmic Consciousness 363
    Julian Jaynes and the Breakdown of the Bicameral Mind................364
    Psychedelic Experience 365

Appendix 3..366
Chapter 3 Elaborations 366
    Orality in Psychoanalytic Theory 366

Appendix 4 ... 371
Chapter 4 Elaborations ... 371
   Primate Ritualizations and Social Instincts ... 371
      Greeting Behavior and Mother-Infant Bonding: Orality ... 371
      Dominance and Submission: Anality ... 375
      Copulation Interference: The Oedipus Complex ... 376
      Sexual Inhibitions and Incest Taboos: The Latency Phase ... 379
      Displaying, Battling, and Mating: Adolescent Genital Stage ... 380
   Konrad Lorenz and Aggression ... 382
   The Human Symbolic Function ... 383

Appendix 5 ... 388
Chapter 5 Elaborations ... 388
   The Killing of the Beast ... 388

Appendix 6 ... 394
Chapter 6 Elaborations ... 394
   Panare Hunting, Gathering, and Tending the Garden ... 394

References ... 405

Photo Credits ... 424

Index ... 445

About the Author ... 484

Introduction

Speculation on the relationship between psychological development and cultural evolution played an important role in Sigmund Freud's theorizing about universal symbolism and the origins of the Oedipus complex. Although this aspect of psychoanalysis was never completely rejected, it was neglected over the years as analysts became more attentive to clinical concerns and as the assumptions underlying Freud's psycho-Lamarckian speculations collapsed when faced with the discoveries of modern science.

Nonetheless, if asked about the origins of the Oedipus complex, the recurring symbolism in dreams, or the relationship between dreams and myth, most clinicians with a psychoanalytic orientation would probably offer up, or at least mention, Freud's outdated speculations. These include the individual's biological inheritance of a cultural memory of repeated events in our prehistoric past, such as a matriarchy preceding a patriarchy, a primal father who kept all the females to himself, the castration or expulsion of young men who threatened the primal father, the killing of the primal father by the fraternal clan, the totemic feast in celebration of and in atonement for the murder of the primal father, and so on. These ideas are found throughout Freud's writings and were featured prominently in his *Totem and Taboo* (1913/1955h).

Freud built his prehistoric reconstruction on 19th-century assumptions that were outdated even at the time he wrote them, but he wrote them with conviction and maintained them to the end of his days. Because his basic assumptions were wrong, his conclusions were as well. Nonetheless, *Totem and Taboo* still won't leave us. It might be erroneous, but it remains compelling.

Freud speculated that our psychodynamics originated in the intentional behaviors of our ancestors, which were enacted countless times in our prehistoric past until they became encoded in our modern minds as inherited memories of these ancestral experiences. In contrast to this view, I assert that *the symbolization of our primate social instincts is what gives rise to our psychodynamics*. Beyond this, our psychodynamics coevolved with prehistoric culture from the Paleolithic period, to the Neolithic, to the High Neolithic, to the Urban Revolution in such a way that it left derivatives of libidinal and object relations development in myth, ritual, and other manifestations of culture.

The book before you presents this new set of speculations on the relationship between psychological development and cultural evolution. It is a metapsychological work in that it deals with fundamental assumptions about the structure of the psyche. While this work is speculative in nature, I have attempted to deal with the psychological and cultural material in a disciplined manner. The difference between my speculations and those of Freud are that I had the benefit of Freud's genius, his courageous spirit, his brilliant connections between seemingly disparate phenomena, his understandable errors, and an additional 100 years of research findings in psychoanalysis, anthropology, archeology, and primatology.

I use the term "cultural evolution" not to describe fixed evolutionary stages that all cultures pass through and mark some cultures as more "advanced" than others, but rather as a somewhat inevitable set of changes in cultural structure that are associated with population size, technological development, and associated cultural concerns. The four cultural periods that I address in this qualified "cultural evolution" are the Paleolithic, Neolithic, High Neolithic, and Urban Revolution. These terms are somewhat out of date, as most modern archeologists and anthropologists prefer to examine the relativity and uniqueness of cultures within their historical contexts rather than group them in terms of broad similarities and universals. Nonetheless, I think there is something to be gained in looking at these broad culture forms and their relation to psychological structure. Paleolithic peoples were nomadic hunter-gatherers. Neolithic peoples were the first to build permanent houses, and most of them domesticated plants and animals. The people of the High Neolithic period (sometimes referred to as Upper Neolithic or Chalcolithic period) lived in larger, more complex Neolithic settlements that constructed large earthworks and crude stone monuments and also developed the technology to forge metal. The peoples of the Urban Revolution stepped out of prehistory and began history with the inventions of the calendar, the written word, and kingship. These four cultural periods are associated in this book with the stages in psychosexual development or libido development. I regard libido not as "sexual energy" but as an energic metaphor for the intensity, bodily localization, aim, direction, and goal of sexual excitation in the most specific and broadest definitions of that term.

This book examines how libido development influenced cultural evolution and gave rise to symbolic representations that were then projected into mythical and religious thought throughout our cultural evolution. To be more specific, it considers how libido development, ego development, object relations, the symbolic function, and our primate social instincts gave rise to spiritual beliefs, myths, rituals, technology, social structure, and psychic structure in these four stages of cultural evolution and how those stages correspond sequentially to Freud's four stages of libido development: the oral, anal, phallic, and adolescent genital stages. Furthermore, it investigates how the metaphors embedded in cultural evolution have been inherited as a part of psychic structure—not through our genes, archetypes, or an archaic cultural memory in the brain, but through language, technology, customs, beliefs, architecture, and more.

Our psychological development, rooted in our anatomy, physiology, social instincts, and central nervous system, grants us cognitive abilities such as memory, object constancy, abstract thinking, and a symbolic function that enable us to symbolize, speak, and create psychological and cultural structure clothed in metaphor. Culture, and the metaphors it carries, shapes our psychological structure, and by contributing to culture we further modify the cultural surround into which subsequent generations are born and given shape. Thus, throughout cultural evolution from the Paleolithic period to modern times, and throughout the life cycle from infancy to old age, an ongoing interchange of metaphors is taking place between the individual and culture. These are the metaphors of the body, technology, the world, and the cosmos. An understanding of these metaphors allows us to listen more deeply to our patients and ourselves and to observe culture as a social phenomenon that is influenced significantly by the derivative material of individual experience.

In this book we will delve into a complex set of ideas, each built one on top of the next, which may at times leave us feeling dizzy. We'll try to resist the fascination of metaphors, symbols, and religious ideas as well as the temptation to simply back away from it all and abandon the project. We will explore boldly but carefully. We will see how Freud took his initial inspiration from Charles Darwin, Ernst Haeckel, Jean-Baptiste Lamarck, James George Frazer, and others. Based on these influences and more, Freud offered a reconstruction of humanity's primordial past. He brought together psychological development, psychopathology, cultural evolution, myths, and rituals into a convergence of phenomena that offered a first step toward a kind of unified theory of human development. We will examine Freud's magnificent latticework of speculation to see where errors were made and to find out which aspects are still useful. We will then reapproach what I call the "phylogenetic project of psychoanalysis" with more data and different understandings in order to arrive at an updated reconstruction of the relationship between psychological development and cultural evolution. Below is a summary of the chapters to follow:

Part 1. The Phylogenetic Project of Psychoanalysis

In chapter 1, "The Phylogenetic Fantasies of Charles Darwin and Sigmund Freud," we will explore Darwin's ideas on anatomical and cultural evolution and the functions of natural selection and sexual selection. We'll reflect on Jean-Baptiste Lamarck's ideas on the inheritance of acquired characteristics, including the notion of *psycho-Lamarckism*, in which experiences repeated throughout prehistory were thought to make such an impression on people, and their brains, that these experiences of past generations would be recalled as species-specific memories—memories inherited by subsequent generations of the species. We'll consider Ernst Haeckel's idea that "ontogeny recapitulates phylogeny"—that is, that the early development of the individual repeats the evolution of the species. We'll see how Freud used these ideas to understand how ego development and libido development have their roots in our cultural evolution and to account for what he called the "points of agreement between the mental lives of savages and neurotics." Freud saw neurotics as fixated at earlier stages of psychological development, making them appear in some ways like caricatures of stages in our ancestral prehistoric past.

Freud was in search of the origins of the Oedipus complex and universal symbolism. He found clues in psychopathology, dream symbolism, libido development, mythology, and comparative religion. Then, in *Totem and Taboo,* he speculated on the deeds of our ancestors in our prehistoric past and imagined a primal father guarding the women for himself and driving off his sons, who later returned as the fraternal clan to murder and cannibalize the primal father and develop a more equitable culture. This happened innumerable times until it became a part of our archaic inheritance—a set of species-specific memories. Freud found analogous relations between the *phallic stage* of normal psychological development, *obsessional neurosis* as a psychopathological fixation, the *fraternal clan* as a cultural stage in prehistory, the *legend of Oedipus Rex* as a mythic analogue, and the *totemic feast* as an analogous ritual. We will examine both the strengths and the weaknesses of Freud's reconstruction.

In chapter 2, "Brief Psychotic Disorder and the Myth of Sacral Kingship," we will reexamine Freud's model of associating (1) a normal stage of psychological development, (2) a psychopathological fixation, (3) a stage in cultural prehistory, (4) an analogous myth, and (5) an analogous ritual. Then, while maintaining our Freudian viewpoint, we will draw on the clinical work and scholarly research of John Weir Perry, a Jungian analyst who tracked the recurring images and themes in his patients' delusions, hallucinations, and drawings while they were undergoing brief psychotic disorders. Perry found extraordinary analogues (points of agreement) between the images and themes in the delusions and hallucinations of his patients with *brief psychotic disorders* and the images and themes found in the *myths of sacral kingship* and the *ritual of the ancient New Year festivals* in cultures around the world at the time of their respective *Urban Revolutions.* Perry illuminated the myths, rituals, politics, and history of cultures on the threshold between the High Neolithic and the Urban Revolution and found them to be in some ways analogous to the personal experiences of those undergoing brief psychotic disorders.

The ten recurring images and themes common to the myths of sacral kingship, the rituals of the ancient New Year festival, and the delusions and hallucinations of Perry's patients undergoing brief psychotic disorders are the center, death, return to beginnings, cosmic conflict, threat of the opposite sex, apotheosis, sacred marriage, new birth, new society, and a quadrated world. They are the same images and themes present in the visions of the founders of many religions as well. Perry's work did not contradict Freud's. While Freud had addressed the obsessional neurosis and a prehistoric stage in cultural evolution, Perry addressed the brief psychotic disorder and the Urban Revolution, the first historical stage in cultural evolution marked by the emergence of the written word. We will examine Perry's formulation from a Freudian perspective in order to determine lines of agreement and disagreement. I will further associate the material Perry presented with the challenges of the adolescent *genital stage* of libido development.

In chapter 3, "Infantile Autism and the Myth of Death and Rebirth," I present my work with a profoundly disturbed child on the autism spectrum who, for several years, drew circles he called "mouths." I explore the themes of orality and the image of the mouth in myth and ritual. Reflecting on autistic dynamics, I formulated that the child with autism is, poetically speaking, a disembodied soul with the spiritual task of embodying—that is, entering and being swallowed by the mouth of the body, the family, and the world. If the spiritual task is embodiment, then the psychological task is one of leaving autistic encapsulation and then bonding and attaching to a mother. *Autism* has been associated with the *oral stage*, and based on my exploration into myth and ritual, I propose that the mythic analogue to the autistic syndrome is not the myth of Oedipus or the myth of sacral kingship but rather the *myth of death and rebirth*, and that the ritual correlate is not that of the totemic feast or the ancient New Year festival but that of the *funerary ritual*, in which the soul reunites with the (m)other on the other side of death. I further elaborate this theme by exploring some of the psychoanalytic understandings of autism and orality and tracing the roots of the ancient funerary ritual back 100,000 years into the *Paleolithic period*.

In chapter 4, "Human Evolution: How We Got to Be the Way We Are," we examine the ritualizations, or social instincts, of the higher primates, particularly chimpanzees. We find in these social instincts the seeds of human psychodynamics, which later became metaphorized in culture. These social instincts include greeting, dominance and submission posturing, copulation interference, and alpha male dynamics. This view will help us to see more clearly how our *primate social instincts*, or *ritualizations*, when symbolized, gave rise to our loftiest spiritual ideas emerging throughout our prehistoric cultural evolution. We then review the current status of human evolution, and trace the developments through the Australopithecus and Homo lines up into the Lower and Middle Paleolithic periods (Benveniste, 2020).

Part 2. From Infancy to Adolescence, From the Paleolithic to the Urban Revolution
In chapter 5, "The Upper Paleolithic Period and the Oral Stage of Libido Development," I restate my formulation of the myth and ritual analogues to the autistic syndrome and John Weir Perry's formulation of these analogues to the brief psychotic disorder. With these formulations as points of orientation, which I associate with the oral and genital stages, respectively, we will examine the stages of libido development—from the oral, to the anal, to the phallic, to the adolescent genital stages—and find their analogues in the four stages of cultural evolution from the Paleolithic, to the Neolithic, to the High Neolithic, to the Urban Revolution, including their various myth and ritual analogues.

While all of this may sound rather odd, I hope to make it clearer as we get deeper into it. But for now it should be enough to say that our Paleolithic ancestors were nomadic hunter-gatherers who feasted or starved at Mother Nature's whim. The Paleolithic period and the oral stage are about oneness. Paleolithic culture was embedded in the unity of nature, just as the infant's psyche is embedded in the unity of the early mother-infant relation. And just as the mother-infant dyad constellates a subjectivity in the infant, the spiritual innovation of the Paleolithic was the concept of the "soul," which is implied in the then newly emerging traditions of the *funerary ritual* and its associated *myth of death and rebirth*, in which the body dies and the community says "good-bye" to the soul that presumably carries on. The concept of the soul is also inherent in other Paleolithic spiritual innovations, such as ritual cannibalism, in which the soul of the other is internalized by being eaten; the use of amulets, which house the souls of ancestors; cave paintings, which contain the souls of the represented; and carved maternal figurines, representing perhaps the very soul of motherhood.

Chapter 6 is titled "The Neolithic Period and the Anal Stage of Libido Development." If orality and the Paleolithic are about oneness, then anality and the Neolithic period are all about two-ness. The toddler separates from mother by saying "no" and moving away from her, and in the Neolithic period human culture separates itself from nature by building walls around the village, walls for the first permanent houses, and walls that transformed the hearth into an oven and a kiln. And in the kiln they fired ceramic pots and ceramic female figurines. They even contained their newly domesticated crops and livestock within bounds. The separation of infant from mother was reflected in the separation of culture from nature. Agriculture, animal husbandry, permanent houses, and stable villages afforded the possibility of gathering wealth and developing trade with neighboring communities. No longer victims of Mother Nature's whims, Neolithic communities took control over food production, and when nature resisted, they made a one-sided contract to trade with her in the form of a simple *ritual sacrifice*, which I propose was the spiritual innovation of the Neolithic period. This ritual sacrifice ostensibly protected inhabitants of the house and assured the success of the hunt. But, psychologically, ritual sacrifice defends us against our feelings of powerlessness by granting a magical means of appealing to the goddess. The themes of separation from nature and two-ness suggest that the corresponding myth might pertain to the *fall from grace*—from oneness—or the expulsion from Paradise.

In chapter 7, "The High Neolithic Period and the Phallic Stage of Libido Development," we see how both the High Neolithic and the phallic stage are about ambition, power, and the myth of the hero. In the High Neolithic period, the small villages of the previous Neolithic period were transformed into much larger settlements. Ceramic mother goddess figurines of the High Neolithic sometimes appeared alongside figurines of children or male consorts, and images of stars and suns were etched into the rocks, signaling the beginning of a changing orientation from the bountiful earth goddess to the fertilizing sky gods. The Oedipus complex of the phallic stage is organized around a child, a mother, and a father. In the High Neolithic, agriculture and religion appear to have been organized around another oedipal triangle— the mythic hero, the mother goddess, and the emerging father god. High Neolithic sites are commonly associated with large earthwork ditches and mounds; large stone structures, such as Stonehenge; carved phalli; and metallurgy, which gave rise to metal plow tips that transformed farming, and metal spear points that revolutionized warfare. The oedipal struggles and ambitions of the High Neolithic lead me to speculate that the mythic analogue might be the hero's battle with the dragon. And, of course, *hero mythology* is the basis for legends like that of Oedipus Rex. The ritual innovation of the High Neolithic was the elaborated sacrifice of the primal being to bring fertility to the women and the fields as was seen in *planting and harvesting rituals*. These rituals were based on their newly discovered sexual knowledge but at the same time employed magical control over the gods by offering sacrifices. In this way, they both recognized and defended against their awareness of sexual knowledge, the role of the father in reproduction, and patricidal wishes.

In chapter 8, "The Urban Revolution and the Genital Stage of Libido Development," we recognize that adolescence marks a full shift in orientation from the mother of childhood and the home to the father of adulthood and the world. The genital-stage dynamics of the adolescent are analogous to the Urban Revolution, when cultures around the world repositioned themselves in relation to male gods, liberated themselves from the circularity of time by inventing calendars, and entered history with the invention of writing. Leadership of the group was bestowed upon the visionary, the human god-king in relation to a king-god deity, as described in the *myth of sacral kingship* and the *ancient New Year festivals* that commemorated it. The god-king's mission was to create a kingdom on earth in accordance with God's kingdom in heaven. In the king's heroic battle with the chaos-dragon, we can see, in myth and ritual, a reflection of the earlier oedipal battle. Beyond that, the mythic union of the king and queen parallel the adolescent's new relation to adult sexuality. And the god-king's vision of a new world order is analogous to the adolescent's establishment of an identity and a worldview. The ancient New Year festival grants a sense of meaning and naturally defends us against the awareness of the ultimate meaninglessness of our finite, mortal existence by granting us a special relationship to God or godhood itself.

We will see in this chapter how each stage of psychological development is associated with its analogues in psychopathology, cultural evolution, myth, and ritual. We conclude chapter 8 with a schema of four sets of metaphors, each set associated with a stage of psychosexual development and a stage in cultural evolution. I describe these four constellations of metaphors as stages in *psychomythic* development, referring to the tendency of psychology to be projected into myth. I've named these four stages after their recurring images and themes: (1) Death and Unity, (2) Birth and Separation, (3) Ascension and Conflict, and (4) Transformation and the Establishment of Order. Each of the four stages is associated with a cluster of metaphors that can be useful in informing our clinical listening. These clusters or sets of metaphors allow us to recognize psychomythic (developmental) themes in our patients' clinical material. The term psychomythic stages is based on Freud's term "psychomythology," referring to the vague perception of one's own psychic apparatus, which creates illusions that are projected onto the world, into the future, and out into the beyond—in other words, psychology projected into religious, philosophical, and political thought.

There are those who will say each culture is distinct and broad groupings of culture ignore kinship structure, language, unique history, and local economics. To this I say yes, and no. Yes, cultures are unique, but viewed from an appropriate distance their uniqueness blurs and some of their similarities come into higher relief. Others will say that libido development (and ego development and object relations) cannot be found sequentially represented in cultural evolution, as psychological development and cultural evolution are completely different kinds of phenomena. To this I say again yes, and no. They are different phenomena, but from my perspective they are analogous human experiences in the realms of childhood and society. (Benveniste, 2020).

Part 3. Libido, Culture, and Consciousness

In chapter 9, "Cosmogony and Cosmology, Anamnesis and Psychic Structure," we will see reflections of the previously described four stages of psychomythic development and cultural evolution in the images and themes embedded in cosmogonies (creation myths) from cultures around the world. These cosmogonies typically begin with a unity, which is divided into a duality. The two aspects of the duality interact, giving rise to a trinity that intensifies into a transformative and stable quaternity—a four-fold world for example. In other words, they parallel the four stages described above. We will see how these creation myths are not about the creation of the external universe but are metaphors for the creation of a psychic universe and a cultural universe, which are subsequently projected onto the walls of the external universe. In addition to cosmogonies, we will examine a number of cosmologies (descriptions of the order of the universe) and again see reflections of the four stages previously described. Some of these cosmologies have seven aspects. Their order climbs from unity, to duality, to trinity, to quaternity like steps up a small pyramid reaching the top in the quaternity—stability, order, and the vision. When they move to the fifth stage, they revisit the trinity from a different perspective—the other side of the pyramid. If the third stage was from the perspective of the oedipal child in relation to the mother and father, the fifth stage is about the oedipal triangle from the perspective of a parent. In the sixth stage, there is a return to a duality but instead of separating the opposites as in toddlerhood, it is all about the opposites coming together—the reconciliation of the opposites. And the seventh stage, of old age and death, is about a return to unity from which the infant's psyche had originally emerged.

Freud's *psychosexual* stages of development pertain to the intrapsychic experience of the body and its drives and instincts in relation to pleasurable experiences and the frustrations of cultural prohibitions. Erik Erikson's (1963) *psychosocial* stages of development pertain to the experience of the body in direct relationship to others—that is, in societal context. The *psychomythic* stages of development pertain to the experience of the body in the context of society and projected onto the walls of the universe in the form of religious, political, and philosophical ideas. The psychosexual, psychosocial, and psychomythic are all intrapsychic perspectives. The difference is that Freud's psychosexual schema begins with drives and instincts and extends out to the skin, Erikson's psychosocial schema extends out to the social world, and the psychomythic schema extends—or is projected, as I say—onto the walls of the universe.

In chapter 10, "Psychomythology: Projections onto the Walls of the Universe," we will explore how the metaphors of the body are projected not only into bodily experience, symptoms, and social relations but also into religion, politics, and philosophy (Benveniste, 2020).

❖ ❖ ❖

On May 3, 1987, Erik H. Erikson and his wife, Joan, were featured in the conference "Vital Involvement in Old Age" in San Francisco. I arrived early and sat in the center seat of the front row. As the crowd was filing in, I saw a majestic old couple enter the auditorium—Erik and Joan Erikson. Professor Erikson, at 86, was tall, slender, yet somehow weary, as if near the end of a very long journey. His white hair was combed back like strands of silk in the wind. His eyes were small, as if he were looking at the world from a great distance. And true to the riddle of the Sphinx, in old age he was walking on three legs—that is, with cane in hand. It was to be his last public presentation.

At the front of the auditorium were four chairs for the presenters—the Eriksons, Robert Wallerstein, and Mort Lieberman. Professor Erikson, a great man whose work I had studied for years, neared the front of the auditorium, walked directly in front of me, turned, and sat down—right next to me! He was too weary to sit up front facing the audience. His eyes had looked into Freud's eyes long ago, and now he was looking into my eyes as we greeted each other politely.

Robert Wallerstein described Professor Erikson as the greatest living proponent of psychoanalysis and said that after Freud, no single psychoanalyst has had a more profound impact on our 20th-century culture and the world than Professor Erik Erikson. After that Joan Erikson and Mort Lieberman spoke a bit about old age. When finally it was Professor Erikson's turn to speak, he stood up, walked to the podium, and, standing before us, spoke in an almost free-associative style. I felt I was gazing upon a great old cypress tree with windswept branches, its roots slowly losing their hold on the ground below.

He spoke of the hope that comes with the relatively successful passage of the first stage of development—basic trust versus mistrust—and likened the infant's trust and hope to that of the older person looking forward to the world beyond. It was surprising to hear this famous psychoanalyst speaking obliquely of an afterlife. Soon he commented that he should stop before he bored or disappointed us. He returned to his seat, and then the floor was opened up for questions and comments.

After a number of questions, I raised my hand with the hope of getting some clarification on the point Erikson had made about the infant and the elderly person. "I have long seen a similarity between the first and last stages of psychosocial development and have heard that the two of you [Joan and Erik Erikson] do as well," I said. "I wonder if you could say something about that similarity." Joan loved the question and talked about how the infant and the older person are much more dependent on others than those in the middle stages of development. The other panelists also emphasized the higher levels of dependence associated with the first and last stages of development. Erik Erikson was silent in response to the questions from the floor but appeared to be carefully following the interchange.

Well, I was not satisfied with the answer I was given, so even at the risk of appearing impertinent, I resubmitted my question with more of a focus. "Yes, dependency is a common feature of these two stages," I said, "but what I am particularly interested in is the way the infant enters the world with a unified and undifferentiated psyche and enters consciousness by separating reality into opposites—subject and other, good and bad, inside and outside, here and there, now and then, male and female, adult and child—and the way the older person is involved in reconciling the opposites toward a reunified worldview. Then there is also the way the infant is moving from nonbeing into being and the way the older person is being and yet gazing toward death into nonbeing. And I wonder if you might comment on that." At this point Erik Erikson, still sitting at my side, moved forward, eye-to-eye with me, and said in his thick German accent, with great animation and comedic timing, "A comment or a *book*?"

The audience roared with laughter. Professor Erikson smiled at me, reached out, and reassuringly patted my hand with his. I smiled, recognizing that my question involved more than what a brief comment could address. I then turned to him and promised, "I'll work on the book." This is that book.

Erik H. Erikson (May 3, 1987)

PART 1

The Phylogenetic Project of Psychoanalysis

CHAPTER 1

The Phylogenetic Fantasies of Charles Darwin and Sigmund Freud

> I am now writing about the totem [*Totem and Taboo*] with the feeling that it is my greatest, best, and perhaps my last good thing. Inner certainties tell me that I am right.
> –Letter from Sigmund Freud to Sándor Ferenczi, May 4, 1913

Charles Darwin (1809-1882), who gave us evolutionary theory, and Sigmund Freud (1856-1939), who gave us psychoanalysis, were fascinated by the relationship between psychological development and cultural evolution. Darwin and Freud pieced together bits of seemingly disconnected data concerning the evolution of the species, the development of the individual, embryology, aberrations and fixations in development, anthropology, primatology, and more. As they sifted through the data, they recognized converging patterns, speculated on our early cultural evolution behind the veil of prehistoric amnesia, and constructed their respective phylogenetic fantasies—that is, their fantasies of the cultural evolution of our species, their fantasies of our prehistory at the dawn of human culture, at the dawn of human consciousness.

Charles Darwin: Natural Selection, Sexual Selection, and Cultural Evolution

Charles Darwin, born in 1809 in Shrewsbury, England, enjoyed the study of natural history and pursued it eagerly from an early age. He went to Christ's College, Cambridge, to study theology, though it held little interest for him. After graduating in 1831, he immediately took a job as a ship's naturalist on the *HMS Beagle* and set out for a five-year expedition along the coasts of South America. Returning in 1836, Darwin began developing ideas based on observations he'd made during his expedition and published them in 1859 in his classic *On the Origin of Species by Means of Natural Selection; or, The Preservation of Favored Races in the Struggle for Life*.

In this revolutionary text, *On the Origin of Species*, Darwin found useful the ideas of Sir Charles Lyell, the great geologist of the time, who had stated that the world was not a mere 6,000 years old and created by the hand of God through a cataclysmic history, as was commonly believed at the time, but was actually millions and millions of years old and that the small geological changes that made it what it is are still active today. With Lyell's notion of the great antiquity of the earth, Darwin demonstrated, using modern biological specimens, fossil evidence, and the variations between species, that all the species of our world were not divinely created once and for all in the Garden of Eden but rather were related, mutated over time, belonged to their own separate ecological niches, and were continuing to mutate via the process of natural selection. Those mutations most suitable to their environment survived, and those that were not became extinct. In speaking of natural selection, Darwin referred to the "struggle for existence" and later adopted Herbert Spencer's phrase "survival of the fittest" (Burrow, 1968, p. 35).

Charles Darwin (1881)

Based on fossil evidence, comparative anatomy of contemporary animal species, the elongated notion of geological time spanning millions of years, and the notion of the mutability of species, Darwin concluded that similar animals have a common ancestor. He also recognized humans not as unique divine creations of God but as a species of animal, like any other, and suggested that we too must have an evolutionary past peopled with ancestors some of whom were not people! Darwin said that humans and modern-day monkeys and apes are cousins with a common ancestor in the distant past and that the ancestor was itself descended from a long line of more primitive animals. He did not claim to know who or what those ancestors were, but in a letter to Sir Charles Lyell the power and playful creativity of Darwin's mind is revealed: "Our ancestor was an animal which breathed water, had a swim bladder, a great swimming tail, an imperfect skull, and undoubtedly was a hermaphrodite. Here is a pleasant genealogy for mankind" (Burrow, 1968, p. 16). The creator of this vision was the man upon whose shoulders Sigmund Freud was to stand.

Prior to *On the Origin of the Species* there were other theories of evolution, and one of the more popular ones was that of Jean-Baptiste Lamarck (1744-1829), who put forth the theory of the inheritance of acquired characteristics. Lamarck's theory has two fundamental points: (1) individual members of a species change their shape and functioning by learning, striving, and trying to adjust to their environment; and (2) these changes are passed on to their offspring. Thus, the giraffe's long neck came from generation after generation of its ancestors stretching their necks and then passing on their accomplishments to their offspring. This passing on of the acquired characteristics could be accomplished only if the body somehow remembered or recorded the changes in the lives of the ancestors and somehow passed that memory-trace on to the next generation. It seems quaint now, but this was a well-received and popular idea in its day, which, we should add, was long before the theory of genetics and the discovery of DNA (Edey & Johanson, 1989, pp. 22-26).

In *The Descent of Man, and Selection in Relation to Sex* (1871), Darwin described the mechanism of "natural selection" in the evolution of species in relation to long periods of time, the mutability of species, and the environmental influences that determine which mutations will survive and which will be extinguished. These environmental influences include factors such as food availability, climate, predators, and competition for resources. But Darwin also identified the selective factor of "sexual selection," in which males compete for access to the female of the species and the opportunity to mate and pass on their traits (i.e., strength, speed, attractiveness, aggressiveness, etc.), while females determine which males they will allow to mate with them. In this way, certain characteristics, including secondary sex characteristics, evolve and become established in the species. While *On the Origin of Species* was devoted primarily to an explication of natural selection, *The Descent of Man* was devoted primarily to an explication of sexual selection.

In *The Descent of Man*, Darwin (1871) noted that humans, monkeys, apes, and mammals in general endure a lengthy period of helplessness after birth, that the appearance of the human ovule (a small or immature ovum) and human fetus appear similar to those of other animals, and that the bodies of many animals have rudimentary features and functions that are echoes of a utility in the distant past but are vestigial in contemporary times. Using man as an example, Darwin pointed to the presence of scalp muscles, an inward bump on the edge of the outer ear, the atrophying sense of smell, the third eyelid, and the fine wool-like hair, or lanugo, that many children come into the world wearing (vol. 1, pp. 13–26). He asserted that the similarity of fetal structures between animals and the presence of rudimentary features and functions of the body indicate that a progenitor possessed these features and functions in perfect condition and that they became reduced through disuse or through natural selection when no longer required by the various species that evolved from this progenitor (vol. 1, p. 32). He noted, "From the presence of the wooly hair or lanugo on the fetus, and of rudimentary hairs scattered over the body during maturity, we may infer that man is descended from some animal which was born hairy and remained so during life" (vol. 2, p. 375).

Jean-Baptiste de Lamarck (1802)

Darwin says that since we have the same senses as many lower animals, our fundamental intuitions must also be the same: "Man has also some few instincts in common, as that of self-preservation, sexual love, the love of the mother for her new-born offspring, the power possessed by the latter of sucking, and so forth" (vol. 1, p. 36). Beyond self-preservation Darwin points out that there are social instincts as well, which give rise to moral behavior above and beyond the motivating forces of pleasure and pain. He recounts the social and frankly altruistic behavior of animals and considers the inheritance of moral behavior. However, he also points out that the acquisition of the social instincts is not a calm elevation of the spirit but a constant conflict for each member of the group, whether it is a human or a member of the lower animal world: "As a struggle may sometimes be seen going on between various instincts of the lower animals, it is not surprising that there should be a struggle in man between his social instincts, with their derived virtues, and his lower, though at the moment, stronger impulses or desires" (vol. 1, pp. 103–104). I think this struggle between the social instincts on the one hand and the impulses and desires on the other could fairly be called a conflict in the psychoanalytic sense of the term, and Darwin's observation of moral behavior beyond the motivating forces of pleasure naturally reminds us of Freud's book *Beyond the Pleasure Principle* (1920).

Referring to physical development, Darwin (1871) described cases of arrested development and reversions in development that corresponded to earlier stages in evolution (vol. 1, pp. 121–22). He was addressing anatomy, but the psychoanalytically sophisticated will naturally be reminded of psychological parallels and will describe arrested psychological development as a "fixation" and a reversion in development as a "regression." Darwin observed that the most distinctive characteristics of man were acquired through natural selection and that while the brute-like powers were gradually disappearing, the intellect and social instincts were developing (vol. 1, pp. 151, 157).

Darwin demonstrated that "some extremely remote progenitor of the whole vertebrate kingdom appears to have been hermaphrodite or androgynous" and did not have secondary sex characteristics (vol. 1, p. 207). Sexual differentiation took place after that phase. And then via "sexual selection," sexual differentiation elaborated such that size, strength, and skill in battle became traits that were passed on to the next generation from those males who were successful in battle with rivals for possession of the females. The females were not passive in all of this, however, as they were the ones to select males based on aesthetics such as shape, coloring, voice, physical displays, and other charms. Thus, "the more attractive individuals are preferred by the opposite sex," and in this way their characteristics are passed on to the next generation (vol. 1, p. 421).

Darwin described the differences between men and women in relation to strength, beauty, mental powers, and voice. He also offered an interesting discussion on the social instincts, the development of morality, the belief in God, and the concept of the soul.

Finally—and here we come to our main point—Darwin (1871) mused on our prehistoric past:

> We may indeed conclude from what we know of the jealousy of all male quadrupeds, armed, as many of them are, with special weapons for battling with their rivals, that promiscuous intercourse in a state of nature is extremely improbable. The pairing may not last for life, but only for each birth; yet if the males which are the strongest and best to defend or otherwise assist their females and young offspring were to select the more attractive females, this would suffice for the work of sexual selection.
>
> Therefore, if we look far enough back in the stream of time, it is extremely improbable that primeval men and women lived promiscuously together. Judging from the social habits of man as he now exists, and from most savages being polygamists, the most probable view is that primeval man aboriginally lived in small communities, each with as many wives as he could support and obtain, whom he would have jealously guarded against all other men. Or he may have lived with several wives by himself, like the gorilla; for all the natives "agree that but one adult male is seen in a band; when the young male grows up, a contest takes place for mastery, and the strongest, by killing and driving out the others, establishes himself as the head of the community." (vol. 2, pp. 362-63) [The quote within the quote is from an article by Dr. Savage in the *Boston Journal of Natural History*, 5 (1845-1847), 423.]

This scenario of a jealous primeval man battling with his rivals, and even killing them in order to obtain and guard his women against all other men and thereby become head of the community, fit in so nicely with Freud's concept of the Oedipus complex that he quoted in full the above citation in his *Totem and Taboo* (1913/1955h). But in truth Freud learned of Darwin's musings on our prehistoric social life long before formulating the Oedipus complex, in fact probably in his late adolescence.

The great revolution that Darwin (1871) brought forth is his recognition that man is descended from a "lowly-organized form"; that "he still bears in his bodily frame the indelible stamp of his lowly origin" (vol. 2, pp. 404-405); and that one can see traces of our common past in arrested development, reversions, embryological structure, the behavior of the mentally impaired, and the social structure of contemporary aboriginal peoples. Darwin wrote, "The astonishment which I felt on first seeing a party of Fuegians [aboriginal people on the southern coast of Chile] on a wild and broken shore will never be forgotten by me, for the reflection at once rushed into my mind—such were our ancestors" (vol. 2, p. 404). Darwin and his colleagues were clearly onto something—the evolution of the species is in some way related to the development of the individual—not just in relation to biological structure but at the cultural and psychological levels as well. But the relationship of the evolution of the species to the development of the individual was left to Ernst Haeckel to elaborate.

Ernst Haeckel: Ontogeny Recapitulates Phylogeny

Ernst Haeckel (1834-1919) was a professor of zoology and comparative anatomy at the University of Jena, in Germany. He coined the terms "ecology," "ontogeny," and "phylogeny" and is best known for his formulation of the *biogenetic law*, which states "ontogeny recapitulates phylogeny"—that is, ontogeny, the development of the individual, is driven to repeat the most important changes in phylogeny, the evolution of its species (Gould, 1977, pp. 76-77). This formulation was based on comparative anatomy, paleontology, embryonic structure, and a good bit of speculation in the traditions of ancient philosophy, religion, mysticism, and alchemy, which recognized truths in the relationship between the microcosm and the macrocosm.

Ernst Haeckel (1895)

Haeckel asserted that as embryos we go through stages that resemble those of the animal ancestors of our primordial past. As embryos we have tails, limbs that look like those of a quadruped, and even gill-like structures similar to those of fish. Haeckel's biogenetic law stated that phylogenesis is the mechanical cause of ontogenesis and that it is based on "the principle of terminal addition" and "the principle of condensation." The principle of terminal addition means that evolutionary change occurs by adding stages to the end of ontogeny. The principle of condensation means that the length of ancestral ontogeny must continually be shortened and the added stages must be telescoped into the life cycle. As new features are added onto the end of ontogeny, condensation makes room for them by shortening or deleting previous stages. Thus, phylogeny is the mechanical cause of ontogeny (Gould, 1977, pp. 4, 7, 80, 85).

Mendelian genetics, however, disproved the two laws of recapitulation (Gould, 1977, p. 202). From the Mendelian perspective, genes exist from the beginning, so new features cannot be added terminally—that is, at the end of the adult life. New features can appear only as mutations, thus there is no "terminal addition." Furthermore, genes act by controlling the rates of processes, thus the law of condensation became untenable. If genes control the release of enzymes and enzymes control the rates of various processes, there can be no basis for the hypothesis of a universal acceleration in phylogeny; furthermore, there were slowed rates of change in phylogeny as well (pp. 202-205). Haeckel's biogenetic law was incorrect, but the biogenetic metaphor had captured the imagination of many, especially in the social and psychological sciences.

While phylogeny may not cause ontogeny, there appears to be an analogous relation. The human fetus has gill-like structures before losing them entirely. Are those holdovers from our fish ancestors? The infant walks on four legs and then on two. Does that say something about our evolution from quadrupeds to bipeds? And the young child's thinking is animistic before becoming rational. Is that a holdover from our animistic past?

Sigmund Freud and the Phylogenetic Project of Psychoanalysis

Speculating on the relationship between psychological development and cultural evolution can lead us to new understandings or leave us mired in confusion. In Freud's (1923/1961a) view, "With the mention of phylogenesis... fresh problems arise, from which one is tempted to draw cautiously back. But there is no help for it, the attempt must be made—in spite of a fear that it will lay bare the inadequacy of our whole effort" (*Standard Edition* [hereafter, SE] 19, pp. 37-38).

Long before Freud formulated psychoanalysis, Darwin wrote about the centrality of sex and aggression, the role of rivalry in mating, and the matter of incest in relation to evolution. He addressed developmental arrests (fixations) and reversions (regressions), behaviors motivated by pleasure and others not motivated by pleasure, the conflict between the survival instincts and the social instincts, and the evolution of a sense of morality.

Sigmund Freud was born in 1856, just three years before the publication of Darwin's *On the Origin of Species*. His sister Anna recalled that as an adolescent her brother "was an enthusiastic walker and nature lover, and would roam the forest and woods near Vienna with his friends, bringing back rare plant and flower specimens" (Freud Bernays, 1973, p. 141). Freud's oldest son, Martin, also recalled his father's great love of nature, particularly the mountains. On vacations they went on hikes almost every day, observing nature and hunting for edible mushrooms (M. Freud, 1958, pp. 51, 55). Freud passed on his love of nature to his grandchildren by taking them on nature walks in the woods. His oldest grandson, W. Ernest Freud, recalled, "When my grandfather and I went on walks, he always carried this geological hammer in his coat—to chisel [ammonite fossils] out of the rocks" (Benveniste, 2015, p. 84).

Sigmund Freud (1921)

As a child Freud was deeply interested in the Bible, and as an 18-year-old he developed interests in philosophy, anatomy, zoology, physics, mathematics, and the theories of Charles Darwin and Ernst Haeckel, whom he described as "modern saints." He was fascinated by what he called "the major cosmic and physiological problems" (Boehlich, 1990, pp. 86, 87) and early on decided to pursue his "Ph.D. in philosophy and zoology" (pp. 95, 96). These were the earliest stirrings of what was to become Freud's passion for the phylogenetic origins of consciousness, in which he would try to come to terms with the universality of the Oedipus complex and castration complex, the archaic inheritance of dream symbolism, and the way our prehistoric past may have shaped our modern psychic structure.

Freud wondered how the structure of a patient's psyche came to be in the context of a personal life and what that could tell us about how the human psyche got to be the way it is in the context of human evolution. He admired Darwin, but when it came to psychodynamics, he was psycho-Lamarckian and Haeckelian. He saw the human as an animal that *acquires* experiences and passes them on to the next generation as species-specific memories. And each individual *recapitulates* the cultural evolution of its species in its own psychological development. Thus, the *experiences of pre-history* that occur in cultural evolution get passed on and recapitulated as *archaic memories* in the minds of individual members of the species.

In coming to terms with recurring dynamics in human behavior, Freud (1916/1963a) recognized that humans, like other animals, have inherited predispositions. He further attributed universal sexual symbolism and primal fantasies to inherited phylogenetic memories, our archaic inheritance. Then, based on the overwhelming clinical evidence of the Oedipus complex, he reconstructed, in outline, the events of our prehistoric past, the memories of which, he asserted, we have inherited phylogenetically. He concluded, "The prehistory into which the dream-work leads us back is of two kinds—on the one hand, into the individual's prehistory, his childhood, and on the other, in so far as each individual somehow recapitulates in an abbreviated form the entire development of the human race, into phylogenetic prehistory too" (SE 15, p. 199).

Though Freud did not mention the repudiated Haeckel, his assertion echoes the biogenetic law. Freud (1915/1957) further asserted that instinctual ambivalence (SE 14, p. 131), the ego ideal, religion, morality, a social sense, and the Oedipus complex are all inherited—that is, acquired phylogenetically (S. Freud, 1923/1961a, SE 19, pp. 36-38). Furthermore, "the archaic heritage of human beings comprises not only dispositions but also subject-matter—memory-traces of the experience of earlier generations" (p. 99). He later went on to say, "Furthermore, dreams bring to light material which cannot have originated either from the dreamer's adult life or from his forgotten childhood. We are obliged to regard it as part of the archaic heritage which a child brings with him into the world, before any experience of his own, influenced by the experiences of his ancestors" (S. Freud, 1940/1964a, SE 23, pp. 166-67).

Freud (1923/1961a) saw that the memories of our forgotten ancestors also gave shape to psychic structure itself:

> The experiences of the id seem at first to be lost for inheritance; but, when they have been repeated often enough and with sufficient strength in many individuals in successive generations, they transform themselves, so to say, into experiences of the id, the impressions of which are preserved by heredity. Thus, in the id, which is capable of being inherited, are harbored residues of the existences of countless egos; and, when the ego forms its superego out of the id, it may perhaps only be reviving shapes of former egos and be bringing them to resurrection. (SE 19, p. 38)

Beyond dream images and psychic structure, Freud (1918/1955d) wrote of the primal fantasies as being a part of our phylogenetic inheritance: "These scenes of observing parental intercourse, of being seduced in childhood, and of being threatened with castration are unquestionably an inherited endowment, a phylogenetic heritage, but they may just as easily be acquired by personal experience" (SE 17, p. 97). In recognizing primal fantasies as inherited from our phylogeny and also "just as easily acquired by personal experience" (ontogeny), Freud was suggesting two different origins for these recurring experiences: phylogeny and ontogeny.

Robert Paul (1976), defending Freud from his detractors, said, "Whether one accepts Freud's argument or not, it is in any case clearly a grave injustice that general opinion has it that *Totem and Taboo* is marred by Lamarckian heresies, when in fact no such arguments even put in a serious appearance, much less play a crucial role in the argument" (p. 319). What Paul is referring to here is the fact that Freud never mentions Lamarck's name in *Totem and Taboo* and that ontogeny could easily account for what might also be accounted for by phylogeny. But then Paul admits that "while Lamarckian arguments play no role in the essay *Totem and Taboo*, shortly after he published it, Freud noticed the apparent relevance of Lamarck's theory of the inheritance of acquired characteristics to his own work, and the rest of his career is marked by an indisputable adherence to the Lamarckian theory" (p. 319).

Freud saw myth as derived from the dream and the dream derived from the deeds of our ancient past. Karl Abraham (1909/1955a) wrote, "Thus the myth is a surviving fragment of the psychic life of the infancy of the race whilst the dream is the myth of the individual" (p. 208). "The myth survives from a remote period in the life of a people which we might call its infancy.... It contains, in veiled form, their infantile wishes originating in pre-historic times" (p. 180). Elaborating on this theme, Abraham quoted Freud, saying, "Paradise is nothing but the collective phantasy of each individual's infancy" (p. 181).

Otto Rank (1932/1959) linked myths to fantasies: "Myths are, therefore, created by adults, by means of retrograde childhood fantasies, the hero being credited with the mythmaker's personal infantile history" (p. 84). Daniel Merkur (2005), in his study on psychoanalytic approaches to myth, explains that Hungarian psychoanalyst and anthropologist Géza Róheim linked myth to the dream of the primal scene and also to the daydream (pp. 45-47) and that "[Jacob A.] Arlow treated myths as public expressions of communal fantasies" (p. 65). Without contradicting the others, I would add that many myths were probably originally derived from visionary experience—that is, from hallucinations and delusions.

If dreams, memories, free associations, and symptoms provided material for the reconstruction of early infantile experience, archeological artifacts, myths, and rituals were seen as the raw material for the reconstruction of our prehistoric past. Freud's office was filled with more than a thousand antiquities that he collected over the course of decades. They recalled for him another time and another way of being. While he speculated on human prehistory, his collection of artifacts belonged almost entirely to human history. They were from the early literate civilizations like those of ancient Egypt, Greece, Rome, and China, not from the Paleolithic, Neolithic, and High Neolithic periods.

As far as I have been able to determine, Freud's only artifacts from the nonliterate prehistoric periods are a large crude hand axe of unclear origin and a small polished stone chisel with a bone handle from a Neolithic site in Saint-Aubin-Sauges in Switzerland. Freud collected the little chisel in 1897, and it appears to be either the first antiquity he ever collected or at least one of the first (Spankie, 2015, pp. 144-45).

Freud generally resisted his own speculative impulses in favor of more careful, rational thinking. But in *Totem and Taboo*, *Moses and Monotheism*, and in the latter portion of many of his other scientific works, he speculated boldly: "Man's archaic heritage forms the nucleus of the unconscious mind" (S. Freud, 1919/1955a, SE 17, pp. 203-204).

Freud (1919/1955g) observed that because human offspring have a particularly long period of dependence on their parents, love passes a complicated course: "Consequently, the overcoming of the Oedipus complex coincides with the most efficient way of mastering the archaic, animal heritage of humanity" (SE 17, p. 262). Thus, the animal heritage of incestuous desire, jealousy, bitter rivalry, and murderous impulses is mollified and modified under the influence of the Oedipus complex, wherein gender and generational differences are secured, identifications are made, the superego is established, and fraternity becomes a part of the foundation of culture. Every child passing through the Oedipus complex must relive this primordial past in the context of family and in relation to parents and siblings. It is our phylogenetic heritage, taking place on the stage of family relations as a personal intrapsychic conflict.

Freud recognized the Oedipus complex in his self-analysis and in the dreams and free associations of his patients, but he needed to understand the prehistoric origins of this universal complex. He discovered the themes of love for the mother and murderous wishes directed at the father in Sophocles's play *Oedipus Rex*, as well as in myths, legends, and works of art. Was it just an interesting analogy? Or could those myths and legends of our ancient past actually be archaic memories of events that really happened?

While Freud addressed his phylogenetic speculations before and after *Totem and Taboo*, that essay was where he gave the fullest explication of his ideas on the matter. Of *Totem and Taboo* he wrote, "I haven't written anything with so much conviction since *The Interpretation of Dreams* [1900/1953a], so I can anticipate the fate of this essay" (Brabant et al., 1993, 483).

Polished stone chisel with a bone handle from a Neolithic site in Saint-Aubin-Sauges, Switzerland. One of the few pre-historic antiquities in Freud's collection. Purchased in 1897. Now on display sitting in a stone ashtray in the Freud Museum London.

Totem and Taboo

Freud's *Totem and Taboo: Some Points of Agreement between the Mental Lives of Savages and Neurotics* (1913/1955h) contains four essays: "The Horror of Incest"; "Taboo and Emotional Ambivalence"; "Animism, Magic, and the Omnipotence of Thoughts"; and "The Return of Totemism in Childhood." As we review each of these essays, it should be noted that contemporary indigenous aboriginal people living close to nature and with low levels of technology have historically been referred to as "savages," "primitives," and "Indians," and when quoting other authors I use the terms they have used. Otherwise, I refer to such people as "aboriginal" or "indigenous" people, as these seem to be the most descriptive and respectful terms and the least likely to be viewed as pejorative.

In "The Horror of Incest," Freud addresses the universal abhorrence of incest and seeks to understand it in the context of tribal life among some of the aboriginal people of Australia. Freud believed that an understanding of these people could give us a glimpse into the lives of all our ancestors and our primordial past. He described the Australian aborigines' social and religious institution of "totemism" based on ancestor worship, in which the primal ancestor is seen as an animal or plant and is said to be the father of the clan. The totem animal or plant must not be killed or eaten except on special occasions, and members of one clan must avoid sexual relations with members of the same clan. Thus, one must always marry outside of one's clan. This is called *totemic exogamy*.

Freud described the restrictions against marriage within one's clan and the intricate steps taken by the Australian aborigines to avoid any chance of sexual relations with one's mother, sisters, or mother-in-law. While the restrictions were elaborate, the punishment for transgressing the restrictions were harsh: death, or almost death, by stoning or being speared. Freud (1913/1955h) noted that the incestuous wishes that posed an immediate peril to these aboriginal people had become unconscious in modern individuals (SE 13, p. 17). Freud's point was that within their psychic makeup, cultural traditions, behaviors, and ways of thinking modern humans possess *survivals*—that is, the remnants or traces of collective early experiences of our ancient ancestors along the road of cultural evolution. Based on clinical experience, Freud concluded that the horror of incest is not innate. It is a defensive strategy that was exerted consciously and with great effort in our prehistoric past in order to manage the socially disruptive incestuous desires. Thus, for Freud, the horror of incest is a *survival*, a remnant of our collective early experiences. In the modern world, these desires and repressive efforts rarely even become conscious without interpreting them. Thus, under every incest taboo there reside incestuous desires.

In his second essay, "Taboo and Emotional Ambivalence," Freud described taboos as restrictions or prohibitions on behavior to avoid calamitous occurrences. That is, if one touched something belonging to a shaman or touched a menstruating woman, death, illness, or disaster would befall the person or the community. Thus, elaborate taboos existed against touching or having anything to do with certain objects, people, and the totem of the clan. Freud noted the extraordinary resemblance of taboos within totemic and formal religions and the obsessions of obsessive-compulsive patients who develop rules and "rituals" to avoid causing damage or death to themselves or others. There is fear and danger in both, an object of fear and danger as well as an extraneous other object onto which the fear and danger has been displaced.

Both the totemic and obsessive-compulsive rituals associated with their respective cultural and personal taboos are employed to avoid danger. Behind the taboo is desire, and behind the danger is temptation. There may be rituals of avoiding certain foods, wearing certain clothes, saying a prayer (magical words) four times, always taking an even number of sheets of toilet paper, walking seven times around the bride, checking four times to be sure the stove is off or the door is locked, cleansing rituals, repeated hand washing, prayers in the four directions, excessive housecleaning, and so on. The ritual associated with the taboo object is a compromise between the socially imposed prohibition and the instinct. It is a compromise to manage the ambivalent feelings toward the object. In other words, the taboo manages and covers the desire to act out the impulse.

Freud noted that, historically, chiefs and kings have been seen as figures of great power, and taboos were established to avoid touching them, and even their belongings, for fear of death. Similarly, the chiefs or kings were also limited by taboos that constricted their lives in order to magically manage their great power over the well-being of their clan or kingdom. Beneath all the ceremonial taboos of veneration and idolization the kings received from their subjects was an intense undercurrent of hostility. Freud (1913/1955h) noted that the taboos had a double meaning derived from the ambivalent impulses. They exalted the king and at the same time tormented him. Thus, the ritual suppressed the impulse and at the same time gratified it.

Freud observed that taboos related to the treatment of the dead have the function of covering or repressing the death wishes of the mourner. He associated the taboos of totemic clans with those of modern religious people on the one hand and with the neurotic ritualistic behavior of obsessive-compulsives on the other. The social taboo and personal ritual both serve to hide or disguise ambivalent feelings.

In the third essay, "Animism, Magic, and the Omnipotence of Thoughts," Freud reconstructed the prehistory of cultural evolution and the origins of the human psyche. He linked the omnipotence of thoughts—a common neurotic mechanism for managing overwhelming experience—with the magic and animism of aboriginal people. Animism is a philosophical system that explains much of the world by filling it with a belief in spirits, demons, and souls that inhabit animate and inanimate objects and are the cause of natural phenomena. Most important, they inhabit humans as well. The notion of the soul is said to have originated in the observation of and attempts to explain sleep, dreams, and death. Following James George Frazer and others, Freud (1913/1955h) wrote that humanity developed "three great pictures of the universe: animistic (or mythological), religious and scientific" (SE 13, p. 77).

The animistic system of the universe provides explanatory power but is also accompanied by two techniques for controlling spirits, demons, and souls. Those techniques are magic and sorcery. Magic, the older of the two, makes use of objects and manipulates them to affect outcomes at a distance, such as an assault on an enemy by attacking an effigy. Other examples are pouring water or dancing to bring rain and the dramatic representation of intercourse to bring fertility to the fields. As we can see, magic and superstition are intimately linked. Sorcery, a later development, is a very human way of dealing with spirits by, for example, appeasing them, intimidating them, and making amends to them.

Along these same lines, cannibalism is based on the magical principle that the qualities of a person can be incorporated or internalized by another when that person's flesh is eaten. This has also given rise to various food taboos that avoid the incorporation of undesirable or even malevolent qualities. Magic is organized along the lines of formal similarities (things that look alike or sound alike), associations of contiguity (things that touch or are associated in the contiguity of time), and, above all, on the power of wishing—or as Freud's analysand, the "Rat Man," called it, "the omnipotence of thoughts." (See S. Freud, "Notes Upon a Case of Obsessional-Neurosis" [1909/1955f].)

Freud (1913/1955h) recognized this magical thinking or omnipotence of thoughts in the thinking and play of children, the magical animistic world of aboriginal adults, and the thought processes of the neurotic. Furthermore, he traced it through cultural evolution, saying that in the animistic phase, our ancient ancestors attributed the omnipotence of thought to themselves. In the religious phase, this omnipotence was transferred to the gods, but a piece was retained for us. In the scientific view, where there is no room for human omnipotence, it "still survives in men's faith in the power of the human mind, which grapples with the laws of reality" (SE 13, p. 88). In an attempt to bridge psychological development with cultural evolution, Freud declared, "The animistic phase would correspond to narcissism both chronologically and in its content; the religious phase would correspond to the stage of object-choice of which the characteristic is a child's attachment to his parents; while the scientific phase would have an exact counterpart in the stage at which an individual has reached maturity, has renounced the pleasure principle, adjusted himself to reality and turned to the external world for the object of his desires" (p. 90).

Freud asserted that spirits and demons are the projections of man's own impulses and wondered about the origin of this tendency to project these impulses and mental processes into the outer world. He agreed with others in attributing the origin of spirits and demons to early man's experience of the deaths of loved ones. Freud saw it not primarily as an intellectual challenge to come to terms with but as an emotional conflict. The magical actions designed to ward off the danger of the taboo object—the dead person, for example—protected the living from the ghost of the dead and from the ambivalent feelings of sorrow for the loss on the one hand and the repressed death wishes on the other. As a function of the magical actions, the repression was facilitated, making possible the earliest instinctual renunciations of our ancient ancestors. And instinctual renunciation is the basis of the development of both the ego and culture.

In the fourth essay, "The Return of Totemism in Childhood," Freud gathered the observations and insights of evolutionary anthropology, brought them together with his clinical observations and insights, and then took a speculative leap of majestic proportions.

He would not call this speculative leap a hypothesis but rather a "vision" (1925/1959a, SE 20, p. 68). Freud employed psychological Lamarckism, Haeckel's biogenetic law, and Darwin's hypothesis regarding the earliest social state of aboriginal peoples. Observing the habits of the higher apes and man, Darwin deduced that in our prehistoric past, we humans lived in small groups or hordes under the domination of the oldest and strongest male, who kept as many wives as he could support and jealously guarded them from the sexual promiscuity of the younger, weaker males. Drawing on the work of Dr. Thomas Staughton Savage, an American naturalist, Darwin added that among gorillas there is typically only one adult male per band. When the younger males grow up, there is a contest of strength in which the stronger drives out the other, weaker ones. Freud then noted that it was James J. Atkinson who recognized that when the others moved on, they tacitly established a tradition of exogamy. And Andrew Lang then made the connection between exogamy and the tradition of totemism that Freud found so useful (S. Freud, 1913/1955h, SE 13, pp. 125-26).

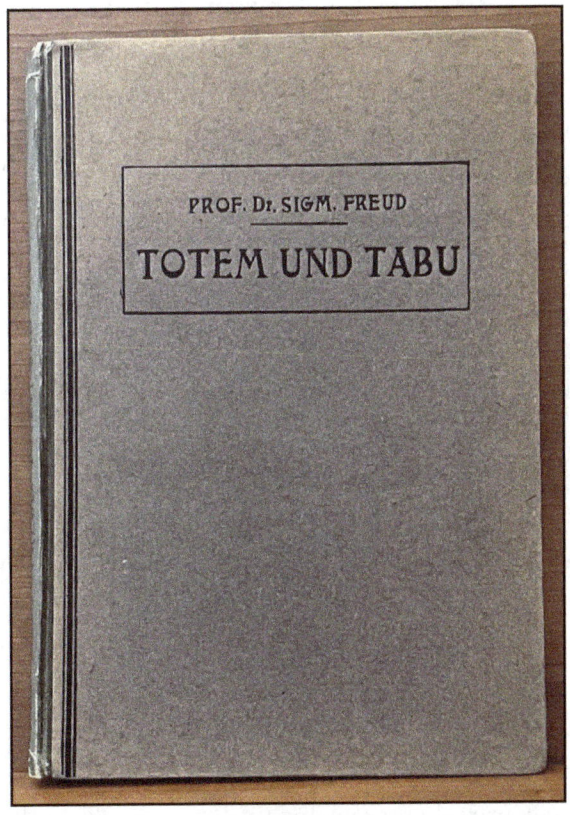

Totem und Tabu: Einige Übereinstimmungen im Seelenleben der Wilden und der Neurotiker (1913) German first edition of Freud's 'Totem and Taboo'.

This exogamy, or marrying outside one's group, whatever its merits might be genetically, is a tradition based on the horror of incest, which, as we learned, is a thin cover for incestuous desires. The taboo against incest confirms such desires by the need for the prohibition. There is no need for a prohibition where there is no desire, and in the family and the clan there are always temptations. Thus, the prohibition against incest was a taboo established by the totem figure of the group in order to maintain social harmony.

Freud (1913/1955h) drew on Frazer's definition of the totem as a class of objects (usually a plant or animal) that has a special relation to a group of people—a clan—and to the individual members of that clan. The people show respect for the totem by not killing it, and in return the totem protects the clan. While a fetish is a particular object, a totem is always a class of objects, a kind of animal, or a kind of plant. The people of the clan see themselves as descendants of a common ancestor—the totem—which is said to be the creator and protector of the clan (SE 13, p. 104).

The two principal taboos of totemism are the taboo against harming the totem and the taboo against sexual relations within the clan (p. 144). Freud further supported William Robertson Smith's hypothesis that the periodic sacramental killing and feasting on the body of the totemic animal, which was strictly taboo at all other times, was an important feature of totemic belief systems (SE 13, p. 139). To conclude, Freud introduced the psychoanalytic interpretation that the totem animal is a substitute for the primal father of the primal horde, killed in primeval times by the band of brothers who transformed the dead father into a totem in order to worship him and to periodically recall his murder and mourn him again in the sacrificial totemic meal (p. 141): "The totem meal, which is perhaps mankind's earliest festival, would thus be a repetition and a commemoration of this memorable and criminal deed, which was the beginning of so many things—of social organization, of moral restrictions and of religion" (p. 142).

Freud was building a schema of cultural evolution from the patriarchal horde, to the totemic fraternal clan, to the religious world, to the modern scientific *weltanschauung* (worldview). His focus was on the first two stages, particularly the transition from the patriarchal horde to the totemic fraternal clan. Freud mused that after the brothers banded together and slew the hated primal despotic father, they felt triumphant at first, but then their love, admiration, identification, and affection for the primal father reemerged in the form of remorse, guilt for the original sin. To manage these feelings, they brought the father back to life, so to speak, in the form of the totem. To ensure his longevity, he became a class of animal or plant rather than just one being. The brothers attempted to undo their primal crime by making it forbidden to kill the totem plant or animal and resigned any individual's claim to all the women by establishing sexual taboos and the principles of exogamy (p. 143).

Freud wrote that there is always the return of the repressed, and in totemism the repressed crime of the murder and cannibalizing of the primal despotic father is reenacted and commemorated in the ceremonial sacrificial killing of the totem and the communal feasting upon its flesh. In sacrificing (killing) and ceremonially eating (cannibalizing) the flesh of the totem and drinking its blood, the clan incorporated the spirit of the totem and reconfirmed the bonds of kinship, fellowship, and social obligations among the members of the clan. The communal totemic feast sanctified the clan and reconfirmed the identification between the members of the clan and their totem, who also took part in the feast (pp. 133-47).

Freud's analogous linkage of the totemic feast with an oedipal-type myth was based on the theory of the myth and ritual school. Some in this group said that myth is primary and ritual enacted it, others said that ritual came first and myth described it, and still others said the two appeared together. But the analogous linkage was common to them all. William Robertson Smith, James George Frazer, Jane Ellen Harrison, and Francis Cornford were among the leading lights of the myth and ritual school. They used the comparative method to see analogous relations between myths and rituals. Their work in the late 19th and early 20th centuries influenced Freud's thinking significantly. But as 20th-century anthropology advanced, the comparative method was discarded, as it seemed their search for universal psychological meanings ignored social contexts. Their assumption of cultural evolution from animism, to religion, to science was also seen as false and ethnocentric (Ackerman, 1991, pp. 46, 63-65, 83). While modern anthropology considers myth and ritual to be independent of each other, a psychological view still finds compelling the comparative method and the analogous relations between myth and ritual.

Within his reconstruction Freud struggled to understand how the patriarchal horde was followed by a fraternal clan organized under matriarchy or the great mother goddesses and was subsequently followed by yet another patriarchal phase of a character different from the first. Nonetheless, the patriarchal phase following the phase of the great mother goddesses left abundant traces of the worship of father deities, divine kings or god-kings, and king-gods. According to Freud (1913/1955h):

> As time went on, the animal lost its sacred character and the sacrifice lost its connection with the totem feast; it became a simple offering to the deity, an act of renunciation in favor of the god. God Himself had become so far exalted above mankind that He could only be approached through an intermediary—the priest. At the same time divine kings made their appearance in the social structure and introduced the patriarchal system into the state. (SE 13, p. 150)

As the relation between the divine kings and the king-gods was established, the death of the father, the king, continued to be an important feature and was reenacted as the literal death of the king, the death of a substitute for the king, or a symbolic death of the king. Freud noted:

> In his great work, *The Golden Bough*, Frazer (1911a, 2, Chapter XVIII) puts forward the view that the earliest kings of the Latin tribes were foreigners who played the part of a god and were solemnly executed at a particular festival. The annual sacrifice (or, as a variant, self-sacrifice) of a god seems to have been an essential element in the Semitic religions. The ceremonials of human sacrifice, performed in the most different parts of the inhabited globe, leave very little doubt that the victims met their end as representatives of the deity; and these sacrificial rites can be traced into late times, with an inanimate effigy or puppet taking the place of the living human being. (SE 13, p. 151)

Freud was building an evolutionary sequence for human culture beginning with a primal father and primal horde, followed by a fraternal clan in a totemic culture with its totems and animistic thinking, then a religious worldview organized around gods that lost their animal forms and reattained human form, followed by the unification of the multiple gods into a single god, and finally to our modern world with its scientific worldview (SE 13, p. 77). He saw traces of this primordial past in the religions of ancient times as well as in our modern religions of the father, in the myth of the dead and reborn god, the sacramental drinking of wine as the blood of the dead god, in food prohibitions, and so on.

Psychoanalysts, who are generally less familiar with anthropology, archeology, ancient history, mythology, and comparative religion, often overlook the phylogenetic aspect of Freud's work. But when we follow the thread of these interests throughout his collected works and gaze upon his enormous collection of antiquities, now on display at the Freud Museum in London, one becomes acutely aware that Freud's interests in such subjects were neither passing nor parallel. They were integral to his thinking about dream symbolism, psychopathology, the structure of the psyche, the evolution of psychic structure, and the nature of the Oedipus complex.

Considering the universal nature of the castration complex, Freud mused in *Moses and Monotheism* (1939/1964b), "The possibility cannot be excluded that a phylogenetic memory-trace may contribute to the extraordinarily terrifying effect of the threat—a memory-trace from the prehistory of the primal family, when the jealous father actually robbed his son of his genitals if the latter became troublesome to him as a rival with a woman" (SE 23, p. 190n). This phylogenetic memory-trace, Freud (1913/1955h) suggested, exists in a hypothesized "collective mind": "Without the assumption of a collective mind, which makes it possible to neglect the interruptions of mental acts caused by the extinction of the individual, social psychology in general cannot exist" (SE 13, p. 158).

Although Freud (1939/1964b) held the concept of a "collective mind," he specifically repudiated Jung's concept of the "collective unconscious." He saw the content of the unconscious as "a collective universal property of mankind" (SE 23, p. 132) but could not go along with Jung's project, which Freud believed was an effort to understand the individual from the perspective of history and culture. For Freud, it was the other way around: he sought to understand history and culture from the perspective of the individual.

In his autobiographical study, Freud (1925/1959a) summarized his vision in *Totem and Taboo* as follows:

> The father of the primal horde, since he was an unlimited despot, had seized all the women for himself; his sons, being dangerous to him as rivals, had been killed or driven away. One day, however, the sons came together and united to overwhelm, kill and devour their father, who had been their enemy but also their ideal. After the deed they were unable to take over their heritage since they stood in one another's way. Under the influence of failure and remorse they learned to come to an agreement among themselves; they banded themselves into a clan of brothers by the help of the ordinances of totemism, which aimed at preventing a repetition of such a deed, and they jointly undertook to forgo the possession of the women on whose account they killed their father. They were then driven to finding strange women, and this was the origin of the exogamy which is so closely bound up with totemism. The totem meal was the festival commemorating the fearful deed from which sprang man's sense of guilt (or "original sin") and which was the beginning at once of social organization, of religion and of ethical restrictions. (SE 20, p. 68)

The subtitle of *Totem and Taboo* is *Some Points of Agreement between the Mental Lives of Savages and Neurotics*. It is a long subtitle but does not say all that it could, as the points of agreement are between more than just "savages" and "neurotics." Freud was establishing analogous relations between a stage of normal development, a form of psychopathology (neurosis), a stage in cultural evolution (including "savages"), a myth, and a ritual. While he did not present these analogous phenomena in a schematic form as I do, these points of agreement were all present.

With regard to a stage in normal development, Freud wrote almost exclusively about the oedipal stage (phallic stage) in his discussion of his phylogenetic project. The psychopathological correlate or fixation to this stage was the obsessional neurosis. As Freud stated in *The Future of an Illusion* (1927/1961b), "Religion would thus be the universal obsessional neurosis of humanity; like the obsessional neurosis of children, it arose out of the Oedipus complex, out of the relation to the father" (SE 21, p. 43). With regard to a stage in cultural evolution, Freud wrote at length about (1) the primal horde, (2) the fraternal clan, and (3) the emergence of gods and religion. But his focus was on the fraternal clan and the development of totemism. Freud did not explicitly assign a myth to this stage but wrote at length about the oedipal components of totemism (the taboos against killing the father and against incest), so we might say the analogous myth is the totemic myth, the myth of the ancestor, the myth of Oedipus, or the myth of the hero. Freud was explicit about the corresponding ritual; it is the sacrificial totemic feast in which the killing of the totem (father) is commemorated.

1. A stage of normal development — The phallic stage
2. A form of psychopathology — Obsessional neurosis
3. A stage in cultural evolution — Fraternal clan
4. A myth — Totemism—myths of the great ancestor, of the hero, of Oedipus
5. A ritual — Sacrificial totemic feast

The "points of agreement" between these seemingly disparate phenomenon are the two themes, or metaphors, they hold in common: (1) erotic desire for the mother and the horror of incest, and (2) desire to kill the father and the adoration of the father.

The idea that a stage in normal *physical* development could be associated with a *stage in the evolution of the species* is based on the structural similarities between ontogeny and phylogeny. The idea that a stage in normal *psychological* development could be associated with a *stage in cultural evolution* is based on individual cognitive structures and functioning that are analogous to cultural structures and functioning. The idea that a stage in normal *psychological* development could be associated with a *form of psychopathology* is based on the Darwinian notion that an earlier stage in normal anatomical development can be seen in the pathology of arrests and reversions in otherwise mature individuals.

Totem and Taboo is a grand unified theory of human development. It is the jewel of Freud's genius, integrating his clinical observations; his theoretical understandings of psychological structure, psychological development, and psychopathology; and his speculations on cultural evolution. His vision was bold, inspired, and courageous, but his psycho-Lamarckian assumption meant it was also wrong. We do not biologically inherit the memories of our ancestors' experiences. But we need not be harsh in our criticism or dismissive of Freud's creative effort to integrate such diverse aspects of human experience. Even with its inadequacies, his vision is majestic.

Freud and Anthropology

To read Darwin is to walk in the footsteps of a genius and understand Freud's appreciation of his work. Freud (1907/1959c) wrote that Darwin's *The Descent of Man* was, for him, one of the "ten most significant books" (SE 9, p. 245). Edwin Wallace's *Freud and Anthropology: A History and Reappraisal* (1983) offers a thorough analysis of the ideas in *The Descent of Man* that are fundamental to or borrowed from "evolutionary anthropology." These are:

1. The unity of the mind of man—the idea that the mind of *Homo sapiens* is basically the same for all members of this species.
2. The equating of prehistoric people with contemporary aboriginal people who share a similar level of technology.
3. The notion of *survivals* in human behavior. Survivals are certain behaviors, customs, ways of thinking, etc. formed in our ancient past that remain in various forms to the present day.
4. The belief that the tenets of evolutionary theory in biology can be applied to ethnology: the study of human behavior in various parts of the world.

Some of Darwin's other ideas that were not fundamental to evolutionary anthropology but were adopted by Freud were these:

1. All peoples believe in spirits.
2. The sexual instinct plays a role in language formation.
3. There is a sexual element in religion.
4. The incest taboo is not instinctive.
5. Female infanticide was very prevalent in our early prehistory.
6. Man was originally promiscuous and was organized around group marriage.
7. Psychological Lamarckism—The notion that humankind inherited complex behavior patterns that were originally performed in previous generations.

8. The biogenetic law as applied to psychic life—The individual human being repeats the acquired experiences of the evolution of the species in its own life, and this includes its cultural evolution. (Wallace, 1983, pp. 10-11)

Wallace explained that beyond Darwin, several key philosophers and evolutionary anthropologists significantly influenced Freud's work on *Totem and Taboo*. David Hume said people conceive of their gods as having qualities like their own. Hume also held euhemerist views, the idea that ancient myths were based on real people and real events of the past. He also addressed the ambivalent relationship between people and their gods, as did Freud (Wallace, 1983, pp. 13-14). Ludwig Feuerbach said, "Theology is anthropology." He saw religion as infantile and based on projection and a function of dependency. He believed that animal worship preceded the worship of the anthropomorphic gods and that religion was a necessary stage in the development of man's self-consciousness (Wallace, 1983, pp. 14-15). Friedrich Nietzsche believed that authority is the source of conscience and that the voice of God in men is actually the composite of multiple voices of various men in man. He considered souls, spirits, and gods as primitive misunderstandings of dreams and linked the dreams of modern adults to contemporary "primitives," to our prehistoric ancestors, to poets, and to artists (Wallace, 1983, pp. 16-17). Henry Thomas Buckle subscribed to the notion of psychic unity—the idea that the human mind is the same wherever it is in different cultures and across time, that there are laws of history, and that cultures can by ranked evolutionarily (Wallace, 1983, p. 18).

Wallace stated that Freud also read the evolutionary anthropology of Herbert Spencer, Edward B. Tylor, and John Lubbock and was probably familiar with Lewis H. Morgan, John Ferguson McLennan, and Johann Jacob Bachofen as well. Spencer interpreted mythology and religion figuratively, allowing for a metaphorical interpretation of meaning that not infrequently led into the past. He saw contemporary aboriginal peoples (hunter-gatherers and Neolithic people) as equivalent to our early ancestors. He believed in recapitulation—specifically, that modern-day children demonstrate behaviors that are common to modern-day "primitive" adults. His psycho-Lamarckism permitted him to think that personal experiences can accumulate into thoughts, change psychic structure, and be passed on to the next generation. But religion and the avoidance of incest, he believed, were not innate. Spencer believed that religion serves social cohesion, suspends hostility within the group, encourages discipline and respect for authority, and supports people in the delay of gratification. He was a euhemerist who, as Wallace said, "derived the Heavenly Father from the earthly one, viewing ancestor worship as the prototypic religion and the funeral as the prototypic ritual" (Wallace, 1983, pp. 21-22).

Tylor emphasized the role of conflict in cultural evolution and pointed out the myth-making function in contemporary aboriginal peoples, in the ancients, in children, in poets, in the insane, and even among the deaf and mute (Wallace, 1983, pp. 24-27). Lubbock subscribed to the notion of the survival of ancient behaviors in the behavior of modern man. Bachofen elaborated the theory that the first period of human social development was matriarchal—that is, politically ruled by women—and that in a later stage it became patriarchal. Based on his studies of marital contracts, anthropology, archeology, contemporary aboriginal people, mortuary symbolism, and more, Bachofen described several stages of cultural development including two matriarchal stages leading to two patriarchal stages (George Boas, in Bachofen, 1967, p. xix; Joseph Campbell, in Bachofen, 1967, pp. xlvii, xlviii; Bachofen, 1967, pp. 106, 107, 132, 134, 179).

From all of these influences and many more, not the least of which was his clinical work, Freud began to piece together a phylogenetic fantasy of psychological development and cultural evolution. With Freud's biogenetic-psycho-Lamarckism, psychological development was seen as a recapitulation of cultural evolution, and psychopathology, dream symbolism, and the universal complexes (Oedipus, castration, etc.) were seen as *survivals*—that is, remnants of collective experiences of our distant past (Wallace, 1983, pp. 42-51).

Wallace (1983) summarized the multiple critiques of *Totem and Taboo* by modern anthropologists from the 1920s to the early 1980s (pp. 113-328). The first critiques were leveled at Freud's psycho-Lamarckian assumption of the inheritance of memories from one generation to the next and his use of the defunct biogenetic law for understanding the ontogenetic reappearance of the Oedipus complex, castration complex, and archaic symbolism as a function of phylogenetic inheritance. They criticized Freud and the evolutionary anthropologists for their broad generalizations about the formal similarities between different cultures and for not recognizing that many of the observed similarities were not a function of the unity of the human mind and our phylogenetic memories but simply a result of diffusion—that is, of direct contact between one group and another.

This new wave of anthropologists was less interested in the similarities between cultures and found more useful understandings in recognizing the unique differences between cultures and the influence of their respective histories. Thus, the overarching cultural pattern of totemism broke down under closer examination of individual cultures,[1] and the thought of comparing a contemporary aboriginal culture with our primeval ancestors became completely untenable.

---

[1] An outstanding analysis of totemism can be found in Gerard Lucas's *The Vicissitudes of Totemism: One Hundred Years after* Totem and Taboo (2015).

The modern 20th-century anthropologists found that Bachofen's idea that matriarchy preceded patriarchy had no basis in fact, since no one really knows the political structure of prehistoric peoples, and the same held for the notion that matrilineal descent preceded patrilineal descent. The constellation of characteristics defining totemism were found to be illusory, and the same was said about taboos. Robertson Smith's reconstruction of the totemic feast was disassembled and found to be lacking in ethnographic data—in other words, there was no evidence for it.

Cultures were increasingly found to be more different than they were similar, and their differences and unique histories became increasingly important to the modern anthropologists. The lumping and clumping and generalizations of Freud and the evolutionary anthropologists were giving way to the slicing and dicing and deconstruction of the modern anthropologists. Freud could not see the trees for the forest, and, if I may say so, those making the modern anthropological critiques could not see the forest for the trees. Freud did, however, make a good name for himself, even among anthropologists, for paying such close attention to personal history in the analysis of individuals, but when it came to speculation about cultural phenomena, he showed himself to be startlingly ahistorical.

While Freud privileged the instinctual determinants, psychoanalysts Abram Kardiner, Harry Stack Sullivan, Karen Horney, and Erich Fromm saw sociocultural determinants of greater significance than Freud would attribute to them. Furthermore, both Kardiner and Géza Róheim would dismiss Freud's phylogenetic thinking about the origins of the Oedipus complex and instead locate the Oedipus in biological, social, and psychological structure. Derek Freeman (1967) wrote that the sacramental totemic meal is far from universal, and in fact there are very few examples of it. Anthropological evidence shows there is nothing to suggest that human societies ever lived in cyclopean families (primal hordes). And, finally, according to Freeman, psychoanalytic and anthropological evidence suggested that the rituals of aboriginal people are derived from dreams and fantasies, not from "the repetitive performance of actual deeds" (pp. 11, 15, 21, 27).

Freud's speculations were repeatedly challenged over a period of decades by the giants in anthropology—Franz Boas, Alfred L. Kroeber, Robert Lowie, Edward Sapir, Margaret Mead, Paul Radin, Bronislaw Malinowski, R. R. Marrett, Klyde Kluckhohn, Claude Lévi-Strauss, and others. But the number and stature of these anthropologists and the continuing preoccupation with Freud's ideas revealed that as wrong as Freud was, he was still offering something that was very compelling. Wallace (1983) wrote, "Much of the negative criticism has been directed against Freud's explanation of totemism, where his ahistoricism is most marked and where he broaches the parricide idea. By contrast, his ideas on the incest taboo, on spirits as projections, on magic as wish fulfillment and omnipotence of thoughts, and on ambivalence toward the dead have been favorably received" (p. 169).

Freud discovered the Oedipus complex in his own early childhood memories, in his patients' free associations, in Sophocles's play *Oedipus Rex*, and in other literary and artistic cultural expressions. When he declared the Oedipus complex universal, his theory was based on startling examples of blatant oedipal wishes but also on many examples of disguised representations in which the oedipal dynamics only became apparent from behind a veil of metaphor.

Some psychologists who rejected the universality of the Oedipus complex found that many people did not fit the concrete pattern. What they failed to see, and what Freud perhaps failed to emphasize, was that oedipal fantasies accompany strong infantile emotions and that in most cases we detect them only in the well-disguised metaphorical representations of the Oedipus complex. Maybe the love object is a mother, an aunt, a father, a nanny, a sister, or a brother. And the one who is hated to the point of murderous wishes is the father figure—maybe father, maybe not—but it's typically the one who installs the taboo, the prohibitions, and generally manages the day-to-day limit-setting strategies for the child. The Oedipus complex is how the child demands gratification of wishes and comes to terms with the prohibitions of society.

Franz Boas was fundamental in setting the course for 20th-century North American anthropology. He found that the structure of any given social group was more influenced by its unique culture, history, language, and foreign influences than by psychological necessity. The universality of totemism, taboos, parricide, parent-child incest, ritual cannibalism, and more seemed to break down when anthropologists searched for specific examples of such behavior that would fulfill all the criteria that Freud attributed to each. Boas was also skeptical of Freud's ideas about a universal symbolism in folklore (Smadja, 2018, pp. 42-45).

Alfred L. Kroeber, a student of Franz Boas and a representative of historical ethnology, valued many of Freud's contributions, but he critiqued the ahistorical and universalist claims of *Totem and Taboo* (Smadja, 2018, pp. 45-48). Another distinguished anthropologist of that time was Bronislaw Malinowski, who set out to test the validity of Freud's assertion that the Oedipus complex is universal by studying the Trobriand Islanders. He discovered that Trobriand boys don't want to marry their mothers and kill their fathers; rather, they want to marry their sisters and kill their uncles. Any Freudian who understands the concept of displacement would see Malinowski's findings as further confirmation of the Oedipus complex, but, concretely speaking, the sister is not the mother and the uncle is not the father. Malinowski concluded that there is a universal family complex and that the Oedipus complex belongs to patriarchal society, while the Trobriand pattern of love for the sister and hatred toward the uncle pertains to matrilineal society (Smadja, 2018, pp. 23-29).

If "mother" is a metaphor for pleasure, the unimpeded instinctual life, nature, need gratification, fusion, merger, and unlimited access to love, and "father" is a metaphor for taboos, prohibitions, laws, limits, rules, institutions, and societal structure, it becomes easier to recognize the Oedipus complex as a metaphor for socialization in patriarchal societies, matrilineal societies, single-parent families, communal living, and families with gay and lesbian parents.

In the introduction I noted that *Totem and Taboo* was neglected over the years as clinical concerns took the attention of analysts away from other psychoanalytic interests and as Freud's psycho-Lamarckian speculations collapsed under the discoveries of modern science. In this regard I find useful William I. Grossman's 1998 article "Freud's presentation of "The psychoanalytic mode of thought" in *Totem* and *Taboo* and his technical papers," which specifically addresses Freud's "The Dynamics of Transference" (SE 12, 1912/1958c) and "Recommendations to Physicians Practicing Psychoanalysis" (SE 12, 1912/1958b). Grossman's assertion was that they all demonstrate "the psychoanalytic mode of thought" as applied to both clinical and cultural material. He pointed out, "In the technical papers that appeared concurrently with his [Freud's] book, he applied to the clinical situation the ideas on transference, narcissism, primitive mental mechanisms, and unconscious communication that he had explored in *Totem and Taboo*" (Grossman, 1998, p. 469). But because of the focus on the anthropological critiques, he noted, "readers have often overlooked the significance of *Totem and Taboo* as an example of Freud's application of psychoanalytic thinking that is much like the thinking employed in understanding clinical material. In both cases, his goal was the reconstruction of early mental life" (Grossman, 1998, p. 469). He was addressing specifically the stratification of psychic material being subjected to rearrangement or retranscription. Grossman noted, "According to this principle, the processes of defense lead to compromise formations and the progressive build up of complexity" (p. 471). There is also the complemental series, which finds application in both clinical and cultural material in which disposition and environment interact. Grossman noted that for Freud, "the disposition to neurosis was the result of the variable interplay of constitution and experience. The outcome of this interaction in turn interacted with further experience to produce neurosis, a new structure" (pp. 471–72). And then Grossman quoted Freud: "The neuroses themselves have turned out to be attempts to find individual solutions for the problems of compensating for unsatisfied wishes, while the institutions seek to provide social solutions for these same problems" (1913/1955h, SE 13, p. 186).

Freud's Phylogenetic Fantasy

In 1915 Freud wrote "Overview of the Transference Neuroses" and sent his draft to Sándor Ferenczi (Grubrich-Simitis, 1987, pp. xv–xvii). In this paper, Freud linked the sequential themes of ontogenetic development with stages in cultural evolution and linked those with specific forms of psychopathology. As Freud explained to Ferenczi, "What are now neuroses were once phases in human conditions" (S. Freud, 1987, p. 79). This previously unpublished paper was discovered in 1983 and published in English in 1987 as *A Phylogenetic Fantasy: Overview of the Transference Neuroses*.

Referencing Fritz Wittels, Freud (1987) imagined the primal human animal living in a rich environment where all needs were easily satisfied. This primordial existence subsequently became memorialized in myths of Paradise. Citing Ferenczi, Freud suggested that the perils and privations of the Ice Age brought realistic anxiety in normal ego development and the transformation of unsatisfied libido into an external danger, as in anxiety hysteria (pp. 13–14). With the hardships of the ice ages there emerged a conflict between self-preservation and the desire to procreate. A lack of food and the need to limit procreation gave rise to perverse satisfactions and a regression of the libido to levels previous to genital primacy. Mankind was still speechless, and the preconscious had not yet been established over the unconscious. The situation corresponded to conversion hysteria (pp. 14–15).

Mankind economized on libido by regressing in sexual activity to earlier phases, activating its intelligence, learning how to investigate the hostile world, inventing new technologies with which to master the surroundings, and creating language. Language was magical and thoughts omnipotent, and the worldview was animistic. Humanity disintegrated into primal hordes each dominated by a strong, wise, and brutal man who was seen as invulnerable, and his possession of the women was not to be challenged. This marked the end of the Ice Age. Obsessional neurosis recapitulates this stage in its overemphasis on thinking, the tendency toward omnipotent thoughts, the inclination toward inviolable laws, and the struggle against brutal impulses that want to replace the love life only to result in compulsion (pp. 15–16).

Freud further speculated on stages of cultural evolution and the analogous psychopathologies: the sons being driven off by the father—dementia praecox (pp. 16–17); the brothers joining with one another in the struggle for survival—paranoia (pp. 17–18) and the brothers killing the primal father, triumphing over his death, and, because of their identification with him, mourning him as the revered father that he was—melancholia-mania (pp. 18–19). Freud asked his readers to be patient with the presentation of unconfirmed ideas if only they might be stimulating and useful in opening up distant vistas: "In sum, we are not at the end, but rather at the beginning, of an understanding of this phylogenetic factor"

(p. 20). He later reevaluated this part of his work ("Overview of the Transference Neuroses") more critically, discarded it, and hoped we would never find it.

Other depth psychologists contributed significantly to the phylogenetic project of psychoanalysis, but they typically made the same psycho-Lamarckian errors that Freud had made. Géza Róheim, however, replaced Freud's psycho-Lamarckian assumptions with an ontogenetic formulation for the repetition of universal psychodynamics, and his contribution is worth reviewing here.

Géza Róheim and the Shift to the Ontogenetic Explanation

Géza Róheim (1891–1953), conducted psycho-anthropological field studies among the aboriginal peoples in central Australia, on Normanby Island in Melanesia, Sipupu Island in Somaliland, and among the Yuma indigenous people of Arizona. He modified Freud's vision of our ancient past by eliminating the psycho-Lamarckian assumption that the murder and cannibalizing of the primal father, repeated on innumerable occasions, became a part of our phylogenetic inheritance. In its place he offered an ontogenetic perspective: people did what they did over and over again not because they remembered it from their phylogenetic past but because it was in the structure of their beings and in response to the childhood traumata of their personal lives. Róheim (1934/1974) explained, "Humanity has emerged, as a human being emerges today, by the growth of defense mechanisms against the infantile situation, by the development of the unconscious" (p. 196).

Géza Róheim (1930)

Róheim observed the widespread belief in demons with "protruding teeth, nose and chin, hairiness, a preference for holes and cannibalistic habits" (p. 11). He attributed this belief to the extended dependency of the human child on its mother and father, which exposes the child to seductions, rejections, sexual excitements, threats, and primal scenes. Consequently, mother is experienced as a cannibalistic demon (pp. 17–18): "We must stress the fact that in boys the primal scene is not the only cause of the belief in 'wild' cannibalistic women with magical and deadly vaginas. Every trauma for which the mother is responsible contains within it the danger of unsolved tasks and disappointed wishes and therefore may help to build the sinister conception of the mother as a 'wild' cannibal with a poisonous, that is, dangerous, genital organ" (p. 14). Thus, we do not remember demons from our phylogenetic past but rather create them anew through the vicissitudes of infancy: "Demons originate in the nursery and reflect the primary ontogenetic situations of love and fear" (p. 14). Sexual seductions of children are very real events and often have terrible consequences, but not every child is overtly sexually seduced. That said, all children, throughout the course of child-rearing, may be cuddled, bathed, diapered, put to bed, soothed, dressed, undressed, cleaned, comforted, frustrated, and disappointed, and quite naturally they develop feelings and fantasies about all of that.

Róheim presents an impressive series of what he calls "primal horde myths" from Australia, South America, and Africa. In each myth there is a big and powerful father, man, woman, giant, or other being who oppressively ruled over the people and may have been a cannibal. The people banded together and killed the being and may have eaten him or her as well (pp. 161–79). Developing the theme further, Róheim rejects the idea that these represent phylogenetic memories and instead offers some stunning observations of nonhuman primates in which males instinctually battle for dominance of a monkey or ape group in a way very reminiscent of Freud's reconstruction of the primal horde (Róheim, 1974, pp. 178-84).

Central to Róheim's (1943) thesis is that the slower maturation of humans in relation to other animals naturally prolongs the dependent infantile situation, and this dependence on the parents has the effect of amplifying the vicissitudes of development. These vicissitudes (traumata) are then defended against, and the defenses become part of the character formation. Thus, we evolved from our simian ancestors and became human partly because of our slowed development: "In a non-retarded species everything depends on inheritance and the importance of ontogenesis increases with the degree of retardation" (p. 19).

Róheim recalled the association Freud made between paranoia and philosophy, between religion (ritual) and the compulsion neurosis, and between hysteria and art. In exploring the earliest professions of mankind, Róheim found defenses for warding off helplessness: the soldier reenacts bodily destruction fantasies or the Oedipus complex; the lawyer lives out the intrapsychic struggle between id, ego, and superego; the scientist is a voyeur looking in on the secrets of Mother Nature; the painter plays with feces; and the fiction writer never renounces his daydreams. Róheim linked paranoia with projection, compulsion neurosis with isolation, and melancholia with introjection. Finally, he demonstrated that the basis of totemism is in isolation, primitive magical medicine in introjection, and the scapegoat ritual in projection. Suddenly we begin to see how the institutions of culture—and indeed culture itself—are defensive structures for managing all the primitive fears of the child and the community (pp. 25, 72–73): "Civilization originates in delayed infancy and its function is security. It is a huge network of more or less successful attempts to protect mankind against the danger of object loss, the colossal efforts made by a baby who is afraid of being left alone in the dark" (p. 100).

Other depth psychologists, such as Carl Gustav Jung, Erich Neumann, Sándor Ferenczi, and Theodore Reik, contributed significantly to the phylogenetic project of psychoanalysis; summaries of their contributions can be found in appendix 1.

In addition, Esther and William Menaker (1965) took a decidedly more cognitive approach and addressed the evolution of ego functions. Before them Charles Darwin explored the evolution of innate behaviors, facial expressions, social behavior, morality, and mental faculties (Darwin, 1871/1981; Darwin, 1872/1873). George John Romanes (1889) compared the cognitive functions of animals and man as well as the ontogenetic development of those functions. William James (1890/1950) offered reflections on the evolution of elementary mental categories such as sensation, feelings of personal activity, emotions, desires, instincts, ideas of worth, aesthetic ideas, and ideas of time and space and number. More recently sociobiologists Charles J. Lumsden and Edward O. Wilson (1983; see also Wilson, 1975) reflected on our hominin evolution and considered the genetic basis of social behavior, sensory capacities, cognitive abilities, sexual orientation, susceptibility to alcoholism, nervous disorders, and much more. Evolutionary psychologists, including Merlin Donald (1991), Steven Mithen (1996), and Leda Cosmides and John Tooby (1997), have made other creative contributions to this discussion of the evolution of mental functions focusing on cognitive development, neurosciences, genetics, natural and sexual selection, while employing the metaphors of mechanics and information processing. As interesting and related as their work is to the phylogenetic project of psychoanalysis, sociobiologists and evolutionary psychologists naturally tend to be more focused on the evolution of cognitive functions, information processing, and consciousness than on some of the typical psychoanalytic concerns such as instincts, defenses, object relations, libido development, derivative material, symbolism, complexes, myth, ritual, and art.

Basic Ideas upon which to Advance the
Phylogenetic Project of Psychoanalysis

Totem and Taboo addressed, in a sense, the question, *What happened in our prehistory for us to develop our modern psychodynamics?* Freud's answer was his phylogenetic fantasy being repeated generation after generation until it became a racial memory recognized today in the Oedipus complex and universal symbolism. But memories of individuals are not genetically passed on from one generation to the next as "racial memories." The Haeckelian biogenetic law also collapsed because not all ontogenetic stages are represented in phylogeny, not all phylogenetic stages are represented in ontogeny, and phylogenetic evolution is not a "cause" of ontogenetic development. The formal similarities between cultural evolution and psychological development are due to the common factor of human psychological structure being present in both fields and a variety of other parallel modes of information transmission other than DNA. Those other modes include language, technology, architecture, myths, rituals, and traditions, among others.

The idea that an original matriarchy was followed by patriarchy fell hard when the literal definitions of these terms met the facts of field anthropology. But if we think of matriarchy not as political rule by women but as a culture form oriented to giving birth, feeding, caring, protecting, and the fabrication of female figurines (goddesses?), and we think of patriarchy as a culture form oriented to human control, the word, the law, and the fabrication of male figurines (gods?), we resuscitate these concepts and their relation to individual development and cultural evolution.

Géza Róheim's contribution to the phylogenetic project of psychoanalysis was to replace the psycho-Lamarckian assumption and biogenetic law with the notion that the recurring symbols, myths, and rituals were based in ontogeny. They were reconstructed anew in every individual and every culture around the common experiences of anatomy, physiology, and the inevitable vicissitudes and traumas of child-rearing by way of the human symbolic function.

When Róheim said we recreate our symbols anew, it begged the question, *If our psychodynamics are created anew in our ontogeny, why is there such uniformity in our psychodynamics?* For this Róheim pointed to something Freud and even Darwin knew very well: primate social behavior. Throughout this work I often refer to "ritualizations" as "social instincts." Ritualizations are genetically based, innate fixed-action patterns that have a communicative function and serve the survival needs of the individual and the species. We don't have an Oedipus complex because of what happened in human prehistory; we have an Oedipus complex because that is what naturally and inevitably emerges between our human symbolic function and the genetically inherited primate alpha male ritualizations. We will get into this more deeply in chapter 4, "Human Evolution: How We Got to Be the Way We Are," but for now it is enough to say that when the human symbolic function symbolizes the primate social instincts, what we end up with are our psychodynamics.

Returning to the basic ideas upon which to advance the phylogenetic project of psychoanalysis, we find that the equivalence of contemporary aboriginal peoples with our ancient ancestors is incorrect when the equivalence is viewed concretely. No two contemporary aboriginal cultures are the same, so why should a contemporary aboriginal community be equated with our ancient ancestors? If we are thinking concretely about those similarities, they could not possibly be the same. But if we examine the similarities of technology, relation to nature, and cultural artifacts, we may indeed be able to make some general comments linking contemporary aboriginal people with all of our ancient ancestors, including the ancient ancestors of contemporary aboriginal people.

The shared symbols and analogical associations between psychological development and cultural evolution are often a function of the interplay between the vicissitudes the individual meets in its developmental challenges and the corresponding vicissitudes the culture meets in its evolving challenges. The individual psyche manages threats to its integrity with a set of unconsciously determined defensive strategies, and a culture defends itself from those things that threaten it with language, customs, politics, religion, myths, rituals, and other manifestations of cultural life. As culture evolves, the defensive strategies of the community are passed on to the children born into it, and the children transform them and hand them back to the culture. In this way, a dialectic emerges between the developmental challenges of the individual and the challenges of an evolving culture.

Freud's phylogenetic project sought to understand what our ancestors did in our ancient prehistoric past, how they ritualized and mythologized those deeds, and how they laid down symbols and complexes that became part of our archaic inheritance. He associated (1) a stage of normal development, (2) a form of psychopathology, (3) a stage in cultural evolution, (4) a myth, and (5) a ritual based on two "points of agreement" they held in common: the erotic desire for the mother and the horror of incest; and the desire to kill the father and the adoration of the father.

If we think of *Totem and Taboo* as a brick house held together with a mortar of faulty assumptions, I would like to keep the bricks—the data and observations—in place and exchange the faulty assumptions with better ones. Those new assumptions include:

1. The assumption that the roots of our psychodynamics are not in the deeds of our prehistoric ancestors but in our social instincts—that is, the social innate fixed-action patterns (ritualizations) of our primate nature.
2. The assumption that our innately determined social instincts are transformed into psychodynamics as a result of being processed through our human symbolic function.
3. The assumption that matriarchy did precede patriarchy if we can define these terms not as political leadership by one gender or the other but as orientation to food, care, protection, and the goddess representations in the case of "matriarchy" and power, the law, the word, and the gods in the case of "patriarchy."
4. The assumption that psychopathology, stages in normal child development, "levels" of cultural sophistication, myths, and rituals are not equivalent to one another but can be associated analogically by virtue of sharing metaphors in common.
5. The assumption that the vicissitudes of early infantile sexuality find parallel challenges in cultural contexts resulting in myths and rituals that defend culture similar to the way defensive strategies defend the individual.
6. The assumption that recurring symbols and complexes are not attributable to an archaic inheritance but are largely due to common human experiences of the body, its functions, and human relations being processed through the human symbolic function. Beyond that, many specific representations need not be created anew, as they can also be passed on through culture in language, acquired knowledge, architecture, technology, myth, ritual, belief, traditions, and so on.

❖ ❖ ❖

In the next chapter, we will reapproach the phylogenetic project of psychoanalysis in order to understand how ancient experience was ritualized and mythologized at the time of the Urban Revolution—the birth of civilization. We will use this example as our point of entry and later as our model for elaborating our inquiry into the relationship of psychological development and cultural evolution. This point of entry will be through the work of John Weir Perry, who studied the hallucinations, delusions, and drawings of a number of patients undergoing brief psychotic disorders. He recognized ten recurring images in the content of their psychotic material and analogically associated them with a particular myth, ritual, and stage in cultural evolution. While Perry's formulation is embedded in Jung's archetypal theory, the material itself is clinical and cultural in nature and easily lends itself to a Freudian reformulation.

CHAPTER 2

Brief Psychotic Disorder and the Myth of Sacral Kingship

> Fools, visionaries, sufferers from delusions, neurotics and lunatics have played great roles at all times in the history of mankind and not merely when the accident of birth had bequeathed them sovereignty. Usually they have wreaked havoc; but not always. Such persons have exercised far-reaching influence upon their own and later times, they have given impetus to important cultural movements and have made great discoveries.
>
> –Sigmund Freud, *Introduction* to *Thomas Woodrow Wilson: A Psychological Study*

In *Totem and Taboo* (1913/1955h), Freud called attention to the recurring images and themes of the phallic stage and Oedipus complex in child development, obsessional neurosis, the fraternal clan of ancient prehistory, totemism, and the totemic sacrificial feast. But he purposely left these analogous points of agreement and their relation to one another somewhat imprecise, explaining, "The lack of precision in what I have written in the text above, its abbreviation of the time factor and its compression of the whole subject matter, may be attributed to the reserve necessitated by the nature of the topic. It would be as foolish to aim at exactitude in such questions as it would be unfair to insist on certainty" (*SE* 13, pp. 142-43).

"Exactitude" and "certainty" are hard to come by when speculating about our prehistoric past. But in the mid-1970s there emerged a clue of considerable value in advancing the phylogenetic project of psychoanalysis. The clue was embedded in John Weir Perry's Jungian formulation of the brief psychotic disorder. Perry was not directly engaged in the phylogenetic project of psychoanalysis; he was interested in his Jungian formulation of "schizophrenia," the treatment considerations implied, and the insights his formulation had for understanding the Urban Revolution, visionaries, visionary experience, and visionary movements. The clue that helps us take a step forward was his emphasis on myth and ritual analogues. Perry explicitly denied a platonic, a priori definition of archetypes and also denied psycho-Lamarckian and biogenetic assumptions, but he tended to employ these old assumptions, even if only as a poetic way of talking about what he observed.

In this chapter, we examine Perry's formulation of the brief psychotic disorder with attention to the recurring images and themes in the delusions and hallucinations of his patients. We will look at the curious similarity that those recurring images and themes have to those found in the myths of sacral kingship and the ancient New Year festivals that emerged in cultures around the globe as they transitioned from the preliterate High Neolithic into the literate Urban Revolution. Where Freud had been necessarily imprecise in his prehistoric reconstruction, Perry offered us a precise, one-to-one association between a form of psychopathology, a stage in cultural evolution, a myth, and a ritual, all based on the images and themes they hold in common. Perry's method of linking these disparate phenomena was not a new strategy. Freud had already done something very similar in *Totem and Taboo*. But unlike Freud, who speculated on what may or may not have happened in prehistory, Perry drew on written historical data—the earliest texts describing the lives, myths, and rituals of people at the beginning of the Urban Revolution.

John Weir Perry (1982)

John Weir Perry (1914–1998) was the son of an Anglican bishop. He studied history and literature at Harvard, but his deeper interests were in psychology and religion. In 1936 Carl Gustav Jung gave a tercentenary address at Harvard University. During his visit he stayed at the home of Bishop Perry and provided John, 22 years old at the time, with a private tutorial in Jungian psychology (Perry, 1963, p. 214). Perry graduated from Harvard with a degree in history and went on to Harvard Medical School. During the Second World War he served as a war surgeon in the Friends Ambulance Unit in the Chinese interior. From 1947 to 1949 he studied in the first class of the newly formed C. G. Jung Institute in Zurich, where he was analyzed by Toni Wolff and C. A. Meier and was supervised by Jung himself. In 1950 Perry moved to the San Francisco Bay Area, where he began a private practice and worked in a hospital with psychotic patients (Benveniste, 1999).

Based on this work, Perry began piecing together a Jungian formulation of schizophrenia. In his first book, *The Self in Psychotic Process: Its Symbolization in Schizophrenia* (1953/1987b), Perry presented a detailed case study of a hospitalized woman undergoing a schizophrenic episode. He described the patient's family background, the circumstances leading to her hospitalization, the use of medications, her relations to others, the nature of her transference to Perry, his role in the therapy, the patient's changing mental status as the therapy progressed, her delusional world, her drawings, and the evolving process of the therapy. Perry described psychosis as a process of self-healing involving fantasy themes of death and rebirth. Based on the content of the patient's fantasy life, he concluded that the psychotic process is aimed at the reorganization of the "Self," or what he called the "center." With this reorganization comes the integration of a new personality and with it a new worldview, which commonly appears as a fourfold world, quadrated circle, or mandala in the hallucinations, delusions, and drawings of schizophrenic patients.

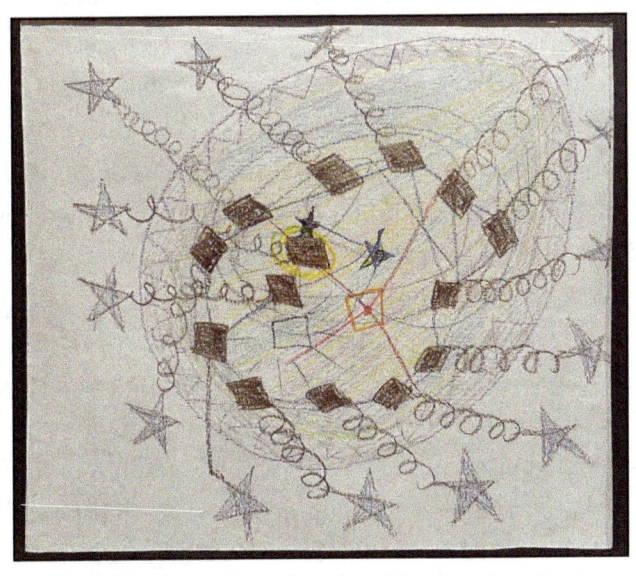

Mandala drawn by a chronic schizophrenic patient

Throughout the 1950s, Perry continued to work with psychotic patients and found not only the recurring themes of death and rebirth but also a recurring constellation of eight other images and themes in the hallucinations, delusions, fantasies, and drawings of almost all of his psychotic patients. Curiously enough he then recognized the same ten images and themes in the mythology of sacral kingship and its associated ritual of the ancient New Year festivals, which coincide with the emergence of the god-kings and king-gods of the Urban Revolution.

In *Lord of the Four Quarters: Myths of the Royal Father* (1966), Perry traced the changing image of the father figure as it evolved in the mythologies of cultures transitioning from prehistoric High Neolithic economies and lifestyles into the economies and lifestyles that were characteristic of the historic Urban Revolution—the beginning of civilization. In one culture after another, he traced the evolving figure of the father from the divine ancestral chthonic father below to the spiritual sky father above, with the sun gods as the embodiments of the right order and the storm gods as the violent upholders of that order. The shift in focus from the mother goddesses of the High Neolithic to the king-gods of the Urban Revolution brought with it a new ethical order established by the king-god and maintained on the earthly plane by his representative, the god-king.

Perry traced the fate of the father figure in 16 ancient cultures. He explained that myth serves as a set of guidelines concerned primarily with governance and ethical order in times of uncertainty, such as those that prevail in the midst of cultural change. The myths of sacral kingship, Perry asserted, were born of the personal visions of extraordinary individuals such as prophets, visionaries, and culture reformers. He noted that these visions bear an uncanny resemblance to the hallucinations and delusions of individuals undergoing brief psychotic disorders.

In *The Far Side of Madness* (1974), Perry brought together his clinical and cultural interests into a formulation of the myth and ritual analogues to the schizophrenic episode. When he started his work, he believed his most successful cases were schizophrenic patients. In retrospect he discovered that although his observations of symbolic content often applied to schizophrenics, his successful treatments were with those who were later diagnosed as having brief reactive psychoses, or what we refer to today as "brief psychotic disorders" (*DSM-5*) (John Weir Perry, personal communication, February 22, 1987). Perry described the brief psychotic disorder as a "visionary state" in which a "renewal process" is under way to bring about the death of an old, emotionally constricted worldview and to facilitate the emergence or rebirth of a new, more humanly related worldview. It is important to recognize that while his clinical work dealt with the ontogenetic components of each patient, Perry's formulation brought the phylogenetic components into high relief. And those phylogenetic components or analogues were the myth of sacral kingship and its associated ritual: the ancient New Year festival. While Perry recognized the mythic pattern of sacral kingship in 16 different cultures, it is important to remember that there were differences from one culture to the next, and not all demonstrated the full set of images and themes. In some cultures the king didn't even have a sacred character, but the pattern still remains and is compelling.

The myth of sacral kingship is like a typical hero myth in that the hero battles a monster or triumphs over great odds and in victory becomes a culture hero. But in the specific case of the myth of sacral kingship, the hero's victory means ultimately becoming a god-king with a special relationship to the king-god. Furthermore, the hero's cultural reformation facilitates a transition from the "matriarchal" society of the High Neolithic to the "patriarchal" society at the beginning of the Urban Revolution. Perry used the term "matriarchal" to describe the earlier prehistoric cultures organized around the worship of the goddess and "patriarchal" to describe the later historic cultures organized around the worship of the male gods.

Perry (1974) described the psychotic experience in the following way:

> A negative self-image at the ego level presents itself, along with a compensatory overblown self-image at the fantasy level, in mythological and delusional form (negative: clown, ghost, witch, puny outsider; positive: hero, saint, one chosen for leadership).
>
> There are feelings of participating in some form of drama or ritual performance (playing parts on radio, television, or stage; dancing, chanting, mimetic or ceremonial motions). (pp. 29-30)

He then described the images and themes found in common with the myth of sacral kingship, the ancient New Year festivals, and the delusions and hallucinations of psychotic patients. They are as follows:

A. Center: A location is established at a world center or cosmic axis (point where sky world, regular world, and underworld meet; between opposing halves of the world; center of attention).

B. Death: Themes of dismemberment or sacrifice are scattered throughout and make themselves evident in drawings (crucifixion, pounding or chopping up, tortures, limbs or bones rearranged, poisoning). A predominant delusional statement is that of having died and of being in an afterlife state (people look like living dead; in hell or heaven; or in prison as equivalent to death).

C. Return to Beginnings: A regression is expressed that takes the person back to the beginnings of time and the creation of the cosmos (Garden of Eden, waters of the abyss, early steps of evolution, primitive tribal society, creation of planets). There is a parallel regression, of course, to emotions, behavior, and associations of infancy (surrounded by parent figures; crawling, suckling; needs for touch and texture; oral needs).

D. Cosmic Conflict: There arises a world conflict of cosmic import between forces of good and evil, or light and darkness, or order and chaos (surprisingly often expressed nowadays as democracy and communism; Armageddon, or the triumph of the Antichrist; destruction or end of the world, or the Last Judgment; intrigues, plots, spying, poisoning—all to gain world supremacy).

E. Threat of Opposite: There is feeling of a threat from the opposite sex, a fear of being overcome by it, or turned into it (drugs to turn one into the opposite; identifications with figures of the other sex; supremacy of the other sex; moves to eradicate the other sex).

F. Apotheosis: The person experiences an apotheosis as royalty or divinity (as a king or queen, deity or saint, hero or heroine, messiah).

G. Sacred Marriage: The person enters upon a sacred marriage of ritual or mythological character (royal marriage, perhaps incestuous; marriage with God or Goddess; as a Virgin Mother, who conceives by the spirit).

H. New Birth: A new birth takes place or is expected of a superhuman child or of oneself (ideas of rebirth; Divine Child, Infant Savior, Prince, or Reconciler of the division of the world).

I. New Society: A new order of society is envisioned, of an ideal or sacred quality (a New Jerusalem, Last Paradise, Utopia, World Peace; a New Age, a New Heaven and New Earth).

J. Quadrated World: A fourfold structure of the world or cosmos is established, usually in the form of a quadrated circle (four continents or quarters; four political factions, governments, or nations; four races or religions; four persons of the godhead; four elements or states of being).

(pp. 29-30)

Perry saw the emergence of these images and themes as a spontaneous psychological attempt at renewal directed by the Self, or psychic center, drawing on the archetypes (or "affect-images" as Perry called them) of the collective unconscious to address the personal conflicts, which routinely included the lack of eros, or relatedness, in the life of the patient. He developed a treatment strategy that regarded this particular psychopathological process as one that required receptivity, therapeutic support, and a permissive stance in relation to much of the perceived madness. Rather than dismissing his patients' delusions, hallucinations, and fantasy preoccupations as "word salad," or nonsense, Perry looked into the personal meaningfulness of the patients' psychotic material. He regarded hallucinations and delusions as "visions" worthy of being listened to, honored, and interpreted within their personal contexts.

Several residential treatment homes were established along the lines of Perry's clinical recommendations. They allowed patients to go through their psychotic processes safe from psychiatric control and interference. Patients were provided with a warm, supportive, and encouraging staff and a homelike setting to work through their conflicts. Perry's approach was successful. He found that patients in these environments reconstituted more quickly and were often able to do so without medications and without the damning effects of institutionalization.

Clinically, Perry paid attention to his patients' narratives and their ontogenetic symbolic significance. He saw the underlying phylogenetic structure cloaked in ontogenetic concerns. Perry abstracted that phylogenetic structure from the common imagery described by his many psychotic patients, and he further recognized it in the myth of sacral kingship and its associated ritual of the ancient New Year festival. He also found it in the visions of prophets, culture reformers, and visionaries throughout history whenever the cultures they resided in became stale and lifeless, power-ridden, and devoid of relatedness. These culture reformers offered their visions as a way to facilitate cultural renewal through their leadership of a counterculture bringing love as their message.

The following are two of Perry's case vignettes. The details are unique to each patient, but the recurring images and themes will be recognizable to anyone familiar with psychotic patients.

Case One

The patient was a 23-year-old single Irish Catholic woman in an acute schizophrenic episode: "On admission [to the hospital] she presented the characteristic picture of a hyperactive young catatonic, carrying on a stream of 'bizarre' and disconnected talk, posturing, dancing, and pausing at intervals to listen to voices" (Perry, 1976, p. 56). Perry provided all the personal data regarding her family, her history, and her psychological structure, but for our purposes I will focus on the "visionary" material—the hallucinations and delusions. To this end, I quote Perry at length:

She felt that there was a cosmic struggle. The Devil was hatching a plot to destroy the world by an explosion of radioactive substances with which he was experimenting. Opposing him was Christ, who was struggling against him to save the world. Each had followers, thus dividing the world into two camps: the communists, in league with the Devil, aimed at bringing about the final disintegration of everything, and the democracies, under the banner of Christ, aimed at keeping the world intact. She said she also felt these camps to be two sides of her own nature, masculine and feminine sides in conflict. In another polarity, both the Devil and God were constantly speaking with conflicting voices in her ear. God's voice was always hilariously funny cracking jokes and laughing. The Pope was possessed by the Devil, just as she was, and was in hell, as she was. The Pope's hat (the threefold tiara) was torn into little triangular bits of paper that were scattered about the earth, and at the same time the Holy Trinity was separated on earth in the same way, so work had to be done to reunite the Pope's hat and thus the Trinity.

Then she felt herself to be going through a whole drama of her own. She was in hell, which was a crazy place or a jail; it was a single room like those in the hospital. Around her were various friends, wearing huge masks of animals' heads. She had a severe task to perform as a test: to crawl through a skeleton from bottom to top without breaking it, and come out of the mouth. This she achieved successfully. The Devil was in her bones, and she had to turn these around one by one, reversing all but the head and neck back to front. The hands, meanwhile, became claws. At the same time, another trial she had to perform was to repeat creation and evolution again. She was under the sea for a long time, in the presence of primordial monsters. Then she came on land and saw the age of reptiles. Finally she lived among primitives and took part in their rituals and dances and chants. Also, she had to return to her own beginning—that is, her own birth—and repeat her childhood and growth to her present age; in this repetition of her life everything had to be done precisely and without error, otherwise she had to go back to the beginning and start over each time. She only reached the age of sixteen in this performance.

Now the central drama running through all of this conflict and resolving it concerned the birth of a divine child. She felt herself to be in the middle between the Devil's and Christ's sides in the struggle to destroy or save the world. She was to give birth to a baby as an outcome of having intercourse with God every night, God appearing either in the form of her father or the man of her infatuation. The baby was to be a savior child, like Christ, but in a new form, with a special function in saving the world from the conflict described. This birth made of her a kind of Virgin Mother. Now, it was to the interests of the communists to steal this child and do away with it, and there was a critical question of how to rescue it. The solution lay in a certain patient on the ward, a motherly sort of a woman who reminded her of a neighbor who had been as warm to her as her own mother had been cold. This woman appeared in the drama as Queen of the Sea, who had magical ways of protecting the life of the child and thus saved it from destruction.

Along the way through this fantasy drama occurred a few impressive visions that the patient found deeply stirring. One was of the world as a mountain, with a plane circling around it going to four planets, which were called God, Mercury, Mars and Venus. On another occasion she and a lover stood each on a globe, with another couple looking on from two other globes. The spheres were planets, and her lover and she were King and Queen of the Universe, and were also twin brother and sister or Prince and Princess. They adopted foster parents, the kindly mother who lived near her as a child, and that mother's husband. Finally, and most fraught with meaning, was the vision of a pair of gold rings flanking a vertical gold staff, which she understood as a symbol of marriage; to the right was the standing figure of Christ. The virgin appeared to her to give her a message of import to the world, that the women of the world were not keeping their marriage vows and the sacrament of marriage was not being respected; this message was given to her to correct this evil. (pp. 63-65)

In this example, we see cosmic conflict, death, rebirth, sacred marriage, and so on. The content is explicitly Christian, but that is only because the woman's psyche used Christian imagery, with which she was familiar, to meet the psychological crisis in which she found herself. Others undergoing psychotic episodes employ other religious, mystical, philosophical, or political themes to express their very personal concerns. But in one way or another the themes generally come back to the world, society, the universe, and universal concerns, because in the psychotic episode we are dealing with a psychological collapse, and as the psyche collapses, so does the worldview. And to the extent that the worldview is projected into the world, a psychic collapse is experienced as the end of the world. Conversely, the recompensation of the psyche is also projected and experienced as the recreation of the world.

Case Two
The next case is of a 19-year-old male who entered the hospital in a state of confusion and was behaving in a bizarre fashion. Again, I quote Perry (1974):

I held interviews three times a week with him in which I listened attentively to the free flow of his symbolic content. Most predominant in his ideation were his inflated identifications with superlative figures of three main types—governmental, religious and heroic; in each role he single-handedly conducted an attack on enemies appropriate to the same three groups: that is political systems, forces of evil, and monsters of various sorts. The three overlapped of course.

In the governmental idiom, he was an ace airman ("ace-high"), and a second George Washington leading the defense of the country against the Russian communists, who were trying to capture the world. Russia was on hell's side and under Satan's rule, and his own death was to be a sacrifice for his people. At other times he thought he would be made ruler of the Russians, a nation of darkness and slavery. As Prince Valiant, king of the country, he sent 300 youths, members of his club, to their sacrificial deaths in the Korean War. Later in the process, the imagery shifted to a plot by the Germans to conquer the world and raise him up as universal emperor; the Germans were to be heroic superscientists and masters of the heavenly world through astronomy; they would shoot him in a rocket to the moon, where only he could survive.

The religious imagery described the patient as another Christ, leading the fight against the Devil; like Christ, he was to be crucified and rise again. The Garden of Eden figured prominently: It was once occupied by Father, Son, and Holy Ghost, but then taken over by the Devil. Interwoven with this were stories of four kings of the four directions, and a major world conflict between the king of the North and the king of the South.

As a mythical hero the patient found himself performing great wonders. As King Richard the Lion-hearted, he killed a tiger and strangled a serpent just after he was born. As a Japanese-born hero he took on the form of a serpent and acquired a "vicious power to strike back"; he killed a tarantula who was a Japanese mother dressed for battle, and he overcame several monsters. (pp. 124–25)

These delusional preoccupations are common enough among psychotic patients, but we usually use our analogical reasoning to interpret only the personal meaning embedded in the narrative, which is where the treatment takes place. Perry saw in the "visions" of his psychotic patients not only a personal ontogenetic narrative but also a parallel phylogenetic narrative. Jung (1953/1987), in his foreword to Perry's *The Self in Psychotic Process*, wrote, "The psyche, like the body, is an extremely historical structure" (p. vi).

In *Lord of the Four Quarters* and again in *Roots of Renewal in Myth and Madness* (1976), Perry summarized the myths and rituals of kingship at the time of the Urban Revolution—that is, the beginnings of civilization—in 16 different cultures. "Civilization" in this context is defined by the political structure of kingship, the invention of the calendar and writing, large-scale armies and war, city living, and the emergence of the gods associated with the Urban Revolution over the goddesses of the High Neolithic period. Perry described the myths of sacral kingship and the New Year festivals in ancient Egypt, the Shilluk, Mesopotamia, Canaan, Israel, India, Iran, the Hittites, Mycenae, Athens, early Rome, Etruria, classical Rome, the Norse Lands, the Toltecs, the Aztecs, and China.

The following are four examples of the New Year ritual dramas of renewal from ancient Egypt, ancient China, the Toltecs of ancient Mexico, and the Israelites.

Kingship in Ancient Egypt

There were several different ancient Egyptian New Year festivals—one at the start of each of three seasons and each involving enthronement. They were the sacred marriage of Edfu, the Summer Festival of Minh, and the Sed Festival of the king's renewal. It is believed that the latter was the main enthronement and New Year ritual of the earliest dynasties 5,000 years ago. The time was the beginning of spring, coinciding with the subsiding of the Nile floods. The exact order of the proceedings of the enthronement festival can be reconstructed only from unclear accounts:

1. Establishing a world center as the locus

The place was the city of Memphis, the center of the "union of the two lands"—that is, of Upper and Lower Egypt—and thus of the ordered world. The throne was placed on a raised podium that represented the Primeval Hill, the first land to appear at the creation, and the center of the world, charged with vital power that radiated out into the whole kingdom. On the eve of the ceremony, the king made a circumambulation around the white walls of the city.

2. Undergoing death

In the last few days of the Season of Inundation occurred the ceremony of the Raising of the Djed Pillar, a column of bound stalks resembling a tree trunk, and there was enacted the burial, in the column, of the Dead King Osiris, drowned by his brother Seth in the flood of the Nile. The theme of death prevails at this turning of the year, when the powers of chaos gain the upper hand and when there is a temporary disruption of the union of the two lands and of the normal order of the realm. The dead king, father of the living king, becomes Osiris through a ritual purification and transfiguration and rebirth into a new life in the Beyond as Lord of the Kingdom of the Dead, and his son is enthroned as the sky god, Horus, Lord of the Kingdom of the Living. The vital force that gives life to the kingdom is transmitted from the ancestral realm of the dead, through Osiris in his embrace of his son, the living king, and thus into the realm. After the funerary rites and on the first day of spring, the king is crowned as the living embodiment of Horus.

3. Return to the beginnings of time and the creation
The ritual time is the moment of the creation. As the king stands high over the land on his dais, he is personifying the first divine king and creator, Atum, standing on the Primeval Hill as it arose from the waters of Chaos (represented as the Goddess Nun). These waters were the source of the life-giving subsoil waters of the abyss and of death and of the Nile flood, while the hill was the place of the creation, and of rebirth and resurrection. The king was put through baptismal lustrations and purifications in these waters and dressed in brilliant vestments representing the first sunrise and first shining forth of the light over the newly risen land.

4. Cosmic conflict as a clash of opposites
As the myth tells of Horus avenging the death of his father Osiris by doing battle with his uncle, Seth, the ritual represents the sacred combat as a mock fight between the men of two cities of the Delta, designating the forces of death as against those of the living. Seth personifies the King's Enemy, in the form of a boar, as the pretender to the throne against the legitimate heir.

5. Threat of the reversal of opposites
For a while death and the enemy hold the upper hand, and there is a period of chaos in which there is a suspension of the normal order of the realm (it is not clear how this phase was dramatized).

6. Apotheosis as king or messianic hero
The coronation and investiture of the king as the Living Horus extols him as victor, as one with the first king-god, Atum, and as partaking of the nature of the sun god, Re, ruling over the entire ordered world. There takes place first a procession of the gods in the form of their standards and emblems, and then a Dedication of the Land, in which the king performs a dance circumambulating a field that represents the realm, holding in his hand the will that assures his legitimate claim to the throne of Horus.

Egyptian Pyramids and Sphynx.

Ramses II from the 19th dynasty. Egyptian pharaoh
1279–1213 BCE. Luxor, Egypt

7. Sacred marriage as a union of opposites
The occurrence of a sacred marriage is not certain in this particular ceremony, but at the other New Year festivals there are well-documented marital rites. Notably, at Edfu there was a summer harvest festival, at which the effigy of Horus was brought to the temple of his mother and consort, Hathor, to cohabit with her for two weeks; a sacred combat and funerary rites for the ancestors were also performed.

8. New birth as a reconciliation of opposites
The motif of rebirth and resurrection runs through the entire series of rituals as a dominant theme; it primarily concerns the transfiguration of the dead king, Osiris. On the one hand the Goddess of the Night Sky, Nut, is represented as his mother, through whom he is reborn, and she is ritually identified with the sarcophagus or coffin as the body of the mother. On the other hand the Djed Pillar is also a representation of the mother of Osiris as Hathor, as the tree pregnant with the king Osiris, surrounded by the wings of Nut.

9. New society of the prophetic vision
The coronation rite signals the creation of a new epoch, after the dangers of the interruption by death and chaos, a new time of harmony between society and nature, yet partaking of the qualities of the original time of creation. In his achievements the king only makes manifest what has been potentially present in the plan of creation. The world order, as established at the beginning of time, remains the normative order, whose champion is the king; he maintains justice as the representative of Re, the sun god.

10. Quadrated world forms
The representation of the quadrated world recurs throughout the rites. In his baptismal purification rites at the start, the king is given water by the four gods of the cardinal directions, conveying their life and power to him. At the enthronement he is seated four times on four thrones, in the cardinal directions, conveying their life and power to him, and he is proclaimed to each of the quarters of the world as an arrow is shot by him into each one.

(Perry, 1976, pp. 82-85)

The Chiao: A Taoist Ritual in Ancient China

In ancient China there is the king-god and his son, the god-king. The cosmic conflict is against the Barbarians or between the king and the demon of chaos. The religious life is oriented around a cosmic center and the four cardinal directions. Renewal came in the form of changes from one dynasty to the next (Perry, 1966, pp. 204-218). In the *chiao*, a Taoist ritual derived from the late Han Dynasty (207 BCE–220 ACE), the cosmos was renewed and cleansed of all impurities brought on by the dark forces over the intervening years since the last chiao. The priest wields a magical sword to fight the malevolent forces and lock them out. He also summons the benevolent spirit armies to assist in this cosmic combat. Dressed as a royal figure, the priest establishes a cosmic center, where he performs a dance. He imagines a mandala, or four-quartered image, of the universe and draws into himself the cosmic agencies in the form of opposite pairs, which marry and then give birth to what is called the "red infant." Through a return to the beginnings, the world's original condition is recreated and thereby renews the cosmos (Perry, 1987a, p. 94).

"This is me." A mandala spontaneously drawn by a six-year-old boy. Mandalas are commonly drawn by children in the pre-pictorial phase of drawing development (See Rhoda Kellogg, 1970) and later in the religious art of cultures around the world.

A Tibetan Buddhist mandala upon which monks would meditate.

Quetzalcoatl among the Toltecs

Among the Toltecs there was an ancestral founding king named Quetzalcoatl, with whom the priest-king, or sacral king, identified. In their cosmology, they recall the Flowering War between the opposites of fire and water and another conflict between the heavenly and earthly forces. Quetzalcoatl dies and is reborn. Their religious life was oriented to the four cardinal directions (Perry, 1966, pp. 194-99).

The Festival of Sukkoth in Ancient Israel

Israel's New Year festival was grafted onto an autumnal agricultural rite of the land, the Feast of Ingathering (Perry, 1976, p. 88). This ritual was Sukkoth, the ritual of the tabernacles. It took place in a royal temple seen as Yahweh's Holy Mount of Zion. The mount itself was seen as an *axis mundi,* or world axis, whose top touches the sky and whose base touches the waters of the underworld abyss. In the ritual drama, the king is humiliated by his enemies, is forsaken by his father, and sinks into the abyss—the waters of death. Time becomes mythical time, and in the ritual there is a return back to the time of creation and Yahweh's heroic battle with the waters of chaos. The king becomes the primordial man, Adam, the first ancestor. The king enters into a sacred combat and cosmic conflict with Yahweh's enemies: darkness, chaos, death, and the waters of the abyss, as embodied by threatening foreigners. The king succumbs temporarily. Death gets the upper hand. The king is humiliated. Then Yahweh comes and lifts the king from the abyss. Yahweh is enthroned, and the king is anointed priest forever and granted universal rule over all kings. A sacred marriage may have been performed. The king is reborn and transformed. He is promised a reign of righteousness, justice, and peace. The world mountain with four rivers moving outward to the far reaches of the circle of the world form a great mandala (pp. 88-91).

John Weir Perry, Sigmund Freud, and the Phylogenetic Project

We now examine Freud's discussion of psychosis in the Schreber case to see how it compares to Perry's formulation of the ten recurring images and themes in the psychotic material and sacral kingship. Freud's case can be found in *Psychoanalytic Notes on an Autobiographical Account of a Case of Paranoia (Dementia Paranoides)* (1911/1958a). Daniel Paul Schreber (1842-1911) was a successful judge and the *Senatspräsident* of the High Court of Saxony when in 1893 he began suffering sleeplessness, hypochondriasis, depression, paranoia, and, eventually, debilitating psychotic episodes, for which he was hospitalized involuntarily for years at a time. During his extended hospitalization (1893-1902), Schreber wrote his memoirs, together with an appeal for his release from involuntary hospitalization. Freud used the memoirs as a way to elaborate his ideas about the relation of paranoia to homosexuality. For our purposes here, it is enough to say that in Schreber's memoirs Freud was in the position to see many of the same images and themes that Perry recognized in his patients' psychotic material. Schreber was not suffering a brief psychotic disorder or even schizophrenia. Zvi Lothane (1992) has demonstrated that while Schreber was clearly psychotic and paranoid, it was depression that dominated the diagnostic picture. Nonetheless, using Perry's categories we are able to recognize the following images and themes in Schreber's delusions and hallucinations:

1. Center: Schreber believed that his ego was attracting the rays of God to himself (S. Freud, 1911/1958a, SE 12, p. 78). His auditory hallucinations named the hospital he was in "The Devil's Castle" (Lothane, 1992, p. 59).

2. Death: Schreber believed he was dying, dead, and decomposing (S. Freud, 1911/1958a, SE 12, p. 13). He also had delusions of the end of the world (p. 70). He felt his soul had been murdered by the psychiatrist in charge (p. 14).
3. Return to Beginnings: Schreber had a mission to restore the world and return it to its lost state of bliss (p. 16).
4. Cosmic Conflict: There was a struggle between Schreber and God (p. 28) and between the upper God and the lower God (p. 24).
5. Threat of the Opposite Sex: Schreber felt he was being transformed into a woman who would be impregnated by God. It was a threat that he embraced and to which he happily submitted (pp. 16-17).
6. Apotheosis: Schreber believed he was in direct communication with God (p. 14) and became the redeemer of the world (p. 18), who would save the world from misery and destruction. He identified himself with Jesus Christ (p. 28).
7. Sacred Marriage: Schreber felt that he was God's wife (p. 32).
8. New Birth: Schreber believed that by becoming a woman and being impregnated by God he would give birth to a new race of men (p. 17).
9. New Society: Schreber believed he would give birth to a new race of men, who would regain a state of bliss in the world (p. 17).
10. Quadrated World: Schreber, so far as I know, made no reference to the renovated world being quadrated.

Perry found something constructive and progressive in his patients' hallucinations and delusions, and Freud did too. Freud (1911/1958a) wrote, "And the paranoiac builds it [his shattered world] again, not more splendid, it is true, but at least so that he can once more live in it. He builds it up by the work of his delusions. The delusional formation, which we take to be the pathological product, is in reality an attempt at recovery, a process of reconstruction" (SE 12, p. 71). Perry would agree but would also assert that the person's rebuilt world could, in some circumstances, be "more splendid" than before.

While Perry emphasized the creative potential of the psychotic experience, Freud (1911/1958a) focused on the defensive function of the delusions. Freud saw Schreber's megalomania as a compensation for his dejected ego, and his fear of emasculation was delusional and defensively transformed into a desire to be a woman and impregnated by God (SE 12, p. 48).

Schreber developed ideas about the imminence of a great catastrophe—caused by glaciation following the withdrawal of the sun, by earthquake, or by the magic arts of his psychiatrist, Dr. Paul Flechsig, whom he said brought fear and terror among men, destroyed the foundations of religion, and brought nervous disorders and immorality to the world. Freud (1911/1958a) observed, "A world-catastrophe of this kind is not infrequent during the agitated stage in other cases of paranoia" (SE 12, p. 69). He explained that these were thoughts associated with the withdrawal of libido from the world. In Freud's interpretation, "The end of the world is the projection of this internal catastrophe; his subjective world has come to an end since his withdrawal of his love from it" (p. 70).

Schreber had much to say about the sun, which he identified with God. Freud wrote that the sun is a symbol of the father, its counterpart is Mother Earth, and the fantasies of neurotics frequently confirm these assertions. He then added, "I can make no more than the barest allusions to the relation of all this to cosmic myths" (SE 12, p. 54). Freud confirmed Jung's assertion that the mythopoeic (myth-making) forces of the ancient past are alive today and seen in the psychical productions of neurotics: "'In dreams and in neuroses,' so our thesis has run, 'we come once more upon the *child* and the peculiarities which characterize his modes of thought and his emotional life.' 'And we come upon the *savage* too,' we may now add, 'upon the *primitive* man, as he stands revealed to us in the light of the researches of archeology and of ethnology'" (p. 82; Freud's italics).

Another early psychoanalytic study of schizophrenic thought process was reported by Alfred Storch (1888-1962) in *The Primitive Archaic Forms of Inner Experiences and Thought in Schizophrenia* (1924). Storch recognized analogies between the magical world of aboriginal indigenous people and the delusional world of the schizophrenic, especially with regard to magical change of sex, mystic union, cosmic identification, and themes of death and rebirth. He asserted, "In many tribes the boy, before his initiation, has the same value as a woman and he must prove he is a man by performing certain tests. In some African tribes the boy who has just been circumcised is called 'No longer a girl'" (p. 67). Among schizophrenics, Storch observed, men often seem to feel they are becoming like children again, or they are being feminized or turned into women.

Storch cited biblical, Babylonian, and Buddhist references to the relationship between man and the universe and the shared identity between man and the universe:

> At a remotely earlier level man felt himself to be the immediate center of the universe; he did not discriminate between himself and the all; it was only through repeated experiences of obstacles and resistances that he became conscious of his limitations.... Mysticism also affords a means to many even today of reestablishing the lost identification with the universe. In schizophrenics, on the other hand, there is a direct demolition of the limits of the self and therewith a cosmic extension which resembles the original identification with the cosmos. (pp. 78-79)

Storch cited examples of death and rebirth as a theme common to initiation rites around the world. In New Guinea, for example, the initiate is led into a hut, where he is swallowed by a monster that then gives birth to him again. Primitive and ancient mysteries find parallels in schizophrenic thought, where one frequently encounters rebirth after a primal battle as well as "the idea of passing through the region of death, of regeneration and finally of apotheosis" (p. 90).

Storch observed that puberty is what often brings about the first schizophrenic episode. He said the schizophrenic youth is caught between his enthusiastic impulses to enter the world and his moody, gloomy, autistic reserve. The pressure rises and soon reason gives way: "From the substrata archaic elements swell up, an intoxicating Dionysiac cosmic consciousness, a grandiose world phantasy; the person feels himself the center of the universe; he is the master of wonderful magic power; he expands into the cosmic whole; becomes Mythos; he wars with the demons of his fate; in the mystical ecstasy of his introversion he attains to a knowledge of the infinite; he is God" (p. 106).

Silvano Arieti's (1914–1981) attention to the cognitive thought processes in schizophrenia led him into questions of the phylogenetic aspects of cognitive development, including the cognitive processes of aboriginal peoples and those who have had religious experiences. In addition to addressing the role of projection and rationalization in schizophrenic thought processes, Arieti called special attention to "paleologic thought" and its distinction from Aristotelian thought. Paleologic thought was referred to by Eilhard von Domarus as "paralogical thought" and by Lucien Lévy-Bruhl as "prelogical thought" (Arieti, 1974, p. 229). To a great extent, paleologic thought is based on the principle, first presented by von Domarus, that "whereas the normal person accepts identity only upon the basis of identical subjects, the paleogician accepts identity based on identical predicates" (p. 230). Arieti defined "predicates" as "qualities." Paleologic thought allows the identity of one thing to become the identity of another on the basis of a single common attribute; for example, *I suffer + Christ suffers = I am Christ*.

In the following example the phoneme "ton" became a linking predicate. A man I once knew, who was profoundly psychotic, became interested, in a sense, in the word/phoneme "ton." It was for him a word of substance, a weighty word, a word that implied a heavy reality. He'd walk through the house and say in a loud voice, "Thirty-six tons of rock" and then keep walking through. He would marvel at the sign near a local bridge that said, "No trucks over ten tons." Or he would strike up a kind of conversation and reflect on how marvelous it was that *Washington, Hamilton, simpleton, plankton*, and other such words had "ton" in them. He was an extremely heavy smoker, maybe five packs a day. One evening he explained to me that he smoked Tareytons for the "tons," smoked Carltons for "tons" of Carl Jung, and smoked Winstons because he believed that he who smokes Winstons "wins tons." This sort of paleologic thinking plays a significant role in mythological, religious, and mystical thought, as well.

Children between 1 ½ and 3 ½ have a tendency to think paleologically, though not at all times. Similarly, we find paleologic thought common to dream thought and to the communal thinking and beliefs of aboriginal peoples; it is also well established in modern organized religious thinking and belief. Freud's concept of primary process thinking overlaps significantly with paleologic thinking. Phyllis and Robert L. Tyson's (1990) summary statement on this subject reads as follows:

> Primary process thought is characterized by concretism, condensation, displacement, visual imagery, and symbolism. Primary process thinking is manifest through conscious and unconscious fantasy, fantasy play, day and night dreams, magical thinking, slips of the tongue, jokes, and artistic and creative activity.... Thinking governed by secondary process can be conscious or unconscious. It is characterized by rationality, order and logic. It relies heavily on verbal symbolism and functions chiefly in adaptation to reality. (p. 164)

Primary process thought, in the Tysons' view, is sometimes seen as subjective, chaotic, and pathological, while secondary process thought is seen as objective, orderly, and reality-oriented (p. 167). This view, they explain, overlooks the interpenetration of the two modes of thought and their respective contributions to human cognition.

Arieti speculated that early hominins, 2 to 3 million years ago, had no capacity for secondary process thinking. And while Cro-Magnon people (10,000–80,000 years ago) may have thought more paleologically than we do today, they left ample evidence of their highly symbolic and Aristotelian thinking as well (pp. 292-94).

Arieti cautioned that when we hear of a group of Pacific Islanders or Native American or African tribes in which all members have a paranoid and delusional attitude toward other people or groups of people outside their tribe, we cannot conclude that these people are schizophrenic or that their culture is schizophrenic. Their myths, rituals, religion, belief systems, magic, and daily customs are transmitted from generation to generation and accepted as true. While it may all seem rather delusional to us, Arieti points out, "We have our own, not less irrational beliefs and traditions" (p. 288): "By using paleologic conceptions, he [the aboriginal person] does not withdraw behind an autistic barrier, as the schizophrenic does, but, on the contrary, he becomes more intimately a part of his tribe" (p. 290).

By introducing Freud's thoughts on Schreber and the observations of Storch and Arieti, I am making linkages between Perry's observations and the observations of others from the psychoanalytic perspective. While Perry was able to recognize these recurring images and themes in the clinical material of his psychotic patients and link them to the mythology of sacral kingship, others have previously observed the same recurring images and themes in the inner worlds of psychotic patients and created similar or alternative interpretations. (For a parallel discussion of the phenomena of psychotic experience and religious experience, see appendix 2 sections "Anton T. Boisen and His Exploration of the Inner World," "Chronic Schizophrenia," "Richard Bucke and Cosmic Consciousness," "Julian Jaynes and the Breakdown of the Bicameral Mind," and "Psychedelic Experience.")

When John Weir Perry established a parallel between the Urban Revolution and the brief psychotic disorder, he did so in a way that was not so different from Freud's phylogenetic project. However, three problems arose when I tried to apply his discoveries to the phylogenetic project of psychoanalysis. The problems pertained to the specificity of the diagnosis, the relative lack of attention to a corresponding stage in normal development, and the specificity of the stage in cultural evolution.

Diagnosis: The ten images and themes associated with the diagnosis of the brief psychotic disorder were specific enough but are not uncommon in other psychotic states, such as schizophrenia, bipolar affective disorder, psychotic depression, chronic schizophrenia, and even hallucinogen intoxication. But the full ten images and themes, as well as positive prognosis, were clearly identified with the brief psychotic disorder.

A stage in normal development: Perry rarely, if ever, identified a stage in normal development that corresponded to the brief psychotic disorder. Nonetheless, it makes sense that the stage would be adolescence. While the psychological injuries at the roots of psychosis derive from early infancy, the brief psychotic disorder does not manifest itself so dramatically until late adolescence or early adulthood, when the foundation of the psyche proves too fragile to take on the tasks of adolescence, whether they be identity formation, a first love, separation from home and parents, or the management of adult impulses and responsibilities. If the experiences of adolescent genital-stage love and identity formation were sufficiently challenging and overwhelming to the young person, they might take on a psychotic mythological sheen, stirring visions of death, rebirth, sacred marriage, and a new worldview. When I had the chance to discuss this with Perry, he could easily see my point and agreed with the association I made between the general content of the brief psychotic disorder and the challenges of adolescence.

A stage in cultural evolution: The stage in cultural evolution lost its specificity when, after referring only to cultures on the cusp between the High Neolithic and the Urban Revolution, Perry began recognizing the pattern with other cultures in crisis. These cultures, facing times of troubles, began casting off rigid power structures of the old way of being and started renewing themselves in relation to the principles of love.

Perry recognized this cultural pattern at various turning points in history, such as the appearance of Jesus Christ as a sacral king, the courtly culture of 12th-century France, and even in the North American counterculture of the 1960s and 1970s. Consequently, one is left wondering if these myths and rituals appeared for the first time on the cusp of the Urban Revolution and reappeared subsequently in similar situations throughout history, or if recurring myths and rituals are somehow tied to sociological phenomena that appear and disappear under the proper circumstances independent of cultural evolution.

Schemas Based on Freud's and Perry's Work

In the first chapter, we saw how Freud made analogous linkages between a stage in psychological development (oedipal stage), a form of pathology (obsessional neurosis); a stage in cultural evolution (loosely called the fraternal clan); an Oedipus-type hero myth, or the myth of the great ancestor in totemism; and the ritual of the sacrificial totemic feast. I constructed the following schema based on Freud's work. The column on the left has five categories of human experience: two psychological and three cultural. The column on the right lists the manifestations of those five categories.

SIGMUND FREUD

1. A stage of normal development	The phallic stage
2. A form of psychopathology	Obsessional neurosis
3. A stage in cultural evolution	Fraternal clan
4. A myth	Totemism—myths of the great ancestor, myths of the hero (Oedipus)
5. A ritual	Sacrificial totemic feast

In this second chapter, we have seen how John Weir Perry assembled a similarly compelling set of diverse phenomena with curiously analogous relations. I constructed the schema below, based on his work, to which I added adolescence as the stage of normal development in accordance with my thinking and Perry's agreement when I had the chance to discuss it with him.

JOHN WEIR PERRY
1. A stage of normal development — Adolescence
2. A form of psychopathology — Brief psychotic disorder
3. A stage in cultural evolution — Urban Revolution
4. A myth — Sacral kingship
5. A ritual — Ancient New Year festival

Two obvious differences in the schemas are that Freud and Perry attended to different stages in normal development and different stages in cultural evolution. Another difference is that while Freud was working on a reconstruction behind the veil of prehistoric amnesia, Perry was doing something similar but drawing on data from the beginnings of history and the earliest of written texts.

What can we say about those earlier stages of cultural evolution before the Urban Revolution and the written word? What can we say about those prehistoric stages in cultural evolution and their relation to the stages in normal development before adolescence? Are all the possible linkages lost in the darkness and silence of prehistory?

In the next chapter we will begin an exploration into early childhood and the prehistoric origins of culture. Our point of entry will not be obsessional neurosis or the brief psychotic disorder but a profoundly disturbed boy with autism whom I met early in my career. As we proceed, our interest will be drawn to the images and themes that echo and reflect one another as analogies between the ontogeny of psychological development and the phylogeny of cultural evolution.

CHAPTER 3

Infantile Autism and the Myth of Death and Rebirth

> In order to understand such patients [with autism], it is necessary to be in touch with the nature of the infant's early suckling experiences. This is where relationships begin.
> —Francis Tustin, *Autistic Barriers in Neurotic Patients*

When we look at the schemas I constructed based on Freud's phylogenetic fantasy and John Weir Perry's formulation of the brief psychotic disorder, we recognize that the phallic stage precedes adolescence, and the fraternal clan of prehistory preceded the Urban Revolution.

FREUD	PERRY
1. Phallic stage	Adolescence—genital stage
2. Obsessional neurosis	Brief psychotic disorder
3. Fraternal clan	Urban Revolution
4. Totemism—myths of the hero	Sacral kingship
5. Sacrificial totemic feast	Ancient New Year festival

In this third chapter, we will follow Freud and Perry into the realms of developmental psychology, psychopathology, myth, and ritual back to the dawn of civilization and then step off into the darkness of early childhood experience and cultural prehistory. Freud's psychopathological starting point was obsessional neurosis and conversion hysteria, Perry's was the brief psychotic disorder, and mine is infantile autism. We will explore one aspect of the phenomenology of infantile autism—oral trauma—and meet a profoundly disturbed boy on the autism spectrum who drew pictures of what he described as "mouths." We will also explore the psychodynamics of orality and the symbolism of the mouth in myth and ritual and conclude by constructing a schema that lines up "points of agreement" between early infancy, infantile autism, a stage in cultural evolution, and a corresponding myth and ritual.

In my discussion of autism, I want it to be perfectly clear that I am not making a statement about the etiology or treatment of autism but rather speculating on the psychic dilemma of the child with autism in relation to the experience of orality and oral trauma.

❖ ❖ ❖

I was a 20-year-old psychology student when I began working as a live-in child-care worker in a psychodynamically oriented residential treatment center for 14 autistic children. I lived for three and a half years in the basement of the center and worked with two of the boys every morning, five days a week—waking them up; changing their wet and soiled sheets; and getting them showered, dressed, breakfasted, and off to our in-house school program.

Autism spectrum disorder is a frequent topic of popular articles and television shows. Fashionable cures or new ideas that promise miracles are coming out every few years. The sad truth is that the *classic autistic disorder* is one of the most profound emotional disorders of childhood, and in severe cases the prognosis is bleak. It is characterized by severe speech and eating disturbances, impaired nonverbal communication, idiosyncratic language, emotional isolation, self-destructive behavior, repetitive idiosyncratic gesturing or body movements, odd posturing, twiddling of objects, and hand flapping or finger fiddling. People with autism generally make poor eye contact, and their interpersonal relations are extremely impaired and lacking in social reciprocity. The newer diagnosis of *autistic spectrum disorder* is a wide category that includes profoundly disturbed children as well as those with less severe symptoms, greater accessibility to education and psychotherapy, and realistic hope for much better prognoses as well.

According to a review study by Herbert, Sharp, and Gaudiano (2002), the most probable cause of autism is the combination of genetic predispositions and early environmental insults that affect the developing fetus (pp. 23–43). That does not mean the child with autism has no psychodynamics. While I do not directly address treatment, the psychodynamics are the focus of my exploration into autism.

Treatment strategies for autism have included behavior modification, psychoanalytic interventions, sensory integration therapy, behavioral training programs, and more. While none have offered a cure, the behavioral training programs often help the severely disturbed child to establish a better social adaptation upon which to build healthier relations, which may include psychotherapeutic relations.

Bruno Bettelheim, a controversial figure in the field of autism, was a compelling psychoanalytic theorist and leader in the residential treatment of children on the autism spectrum. In his conceptualization of autism, he drew heavily from the works of Margaret Mahler (1968) and her associates (1975), who focused on the importance of "catastrophic threats," which occur during "critical periods" of development and result in disturbed modes of adjustment. Bettelheim (1967) made the following observations about autism and infancy:

> The autistic *anlage* consists of the conviction that one's efforts have no power to influence the world, because of the earlier conviction that the world is insensitive to one's reactions. (p. 46)

> The infant, because of pain or discomfort and the anxiety they cause, or because he misreads the mother's actions or feelings, or correctly assesses her negative feelings, may retreat from her and the world. (p. 72)

Frances Tustin (1986), another important psychoanalytic clinician and theorist, described the psychology of the child with autism in this way:

> The Fall from the sublime state of blissful unity with the "mother" who, in early infancy, is the sensation-dominated centre of the infant's universe, is part of everyone's experience. However, for some individuals, for a variety of reasons, different in each case, the disillusionment of "coming down to earth" from this ecstatic experience has been such a hard and injurious experience that it has provoked impeding encapsulating reactions. (p. 25)

> Clinical work indicates that the *sensation* of nipple-in-mouth (or teat of the bottle experienced in terms of an inbuilt gestalt of the breast) is the focus for the development of the psyche. Associated with the mother's encircling arms, her shining eyes and the mutual concentration of their attention, it becomes the core of the self. (p. 29; Tustin's italics)

> It has become clear to me that a crucial factor in the precipitation of the autism was the realization that the nipple of the breast was not part of the mouth, but was separate from it and could be "gone." (p. 58)

Tustin described this premature and poorly mediated sense of separateness as the factor that gives rise to the autistic symptomatology, including the use of what she called "autistic sensation objects." These are actual physical objects that are valued by the autistic child not for what they symbolize but for their hardness, which seems to offer a sense of safety to these exceedingly vulnerable children.[1] While the child with autism mediates this premature sense of separateness with autistic sensation objects, the child without autism appears to mediate this separation with symbolic representations—that is, with language. Tustin (1986) explained:

> Autistic objects seem to plug the gap between the couple (the mother and child) so that bodily separateness is not experienced.... Perpetual recourse to autistic objects means that autistic children have remained in a raw, unnurtured state relatively unmodified by the disciplining and humanizing elements of the nursing situation. They are at the mercy of elemental inbuilt patterns which are stereotyped and unmodified by experience. These are unregulated and have not been coordinated in the normal way. They also seem to be affected by atavistic elements. Such children feel threatened by predatory mouths and creatures. (p. 110)

At the time of my work (mid-1970s) with Jimmy, the boy I describe below, the psychodynamic etiology of autism identified severe trauma in early infancy as the causative or precipitating factor of this disorder. Indeed, virtually all of the children I worked with had horrific infancies. One had a profoundly psychotic mother, another had been fed LSD as an infant, and another had experienced severe agonizing constipation during the first nine months of life. When one saw these terribly disturbed children and heard the stories of their early childhood trauma, it was not difficult to imagine a cause-and-effect relationship. But there are three problems with this way of thinking.

In the first place, there are many children who have horrible infancies who do not become autistic. In the second place, there are numerous cases of children who become autistic without experiencing horrible infantile trauma. And in the third place, being a mother, father, sister, or brother of a child on the autism spectrum is extraordinarily difficult, so it is not unusual for such profoundly unresponsive children to have a wrenching effect on family dynamics. However, these dynamics are typically *in response to* the child's unresponsiveness, not the cause of it.

Modern thinking now recognizes autism as a profound neurologically based disorder that can be most effectively addressed through behavioral strategies, speech therapy, special education classes, and other such techniques. Nonetheless, a subgroup of children on the autism spectrum has been recognized by some researchers, most notably Frances Tustin and

---

1 I knew one boy with autism, for example, who carried with him everywhere a hard, heavy plastic toy apple, which he would pat with his hand and knock with his knuckles. Another child found comfort in bringing the cold, ceramic toilet-tank top into his bed with him, and still another collected ceramic insulators used for the electric wires on telephone poles.

those who follow in her tradition, as having a psychogenic autism that can benefit from child psychoanalysis. That said, I must note that the work I did with the boy I will describe was really more of an investigation than any kind of therapy. It was basic research in which my observations within a controlled environment were aimed at simply discovering whatever I might discover.

A Boy Named Jimmy

Jimmy was already rather unresponsive in his first year of life. He was evaluated by a specialist at 11 months, had follow-up evaluations throughout early childhood, and at 7 ½ was diagnosed as having characteristics of infantile autism. He was then admitted to a residential treatment center for severely disturbed children, where I met him a year later.

Jimmy had a slender build, big dreamy eyes, and thick wavy hair. He was quiet, passive, submissive, withdrawn, and spoke in a strange manner when he spoke at all. He was a slow eater, ate small portions of food, drank large quantities of milk, and was enuretic. His lips were often passively parted, with his lower jaw hanging just slightly. When he was between the ages of 8 ½ and 14, I observed him performing a wide variety of repetitive idiosyncratic behaviors such as finger snapping, rocking, and hand flapping. He often pranced back and forth on his tiptoes in a ritualistic fashion. Intermittently he would stop prancing and bite the knuckles of both of his index fingers simultaneously while wiggling the other fingers. Then he would take his fingers out of his mouth, let a viscous string of saliva slide out slowly and dangle a couple of inches below before sucking it back in, and then resume his prancing, after which the ritual would be repeated. Without speculating on their meaning, I note these as examples of Jimmy's day-to-day behavior and now turn to his drawings and commentaries on them as the focus of my attention.

Jimmy's Drawings

I gave Jimmy a sheet of white paper (8 ½" x 11") and eight crayons (red, yellow, blue, orange, green, purple, brown, and black) and invited him to draw whatever he would like. As he drew, I took verbatim notes of his occasional, typically odd comments. I also wrote down my own questions to him, often in the form of incomplete sentences, along with his responses. During the first two years of our work together, I invited Jimmy to draw one picture each day, five days a week. For three years after that, we met once a week and increased the number of drawings

LIBIDO, CULTURE, AND CONSCIOUSNESS

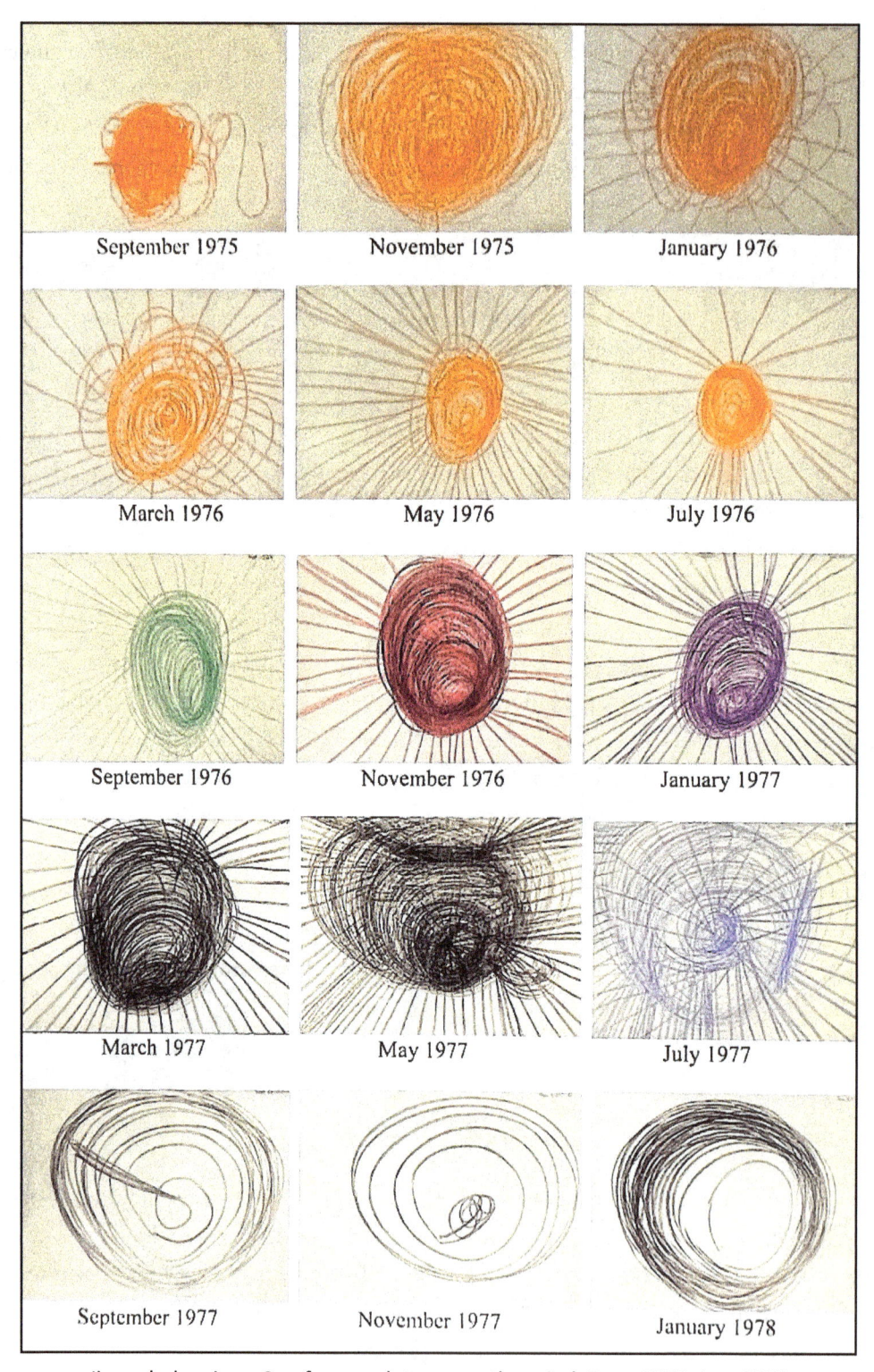

September 1975	November 1975	January 1976
March 1976	May 1976	July 1976
September 1976	November 1976	January 1977
March 1977	May 1977	July 1977
September 1977	November 1977	January 1978

Jimmy's drawings. One from each two-month period. Sept. 1975–Jan. 1978

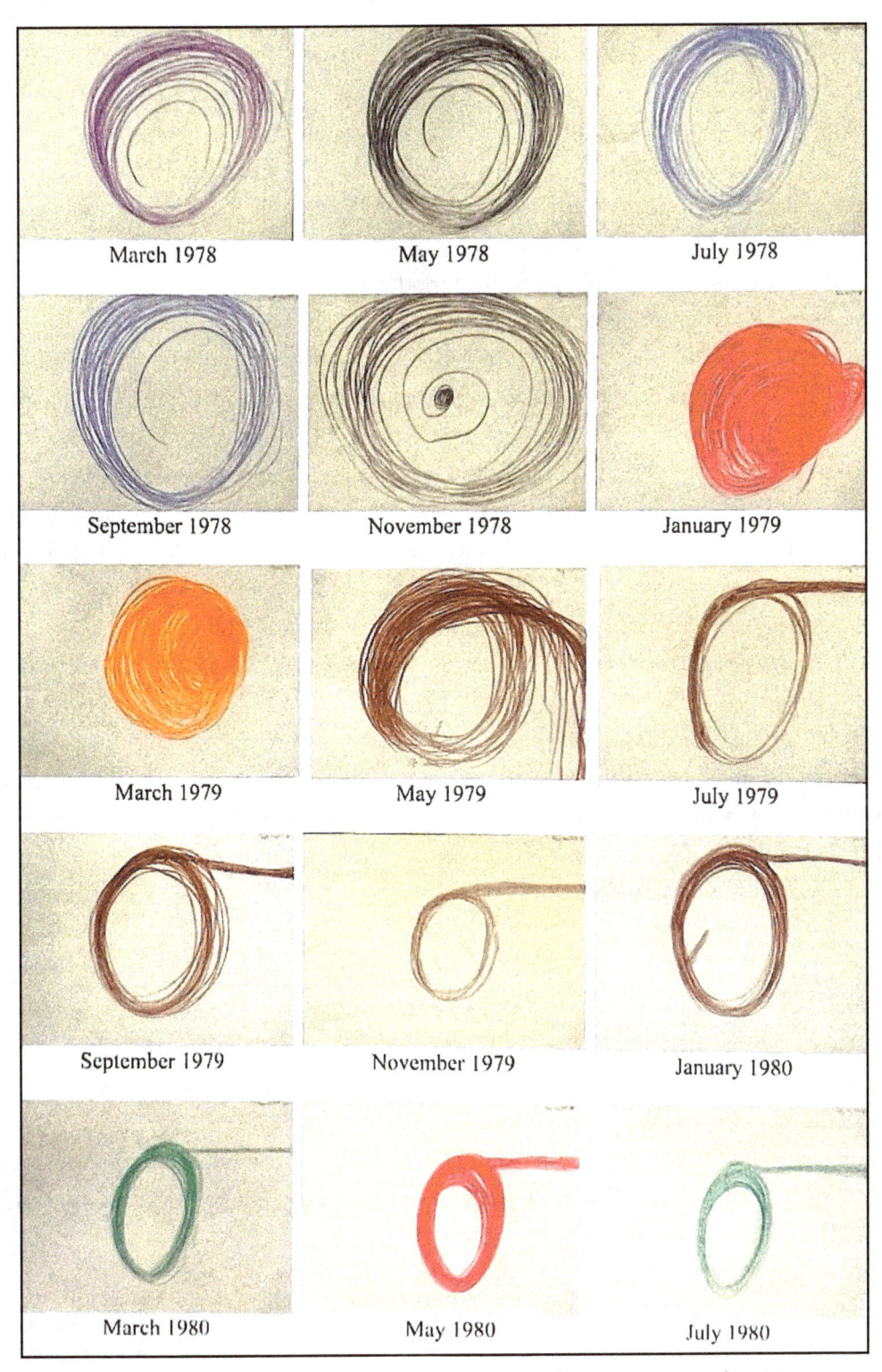

INFANTILE AUTISM AND THE MYTH OF DEATH AND REBIRTH

Jimmy's drawings. One from each two-month period. Mar. 1978–July. 1980

to five per session. We began our work together in September 1975, when Jimmy was 9 years old, and ended it five years later in July 1980. During that time Jimmy created 1,250 drawings.

With the exception of 44 scribbles, all of his drawings were circles or variations on circles (i.e., quadrated discs, suns, spirals, discs, or circles with a line off to the side). In the first three months, roughly half the drawings were scribbles and the other half were discs. Each disc was a circle filled in with a tight spiral and/or crosshatch.

Over the next year and a half, not only were there no scribbles drawn, but Jimmy added rays on the discs, transforming them into sun-like images. Then an even more elaborated phase began in which radials (points out of which lines emanate) were drawn onto these sun-like images. This sun-with-radial phase lasted six and a half months and coincided with an overall improvement in Jimmy's functioning. In a few drawings, two radials were placed on the face of the sun in such a way as to suggest eyes, thus hinting at a potentially emerging human face.

The next phase was a clear regression to the earlier circle or disc forms and coincided with Jimmy's sinking into a profoundly apathetic state and becoming echolalic. This circle phase included all the drawings of the last three years of our work together. The great majority of these drawings were loose spirals, circles, discs, and circles with a line off to the side. All of Jimmy's drawings were pre-pictorial, so even those images that look to us like suns were not, for him, suns at all.[2]

Excluding the last phase of regression, the preceding phases—from scribbles to discs (rudimentary mandalas), to suns, to radials, to hints of the human face—recapitulated the pre-pictorial developmental stages seen in the drawings of toddlers and preschoolers as described by Rhoda Kellogg (1970). It was stunning to see such a recapitulation of images in the drawings of a much older but profoundly disturbed child.

Jimmy's Commentary

Jimmy's speech was composed of sounds, single words, phrases, and single sentences that were either odd or had no relation to the immediate situation (e.g., "Bin-bin," "Horse," "Fight," "Spank your hand," "Who broke the cottage cheese?"). Other comments were appropriate to the situation and communicative (e.g., "Good morning," "I want French toast, Daniel").

---

2 Beyond this developmental consideration is the compelling image of the circle. Eugenio Gaddini (2001) theorized, "It is only at a certain point, after a 'basic mental organization' can be said to have been formed (that is, after the 6th month), that the sense of self is reflected in the mind in a visual image, which may therefore be regarded as the first representation of the bodily self as an image, a first *form* of self. This form is round and will be expressed graphically by a child as a circle, as soon as the scribbling phase is over" (pp. 179–80).

A third aspect was the repetition of previously heard directives (e.g., "Put your plate down," "Hold still," "Chew up your bread").

Jimmy's commentary over the course of years is easily subdivided into four phases. The first phase, from September 1975 through February 1977, was characterized by loose associations, the repetition of previously heard directives, and an increasing accessibility to my inquiry. Each comment was typically separated from the next with a long pause.

December 24, 1976:
"Close your mouth… Relax… Throw it down… Put your plate down… Head… Head hurt… The orange head… You close your mouth… You throw it down."

The second language phase, from March 1977 through June 1977, was when Jimmy offered the largest amount of symbolic material and was most accessible to my inquiry. It closely coincided with the sun-with-radial phase.

March 23, 1977:

My Inquiry	Jimmy
	I am closing the mouth
	Don't hurt me,
	I am closing the mouth.
	Lunch.
The mouth is…	not a mouth.
The mouth is a…	cat.
The cat…	is no cat.
	This is not a cat.
This is not a cat, it's a…	dragon.
The dragon…	live in eh eh.
	Live in a close.
The dragon live in…	the eh eh.
	No oh oh.
	You don't throw it on the floor.
……….	

The dragon's mouth is…	old.
The dragon's old mouth is…	closing.
	I am closing the mouth.
The dragon has…	the mouth.
	This is not it.
When the dragon opens its mouth, it…	bite.
	Don't bite.
	Don't bite.
	Don't bite it.
……….	
The dragon…	has a mouth.
The dragon's mouth…	no mouth.
The dragon's mouth…	has a star in it.
The star…	is shiny.
	The star is shiny.
	Shiny.

The third language phase, from July 1977 through September 1977, was similar to the first except that Jimmy was less responsive to me.

The fourth language phase, from October 1977 through July 1980, was characterized by echolalia, a lack of spontaneous speech, and little if any accessibility to my inquiry. It coincided with the circle phase and Jimmy's deteriorated and apathetic state.

The Mouth

During the first three language phases, Jimmy would often describe his circular drawing as a "mouth." While drawing, he would chant a monotonous "yayayayayayaya," which one might imagine as his own breast-feeding song. Also while drawing, he made references to biting, chewing, and spitting. "The mouth" was most frequently identified with "the cat," but on other occasions with "the lion," "the alligator," "the rat," and "the dragon." "The mouth bites," is "closing," and has "terrible teeth." "The mouth has a star in it," and "the star is shiny," "old," and identified with the "bird." The "star" is also in the "horn" and at the "top of the hill." Jimmy spoke of needing a "ladder" and climbing on this ladder to get something out. He occasionally spoke of biting the mouth, underscoring the confused state of affairs when subject and object are so primitively differentiated.

The Symbolism of Jimmy's Commentary

Psychoanalytic interpretation relies primarily on personal associations and only secondarily on the analyst's knowledge of culture-bound symbolism, but with Jimmy it was impossible to elicit free associations or even a brief a story about his drawing. So I turned to symbolism to obtain whatever insights might be available.

In the brief description above, we saw the "mouth" of the "cat" or "dragon" as a biting organ, which contains within it the "shiny" "star." We might be able to entertain parallels to a witch or devouring mother monster in this mouth-cat-dragon with "terrible teeth." The "star," as a small light in the darkness, might symbolize the fragility of an emerging or fading consciousness. The "bird" symbolizes an airborne soul image, like the "star," and is associated with flights of imagination and dreams. By using the word "soul," I am not introducing a religious agenda but referring to the human mind's tendency to abstract and represent personalities and the tendency to project internal objects into animate and inanimate objects. We name children, animals, and objects and, in doing so, give them a soul. We imagine the river, the thunder, and the rain as possessing souls and having needs and intentions. We even project souls into loved ones that we imagine will carry on even after death. The soul is not a metapsychological concept; it is a spiritual concept. It is poetry. And for our purposes here it is metaphor.

The star, the bird, and other sorts of soul images remind us of the goal in hero mythology. Heroic strategies for attaining a soul image or "treasure hard to attain" are through self-sacrifice, by slaying a "dragon," by journeying to the "top of the mountain," by climbing a "ladder" (stairway, rope, chain of arrows, etc.) to heaven, or by performing a task that is humanly impossible.

The hero's (Jimmy's) task of slaying (biting) a dragon (the mouth) or overcoming some sort of obstacle in order to acquire and be transformed by a "treasure hard to attain" (the star), such as a damsel in distress, a jewel, a magic orb, or some other treasure with transformative properties, is a mythic analogue to Jimmy's commentary on his drawings and, presumably, to his ego development as well.

The analogous relation of the hero myth to ego development is a topic about which Sigmund Freud and Otto Rank wrote extensively. Child therapists are very familiar with these heroic themes in children's drawings and play. We see battles between the gorilla and the lion, sports competitions, the forces of good and evil, and stories borrowed from culture: David and Goliath, King Kong and Godzilla, humans and aliens, and so on. Consequently, it is not particularly surprising to recognize these themes emerging from Jimmy's cryptic comments, as they are also easily recognized in the stories other children tell from their imaginations. What is surprising, however, is that in Jimmy's commentary he did not focus on a blow-by-blow account of the fight or struggle, as we might expect to see with higher functioning children. Instead, he seemed spellbound by the simple yet vivid perception of the "mouth" and its "terrible teeth," as though he were being precariously suspended above that death-dealing organ of destruction and in danger of being swallowed by unconsciousness at any moment.

Jimmy's preoccupation with the mouth is not entirely unlike that of other children with autism. These children don't generally talk about mouths or draw pictures that they describe as "mouths," but it is symptomatic of autism to have both speech disorders and eating disturbances. Bettelheim (1967) described the case of Laurie, whose oral zone had become decathected as evidenced by her total passivity to eating and vomiting (p. 121). For another of his autistic patients, Marcia, "Any lip or mouth sensations seemed to terrify her. She made an effort to bypass the mouth by trying to put water in her ears and nose instead" (p. 174). "When asked what was wrong with the baby [doll], Marcia said, 'Her mouth'" (p. 222).

Addressing the psychogenic factor in autism, Bettelheim wrote:

Step by step they may have defensively withdrawn cathexis from the outer world and from all but the whole of their body; hence their unresponsiveness to what they see, hear, and feel. In parallel process, they concentrate all cathexis, all protection, on some last inner fortress, the very center of their life, as they feel it.

If this assumption is correct, and if the origin of infantile autism, the *anlage* for it, has to do with very early, maybe the earliest experiences in life, then both damage around the oral experience, and totally repressed but extreme oral aggression are among the origins of this disturbance. Perhaps these children have some dim recollection that this is the place where the critical damage occurred. (p. 61)

Those of us who have worked with severely disturbed children on the autism spectrum are often impressed by how these children block out their awareness of the rest of the world. Frances Tustin (1986) asked, "But why does the autistic child have this terror of the 'not me'?"

For such a baby, the frustration of the inevitable realization that this [nipple] is not a part of his mouth is a bitter blow from which he does not recover. (p. 61)

Those fortunate individuals who, in early infancy, have been able to enjoy and internalize emotional experiences of a rhythmical, adaptive interaction of the mouth differentiated from the breast are receptive to later experiences such as human sexual love, and aesthetic and religious experiences. (p. 284)

I have found early difficulties in sucking to be characteristic of all the autistic children I have seen, and also of those cases I have supervised. (p. 49)

Does Jimmy's "star" in the mouth allude to the nipple in the mouth? Could it also have something to do with hero mythology? Can the meaning that psychoanalysts abstract from mythology be in any way relevant to the utterances of a child with autism?

The Mouth and Orality

Psychosexual development, or libido development, pertains to the movement of libidinal attention as it shifts from the mouth, to the anus, to the genitalia throughout the course of childhood and into sexual maturity (S. Freud, 1917/1963b, SE 16, pp. 320-38). The first stage of psychosexual development is the oral stage, when the cathexis (attention, investment) of libido is focused on the lips, teeth, and mucous membranes of the mouth. It is named for the oral orifice, the mouth, which Freud identified as the primary site of libidinal gratification for the infant. The infant engages in pleasurable sucking at the nipple, thumb sucking, eating, making gurgling sounds, cooing, mouthing objects, inhaling, exhaling, burping, engaging in mouth play, biting, chewing, spitting, and pursuit of the cannibalistic sexual aim. It is through oral incorporation and oral expulsion that the infant comes to know various aspects of self and the world. Orality is the bodily metaphor of the infant's incorporation of the world, rejection of the world, and the nascent alienation of subjectivity from otherness. Freud observed that sucking is a primary sexual gratification embedded in infancy and tied to the nutritive function. But after teeth appear and food is chewed up, oral eroticism and the nutritive function pursue their goals separately or together.

In Karl Abraham's (1924/1927b) rethinking of the oral stage, he suggested two subphases: the "earlier oral stage" (sucking) followed by the "later oral stage" (cannibalistic). Abraham wrote that in the early oral stage the infant's object relations are such that its love object is totally "auto-erotic" and "exempt from instinctual inhibitions" (p. 496). There is no real sense of otherness in the world. The infant's psychic investment is not out there in an external world separate from and related to itself, but rather in a world of bodily sensations. In this sense, the infant is in a very receptive or incorporative mode, taking the world in and getting to know it, both figuratively and literally, through its mouth.

Erik Erikson (1968) would later write that the newborn infant "lives through, and loves with, his mouth; and the mother lives through, and loves with, her breasts or whatever parts of her countenance and body convey eagerness to provide what he needs" (p. 97). From this perspective Erikson brought to light the importance of the dynamic tension between trust and mistrust as they develop between the mother and infant. This is particularly important in the later phase of the oral stage, when the nursing infant is gathering strength, becoming more active, and, perhaps more important, growing little teeth.

Having weathered the cyclic emotional storms of instinctual need, frustration, and gratification, the infant develops a rudimentary recognition of otherness. The line between mother's milk and mother is thin indeed, so the line between sucking and cannibalism is only a bite away. Thus, feeding and weaning become the arenas for the differentiation of the infant's worldview and the development of object relations. It is the breast that comes and goes, and thereby becomes the primal "other."

Sucking its food in without biting or chewing, the infant settles into a vague and global worldview, taking it all in and swallowing it whole. Later the infant's orality becomes more active, more aggressive—biting off pieces of food and chewing them up before swallowing them. The infant begins to break up the world into smaller (bite-size) pieces that afford the possibility to consider (taste) and get to know them (chew) before fully incorporating them (swallowing and digesting) into a more differentiated worldview. (For more on orality in psychoanalytic theory, see appendix 3.)

When Jimmy drew his 1,250 drawings of the mouth, he was unable to free-associate, so I tried to get a phylogenetic insight by turning to the analogies and symbolism of the mouth in myth and ritual. This might seem at first a dubious effort, as there is a great distance between the idiosyncratic comments of a profoundly disturbed child and the symbolically laden literature and traditions of ancient and modern religions, but my rationale is as follows.

Jimmy's preoccupation with the mouth did not set him apart from other children with autism. While other autistic children might not draw pictures that they describe as mouths, Tustin, Bettelheim, and others have recognized the mouth as the psychosexual site of greatest trauma for the profoundly disturbed child on the autism spectrum, whether the disorder is organically or functionally based. Furthermore, from Jimmy's minimal elaboration, it was possible to recognize that his use of the word "mouth" was in fact referring to what we consensually agree upon as being a mouth. He described it as closing, biting, and having teeth, and he even snapped his teeth together at times while talking about it. If we can make a connection between Jimmy's meaning of the mouth and our meaning of the mouth, between Jimmy's oral preoccupation and the oral preoccupation of other children with autism, and between the orality of autistic children and the orality of early infancy, we can give ourselves permission to explore the meaning of the mouth in myth and ritual. This last linkage is based on the assumption that because these myths and rituals are ultimately derived from the symbolization and elaboration of early infantile experience and early infantile fantasy, they may well have something to do with the orality of the autistic child.

We are exploring autism and orality for a reason that will soon become more apparent in relation to our phylogenetic project of psychoanalysis.

The Symbolism of the Mouth

In an exploration of the symbolism of the mouth as it appears in myth and ritual, we find it to be an image with five basic symbolic meanings. The mouth is (1) the hero's passageway to death, (2) the birth canal of the reborn hero, (3) the avenue through which the soul embodies, (4) the avenue of the soul's disembodiment, and (5) an image of integral consciousness.

The first two meanings pertain to the hero of myth, which can be thought of as being associated with the ego. The personal heroic figure of the private imagination typically performs tasks that no ego could ever accomplish, but in doing so it expresses, in metaphor, the person's wishes, fears, and conflicts. It offers a solution or compensation, a model or inspiration that the ego needs to pursue its own developmental tasks and maintain its equilibrium in response to internal and external pressures. Thus, the paths of the ego, as a metapsychological concept, and the hero, as an imaginary and mythological figure, are distinct yet in some ways parallel.

The mouth as the hero's passageway to death is a symbolic expression of the extinction of ego consciousness, the end of a way of being, or the end of a previously established worldview. The hero being swallowed or engulfed by the dark chaos-dragon of unconsciousness is a mythic or fantasy analogue to the experiences of drifting off into sleep, the weakening of the ego, and psychotic decompensation, wherein the worldview is fractured, melted, dismembered, obliterated. Boundaries are dissolved and ego consciousness is extinguished. While the hero's death and dismemberment may seem final from a literal perspective, it is important to bear in mind that it is taking place in the imagination and, as such, is best viewed from a figurative perspective wherein the hero's death may imply a return to the mouth/womb of the great

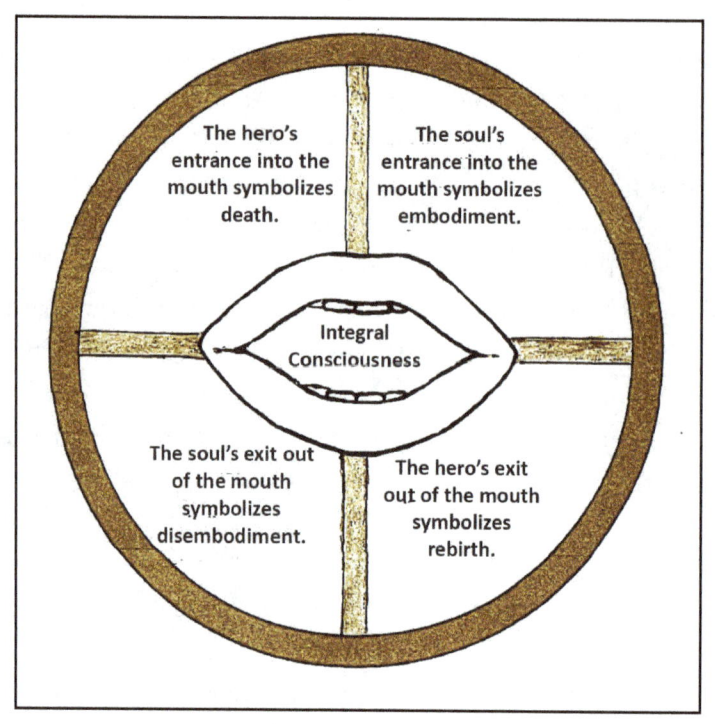

The Five Basic Meanings of the Mouth.

mother, with the potential of spiritual rebirth, the birth of consciousness, or the birth of a new worldview. We see the hero's death not only in stories like Jonah being swallowed by the great fish but also in initiation rites in which the initiate is swallowed by a monster, "dies," and is reborn as an adult member of the tribe.

The mouth as a birth canal for the hero is symbolic of this upper birth. It is the place from which the hero is delivered anew, the center out of which he is resurrected, or the site of his rebirth. The image of the hero being reborn from the mouth is analogous to the experiences of awakening, psychological birth, the reconstitution of the ego following a psychotic episode, a rising up of the ego from unconsciousness or a transformation of status following initiation. It represents the re-membering of the worldview or the establishment of a new worldview, the firming up of boundaries and a rising up toward a more focused stable consciousness. Concerns about the mouth death or mouth birth can also be a displacement upward of hopes and fears about closeness to the vagina, which may be experienced as a vagina dentata—a vagina with teeth. On ancient temples, restaurants, and modern fun houses it is not uncommon for a doorway to be framed by a large open mouth through which one enters and exits.

The third and fourth meanings of the mouth pertain to it as a passageway for the soul. In myth and tradition, as the soul enters the mouth or is swallowed, it leaves the celestial realms and enters into the limited world of human existence. While the hero entering the mouth represents a return to the mouth/womb, the soul entering the mouth represents embodiment. Naturally enough, when the soul leaves the body by way of the mouth, it is a kind of birth, or at least a liberation of sorts, and is associated with the astral flights, travels, and wandering of the soul in dreams, visions, and imagined afterlife journeys. As such, the soul's departure from the mouth represents a disembodiment. In many traditions, illness is also attributed to the soul leaving the body by way of the mouth and getting lost. It seems as though there may even be a complementary relationship that exists between the hero and the soul. When the hero enters the mouth (dies) the soul leaves the body and when the hero exits the mouth (is reborn) the soul enters the body.

The fifth basic symbolic meaning of the mouth is that of integral consciousness. In this context, the mouth may represent a vessel containing the universe, or it simply may be the organ from which divine wisdom comes forth.

The Mouth as the Hero's Passageway to Death

The mouth as a symbol of death, destruction, and dismemberment is the gateway to the underworld, the jaws of hell, the devouring terrible mother, and time itself, the devourer of all things created.

When Lord Krishna, in the Hindu scripture the Bhagavad Gita (c. 500 BCE), reveals to Arjuna his infinite celestial forms, Arjuna is awestruck and filled with terror, for he sees Lord Krishna's many mouths, with their terrible teeth and fearful fangs, in which the heads of mortals are being crushed to powder, and still other fiery mouths destroying all the worlds (Muscaro, 1962, pp. 91–92). In the Epic of Gilgamesh, the great monster Humbaba, guardian of the wilderness, was said to have had breath like fire, and his jaws were equated with death itself (Sandars, 1972, p. 26). In the mythology of the Greeks, there was a prophecy that Cronos, the god of time, would be dethroned by one of his own sons. To circumvent this, he ate his children as his wife bore them (Graves, 1959, pp. 39–40). A shamanic amulet carved in walrus tusk by the Tlingit Native Americans of Alaska depicts a "terrible mother" figure about to devour a person whom she holds in her clutches (Jung, 1912/1956, plate 38b). A picture from a 16th-century Aztec codex depicts Quetzalcoatl, the great plumed serpent, devouring a person in his jaws (p. 299). In an 11th-century drawing from Constantinople, we see a ladder on which mortals are ascending toward an image of Christ while others are seen falling off the ladder toward the open mouth of a dragon waiting below. (This image is numbered 5Dk.

016 in the Archive for the Research of Archetypal Symbolism [A.R.A.S.] located at the C. G. Jung Institute of San Francisco, in California.)

Many cultures have a deity or mythological being that personifies this devouring aspect of the great mother (e.g., Kali, Ta-Urt, Gorgon, the witch, Rangda). These personifications, however, are also found to possess life-giving, nourishing, protective, and nurturing qualities or are at least counterpoised to a positive mother goddess who possesses these qualities. An example of the destructive and life-giving qualities in a male deity is found in a myth of the Manja and Banda of Africa. A hairy black being, Ngakola, was said to live in the bush and was known to eat people. He told the people, "Send me men. I will swallow them and vomit them up renewed." The people did as they were instructed, but Ngakola vomited only half of the men. So the people killed him and established a secret society in which novices are "swallowed"—that is, taken into a house that is said to be Ngakola's body. In the house they are tortured, which represents being digested in the belly of Ngakola. Next they are vomited up renewed and initiated into the group (Eliade, 1958a, p. 75).

The Mouth as the Birth Canal of the Reborn Hero

The image of the mouth as a site of renewal or birth canal for a second birth, a higher birth, or a spiritual birth refers more to a spiritual (psychological) awakening than to a physical birth. This motif of death (swallowing) and rebirth (disgorging) found in the myths of the Manja and Banda is also common in other cultures and often plays an important role in the initiation rituals of adolescents. In these rituals the adolescent's identity as a child is ceremonially killed and swallowed by the deity. In the belly of the god or goddess, the initiate is then spiritually transformed. Following transformation, the initiate is disgorged from the mouth of the deity as a full-fledged member of the adult community. The swallowing represents the death of the old identity, the gestation in the belly represents the regression to the nourishing mouth/tomb/womb, and the disgorgement represents the spiritual birth itself—deliverance! This motif of the swallowing and disgorging deity is common to myths and rituals among the Polynesians, the Australian aborigines, some native North American tribes, and various aboriginal peoples in Africa and South America, just to name a few.

The most familiar version of this motif in Western culture is, of course, the myth of Jonah and the great fish (whale) in the Old Testament. A Polynesian myth tells of a hero named Nganaoa who is swallowed, along with his boat, by a kind of whale. Nganaoa props open the monster's mouth with the mast of his boat and then descends into its stomach, where he finds both of his parents still alive. He lights a fire, kills the monster, and reemerges from its mouth (Eliade, 1967a, p. 222). A 12th-century German painting from the Braunweiler monastery depicts an image of Christ drawing two people out of the mouths of dragons in a representation of salvation (Jung, 1953/1968, p. 332).

The Mouth as the Passageway for the Soul's Embodiment

In a Swahili creation myth with Islamic influences, God was said to have spoken a word that entered through Adam's mouth and spread life throughout his body (Knappert, 1970, p. 23). Briffault (1927/1977, p. 664) noted that women in Germany used to be afraid that a snake could slip into the mouth while sleeping and cause them to become pregnant. Other tales tell of women being impregnated by swallowing a rose petal or a bug. In an ancient Egyptian creation myth, Khepera (he who comes into existence) "had union with [his] clenched hand," poured his seed into his mouth, and spat forth his son, Shu, and his daughter, Tefnut (Budge, 1904/1969, pp. 308-313).

In Chinese and Japanese mythology, it is said that the flaming orb associated with the pearl, sun, moon, crystal ball, hailstone, and star is symbolic of wholeness and that which awakens consciousness. It was originally held in the mouth of the *lung*, or dragon, but was wrestled free by mortals. Ever since that time, the dragon is said to have steadfastly pursued this flaming orb. Depiction of this pursuit continues to be one of the most popular themes in Chinese and Japanese art (Allen, 1917, p. 46) and is commonly seen on porcelain dishes. In Egyptian mythology, it is the Eye of Horus that represents the hero's "treasure hard to attain." This Eye of Horus is a composite image of the "sun in the mouth" (the pupil framed by the rims of the upper and lower eyelids) and is symbolic of the creative word (Cirlot, 1962, p. 99). When the Asian shaman is conducting a healing, he may breathe in deeply in order to take in the souls of his ancestors to help him in his work (Jochelson, 1924, p. 197). When the shaman, journeying in the celestial realms, finds the lost soul of his suffering patient, he inhales it and flies it back home (Jochelson, 1924; cited in Eliade, 1964, p. 248). In some tales, placing the leaf of an herb on the lips of a dead man reunites his body and soul, bringing him back to life. Such was the case when Zeus killed Glankos with a lightning bolt and Asclepius brought him back to life by placing an herb on his lips (Walton, 1894, p. 25).

The Mouth as the Passageway for the Soul's Disembodiment

A 9th- or 10th-century Italian painting illustrates the flight of the soul, in the form of a bird, from the mouth of St. John up to Christ, seen sitting in a circle above (A.R.A.S. 5Ck. 153). In a 12th-century German painting, by Hildegard von Bingen, we see a woman lying on her deathbed while her naked soul slips out of her mouth (A.R.A.S. 5Dk. 196). In the Indian tradition, there is a belief that yawning runs the risk of losing one's soul, and thumb snapping was a precaution taken to prevent this from happening. A report on the religious beliefs of the indigenous people of Nicaragua in 1528 stated, "When they die, there comes out of their mouth something that resembles a person and is called Julio [Aztec *yuli* = to live]. This being goes to the place where the man and woman are. It is like a person, but does not die, and the body remains here" (Eliade, 1967b, p. 178). In a woodcut from an alchemical text, Theatrum Chemicum (Portu, 1613/1659), a man is depicted in the deathly state of the Nigredo, while out of his mouth there have flown two bird-like figures with human heads, symbolic of the soul or spirit (Jung, 1963, plate 10). In addition to the mouth as the departure point of the soul, there are also numerous European paintings illustrating exorcisms in which the exorcised demon is seen departing by way of the mouth (Gilman, 1982, plates 29, 30, 32, 38).

The Mouth as Integral Consciousness

In the I Ching, the Chinese oracular text, the hexagram (Number 27) called "I" or "the Corners of the Mouth" represents an unobstructed open mouth. This oracle is about integration and wholeness and refers to the tasks of nourishing oneself and the spiritual nourishment of others (Wilhelm, 1950/1967, pp. 86-89, 107-111, 489-94, 519-24). There are tales of Pindar, Homer, and Sappho, all of whom, according to legend, acquired their gift of verse by having bees, creatures symbolic of the soul and the mysteries of transformation, alight on their lips when they were young (Gerry, 1961, p. 16). There is also the 15th-century German legend of St. John Chrysostom, who was also known as "John Golden Mouth." As a youth, he prayed every morning before the image of Our Lady to help him in his studies, as he was a poor student and subject to the ridicule of others. One morning while he was praying, the Virgin called him to come close to her and kiss her on the lips. He was afraid, but her image gave him courage. She called out to him again, "Kiss me, John! Come! Do not be afraid!" He was drawn close, kissed her lips, and in that moment was filled with great wisdom, knowledge, and the ability to speak eloquently. It was then that a golden circlet formed around his mouth, and it was said to have shone like a star (Zimmer, 1957, pp. 52-54).

These examples of the mouth as the deliverer of wisdom establish the mouth's relationship to integral consciousness. In the creation mythology of the Ngaju Dayak of Borneo, the cosmic totality was conceived of as originally lying undivided in the mouth of a great, coiled water snake (Scharer, 1946/1969; cited in Eliade, 1969, pp. 77-78). In an ancient hymn (c. 1600 BCE), Ishtar, the queen of heaven and goddess of love and war, is described in all her beauty as filled with enchantment and voluptuous joy and having sweetness in her lips and life in her mouth (Sandars, 1972, p. 71). In an Indian tale, Lord Krishna as a child was eating clay when his foster mother heard of his mischievousness and went to scold him. Upon her arrival, he wiped his mouth clean and denied her accusation. Not believing him, she opened his mouth, looked inside, and saw that it contained the entire universe (Campbell, 1949/1968, p. 328). In an 18th-century Tantric Indian miniature painting, Shiva is depicted lying on his back making love to Mahavidya Chinnamasta. As a Tantrika, he withholds his ejaculation and directs the sexual-spiritual energy, the Kundalini, up the *sushumna*, or passageway through the seven chakras or spiritual energy centers of the body. The seventh chakra, located at the crown of the head, is called the Sahasrara chakra and is associated with higher consciousness, liberation from worldly existence, and oneness with God. The Sahasrara chakra is also called "the Mouth of God," and in this particular painting there emerges from the crown of Shiva's head another tiny head with its mouth open, spewing forth the River Ganges, or river of life—the sexual energy transformed (Mookerjee, 1995, plate 13).

Entering the mouth of death. Detail from the front of Conques Abbey, in southern France, showing the Last Judgement and people entering the Mouth of Hell, 11th century.

The hero is reborn from the mouth. Jonah, of the Bible, is disgorged from the belly of the great fish onto the shore.

PHILOSOPHORVM.

& ficca foluantur, calcinentur, fiue fublimentur fe
cundum quod viderit, & melius iudicatur fecun-
dum fanum fenfum operantis.

Ich bin der war grün vnnd guldifch Löw ohn for-

The soul enters the mouth. The alchemical Green Lion swallowing the sun. Carl Jung said it represented the "spiritual principle" sinking "into the embrace of physical nature" (Psychology and Alchemy, 1968, pp. 331–332) As such, it is an analogue of the soul entering the mouth in order to embody. The Green Lion of European alchemy represents one of several stages in the creation of the Philosopher's Stone. Image from a German alchemical text of circa 1530.

An exorcism: The soul, or in this case, the demon, leaves the body by way of the mouth.

The soul leaves the mouth at the time of death. In the alchemical process,
the death state is known as the Nigredo. In this drawing, a male figure is seen
in a tomb (circle) with his soul and spirit (two human-headed birds), leaving his body
by way of his mouth. Image from Viridarium Chymicum by Daniel Stolcius, 1624.

The mouth as integral consciousness.
A Chinese dragon spewing forth the sacred pearl from its mouth.

The mouth as integral consciousness. Shiva with his kundalini emerging from the seventh chakra, the Sahasrara chakra, which is also called the "Mouth of God". Notice the snake wrapped around his topknot, a small head sticking out, and the River Ganges, the River of Life, spewing out of the mouth of the little head – out of the Mouth of God. Detail from an 18th century Tantric Moghul Chinnamasta – Shiva and Shakti.

The Autistic Child as a Soul Unable or Unwilling to Embody

Recalling Jimmy's drawings of the closing mouth and our review of the symbolism of the mouth, I find that nothing describes the autistic dilemma quite so poetically as that of a soul that is unable or unwilling to embody. It is in the union of the soul and the body that the psyche gives birth to the hero and the ego with it. And the child with severe autism, of course, has an absent, weak, or damaged ego. Thus, it seems to me that the image of the mouth that Jimmy was preoccupied with, and around which all children on the severe end of the autism spectrum have conflict, may be, at a symbolic level, expressive of the soul's inability to fully embody. We can also wonder if the psychomythic gap between the mouth and the soul is equivalent to the psychosexual gap between the mouth and the nipple. I know this kind of formulation threatens to scramble together the body, the psyche, and the soul, yet I ask your indulgence. It is a poetic formulation, to be sure, but it might be useful as well.

When I say the autistic dilemma deals with that aspect of mouth symbolism pertaining to embodiment, I am talking about the mythic task of an incarnating soul. Psychologically speaking, it is about bonding with a mother, attaching to a mother, taking ownership of the body, entering the family, and entering the world. Theodore and Judith Mitrani recalled Frances Tustin's 1981 formulation that the essential process of "rootedness" had failed in these children. They suggested, "This process might be related to (or perhaps is the precursor for) what Bowlby referred to as 'bonding'" (Mitrani & Mitrani, 2015, p. xxxiii).

Thomas H. Ogden, from an object relations perspective, has proposed that an autistic-contiguous organization precedes the paranoid-schizoid organization and the depressive organization of the psyche and forms an ever present foundation of psychic structure. For Ogden (2015), "The autistic-contiguous organization is associated with a specific mode of attributing meaning to experience in which raw sensory data are ordered by means of forming pre-symbolic connections between sensory impressions that come to constitute bounded surfaces" (p. 156). This sensory mode and, particularly, the experiences on the surface of the skin "are the principal media for the creation of psychological meaning and the rudiments of the experience of self" (p. 157). And while the autistic-contiguous position is a mode of organization common to all, it helps illuminate aspects of autism as well: "Although pathological autism can be thought of as constituting an 'asymbolic' realm, the normal autistic-contiguous mode is 'pre-symbolic' in that the sensory-based units of experience being organized are preparatory for the creation of symbols mediated by experience of transitional phenomena (Winnicott, 1953)" (Ogden, 2015, pp. 160–61). "The machine-like predictability of experiences with pathological autistic shapes and objects substitutes for experiences with inevitably imperfect and not entirely predictable human beings" (p. 161). Ogden describes common autistic-contiguous anxieties as feelings of "rotting," "leaking," and falling "into endless, shapeless space" (p. 165).

As I would put it, the child with severe autism, who often appears to be residing in another world, in "endless and shapeless space," clings to autistic shapes and objects and a wordless sensory stability, largely devoid of human relatedness, in order to avoid embodiment. When I say, poetically, that the autistic child is a disembodied or poorly embodied soul, I am using the mythic metaphor of "soul" to help describe a psychological state or process—and, lest we forget, "psyche" means "soul." It would be difficult for us to speak of an identity, a self, or even an ego when discussing these primitive threshold phenomena, but "soul" is a word that approximates some sort of essential or seed potential of psychic organization. When I speak of the child with autism as a soul "unable" or "unwilling" to embody or "avoiding" embodiment, I do not want to suggest there is any will, decision, intention, or even subjectivity involved. It is simply a walled-off retreat.

The autistic child, as a disembodied or poorly embodied soul, has a weak relation to the body, to pleasure, to pain, to the family, to language, to society, to the world. The child with autism does not, in a sense, want to enter the world, or can't enter the world, or feels unwelcome in the world, and the main symptomatology is organized around the mouth: eating, drinking, and speaking. To embody or to incarnate is to be eaten by the world. It is for the soul to enter the mouth and for the child to be swallowed by the world. We all know that every infant explores the world by taking objects and putting them in his mouth. And what I am asserting here is that as the infant is taking the world in through his mouth, he is simultaneously being swallowed and incorporated into the world.

When I speak of the child with autism as not feeling welcome in the world, I am not saying the child is not welcomed by the world but that the child does not *feel* welcomed by the world. That feeling could be derived from an unwelcoming world but also from a child who is neurologically incapable of bonding, attaching, trusting, and feeling welcome. If a child is rejected by a mother, he will certainly feel unwelcome, and if he is neurologically "immune" to his mother's attempts at attachment, he will similarly feel unwelcome.

The Ritual of Opening the Mouth

If autism involves traumatized orality and orality pertains to the incorporation of the world and being incorporated by the world, then perhaps we could say, even if only poetically, that the psychomythic task of both the infant and the child with autism is embodiment—that is, entering and being swallowed by the mouth of the body, the family, and the world. If the psychomythic task is embodiment, then it might correspond to the psychological task of leaving autistic encapsulation and bonding and attaching to a mother. Through my research I discovered that there is an ancient ritual that describes the process of embodiment. However, interestingly enough, it is not a birth ritual but a funerary ritual dating back some 5,800 years to ancient Egypt, and it is associated with the myth of death and rebirth. It is called, of all things, "the ritual of opening the mouth."

If it seems paradoxical that orality and psychological birth would in some way be associated with a funerary ritual, we need only remember Bertram Lewin's (1950) "oral triad of wishes": the wish to devour, the wish to be devoured, and the wish to go to sleep (to die). The function of the ritual of opening the mouth was to reunite the Ka (spirit or character) and the Ba (soul) with the Khat (corpse) in order to be reborn as a Sahu (spiritual being); to purify, sanctify, and revivify the deceased; to guard him against death and decay in the hereafter; to transfer to him the strength, powers, and immortality of the gods; and to open his mouth and eyes so that he might partake in the sepulchral offerings of food and drink. It was through this ritual that the Sahu acquired the ability to speak, eat, breathe, think, see, hear, smell, and walk. His flesh and bones were reunited; his head was reattached to his body; and his arms, legs, feet, and hands were once again under his control. He obtained twofold strength and all-encompassing knowledge and was welcomed into the House of God, where he was to dwell throughout eternity in the presence of the gods.

The ritual of opening the mouth begins by identifying the deceased with Osiris, a hero in Egyptian mythology and the god of the underworld. It recalls in drama and incantation the death and rebirth of that great hero. Throughout the ritual, the Khat, or the statue representing the Khat, was purified, sanctified, and revivified with water, libations, incense, and ointments. The mouth and eyes were "opened" with various instruments, which also transmitted life and power to the Sahu. Interestingly, in Egyptian hieroglyphics the Ba is sometimes represented by the image of a star and other times by the image of a bird, both of which Jimmy said were in the mouth.

Near the end of the ritual, the Sahu was said to have a mouth like that of "a suckling calf on the day it was born." Numerous food offerings were then presented to him. These food offerings, which always began with milk, cheese, or whey and, among other things, always included the presentation of an animal's breast, reflect the Sahu's rebirth and reunion with the mother.

In the event that the Ba was not reunited with its Khat, and thereby not initiated into this new way of being through the ritual of opening the mouth, it was quite simply a disembodied Ba—a disembodied soul. The disembodied Ba was said to be hungry and thirsty, could not speak or breathe, ate filth, and drank polluted water. He was said to have been sad; wandering in the desert; and bringing sickness, disease, and trouble in his path. His flesh and bones were not united, his head was separated from his body, and his body parts were out of voluntary control. He was powerless, isolated from the company of the gods, and, perhaps most important, was not spiritually reborn (Budge, 1909/1972a; Budge, 1909/1972b).

The similarity between the poetry of the disembodied Ba and the torment of the child with autism is striking indeed. Not only can the autistic child be viewed as a disembodied or poorly embodied soul, but he is also known to have profound eating and speech disturbances. He is frequently seen as very sad or depressed and, like the disembodied Ba, often presents a behavior problem for others. He may have limited control over his body, distorted body perceptions, or a poor body image. He lives in emotional isolation from the people around him, including his mother. In poetic terms, he has not left the celestial realms, entered the mouth of this earthly world, and been psychologically born by way of a close relationship with a mothering figure. As Tustin would poetically put it, he has not come down to earth.

Instruments used in the ancient Egyptian Ritual of Opening the Mouth.

The Sem priest conducting the ritual of opening the mouth on the statue representing the deceased. The priest opens the mouth using the Pesh-en-kef instrument.

The Sem priest presenting the breast.

The Sem priest presenting the breast as a funeral offering to the deceased in the ritual of opening the mouth.

Falcon headed God, Horus, performing the ritual of opening the mouth on the deceased Ramses II, an Egyptian pharaoh. 1279–1213 BCE 19th dynasty. Abydos, Egypt.

The Role of the Mouth in the Funerary Ritual

The myth of death and rebirth has long been known to play a central role in funerary rituals around the world, and in my investigations I have found that the image of the mouth as a passageway for the soul also plays an important role in many of these rituals. The funerary rituals of the ancient Aztecs, the Chinese, the early Romans, the Spanish, the ancient Greeks, the Laotians, the Turkish, the Pacific Islanders, some of the tribal peoples in Africa and North America, and many others included some aspect that specifically involved the mouth. In most cases a piece of jade, gold, a pearl, a ruby, some water, a drop of honey, or a coin was placed in the mouth of the corpse. Although each culture attributed a slightly different meaning to this gesture, they all associated it with giving the person strength or assistance in his journey to the world beyond. Several associate the item in the mouth either directly or indirectly with the soul itself.

Examining the imagery associated with the ritual of opening the mouth and comparing it with the imagery associated with funerary rituals from around the globe, I found there to be three common motifs: (1) reunion of the soul and the body, (2) rebirth, and (3) reunion with the mother. These three motifs remind us of the healing task of the child with autism who needs so desperately to (1) embody, (2) be psychologically born, and (3) enter into a warm relationship with a mothering figure.

The funerary ritual, based on the imagery associated with it, represents a ritual analogue to the healing task of the child with autism as well as to the early developmental task of the infant making the transition from being a neonate to being a bonded and attached infant. This psychomythic task of embodiment is best thought of as a matter of degree rather than as a matter of success or failure. The degree to which one embodies is reflected in the degree to which the soul trusts its environment enough to let go, to be swallowed, and to send forth a rudimentary ego that will enter into relationship with a mother and be nourished. The degree to which one trusts is directly related to the degree to which one feels physically and psychically welcomed into the world. Thus, the strength and the integrity of the ego are reflected in the degree to which the soul has "trusted" the world enough to embody.

While it has long been noted that the infant comes to understand and incorporate much of the world by experiencing it through his or her mouth, I suggest that the soul of the infant is simultaneously being incorporated into the "mouth" of the human or earthly world—that is, being incorporated into one's body, family, and culture. Like the alchemical image of the sun being eaten by the lion, which Jung (1953/1968, pp. 345, 350) describes as spirit entering matter, so must the soul of the autistic child enter the mouth of the human world. It is a task not without dangers, for it represents engulfment and means becoming vulnerable to the pleasures and pains of human existence. It means leaving endless and shapeless space; leaving the celestial, or hallucinated, realms; becoming embodied in this earthly world; and being nourished by a mother in a warm maternal attachment. The inability or unwillingness to leave the hallucinated realms and embody represents the "mistrust" of a soul that perceives the world as a hostile environment in which there is more pain than pleasure (whether there truly is or is not). Withholding its trust, the soul cannot embody. Unable or unwilling to embody and enter into a relationship, the child with autism remains separate, aloof, above and outside the world of warm human relations. This leaves him always desiring to enter the world and yet, paradoxically, frozen in fear of being swallowed up by it. And there he remains, alone, disconnected, and figuratively poised above that "mouth" and its "terrible teeth."

Autism and Embodiment

But how can an ancient Egyptian myth written by adults thousands of years ago have anything to do with the primitive mental states of a child on the autism spectrum? It's a good question and we will not want to lose sight of it. In 1983 I shared with Bruno Bettelheim an early version of my ideas on the symbolism of the mouth and its relation to autism. He responded with the following:

Oct. 4, 1983
Dear Mr. Benveniste,

Just a note to thank you for having sent me your very interesting article on your experience with an autistic youngster. The development of his drawings under the impact of your treatment of him is quite convincing. I have my doubts about to what degree myths created by adults out of their unconscious can be likened to the unconscious productions of autistic individuals. But your speculations about it are certainly interesting.

Sincerely yours,

Bruno Bettelheim

I found his cautionary note to be sound and his interest in my speculations very gratifying.

In *The Empty Fortress* (1967), Bettelheim put it this way: "The infant, because of pain or discomfort and the anxiety they cause, or because he misreads the mother's actions or feelings, or correctly assesses her negative feelings, may retreat from her and the world.... Any such retreat from the world tends to weaken the baby's impulse to observe and to act on the environment, though without such an impulse personality will not develop. Retreat debilitates a young ego barely emerging from the undifferentiated stage, and leads to still further psychic imbalance" (pp. 72-73).

While "retreat" is more of a military metaphor and "disembodiment" is a spiritual metaphor, they describe basically the same thing. I have known children with autism who could not feel pain, even one who had gashed his hand on a broken window. I once observed Jimmy rocking his body in a room where some loud rock 'n' roll was playing. He was not only out of rhythm with the heavy beat of the music, but he was also completely into his own autistic rhythm. He was in total retreat.

Tustin (1986), it will be recalled, wrote that "for some individuals, for a variety of reasons, different in each case, the disillusionment of 'coming down to earth' from this ecstatic experience [blissful unity with the 'mother'] has been such a hard and injurious experience that it has provoked impeding encapsulating reactions" (p. 25). In the same work, Tustin also made reference to disembodied states. In 1989 I sent her a copy of the same article I sent to Bettelheim (Benveniste, 1983, p. 110), and she graciously replied:

Feb. 18, 1989
Dear Daniel Benveniste,

How generous of you to write to me, and how interesting to hear about your work with the child whose drawings are reproduced in your article.... How hard you worked, and how well you understood the child you wrote about. You were "on" to important matters concerning his development.... I found your notion of the importance of "embodiment" relevant to these children—they've no notion of "insides," and it's a great progress when they begin to "embody" and to "internalise," and they don't do this until they've begun to trust—but it's devastating if they're let down at this point. Some people talk about projective identification, a la Mrs. Klein, in relation to these children, and it's inaccurate. They "evacuate" not "project"—they "embody" or "imitate"—they don't identify. Thank you for the word "embody." I'll go on thinking about it further, and if I use it in any further writings, I'll of course mention your paper....

Yours sincerely,

Frances Tustin

In *The Protective Shell in Children and Adults* (1990), Tustin wrote:

> They [children with autism] feel they have nothing to hold onto and that they are falling, falling down and down, into nothingness. There seems to be no solid ground beneath their feet. To avoid this feeling of cataclysmic falling, they have resorted to the delusion that they are floating weightlessly, high above the ordinary world of human beings. They have escaped into a non-human realm, where "to be or not to be" is not an issue. Coming down to earth means that they have to face this issue. (p. 45)

> We have to bring them down to earth, whilst preserving but moderating their excessive vulnerability. As the autogenerated encapsulation is modified through the infantile transference, they have more satisfying experiences than they were able to have as a baby. As they embody these experiences, they begin to feel surrounded by a caring ambience. (p. 25)

The work of Frances Tustin has many aspects, but two of her most significant contributions are the recognition of what she calls "autistic sensation objects" and "autistic sensation shapes." The autistic sensation objects start as a hard cluster of tactile sensation, such as hard feces in the anus or a rolled-up tongue, and later are replaced with hard objects, such as hard plastic or metal toys, that are employed not for their symbolic value or even as objects per se but for the hard impression they leave on the body. They are carried, twiddled, or spun. The hardness or impenetrability is perceived as part of the body and as a kind of protection from a dangerous world (Tustin, 1986, p. 110). Autistic sensation shapes, on the other hand, "are auto-generated by such tactile activities as stroking, brushing, rubbing, smearing, and even by drawing and painting on smooth surfaces, both those of the subject's own body and those of outside objects experienced as part of the subject's body surfaces" (Tustin, 1990, p. 41). These autistic sensation shapes are soothing, comforting, and tranquilizing and ward off the awareness of separateness (Tustin, 1986, pp. 120, 146).

In Tustin's view, "Autism is anti-life, but 'anti-life' is not synonymous with death. Dying is an inevitable part of the life process. Autistic techniques are reactions to avoid becoming conscious of the 'black hole' of separation, of partings, of endings, and ultimately of death" (p. 282). Suddenly we are back to death and to death or separation as a way to be born psychologically. On the threshold between autistic shapes and representational shapes, Tustin observed, "The appearance of geometrical forms seems to be an important step in psychic development. Such forms appear at a critical point in the psychotherapeutic process, when the patient is struggling out of the 'tomb-womb' of psychogenic autism to achieve what we, metaphorically, call 'psychic birth'" (p. 167).

So from this very different angle we have found our way back to the myth of death and rebirth as a metaphor of psychological birth. Bettelheim spoke of the autistic child's retreat, Tustin spoke of encapsulation, and I offer the metaphor of disembodiment. I have used the myth of death and rebirth and the ritual of opening the mouth as analogies for the autistic dilemma and the spiritual task of infancy. But could these be more than idle literary metaphors? To answer this, let us begin by asking, *To what extent can we generalize from the ancient Egyptian funerary ritual of opening the mouth to other funerary rites?*

Funerary Rituals, the Mouth, and the Soul

When we examine the literature, we repeatedly find the funerary ritual associated with the concept of the soul. The soul is that most basic spiritual belief that there is some nonmaterial essential aspect of the person residing within the body that will live on beyond physical death. Some funerary rituals may take the form of a recitation of the people, places, deities, and otherworldly phenomena the soul can expect to encounter on its journey to the netherworld. In other rituals, offerings of food and supplies are made to the deceased to nourish and prepare the soul for life in the hereafter. An offshoot of this tradition of sepulchral food offerings is the funerary feast, in which the friends and loved ones participate in the death and rebirth of the deceased by first mourning the loss and then partaking in the food offerings. Another common sepulchral offering is the presentation of bright beautiful flowers, which not only are symbolic of spring, new life, and the cycle of death and rebirth but are often associated with healing as well. Further references to funerary imagery that is symbolic of death and rebirth are found in the funerary boat, crypt, mausoleum, tomb, coffin, and cremation urn, all of which are associated with the womb of Mother Earth.

With the ancient Egyptian ritual of opening the mouth as a model for reuniting the soul with the body, we now turn our attention to a brief cross-cultural examination of funerary rituals. As we do so, notice the recurring importance of the mouth. With regard to this recurring aspect, I must clarify that in the examples that follow:

1. I have reported only those aspects of the rituals that involve the mouth, not the rituals in their entireties.
2. Not all funerary rituals make direct reference to the mouth, but the mouth is clearly a recurring site of interest in many funerary rituals around the world.

3. If we include sepulchral food offerings and funerary feasts as ritual gestures associated with the mouth, we would be hard-pressed to find a single funerary ritual that was not in one way or another associated with the symbolism of the mouth.

For the early Romans it was common practice for the nearest relative to give the last kiss to the dying person at the moment of death in order to catch the soul as it was leaving the body through the mouth with the final breath. The same relative then closed the eyes of the deceased and the body was set on the floor for washing, anointing, and dressing. A coin was then placed in the mouth to pay Charon, the ferryman, for the ride across the river of death (Toynbee, 1971, pp. 43–44).

In ancient Greece, the ritual began with the closing of the mouth and eyes. Then a coin was placed in the mouth as a charm against evil spirits and as the fare for crossing the river of the dead. Clay vessels were broken, and garlands and sepulchral offerings were presented. Offerings included milk, honey, water, celery, wine, fruits, vegetables, and a sacrificial bull, sheep, goat, or fowl (Alexiou, 1974, pp. 4–7, 27, 30). Gold bands were wrapped around the head of the deceased to cover the mouth and eyes. These gold bands have been found to date back as early as the 4th century ACE (Kurtz, 1971, pp. 212–13).

For the ancient Aztecs, going into the afterlife meant facing the hazardous journey of passing through the eight underworlds, the goal of which was to arrive safely in the ninth underworld for eternal rest. To prepare the deceased for the journey, warm blankets, paper flags, water, dogs, and food were provided. The deceased also took gifts to present Mictlantecuhtli and Mictlancihuatl, the lord and lady of the underworld, so as to assure their welcome reception. Mourners placed in the mouth of the deceased a jade bead, which served as a substitute heart and provided the necessary strength to safely proceed on this great journey (Peterson, 1962, pp. 141–42).

The Santee Sioux of North America painted the faces of their dead with red paint. If the deceased had been a great warrior, however, a black hand was painted on his mouth (Habenstein & Lamers, 1963, p. 218).

In the funerary rituals of a Basque village called Murelaga, a woman prepares the corpse for burial. The corpse is washed, its hair is combed, and it is dressed in its finest clothes. Then the eyes are closed with dabs of wax and the mouth is tied shut with a cloth. The closing of the mouth and eyes is to prevent the soul of the deceased from taking other family members to the land of the dead (Douglass, 1969, pp. 24, 222).

In a Jewish tradition, immediately after death mourners say, "Blessed be the true judge." Then a feather is placed on the lips, and for the next eight minutes the corpse is left untouched while everyone assembled watches attentively for the slightest sign of the feather's movement, signaling the departure of the soul (Roth, 1971, p. 1426).

In Turkey a few drops of water are dripped into the mouth of the dying person to quench the thirst and thus render the deceased less vulnerable to the temptations of Satan, who offers a cup of water in exchange for the deceased's confession of a loss of faith in Allah (Habenstein & Lamers, 1963, p. 156).

The Dahomeans of West Africa take special care to see to it that no one steals a hair, a bit of cloth, or moisture from the mouth or any other part of the corpse, which may capture the soul and then be used in necromantic practices (p. 156).

In Ethiopia, when a celibate monk or virgin nun dies, the arms are folded over the chest in such a way that the fingers rest gently on the mouth (p. 249).

The Ashanti tribe of Ghana, in West Africa, believes that at death the "thirsting spirit" has to climb a steep hill that leads to eternity. To assist in this task, family or friends pour a little water into the parched throat of the deceased to relieve this thirst before this great climb (p. 202).

The Marquesans in the South Pacific believe the soul departs through the mouth or nose, so it is the custom to plug them up in an attempt to prolong this inevitable departure (Frazer, 1924, p. 352).

The Balinese believe that in death the soul is reborn with powers perfected. To symbolize this belief, splinters of mirror are laid on the eyelids, steel fragments laid on the teeth, jasmine flowers stuffed into the nostrils, iron nails laid on the arms and legs, and a gold ring set with a ruby is placed in the mouth (Habenstein & Lamers, 1963, p. 686).

In Laos a coin or a small piece of gold is slipped between the teeth of the deceased. The gesture symbolizes the superfluousness of the material world by showing how little the soul needs to take with it to the land of the dead (p. 96).

In northern India, among the Muslim tribes, a few drops of honey are dripped into the deceased's mouth to satisfy the palate and in doing so strengthen the deceased so as not to be tempted by sweetmeats offered by the evil one, who lies in wait for the soul (p. 130).

It will be recalled that in Chinese myth, the dragon, or lung, is frequently seen chasing after a luminescent and transformative pearl, moon, sun, crystal ball, or jewel (Williams, 1974, p. 138). Whatever it might be, it represents the cosmic opposites joined as one (De Groot, 1964, p. 277). In some parts of China, gold leaf and pearls are placed in the mouth of the deceased, and a ball of red paper mixed with ashes of incense is placed between the lips (Habenstein & Lamers, 1963, p. 7). When Chuang-tzu, the Taoist philosopher, was on his deathbed, his disciples promised to provide him with the most beautiful and elaborate funeral. Chuang-tzu replied, "I consider heaven and earth to be my coffin and vault, the sun and moon to be a double piece of jade, the stars and planets to be pearls, and all the products of nature a supply of presents bestowed upon me; are not then the articles required for my burial ready at hand? Why will you add anything to these?" (De Groot, 1964, p. 305).

The concept of some essential aspect of the being—the soul—surviving death and either wandering among the living and causing problems or journeying to the hereafter for eternal life is clearly the recurring theme inspiring the need to put a little something in the mouth, tie the mouth shut, make food offerings, or have a funerary feast. The mythology of a hero entering and exiting the mouth is an inevitable symbolizing and mythologizing of the experience of food entering and exiting the mouth. And the mythology of a soul entering and exiting the mouth is an inevitable mythologizing of the experience of breathing in, breathing out, and the relationship of breath to life itself. With the first breath the soul enters the body and there is life, and with the last breath the soul leaves the body and there is death.

An Iron Age woman's grave from Himlingoeje, Denmark. In her mouth is a little piece of gold – 'Charon's Penny' – From the 3rd century BCE.

Tiny Chinese (Han) jade figurines. As a part of funerary ritual practice, a small figurine would be placed in the mouth of the deceased before burial.

Aztec archeologists at the Great Temple of Tenochtitlan in Mexico City found human skulls with sacrificial knives placed in the mouths and nasal orifices. The flint blades were seen as metaphors for the breath and words of the deceased.

Death and Rebirth and the Phylogenetic Project of Psychoanalysis

Returning to the phylogenetic project of psychoanalysis, we can now create the following schema in which the oral stage in normal development is analogically linked to infantile autism, the myth of death and rebirth, and the ancient funerary ritual, but it leaves us wondering about the corresponding stage in cultural development, which has been left open, for now.

Individual and Cultural Dimensions	Analogous Expressions of Earliest Stages
4. A stage of normal development	Oral stage—early infancy
5. A form of psychopathology	Infantile autism
6. A stage in cultural evolution	——?——
7. A myth	Death and rebirth
8. A ritual	Ancient funerary ritual

To what stage in cultural evolution might we attribute the myth of death and rebirth and the funerary ritual? It's hard to know. But it is clear that we are dealing with the very primitive, pan-cultural denial of death as well as the earliest stirrings of the concept of the soul, which are undoubtedly embedded in our most ancient prehistory.

Now, if autism appears before the brief psychotic disorder and infancy precedes adolescence, then it stands to reason that the myth of death and rebirth and the funerary ritual may well have appeared before the myth of sacral kingship and the ancient New Year festival—that is, before the Urban Revolution. But that reasoning presents us with yet another problem. We know that the ancient Egyptian ritual of opening the mouth was written in full around 2,000 years ago but is clearly a ritual of great antiquity, with origins and historical references in ancient Egypt dating back to the Fourth Dynasty, 5,800 years ago (Budge, 1909/1972b, p. 2; Budge, 1909/1972a, pp. 1-2). That situates it firmly at the birth of civilization, and therefore the ritual coincides with the emergence of the myth of sacral kingship and the ancient New Year festival. Now, sacral kingship can't possibly be older than the birth of civilization, as it mythologizes kingship, the calendar, the god-kings, and the king-gods, but what about the ritual of opening the mouth? There is no aspect of the ritual that would prohibit our considering the possibility of its being older than its first written description.

However, if the definition of civilization includes the beginning of writing and literature, how can we pursue the origins of the funerary ritual any earlier than the birth of civilization?

Well, if we confine ourselves to literature, this pursuit must end before it begins. Yet if we allow the archeological artifacts to speak for themselves—or at least suggest—we may indeed be able to get some ideas about the antiquity of the funerary ritual. For example, in a Bronze Age burial excavated near Nazareth, Israel, a corpse was laid to rest in a large clay pot, symbolic of the womb, and placed in a fetal position (Neumann, 1955/1963, plate 42). The town of Hajji Firuz, in northwestern Iran, was burned and its people massacred in 5152 BCE. Before burying the dead, the survivors sprinkled red ochre over the bodies (Mellaart, 1965, p. 72). This red ochre may well have been intended to ritualistically bring life to the deceased by associating the blood-red color of this powdered stone with the lifeblood in their veins. At Hacilar, located in western Turkey, c. 5600 BCE, the dead were found buried in the fetal position with clay bowls, beads, cups, and bone pins under a house or courtyard (pp. 107-12).

At Çatal Hüyük, in south-central Turkey, c. 5900 BCE, the dead were buried below the platforms of their houses and shrines. The deceased were laid to rest there only after the flesh had been stripped off the bones, the bones placed in a fetal position, and then wrapped up in cloth or skins or placed in a basket. Some of the bones were painted with red ochre or cinnabar. And funerary gifts were items used in daily life (pp. 85-89). It is from the womb-like urns, fetal positioning, revivifying red ochre, and grave goods that we might imagine an accompanying myth of death and rebirth and a ritual that prepares the deceased for life in the hereafter.

At Khirokitia, on the island of Cyprus, c. 6020 BCE, there lived a people who buried their dead among the houses or under them. Women were accompanied with stone bowls and necklaces, while men and children were accompanied with pins and other offerings. All bodies were set in the fetal, or contracted, position (pp. 52-54). At Nea Nikomedeia, on the eastern coast of the Grecian peninsula, an early Neolithic settlement was unearthed (c. 6220 BCE). In the article reporting this discovery, the author marvels at how little regard these people had for their dead. He cites the burial location outside the house walls, the lack of personal adornment or sepulchral offerings, and the way they "were crammed into a barely adequate depression." He then goes on to say that "in one enigmatic instance, however, a skeleton was found with a large pebble thrust between its jaws" (Rodden, 1972, pp. 95-102).

Further back in time, as we trace the origins of the funerary ritual and speculate on the possibility of an accompanying myth of death and rebirth, we note that at Eynan, c. 7000 BCE, in northern Israel, there lived Mesolithic people who used a circular, stone-walled structure as a tomb. This tomb contained at least seven individuals dressed in their finest attire and covered with red ochre (Clark & Piggott, 1965, p. 151). Other burial sites at Eynan were found underneath the houses or under the floors of caves being used as living spaces. In one such burial, c. 8500 BCE, a chieftain was found with his skull propped up so as to be facing the snowy peak of Mount Hermon (Mellaart, 1965, pp. 26–27). The people of Eynan were part of a larger culture, the Natufians. At Tel-es-Sultan, Jericho, another Natufian site, head burials were practiced. In the ritual of head burial, the skull was covered with clay and the clay modeled to return it to its previous lifelike form, and the eyes were inset with seashells. Head burials were also conducted in Mesolithic Germany at approximately the same time, but in these rites no efforts were made to reconstruct the flesh out of clay. Instead, at Ofnet, in southern Germany, nests of up to 27 skulls were found coated with red ochre and buried with personal ornaments and microliths—small stone blades (G. Clark, 1967, pp. 117–119).

The people of the Upper Paleolithic commonly prepared their dead by dressing them in their best clothes and sprinkling them with red ochre. The bodies were contracted into the fetal position or stretched out and placed in a shallow grave under the living space, whether it was a cave or an open site. In some locations, stones or heavy bones served as roofs over the deceased, and in most cases food, jewelry, or stone tools accompanied them in their graves (Chard, 1969, p. 149).

In France, an Upper Paleolithic skeleton was discovered under a rock shelter and found to be in the familiar fetal position and tinged with red ochre. Another five well-preserved skeletons also sprinkled with ochre were found in a cave at San Teodoro, Sicily. Both the French and Italian discoveries were about 17,000 years old (Boule & Vallois, 1957, p. 282).

At Sungir, 130 miles east of Moscow, two Cro-Magnon burials were found. In one of the graves, two boys were found buried together lying on their backs, head to head, with their bodies in opposite orientation. One boy was about 8 years old and the other about 12 or 13. They were dressed in beaded garments and had with them spears made from straightened mammoth tusks, ivory bracelets and rings, and hats of some sort. The other spectacular grave at this site was that of a 55-year-old man. The grave had been sprinkled with red ochre prior to his burial, and still more was sprinkled on the corpse itself after it was set in place. The dead man was dressed in leather clothes that had ivory beads stitched to them. He had with him in his grave two dozen bracelets made of mammoth ivory, a necklace made of pierced arctic fox teeth, and 1,500 bone ornaments. Both this grave and those of the two boys are 23,000 years old (Prideaux, 1973, p. 35).

In the French cave known as Grotte des Enfants, two people were buried in the fetal position, covered in red ochre, and accompanied by perforated shells and decorative objects. This funeral site is 30,000 years old (Boule & Vallois, 1957, p. 287).

As we examine the origins of the funerary ritual deeper into our past, we must keep in mind that the people who left these artifacts were a hunting and gathering people who followed the migratory paths of the big game animals. They had no permanent dwellings or agriculture, but they were spiritually oriented insofar as they buried their dead in a way that suggests a future orientation and perhaps even a myth of death and rebirth.

In the rugged Zagros Mountains of northern Iraq, there is a cave known as the Big Cave of Shanidar. In the floor of this cave, a Neanderthal was found buried on a bed of woody branches and bright colorful flowers. These flowers were identified by the microscopic examination of pollen found in the soil below and surrounding the bones. They were identified as species related to the grape hyacinth, bachelor's button, hollyhock, and groundsel. These all have brightly colored flowers, and contemporary Iraqis use some of them in herbal remedies. The Shanidar flower burial is 60,000 years old (Poirer, 1973, p. 182; Constable, 1973, pp. 135-49). Recent analyses have called into question the flower burial interpretation in favor of the theory that rodents dug holes into the burial site and deposited flowers and other plant matter. In either case, it is an impressive Neanderthal burial site (R. Klein, 2002, p. 194).

Then there is the Skhul Cave on Mount Carmel in Israel, where eight male and ten female Homo sapiens were found, intentionally buried in a site littered with 10,000 Mousterian stone tools. The adult male specimen, known as Skhul V, and nine other adults and children excavated from the cave at Skhul may represent, along with the people from the nearby cave of Qafzeh, the ancestral population of modern humans that later spread out to occupy the globe. The skeleton Skhul V is of a male between 30 and 40 years old. He was laid on his back and turned to the right. His legs were flexed tightly and his chin pressed close to his chest. His left arm was stretched out across his body, and, most significantly, it appears that when he was buried his hand was clasping the jawbone of a wild boar. This intentional burial and apparent funeral were conducted 90,000 years ago (Johanson & Edgar, 2006, p. 258).

Bones have long been said to contain the souls of the dead, and this is especially the case with skulls and jawbones, which often serve as amulets in shamanic ritual. We might imagine that as this man set off for the land of the dead, he was strengthened by the soul or spirit of the wild boar, which he had incorporated into his own being by killing it, eating it, and possessing this jawbone amulet. Or perhaps it was his totem. We may well imagine that he was strengthened by this jawbone amulet in much the same way as a deceased ancient Chinese man is strengthened by having a pearl placed in his mouth or the ancient Aztec by having a piece of jade placed in his. With this skeleton lying in the fetal position and holding on to the jawbone, the Skhul funeral site offers a dramatic statement about the ancient origins of the myth of death and rebirth and reminds us of the recurring association between death, rebirth, and the symbolism of the mouth (the jawbone).

Although it may be challenging for us to understand, it seems as though the earliest experiences of infancy, of surrendering to the care of a mothering figure and being psychologically born into human culture, are reactivated in the emotional challenge of coming to terms with the death of a loved one. In the dance of mother and infant, there is an ongoing encounter between the two—a meeting and a greeting. And in the case of the death of a loved one, the mourning survivor is left with an unanswered greeting, an unreciprocated meeting, an encounter with an absent other. The mourning survivor calls the name of the dearly departed, but there is no reply. This unanswered greeting leaves the mourner distressed and inclined to imagine that this unfulfilled encounter, will find fulfillment on another plane of reality with a god, with a totem, or with an ancestor spirit. Perhaps the deceased and the grieving mourner will even someday meet again in the land of the dead.

While the funerary ritual is a blatant denial of the finality of death and an unconsciously motivated defense against the bitter loss, it is also a socially sanctioned way of defending the group and the individual from the shattering effects of loss by promoting the process of mourning. Although the Paleolithic funerary ritual provides us with the earliest archeological evidence of the spiritual concept of the soul, the object relations required to abstract a soul were probably already elaborate enough in the Paleolithic to be attached to unique relationships with specific people who may well have had names and were able to anticipate absence and mourn their losses. Yet the main point here is that while the ritual of opening the mouth is only 5,800 years old, the funerary ritual itself goes back at least 90,000 years and appears to be associated with a belief in the spiritual concept of the soul and the myth of death and rebirth.

From Darwin's and Freud's phylogenetic fantasies, to Perry's work on the brief psychotic disorder and the Urban Revolution, to my work on autism and the Paleolithic period, we appear to have found our way into the belief systems of our prehistoric ancestors. I will be elaborating this further in the next chapters, but for now we can add the phylogenetic dimension, the Upper Paleolithic, to the schema associated with the first ontogenetic stage—the oral stage—and lay it side by side with that of the schema I created based on John Weir Perry's work. Once again, the two columns each include two aspects of individual phenomena (a developmental stage and a form of psychopathology) and three aspects of cultural phenomena (a stage in cultural evolution, a myth, and a ritual). They are united by sharing analogous points of agreement. The difference between the two columns is that the first column precedes the second in both individual development and cultural evolution:

Oral stage—early infancy	Genital stage—adolescence
Infantile autism	Brief psychotic disorder
Upper Paleolithic	Urban Revolution
Myth of death and rebirth	Myth of sacral kingship
Ancient funerary ritual	Ancient New Year festival

With these two points in the spectrum of cultural evolution established, we are now in a position to wonder what took place in our cultural evolution between the Upper Paleolithic and the Urban Revolution. In what way were those cultural changes related to the stages of psychological development between infancy and adolescence, between the oral stage and the later genital stage? Did the anal and phallic, or early genital, stages leave their traces in cultural evolution?

Hold these questions in mind, as we will be getting into all of this in chapter 5, but first we need to step back even earlier in time. Freud said the Oedipus complex is a psycho-Lamarckian racial inheritance from repeated battles between despotic primal fathers and rebelling fraternal clans over countless generations. But I say the Oedipus complex is the natural outcome of elaborating our higher primate alpha male dynamics by way of the human symbolic function. Instinctual behaviors that are symbolized become our psychodynamics. In order to grasp this idea, we need to acquaint ourselves with human evolution, our chimpanzee cousins, and the higher primate social instincts or ritualizations. We also need to consider the extraordinary evolution of the human symbolic function, which transformed our higher primate ritualizations into our human psychodynamics. This is what we will be addressing next in chapter 4.

CHAPTER 4

Human Evolution: How We Got to Be the Way We Are

> Every civilized human being, whatever his conscious development
> is still an archaic man at the deeper levels of his psyche.
> —Carl Gustav Jung, *Modern Man in Search of a Soul*

We're now going back in time to the beginning of the universe, the appearance of life on earth, and the evolution of man in order to better understand the facts of the body and the emergence of the symbolic function, which allowed us to symbolize our universe. We will look into the ritualizations, or social instincts, of chimpanzees in particular to understand how we transformed those social instincts into human psychodynamics.

The big bang origin of the universe occurred 13.8 billion years ago, the physical origin of the earth 4.5 billion years ago, and the first evidence of life on earth about 3.8 billion years ago. The first protozoa and algae appeared 2.5 billion years ago, and the first vertebrates (jawless fish) appeared 505 million years ago. Then came the fish with jaws, amphibians, and reptiles. The first mammal-like reptiles appeared 290 million years ago, followed by an explosion of life that gave rise to dinosaurs, birds, and mammals. The first primates appeared 65 million years ago, followed by the appearance of the monkeys and gibbons. The great apes made their appearance 10–20 million years ago, and from them evolved the chimpanzees, orangutans, and gorillas. Chimpanzees have evolved very slowly, and because of this, modern chimpanzees bear a striking resemblance to their 6-million-year-old ancestors. But from those chimpanzee-like apes 6 million years ago there also emerged a fast-evolving line of chimpanzee cousins called the *hominin* line.

As this hominin line evolved, so did its primate social instincts. It is my proposal that these primate social instincts became human psychodynamics after the human symbolic function underwent a dramatic transformation around 50,000 years ago. This naturally raises our curiosity about those primate social instincts, and in this chapter we'll explore them to learn a little more about how we got to be the way we are.

Primate Ritualizations and Social Instincts

Oral stage dynamics found expression in the cultural challenges of the Paleolithic with its orientation to food and feeding, the fusion of culture with nature, the emergence of subjectivity and the concept of the soul, and the innovations of ritual cannibalism, and funerary rituals involving orality (food offerings and jawbone amulets). But we certainly couldn't say orality emerged during the Paleolithic. No, it would be much safer to say that orality appeared about 65 million years ago when the mammalian line began to diversify and milk provisioning became a distinguishing characteristic (Matsuzawa et al., 2006, p. 128). Even the earliest mammalian offspring were born prematurely, had long periods of dependence on their mothers, and, most significantly, also needed to suck at the breast for their initial sustenance. This, we could imagine, would have been the beginning of orality and mammalian bonding and attachment.

Human orality no doubt shares much in common with mammalian orality in general and even more so with animals closer to our own species, such as chimpanzees. It would not be surprising to create anxiety, mistrust, or distress in a nonhuman mammal by disrupting this oral stage with erratic or unsympathetic feeding strategies. But the pleasures and vicissitudes of the mammalian oral stage take on a unique quality in the human infant: they take on "meaning." The mouth becomes symbolized and socialized, as does the breath, food, drink, and the words that pass through it.

Anal-stage dynamics are evident in the way mammalian infants are controlled in some ways and granted freedoms in others by their mothers, in the management of feces and urine and also in their overall movements and behavior. The anal and phallic stages and the latency phase might in some ways be less obvious in some mammals, but as we get closer to animals that are more similar to ourselves, we begin to see behaviors that might be fundamental to our own innately determined social instincts. One could well imagine that reaching sexual maturity (adolescence—the genital stage) is a universal stage in mammalian development. Yet there are many different solutions to power dynamics and mating behavior within the mammalian world. And again, what makes these solutions so different in humans is that the entrance into sexual maturity is symbolized, ritualized, mythologized, and given personal and cultural meaning within the context of initiation rituals and other social conventions.

Imre Hermann (1926), in "Oedipus and Castration Complex Models in Monkeys," maintained that we should not look for the Oedipus complex in monkeys but for components of monkey behavior that become organized into the Oedipus complex in humans. Toward this end, Hermann examined several aspects of primate behavior as prototypes, forerunners, or constituent parts of the Oedipus and castration complexes, such as the strict father who stops the son's sexual intercourse with the mother; the fight between father and son in which the father is killed; the victorious son having intercourse with the mother; and so on (p. 61).

Reijo Holmström (1991), in his article "On the Phylogeny of the Oedipus Complex: Psychoanalytic Aspects of the Ethology of Anthropoid Apes," recognized forms that the oedipal constellation has taken in the African anthropoid apes. He noted that in both chimpanzees and gorillas "we find primal scene situations, homosexual practices, powerful rivalry between males over females, the overthrowing (though not necessarily killing) of the former leader, and the formation of male groups.... The ritualized killing of the infants in the battle over a desirable female is common in both species" (p. 297).

Holmström also made an interesting point concerning the function of the mother-son incest taboo among chimpanzees and gorillas:

> The incest inhibition forces the young male to seek a sexual partner from outside the circle of his nearest relatives. The temporary alliance between the leader and the young male strengthens the defensive capability of the group and the safety of the offspring, which is of fundamental importance for the preservation of the species. The process whereby the young male moves from the mother's company to that of a male (gorilla) or males (chimpanzee) is important in terms of the training of the young animal; at the same time it diminishes his dependence on the mother. (p. 295)

Social instincts, those complex innate communicative behaviors that serve a basic survival function for the individual as well as the species, are called *ritualizations*. Sir Julian Huxley (1966) sees "ritual" and "ritualization" as very different phenomena with some extraordinarily similar qualities that warrant the discussion of the two together:

> Ritualization may be defined ethologically as *the adaptive formalization or canalization* of emotionally motivated behavior, under the teleonomic pressure of natural selection so as: (a) to promote better and *more unambiguous signal function*, both intra- and interspecifically; (b) to serve as more efficient stimulators or releasers of more efficient patterns of action in other individuals; (c) *to reduce intra-specific danger*; and (d) to serve as *sexual or social bonding* mechanisms." (p. 250; my italics)

"Teleonomic pressure," I must note, refers to the quality of purposefulness and goal-directedness of a function, a ritualization in this case, based on the evolution of that function and its reproductive success. Ritualizations are behaviors seen in many animal species. A ritualization begins as an innate behavior with a particular function that, through evolution, is modified in one way or another (intensity, strength, or direction) and takes on a separate communicative function that reduces intra-group damage or improves intra-group bonding (p. 258). Ritualizations support social interactions such as bonding, threat behavior, and courtship.

Huxley noted that animal ritualizations and human rituals function in a somewhat similar way, although the behavior is encoded and transmitted genetically for ritualizations and culturally for rituals. The learning capacity of Homo sapiens accelerated the complexity and variety of rituals and the speed of acquisition. Rituals develop in psychosocial evolution with a primarily ontogenetic basis rather than a phylogenetic basis. Rituals are derived through psychosocial selection, not natural selection, and they develop in decades not millennia (p. 258).

Huxley observed that "most human rituals and ceremonies are preponderant symbolic and non-genetic, a few have an innate genetic basis and act as signals or automatic releasers of behavior in others" (p. 259). As an example of a human ritualization, he points to the smile signal between infant and mother (p. 264). I would agree but argue that the genetically based ritualizations (innate primate social instincts) residing at the heart of human rituals are actually stronger than Huxley might have imagined. It is just that the symbolic non-genetic components of language and culture are what cover over our ritualizations, obscuring them and bringing into higher relief all the cultural differences.

Erik Erikson (1966/1987b) also called our attention to the smile signal between infant and mother. He wrote, "Ritualization in man seems to be grounded in the preverbal experience of infants while reaching its full elaboration in grand public ceremonies.... The theme of ritualization... can help us to see new connections between seemingly distant phenomena, such as human infancy and man's institutions, individual adaptation and the function of ritual" (p. 576). Erikson suggested that the "greeting ceremonial" is the ritualization, in human behavior, between mother and infant that supports the oral stage of psychosexual development and the stage of trust versus mistrust in psychosocial development: "The 'greeting ceremonial' is the way mother and infant greet one another in the morning. The infant signals he is awake, the mother calls him by name and they respond to each other again and again in a dance based on a 'mutuality of recognition.'... I would suggest, therefore, that this first and dimmest affirmation, this sense of a hallowed presence, contributes to man's ritual-making a pervasive element which we will call the 'Numinous'" (pp. 577–78).

Erikson recognized this attitude in the believer who confesses his dependence upon and childlike faith in the supernatural being who lifts up and uplifts the believer to a benign faint smile: "The result is a sense of separateness transcended, and yet also of distinctiveness confirmed" (p. 578). The "Numinous" is the "aura of a hallowed presence" (Erikson,

1982/1997, p. 45) between the "I" and the "other" of the infant and mother, which forms the basis of subsequent encounters of the numinous in love, religion, and art.

To my way of thinking, this numinous experience corresponds directly to the naked encounter with being and nonbeing, which our Paleolithic ancestors contained with the invention of the funerary ritual—a ritual created after the death of a loved one who no longer participated in the greeting ceremonial. Thus, the ritualization of the greeting ceremonial helps to contain the ambiguity of the awe and the awful, the love and the threat experienced in the encounter between mother and infant. This ritualization also creates a psychosocial connection to contain the promise of benevolence and ward off the threats of wrath and abandonment (Erikson, 1966/1987b, p. 579). In Erikson's (1982/1997) view, "A lack of such early connection can, in extreme cases, reveal an 'autism' on the part of the child that corresponds or probably is responded to by some maternal withdrawal" (p. 45).

While Erikson associated the first stage of development with a specific behavioral ritualization—the greeting ceremonial—the subsequent stages he offered were not behaviors as such; they were qualities or abstract concepts. He associated the anal stage and autonomy versus shame and doubt with the ritualization of "the judicious." The phallic stage and initiative versus guilt were associated with the "dramatic." The latency phase and industry versus inferiority were associated with the "formal" or "technical." But then with the genital stage and identity versus identity confusion, Erikson (1966/1987b) returned to specific behaviors such as the rituals created spontaneously by adolescents to mark them as separate from the children below and the adults above (p. 582). One is reminded here of adolescents who spontaneously invent initiation rites or rites of passage by taking drugs together, taking risks together, becoming "blood brothers," forming secret clubs or gangs, getting pierced or tattooed, creating pacts, and other practices to draw the young person into something of a "tribe."

If we are to recognize ritualizations (innately determined social behaviors) associated with each stage of development, we need to closely examine small, recurring behaviors that we would expect to be present cross-culturally. Trying to look for such behavior in children, however, is fraught with all sorts of confounding variables, not the least of which are language and culture. That said, there are more obvious ritualizations (social instincts) in chimpanzee behavior, and it stands to reason that these ritualizations are the simian foundations of ritualizations in Homo sapiens.

When we begin to think about psychoanalytic instinct theory in relation to primate ritualizations, some interesting new considerations come into view. While Freud suggested an archaic inheritance in a collective mind, Kleinian theory suggested a phylogenetic inheritance of ideas related to instincts. Thomas H. Ogden (1986) more recently proposed "a theory of inborn, organizing codes (associated with life and death instincts) by which perception is organized and meanings are attached to experience in a highly determined way" (p. 4). In this way, Ogden formulated instincts as psychological deep structures. This is a useful reformulation.

I would like to further unpack the life and death instincts in relation to our primate ritualizations and the consequences that come about in response to their being frustrated, gratified, or transformed through the vicissitudes of development. This would mean speaking of these instincts in relation to the ritualizations of greeting, suckling, mother-infant attachment, and weaning. By thinking of human instincts in relation to ritualizations, we link ourselves to our primate cousins and recognize specific instincts that are not socially acquired but are essentially human. Each of our primate cousins demonstrates species-specific ritualizations, so we cannot assume ours are identical with any other primate. That said, we share 98.8 percent of our DNA with chimpanzees, which is more than we share with any other animal.

The ritualizations of the solitary orangutan or the silverback gorilla with its harem will no doubt be informative in an exploration of primate ritualizations, but the orangutan and gorilla are genetically and behaviorally more distantly related to us than are the chimpanzees. So, without further delay, I offer the following very preliminary developmental schema of chimpanzee ritualizations, which I suggest represent another way of thinking about our human social instincts. In this sense, ritualizations, as social instincts, are the seeds of our human psychodynamics (Benveniste, 2021. pp. 33-50). They are the innate fixed-action patterns that have a communicative function, which we, as humans, elaborate by way of our symbolic function and then use as further scaffolding to construct personality and culture.

When our primate ritualizations were symbolized by our evolving symbolic function, during the last 100,000 years (and most dramatically 50,000 years ago), they transformed into our human psychodynamics laden with personal and cultural meaning, object relations, and personality dynamics. Our human psychodynamics were then ritualized and mythologized throughout our subsequent cultural evolution. The symbolic function had to have been evolving all along, but heightened capacities did not emerge and leave traces in the archeological record until the Paleolithic period, when there was an expansion of technological, artistic, and spiritual innovations. But before getting into all that, let's look at the following list of primate ritualizations in chimpanzee behavior and a brief discussion of each:

1. Greeting behavior and mother-infant bonding
2. Dominance and submission
3. Copulation interference
4. Sexual inhibitions and incest taboos
5. Displaying, battling, courtship, and mating

There is much that can be said about primate ritualizations and there is much to be worked out with our colleagues in primatology, but this is a preliminary attempt to approach the subject. The interested reader will find further elaborations on this topic in appendix 4.

Greeting Behavior and Mother-Infant Bonding: Orality

Jane Goodall (1986) and her colleagues have witnessed the importance of mother-infant greeting in chimpanzees, including eye-to-eye gazing, touching, kissing, hugging, soothing, grooming, and suckling. They have observed the distressed searching behavior, whimpering, or crying that occurs when there are separations as well as the obvious emotional damage that occurs as a result of the early death of a young chimpanzee's mother who can no longer return the infant's greeting (p. 203).

Tetsuro Matsuzawa created an evolutionary stage model of the mother-infant relationship in which the mammalian provision of milk is shared with 4,500 species, primate infant clinging is shared with 200 species, simian embracing by mother is shared with 80 species, and hominoid mutual gazes and smiling are shared by 2 species: chimpanzees and humans (Matsuzawa et al., 2006, pp. 128, 140).

Chimpanzee greeting behaviors begin in infancy and are elaborated throughout the life cycle. They are integrated into dominance and submission behavior, courtship, copulation, alpha male dynamics, and more. When chimpanzees separate and don't see each other for an extended period of time, they reunite with great excitement and greet each other with kisses, hugs, and grooming. Deaths of loved ones are met with attempts to elicit greeting responses, and when no response is forthcoming, the surviving chimpanzees grieve their loss bitterly.

After studying greeting behavior in several books on chimpanzees, I made a startling discovery of my own. I discovered something that was not there! Chimpanzees do not "say good-bye." They celebrate reunions and grieve their losses but do not anticipate absence and signal it. When I had the opportunity to very briefly meet Jane Goodall, after one of her public lectures, I quickly put forth my question: "Do chimpanzees have any way to say good-bye?" She quickly replied, "No, they don't. They just walk away. Isn't that funny?" (Jane Goodall, personal communication, October 28, 2010, Seattle, Washington). Well, yes, that is "funny" and very interesting too, because while chimpanzees "just walk away" and humans "say good-bye," this "saying good-bye" is the very basis of the funerary ritual that initiated the spiritual life of Homo sapiens 100,000 years ago.

Dominance and Submission: Anality

Holmström (1991) observed that chimpanzees and gorillas have a maturation process very similar to humans but then added, "The significant difference—admittedly an important one—is the absence or relative unimportance of the anal stage in these apes" (p. 277). I suspect that in terms of the management of feces, anality is of "relative unimportance" for gorillas and chimpanzees, as it would be even for our nomadic Paleolithic ancestors. But once our ancestors started living in permanent houses and were no longer content to evacuate their bowels wherever they just happened to be, anality probably took on a new character. While anality in terms of the management of feces is not so evident in gorillas and chimpanzees, the dynamics of control or dominance and submission around which human anality is organized certainly are, and these dynamics are naturally first established between mother and infant.

When two chimpanzees meet, they greet each other in a way that negotiates, establishes, or, more commonly, confirms the hierarchy between them. The lower-ranking individual submitting to the dominant individual will "not only reach out his hand toward his superior, as in supplication, but may actually make contact. The dominant, in response to submissive gestures, will in many instances respond by touching, kissing, embracing, or mounting. The lower-ranking individual may actually beg for a reassuring touch. Once the desired contact has been made, the subordinate visibly relaxes" (Goodall, 1986, p. 124).

Submissive ritualizations include presenting one's rump to the dominant chimpanzee, reaching out a hand, crouching down low to the ground with slicked-back hair, and bobbing up and down. These are the actions of a submissive or simply frightened animal (pp. 122-23). Frans de Waal (1982/2007) adds to this list short pant-grunts and deep bows: "Sometimes 'greeters' bring objects with them (a leaf, a stick), stretch a hand out to their superior, or kiss his feet, neck or chest. The dominant chimpanzee reacts to this 'greeting' by stretching himself up to a greater height and making his hair stand on end.... The one almost grovels in the dust, the other regally receives the 'greeting.'... 'Greeting' is a kind of ritualized confirmation of the dominance relationship" (pp. 78, 79). We might wonder if the gift of a leaf or stick is a kind of ritual offering, a love offering or even a sacrifice.

The submissive presentation of the rump, the dominant chimp mounting the submissive chimp, the ingratiating efforts of the submissive, and the dominant's brutal or benevolent control over the submissive all remind us of the dominance and submission, sadism and masochism, lording over and humiliation of anal-stage dynamics which originate in the toddler's attempts to dominate the feces and sphincter within and the controlling mother without.

Copulation Interference: The Oedipus Complex

The Oedipus complex is a set of relationship dynamics involved in the socialization of the human child. Chimpanzee society also has its relationship dynamics—its rules, alliances, and identifications—and there is even a chimpanzee ritualization that stands as a compelling precursor for one aspect of the Oedipus complex. It is "copulation interference."

When adult chimpanzees copulate, both male and female infants try to intervene and push the male away or shove at his face. Interestingly enough, the male suitors demonstrate extraordinary tolerance of these efforts. Young males intervene in all copulations, whereas young females intervene only when their mother is being mated. On those few occasions when an adult male does become irritated by the interveners and strikes out, the victim is always a young male. Copulation interference begins to subside at age four when they enter the juvenile stage and are weaned (de Waal, 1982/2007, p. 158-60).

De Waal observed, "When adults start a mating session the young come rushing up. They jump on the female's back so as to be able to push her partner away or touch him, or they wiggle between the couple. They throw sand at them or, despite their size, conduct intimidation displays. In one instance, Franje's son, Fons, interfered when Nikkie mounted Franje. In this instance, Fons actually bit Nikkie's testicles. And on another occasion, involving the same triad, Fons simply approached, embraced the two and gave Nikkie a kiss" (pp. 156-58).

In 2008 my wife, Adriana Prengler, assisted me in conducting a small investigation into one particular human ritualization. We approached the parents of young children and asked for their cooperation in a little study. Half of the subjects in this informal study were sunbathers at a Caribbean beach club, and the other half were parents at an elementary school in Caracas, Venezuela. To each we asked the following question: "What is the reaction of your child when he/she sees you and your spouse hugging and/or kissing?" We collected data on 30 children (22 boys and 8 girls). When parents were hugging or kissing, 18 of the children intervened between the two parents. Of those 18, there were 9 who actually pushed out one of the parents. Of those who hugged their parents or just tried to get closer to their mother, 17 were boys and 1 was a girl. Of the 6 children who hugged their parents and tried to get closer to their father, 1 was a boy and 5 were girls. The following are a few examples of the parents' replies:

Mariam Girl, 4 years old
She gets closer to us and she hugs both of us and says that the three of us have to give kisses to each other. Sometimes she is jealous with her father. She says, "No, no only me." She wants to push me out and stay with her father.

Jeff Boy, 3 years 6 months
When we are kissing, he comes in between us or he says, "Give my father to me because he is mine." And he hugs and kisses his father.

Anne Girl, 7 years 2 months
She comes in the bed with us and in the morning, we wake up hugging. But she has a tendency to go more to the father but also to come in between us.

Eric Boy, 2 years 1 month
When the mother kisses the father, he [the boy] says to his mother, "It's not good to kiss Daddy." "Don't give kisses to Daddy." And then he pulls me and takes me.

Joan Girl, 5 years old
She hides. She smiles. She gets embarrassed. She gets very embarrassed. She says, "First me, Daddy." She hugs the two of us. She says, "I am here and I share." She doesn't separate us but hugs us both.

Sam Boy, 3 years 10 months
Sometimes nothing but often he comes between us and separates us or uses his index finger and middle finger as if he was cutting the two of us apart with scissors. When we haven't hugged or kissed in a while he watches with satisfaction. If we are in bed and I [Father] am lying on top of her, this is when he is his most offensive. He kicks and punches me and then he gets on top of her.

Interestingly enough, Sigmund Freud's oldest grandson, Ernst, son of Sophie (Freud) and Max Halberstadt, was 2 years, 4 months old when his mother recorded the following in her baby diary: "He [Ernst] is really jealous of Max; on July 22 [1916], when he sees that Max kisses and hugs me, he pulls me away and says very angrily: 'Mommy love me so much'" (Benveniste, 2015, p. 581). The hugging interference behavior of children offers a striking parallel to chimpanzee copulation interference. It seems reasonable to assume that the hugging interference behavior is a human ritualization with a genetic basis derived from our primate ancestors.

The chimpanzee doesn't have an Oedipus complex; it has a copulation interference ritualization. Humans, however, have the instinctually based copulation interference ritualization but also a highly developed symbolic function and are born into language and culture. It is this convergence of factors that gives rise to the Oedipus complex and the elaborate nature of the human psyche and human culture. One cannot overlook the fact that chimpanzees are also social animals and have elaborate cultures, complete with expressions of altruism and morality. Nonetheless, they have nonverbal cultures, nonverbal identifications, and a nonverbal morality.

Sexual Inhibitions and Incest Taboos: The Latency Phase

Anne Pusey (2005) has noted that, in primates, inbreeding between first-order relatives rarely occurs, that there are dispersal patterns in which male or female individuals tend to leave the groups they were born into and join other groups, and that adults who are close relatives residing in the same group usually do not mate (p. 62).

In early life, male chimpanzees enjoy a lengthy period of tolerance, indulgence, and sexual satisfaction with primary love objects. In the subsequent phase, sisters and mothers withdraw cooperation in sexual games, adult males grow less tolerant of juvenile sexuality, and aggression reinforces the limitations imposed, thus creating genuine inhibitions. In the next phase, incestuous sexuality remains minimal, but adult sexuality becomes permissible within the context of hierarchies and alliances (p. 68, 70). The middle period of inhibition and intolerance of infantile sexuality in middle childhood is a stunning chimpanzee prototype for the latency phase in Homo sapiens.

Displaying, Battling, Courtships, and Mating: Adolescent Genital Stage

Chimpanzee alpha male dynamics include displaying, battling, courtship, and mating behavior. All of these have their playful antecedents in earlier stages of development, but when the chimpanzee reaches physical maturity, the playful quality diminishes and the establishment of the chimpanzee's place in the power hierarchy of the group becomes serious business.

Display behaviors are intended to intimidate others, establish rank, and solicit sexual relations. We might consider them as prototypes of human exhibitionism. Aggressive display ritualizations are a part of dominance strategies and include threatening behaviors such as arm raising, hitting out toward the other, slapping movements in the air and on the ground, hunching the shoulders with the arms held out from the body, throwing rocks, bipedal swaggering, charging, screaming, barking, hair erection, foot stamping, drumming on a tree, shaking branches, leaping from branch to branch, and other similar sorts of behaviors (Goodall, 1986, pp. 314–16).

But beyond threats, there are also full-contact battles that include "hitting, kicking, stamping on, dragging, slamming, biting, scratching, and grappling" (p. 317). Threats and attacks are typically between males establishing dominance within the group, which is organized around an alpha male—a physically dominant male who has sexual liberties with the females and exercises a leadership and enforcing function within the troop. There is typically one alpha male in the group, and the other chimpanzees are at various levels in the hierarchy depending on their strength, ferocity, and alliances.

Violence and alliances establish the hierarchy, and threats and alliances maintain the hierarchy and are the leading edge toward the construction of what we might call "culture." A threat is an indicator of strength, and alliances are agreements in place of fighting. Goodall notes that threats maintain or challenge the hierarchy while changes in the hierarchy are almost always the result of real fights.

Behaviors of younger males toward the alpha male include imitation, identification, and even identification with the aggressor—a defense mechanism to manage the threat of older males. Goodall (1990) observed, "Sometimes an adolescent male selects one of the senior males as his 'hero'" (p. 56). He will apparently identify with him and imitate him with ambitions to move up the hierarchy. But not every male becomes an alpha male, and no alpha male remains in that position forever. To stay in power requires threats, alliances, and displays. To maintain his position, Figan, a chimpanzee at the Gombe Reserve in Tanzania, put on magnificent displays in the early dawn, leaping from branch to branch, shaking and snapping limbs, and pounding on subordinates: "And then when it was all over, their new alpha, all bristling magnificence, would sit on the ground and, like some great tribal chief, receive the obeisance of his underlings" (p. 54).

Goodall's references to "heroes" and "tribal chiefs" are not simply colorful language. We are dealing with chimpanzee ritualizations, which are the seeds of our own individual and group behavior. When the alpha male ritualizations of chimpanzees are performed by human primates, with their extraordinary symbolic functions, the older male becomes a hero for the younger male, dominance battles become battles between chaos and order within the community, and alpha males do become tribal chiefs—and even kings!

What are all of these threats and dominance battles about? Sex. Chimpanzees typically copulate after a male courtship display (Goodall, 1986, p. 447). Mating displays are quite similar to aggressive dominance displays. When a female becomes aware of a male's mating display, she will calmly or with fear approach him, crouch down, and present her rump. He will then sit in a squatting position and copulate with her from behind, ejaculating after, on average, 8.8 pelvic thrusts. A female in estrus is likely to copulate 20 to 30 times a day. In addition to these copulations in the group settings, there are also what Goodall and her colleagues refer to as "courtships." An individual male will look at a female in estrus and shake a branch, which is a signal for her to come with him. He will lead her away from the group for a number of days and they will peacefully walk together through their group territory, and maybe even beyond it, foraging, grooming each other, resting, and copulating maybe four or five times a day (Goodall, 1990, pp. 85–89; Goodall, 1986, p. 450).

The coming-of-age ritualizations associated with chimpanzee adolescence (mature battling and mature sexual behavior) are the foundation upon which Homo sapiens constructed initiation rites for the individual to enter the adult social world. Similarly, extended courtships between male and female chimpanzees and the sexual act itself offer a prototype for marriage. And, of course, the dominance battles for position as alpha male are the basis for the ascension of human "tribal chiefs" and kings. (A more extensive discussion of primate ritualizations and social instincts can be found in appendix 4.)

❖ ❖ ❖

As humans we have transformed our greeting ritualization into the encounter between I and thou. Its opposite, the good-bye ritualization, is virtually nonexistent in the chimpanzee and yet so highly developed in the human that it forms the basis of the funerary ritual. We have elaborated our dominance and submission ritualizations into obedience and faith, sacrifice, and the renunciation of instinct. Our copulation interference ritualization has been sublimated into the mythologies of the dragon fight and the myth of Oedipus. Male dominance battles and mating ritualizations have transformed into initiation rites, marriage, and kingship. Alliance ritualizations of mother-infant bonding, male bonding, and female bonding have transformed into fraternity, cooperation, and even democracy.

Konrad Lorenz and Aggression

Konrad Lorenz (1963) observed the role of ritualizations in aggression-neutralizing behaviors throughout the animal kingdom. He demonstrated how aggression within a species exerts a pressure toward the selection of certain adaptations to improve the distribution, strength, and protection of the species but can also pose a threat to the species (pp. 43, 116, 120, 123, 130). Lorenz found aggression-neutralizing behaviors in cross-species phenomena such as mother-infant bonding, submissive behavior, redirected attack, threat behavior, and other strategies for managing the threats to the species that aggression posed while at the same time preserving those aspects of aggression that contribute to its survival.

These innate aggression-neutralizing behaviors or "ritualizations" are the movement patterns that may have a certain pragmatic function by themselves but, through the course of phylogeny, are repeated, elaborated, joined to other movements, lose their original part functions, and become purely symbolic acts that signal (communicate) readiness to greet, submit, fight, mate, and perform other functional acts.

Lorenz explained that the phylogenetic origins of innate ritualizations are embedded in aggression inhibition (p. 73). Between the aggressive instinct and survival instinct there is created a ritualization, which functions as "a very special inhibitive mechanism" (p. 110). In fact, a wide variety of animals have transformed threat behavior into greeting ritualizations, gestures of appeasement, and even into love ceremonies (p. 172-73).

Lorenz also said that habit plays an important role in the establishment of ritualizations and rituals: "Indubitably it is habit which, in its tenacious hold on the already acquired, plays a similar part in culture as heredity does in the phylogenetic origin of rites" (p. 68). Here Lorenz was likening habit, as a basis for the repetition in ontogeny, to heredity, as the basis for repetition in phylogeny:

> Though governed and sanctified by the superindividual, tradition-bound, and cultural super-ego, the ritual has retained, unaltered, the nature of a habit which is precious to us and to which we cling more fondly than to any habit formed only in the course of an individual life.... The formation of traditional rites must have begun with the first dawning of human culture, just as at a much lower level, phylogenetic rite formation was a prerequisite for the origin of social organization in higher animals. (pp. 74-75)

From Higher Primate Ritualizations to Human Psychodynamics

Freud speculated that the repeated deeds of the primal fathers and the fraternal clans became encoded in our "archaic memory" as the castration and Oedipus complexes. I, on the other hand, suggest that Homo sapiens inherited a constellation of higher primate social instincts and that the critical difference between earlier hominins and Homo sapiens is our human symbolic function, which symbolized those instincts and gave rise to the Oedipus complex, myth, ritual, and our elaborated human culture. The neurological mutations necessary for the human symbolic function to take that monumental leap forward left no detailed anatomical fossil record, but the startling abundance of archeological evidence, including tools, art, and artifacts of a spiritual life, make it clear that something extraordinary happened in our brains about 50,000 years ago. We will now examine the nature of the human symbolic function, trace its evolution, and muse on how the higher primate ritualizations (social instincts) when symbolized, became our psychodynamics.

The Human Symbolic Function

The human symbolic function is the cognitive activity that enables us to represent one thing with another—to transform, displace, and condense elements of subject and world onto and into one another via processes of representation. A symbol is a signifier, representative, or substitute for a person, thing, idea, or quality. This uniquely well-developed ability to construct, recognize, and respond to symbolic meaning is what enables humans to communicate, think, become self-aware, and be creative in so many ways. It plays a significant role in the construction of our language, art, play, culture, dreams, fantasies, personality styles, psychological symptomatology, and sense of self. Freud (1923/1961a) said, "The ego is first and foremost a bodily ego; it is not merely a surface entity, but is itself a projection of a surface" (SE 19, p. 26). And in a footnote, he elaborated: "The ego is ultimately derived from bodily sensations, chiefly from those springing from the surface of the body. It may thus be regarded as a mental projection of the surface of the body, besides, as we have seen above, representing the superficies of the mental apparatus" (p. 26).

This ego is a psychological construction fashioned out of symbolic representations of sensory experience. As sensory experiences are organized into psychic configurations, ever widening experiences of the world become organized along similar lines. As Ferenczi (1913/1956) would say, "Thus arise those intimate connections, which remain throughout life, between the human body and the objective world that we call symbolic. On the one hand the child in this stage sees in the world nothing but images of his corporeality, on the other he learns to represent by means of his body the whole multifariousness of the world" (p. 194).

Ernest Jones (1948) observed that "all psycho-analytical experience goes to show that the primary ideas of life, the only ones that can be symbolized—those, namely, concerning the bodily self, the relation to the family, birth, love, and death—retain in the unconscious throughout life their original importance, and that from them is derived a very large part of the more secondary interests of the conscious mind" (p. 116).

Many of the early analysts viewed the recurrence of symbolic forms as due to a collective mind, a collective unconscious, an archaic memory, or a phylogenetic inheritance. Subsequent theorists have toppled these notions and recognized symbolic representations constructed entirely within the dialectic of the personal and social bodies. Jones reflected that "some writers—e.g., Jung—hold that anthropological symbolism is inherited as such, and explain in this way its stereotyped nature. For reasons I have developed elsewhere, I adhere to the contrary view that symbolism has to be re-created afresh out of individual material, and that the stereotypy is due to the uniformity of the human mind in regard to the particular tendencies that furnish the source of symbolism—i.e., to the uniformity of the fundamental and perennial interests of mankind" (p. 98).

Harold P. Blum (1978) explained that "symbolism may have a phylogenetic basis in a basic human capacity, but economy of explanation in terms of the common human interest experiences and the universal conditions of ego immaturity, and libidinal-aggressive conflict in early life would ontogenetically account for the cross-cultural ubiquity of unconscious symbolism" (p. 467).

Freud, Ferenczi, Jones, and Blum were all referring to psychoanalytic symbolism or unconscious symbolism as distinct from (1) Silberer's (1917) anagogic symbolism, which pertains to abstract thoughts and metaphorical meanings aiming at a goal, ideal, or potential; (2) the symbolic nature of language; and (3) cognitive symbolism. Blum offers a number of points of distinction to clarify the nature of psychoanalytic symbolism, such as the way psychoanalytic symbolism is spontaneous, not learned, and is embedded in primary process thinking, while language and metaphor come to us in the mother tongue and are largely managed through secondary process thinking. That said, there is overlap in the origins of psychoanalytic symbolism and the symbolic nature of language, and clinically we also draw heavily on both psychoanalytic symbolism and metaphor in the interpretation of dreams and other derivative material. (For more on the human symbolic function, see appendix 4.)

Chimpanzees, Humans, and the Symbolic Function

The things that makes us different from chimpanzees are not mother-infant bonding, kissing, affection, battles for male dominance, play, male bonding, female bonding, or lethal territorial raiding (war). These are common to both chimpanzees and humans. What makes us different, or one of the things that makes us different, is that we have a human symbolic function that transforms our primate instincts and social relations into symbolic behavior—meaningful behavior—in an elaborate worded latticework of psychic and cultural experience.

As mentioned before, early in my career I worked with a group of profoundly disturbed children with autism who had little capacity to symbolize in language, representational art, or play. A 10-year-old boy used to hold a doll by its head and twiddle it. It was startling to watch, as to him it clearly wasn't a doll; it was a shape, a weight, a color, and a texture—pure sensation without much if any perception of its symbolic significance. It would be almost impossible for most people to look at a doll and not see it as representing a person, but the profoundly disturbed child with autism may not see the doll as a person, may not see the child-care worker as a person, and may not even see himself as a person. The profoundly disturbed child with autism is a human with a severely impaired symbolic function. And what could we say about the symbolic capacities of our nearest cousins—the chimpanzees?

In May 1993, William Wrangham, a primatologist doing field studies of chimpanzees in Africa, was observing Kabarole, a chimpanzee pregnant with her second baby and walking along with her 6-year-old son, Kakama. As they made their way from one fruit tree to another, Kakama tried in vain to get a reaction out of Wrangham, who followed at a distance. The chimpanzee slapped the ground, displayed, retreated, and then somersaulted away, coming to rest on a small log, which he picked up and then carried with him: "While he fed, the log lay next to him. When he moved, he picked the log up. He took it with him wherever he went, perhaps five or ten moves. Then it was rest time." Kakama made his nest in the trees, and Wrangham "could see that he was holding the log over him. Just as some mothers do with their babies, he slowly juggled and balanced the piece of wood with his hands and feet. Then his limbs and the wood disappeared into the nest, and I saw no more movement for a while." Kakama with the log and Kabarole left their nests and a little later made new nests: "Completing it, [Kakama] put the log into the nest, and sat next to the nest. Two minutes more, and he climbed in, too, and disappeared from view" (Wrangham & Peterson, 1996, pp. 253-54). "My intuition suggested a possibility that I was reluctant, as a professionally skeptical scientist, to accept on the basis of a single observation: that I had just watched a young male chimpanzee invent and then play with a doll in possible anticipation of his mother giving birth. A doll!" (p. 254-55).

Four months later two other primatologists, Elisha Karwani and Peter Tuhairwe, knowing nothing of Wrangham's original observation, witnessed Kakama carrying a log with him for three hours as he fed. After a time he abandoned the log, but it was picked up by the researchers, who brought it back to camp and put a label on it: "Kakama's Toy Baby." Five weeks later Kakama had a baby sister, Omugu.

Bill Wallauer (2002), the videographer of wild chimpanzees at Tanzania's Gombe Reserve, elaborated on the theme:

> The only case of possible projected "animation" on an inanimate object is that of a young female chimpanzee carrying and cradling rocks and sticks in mimicry of nurturing behavior. I cannot be sure that this is exactly what I was seeing, but Gaia on several occasions has shown what appeared to be mothering behavior toward objects, much as human children care for dolls. There is a fine line between hugging and holding on, but I have seen Gaia groom both rocks and sticks as she held them

in her lap. A similar observation was made of a young female baboon at Gombe who was observed mothering a rock.

Evolution of the Symbolic Function

The symbolic function is a complex set of cognitive operations based in brain anatomy and physiology that evolved over millions of years. Terrence W. Deacon (1997) has studied the evolution of the symbolic function and finds useful Charles Sanders Pierce's (see Hartshorne & Weiss, 1978) three categories of referential associations: the icon, the index, and the symbol. An "icon" is a recognizable resemblance. Things are recognized for what they are or what they resemble. This enables a nonhuman animal to recognize food or for a person to recognize an image in a picture. An "index" is an indicator of any kind: a thermometer indicates temperature, a weathervane indicates the direction of the wind, the smell of smoke indicates a fire nearby. A "symbol" is a socially agreed upon convention that establishes a relationship between an image or vocalization and what it stands for. For example, a ring means marriage, a word is tied to a meaning, a flag represents a country, and a totem figure represents a clan (Deacon, 1997, pp. 70-71).

The vast majority of nonhuman communication (greetings, warnings, threats) uses icons and indexes. Some of the higher primates, most notably chimpanzees and gorillas, have been taught American Sign Language (ASL) or other means of nonvocal speech, and some have achieved the language sophistication of a 3-year-old human. But developing any further sophistication is limited by their cognitive abilities (Deacon, 1997, p. 255).

In 1967 a chimpanzee named Washoe became the first nonhuman primate to learn ASL. She learned 350 signs that she used correctly and appropriately in social contexts. Subsequently, other chimpanzees were taught ASL. In the 1970s, Francine "Penny" Patterson taught ASL to Koko, a gorilla, who also developed an impressive but also limited vocabulary (Patterson & Linden, 1981). In the early 1980s, I visited Penny Patterson at her research center in Woodside, California, and met Koko. I took with me some tomatoes for her to eat and a barrette for her hair, as I had read that she liked these things. When I arrived, Koko immediately began signing and Penny began translating. The first thing Koko asked was to see inside my mouth. She once had a trainer with a gold filling, and ever since then Koko checked the insides of visitors' mouths to see if there were any gold fillings to be found. She ate the tomatoes I brought with great pleasure. I had read that she liked signing the words "red," "mouth," "lip," "lipstick," "toothbrush," "corn," "eat," "drink," "quiet," and "orange." She was afraid of a toy alligator, spoke of the teeth of a toy animal, put her finger in its mouth, and made her toy animals bite. It's difficult to know what to make of all of this gorilla orality, but even more evocative was her frankly coquettish response to having the barrette I had brought placed in her hair. It was dazzling to witness the transformation of this massive gorilla into a seemingly coquettish little girl. No, I didn't put it in her hair. Penny did! Koko was a young female but she sure looked like King Kong to me.

In 2011 I visited the Chimpanzee and Human Communication Institute in Ellensburg, Washington, to observe Tatu (female), Dar (male), and Loulis (male), three chimpanzees who communicate in ASL. It was the former home of Washoe, but she had died four years before my visit. I found the nonhuman primate communication research to be convincing, but gorillas and chimpanzees often sign rapidly and do so while running or moving around, so one needs to know sign language, know the individual, and know what to look for to recognize anything that looks like communication. What was clear was that Loulis was exceedingly interested in my wife's shoes, and most everyone else's shoes, for that matter! (And I have no idea what that was all about!)

According to Deacon (1997), for the last 2 million years, from our late australopithecine ancestors through Homo habilis and Homo erectus down to Homo sapiens, four aspects were evolving or developing simultaneously: (1) laryngeal descent and syntactic complexity; (2) brain restructuring for speech and symbols; (3) stone toolmaking and group hunting; and (4) male provisioning, pair bonding, and mating contracts (p. 409). Then, about 50,000 years ago, something extraordinary happened when speech and the symbolic function took on a form that must have been quite similar to the speech and symbolizing capacities we have today. It was then that stone tool manufacturing diversified dramatically into an expanded tool kit, and tools began to be constructed on the basis of local traditions. Cave walls were painted and sculptures carved. Homo sapiens spread out across the world, adapting to different climates and geographies, and a rudimentary religious life became apparent in the archeological evidence of funerary rites, amulets, skull "worship," and ritual cannibalism.

Why do humans have the neurological equipment to symbolize as elaborately as we do when the other apes do not? The answer is evolution, but not just an evolution based on changing environmental conditions, mutations, natural selection, and sexual selection. No, there is also Baldwinian evolution. James Mark Baldwin said that learning and behavioral flexibility in a species could lead individuals and entire species to move into different environmental niches, which could then exert evolutionary pressures to tolerate colder or hotter environments, saltwater or freshwater, and so on (Deacon, 1997, p. 322). Considering alarm calling from a Baldwinian perspective, Deacon suggested that the dangers in nature "can produce consistent and powerful selection for calls that can be unambiguously distinguished, and selection for consistent linkage of these calls with a set of highly specific sensory, motor, and attentional predispositions" (p. 331). Thus, the more accurate and differentiated the alarm signal is, the higher the survival rate and the greater the possibility for further differentiation: "The evolution of these alarm call systems created a kind of innate 'foreknowledge' of useful stimulus-response associations appropriate to the environment. These are the sorts of built-in predispositions that we would feel comfortable calling 'instincts,' and they have many of the features that might lend themselves to a genetic assimilation interpretation that parallels Lamarckianism" (p. 331). He later stated, "In the classical terminology of ethology, the process whereby some behavior became progressively modified and specialized for its communicative function was called 'ritualization,' by analogy to human ritual and ceremonial embellishments of communication" (pp. 379-80).

Deacon recognized that Baldwinian evolutionary change is slow, gradual, and needs support in order to keep moving in one direction or another—in this case, toward symbol making. He asked, *What could possibly have provided the necessary support to establish and maintain symbol-learning societies?* Responding to his own question Deacon wrote, "In a word, the answer is ritual" (p. 402).

Deacon was jumping from "ritualization" to "ritual." He described the learning process of chimps to understand sign-sign associations as requiring numerous repetitions of the task and says that similar repetitions are involved in ritual behavior by humans all around the world. So perhaps we could say ritualizations are *genetically determined* complex social behaviors, rituals are *culturally encoded* complex social behaviors, and both of them support the growth and development of the individual and the species. Ritualizations are encoded in DNA, and rituals are encoded in culture—language, custom, belief, religion, and so on. Deacon did not imagine that our australopithecine ancestors had marriage ceremonies or puberty rites. To the contrary, he says there probably weren't any words or their equivalents at all until Homo erectus came along. But presumably there were ritualizations for establishing fidelity in pair-bonding hominids with male provisioning in large multi-male and multi-female social groups (p. 407). Deacon described the power and influence of the symbolic function thusly:

> One of the essentially universal attributes of human culture is what might be called the mystical or religious inclination. There is no culture I know of that lacks a rich mythical, mystical, and religious tradition. And there is no culture that doesn't devote much of this intense interpretive enterprise to struggling with the very personal mystery of mortality. Knowledge of death, of the inconceivable possibility that the experiences of life will end, is a datum that only symbolic representation can impart. Other species may experience loss, and the pain of separation, and the difficulty of abandoning a dead companion; yet without the ability to represent this abstract counterfactual (at least for the moment) relationship, there can be no emotional

connection to one's own future death. But this news, which all children eventually discover as they develop their symbolic abilities, provides an unbidden opportunity to turn the naturally evolved social instinct of loss and separation in on itself to create a foreboding sense of fear, sorrow, and impending loss with respect to our own lives, as if looking back from an impossible future. No feature of the limbic system has evolved to handle this ubiquitous virtual sense of loss. Indeed, I wonder if this isn't one of the most maladaptive of the serendipitous consequences of the evolution of symbolic abilities. What great efforts we exert trying to forget our future fate by submerging the constant angst with innumerable distractions, or trying to convince ourselves that the end isn't really what it seems by weaving marvelous alternative interpretations of what will happen in "the undiscovered country" on the other side of death. (pp. 436-37)

Hominin Evolution

While there were many different hominins that evolved and died out, there were times during the last 6 million years when several different types of hominins coexisted on the planet. We humans are not descendants of all of them. Some were cousins that went extinct, presumably without passing on their genes to the next evolving species. With those cousins we share only a common ancestor, not direct lineage. Based largely on morphology, Donald Johanson and Blake Edgar (2006) tentatively traced the following line of direct descent as one possibility. It, of course, excludes those hominins that went extinct and were outside of our direct line of descent.

Ardipithecus kadabba	5.8-5.2 million years ago
Australopithecus ramidus	4.5-4.3 million years ago
Australopithecus anamensis	4.2-3.9 million years ago
Australopithecus afarensis	3.9-3 million years ago
Homo habilis	2.3-1.6 million years ago
Homo ergaster	1.8-1.5 million years ago
Homo antecessor	800,000 years ago
Homo heidelbergensis	700,000-200,000 years ago
Homo sapiens	200,000 years ago-present

(p. 38)

There are naturally gaps in this family tree, and Johanson and Edgar suggest that it was either *Homo antecessor* or *Homo heidelbergensis* that stood as the link between *Homo ergaster* and *Homo sapiens*. The elaboration of our evolutionary tree is a work in progress that has changed many times since Darwin; it will continue to change with new discoveries until we arrive at a consistent and stable reconstruction of our evolutionary past.

Our hominin ancestors were definitely bipedal—walking on two feet—4 million years ago, maybe even before. They made and used tools 3.4 million years ago and used fire 1.5 million years ago. As descendants of a chimpanzee-like creature, the hominins already had the capacity to problem-solve, play, communicate, and make and use tools. Based on the behavior of chimpanzees, we can extrapolate that our hominin ancestors had elaborate social structures, including mother-child bonding, dominance and submission behavior, alpha male battles, male bonding, territorial patrolling, and raids on neighboring troops. They lived a relatively long time (20-30 years) in stable social groups with individuals of different ages and both sexes. They were born very dependent and required a long period of maternal care before being able to fend for themselves within the context of the group. Individual members of the group were complex enough that interactions between members were highly individualized. There was a separation of roles between the sexes and between adults and the young. A brief glance at this list of primate behaviors reminds us not only of ourselves but also of Freud's understandings of the dominant themes in infantile sexuality and their role in the construction of personality.

Through the evolution of the hominin line of descent, brain size grew significantly as did our cognitive functioning. The table below presents this expansion of brain size in cubic centimeters.

Modern chimpanzee (similar to its 6 million years old ancestor)	395cc
Australopithecus afarensis—3 million years ago	530cc
Homo habilis—2.4 million years ago	650cc
Homo erectus Java man—1 million years ago	940cc
Homo sapiens archaic—200,000 years ago	1,120cc
Modern human	1,450cc

(Lancaster, 1975, p. 66; Johanson & Edgar, 2006, pp. 137, 201, 250, 124; Wragg-Sykes, 2016, p. 189)

Darwin's project of tracing the origin of species was challenging in itself, as it contradicted the Judeo-Christian cosmogony, or creation myth, of a world created in seven days by the hand of God. But what really stirred the controversy was Darwin's assertion that humans are animals and not in any way a privileged species chosen by God. That being the case, Darwin concluded that we too descended from other animal forms and that if we searched, we would find in the fossil record the story of our evolutionary descent.

The fact of the matter is that the data were coming in, even in Darwin's time, with the discoveries in 1848 and 1856 of skulls belonging to what is now referred to as *Homo neanderthalensis* (Johanson & Edgar, 2006, pp. 242, 244). And in 1868 the skull of Cro-Magnon man was discovered in southern France (p. 260). But at the time of Darwin's death, in 1882, the project of plotting our evolutionary lineage in the fossil record was still speculation based on a new theory with few hominin fossils to support it. With rising interest, new scientific methods, and increased funding, one discovery followed another, and the evolutionary tree was elaborated into its current form, which is, of course, changing all the time with extraordinary new discoveries in Africa, Europe, the Middle East, and Asia.

As this new field of paleoanthropology developed, names like Raymond Dart, Robert Broom, and Louis S. B. Leakey gained notoriety. Donald Johanson and Blake Edgar (2006) stated, "Louis Leakey, virtually the embodiment of human paleontology, believed that humans, large brained and tool making, originated millions of years ago" (p. 168). And it was Leakey who set out to prove Darwin's theory that Africa was the birthplace of humanity.

Louis Leakey (1903–1972), the son of British parents, was born in Kenya and initiated as a member of the Kikuyu tribe. At 13 he discovered his first ancient stone tools and became determined to find out who made them. Based on his research and excavations in East Africa, he was awarded his PhD in anthropology in 1932 at Cambridge University. After years of research at Olduvai Gorge in Tanganyika (Tanzania), he and his second wife, Mary, collected an enormous number of ancient stone tools, as well as a skull they named "Zinjanthropus boisei" (*Australopithecus boisei*), and found many fossils of a species they called, along with Phillip Tobias and John Napier, *Homo habilis*. Leakey was known for his passion, perseverance, and uncanny intuition. In addition to the paleoanthropologists he inspired, he was influential in launching the careers and field research of Jane Goodall, who observed chimpanzees in the wild; Dian Fossey, who observed gorillas; and Biruté Galdikas, with her field research on orangutans (Foley, 1998; Anonymous, 2000).

❖ ❖ ❖

Leakey's *National Geographic* articles excited my imagination when I was still a very young boy. I collected my first fossilized mussel shells when I was 9 years old and as an adolescent developed a nice collection of Pleistocene fossil clams, snails, sand dollars, and worm tubes.

In the early 1970s, Louis Leakey gave a lecture in Walnut Creek, California, not far from Danville, where I lived and collected my fossils. I attended and got a chance to hear and see the man referred to as "virtually the embodiment of human paleontology." I was excited to see Leakey and hear him speak about the fossils of early hominids he had been finding during the course of his life's work as a paleontologist in Africa. One hundred years after Darwin's *On the Origin of Species*, Leakey was the man literally on the ground, carrying on the work, with his wife Mary and other colleagues, finding fossils of Paranthropus boisei (an australopithecine), Homo erectus, Homo habilis and their ancient stone tools. After his lecture I introduced myself, shook his hand, and got his autograph. It was an honor and an inspiration to have met him. Louis Leakey died shortly thereafter, in 1972.

❖ ❖ ❖

Darwin predicted that the earliest stages of man's evolution would be found in Africa, and the data coming in slowly over the next century would prove him correct (Johanson & Edgar, 2006, p. 154). The early discoveries were awe-inspiring and offered the promise that there was clearly much more to be found in Africa.

In Africa, apelike beings with hominid features appeared 6-7 million years ago as *Sahelanthropus tchadensis* and then 6 million years ago as *Orrorin tugenensis*. Between 5.2 and 5.9 million years ago *Ardipithecus kadabba* appeared (pp. 116-20). Then came *Ardipithecus ramidus* (4.3-4.5 million years ago) and *Australopithecus anamensis* (3.9-4.2 million years ago). Throughout our evolution and up to this point, our chimp-like ancestors were still small-brained but becoming increasingly bipedal—that is to say, developing anatomical characteristics that would promote locomotion on two legs without necessarily being primarily bipedal. With *Australopithecus afarensis* (3-3.9 million years ago), however, we have our first undeniably bipedal ancestor (pp. 37-38). The first fossil of this species was found by Donald Johanson and it is commonly known as Lucy.

It is hard to know what to say about the australopithecines, but some of the data excite the imagination. Consider for a moment the following reconstruction of events: About 3.5 million years ago on a nameless stretch of land near Laetoli, in what is now called Tanzania, a nearby volcano erupted and spewed forth ash like fine beach sand. When the ash settled, a light rain turned it into an impressionable mud. Then along came a couple of australopithecines walking, perhaps separately, perhaps together. One was larger than the other, perhaps a male and female, or perhaps an adult and child. They walked northward, stopped a moment, turned westward, and then continued on their way north, leaving the trail of their footprints and brief interlude impressed in the wet ash. The sun came out, dried the wet ash into a hard mud, and preserved the footprints. When the next layer of ash spewed forth, the footprints were covered over and preserved for the next 3.5 million years until their excavation in 1978 by Mary Leakey (Johanson & Edgar, 2006, p. 142).

Australopithecines have a larger cranial capacity than chimpanzees and are bipedal, which naturally frees their hands to manipulate objects. Though no stone tools have been found in association with australopithecine fossils, in 2010 Shannon McPherron and her colleagues found "unambiguous stone-tool cut marks for flesh removal and percussion marks for marrow access" associated with 3.4-million-year-old *Australopithecus afarensis* fossils (IHO, 2010). In 2015 researchers Sonia Harmand and Jason Lewis, in Kenya, at the Lomekwi 3 excavation site, found early stone hammers and cutting instruments that are 3.3 million years old and possibly the work of *Kenyanthropus platyops* (Earth Institute, 2015).

The Lower Paleolithic

For quite some time, the Lower Paleolithic was said to have begun 2.6 million years ago with the appearance of the first stone tools (Johanson & Edgar, 2006, p. 90). That start date is now probably being revised following the recent discoveries of 3.4-million-year-old stone tool cut marks on bone and 3.3-million-year-old stone tools.

Without stone tools or other artifacts, it is hard to say much about the early hominin psyche or culture. It would clearly be an error for us to project our psyche into their lives and imagine that the australopithecines and early Homos were just like us. But it would be just as much an error to assume they were like chimpanzees. When we imagine a bipedal hominin leaving behind a stone tool 3.3 million years ago, we should not imagine an elaborate collection of other tools for which there is no evidence, but we should also not assume that the only tools they made were stone tools. If the early hominins were smart enough to make stone tools, we could easily imagine that other tools were made of wood, plant fiber, animal skins, bone, horns, seashells, and other natural materials. We have no reason to think that *Homo habilis*, for example, had totemic beliefs but also no reason to think their social organization was identical to that of the chimpanzees. While speculation on early hominin culture is an open projection screen, it is easy to assume that mother-infant bonding, dominance and submission behavior, copulation interference, and alpha male social dynamics remained and were being elaborated.

A 2.3-million-year-old Homo upper jaw was found in association with stone cores from which flakes were broken with a separate hammerstone (Johanson & Edgar, 2006, pp. 90, 180). From that point on, stone tools became more common in the fossil record associated with the various Homo species. In 1964 Louis Leakey announced the discovery of Homo habilis (1.6–2.3 million years ago), named for its distinctive toolmaking ability. The first specimen was found at the Olduvai Gorge in Tanzania along with tools from what is called the Oldowan tool kit (p. 174). These included hammerstones for striking flakes off of stone cores, crude unifacial and bifacial choppers, flakes for cutting, heavy-duty and light-duty scrapers, and spheroids. The Oldowan tradition, from 1.5 to 2.4 million years ago, marks a period not when the stone tool tradition began and ended but rather when it began and when a new stone tool tradition started up: the Acheulean tradition (p. 266).

When *Homo georgicus*, which had affinities to Homo erectus and Homo ergaster, was found in Dmanisi, Georgia, with flakes and cores dating back 1.8 million years, it provided unequivocal evidence of Homo's departure from Africa. But perhaps even more startling was the discovery that one of the skulls was of an older man who was missing all of his teeth. How did he eat? How did he survive? David Lordkipanidze has suggested that the old man was cared for by others! Compassion. Altruism. It is extraordinary to consider the implications (Johanson & Edgar, 2006, p. 192).

Early use of fire dates back to 1.5 million years ago in Swartkrans, South Africa, and to 1.4 million years in Chesowanja, Kenya. Although multiple hominin species existed at that time, both sites suggest that Homo erectus was the one using the fire. So we now have a toolmaking, compassionate hominin who, unlike every other animal before it, did not run from the flame. We could imagine that Homo erectus studied the fire originating from lightning strikes, volcanic activity, or spontaneous combustion as if it were some sort of mysterious being that destroyed all living and dead things in its path. They attempted to tame it and draw it under their control. These fires, and others that left evidence in Israel and China, may have been derived from lightning strikes and used in opportunistic fashion, for example, finding dead and cooked animals in the path of the fire or placing meat into the wild fire. A site where evidence for the controlled use of fire in a hearth to cook rhinoceros meat is between 380,000 and 465,000 years old and was found at Menez-Dregen on the southern coast of Brittany. In other hearth-like depressions, burned mussel shells and charcoal were found on the coast of the French Riviera and dated to between 200,000 and 400,000 years old. Hearths became common during the Middle Paleolithic period (40,000–100,000 years ago) in Africa, Europe, and the Near East (Johanson & Edgar, 2006, pp. 96–97).

The Acheulean stone tool tradition was named after an archeological site at Saint Acheul in France. The typical Acheulean hand axe is a heavy, somewhat flat, bifacial, sharp-edged tool that is typically in the shape of a teardrop, pear, or ovate. Some are heavy and crude; others are elegant and skillfully executed. The tradition lasted over a million years and stretched from Africa to Europe, the Near East, and India (p. 270).

Homo sapiens appeared in Africa 200,000 years ago. But between 123,000 and 195,000 years ago, cold and dry climate conditions left much of Africa uninhabitable for Homo sapiens. A small group survived on the southern coast of Africa eating shellfish and edible plants, including, most probably, tubers, bulbs, and corms, which are carbohydrate-rich root foods. Marine foraging at this site has been dated to 164,000 years and is associated with stone bladelets used in the construction of composite tools. Researchers also discovered that the rocks in the area that were used for making stone tools were in fact not conducive to stone toolmaking in their natural state. Through a series of examinations, it was discovered that the stones were heat-treated by our Paleolithic ancestors before being crafted into stone tools and that heat treatment made the stones more conducive to skilled crafting. Also at this site were "dozens of pieces of red ochre (iron oxide) that were variously carved and ground to create a fine powder that was probably mixed with a binder such as animal fat to make paint that could be applied to the body or other surfaces" (Marean, 2010, p. 46).

Meanwhile the Neanderthals had already arrived and were flourishing in Europe, where they were making stone tools and hunting. Then, 176,000 years ago in southern France, Neanderthals with flames they could carry entered 1,000 feet into Bruniquel Cave. There they broke off 400 stalagmites and stacked them in heaps, constructed semicircles, and built one large circular structure 22 feet in diameter. Fires were lit atop the stalagmites, which were left with red and black discoloration, and charred bits of bone were left near a smaller circle (Drake, 2016). What was this site used for? What could it mean? We still don't know.

About 200,000 years ago the Mousterian tool tradition began and lasted until about 40,000 years ago, at which point a new technology began and predominated. The Mousterian tradition is named after the site where these tools were first found, Le Moustier, France. In the Acheulean tradition, the toolmaker chipped away at a large stone until the axe or cleaver had been formed. In the Mousterian tradition, a large stone core was prepared, and then, with one well-placed blow, a long thin flake was peeled off and subsequently shaped into any one of a wide variety of tools. Toolmakers used the Levallois technique of retouching, or removing small flakes around the edges, to obtain a sharp, clearly defined tool, whether it be a scraper, a knife, or a sharp spear point. Using the Mousterian technique, the large stone core yielded dozens of fine flake tools rather than just one heavy Acheulean hand axe.

The Middle Paleolithic

The Middle Paleolithic began 100,000 years ago with several different hominin species (Homo sapiens, Homo neanderthalensis, Homo erectus, Homo denisova, and Homo floresiensis) inhabiting the earth simultaneously. It was characterized by rapid technological and cultural developments among the Homo neanderthalensis and modern *Homo sapiens* communities.

And then something truly extraordinary happened: after millions of years of animals leaving their loved ones to die on the ground and rot in the sun or be scavenged by animals, Homo sapiens began burying their dead. Perhaps they were repelled by the stench of rotting flesh, the gaping mouth, the horror of rigor mortis, or the sorrow of seeing a loved one devoured by hyenas, vermin, or vultures. Perhaps they were overcome with grief at the loss of a loved one who had long since become established as a significant internalized other within the hearts of every member of the community. Perhaps their evolving intellect and symbolic function had reached a point at which they could begin to both confront death head-on and at the same time deny it through the funerary ritual, which, in a way, also permitted them the opportunity to mourn their losses. One thing is for certain: the symbolic function took an enormous evolutionary step forward and changed the human condition forever. Philosopher Ernst Cassirer (1944) described the symbolized human condition as follows: "No longer in a merely physical universe, man lives in a symbolic universe. Language, myth, art, and religion are parts of this universe" (p. 25). And with that symbolic function, Homo began to consciously come to terms with death, ritualize it, and mythologize it.

At Qafzeh Cave in Israel, between 90,000 and 100,000 years ago, a 20-year-old woman was intentionally buried on her left side with her legs flexed and with the skeleton of a young child at her side. They were Homo sapiens (Johanson & Edgar, 2006, p. 255). Why were they buried? Perhaps the burial unconsciously served a defensive function to manage the persecutory fantasies that arose in response to death wishes and survivor guilt in the hearts of those left behind. Perhaps it was a way to ritually put the corpse underground and thereby symbolically push the painful thoughts and conflicts into unconsciousness. Perhaps if they were out of sight, they might also be out of mind. Perhaps a journey to the underworld is facilitated by taking a first step underground. Why was the woman buried with her legs flexed in the fetal position? Perhaps she had died to be reborn. Perhaps in death she was as helpless as a baby. Perhaps she was buried in the womb of Mother Earth. And why did the woman and child need to be buried together? Perhaps it was awful enough that these two had separated from the community in death and it was just too overwhelming to think of now separating them. Perhaps they were mother and child and the thought of sending a small child off to the land of the dead all alone was just too unbearable.

Cassirer (1944) speculated that after the terror of death, came "the wish to detain or to recall the spirit of the dead.... The ghosts of the deceased become the household gods; and the life and prosperity of the family depend on their assistance and favor" (p. 87). Cassirer reminded us that Herbert Spencer "propounded the thesis that ancestor worship is to be regarded as the first source and the origin of religion" (p. 84).

Then there is the Skhul Cave on Mount Carmel in Israel, discussed earlier, where a man in the fetal position was buried 90,000 years ago with his hand clasping the jawbone of a wild boar (Johanson & Edgar, 2006, p. 258). The jawbone wouldn't have provided much sustenance for the journey off to the land of the dead, so maybe it was a protective amulet of an ancestor spirit or totem.

But perhaps we're getting ahead of ourselves. We've just identified the second intentional burial in human prehistory with funerary evidence, and suddenly I'm suggesting the possibility of the myth of death and rebirth, journeys to the land of the dead, amulets, spirits, and totems. It's difficult to conclude anything, but as psychologists we can certainly speculate and carry on with the exploration. Cassirer (1944) suggested, "In a certain sense the whole of mythical thought may be interpreted as a constant and obstinate negation of the phenomenon of death" (pp. 83–84).

Then 70,000 years ago a 9-year-old Homo neanderthalensis boy died at Teshik-Tash, Uzbekistan, and was intentionally buried in a cave with his feet pointed toward the cave entrance. Six pairs of large, bony horn cores from Siberian ibex, or mountain goat, were placed points-down in a circle surrounding the boy's skull and a few other bones. A small fire was lit beside the body (Johanson & Edgar, 2006, p. 229), and though the tiny flames were extinguished 70,000 years ago, they can still ignite our imagination.

At the Amud Cave in Israel, the skeleton of a 10-month-old infant Homo neanderthalensis was found lying on its side in an intentional burial, with the upper jaw of a red deer leaned up against the infant's pelvis. This burial took place between 50,000 and 60,000 years ago (Johanson & Edgar, 2006, p. 236). What can we make of another upper jawbone associated with an apparent funerary ritual?

Additional graves were excavated at La Ferrassie, France. The deceased are Homo neanderthalensis and 50,000 years old. An adult male and adult female were found buried head to head, and a series of other graves included the bodies of five children, who ranged in age from prenatal to 10 years old. The skull of one child was separated from the rest of the skeleton and buried beneath a stone marked with curious depressions in it (p. 240). Perhaps the stillborn child gave rise to heartache and inspired the community to honor it with a burial. Perhaps the skull under the rock represented special treatment for a special child—a gifted child or even a problem child.

Fifty thousand years ago Homo erectus was going or had gone extinct, the Middle Paleolithic was coming to an end, and one of the three remaining hominins was becoming increasingly human when suddenly a cultural explosion of unprecedented proportion took place. It was the threshold crossing development in our symbolic function that could not have happened without a corresponding mutation in the human brain. When our symbolic function achieved modern proportions some 50,000 years ago, language, art, religion, and technology proliferated, and Homo sapiens spread out on an adventure to discover the world. In the next chapter, we will explore the way psychological development influenced cultural evolution. We will see how libido development, with its roots in mammalian evolution, became symbolized and began echoing off of social structure, cultural concerns, and inspiring the creation of myths, rituals, and religious beliefs from the Upper Paleolithic period, to the Neolithic, to the High Neolithic, to the Urban Revolution.

As mentioned in the introduction, these terms, describing different levels of cultural sophistication, are somewhat out of date. Most modern archeologists and anthropologists prefer to examine the uniqueness of individual cultures within their own historical contexts rather than grouping them in terms of broad similarities and universals. Nonetheless, I think there is something to be gained in looking at this broad cultural pattern and the relations between these culture forms and psychological development. The following is a summary of the culture forms to which I am referring.

Upper Paleolithic Period—Nomadic hunter-gatherers; first paintings and sculptures of female figures and animals; elaborate burials; and a diversified stone and bone tool kit. It began about 50,000 years ago, but in some places it continues up to the present.

Neolithic Period—Permanent homes; hunting and gathering plus agriculture and domestication of animals; ceramics; trade; and sacrifice. It began 10,000 years ago in some places, and later elsewhere, but continues up to the present in some isolated parts of the world.

High Neolithic Period—Large Neolithic settlements; domestication of plants and animals; metallurgy; megaliths; and perhaps fertility rituals associated with planting and harvesting. It began 7,000 years ago, but in some places High Neolithic cultures existed into more recent history.

Urban Revolution—Large kingdoms; kingship; occupational specialization; large-scale warfare; writing; calendar; and New Year festival. It began 5,500 years ago in the Middle East but at later times in other parts of the world.

We are always curious about data that do not fit the cultural patterns we create. An interesting exception to the Neolithic pattern is found among the Pacific Northwest indigenous peoples, who developed an extraordinarily rich and elaborate culture that was fully Neolithic, if not High Neolithic, without ceramics becoming a significant part of their culture and without farming either. They were complex hunter-gatherers living in permanent houses and became masters at working with wood, stone, and bone, and with weaving baskets (Ames & Maschner, 1999, pp. 13, 24-27).

Another exception to the pattern is a fascinating megalithic monument that was not built in the High Neolithic as we might expect. It is a cromlech, a circle of large stones, at Göbekli Tepe in southern Turkey. Hunter-gatherers built this apparent temple site 11,600 years ago on the cusp of the Paleolithic and Neolithic (Mann & Musi, 2011, pp. 34-59). It doesn't fit the pattern and therefore gives us much to wonder about. Nonetheless, I find the overall pattern useful. If others can find a more effective way to organize the data that yields greater insights, I'll be most interested, and the phylogenetic project of psychoanalysis will take yet another step forward.

A chimpanzee family (Pan troglodytes) sitting close together in the Muenster Zoo in Germany.

Skull of Homo erectus between 350,000 and 500,000 years old. Yunxian Man was found in Yunxian County, China.

Acheulean hand ax from ancient Paleolithic site in South Africa.
Given to John Weir Perry as a gift when he gave lectures in South Africa at the invitation of Sir Laurens van der Post.

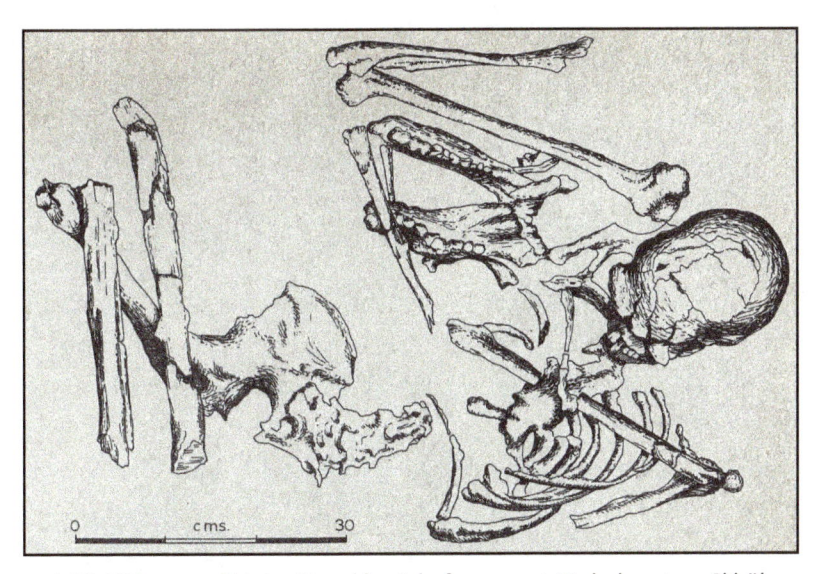

A 90,000-year-old intentional burial of a man at Muhgharet-es-Skhül, Mount Carmel, Israel. He was buried with his legs tightly flexed and his arm clasping the jawbones of a wild boar.

PART 2

From Infancy to Adolescence, From the Paleolithic to the Urban Revolution

CHAPTER 5

The Upper Paleolithic Period and the Oral Stage of Libido Development

> What, we ask, is the attitude of our unconscious towards the problem of death?
> The answer must be: almost exactly the same as that of primaeval man.
> In this respect, as in many others, the man of prehistoric times
> survives unchanged, in our unconscious.
>
> —Sigmund Freud, *Thoughts for the Times on War and Death*
>
> My interest, after making a lifelong detour through the natural sciences, medicine
> and psychotherapy, returned to the cultural problems which had fascinated
> me long before, when I was a youth scarcely old enough for thinking.
> At the very climax of my psycho-analytic work, in 1912, I had already
> attempted in *Totem and Taboo* to make use of the newly discovered findings
> of analysis in order to investigate the origins of religion and morality.
> I now carried this work a stage further in two later essays, *The Future of an Illusion*
> [1927] and *Civilization and its Discontents* [1930]. I perceived ever more clearly that
> the events of human history, the interactions between human nature, cultural
> development and the precipitates of primeval experiences (the most prominent
> example of which is religion) are no more than a reflection of the dynamic
> conflicts between the ego, the id and the superego, which psycho-analysis studies
> in the individual—are the very same processes repeated upon a wider stage.
>
> —Sigmund Freud, *An Autobiographical Study*, Postscript

As soon as evolution granted Homo sapiens a superior symbolic function, about 50,000 years ago, our psychodynamics and cultural dynamics began a dance that gave rise to new forms of technology, art, spiritual life, and cultural structure. When personal psychodynamics were projected into the world and symbolized, they shaped cultural structure, which subsequently shaped psychic structure, and this psyche-culture coevolution then made its way from prehistory into history. In other words, the unconsciously determined defensive strategies that had been developed to meet the vicissitudes of infancy were called upon to meet the parallel challenges of cultural evolution. And that cultural evolution, in turn, elaborated individual experience. This is not particularly surprising, as it really couldn't be any other way. But what is surprising is how cultural structure and spiritual life seem to have drawn on individual psychodynamics and expressed them in a diachronic fashion—that is, one stage following the next.

At the end of chapter 3, I presented the following two schemas of parallel phenomena, each schema being internally organized around a different constellation of metaphors. These parallel phenomena are a stage in normal development, a form of psychopathology, a stage in cultural evolution, a myth, and a ritual:

Oral stage—early infancy	Genital stage—adolescence
Infantile autism	Brief psychotic disorder
Upper Paleolithic	Urban Revolution
Myth of death and rebirth	Myth of sacral kingship
Ancient funerary ritual	Ancient New Year festival

In part 2 we will be linking stages in libido development with periods in early cultural evolution using analogical reasoning to find "points of agreement" between parallel phenomena. More specifically, we will associate the oral stage with the Paleolithic period, the anal stage with the Neolithic period, the phallic stage with the High Neolithic period, and the genital stage of adolescence with the Urban Revolution or birth of civilization.

The Paleolithic was a cultural echo of the oral stage, when life was oriented around bounty and starvation and the projection of an all-powerful mother goddess whose whims determined the fate of culture. The infant's personal encounter with the mother and periodic loss of the mother facilitated the emergence of subjectivity and in the paleolithic, gave rise to the concept of the soul, along with the capacity to represent it, recognize it, and mourn its loss when a loved one died. And just as the lonely infant longs for reunion with the mother, our Paleolithic ancestors may well have imagined their dearly departed to be returning home to a great mother goddess. What we are dealing with here is the awe of encounter and the awful terror of death, with their roots in mother-infant bonding, attachment, separation, and bitter loss.

The Neolithic was a cultural echo of the anal stage. The separation of self from other informed the separation of culture from nature. The articulation of boundaries came with the invention of permanent walls that established the inside and outside of the village, the house, the stove, and the ceramic pot under the ongoing supervision of the female goddess. No longer entirely at the mercy of the mother goddess, culture began to exercise control over her—over nature—architecturally, agriculturally and spiritually.

The High Neolithic was a cultural echo of the phallic stage, with its heroic ambitions, competition, and phallic striving inspired by the fertilizing male sky gods but still oriented to the goddess. We are reminded of the High Neolithic's phallic stone pillars, stone circles, and the dawning of sexual enlightenment.

Finally, the Urban Revolution was a cultural echo of the genital stage, adolescence, and identity formation. It was in the Urban Revolution that there emerged the written word, the calendar, large city-states, and the rise of the god-kings oriented to the distinctly male king-gods. The links between the psychological stages and cultural periods will now be elaborated each in turn beginning with the Paleolithic.

❖ ❖ ❖

During the Upper Paleolithic, from 10,000 to 50,000 years ago, there were four hominin species inhabiting the earth: Homo neanderthalensis, Homo floresiensis, Homo denisova, and Homo sapiens. But the cultural explosion was primarily the work of Homo sapiens. In the Upper Paleolithic, brain size and mental capacities appear to have reached modern proportions. In fact, some make the case that our brains have not physically evolved in any significant way in the last 50,000 years.

Terms like "Paleolithic" and "Neolithic" refer to the technological sophistication of a culture; consequently, start dates and end dates for these periods are variable. In the Upper Paleolithic, tools became increasingly specialized. Homo sapiens at that time were hunter-gatherers who lived a nomadic life, building temporary shelters and following the herds of animals, the seasonally ripening plant foods, the fluctuating weather conditions, and their curiosity. As mentioned earlier, modern humans emerged in Africa 200,000 years ago, and with their migratory spirit and extraordinary adaptability they soon began spreading out and peopling the world. They arrived in Israel 100,000 years ago; throughout the Middle East 50,000-70,000 years ago; in Australia 50,000 years ago; in Europe 30,000-40,000 years ago; in Asia 40,000 years ago; in North America 20,000 years ago; and in South America 15,000 years ago (Shreeve, 2006, pp. 64-65). These are conservative dates, and subsequent research is likely to extend these arrival dates somewhat further into the past.

Religious life burst forth in the Upper Paleolithic with the emergence of the most basic of spiritual concepts—the concept of the soul, which is reflected in the traditions of the funerary ritual, ritual cannibalism, the use of amulets, the worship of animals, and the sudden appearance of cave painting and sculpture. It is my assertion that embedded in these emerging cultural phenomena are the echoes of the elaborate object relations, associated with the oral stage, that are constellated in the process of mother-infant bonding and attachment. As can be seen, I am using the term "oral stage" in the broadest sense, including orality, erotic and aggressive drives, bonding, attachment, separation, individuation, and the development of defenses and object relations in infancy.

Paleolithic cultures were not oral cultures, nor were they devoid of anal, phallic, or genital dynamics, but the earliest spiritual concerns of human culture were parallel to the earliest psychological concerns of the infant: psychological (spiritual) birth and the encounters with otherness and with death. It is very important for the reader to keep in mind, throughout this entire book, that the symbolic acts and defensive strategies of myth, ritual, and religious life were no doubt conscious acts, but much of their symbolic nature and defensive function was unconsciously determined.

Freud's theory of human development proposed both an ego development and a libido development. But these developmental processes are interwoven and are separated abstractly only for theoretical purposes. *Ego development* pertains to the maturation of cognitive functioning, which addresses (1) the progressive differentiation of ego consciousness out of the matrix of narcissism, (2) the development of the reality principle, (3) the progressive increase of secondary process thinking, (4) the development of psychological defense mechanisms, and (5) a progressively more differentiated approach to interpersonal relations. *Libido development*, on the other hand, pertains to the transformations of psychosexual development. It addresses the sites of libidinal gratification as they shift from the mouth, to the anus, to the genitalia (S. Freud, 1917/1963b, SE 16, pp. 320–38; Baldwin, 1967, p. 350). The erogenous zones are those highly sensitive openings in the human body rimmed with mucous membrane and subject to intense socialization processes. As I say, ego development and libido development are interwoven, but, lest I be misunderstood, I use the terminology of libido development to anchor the stages of child development to cultural evolution.

Having previously discussed the oral stage, I'll simply emphasize that the nursing encounter between mother and infant is one in which the mother's nipple enters the infant's mouth, and while the baby is sucking, the two greet each other eye-to-eye. The oral stage is about breast-feeding, the encounter between mother and baby, the reciprocal greetings, and the progressive congealing of the infant's psyche into a subjectivity—into a soul. When the greeting is not returned on one side or the other, for whatever reason, the result can be emotional disconnection and failed attachment in the direction of autism. The oral stage is the psychological backdrop that helped shape the spiritual and social life of our Paleolithic ancestors, who met the challenges of Paleolithic life with the oral dynamics, traumas, and traditions that were shared to a certain extent among all the people and became embedded in their solutions to the threats against culture.

Freud observed that the typical traumas of childhood generate various fantasies and psychopathologies. Róheim (1934/1974) noted that when a homogeneous culture has a stable tradition for child-rearing, the group will end up sharing some typical traumatic experiences and as a result will join individual fantasies into a myth of the group (pp. 11-18, 196). I am extending this formulation to an entire culture form—the Paleolithic—and without going into the details of this funerary ritual or that, I am simply recognizing the recurring strategies that Homo sapiens invented and embraced as a way of dealing with the traumas associated with facing death—that is, the traumas of presence and absence, the traumas of being and the confrontation with nonbeing.

Deaths of loved ones were traumas that inherently engaged and stimulated the oral dynamics of attachment and loss, embodiment and disembodiment. In other words, the earliest stirrings of religious feeling, social structure, and technology in the Upper Paleolithic were not only positive assertions of a developing culture but also defensive strategies against the overwhelming terror and divine awe with which our Paleolithic ancestors met the world. The experiences stirring terror and awe in the Upper Paleolithic were not new, but Homo sapiens met them in a new way owing to a dramatically expanded capacity to symbolize, represent, experience, and speak about their world. At times I imagine they met the experience of being and nonbeing with nothing short of terror and other times the conscious perception of being and nonbeing must have filled them with awe.

The Paleolithic Funeral and the Awareness of Death

Archeological sites containing evidence of the first funerary rituals reveal the first indications of a spiritual life and all that it implies: the bitterness of a painful loss, a recognition of self and otherness, an idea that the subjectivity of the deceased loved one remains constant and survives death (in the beyond or in our memories), and a reverence for the ineffable and the mysterious. After millions of years of evolution, the Paleolithic funerary ritual stands out as a dramatically new form of animal behavior. Birds become obviously upset by the deaths of their chicks and mates, and many mammals suffer bitterly the loss of family or group members. But there is no animal, other than the human animal, that conducts a funeral and creates an accompanying myth of death and rebirth.

As seen in chapter 3, the tradition of the funerary ritual began in the Middle Paleolithic, 100,000 years ago. It then flourished in the Upper Paleolithic. The skeleton of a Homo neanderthalensis (36,000 years ago) found at Pierrot's Rock, Charente-Maritime (Saint Césaire), in France, "was found flexed into a small oval burial posture" (Johanson & Edgar, 2006, p. 246). We could say that the flexed position is a natural position for a person in pain to curl into before death, or that it is a way to save space and economize on digging, but it requires very little speculation to see the flexed position as a fetal position and attach to it the notion of returning to the womb, returning to the mother.

In 1868 the skeletons of three adult males, one adult female, and one infant were found intentionally buried at Abri Cro-Magnon at Les Eyzies in southern France. They were Homo sapiens of the Cro-Magnon type (30,000-32,000 years ago) and were buried together along with necklaces of pierced shells and animal teeth. Also included were stone blades and knives and the bones of reindeer, bison, woolly mammoths, and other animals (p. 260). Why would a hominin wear pierced shells? What was the significance of wearing an animal tooth? Other animals don't wear animal teeth. Is an animal tooth in some way symbolically related to an animal's jawbone? They both derive from the oral cavity. Were the other animal bones amulets or food? Why would a dead person need food or tools? It seems the survivors recognized their loved ones to be dead yet at the same time prepared them for a journey to a place where they would need food and tools.

A teenage Homo sapiens was buried 20,000 years ago at Arene Candide, Italy, wearing a shell bracelet and adornments of mammoth ivory and carrying a flint knife in his hand. His body was sprinkled with red ochre (pp. 101-102). The most common interpretation of the red ochre is that it was associated with blood and therefore with life and may have functioned magically to reanimate the body.

About 11,500 years ago a female shaman was ritually buried in the Galilee region of Israel and later discovered by researchers Leore Grosman and Natalie Munro. The burial is an oval-shaped basin cut into the cave floor. At the site were found the butchered bones of 3 wild cattle and 71 tortoises, indicating that the burial had included a feast for 35 or more people—the first of its kind ever found. Could this have been what Freud described as a totemic feast? (Buckley, 2010).

The technological and cultural explosion of the Upper Paleolithic could not have taken place without significant genetic mutations permitting the development or refinement of the symbolic function and capacity to speak. Randall White, cited by Richard Leakey, presented seven aspects of archeological evidence that suggest the large and significant role that language played in the Upper Paleolithic. Those aspects are (1) artistic expression, (2) technological innovation, (3) the appearance of regional differences, (4) long-distance contacts and trading, (5) an increase in the size of living sites, (6) the development of different toolmaking materials other than stone, and (7) the intentional burial of the dead. The highly distinguished archeologist Lewis Binford, also cited by Richard Leakey, said, "I don't see any medium through which such a rapid change could occur other than a fundamentally good, biologically based communication system" (R. Leakey, 1994, p. 126).

Richard Leakey himself wrote, "Ritual disposal of the dead speaks clearly of an awareness of death, and thus an awareness of self.... Neanderthals, as I've suggested, and probably other archaic sapiens, did have an awareness of death and therefore undoubtedly a highly developed reflective consciousness. But was it of the same luminosity as we experience today? Probably not. The emergence of fully modern language and fully modern consciousness were no doubt linked, each feeding the other" (pp. 155-56). Elsewhere Leakey (1977) asserted, "The fact of deliberate burial is interesting enough, for it betrays a keen self-awareness and a concern for the human spirit" (p. 125).

Ernest Becker (1973) noted that Homo sapiens is a creature with a symbolic function, and because of this, unlike other animals, we are able to become aware of our own creatureliness and mortality. It is the human paradox that we can symbolize the beyond and be aware of our own limit—our own death. We are half animal and half symbolic. We are "out of nature and hopelessly in it" (p. 26). We stand above nature in all our glory and then go to the ground and rot. Echoing others, Becker stated simply, "Death is man's peculiar and greatest anxiety" (p. 70). Following Otto Rank, he asserted, "Consciousness of death is the primary repression, not sexuality" (p. 96). For Becker, culture is Homo sapiens' protest against creatureliness and death (pp. 32-33).

It is fascinating to consider one hominin becoming simply distressed by the lifeless corpse of a deceased family member and another placing the body in a grave, sprinkling on red ochre, putting adornments on the corpse, placing food and tools in the grave, lighting a commemorative flame, and burying the body. For millions of years, animals have been evolving their awareness of the outside world. They developed sense organs and defensive strategies for survival. The evolving human strategies included the development of bipedal locomotion, the opposable thumb, our social instincts, and the ability to communicate. With the development of the symbolic function came the capacity to represent pictorially and to speak.

We imagine that with language a Homo sapiens might have stood watch on the savannah, named the things in his world, named himself, and maybe even had the dawning awareness that he existed. He named the trees and the animals in order to be able to communicate about them. He named his loved ones—his mother, his father, the men and women of his tribe, his siblings, his children, his friends—and his enemies. He called them by name. They came. They greeted one another. He cooperated with them, worked, loved, and huddled together with them against the cold dark night and a world of dangers. For our imagined Homo sapiens, a name represented a face, a personality, a constellation of experiences associated with the person who carried that name. The name became a part of the person. To intone the name when the person was absent was to make the person present in a way. Saying the name of a person who was not present was enough to stir emotions in those who missed the absent other. Chimpanzees and gorillas have elaborate personal relationships, but they do not name each other. Only humans do that.

When we name someone, we abstract the person. To name someone is to make them less threatening. We reduce them to a name, define, disarm, and explain them with a name. We confuse the part for the whole, and in doing so we kill them, in a sense, with a name. This little murder enables us to relate, to communicate, and to defend against the overwhelming anxiety of being and the encounter with the other. With speech and the symbolic function, our object relations and the internalization of our experiences and relationships help us to elaborate an internal world and an intrapsychic culture of introjects.

When we imagine an early Homo sapiens dreaming, as surely he did, he had to come to terms with his apparent travels to strange worlds that were markedly unlike those of his waking life. It was entirely too much to imagine a dreamscape within, where an intrapsychic culture of personal introjects was playing out personal conflicts, hopes, and fears in wish-fulfilling dramas. No, it took Freud to see that. It would have been much easier for our Paleolithic ancestors to see the dream as another world—a dreamworld—or to see the dream as related to phenomena in the waking world. One also has to remember that the waking world of our early Homo sapiens ancestors was a world full of monstrous physical threats but also full of demons and spirits, acausal relationships, magical thinking, and frequent inundations of primary process thinking into secondary process thinking. So just as waking life left its day residues in the dream, so too did the dreamworld invade waking reality with its night residues. But in addition to coming to terms with his dreams, our imagined Homo sapiens had to come to terms with the relative lifelessness of his loved ones every night as they curled up in a fetal position on the floor, slept, and dreamed.

❖ ❖ ❖

Let us imagine that one day at dawn, a Homo sapiens is standing amid the hills and caves of what is now Israel. He is sunk in natural beauty, safe in his position within his group, feeling the cool breeze wafting through his hair and awakening his senses. A friend in a tree looks out for danger and the group's next meal. Suddenly the friend slips, falls to the ground, hits his head on a large stone, and appears to be sleeping—perhaps dreaming—but when shaken, he doesn't wake up. He is dead. But what is death? Our Homo sapiens looks upon his friend and thinks, "I remember him moving, so why doesn't he move now? How can he no longer be? Is he this lifeless corpse? Where has the life gone? I remember him. I know his name. If I call his name, perhaps he will come back. I call and call, but he doesn't come back. He doesn't answer. Where is he? He looks asleep. Perhaps he is dreaming. Perhaps he has gone to the land of dreams." Our Homo sapiens is distressed and frightened by the sight of his dear friend—his now dead friend. He can't leave him there to rot and be eaten by scavengers, nor can he accept that his friend's body has become trash. He is confronting the absence of his friend, the loss of his friend, the death of his friend, and confronting his own life in the face of death. He is met with the anxiety of being in the face of nonbeing.

Confronted with existential terror, he pushes the reality away and, at the Skhul Cave on Mount Carmel in Israel, 90,000 years ago, he intentionally buries his friend with his legs tightly flexed and places in his friend's hand the jawbone of a wild boar. But why with legs flexed in the fetal position, and what is the meaning of the jawbone? If he is dead, he is dead. Or is he? If the life of the friend, which our Homo sapiens remembers, is no longer here, what was it and where is it?

One clue is that even after his friend died, our Homo sapiens heard his friend's voice in the winds and rustling leaves. His friend visited him in dreams, and just saying his name evoked emotion even years after his death. So where do the souls of the dead go? Sometimes they go, accompanied by food offerings, to an orally gratifying world where all needs are satisfied. Other times they go to an orally depriving world of hunger, thirst, pain, desperation, and aimless wandering—or so the modern traditions tell us. There is no way to know about the specific mythology behind the Paleolithic burials. What we do know is that food offerings, tools, and amulets are common, and they give the impression that the person is going someplace where he or she might need those things.

Róheim (1934/1974), we recall, explained that "humanity has emerged, as a human being emerges today, by the growth of defense mechanisms against the infantile situation, by the development of the unconscious" (p. 196). In the confrontation with death—the confrontation with being and nonbeing—humanity developed defensive strategies that served as the unconscious foundations for culture and for consciousness. The dead are not dead. They went somewhere else. They went down below. They went up above. They went away. They went to the dreamworld. The dead are not dead; they are reborn. The dead were in terrible pain while dying, but now they are made whole. They are gone forever but will live for eternity. We are sad, but they are happy now. We have lost our loved ones; now they will watch over us. I want to take my friend's spear, but if I do so, he will persecute me in my sleep, so I will give to him his spear to use in the hereafter. And on and on it goes. With the ability to symbolize, speak, and create traditions, a whole array of new defensive strategies became possible: negation, displacement, doing and undoing, turning passive into active, projection, and so on.

We have seen that the mouth has been repeatedly closed, opened, or filled with objects in funerary rituals around the world and throughout time. In other cases, food offerings and the jawbones or teeth of other animals were buried with the deceased. We also see how the baby's first act is to inhale and the dying person's last act is to exhale. Thus, the spirit enters with the first inspiration and exits with the final expiration. All animals do the same, but humans mythologize these phenomena into the embodiment and disembodiment of the soul. In historic times, the earth has been seen as a mother and death as a return to her, giving rise to the tradition of burying the loved one in a box, urn, tomb, or other such womb-like substitutes.

Similar to the mythologizing of the breath, the idea of going into another world at death or returning to the mother may have some rather natural origins in the phenomenology of dying. In the days leading up to my dear mother's death, at the age of 96, she started losing contact with the outer world, became more attentive to waking dream states and occasionally called out, as if to her mother in the next room, "Mom… Mom… Mom…" It turns out that calling for one's mother when nearing death is a rather common phenomenon and so are the waking dream states. This makes obvious sense from a psychoanalytic perspective, but it is impressive to see, nonetheless. My mother's mother died over fifty years before. So maybe the notions of an afterlife and a return to the mother are actually rather natural conclusions to draw from the experiences of dying.

Often accompanying the notion of the return to mother, or to Mother Earth, is the idea of rebirth and the need for food offerings or for those attending the funeral to partake in the funerary feast. Our Paleolithic ancestors were not orally fixated and were not acting like infants, but their culture, spiritual life, and psychology were oriented, by necessity, to the most basic facts of life: birth, the search for food, eating, meeting each other, protection of the group, and death. The most basic spiritual concept, which laid the foundation of our modern psychological structure, was that of the spirit or soul—an intangible reified essence of being. It was projected into water spirits, tree spirits, the spirits of ancestors, and the spirits of the living. The funeral was a ritual that consciously reaffirmed the group and unconsciously defended the group against the overwhelming confrontation with death and life, nonbeing and being. It also gave us a myth with which to defend ourselves against the terrors of death: the myth of death and rebirth.

This myth is one of doing and undoing; it's a defensive strategy to manage the feelings and impulses liberated by the terrors of death. The feelings are those of abandonment and of loneliness in facing the dark, angry death wishes directed toward the deceased, survivor guilt, and fear of reprisals, to name but a few.

When I imagine a soul or spirit entering the mythology of the Paleolithic, I am in danger of committing an error, as it is a speculation based on modern traditions that I am projecting into our prehistoric past. The projections of modern fantasies into our prehistoric past have been responsible for many of the errors in our thinking about the Paleolithic, but fortunately many of those have been corrected with increasing methodological rigor. In 1981, when Lewis Binford called for methodological rigor in the investigation of Pleistocene hominin behavior, he noted that assumptions led to inferences about artifacts found in association with other artifacts, and then came the interpretations. These interpretations were deemed probable or plausible, and then the doubtful reconstructions were established (pp. 31–32). But the question remained, Was it a reconstruction of the past or a reconstruction of the present projected into the past? Were cavemen violent promiscuous brutes, or have modern men projected their repressed instincts into the data? Did our Paleolithic ancestors live peacefully in the Garden of Eden, loving one another under the watchful eye of the great mother and leadership of the tribe's women, or is this too a projection of modern fantasies? As a clinical psychologist, I grant myself more room to speculate on these matters than a paleoanthropologist would. But I find that even when I am disciplined and parsimonious in my speculations, the data insists on the presence of the concept of the soul.

The psychomythic innovation of the Paleolithic was this concept of a soul, a spirit, an anima that was projected into and embodied various aspects of nature. Family members project a soul into the infant at the time of birth, and that soul is left hanging in the air at the time of death. The soul is greeted at birth and then again every day after in the "good morning" greeting ceremonial. We further salute it on saying "good night," "good-bye," and at death when we say, "fare thee well." Without ever being able to really know, I suggest that the predominant myth of the Paleolithic was the myth of death and rebirth and its corresponding ritual: the funeral ceremony.

If the speculative leap from historic anthropological data to prehistoric archeological data seems too great, perhaps this tapestry of speculations will find further support by weaving into it evidence of Paleolithic cannibalism, skull worship, the use of amulets, and magical artistic representation. Embedded in all of these is the basic spiritual idea of the spirit or soul. It originated in the Paleolithic and became the basis upon which we name our children and develop subjectivity, a sense of self, and a sense of the other. It is the way the mother draws out her infant and conjures its soul in the daily, mother-baby eye-to-eye greeting ritual.

Paleolithic Cannibalism and the Internalization of the Other

Human cannibalism is an impulse buried so deeply in the human psyche that it is seen primarily at the earliest levels of child development (the baby's desire to "devour" the mother by drinking her milk and biting her nipple), in some of the most severe forms of psychopathology, in some warring tribes, and in the fantasized deeds that we attribute to our most hated enemies, even when there is no evidence for their cannibalism.

Darwin (1871/1981) speculated that among our primeval ancestors, the strongest male jealously guarded and protected his females and used his strength and violence to kill or drive off competing males (vol. 2, pp. 362-63). Freud's (1913/1955h) phylogenetic fantasy imagined the competing males returning to kill and cannibalize the primal father. In their remorse, they created a fraternal clan under the protection of the totem father/animal, whose life and murder were celebrated in the totemic feast (SE 13, pp. 133-47).

How do we reconcile such speculations with the paleoanthropological record? Tim D. White (2001), of the University of California at Berkeley, studied man-made cut marks, fractures, and signs of intentional crushing on human bone and learned to distinguish them from human bones that have been crushed by falling rocks, chewed on by wild animals, damaged by natural forces, damaged by modern archeologists, and so on (pp. 58-65). White looked for stone tool cut marks on bone indicating the disarticulation of muscle and tendon, fractures, and hammering damage that would suggest the extraction of brains from the skull and marrow from long bones, burn effects indicating the cooking of flesh, and more. Using electron microscopy, he learned to distinguish cut marks made by stone tools from similar marks caused by erosion (pp. 58-65). And even when it was determined that damage to human bones was indeed caused by human hands, it was still difficult, if not impossible, to determine if those bones were left over after a nonreligious meal or prepared for skull worship, prepared as a trophy, modified as a part of funerary practices, or involved in some sort of formal ritual cannibalism.

The earliest evidence of hominin cannibalism is attributed to Homo antecessor 800,000 years ago and was found in the foothills of Sierra Atapuerca in northern Spain. It was there that the remains of six individuals were found with evidence that they had been butchered with stone tools and skinned, and that their brain cases had been opened and the long bones processed for extracting marrow (White, 2001, pp. 58-65).

Cut marks on the Bodo cranium from Ethiopia indicate that this Homo (erectus?) individual was defleshed 600,000 years ago (Pickering, White & Toth, 2000, pp. 579-84). But White reminds us that, based on this evidence, we are not able to tell if the Bodo cranium came from a victim of mortal combat and was defleshed in preparation for a meal, a meal and trophy, or just as a trophy. Similarly, we cannot tell if he was a venerated ancestor who was ritually cannibalized, ritually curated, or both (White, 1986, pp. 503-509; White, 1985, pp. 20-21). At Herto, Middle Awash, Ethiopia, three Homo sapiens crania dated to between 154,000 and 160,000 years old have evidence of postmortem mortuary practice, specifically cut marks associated with defleshing (White et al., 2003, pp. 742-47; Clark et al., 2003, pp. 747-52).

Neanderthal bones found at sites in Krapina and Vindija in Croatia bear signs of stone tool cut marks and crush fractures indicating they were also cannibalized. Their inexact age is between 35,000 and 150,000 years old (White, 2001, pp. 58-65). Another Neanderthal site, 100,000 years old, reveals evidence of cannibalism at the cave of Moula-Guercy on the banks of the Rhone River in southeastern France (pp. 58-65). On the banks of the Solo River in Java, further evidence of cannibalism was found when 11 Neanderthal skulls, 100,000 years old, were dug up with no trace of any other skeletal parts other than two leg bones. The facial bones were shattered off of each skull. All of the jaws and teeth were absent, and the *foramen magnums* (the large opening where the skull articulates with the vertebral column) of all but two of the skulls were enlarged (Constable, 1973, p. 105).

But something different was found on Monte Circeo near Rome, Italy. There, on the floor of a cave, a single skull was found. It was the skull of a Neanderthal man who had been killed by a blow to the temple. The foramen magnum was enlarged and the skull itself surrounded by an oval ring of stones. Indications of cannibalism, by themselves, do not imply ritual cannibalism. Sometimes the only thing we can say is that people ate people. But when the skull is set within an oval of stones, we can see something else is going on, something symbolic. Is this a remnant of a ritual? Was this a way to honor the deceased? Did the cannibals internalize the spirit of the deceased by eating its flesh? Analysis of the Monte Circeo site indicates that this apparent cannibalistic ritual took place about 60,000 years ago (Constable, 1973, pp. 105-106). The technique of enlarging the foramen magnum to scoop out and eat the brains is a practice still in use today among modern cannibals.

Cannibalism is observed in various other species throughout the animal kingdom, including chimpanzees. But it would be incorrect to attribute to these species the significance of ritual cannibalism. In fact, one could even question quite seriously whether cannibalism among hominins before 90,000 years ago had any of the ritual (magical) significance we commonly attribute to it in contemporary times—that is, the significance of incorporating the spirit, soul, strength, wisdom, and other characteristics of the enemy or loved one. We can speak of ritual cannibalism or ancestor worship only if we have some reason to believe that the cannibals had some basic spiritual concept of soul that they sought to magically incorporate by eating the deceased.

Joshua A. Hoffs (1963), in his article "Anthropophagy (Cannibalism): Its Relation to the Oral Stage of Development," wrote, "Human flesh has been eaten with the magical idea that the attributes, virtues, qualities, strength, or the soul of the person eaten could be acquired by the anthropophagist through a process of literal incorporation.... According to animistic thinking, a man's spirit could be possessed, just as his strength could be possessed, by eating part of his flesh.... Furthermore, enemies were eaten in the belief that by possessing their spirit one could render it harmless" (p. 35). Hoffs also explains that in honorific cannibalism "the dead were honored by being eaten by their relatives, thus insuring proper burial and the prevention of corruption of body and soul by decay" (p. 36).

The early Spanish explorers of the Americas encountered aboriginal peoples on the northern coast of South America who were a man-eating tribe. They were called the Carib or the Caribal. In time the Spanish called them the Canibal, and the name for this one group became a name for a wider category of people—the cannibals. Cannibals were encountered among the Fiji Islanders; the Tupis in South America; the Maori of New Zealand; indigenous peoples in central and east central Africa, New Guinea, Central Australia and China; in New Caledonia, Mexico, Peru, Greece, Polynesia, and Sierra Leone; among the Mau-Mau; and among many other peoples as well. Hoffs saw the funeral feast as a tradition derived from cannibalism:

> For purposes of illustration, the "funeral feast" may be cited as an overt cannibalistic derivative. In England, feasts occurred across the dead body, and in ancient Greece and Rome, they occurred at the graveside. In Bavaria, "corpse-cakes" were eaten, and in Albania, cakes were eaten which had on them the impression of a human form; this practice was called "eating the dead." It was believed that the "corpse-cake," or other food, actually contained the virtues and strength of the deceased, which could be acquired by the eater who simultaneously was honoring the dead. These feasts were identical in every way to cannibalistic funeral feasts, where the body of the deceased was actually eaten. (p. 40)

Cannibalism and derivatives of cannibalism have made their way into mythology (Zeus, Baba-Yaga, the vampire, Humbaba, Ngakola, Chronos, etc.), fairy tales ("Little Red Riding Hood," the witch), nursery rhymes, literature, and religion (Holy Communion, food restrictions). While trekking in the Himalayas in 1983, I saw numerous old Tibetan Buddhist ritual skullcap cups. It was explained to me that anything placed in these cups, whether it was beer or water or rice, was said to become sanctified by virtue of the fact that the cup was itself made from the skullcap (the top of the skull) of a high monk. In this way, it offered an unending magical cannibalistic feast where one could take in the sacred character of the high monk by eating or drinking anything that had been placed in the bowl.

Of course, cannibalism and derivatives of cannibalism are also common in dreams, fantasies, jokes, common expressions, terms of endearment, perverse and psychotic symptomatology, erotic play, gingerbread men, and so on (Hoffs, 1963, pp. 39-45). And what child does not enjoy being eaten up by a mother or father in the guise of "the cookie monster"?

Amulets: Homes for the Souls of the Ancestors

Amulets are sacred objects with no apparent utilitarian value but imbued with spiritual significance. Amulets might be stones, carved objects, pieces of bone, skulls, or any other object into which a spirit or the spirits of ancestors are projected. Some amulets may have a utilitarian value, but if so, it is parallel to their spiritual significance.

The skull, as the least corruptible part of the body, was worshiped or consulted as an object that brought the living closer to a wise and helpful ancestor/totem residing in the other world. Our Paleolithic ancestors went to their graves with the jawbones of animals (totems?), wore necklaces made of animal teeth, and even carried with them stones, bones, or shells that had been marked or purposefully modified, not for use as tools but for some aesthetic or possibly spiritual purpose.

In Paleolithic Hungary, in Tata, 60 kilometers west of Budapest, numerous Paleolithic scrapers were found as well as a rounded fragment of mammoth ivory with no apparent utility but with traces of red ochre all over it. In the same 50,000-year-old site was found a disc-shaped stone with an X etched into it (Bordes, 1968, p. 111). A piece of carved reindeer antler from Teyjat in southern France was engraved with images of animals. Also found were a carved bison missing its head, a goat sculpted from bone, a horse of ivory, and the image of a reindeer engraved on a small piece of limestone (Maringer, 1960, plates 20, 39, 40, 43).

Jan Jelínek (1975) provides drawings and photographs of dozens of Paleolithic amulets. They include objects with carved representations of vulvas, stylized pendants of women's breasts, animal teeth with holes drilled into them to be worn as beads on a necklace or as pendants, a swan carved from ivory, pebbles engraved with animals, and pieces of antler with geometric designs engraved into them (pp. 373, 407, 409, 419, 420, 425, 429, 440, 442, 453). Johannes Maringer (1960) described graves that included animal skulls, horns, and amulets (pp. 52, 54). And at Grottes du Placard in France, nine skull fragments were unearthed and on close examination found to be skullcap cups similar to those found in other Paleolithic sites from Spain to the Czech Republic. Maringer cites the claim of Herodotus that the

Issedones prepared gold-mounted skulls of their ancestors from which to drink. The Tibetans and Bengali are known to line ritual skullcap cups in silver. In the Christian Middle Ages, the skullcaps of saints were used as memorial drinking cups, and a 19th-century traveler in Australia reported seeing a 10-year-old aboriginal girl in southern Australia who carried with her a piece of her mother's skull from which she would drink (pp. 54, 55). As a drinking cup it had a utilitarian function, but being made of the skull of her mother it was also an amulet with a parallel spiritual function. The mother was feeding her daughter and the girl was drinking from her mother.

An amulet can be a stone with tiny markings on it, a skull venerated as a totem figure, a saint's bone established in a reliquary, the tooth of a shark on a necklace, a baseball signed by Babe Ruth, or a book signed by its author. All are believed to carry some sort of power, magic, or spirit. The Venezuelan Yanomami of today still live a lifestyle that is somewhere between the Paleolithic and the Neolithic. They are seminomadic hunter-gatherers who tend gardens. But after decades of contact with outsiders, they no longer make stone tools. Sometimes, however, they find ancient stone tools or amulets in their gardens, which they recognize as gifts from their ancestors. A Yanomami amulet that I saw on one of my expeditions up the Orinoco River was shaped like an elongated, slightly flattened meatball with small man-made indentations on the top and bottom. On the sides were four purposefully flattened surfaces. It was an ancient amulet being used as a modern-day amulet in Yanomami ceremonies when taking hallucinogenic drugs (*yopo*). At the heart of their ceremonial space, the amulet facilitated communication with their animal spirits (*hekuras*).

One of the things implied in totemism and the worship of amulets is the veneration of the ancestor, which is also a part of hunting magic and the spirit of the hunt. Paleolithic hunters in the Swiss Alps had primitive tools but hunted the giant cave bear, which stood 8 feet tall on its hind legs. It must have been seen as a spiritual being at least equal to the Paleolithic hunter, if not a god, or maybe a monster with a great spirit. To kill it required hunting magic, to eat it was to incorporate its spirit, and afterward they curated the skull and venerated it as an amulet in order to assure a good hunting season.

In May 2009 I took a two-week expedition up the Orinoco River to visit a small indigenous village in the Venezuelan jungles. During the course of my stay with the Hoti, I saw the skulls of various hunted animals scattered on the grounds of the village, tucked into notches between tree limbs, and stashed in corners of the homes. After witnessing the butchering of a tapir, I saw the chief cook the animal's head for soup and prepare the skull to be left out on the grounds of their village. This seemingly casual tradition shows respect for the spirit of the hunted animal and, as hunting magic, assures continued success in the hunt. (An account of my visit to this village and the story of the butchering of a tapir can be found in "The Killing of the Beast" in appendix 5.)

When our Paleolithic ancestors went hunting for the Pleistocene beasts of their day, they didn't simply kill them and eat them any more than the Hoti did. After butchering the huge animals, they too felt an impulse to do something with those massive skulls. In Drachenloch in the Swiss Alps, there is a tunnel-cave 200 feet deep. Halfway into the chamber, a pile of Paleolithic cave bear leg bones and skulls was found, and each skull was missing a small piece, leaving a hole in every one of them and no evidence of where the missing piece went. Did the missing pieces become amulets? In another part of the cave, there was a rock chest covered by a large slab of stone. Inside the chest, seven cave bear skulls were discovered, all facing the mouth of the cave. F. Clark Howell (1965) pointed out that in addition to this site, there are literally dozens of other sites throughout the region where curated bear skulls have been found (pp. 126, 127, 153, 154).

How could a hominin culture suddenly start imbuing objects with spirit, with meaning, with power? It is clear that the cultural explosion of the Upper Paleolithic could not have occurred without a dramatic genetic mutation permitting the development of our symbolic function. It was this mutation that turned anguish over a loss into mourning, the confrontation with death into the funerary ritual, alimentary cannibalism into ritual cannibalism, and inert objects into amulets.

One might be inclined to see amulets as the cultural parallel to transitional objects, or the first "not me" possessions, but transitional objects are neither parts of the baby's body nor dolls or teddy bears. Transitional objects are things like a corner of a blanket, a bit of wool, a corner of a sheet, and other "not me" possessions that provide comfort to the infant (Winnicott, 1953, p. 90). Establishing the developmental position of the transitional object, Donald W. Winnicott contended, "The first possession is related backwards in time to autoerotic phenomena and fist and thumb sucking, and also forwards to the first soft animal or doll and to hard toys. It is related both to the external object (mother's breast) and to internal objects (magically introjected breast), but is distinct from each" (p. 97). Thus, the amulet is not a transitional object but more of a spiritual toy or spiritual doll. The amulet is a spiritual doll for remembering the deceased, worshiping the ancestor, and consulting the spirits. The amulet is like the wooden spool of the *fort da* baby (S. Freud, 1920/1955b, SE 18, pp. 14–15), which was an amulet, so to speak, in remembrance of the absent mother.

The only thing that comes close to being a predecessor to the amulet is the stone tool, which appeared more than 3.3 million years before the amulets. Stone tools and the survival factor that they afforded humans no doubt played an enormous role in the selection of genetic mutations leading to the development of the uniquely human symbolic function. That is to say:

Stone tools provided a distinct survival advantage.

Those who were good at making stone tools had a better chance of surviving.

More sophisticated tools required greater intelligence to make and use.

The fabrication of these tools required planning and skill.

Passing on that higher technology from one generation to the next required intelligence, language, education, and tradition.

Intelligence provided a survival advantage, and this drove the genetic mutations to make us who we are today.

Those with the intellect to look at a hunk of stone and see a potential stone tool residing within it were only a short intellectual leap away from imbuing that stone with personality, power, or spirit. Nonetheless, while the amulet is sacred, the stone tool made prior to the Upper Paleolithic was for the most part an extension of the human body—a practical and profane object.

Stone Tools and Technological Evolution

Approximately 3.4 million years ago *Australopithecus afarensis* left evidence of cutting, scraping, and percussing on goat and cattle bones for flesh removal and marrow extraction (IHO, 2010). Then came the crude choppers, flake knives, scrapers, and hammerstones followed by unifacial and bifacial choppers, cleavers, and picks. Then came the bifacial hand axes. With the Upper Paleolithic came the fine blades struck from blade cores, finely worked spear points and knives, tools composed of microliths, borers, sewing needles, barbed harpoons from bone and antler, and other tools.

The Upper Paleolithic technological revolution enabled Homo sapiens to kill and eat the megafauna (large mammals) of the Pleistocene epoch: giant cave bears, woolly mammoths, saber tooth tigers, giant armadillos, giant sloths, and more. Being nomadic and suddenly developing new technologies to master their environment, the Upper Paleolithic peoples began to make their way around the world adapting to new environments.

Current scientific data suggests that Homo sapiens reached Australia 50,000 years ago; Western Europe 30,000 to 40,000 years ago; and the Americas about 15,000 to 20,000 years ago (Shreeve, 2006, pp. 64-65). The date of the arrival of Homo sapiens to the Americas is highly controversial. Genetic evidence suggests the date was between 15,000 and 20,000 years ago, and the earliest reliably dated archeological sites cluster around 11,000 to 12,000 years old. But there are other sites that are believed to be 12,500 years old at Monte Verde in Chile; 12,800 years old at Taima Taima in Venezuela (Adovasio & Page, 2002, p. 203); 14,000 years old at Saltville in Virginia; 15,000 years old at Cactus Hill in Virginia; and 17,000 years old at Meadowcroft Rockshelter in Avella, Pennsylvania (Begley & Murr, 1999, pp. 40-47). More recently a cache of flake stone tools was found deep in Chiquihuite Cave in Zacatecas in central Mexico by Ciprian Ardelean and his team. Scientific dating techniques indicate these stone tools are a startling 27,000 years old (Strickland, 2020).

When we consider that the immigrants presumably came to the Americas from Asia across the Bering Strait, that the Meadowcroft Rockshelter is on the eastern coast of North America, that Zacatecas is in central Mexico, that Monte Verde is on the southern tip of South America, and that there is no reason to think archeologists have already found the oldest evidence of human occupation in the Americas, it is easy to see that in the coming years scientific research is sure to push back the date of the earliest arrival of Homo sapiens to the Americas.

Radiocarbon dates are in dispute at sites in both North and South America, with some scientists arguing for the extreme antiquity of Homo sapiens in the Americas and others with more conservative interpretations. Vance Haynes, a conservative interpreter of the data, examined the evidence at Monte Verde in Chile and noted that a bifacial projectile point found there was very similar to those found at Taima Taima in Venezuela (Adovasio & Page, 2002, pp. 203-204, 216). José Maria Cruxent (1911-2005), the father of Venezuelan archeology, excavated the site at Taima Taima in 1962. One of Cruxent's colleagues, with whom he subsequently worked in the field, was Miklos Szabadics Roka. A self-taught archeologist with years of field experience, Szabadics Roka assembled an enormous collection of thousands of Paleolithic stone tools from surface finds, rather than excavations, on expeditions all across Venezuela. He wrote about this collection in *Archeology of the Prehistory of Venezuela* (1997).

❖ ❖ ❖

In February 2006, my wife and I accompanied Miklos Szabadics Roka and his wife, Eva, on a surface-find expedition in search of stone tools in Paleolithic Venezuela. Here's how it went: We drive from Caracas to Coro and then out to Tara Tara, not far from Taima Taima, to meet Miklos and Eva. From there we head out in their jeep to an isolated stretch of desert 100 kilometers away. Making our way in the jeep, we leave the highway for a back road, the back road for a dirt road, and the dirt road for the open desert. We make our way slowly over small hills and ditches, dried streambeds, and sparse brush until Miklos stops the jeep, jumps out, picks up a rock, and declares he has found a Paleolithic stone flake scraper! It looks like a rock to me. He finds one so-called Paleolithic scraper after another, and I am beginning to wonder what we were doing out in the middle of nowhere under the hot sun. Then he shouts, "Spear point!" And there in his hand is an ancient Paleolithic spear point that even

I am able to recognize as such. We all jump out of the jeep and the search is on. Soon all of us are finding Paleolithic scrapers, spear points, hand axes, and grinding stones. The ground is littered with them. Some sit on the ground where the floods last exposed them; others are half embedded in the earth. Most are crudely fashioned, but others have been made with great skill and refinement. Most are broken. A few are intact. It is a stunning experience to find a Paleolithic stone tool and realize that the last person to hold it was the person who made or used it, perhaps 8,000 years ago.

❖ ❖ ❖

On subsequent expeditions with Miklos, Eva, and Miklos's daughter, Jenny (a university-trained archeologist), we found more of the same but also shell mounds where Paleolithic Venezuelans had gathered clams and sea snails to extract the meat. We found seashells that appeared to be intentionally perforated, probably for use as jewelry. And, most impressively, we found stone hearths eroding out of the sand. The Paleolithic peoples of this area had set up rings of stone within which they built fires to cook their food. The stones, blackened and reddened by fire, sat right where they had been placed. Over the years, shifting sands and dirt had covered up these ancient hearths. Then, more recently, the sand began eroding away under Venezuela's torrential rains, revealing these circular stone hearths that had been hidden from view for thousands of years. To be out in the middle of the desert and come upon an unattended stone hearth eroding out of the sand at my feet was like being transported back to the Paleolithic.

The animals hunted by the Upper Paleolithic Venezuelans included mastodons (10 feet high at the shoulders), giant sloths (15 feet tall and weighing up to 4 tons), and giant armadillos (about 1-2 tons in weight). On a visit to Taima Taima with Miklos, we saw a touristic presentation of an earlier excavation by a group of archeologists, including Cruxent. On display was a mastodon skeleton, including its pelvis, with a stone spear point, similar to the ones we had found ourselves, resting at its center. The guard at the site also showed us the recent find of a fossil scale from the shell of a giant armadillo or Glyptodon. In neighboring Colombia, in 2020, archeologists reported finding a rock wall, deep in the jungle, with thousands of ancient paintings of designs, people, and animals including extinct species like mastodons and giant sloths. The images were painted between 12,600 and 11,800 years ago (Gershon, 2020).

Our Paleolithic ancestors used stone tools to take down large animals, and there was nothing casual about it. The hunt required great intelligence, knowledge, planning, teamwork, physical strength, skill, and emotional preparation. These animals must have appeared to the hunters as nothing less than giant monsters or great spirits. Many of the European Upper Paleolithic amulets and bone tools have images of animals engraved into them, with holes bored through them or images of arrows piercing them. This is widely interpreted as hunting magic, the formula being if one graphically or sculpturally represents the animal, this representation contains the animal's spirit, and if one practices killing the amulet, it will magically help when the actual hunt takes place.

The transformation of stone tools into amulets occurred at the same time nonfunctional amulets appeared, and the appearance of both coincided with the first funerals, ritual cannibalism, and the wider arts explosion of the Upper Paleolithic when humans for the first time began to sculpt, engrave, and paint.

Painting and Sculpture: Projections into the World

Photographs of the Upper Paleolithic cave paintings are certainly interesting to see, but when we consider these images as the first of their kind after millions of years of animal evolution, we are filled with awe. They do not simply represent horses and bison; they are testaments to the then recently evolved cognitive capacity to create a graphic representation. Imagine a highly evolved chimpanzee crawling deep into a cave and painting a picture of a horse. It fills us with wonder just to muse on the possibility, yet that is exactly what our ancestors did.

We colloquially refer to our Upper Paleolithic ancestors as "cavemen." Some of our Paleolithic ancestors did live for periods of time in caves or, more correctly, under rock ledges, but certainly not all of them and not always. Most of the famous painted caves were not dwelling places but shrines, temples, or places for special ritual functions. The reason we focus on the cave paintings is that they are the paintings that survived. One could easily imagine our ancestors painting on trees, open rock surfaces, wood, leather, broad leaves, and even on their own bodies. But if such paintings ever existed, they would have been washed off or deteriorated long ago. Thus, what we are left with are those paintings that by virtue of being painted deep inside caves have managed to survive for millennia.

There are numerous rock walls and caves with Paleolithic paintings located throughout much of the world. Many of the caves in Europe were carved out by water in massive limestone deposits. They were entered at great risk by our Upper Paleolithic ancestors, who crawled on their bellies, naked, into dark holes where they could easily get trapped, drown in cave rivers, or be attacked by cave bears or other wild animals that might be living inside. It is doubtful our ancestors were looking for food or shelter when they entered these caves. Curiosity was likely a strong motivating force, and this curiosity to enter a dark and dangerous cave was certainly mixed with fear and reverence for the mysterious.

These early explorers carried stone cups as oil lamps to illuminate the cave with a flickering flame. The rough texture and irregular warping surface of the walls caught that flickering light and stirred the imagination of this new animal—this human—with a symbolic function that was second to none. Suddenly they were seeing percepts (impressions, illusions) on the walls like the images we project into a Rorschach inkblot. In addition to the visual percepts, these explorers were subject to the audio percepts of the cave born of the whispering breeze, the muttering of trickling water, and the sounds of their own echoing voices and shuffling feet. How could these visual and auditory percepts saturating the darkness of a mysterious cave be perceived as anything other than spiritually imbued? Frightened in one moment, in awe the next, the explorers couldn't put the inkblot down, ignore the echoes, or just disregard it all as a product of their imagination. Their projected psychological reality was a part of their external reality. They highlighted their percepts with their fingers in the soft clay, used stones to scratch lines into the impressionable limestone, and then retreated to the light of day.

Moved by the experience of this remarkable place, our early ancestors may have seen it as a sacred space, a *temenos*, or temple, and the experience they had there called them back. They gathered colored pigments and returned to the cave, where they once again projected their thoughts, feelings, and memories onto the walls and with their pigments painted them into place: bison, horses, lions, elephants, rhinoceroses, bears, birds, deer, ibex, fish, vulvas, lines, geometric forms, handprints. While the animals, appearing in great numbers, were typically executed with fine artistic sensibility, the human figures, far fewer in number, were generally drawn in a cruder fashion. Human figures that have been found include images of women, fewer of men, and some humans with animal heads, which have often been interpreted as shamans officiating over ritual healing and hunting magic. Some of the animals painted onto the walls have spears painted onto them, giving rise to the interpretation that they served a role in hunting magic. Other paintings of animals were used as objects of target practice with real spears; the paintings show evidence of damage from spears actually being thrown at them.

In Harold P. Blum's psychoanalytic approach to prehistoric cave art, he wrote that the cave is symbolic of "the womb, the birth canal, and the primal cavity of self-object relationship... Entering and leaving the cave could also represent coitus but on a deeper level, attachment and separation. The cave had magical and developmental significance, a transitional space between internal and external, fantasy and reality, death and rebirth" (Blum, 2011, 196).

Some of the more famous caves, such as Altamira in Spain and Lascaux in southern France, have been closed to the public or have had limited access for decades in order to protect them. But others, such as those in Les Eyzies in southern France, are open to the touring public. Les Eyzies calls itself the "Capital of Prehistory," with many prehistoric sites open to the public, such as the flint toolmaking site at Laugerie-Basse and the magnificent cave paintings of bison at Grotte de Font-de-Gaume. To see the bison in the Grotte de Font-de-Gaume is to witness a human creation of extraordinary antiquity. These images were created between 11,000 and 17,000 years ago. The cave at Lascaux, referred to as the "prehistoric Sistine Chapel" or the "Louvre of the Paleolithic," is one of three of the most extraordinary examples of Paleolithic art along with Altamira and Chauvet. The paintings at Lascaux were created about 20,000 years ago.

In 1992 scuba divers in the Mediterranean off the coast of France found the entrance to the Cosquer Cave 121 feet below sea level. They swam into this dark, narrow tunnel and made their way 574 feet into it. The tunnel was inclined such that the farther they swam, the higher they went until they reached a large chamber at the end, fully at sea level and filled with air. It turns out that during the ice ages, sea level in the Mediterranean was about 400 feet lower than it is today due to all the water frozen up in glaciers. This meant the cave entrance was actually well above sea level during the ice ages, giving Paleolithic people easy access to the cave. After the last ice age ended, the waters covered the entrance and rose an additional 121 feet. When the scuba-diving explorers arrived at the chamber at the end of the cave, above sea level they found stone tools and cave paintings. There were handprints stenciled onto the walls as well as paintings of horses, bison, deer, ibex, chamois, a feline, ten seals, and three penguins (Simons, 1992, pp. B5–B6). Radiocarbon dating has determined that the paintings in the Cosquer Cave are about 18,000–19,000 years old, and some of the handprints are a mind-boggling 27,000 years old (Chauvet et al., 1996, p. 131). And yet the images painted onto the walls at Chauvet Cave are even older.

❖ ❖ ❖

In the fall of 1994, I registered to attend a symposium on Paleolithic cave paintings at the California Academy of Sciences in San Francisco. The symposium took place in March 1995. But on December 18, 1994, between my registration and the symposium itself, three cave explorers in southeastern France discovered the Chauvet Cave. The program for the March symposium had been arranged months before, and it was a rich presentation, but the 500 people in attendance were eager to learn more about the recently discovered paintings at Chauvet. Fortunately, at the end of the symposium, Dr. Jean Clottes of the Comité

International d'Art Rupestre gave a brief report on the Chauvet Cave and presented slides of the cave art, including paintings of horses, buffalo, rhinoceroses, lions, deer, and more. I believe it was the first time the images had ever been shown publicly.

Clottes showed a beautiful selection of slides of the cave paintings, but when he showed an absolutely spectacular slide of four horse heads in profile looking toward the left, I heard 500 people in unison gasping on the inhale, in total awe. One simply cannot look at these images without being impressed by their extraordinary beauty and overwhelming grace. In the Chauvet Cave, one of the ancient artists drew a buffalo in profile facing to the right but the neck terminates at the corner of the wall. To the right, on the other plane of the wall at the corner, one sees the face of the buffalo not in profile as if turning away from the viewer, but full face, head-on.

There are also 30 cave bear skulls that were purposefully arranged on the floor and now covered in a frosty coating of calcite crystals: "In the middle of the chamber, on a block of grey stone of regular shape that had fallen from the ceiling, the skull of a bear was placed as if on an altar. The animal's fangs projected beyond it into the air. On top of the stone there were still pieces of charcoal, the remains of a fire place" (Chauvet et al., 1996, p. 131). Radiocarbon dating determined that the paintings in Chauvet are between 29,000 and 36,000 years old.

In 2019 a new discovery was announced—cave paintings located on Sulawesi, a large island in central Indonesia. The painted images depict eight human figures approaching wild pigs and buffalo. But the figures are not just your typical hunters, as one has a large beak and another has what appears to be a tail. Figures incorporating human and animal characteristics are found in other cave paintings and are often seen as mythological beings, animal spirit helpers, or shamans. The paintings on Sulawesi are 44,000 years old (Ferreira, 2019).

I'd like to take a moment to say a bit about shamanism, to which I have already made a few references. To begin with it is important to understand that human consciousness includes more than wakefulness, sleep, dream, and drunkenness. There are numerous states of consciousness, some of which give the person feelings of cosmic unity, oceanic feeling, or empathy with all plants, animals and even inanimate objects. There are high arousal states that offer acute awareness of the now, which transcends time and locates the person, emotionally, at the cosmic center of the universe. The shaman is often immersed in a state of consciousness similar to a vivid dream state with the eyes open in which the inner and outer worlds merge in metaphors that fill life with poignancy, meaning, and give rise to visions that contribute to local mythologies. It is in these states that being, knowing, and loving become aspects of a tangible unity to such an extent that the visionaries of many religions have focused on these themes in their teachings. Shamans, in cultures all around the world, experience visions spontaneously or under the influences of psychedelic drugs, meditation, mystical traditions, or initiation rituals. In these altered states of consciousness shamans gather wisdom to heal the sick and spiritually guide their communities. These are experienced as unusual and remarkable states of consciousness but they are really very human and even quite common.

It is useful to think of the cave paintings of shamans and great animal spirits along with the other Paleolithic innovations in order to understand more fully their symbolic and spiritual significance. Funerary rituals, cannibalism, and amulets all involve soul or spirit, the abstraction and projection of some essential quality. The person is dead, but through the funerary ritual the spirit carries on. In cannibalism one incorporates the spirit, soul, or characteristics of the other by eating their flesh. With an amulet a dead object is imbued with life, spirit, soul, meaning, and power. And with graphic representation we point to a drawing on a wet, cold cave wall and say, "That *is* a bison." The illusion that the representation is equivalent to the thing itself is based in animism, magical thinking, and the omnipotence of thoughts, words, and gestures. Thus, it is amusing and thought-provoking to think that in 1929, 36,000 years after Chauvet, René Magritte painted a picture of a pipe and wrote beneath it, "*Ceci n'est pas une pipe*" (This is not a pipe). It seems that after 36,000 years we needed Magritte to tell us that the image is not the actual thing it represents.

In the Paleolithic, the thing could be represented and then remembered in the absence of the thing. The representation became the thing, and one could act on it symbolically—that is, use it to perform magic, to stimulate the fertility of the animals, and to assist in the success of the hunt. A drawing is like a concrete memory to be shared with someone else. A chimpanzee can communicate quite a lot but cannot communicate with another chimpanzee to say, "Yesterday I saw a bird." In chimpanzee communication, everything is in the now. With a drawing one can represent something as here, even if it is not here.

On September 8, 1940, the Second World War was on, France was under German occupation, and a teenager in Montignac, France, was taking his dog for a walk when the dog slid into a hole created by a tree uprooted in a recent storm. The teenager, Marcel Ravidat (17 years old), went into the hole to save his dog and found a large cavern. He returned to the spot four days later with three of his friends to widen the hole. They entered the cave and discovered Lascaux. The extraordinary paintings, 17,000 to 20,000 years old, were executed in brown, reddish-brown, yellow, black, and white pigments brought in from the outside and painted on the walls and ceiling with apparent playfulness and solemnity. The floor was littered with scrapers, engraving tools, flint blades, spear points, eyed needles, perforated seashells, bones of animals that the artists seem to have eaten within the cave, torches from the branches of coniferous trees, limestone slabs used as animal fat lamps, and scaffolding for reaching high portions of the walls and ceilings. The paintings are among the most elegant expressions of art the world has ever seen. After visiting Lascaux, Pablo Picasso emerged from the cave and exclaimed, "We have invented nothing!" (Rigaud, 1988, pp. 482-99).

The cave at Lascaux contains various sections or rooms and is filled with 600 paintings, 1,500 engravings, and a multitude of dots and geometric figures. Various theories have arisen about the purpose of this and other Paleolithic caves, but it is fairly well agreed that these caves were not occupation sites and that their purpose was probably spiritual in character in order to ensure the fertility of the animals they hunted, to conduct rituals of hunting magic, and to provide a sacred space for the spiritual work of Paleolithic shamans. Identified with animal spirits, a shaman may dress in a costume of the spirit, wear a mask, act like the animal spirit that possesses him, or carry amulets of the totem.

At Lascaux there is one crudely executed image of a man with an erect penis and a birdlike head, who is seemingly falling backward in front of a large wounded bison with a staff close by, surmounted by a bird. The German archeologist Horst Kirchner, who studied this painting at Lascaux, interpreted this scene as a shaman in a trance, wearing a bird mask. The bison, he said, is a sacrificial animal, and the bird on the staff is a tutelary spirit. The reason for the representation, he suggested, was to ensure the success of the hunt. It is a grand interpretation, highly speculative and reinforced with contemporary ethnology, but continues to be evocative and highly regarded by people such as Maringer (1960, p. 61) and Joseph Campbell (1969/1976, p. 258).

❖ ❖ ❖

Modern interpretations of ancient prehistoric art are vulnerable to error when there is an absence of data that could disconfirm the interpretation or when the projections of those making the interpretations distort our view of the artifacts and extend too far beyond the data. Two paleoanthropologists who promoted methodological rigor in the interpretation of Paleolithic sites were Sally and Lewis Binford. In 1992 I had the honor of meeting Sally R. Binford (1923-1993). She specialized in Neanderthal sites in Europe, the modern analysis of archeological data, and the development of modern methods of archeological exploration. She had been to the cave at Lascaux on numerous occasions and loved the place, so when I told her of my interest in her trips there, she offered to facilitate my visit to the original cave at Lascaux, which has been closed to the public since 1963. The next time we met was a couple of months later in southern France, where she introduced me to Jean-Philippe Rigaud, director of the Institute of Prehistory and Quaternary Geology at the University of Bordeaux in Aquitaine and the keeper of the caves in southern France at that time. He knew I was in France for just a few days and graciously arranged for me to enter Lascaux that afternoon. Before entering the cave, each member of our small group of five or six (mostly archeology students) stepped into a tray containing a solution that would kill any fungus spores or algae that may have attached to the soles of our shoes. We walked together in the dark, but intermittently a light would be turned on for a few seconds, permitting our viewing of the paintings. A constant light would have promoted the growth of algae on the walls and the destruction of the paintings. Having studied the cave paintings in books, I recognized the images immediately, but I was not fully prepared for their extraordinary beauty.

I don't think the artists in the cave at Lascaux gathered their paints together and said, "Gee, I think I'll paint a horse today." No, I think they entered the cave with flickering oil lamps and solemnly projected their psyches onto the limestone walls as light and shadows from their oil lamps danced across the irregular surfaces. As sacred percepts appeared before them as images outside themselves, the walls spoke to them, giving them ideas of what to paint. A crack in the wall became the line of a horse's back; a concavity became an animal's belly; a bulge in the wall was used to emphasize an animal's hip; a ledge became the ground line for running horses; a broad horizontal patch of discolored wall was configured as water, permitting the artist to paint only the heads and necks of deer above it, giving the impression of four deer swimming through a stream. The age of these paintings is mind-boggling, but independent of their great antiquity they are absolutely stunning pieces of art.

The images at Lascaux are painted on highly irregular surfaces. Because of this, some of the larger animals could not be seen entirely by the artist painting them, as these warped surfaces actually blocked the artist's view from seeing the entire animal unless the artist were to step back from it. And as the artists painted, the spirits of the cave whispered to them from deep in the darkness. For visitors to the cave who have spent a lifetime in rectangular rooms with flat walls and right angles at every corner, the undulated surface of the cave provides a unique experience. The rolling walls, the rising and falling ceiling, and the constricting and opening spaces give extraordinary impressions psychologically. And the paintings are not even painted at eye level but rather on the warped and irregular walls at lower and higher levels all the way up and fully onto the ceiling. One's experience of the art also varies based on the angle of the neck. It is quite different to look straight out at a painting placed at eye level than it is to look up at one. And when the action in the whole room seems to rise and fall, float into the air, and dance across the sky, it is really something to behold. It is so completely different from anything else we usually see in our world, and yet it appears so exceedingly human. Gazing upon these magnificent paintings I had a strange but fantastic feeling that a piece of communication sent thousands of years ago had arrived in the present and I had just received it.

❖ ❖ ❖

Not surprisingly, some psychoanalysts have found inspiration for their theoretical thinking in these ancient cave paintings. Facing the title page of Arnold Modell's *Object Love and Reality: An Introduction to a Psychoanalytic Theory of Object Relations* (1968) is a painting of a horse from the cave at Lascaux. Observing the phylogenetic parallel to ontogenetic development, Modell noted that our Paleolithic ancestors, sunk in magical thinking, did not paint a horse, for example, to denote a horse, but rather the image and the object became fused into one: "The painting of the Paleolithic hunter does not represent a horse, it is a horse" (p. 19). Drawing on the work of Ernst Cassirer, Modell makes a distinction between "the symbol that denotes the object and the symbol that is the object" (p. 161). Addressing this magical view of the world where symbols are the thing they symbolize, where there is an omnipotence of thought, and where there is an interpenetration of the inner world and the outer world, Modell finds useful the perspective of Winnicott and his concept of the transitional object. Modell says that, like the Paleolithic hunter, the infant at 12 months substitutes the mother for an external inanimate object infused with his own creative illusion:

> That is, he is able to invest an inanimate object with the qualities of life. Winnicott terms this object a transitional object; it is the child's first possession, the familiar blanket or Teddy bear. This is an object; it is part of the environment; it is something, not a hallucination. According to Winnicott it is a thing created by the infant and at the same time provided by the environment. As with Paleolithic paintings the inner process interpenetrates the objects of the environment and gives them life. (Modell, 1968, pp. 32–33)

For Modell, the mentality of our Paleolithic ancestors was magico-religious and their environment full of very real dangers: "We are led to the unmistakable conclusion that the cave art served a religious function arising from this primitive society's proximity to death" (p. 14).

Noel Bradley, in "Primal Scene Experience in Human Evolution and Its Phantasy Derivatives in Art, Proto-Science, and Philosophy" (1967), noted that until only very recently people have been living in conditions in which observation of the primal scene (the parents engaging in sexual intercourse) was indeed very common. Bradley observed that the Paleolithic caves are filled with paintings of male and female animal pairs, male animals smelling the genitals of females, and scenes of copulating animals. He suggests that the scenes of copulating animals, in addition to being magically linked to ensuring the fertility of an animal important to their diet, were "partly aimed at giving expression to primal scene fantasy" (p. 41).

Other indications of the spiritual life of our Upper Paleolithic ancestors are the engravings or drawings of vulvas, amulets of a woman's breasts, drawings of women, and small sculptural representations of women. The Venus of Willendorf is a limestone statuette (11 centimeters high) of an ample, naked woman with large breasts, belly, buttocks, and thighs; diminutive arms and hands; diminutive calves and no feet; no facial features; and her hair in what appear to be cornrows in concentric circles from the top of her head down. The sculptor belonged to a group of mammoth hunters 20,000 to 30,000 years ago, in what is now Austria (Jelínek, 1975, p. 375; Maringer, 1960, plate 33).

While the Venus of Willendorf is the most famous of the "mother figures," she is not the only one. There is the Venus of Lespugue, carved in mammoth ivory, with large breasts and buttocks, a featureless face, diminutive arms and legs, and no feet. There are the three Venuses of Mentone, carved in soapstone, with large breasts, bellies, and buttocks and no feet, hands, or facial features. The Venus of Laussel is a bas-relief carved in stone. Her breasts, hips, and belly are emphasized, and while the face appears damaged, it is unlikely that it ever had any facial features. Her left hand rests on her belly, and in her right hand she holds up what appears to be a bison's horn. There are other Venus figurines from Malta, Siberia, the Czech Republic, Savignano and Parabita in Italy, and many more sites (Jelínek, 1975, pp. 372-95; Maringer, 1960, plates 27-35).

Much has been made of these Venus figurines and disembodied vulvas and breasts. Many people have imagined a great mother goddess cult, and others have said such items were aids in fertility magic. When we look at the ratio of female to male representations, we are impressed by the overwhelming majority of female figures. When we look at these female figurines themselves, we see that they are not positioned for war, for walking, for running, for hunting, for gathering fruits and nuts, for cooking, or for tending a fire. They are simply being. They are faceless and have no specific personality or identity. Instead, their nutritive breasts and reproductive bellies and hips are emphasized. For this reason, many have concluded that there may have been a mother goddess cult in the Upper Paleolithic, which not only spread out across Europe, Asia, and Africa but became very much a part of the subsequent Neolithic traditions as well.

Speculations on a mother goddess cult are built on Johann Jacob Bachofen's notion that a matriarchy preceded a subsequent patriarchy. These Venus figurines became "proof" of the Upper Paleolithic matriarchy, and the idea was picked up by Freud, Jung, Neumann, Perry, and many others. Then in the 1970s, '80s, and '90s, millions of people subscribing to New Age philosophies and traditions accepted the idea of the matriarchy as fact. In 1989 Marija Gimbutas, an archeologist who specialized in prehistoric Europe, published *The Language of the Goddess*, an amply illustrated survey of female representation in prehistoric art. Though she did not speak specifically of the matriarchy, Gimbutas became popularly associated with this idea and enjoyed a certain degree of notoriety in New Age circles.

I don't know why she didn't mention the idea of the prehistoric matriarchy, but it is likely she knew full well that this had been a discredited idea for decades: a matriarchy did not precede the patriarchy. Two distinctive pieces of information lead us to this conclusion: (1) other than female figurines, we have no way of knowing and no reason to believe that prehistoric cultures were governed by women, and (2) our knowledge of contemporary aboriginal cultures reveals that the vast majority of cultures are not at all matriarchal.

In "The Cult and Mythology of the Magna Mater from the Standpoint of Psychoanalysis" (1938), the Freudian psychoanalyst Edith Weigert-Vowinkle examined the cult worship of the great mother goddesses, religions oriented around goddess worship, and mythology of the goddesses. Her analysis accepted the old assumptions about matriarchy being associated with prehistory, and she supported her position with mother goddess cult practices and mythology from ancient history, which, of course, are embedded in the world of the male gods and patriarchy.

The mother goddesses and matriarchy presented Freud with a real problem: How was he to reconcile the Oedipus complex, the murder of the primal father, and this idea that a matriarchy preceded a patriarchy? Freud's (1913/1955h) reconstruction included a primal father, followed by a great mother goddess, in turn followed by the father deities:

> I cannot suggest at what point in this process of development a place is to be found for the great mother-goddesses, who may perhaps in general have preceded the father-gods. It seems certain, however, that the change in attitude to the father was not restricted to the sphere of religion but that it extended in a consistent manner to that other side of human life which had been affected by the father's removal—to social organization. With the introduction of father-deities a fatherless society gradually changed into one organized on a patriarchal basis. The family was a restoration of the former primal horde and it gave back to fathers a large portion of their former rights. There were once more fathers, but the social achievements of the fraternal clan had not been abandoned; and the gulf between the new fathers of a family and the unrestricted primal father of the horde was wide enough to guarantee the continuance of the religious craving, the persistence of an unappeased longing for the father. (SE 13, p. 149)

It may well be important to make the distinction that Freud's primal father was not a god per se. In 1921 Freud wrote, "The series of gods, then, would run chronologically: Mother

Goddess—Hero—Father God" (1921/1955e, SE 18, p. 137). At the very end of his life, in *Moses and Monotheism* (1939/1964b), Freud returned to this theme:

> The first step away from totemism was the humanizing of the being who was worshipped. In place of the animals, human gods appear, whose derivation from the totem is not concealed. The god is still represented either in the form of an animal or at least with an animal's face, or the totem becomes the god's favorite companion, inseparable from him, or legend tells us that the god slew this precise animal, which was after all only a preliminary stage of himself. At a point in this evolution which is not easily determined great mother-goddesses appeared, probably even before the male gods, and afterwards persisted for a long time beside them. In the meantime a great social revolution had occurred. Matriarchy was succeeded by the re-establishment of a patriarchal order. The new fathers, it is true, never achieved the omnipotence of the primal father; there were many of them, who lived together in associations larger than the horde had been. They were obliged to be on good terms with one another, and remained under the limitation of social ordinances. It is likely that the mother-goddesses originated at the time of the curtailment of the matriarchy, as a compensation for the slight upon the mothers. The male deities appear first as sons beside the great mothers and only later clearly assume the features of father figures. These male gods of polytheism reflect the conditions during the patriarchal age. (SE 23, p. 83)

In attempting to bring order to his prehistoric reconstruction, Freud was tripping over Bachofen's outdated thesis. But the idea was wrong. We have no reason to believe that females ever led prehistoric communities.

When Sally R. Binford (1979) took up this issue in "Myths and Matriarchies," she said there is a popular idea that long ago "society was organized along matriarchal lines, and political decisions were made according to female principles that, as we all know, are sensitive, just and loving" (p. 63). She explained that according to this popular idea, women had nontoxic and reliable birth control and therefore loved the babies they chose to have and had relaxed and loving relationships with them: "We worshipped the Goddess in temples of great beauty, and priestesses conducted rites celebrating our sexuality. The world was at peace" (p. 63). Then, warring patriarchal males destroyed the temples and suppressed women's rituals and replaced the goddess with a vengeful God. The patriarchal males took away the knowledge of reliable nontoxic contraception, forced women into motherhood, and taught women to be ashamed of their sexuality. Binford, an active and dedicated feminist, saw these popular feminist New Age ideas as complete hogwash and said that trying to talk to these people about the facts was like trying to talk to a hard-core religious fundamentalist about the theory of evolution. Their faith, she said, "renders them impervious to information" (p. 64).

Binford wrote that in addition to the fact that there was no evidence to support the idea that matriarchy (political rule by women) preceded patriarchy (political rule by men), its proponents used mythology to make their case. She added that just because a culture is matrilineal does not mean it is matriarchal, referring to the Iroquois, who were warlike, patriarchal, and also strongly matrilineal. Binford saw the Venus figures of the Upper Paleolithic as indicative not of matriarchal power but of "a common human fascination with the female form" (p. 66). She noted that while others might see the vulva images in Paleolithic caves as evidence documenting the existence of the mother goddess, these "representations of female genitalia... would be right at home in any contemporary men's room" (p. 66). She also wrote that there is no reason to assume that similar images, created in widely different contexts, have the same meaning. She concluded, "The overwhelming body of hard evidence from anthropology and from history argues against a universal stage of matriarchy" (p. 66).

No, prehistoric culture was not matriarchal, and the female figurines might not be mother goddesses, but perhaps they reflect the *maternal instincts*. The Upper Paleolithic female figurines are numerous, appear throughout wide temporal and geographic contexts, and emphasize the nutritive and reproductive aspects of woman. We also see the nutritive theme in hunting magic (paintings and amulets of animals pierced with spears) and the reproductive theme in paintings of copulating animals. So perhaps it would be enough to say that our Upper Paleolithic ancestors seemed to be particularly interested in the mother spirit or maternal spirit with an emphasis on her nutritive and life-giving aspects. After all, if one is to look at the archeological record, it seems that our Upper Paleolithic ancestors lived very close to nature, were surrounded by dangers, and as their budding human consciousness emerged, they paid particular attention to birth, nutrition, and death. Bachofen suggested that early humans were matriarchal (governed by women) but Robert Briffault saw the primitive human group as metaphorically "matriarchal" in the same way that the animal group is "matriarchal." It was not that females dominated and governed males but that the culture was oriented to the maternal instincts (Briffault, 1927/1977, p. 96).

The Paleolithic was "oral" in the sense that it was a way of living devoted primarily to finding food and eating. Nature, and her personification in mother figurines, fed them, starved them, gave birth to them, and in death received them back into her womb in the fetal position and with food offerings. The interpenetrating "participation" of the ego and the world in infancy parallels the "participation" of culture and nature in the Paleolithic.

A Kind of Garden of Eden

Despite the dangers and difficulties of Upper Paleolithic life, it was, poetically and psychologically speaking, a kind of Garden of Eden in the sense that our ancestors lived in nature with little distinction between themselves and the rest of the natural world. Yes, they had tools, and, yes, they were efficient killers, and, yes, they were increasingly aware of themselves, but they were still nomadic, following the herds of big animals; the newly ripening fruits, nuts, and seeds; and looking for places with more hospitable temperatures with each new season. They were very much a part of nature. They organized large-scale hunting of cave bears, mammoths, and other megafauna, but when they met these big animals face-to-face, it was not with a high-powered rifle between man and beast. Instead, the men and women killed such megafauna at close quarters with spears, rocks, hand axes, stone knives, and trickery. They did not even live in permanent dwellings. Homes were temporary campsites—primitive nests, rock shelters, or makeshift tents of leather or plant material anchored with stones or elephant bones.

In describing the Upper Paleolithic as a Garden of Eden, I want to be clear about the meaning and limits of this metaphor. Life in the Garden of Eden for Adam and Eve is a metaphor for a world without distinctions between good and evil, male and female, and the inside and outside of the garden. It is, in a sense, unitary and full of grace. Human consciousness in the Upper Paleolithic lacked the myriad distinctions marking humanity apart from nature that would characterize later cultural developments. Technological innovations were few, and architectural separation from nature was at a minimum. In these ways, the Upper Paleolithic was a kind of unitary state or culture form embedded in nature. Human consciousness was budding, object relations were forming, and language was no doubt developing, but I suspect it would be unlikely that our Upper Paleolithic ancestors saw themselves as separate from, above, outside of, better than, or alienated from nature. If they saw a spirit or soul in their loved ones, it is most likely they projected the same into the plants, animals, landscape, and the forces of nature around them.

This grace and unity with nature should not be taken as a description of a blissful everyday life for our Upper Paleolithic ancestors. Nor should it be seen as my attempt to reinvigorate the outdated concept of the noble savage living in a primordial paradise. No, the Paleolithic was not a Garden of Eden in the sense of a happy, harmonious, orally gratifying ideal. It was probably often a rather hellish existence with dangers, discomforts, high infant mortality, illnesses, injuries, and early deaths. My Garden of Eden metaphor begins and ends with the notion that there were minimal distinctions between human culture and nature.

I previously mentioned my May 2009 visit to a Hoti village, deep in the Venezuelan jungles. The Hoti are seminomadic hunter-gatherers who tend gardens, or *conucos*, growing plantains, bananas, yucca, tobacco, papayas, hot and sweet peppers, rice, and yams. They spin cotton to make hammocks and loincloths. They still make ceramic bowls to contain their curare, a neurotoxic poison, and they hunt with spears, shotguns (when they have cartridges), and with blowguns equipped with *curare*-tipped darts. They fish for pavon, piranhas, and other river fish. They hunt large rodents, bush pigs, birds, tortoises, deer, anteaters, and tapirs. They trade for machetes, shorts and T-shirts, flashlights, metal knives, fishing hooks, and plastic bowls, but they make their square and round houses with mud and stick walls, dirt floors, and thatched roofs. Their world is about as close as one could get to living at one with nature, living in a Garden of Eden. But it is a Garden of Eden with mosquitoes, tarantulas, stinging ants, poisonous snakes, piranhas and caimans, skin infections, respiratory problems, dengue fever, malaria, and a lifestyle devoid of germ theory; thus, not surprisingly, the Hoti have a short life expectancy. The feeling of being at one with nature is not the same as the material reality of living at one with nature.

While visiting the Hoti, several observations related to living at one with nature captured my attention. To begin with, their village was full of dogs, birds, turtles, large rodents, and pigs. Of these, only the turtles and a couple of large rodents were enclosed in pens. The rest walked and flew freely around the village. Even the birds walked in and out of Hoti homes. It is a world in which plants and animals and people interpenetrate one another's living spaces. Baby toucans and parrots had been taken from their nests and were domesticated. Aurora, the chief's sister-in-law, chewed a bit of banana, brought a parrot close to her mouth and extruded the banana mush directly from her mouth into the parrot's beak to feed it. Then she did the same for a baby toucan, extruding chewed-up banana between her pursed lips into the eager beak of the toucan chick as if from the beak of its own toucan mother.

Stanford and Egleé Zent (2008) did extensive anthropological work concerning the Hoti and wrote, "In virtue of the fact that men and animals are ontologically equivalent (they share the human condition), the communication between them is not only possible but indispensable for existing" (p. 565; my translation). Because of the absence of mirrors, the Hoti people are often found grooming each other. When everyone grooms everyone else, the unity of the social intersubjective field becomes all the more obvious.

❖ ❖ ❖

THE UPPER PALEOLITHIC PERIOD AND THE ORAL STAGE OF LIBIDO DEVELOPMENT

In December 2009, I went on another expedition up the Orinoco and then farther up the Caciquiare River in the Venezuelan jungles with the specific intention of witnessing the *yopo* ceremony of the Yanomami. In this ritual, the shamans take a hallucinogenic drug, yopo, to communicate with their *hekuras*, or animal spirits, in order to attend to the spiritual needs of the community. After navigating the river for seven days, we arrived at a Yanomami village. "¿Donde esta Enrique? [Where is Enrique?]" my guide asked a man on shore. "*Esta yopoeando* [He is taking yopo]." We entered the open space of the circular village and arrived at the shamans' meeting place, a rectangular structure with no walls but a series of machete-cut poles holding up a thatched roof over a slightly raised floor of packed dirt.

The six shamans are wearing only lightweight shorts. Their faces and bodies are painted with reddish-brown body paint in lines, arcs, and circles. Some wear feather earrings, bead necklaces, or shamanic upper-arm bracelets with dangling feathers. The men sit on their haunches or on little stools. Each shaman chews a large wad of tobacco. We arrive just as they are beginning the ceremony. On the ground before them sits a round piece of sheet metal; on it is a piece of plastic bag containing the hallucinogenic light-greenish-brown yopo powder made from specially prepared seeds and bark. There is a wooden tube about 3 feet long that narrows at one end and has a ring of bitumen about half an inch from the end. One places this end in the nose when snorting yopo. The tube has an unmistakable and distinctly phallic shape. There is also a large Stone Age axe sitting next to the yopo. The Yanomami find ancient stone tools like this when tending their gardens and see them as gifts from their ancestors that are then used as amulets by the Yanomami.

After being introduced to the shamans and invited to join them, I remove my hat and shirt and sit down with them. There isn't much talking at this point, and whatever is said is spoken in the Yanomami language rather than Spanish, but there is an easygoing feeling of just being together. One after another the shamans insufflate the yopo. The yopo powder is placed in one end of the tube, and then one shaman blows the yopo through the tube and into the nostril of the other shaman. The one receiving the yopo blast typically gags, grabs or hits the back of his head, and scratches his scalp. Yopo has the immediate effect of causing a brief strange pain and itching in the head and scalp. As they all get fairly loaded up on yopo, there is constantly this or that one spitting, snotting, clearing his nasal passages, or hacking onto the dirt floor. Then the men start chanting and dancing. The dance is just a slight jump from one foot to the other with arms bent, elbows slightly raised, and hands raised.

The aboriginal peoples of the Upper Orinoco make little distinction between the animals of the jungles and themselves. Under the influence of yopo, this distinction seems to disappear as the shamans get in touch with their hekuras, which guide them in their efforts to direct the spiritual life of the community and to heal the sick.

As the ceremony continues, the shamans snort more and more yopo and carry on their hacking, spitting, snotting, and drooling. Many have long green strings of mucous oozing out of their nostrils, down across their lips, and hanging there 2, 3, or 4 inches below their chins. They leave the snot hanging off their faces for inordinate amounts of time, only occasionally clearing it with their fingers or the vein of a palm leaf. Large masses of snot and spittle are accumulating on the floor, where they dance barefoot. It's not half as disgusting as it sounds. In fact, I find that it somehow creates a distinctly intimate feeling within the group—an openness, an easiness, a sense of acceptance and warmth in being together. As they dance, each one chants several words and repeats them over and over, then changes the words and repeats those. I don't know what is being said, but it doesn't have the sound of a prescribed text, like a formal prayer, but rather a phrase that comes to each shaman as an inspiration.

As the shamans dance and chant one at a time, the ceremony is building and the chanting becomes screaming and growling as the dancers take on dramatic facial expressions and gesticulations. Sometimes a dancing shaman says something and another sitting shaman answers back responsively, and the two go back and forth like this for a time, occasionally bursting out laughing together. This happens repeatedly between Enrique and Delfin. I would describe Delfin as the lead shaman. Enrique follows Delfin in his dancing, chanting, and in answering him responsively.

It's a hot but glorious day of blue skies, flooding equatorial sunlight, and a few billowing white clouds. In fact, the whole region is in the middle of a severe drought of considerable duration, which is causing everyone a great deal of concern, as the river is going down and becoming increasingly less navigable, leaving communities isolated from each other and making hunting along the river more difficult and fishing holes less accessible. As the ceremony goes on, others in the community go about their business. Bare-breasted women carry buckets of water on their heads. Naked little girls and boys carry younger siblings on their hips. Teenagers walk by eating a sweet fruit that grows wild in the jungle. A woman carries a handmade basket full of wood for cooking.

The spirit of the ceremony is building, and soon Delfin is quite clearly talking and arguing with some spirit. A large black bird, a *pauji*, flies into the shamanic space. A shaman tries to shoo the bird away with his flailing hands, but the pauji keeps flying back in. The interpenetration of people, plants, and animals is profound and undeniable.

Delfin, in contact with his hekura, lifts his shoulders close to his ears, then raises his elbows to shoulder level, bends his arms at the elbows, raises his forearms, and turns in his fists. He's bent his legs so that he is bowlegged and leaning to one side. He turns his head and begins to squawk and scream like some sort of thoroughly crazed bird. At other times he is a mild-mannered and rather timid shaman, and even now he rarely seems to make eye contact with anyone. But he is in contact with his hekura and begins to embody it and be embodied by it. He clucks and squawks and screams. He struts and jumps. He is fascinating to watch, and there is extraordinary humor in it all. He is a brilliant actor, but there does not appear to be any sort of acting intention. He is being acted upon by his hekura. Suddenly I hear another shaman squawking loudly right behind me. I turned around, but no one is there! I look down and find a huge green parrot right behind me. The squawking parrot is actually a bird that is mimicking the man who is squawking like a bird.

Delfin is now arguing with some spirit, and the next thing I know, he grabs his bow, removes its string, and uses it as a spear to attack what seems to be an invisible monster spirit. He is roaring, screaming, and fighting the beast as he jabs at the air with his bow and then thrusts it deep into the dry packed earth. He uses such strength that it penetrates the ground several inches and then stands by itself. Just as quickly, Delfin falls to the ground, next to the bow/spear, and acts out the part of the impaled and wounded beast. It is absolutely overwhelming to watch. Soon Enrique joins in on the dance and the battle, using the yopo tube as a spear to stab at the air. Then Enrique and Delfin jump out of the shamanic space and into the much larger open community circle. They run here and there attacking the unseen forces.

Another shaman, blasted into the spirit world, picks up a huge axe and joins them in their assault on the spirits. The three of them are running around battling the forces. They run this way and that and seem to be having a childlike kind of fun, but there is also a feeling that all of this is deadly serious. The battle goes on. Then suddenly they stop cold and looked intently in the direction of the river. They look and point. I can't tell what they are seeing, if anything at all, as my view is blocked from within the shamanic space by the hut next door. The three of them are still rushing around, and children in the community space are now running scared.

As the shamanic battle intensifies, suddenly there is a huge gust of wind. And I mean huge—enormous! Leaves and the dusty dirt from the wider community space, start flying high into the air and swirling all around. People start running for cover while the three shamans carry on their battle, and a storm of thunder and lightning suddenly descends upon us at close range in a matter of seconds. The thunder explodes, the lightning flashes, and the rain comes pouring down in torrents, soaking the three shamans, who continue stabbing the air with the unstrung bow and yopo tube and swinging the giant axe. The rest of us watch from under the thatched roof. As the rain continues to pelt the ground, Delfin returns to the shamans' space. He leans back against a supporting pole, grabs his genitals through his shorts, and shakes them vigorously, screaming, "Pishee-ee, pishee-ee." It seems like some sort of sympathetic magic gesture uniting urinating with raining and encouraging the rain to keep pouring. Everyone is howling with laughter and the whole thing is absolutely spectacular!

Soon thereafter the rain let up and the ceremony came to a peaceful end. The line between the ceremony and the storm dissolved completely. Did the shamans' ceremony bring the rainstorm, or did the rainstorm bring the shamans' ceremony, or were the shamans' ceremony and the rainstorm somehow part of a whole?

❖ ❖ ❖

If the Yanomami live in a world in which the interpenetration of inner and outer realities pass through gaping holes in the separating wall between the community and the jungle, the hallucinogenic yopo ceremony knocks the wall down completely, turning the dream into an external reality and external reality into a dream. The line between the ceremony and the storm was completely dissolved, giving us perhaps more of an idea of both the blurry line between self and world and what living at one with nature actually involves.

Even in the realms of children's play, I saw that blurry line between self and world. Giggling and laughing, three little Yanomami boys, 4 years old, walked buck-naked with their arms draped over each other's shoulders. They found a large rock in the clearing at the center of the village and took turns lifting it up and throwing it down, trying to break it. Then one stopped and urinated high into the air, much to everyone's delight. The giggling and laughter continued as they wandered off in pleasure. Under the roof of a wall-less Yanomami structure was a naked little 3-year-old sitting on the dirt floor. He drooled a small pool of spittle onto the floor, bent down, carefully placed his lips on it, and gently blew it into a bubble. Then, with the dome bubble sitting on the floor, he locked a pebble between his forefinger and thumb, as one would with a marble, and shot with perfect aim, popping the bubble. He then did it again, and again. The spittle and urine, dirt and stones became the interfaces of self and world.[1]

The Yanomami are more Neolithic than Paleolithic, but their basic technology and close proximity to the forces of nature demonstrate for us this idea of the participation mystique

---

1 Another time I saw one of the old shamans in the middle of the Yanomami village clearing. He was sitting on the ground, cutting small weeds with a machete and seemingly mumbling to himself. When I came nearer, I discovered a large green parrot accompanying him almost like a pet dog and realized it was the parrot that was mumbling, not the shaman. I said to the parrot, "*Toti-hee-tau-way*," which means "Hello" in the Yanomami language. The parrot said nothing. I said it again. The parrot said nothing again. I said it once more and the parrot replied, "*Toti-hee-tau-way*." I burst out laughing, and the parrot started laughing with me! It was another example of the interpenetration of human and animal life.

and living at one with nature. With their orientation to the earth, the river, the weather, the plants, and the animals, it is no wonder their hekuras are seen as animal spirits. Amusingly, during the yopo ceremony on the second day of my visit, one of the shamans named me "*chaman wooshee,*" or "bearded monkey shaman."

From a psychomythic perspective, the Upper Paleolithic was the beginning of a new way of being made possible by meditating on death. With a few critical neurological mutations, we developed the capacity to symbolize, to speak, to form elaborate object relations, to sculpt, to paint, to see spirits in our loved ones and even in those who died, to engage in hunting magic and ritual cannibalism, to imbue objects with souls, to engage in ancestor worship, to see our ancestors in the bones of great animals, and to contact our personal animal spirits. The confrontation with death and the confrontation with being are what marked the Upper Paleolithic—not because there was more death in the Paleolithic than there was before it but because the symbolic function enabled us to be more conscious of being than ever before and therefore more aware of death and nonbeing.

What was it like for our Paleolithic ancestors to confront the awe of being and the terror of nonbeing? I don't know, and perhaps we can't imagine it, but Aldous Huxley (1954) described what I would call his confrontation with being during a mescaline experience he had in 1953: "I was seeing what Adam had seen on the morning of his creation—the miracle, moment by moment, of naked existence" (p. 17). Huxley's naked existence came as a result of hallucinogenic unselving: the pharmacological evaporation of so many of his psychological defenses—personal and cultural.

The confrontation with being and nonbeing filled our Paleolithic ancestors with an awe that had to be defended against with displacements, magical thinking, projection, myth, ritual, and a host of other defensive strategies that became embedded in the technological, linguistic, and religious innovations of the day and passed on from one generation to the next, not as inherited memories but as cultural artifacts and traditions. The Paleolithic was about birth, death, nourishment, and the spirit or soul that entered the mouth. Our Upper Paleolithic ancestors had human consciousness but very little human technology, language, and religion. As such, their world was close to nature, at one with nature, unitary, and in grace. But the Neolithic Revolution would spell an end to all of that and mark our ancestors' expulsion from their Garden of Eden and their fall from grace.

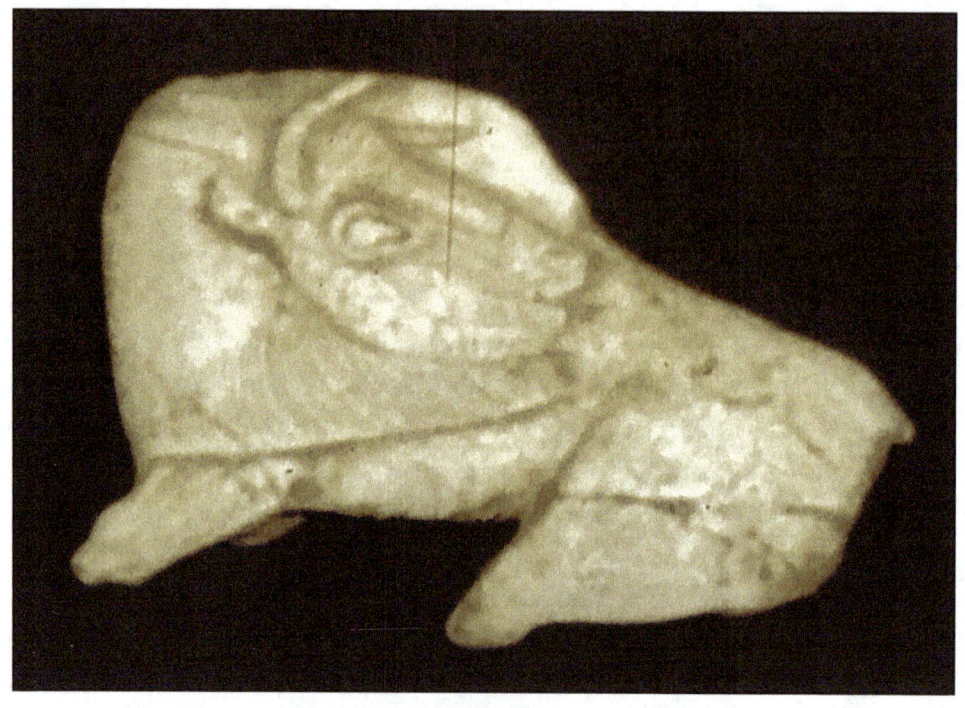

Paleolithic amulet. A bison carved from a piece of antler. 15,000 years old.

This ancient stone ax was found by modern Yanomami indigenous people in Venezuela while working in their garden. The Yanomamis did not use it as an ax but rather as an amulet in their yopo ceremonies to aid them in communing with their ancestors.

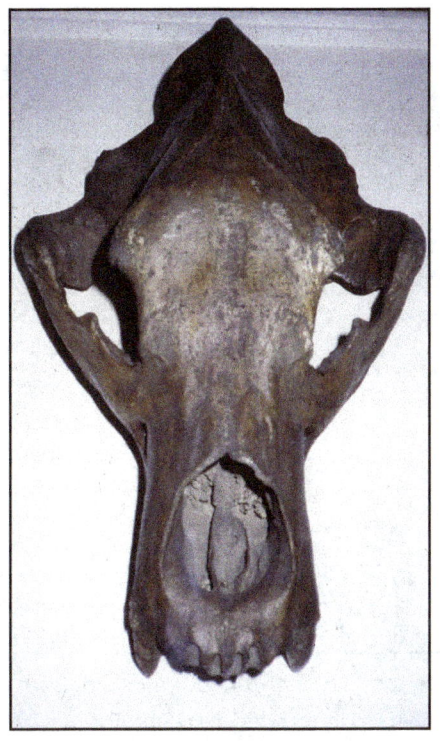

A curated Paleolithic cave bear skull from Les Eyzies-de-Tayac-Sireuil, France.

Curated monkey skulls skewered on a stick through the zygomatic arches. While curating skulls is a Paleolithic tradition, it may still appear at other levels of cultural evolution. This image is from a modern day Panare village in the Venezuelan jungles that is perhaps more Neolithic in its technology and yet also has some metal and plastic tools, shotguns, fishing lines and hooks, and flashlights. Nonetheless, the curating of skulls has the magical meaning of insuring good hunting in the future by showing respect for the deceased.

Paleolithic stone tools (10,000–14,000 years old) from Laugerie Basse, in Les Eyzies-de-Tayac-Sireuil, France

Stone spearpoint on the desert floor in the state of Coro, Venezuela. It is a surface find so the date is uncertain. While similarly made stone tools from the same area have been found to be 9,000 years old, it could just as easily be only a few hundred years old.

Stone tools from Venezuela in the laboratory of Miklos Szabadics Roka.

A stone mortar in Miklos Szabadics Roka's hands. Coro, Venezuela.

Miklos Szabadics Roka with his wife and colleague, Eva Hofle.
Tara Tara, Venezuela.

A previously buried ancient fire ring was under the ground for perhaps
thousands of years until rains and wind more recently uncovered
and exposed it to the light of day in the Venezuelan desert.

Paleolithic engraved representations of vulvas.
National Museum of Prehistory in Les Eyzies-de-Tayac-Sireuil, France.

A Paleolithic or Neolithic engraved representation of a vulva.
La Colonia Tovar, Venezuela.

Paleolithic stone carved bas relief of two bison.

Bison painting in the Altamira Cave in Santander Cantabria, Spain.

Paleolithic stone carved bas relief of a salmon.
From the site, Abri du Poisson. Les Eyzies-de-Tayac-Sireuil, France.

Paleolithic or perhaps Neolithic petroglyphs near La Colonia Tovar, Venezuela.

Paleolithic or perhaps Neolithic petroglyphs near La Colonia Tovar, Venezuela.

Petroglyph of a lizard by the shore of the Ventuari River in the jungles of Venezuela.

A replica of the Paleolithic Venus of Willendorf

Yopo ceremony 1 – Notice the face paint, feather earrings, arm bracelets, yopo tube, and the stone tool amulet on the metal plate on the ground. Yanomami village.

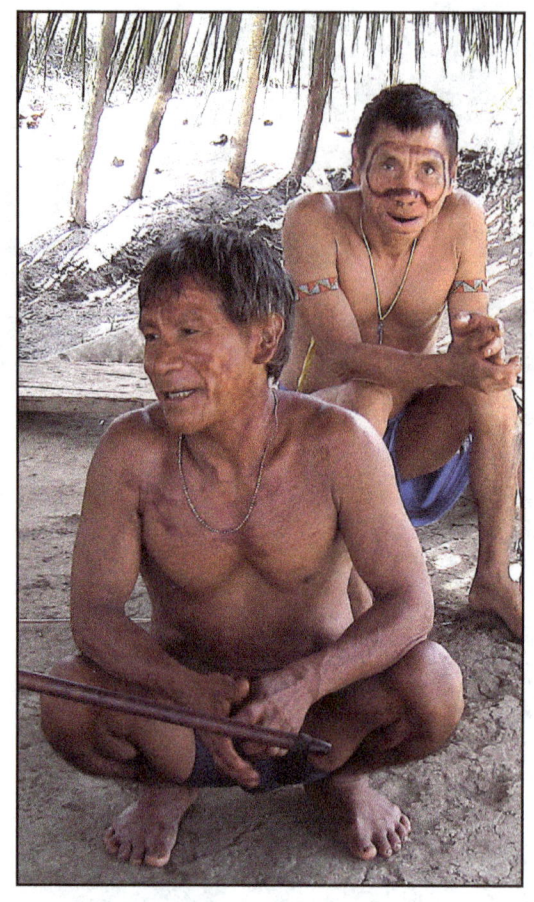

Yopo ceremony 2 – Yanomami village.

Yopo ceremony 3 – Yanomami village.

Yopo ceremony 4 – Notice the feathered arm bracelet. Yanomami village.

Yopo ceremony 5 – Blowing the yopo powder through the tube. – Yanomami village.

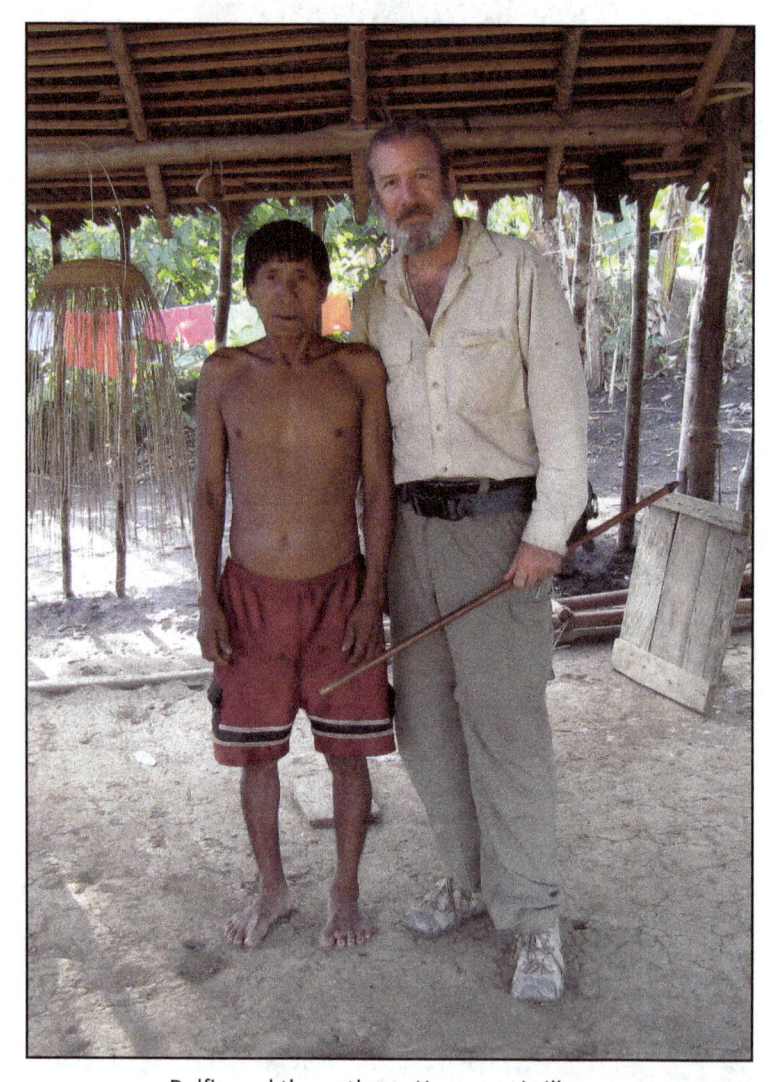

Delfin and the author – Yanomami village.

CHAPTER 6

The Neolithic Period and the Anal Stage of Libido Development

> If we limit ourselves here to what has been learnt about the excretory functions, it may be said that the chief finding from psychoanalytic research has been the fact that the human infant is obliged to recapitulate during the early part of his development the changes in the attitude of the human race towards excremental matters which probably had their start when homo sapiens first raised himself off Mother Earth.
> —Sigmund Freud, preface to John G. Bourke, *Scatalogic Rites of All Nations*

The spiritual, social, and technological innovations of the Paleolithic were shaped by the oral dynamics and early object relations of the infant, which found expression in the context of culture. They were positive cultural assertions as well as socially constructed and sanctioned defensive strategies denying the awe of being and the terrors of nonbeing. By naming and representing the objects of their world, people of that time managed the awe of being. And when confronted with the terror of death, denial was mobilized, allowing the name or the spirit to simply move on. The dead are not dead. They are still with us. They live on and will not die. Beings have spirits that can reside in objects or be internalized by breathing them in or eating them. The themes of birth, eating, encounter, and death dominated Paleolithic life and culture, and the ritual of the funerary ceremony and the myth of death and rebirth, I suggest, were attempts to come to terms with it all. Similarly, the religious, social, and technological innovations of the Neolithic were shaped by the anal dynamics of the toddler and separation from the mother in the context of culture. These innovations include permanent houses and village walls, agriculture, ceramics, weaving, and more, all of which fortified the separation of culture from Mother Nature.

In the anal stage of libido development, the cathexis, or focus of attention and sexual excitation, shifts from the mouth to the anal sphincter without abandoning the oral erogenous zone. In other words, the anal sphincter takes primary importance without the mouth and orality losing their ongoing significance. In the anal stage, the 1-year-old toddler is learning to walk and talk, the neurological pathways between the central nervous system and the anal sphincter become established, and toilet training becomes possible. Without sphincter control during the oral stage, the release of feces and urine takes place whenever and wherever the urge presents itself. The oral stage infant lives in what I call "cosmic space"—that is, at the center of the universe, where "here" is the only place to be. Correspondingly, the infant also lives in "cosmic time"—the "eternal now." But in the anal stage, a highly cathected mother, who has presumably earned her cathexis by attending to the baby's needs for a year now, appeals to the baby to depart from cosmic time and cosmic space and enter the human world of linear time and three-dimensional space. She does this by asking the baby, who is now a toddler, to release the bowel movement not here, but there, and not now, but then. This is generally perceived as a bit of a shock and leaves the toddler with three options: (1) ignore potty training and remain in the oral stage; (2) stubbornly control the bowels and urine, and release them not when and where Mother wants them but when and where the toddler wants to release them; and (3) win Mother's love in a new way by giving her the feces and urine where and when she wants them or better yet negotiating with her on these requests.

On one occasion, in a social setting, I met a child, sorely in need of his afternoon nap. He was giddy and somewhat manic, demanding the attention of everyone in the room. When he climbed onto my lap and continued with his annoying silliness, I told him, "I have bad news and good news." Intrigued, he asked "What?" I said, "The bad news is you're not the center of the universe. The good news is you're not alone." He collapsed sobbing into my arms. It's an example of leaving cosmic space and cosmic time and entering into the human world, no longer at one with the universe but rather at two with the universe, that is, in relation to the universe and in relation to others.

The negotiation between mother and toddler to manage toilet training is one in which there develops a differentiation between the self and the other, the inner and the outer, the passive and the active, the here and the there, the now and the then, the controlled and the out of control, dominance and submission. The anal sphincter defines a limit that declares interiority and exteriority, but the toddler has to determine "Who is in control of this portal? Me inside or someone else outside?" Anality is a bodily metaphor pertaining not simply to a nascent alienation of the subject from the world, as in the oral stage, but to the establishment of a power dynamic between them—a real separation in terms of control. It pertains to the toddler's developing muscular control over its body and its efforts at mastery. The nascent subject, still a victim of its overwhelming helplessness, struggles valiantly to declare itself by controlling the retention and evacuation of its personal products (i.e., urine, feces, flatus, touches, gazes, and vocalizations), presenting them as love offerings or delivering them as warheads. While feeding is seen as the stage upon which the oral drama takes place, toilet training is center stage for the anal drama. But, of course, any curious toddler is sure to be exploring the world and, in the process, getting into mischief and entering into new arenas for power struggles with Mom.

The anal-stage child is also mastering language and developing the ability to use pronouns such as "I," "me," and "you." However, these are not just three more signifiers for miscellaneous objects in the world. These are indicators of a psyche that recognizes its own subjectivity, as well as otherness, and clothes them in language. The achievement of subjectivity and otherness, as reflected in the toddler's use of "I," "me," and "you," is best appreciated in the absence of that achievement. The absence of a separation between subjectivity and otherness is not a philosophical fine point; it is a tragedy of child development with severe psychopathological consequences. Erikson (1968) touched on this matter in the following passage:

> No one who has worked with autistic children will ever forget the horror of observing how desperately they struggle to grasp the meaning of saying "I" and "You" and how impossible it is for them, for language presupposes the experience of a coherent "I." ... No other affliction makes it equally clear that ego psychology alone cannot encompass certain human problems which so far have been left to poetry or metaphysics. (p. 217)

Anal dynamics attach themselves to time, money, and cleanliness. The anal-expulsive character disregards time, spends money irresponsibly, and is messy. The anal-retentive character is prompt, penny-pinching, and fastidious. The overvalued fecal stick given to Mother as a gift can in a moment transform into the most disgusting object imaginable. Anality attaches itself in later life to things overvalued and things rejected, not the least of which are glittering gold and filthy stinking money. (See Freud's *Character and Anal Erotism* [1908/1959b].)

The Wall and Personal Boundaries

The anal stage is about establishing boundaries between the self and other, and the Neolithic Revolution was about establishing boundaries between culture and nature, between the community and the wilderness, between the known and the unknown, between order and disorder, between cosmos and chaos. How did our Neolithic ancestors establish such boundaries? They built walls. They ended their Paleolithic nomadic wanderings in oneness with nature and entered into two-ness by separating themselves from nature. They built permanent walls around their villages, permanent walls for their houses, and even permanent walls around their campfires, transforming them into ovens. The ovens transformed clay into ceramics. And with ceramics they constructed cups, bowls, and pots. Inside the pots, dough was transformed into bread, and juices were transformed into alcoholic beverages. Next to their villages, gardens were established within boundaries, and domesticated animals were guarded within changing but circumscribed limits. (An account of my visit to an indigenous village, in appendix 6, describes Panare hunting, gathering, and tending the garden.)

By creating boundaries to contain themselves, our Neolithic ancestors fashioned a cultural womb and gave birth to increasingly differentiated communities. In doing so, each tribe created its "other" in the shadows, beyond the walls. When our Paleolithic ancestors stopped their nomadic ways and settled down to Neolithic living, they did so in order to be more in control of their food supply through the domestication of plants and animals and to protect themselves from the danger of wild animals and lethal raiding of other tribes with adjoining territorial borders.

The Neolithic Revolution began about 11,500 years ago in what is now called Jericho, a Palestinian city in the West Bank. A visitor there today can see the first permanent village walls, village tower, and some of the earliest house walls ever built. Neolithic Jericho is not the same as the biblical Jericho. They occupied the same place, but the biblical Jericho came much later. To see the wall at Neolithic Jericho is to see something one has seen many times before—a wall. But when we reflect on the fact that there were no permanent walls built before it, we see that wall as a fateful monument to a time when humanity turned a corner and in doing so changed both itself and the world forever. While the Neolithic Revolution began in Jericho, that is not to say that it began everywhere at the same time. In fact, there were a fair number of Paleolithic peoples living their Paleolithic lifestyles up into the 20th century. And even today, despite the rise of civilization 5,500 years ago, there are still a few pockets of aboriginal peoples living basically Paleolithic or Neolithic lifestyles. Sadly, most of them are now on the brink of cultural annihilation.

The construction of the first permanent house was an important cultural event, as the house became a kind of man-made universe; a spiritual device for personal, familial, and cultural transformation; a sacred space, a temenos, a temple. And even if it wasn't built for those purposes, it soon became that for a primate with a well-developed symbolic function. Another way to reflect on the revolution brought by building and living in a house with permanent walls is to try to imagine a chimpanzee, or one of our ancient hominin ancestors, doing such a thing for the first time. It was a turning point in prehistory of dramatic proportions.

The House and the Self

We speculate on the origins of our consciousness by contemplating the stones and bones of our ancestors. In the Proto-Neolithic period, 11,500 years ago, the early Natufian communities in Israel and Jordan were not yet domesticating animals, but tools for the preparation of plant foods were found at Eynan, including sickles, mortars and pestles, and clay-lined storage pits. Evidence of 50 permanent round houses with diameters of up to 7 meters was also uncovered. The round houses were arranged in a circle around a set of storage pits. Each house, sunk 1 meter into the ground, had a plaster stone substructure. The superstructure of the house was probably made of reeds and matting. A central post maintained a conical roof. A stone hearth was set at the house center, or perhaps at the side, and, not incidentally, child and infant burials were often discovered below stone slabs under the floor. They contained necklaces of dentalia shells as burial gifts (Mellaart, 1965, pp. 22-25). Why, of all places, were these children and infants buried under the floor?

Also at Eynan a round house 5 meters in diameter was discovered. In a tomb beneath the floor were found the skeletons of a man and a second person, probably a woman. The head of the man, a Natufian chieftain, was propped up on a stone facing the direction of Mount Hermon. The other person wore a headdress of dentalia shells. The burial was plastered over and a hearth established above it (pp. 22-25).

In the pre-pottery Neolithic A culture of Jericho (9,000-10,000 years ago), round houses were built of mud bricks on stone foundations. Floors and walls were plastered, and the roof was domed with wattle and daub. According to James Mellaart, walls were important for surrounding cities as well: "As the wealth of the settlement grew and powerful neighbors established themselves, city walls became a necessity to protect the town" (p. 33). The thick walls of Neolithic villages offered protection from warring neighbors, but at the same time, these stable settlements permitted the accumulation of wealth and created the necessity of trade. Thus, war and trade became the two primary modes of cultural interaction.

Seven thousand years ago, seafaring Neolithic peoples built a life on the Mediterranean island of Cyprus. The people there built round houses and buried their dead under the floors or among the houses. They wove wool; had sickle blades, querns, and grinding stones; and kept domesticated sheep, goats, and possibly pigs (pp. 52-56).

At the site of Çatal Hüyük, in Turkey, the people built mud-brick houses and shrines of rectangular shape. Domesticated animals were herded into corrals on the edge of the settlement. Although the village appeared as a solid wall to potential marauders, the technology of bows and arrows, slings, and spears provided additional protection for the community. The bones of the dead were buried beneath the platforms of their houses or under their shrines. Women and children were buried with necklaces, bracelets, armlets, anklets, and hoes. When women were buried with children, they were often buried with bone spatulas and spoons. More prominent women were buried with obsidian mirrors, baskets of rouge, and cosmetic spatulas. Males were buried with mace heads; flint daggers; obsidian spears, lances, or arrowheads; clay seals; bone hooks and eyes; and belt fasteners.

The walls of one shrine were decorated with paintings of giant vultures swooping down on headless people. The female figurines represented woman in her three aspects: as a young woman, as a mother giving birth, and as an old woman. In one example, the old woman is accompanied by a vulture. A boy or adolescent is depicted, perhaps the son of the goddess. Another shrine had mounted the heads of bulls and rams, the horns of bulls, and painted images of bulls. There is emphasis on the navel, pregnancy, and the goddess figure giving birth to a bull or a ram. In one shrine, symbols of life (a woman's breasts, the bull's horn) adorned one wall, and symbols of death (lower jaw of the wild boar, skulls of the fox, weasel, or vulture) adorned the other (pp. 81–101).

At the Neolithic site of Hacilar, 7,600 years ago, the people made ceramic pottery and lived in permanent homes with doorways. There are ceramic representations of the goddess, but the male appears as a child or son consort. The dead were typically buried outside the houses, and in some cases under the courtyard, but at one shrine three graves were found under the floor of the building, each containing a woman and child (pp. 102–114).

Three graves under the floor? And each one contained a woman and child? Child and infant burials under the floors at Eynan? A chief and perhaps his wife buried under the floor? Other burials under the floors of houses and shrines? How interesting! What happened that three woman-and-child pairs died? Did they die together or separately? Were they related? Did they die of disease? Accident? Or could there have been a murder involved—a ritual murder, a sacrifice? We don't know. And without written accounts, all we can do is speculate and perhaps consider some historic and more contemporary correlates gathered by Lord Raglan in his book *The Temple and the House* (1964) to see what light it might shed on these questions.

❖ ❖ ❖

When the Arabs, east of the Dead Sea, pitched their tents, they would sacrifice a sheep to send away evil spirits. And at Nebek, in Syria, it is said that a foundation sacrifice must be conducted at the time of the construction of every house or one of the workmen will die. In Lebanon, when a house is finished being built, an animal is sacrificed on the doorstep.

Long ago when a cathedral was built in Shanghai, the city council required human bodies to be buried under the foundation. In Burma, in 1780, the gates of a new city were consecrated by putting one criminal in each of the postholes in order to become protecting spirits. In Thailand, the palaces were built on towers, and when those were replaced, pregnant women were put into the postholes as sacrificial victims who would become powerful monsters that could protect the building from all misfortune. In Japan, the people once believed that for a wall to be secure it needed to be built on the body of a willing victim. The Kammalans of Madras sacrificed a goat at each corner of the house and rubbed the blood of a fowl on the walls and ceiling.

When building a large house, the Milanau of Borneo dug a large hole for the first house post, put a slave girl in the hole, and then crushed her to death with the large post. When the Maori built a house, they dug postholes, killed slaves, and placed their bodies in the holes. In Tahiti, every post supporting the roof of the sacred house was placed into its respective posthole on the body of a man. When the Tonapoo of Central Celebes (now known as Sulawesi) finished building a temple, a person was sacrificed on the ridge of the roof, and the blood was allowed to flow down on both sides.

Among the indigenous peoples of the Canadian Pacific Northwest, when a chief or great man built a house, captives and slaves were killed and the house posts were planted on their corpses. Some North American tribes placed a corpse under the building to see to it that the spirits would protect it. The Chibcha of Peru have what is called the palace of the Bogota, which they say is built on the bodies of maidens. In order for the spirits to protect their buildings, the indigenous people of Guatemala buried a human corpse in every foundation. The Maya consecrated a new house by sacrificing a hen and offering food to the main support poles.

When Take-domu, founder of the kingdom of Dahomey, conquered the Foys in Africa, he killed the king of the Foys and built his palace on the king's body. When an Ashanti town was to be built, a princess was covered in gold dust, dressed beautifully, and sacrificed. Her body was then buried in front of the gate of the king's palace.

There are legends of human sacrifices at major buildings in Wales, Denmark, Serbia, and Thuringia, in east central Germany. In 1871 Lord Leigh was involved in the building of a bridge at Stoneleigh in Warwickshire, England. After it was completed, he was accused of having built an obnoxious person into the foundation of the bridge.

French peasants sacrifice a cock when they move into a new house. The English have a tradition that when they build a church or a public building, they ceremonially place a foundation stone. Under the stone are laid coins, newspapers, and other objects that Lord Raglan (1964) calls "substitutes for the victims in former times" (p. 19). In 1983, while trekking in the Nepali Himalayas, I met a woman living in a mud, stick, and stone round house with a thatch roof. Through my translator I asked if there was a ritual associated with the construction of her house. She said there was no particular ritual except that under the center post she had placed some jewelry.

And, finally, my uncle, Anatol "Ted" Balbach, originally from Lithuania, told me that when his house was built in Los Angeles in the 1960s, his mother came to see his new home and arrived with a live chicken. She sacrificed the chicken and sprinkled its blood on the house to sanctify it.

❖ ❖ ❖

The single most significant innovation of the Neolithic culture was the establishment of permanent houses. It not only marked the end of the nomadic lifestyles of the Paleolithic cultures but also made possible the domestication of animals, the cultivation of crops, and the development of technologies like ceramics and weaving. Mircea Eliade (1958b), professor of the history of religions, explained:

> The creation of the world is the exemplar for all constructions. Every new town, every new house that is built, imitates afresh, and in a sense repeats, the creation of the world. Indeed, every town, every dwelling stands at the "centre of the world," so that its construction was only possible by means of abolishing profane space and time and establishing sacred space and time. Just as the town is always an *imago mundi*, the house also is a microcosm. The threshold divides the two sorts of space; the home is equivalent to the centre of the world. (p. 379)

> To last, a construction (house, technical accomplishment, but also a spiritual undertaking) must be animated, that is, must receive both life and a soul. The "transference" of the soul is possible only by means of a sacrifice; in other words, by a violent death. (Eliade, 1972, p. 183)

The Stone and the Psychic Center

In many cases, the sacred nature of the center around which the house is built is represented by a stone—for example, a foundation stone. The stone is an object that is seemingly changeless and eternal, two qualities that welcome the projections of safe guardian and repository of eternal souls. The foundation stone has its antecedents in the soul stones and amulets of the Upper Paleolithic.

The image of the sacred stone at the ubiquitous center of the universe brings to mind the story of Jacob and his dream recounted in Genesis 28:10–22. Jacob, on his way from Beersheba to Haran, came upon a spot to rest for the night, took a stone for his pillow, and went to sleep. In his sleep he dreamed of a great ladder connecting the earth below with the heavens above and with angels ascending and descending the ladder. The Lord then told of Jacob's future life and work as a father of his people. On waking, Jacob said, "Surely the Lord is in this place; and I knew it not.... How full of awe is this place! This is none other than the house of God and this is the gate of Heaven." He set the stone up as a pillar, poured oil over the top, and called that place Beth-el, meaning the House of God.

As a gateway to heaven, the center, the stone, the Beth-el, and the House of God represent the point at which profane space and time interface with sacred space and time. In the Hebrew tradition, we find that placed on the mouth of the *tehom* (the waters of chaos) and reaching deep into its subterranean waters was the rock of Jerusalem, on which was built the Temple of Jerusalem. Similarly, Babylon was said to have been a *bab-apsi*, meaning the Gate of the Apsu, in which Apsu designated the same subterranean waters of chaos (Eliade, 1954/1971, p. 15). Sometimes the contact between the sacred and profane worlds is a single point, and other times it is at either end of an axis mundi, or world axis, symbolized by a pole, a pillar, a tree, or, as in Jacob's dream, a ladder.

Among the Ngaju Dayak, the house is seen as an *imago mundi,* or image of the world, and is said to be built on the back of a great water snake (Eliade, 1969, p. 79). We see in this reference and in those preceding it, a motif in which the stone, house, temple, or city representing the cosmic center is built or placed directly above the Apsu, tehom, or water snake, all of which are symbolic of the chaos of the underworld.

Covering the underworld waters of chaos and designating the communication point between that underworld below and the upper world above as a suitable place for the construction of a house is also implied in various cosmogonic myths. An Incan creation myth recorded in the mid-1500s tells a story that seems to describe a cultural transition from the Paleolithic to the Neolithic:

> At one time, all the land you see about you was nothing but mountains and desolate cliffs. The people lived like wild beasts, with neither order nor religion, neither villages nor houses, neither fields nor clothing, for they had no knowledge of wool or cotton. Brought together haphazardly in groups of two and three, they lived in grottoes and caves and, like wild game, fed upon grass and roots, wild fruits, and even human flesh. They covered their nakedness with the bark and leaves of trees, or with the skins of

animals. Some even went unclothed. And as for women, they possessed none who were recognized as their very own. (Sproul, 1979, p. 302)

Their father, the Sun, being ashamed of the people, sent forth his son and daughter to teach them to adore him as their god, build houses, live together in villages, till the soil, sow the seed, and raise cattle. As he sent them off, he gave them a rod made of gold that was almost the length of a man's arm and two fingers in thickness. He instructed them to wander across the land with it and thrust it into the ground wherever they stopped to take food or rest for the night. When they reached the spot where the rod passed easily into the ground and disappeared from sight, there they were to establish and hold their court. After much wandering the two reached the Cuzco valley and tested the ground with their golden rod. The rod passed easily into the soil, so the son of the Sun and his sister-bride gathered the people together, built a temple there in honor of the Sun, and taught the people to live as people should (pp. 301–305).

The Neolithic is about the end of our Paleolithic wandering and unity with nature. It is about the establishment of the village, the house, the pot, agriculture, and animal husbandry, so perhaps the analogous myth is that of the separation of the opposites, the fall from grace, expulsion from Paradise, and so on, and the ritual is the house-building ritual in particular and, more generally speaking, the ritual of sacrifice. Sacrifice is a unilateral deal struck with the gods: "I'll give you this for that." Sacrifice is a ritual dedicated to the renunciation of instinct and, as such, facilitates our entry into the reality principle. I'd like to suggest here that when Freud's grandson, Ernst, played the fort-da game (Freud, 1920/1955, SE 18, pp. 14-16), throwing away the wooden reel with a string attached to it and pulling it back by the string, he was playing at making a sacrifice. After observing the game carefully and repeatedly, Freud noted that the interpretation of this game became obvious. "It was related to the child's great cultural achievement—the instinctual renunciation (that is, the renunciation of instinctual satisfaction) which he had made in allowing his mother to go away without protesting. He compensated himself for this, as it were, by himself staging the disappearance and return of the objects within his reach" (p. 15). In essence, his mother, symbolized by the reel, was made to disappear and return at will.

In ancient Mesopotamia (c. middle 3rd millennium BCE), spikes and pegs were driven into the ground, bricks as cornerstones laid, sacrifices made, or sacred fires lit, all in preparation for the building of a house or temple (Ellis, 1968, p. 79). The pegs were said to nail down the building permanently to the earth (Schlossman, 1976, p. 11). The Hittites also used the peg in their building rituals (Ellis, 1968, p. 79). And in Tibetan building rituals, a dagger is driven into the ground in order that it might fight off the demons (pp. 91–92).

In India, an astrologer determines the exact point in the foundation below which there is the head of the great snake. A mason fashions a wooden peg and with a coconut drives it into the appointed spot. The peg is driven into the snake's head, holding it securely in place. If the snake ever really shook its head violently, it would shake the world to pieces. With the peg in place and the head of the snake pinned down, a foundation or cornerstone is placed on top of the peg and construction begins (Eliade, 1954/1971, p. 19).

Sacrifice and the Renunciation of Instinct

Pinning down the head of a great snake, securing the foundation of a building with a peg or dagger, burying the dead in the foundation of a house, making a human or animal sacrifice—all belong to the same class of actions: the renunciation of instinct. Sacrifice is the ritual analogue to the psychological renunciation of instinctual gratification. It's a deal between the one who sacrifices and the spirit or god. It is as though, for example, the person has aggressive impulses but sacrifices them for the good of the group and then projects those impulses into the spirit, demon, or god and says, "I know you want to kill me by destroying my house. I understand you need to kill. I will give you a death—but not mine, someone else's. In return, you will keep my house safe." It all begins with the projected aggressive (destructive, murderous) impulses of the individual. The baby says, in effect, "My cannibalistic impulses compel me to bite the breast, but I sacrifice or renounce the instinct (inhibit it, repress it), and in return for my sacrifice, I get more milk and more of Mother's love." Another renunciation of instinct occurs when the toddler agrees to toilet training in return for Mother's love. Sacrifice is the child's great cultural achievement, the renunciation of instinctual gratification, transformed into a ritual. Thus, we might speculate that in the funerary ritual of the Upper Paleolithic, one dies in order to be reborn and in the Neolithic this evolved into the ritual of sacrifice, wherein one doesn't die but rather gives up something (instinctual gratification) in exchange for the favors, protection, or approval of the deity (the father, the mother, the culture).

The Neolithic house, representing an island of culture in a sea of wilderness, brought with it the dualistic concepts of in and out, cosmos and chaos, us and them, the sacred and the profane, consciousness and unconsciousness. This is not to say that these concepts appeared as concepts but that the technology changed cultural and psychological experience of the world in ways that would lead to a split world and a psyche ever more divided between conscious and unconscious. In the Neolithic period, our ancestors were no longer as dependent upon migrating herds of beasts for their sustenance. They were beginning to cultivate plant foods and to domesticate animals as food sources. In doing so, they fortified their communal center and increased their mastery over the wilderness. Instead of being immersed in nature, they were beginning to manipulate it. It is one thing to collect grains and quite another to cultivate them and learn how to maximize yield by tilling, irrigating, fertilizing, harvesting, and storing. No longer as vulnerable to the whims of Mother Nature, who provided lavishly or starved mercilessly, our Neolithic ancestors developed agricultural technology as a way to control nature and created the ritual of sacrifice as a way to strike a deal with the spirits. Where chaos was, there cosmos shall be. Where wilderness was, there culture shall be.

The independence and control that our Neolithic ancestors exercised over Mother Nature could be seen as analogous to the autonomy the toddler exercises in relation to the mother—that is, the autonomy that Erik Erikson described in the psychosocial stage of autonomy versus shame and doubt.

One day, late in the Upper Paleolithic, a group of people in what is now Meiendorf, Germany, killed a reindeer, opened its thoracic cavity, placed an 18-pound hunk of rock inside, probably sewed it back up, and sank the reindeer to the bottom of the lake. Subsequently, at Stellmoor, two more deer were sunk to the bottom of the lake with stones in their thoracic or abdominal cavities, stones that had obviously assisted in delivering the deer corpses to the depths. Were these sacrifices? Did they aid in hunting magic? Or fertility? Maybe a deal was being struck—something like, "We'll give you our first reindeer of the season if you give us a steady supply of reindeer." It's kind of a trade, but it has a distinctly spiritual aspect in that the one receiving the reindeer was no profane trading partner but quite possibly an ancestor spirit or totemic figure. Archeologist Alfred Rust determined that these sacrifices were conducted in May or June, when the Paleolithic hunters had just moved into their summer settlements. As such, the sacrificial victims were assumed to have been the first or among the first killed of each new season (Maringer, 1960, pp. 67–69). Cassirer (1944) explained:

> Even magic is to be taken as an important step in the development of human consciousness. Faith in magic is one of the earliest and most striking expressions of man's awakening self-confidence. Here he no longer feels himself at the mercy of natural or supernatural forces. He begins to play his own part, he becomes an actor in the spectacle of nature. Every magical practice is based upon the conviction that natural effects to a large degree depend on human deeds. (p. 92)

❖ ❖ ❖

Sacrifice is a magical denial of impotence in the face of nature's overwhelming power and an effort to affect the natural world through an action with no causal relation to the desired outcome. When I visited the Hoti indigenous people in the Venezuelan jungles, I met a people who were living very close to the hunter-gatherer technology of their ancestors. In their village I saw bones, particularly animal skulls, on the ground, wedged between branches of a tree, on the floor in people's houses, hanging from the ceiling, or tucked into the rafters—including a monkey skull, a tapir skull, a bush pig skull, a toucan beak, and the claws of an anteater. I saw the same practice among the Panare and the Yanomami. In a discussion of the Yanomami practice of tucking these bones away in various places around the house, Gabriele Herzog-Schröder wrote, "One bone of the animal killed must always be kept. This respectful attitude towards the game brings future good luck in hunting" (Herzog-Schröder, 1999, p. 52).

A Yavarana man who lived not far from the Hoti and Panare explained that before they were all "civilized" (his word), each group avoided eating one kind of animal. The Yavarana and Hoti did not eat the anteater (taboo), because it was believed to be their grandfather (totem), and the Panare didn't eat the tapir for the same reason. Now everyone eats everything, he said. It was a clear demonstration of the deterioration of the tradition. In the Yavarana community, I saw littered about on the ground ancient pre-Hispanic ceramic figurines of animals and vaguely human forms. "They were made by our grandparents," I was told. And here we can see how grandparents, ancestors, and totems all blur into a conceptual unity. I later discovered the figurines were actually 1,500 years old.

On my expedition up the Caciquiare River, one of my guides, Jesús, caught some fish for us, which we ate in the evening. The next morning, his father, José, of the Amorua ethnicity, left one whole fish on the beach. Seeing it lying on the sand as our boat headed out into the river, I asked about it. José explained that placing a fish on the shore in this way is a common tradition among the indigenous people in the area to show respect for the animal and ensure continued good fishing. He added that even after so many of the indigenous people became Christianized, when hunting they continue to leave a piece of meat for Santa Ines, the patron saint of hunters, and when fishing they leave a fish for San Rafael, the patron saint of fishermen.

Ernest Becker (1973) offered the interpretation that for Homo sapiens, the symbolizing animal, anality means an awareness of physical determinism, creatureliness, decay, and death. He quoted Otto Rank: "The death fear of the ego is lessened by the killing, the sacrifice, of the other; through the death of the other, one buys oneself free from the penalty of dying, of being killed" (Rank, 1945, p. 130, quoted in Becker, 1973, p. 99). "Rank called masochism the 'small sacrifice,' the 'lighter punishment,' the 'placation' that allows one to avoid the arch-evil of death" (Becker, 1973, p. 246).

Up to now I have been speaking as though the Upper Paleolithic gave way directly to the Neolithic Revolution. That is not exactly correct. Actually there was an intermediate period called the Mesolithic when culture was no longer Upper Paleolithic but not fully Neolithic either. During this Mesolithic period, about 10,500 years ago, at the same Stellmoor lakebed, our ancestors were continuing to practice the exact same ritual that was practiced earlier in the Paleolithic. Alfred Rust found there 12 more complete reindeer skeletons, each of which had been submerged into the lake with a stone in its thoracic or abdominal cavity. An additional 30 skulls and miscellaneous bones and large stones were also found, giving Rust the impression that there may have been 45 animals sacrificed in this particular lake (Maringer, 1960, p. 118).

If the funerary ritual was about humanity joining with the spirit, the sacrifice was about humanity saying to the spirit, "Let's make a deal." No longer at one with nature, humanity makes a deal with the spirit, its own spirit, which it has projected into the wilderness along with other aspects of itself. Both the sublime and the terrible became aspects of this spiritual/psychological/cultural shadow. With the sacrifice, humanity strikes a deal with the spirit and fortifies the separation between the two. It is an obsessional resolution to the primitive impulses (incest and murder) that threaten the group. They want to eat the reindeer that they just killed, but instead they renounce the instinct and offer it up as a sacrifice: "If I renounce instinct, I will get something better—Mother's love, Father's approval, a season full of reindeer." The sacrifice involves a doing and an undoing, the isolation of affect, an intellectualization about the crime committed, and a ritual enactment of the deal to ward off aggressive impulses. So perhaps this is where we might entertain the possibility of seeing the obsessional neurosis as the analogous psychopathology to the anal phase and the Neolithic Revolution.

Rust was impressed by the longevity of the ritual sacrifice of reindeer, which had a basic structure that was unchanged for literally thousands of years. Interestingly enough, we see a similar motif in the story of "Little Red Cap" or, as it is more commonly known, "Little Red Riding Hood." A little girl is taking cake and wine to her ailing grandmother. On her way there, a wolf talks with her and learns of her plans for the day. The sly wolf bids her good day, runs off through the woods to Grandmother's house, devours Grandmother, dresses himself in Grandmother's bedclothes, crawls into her bed, and waits for Little Red Cap to arrive. On her arrival, the wolf leaps up out of bed and swallows the child. With a full belly, the wolf settles back into bed and falls asleep, snoring loudly. Just then a hunter passes by and hears the loud snoring. Concerned for the old woman, he stops in at the house to see if she is okay. When he sees the wolf in her bed, however, his fury rises. He prepares to shoot the wolf on the spot but then reconsiders, thinking that perhaps the old woman might still be saved if she were cut free. He grabs a pair of scissors, makes four snips in the wolf's belly, and out comes Little Red Cap followed by her grandmother, both of them alive and well. Little

Red Cap then fetches some big stones and fills the wolf's belly while he continues to sleep. When the wolf awakens, he sees the hunter and tries to run, but the stones in his belly are so heavy that he collapses (Grimm & Grimm, 1972, pp. 139-43). Could we call the murder of the wolf a sacrifice of cannibalistic impulses?

Another tale from the Grimms' collection, "The Wolf and the Seven Little Kids," ends in the same way, with the kids being eaten, the kids being cut free from the wolf's belly, and the wolf's belly filled with stones. But in this tale when the wolf goes to the well to get a drink, the weight of the stones pulls the wolf into the well, where he drowns (pp. 39-42). And what has been sacrificed? A wolf, or the murderous and devouring cannibalistic impulses directed at a mother, a father, a sibling? In creating the light of consciousness, we create a shadow of repressed desires that must be dealt with—that must be controlled. And the personification of those repressed impulses is propitiated with a sacrifice.

Money, Trade, and Toilet Training

The anal-stage toddler is interested in control. While the baby in the oral stage may feel omnipotent, that is more feeling, fantasy, and hallucination than real control. For the anal-stage toddler, sphincter control becomes a psychological variable. Toddlers are interested in control because they have the power to take control. Our Neolithic ancestors were also interested in control, but this is not to say they were toddlers; rather, they were fully integrated communities, which included infants, toddlers, children, adolescents, adults, and the elderly. Their sudden interest in control was due to the fact that their technology had developed to the point that they were able to take more control over their lives than they had in the Upper Paleolithic. And when they met the limitations of their evolving technology, their spirituality evolved and sacrifice became a spiritual innovation.

The toddler says, in effect, "I want to defecate wherever and whenever I want, but I want the love of Mother too. I have a conflict, so I will strike a deal. I will make a sacrifice. I will give her my valuable fecal stick where and when she wants it, and she, in return, will love me." Feces are powerful objects of great interest for the toddler and others as well. They are the child's special creative work. They arrive with fullness and pain, tension release, anal erotic pleasure, warmth, and creative potency. And others respond to these bowel movements with either outrage and disgust or appreciation and admiration. Some children feel a loss after separating from their valued fecal stick and are not enthusiastic about sitting on or flushing the toilet. The whole interaction around toilet training is about passivity and activity, inside and outside, time and space, here and there, now and then, control and loss of control. The anxiety is registered in fears of using the toilet and fantasies of the hand or snake in the toilet that will steal one's feces or genitals.[1]

Freud (1908/1959b) noted that we often recognize the anal disposition in the way a person handles money. If the person is anal expulsive, he spends freely to the point of irresponsibility, and if anal retentive, he is thrifty, penny-pinching, even "a tight ass." Freud explained, "In reality, wherever archaic modes of thought have predominated or persist—in the ancient civilizations, in myths, fairy tales and superstitions, in unconscious thinking, in dreams and in neuroses—money is brought into the most intimate relationship with dirt" (SE 9, p. 174).

The alchemists say the philosophical gold resides in the manure pile, and it's a common expression to say we don't want someone's "stinking money." Tales tell of the goose that laid the golden egg and the ass that defecated gold nuggets. Freud mentions the wealthy spendthrift who was colloquially called a *Dukatenscheisser*—"a shitter of ducats." He also cited the Babylonian doctrine that nuggets of gold are "the feces of Hell." Ferenczi (1914/1976) elaborated on this idea, saying, "The excrementa thus held back are really the first 'savings' of the growing being, and as such, remain in a constant, unconscious interrelationship with every bodily activity or mental striving that has anything to do with collecting, hording, and saving" (p. 82).

We often observe in the clinical situation how some patients equate money with love, care, power, independence, contamination, or control and how the therapy itself can be reconfigured as a kind of prostitution or even as an emotional pay toilet. The association between money and anality has an ancient history and prehistory.

It is difficult to say when money came into being, but it is well known that some Neolithic peoples used cowrie shells as money or traded certain raw materials as units of value. There may have been some limited trade in the Upper Paleolithic, but trade increased significantly during the Neolithic when technology became more elaborate and when people stopped moving around as much and began to collect things and amass wealth. Groups with raw materials in one area would trade for needed raw materials from another area.

Neolithic trade is another way in which humanity renounces or sublimates the gratification of the instincts, particularly the instinct to kill the stranger. It calls to mind those poignant moments in which we see the two-year-old sharing his toys with another child for the first

---

[1] I knew a six-year-old boy who became nervous using the toilet and as a compromise would sit there singing loudly, "It's a grand old flag, it's a high-flying flag," as if to ward off the loss of his feces, the threat to his genitals, or the associated anal erotic stimulation giving rise to his erection—his grand old flag. A little girl had a mother who was anxious about the cleanliness of the daughter's anus after bowel movements. The mother cleaned, cleaned, and cleaned, much to the little girl's annoyance, and the two entered a match of stubborn wills. In therapy the girl invented a game in which we each took turns blowing *our own* noses, and each throwing the Kleenex away *ourselves!*

time. It is a painful compromise in which one abandons the instinct, so to speak, of having the toy all for oneself and accepts the rewards of sharing, learning to play with another, and receiving Mother's love for having done so.

The interchanges taking place in Neolithic trade and in toilet training are fairly obvious: "I give you this for that." But what link can we make between Neolithic trade and the invention of money? William H. Desmonde (1957/1976) offered a clue in his hypothesis that "money in Western culture originated in ancient Greece and Rome in the animal sacrifice, or food communion ritual" (p. 113). Even though we are speaking here of historic Greece and Rome, we suddenly find ourselves back to the sacrifice. Desmonde writes that eating the animal sacrifice was motivated by the desire for union with the mother. He asserts that the first coins were associated with the mother goddess cults that grew up around Astarte, Mylitta, Aphrodite, Artemis, and Hera and that the first coins were religious, heraldic, and commemorative in nature.

The Upper Paleolithic period in Europe saw cults of the cave bear as well as the Paleolithic and Mesolithic rituals of sacrificed reindeer. But in Neolithic Çatal Hüyük, we find evidence of a religion organized around the bovine, which transformed throughout prehistory and history into various representations of the sacred bull in the religious life of ancient Egypt, Mesopotamia, Persia, Crete, Greece, and India. The sacred bull, identified with the god, was, of course, also the sacrificial bull. The better the bull and the more bulls involved, the greater the sacrifice—that is, the size or quantity of the sacrifice came to be associated with the benefits one could expect from it. Thus, the bull became a unit of value in ancient Greece, Rome, and Crete.

The word "fee" is derived from the Gothic word *faihu*, meaning "cattle." The "rupee," the Indian unit of value, is derived from the Sanskrit word for "cattle," *rupa*. "Chattel," "capital," and "capitalism" all have their roots in the word *caput*, meaning "head," in reference to counting cattle by the "head." The sacred bull was identified with the god in classical antiquity, particularly ancient Greece. Desmonde explained, "The intimate connection between the animal sacrifice and the rituals of the cult of the dead in ancient times, coupled with numerous evidences of ritual cannibalism in early Greece, lead us to conjecture that the bull sacrifices originated in the killing of the father" (pp. 118-19).

The sacrifice and communal meal that followed were joined as a community event. The sacrifice was to propitiate the god in order to obtain a good harvest and obtain protection against illness. In ancient Greece, a piece of sacrificial meat was roasted on a spit, or skewer. The spit, on which the sacrificial meat was given to each member of the public, was called an *obolos*: "The Greek coin called obolos hence originated in the portion of the sacrificial flesh roasted on a spit" (p. 121). "A similar origin existed for the tripods and pots which served as units of value in Homeric times: these objects were originally used around the sacrificial altar to hold portions of the sacrificial flesh. The value of these tripods and pots was measured originally in bulls. The iron money of the Spartans, according to [Bernhard] Laum, can be traced back to the sickles used to kill the sacrificial animals" (p. 121).

In ancient Greece, gold, silver, and other metals were considered to be amulets with magical powers. The word "money" is derived from the goddess Moneta, who represented "just distribution" or "equality." Laum suggests that the manufacturing of money is derived from distribution rights in the sacrifice of the sacred bull. The portion of meat or money represented the distribution by the state (temple) of gifts, rewards, or fees to the individual citizens. According to Desmonde, "It must at the outset be stated that the sacrificial bull was often regarded as a fertility spirit or embodiment of the crops emanating from the goddess Earth. The act of eating the bull, therefore, to some extent represented an eating of the goddess, or mother image" (p. 125).

Money is related to sacrifice at its very roots and is even more obvious when it is thrown away (as into a fountain for good luck), donated, given in the name of the god, and so on. But the forerunner of money, embedded in ritual sacrifice, is trade. Trade is the rational interchange of goods between people, and sacrifice is the magical interchange of goods between the people and the gods. It is likely there existed trade in the Paleolithic, but the established sedentary life of the Neolithic made the need to trade all the more urgent.

❖ ❖ ❖

In 2006 my wife and I visited two Yanomami communities in the Venezuelan jungles of the Upper Orinoco. On each visit we were treated to a ritual welcome dance. The dance was conducted by most of the members of the community, who danced and chanted, sometimes individually and sometimes as a group. Both women and men danced, and all danced bare-breasted and bare-footed. The dance was a hopping walk or run from one foot to the next with elbows bent and hands held up or holding on to palm fronds, spears, or bows and arrows. One of the most distinctive features was the brandishing of weapons in the direction of the guests (us!). It was a rather impressive display of ambivalence in the encounter with the stranger. We were welcomed while being reminded that they were dangerous and that we better not try to hurt them.

After the dance, one is expected to give gifts. I had made sure that we had plenty of desirable items to give in exchange for the dance. We brought fishing line, fishing hooks, mosquito netting, and beads, all of which were among the preferred gifts. And yet on both occasions the community became agitated and threatening when it was determined we had not given enough. We found it quite disconcerting, as we felt very grateful for the welcome dance and certainly hoped our gifts would be appreciated. In both cases, the agitation and threatening attitude prompted us to make a somewhat hasty retreat that was then checked by kinder words from our hosts and in fact ended with an invitation to stay the night in the community with them. Our guides then explained to us that this sort of tense exchange happens every time there is a dance and the subsequent presentation of gifts. In the morning I woke up in my hammock to the sound of a chanting shaman wearing a monkey-tail shaman's hat with dangling feathers. He was chanting to protect the community from danger and was paying special attention to where we were sleeping.

A seemingly unrelated anecdote also comes to my mind: I once asked a Spanish-speaking Yanomami shaman about dreams, and he told me that when a shaman has a dream of another shaman, it means the dreamer's life is in literal danger. He told me he had two such dreams, and his brother, also a shaman, conducted the corresponding rituals to protect him from the malevolent spirits of the shaman who appeared in his dream. It was not only a very concrete interpretation of the dream but also characteristic of the highly suspicious Yanomami, who additionally consider all deaths as having been caused by someone out there and because of that the death must be avenged.

The tension related to gift giving, the concrete thinking about the spirit world, and the suspicion of others every time someone gets sick or dies suggest to me a cultural propensity to envy and jealousy. Yanomami groups are always involved in giving and taking things from one another and outsiders. At one point a young Yanomami mother showed her baby to my wife and invited her to hold it. My wife reached out, held the baby, cuddled it, and gave it back to the young mother, who then insisted that my wife was now obligated to give her a necklace. My wife was naturally confused. In the Yanomami community, problems flare up around thefts, desperate desires for objects, and terrible upsets over ruptures in protocol related to the power dynamics of giving and taking. Who has the thing? Who wants the thing? Who took the thing? Who has what I want? Who wants what I have? Who will give me something?

Because of all this, and much more, some people describe the Yanomami as fierce and violent. What is perhaps more to the point are the pronounced characteristics of envy and jealousy, which I assume have roots in their overall social structure. And yet I returned from my visits with the Yanomami overwhelmingly grateful for their generosity. And of course, psychologically speaking, "envy" and "jealousy" are closely related to "gratitude" and "generosity."

What I am getting at here is that the violence of aboriginal cultures is not the free-form gratuitous violence that we are more familiar with in modern societies; rather it is an expression of intense envy and jealousy related to the gifting and receiving of things or reprisals for deaths in the community. Thus, trade as well as gifting-and-receiving rituals seem to be defensive strategies of the group that are unconsciously designed to manage envy and jealousy. And when these strategies break down, violence may erupt. As we shall see shortly, the Yanomami are not unique in these attitudes; I am merely using the example of Yanomami gifting and trading as a mirror to exemplify this component of the human condition in general.

Describing the significance of giving among the Yanomami, Gabriele Herzog-Schröder (1999) explained:

> The request for specific objects, often made whenever Yanomami meet, might easily be interpreted as begging by outsiders. However, such a request gives the one who is asked the opportunity to be generous which in fact makes him feel flattered. (p. 50)

> Although, due to the mobile way of life, a pronounced accumulation of goods would have little advantage, the maxim of the "open hands," as generosity is paraphrased by the Yanomami, is indeed taken surprisingly seriously: thus respected and politically influential personalities frequently own the least goods. (p. 51)

> The necessity to equalize what has been given lies in the rule of reciprocity, fundamental to all exchanges and placing both partners participating in the exchange in an actual relationship with each other or, respectively, reinforcing their already existing relationship. (p. 51)

The giving-and-taking ritual, though tense, makes for a happy relationship, and it is happy because it ritually neutralizes envy and jealousy in a social field. If the gift is not given or if the gift is refused, envy and jealousy are unleashed. Bare-breasted Yanomami women nursing their babies often approached us with their hands outstretched, saying, "*Chupe, chupe,*" literally meaning "Suck, suck," but in this case meaning "Give me candy." Fortunately, we had brought plenty of candy, but, unfortunately, it was never enough.

One of the common items of exchange between Yanomami communities are *rahaka*, bamboo arrow points. "If unknown people appear in the vicinity of a village, they first try to draw attention to themselves in order not to be taken for aggressors. Following this, a small group enters the village. The first stage of the ritual greeting consists of the visitors 'confronting' the hosts. They position themselves standing up straight on the open square in the middle of the village to demonstrate fearlessness while being ritually threatened with bows and arrows by the hosts" (Herzog-Schröder, 1999, p. 53). They are then invited into the communal house: "There the guests remain immobile for about an hour in the host's hammock. In the meantime, the villagers have a chance to get used to the presence of the unfamiliar visitors" (p. 50). The guests are then invited to eat, drink, and "exchange words"—talk. Then the visitors show their arrow points, their rahaka:

> If the group of visitors includes several men, the others then also take out their arrowheads and together they trace the route of the "rahaka." Based on the spectrum of the rahaka shown and the explanation given, the participants in the talk are able to get an idea of their unfamiliar visitors' network of political alliances. Then follows a conversation in the strongly ritualized form of duel-like reciprocal speech where some passages are also sung. At the end of the visit, mostly lasting for one night only, in addition to other goods rahaka are also exchanged between the guests and the hosts. These arrowheads symbolize the confidence that the recipient will not use them against the donor and are a promise of solidarity. (p. 54)

Trade, or the giving and taking of things, establishes all sorts of intratribal and intertribal relations, which form alliances or become the bases for wars, battles, and murders. The giving of things and taking of things forms a large part in the ritual life of many cultures. When it goes well, it instills gratitude, alliances, and bonds of love and fellowship. And when it goes poorly, the envy, jealousy, paranoia, and bitter animosity that are unchecked by the ritual are then unleashed.

Ritual sacrifice and trade are strategies for managing envy, jealousy, gratitude, and alliances, but they are not managed intrapsychically—within the individual. Instead, they are managed interpersonally—within the social surround. In other words, one manages the envy and jealousy of others by giving things to those others. Similarly, one is obliged to reciprocity by accepting things from the other. Thus, in gifting rituals one disowns split-off parts of oneself such as envy and jealousy and projects them onto others. One then relates to those others in a way that forces them to deal with those split-off parts of oneself. This brings us back to the idea that ritual is a defensive strategy of culture and that in cultural evolution we evolved these primal rituals such as the funeral, sacrifice, and ritual trading to help us deal with our primitive impulses while living together in society. Would we be going too far to see in ritual sacrifice, trade, and gifting a kind of cultural parallel to projective identification?

Among the Pacific Northwest Coast tribes of the Haida, Nuxalk, Tlingit, Tsimshian, Nuu-chah-nulth, Kwakwaka'wakw (formerly known as the Kwakiutl), and the Coast Salish, we find the well-known tradition of the "potlatch." The potlatch is a ceremony of giving and taking, or gifting and receiving, in which a leader in the community sponsors a feast and gives his wealth to those invited. The potlatch may be associated with another ritual, such as a birth, initiation rite, marriage, or funeral. In the potlatch ceremony, there may be ritual singing and dancing and the gifting of blankets, dried foods, beautifully worked images on sheets of copper, and other valuables. The ceremony is all about the ritual redistribution of wealth and the customs of reciprocity. Another aspect of the ritual is the establishment of status. In the indigenous cultures of the Pacific Northwest Coast, high status is not based on who has the most but who gives the most. Closely related to the potlatch are the traditions of Kula Ring, Moka exchange, and Sepik Coast exchange among the various indigenous people of Papua New Guinea; the tradition of Koha among the Maori of New Zealand; and many others.

If we want to reflect on the defensive function that any ritual provides its society, all we have to do is imagine that society without the ritual in place. Without the funerary ritual, the shadow of the absent other falls on the community, perhaps in the form of tormenting ghosts, survival guilt, or other unbound affects. Without ritual sacrifice, the group is left to its feelings of guilt and shame for whatever ill fate has befallen them. Without ritual gifting, envy and jealousy are unleashed and social relations become unstable, leading to bitter rivalry, fights, murder, and even warfare. The ritual, as we can see, has its defensive function. It stands to reason that nomadic Paleolithic people would have had few possessions, as they needed to carry all that they owned. But sedentary Neolithic people accumulate wealth, and this naturally intensifies feelings of jealousy and envy.

In *The Gift: The Form and Reason for Exchange in Archaic Societies*, Marcel Mauss (1924/1990) explained that traditional exchanges of goods "are committed to in a somewhat voluntary form by presents and gifts, although in the final analysis they are strictly compulsory, on pain of private or public warfare" (p. 5). Speaking of the indigenous people of the North American Pacific Northwest Coast, he commented, "What is noteworthy about these tribes is the principle of rivalry and hostility that prevails in all these practices" (p. 6). Mauss finds something similar in modern contemporary competitive gift giving at weddings and parties:

> In this system of ideas one clearly and logically realizes that one must give back to another person what is really part and parcel of his nature and substance, because to accept something from somebody is to accept some part of his spiritual essence, of his soul. To retain that thing would be dangerous and mortal, not only because it would be against law and morality, but also because that thing coming from the person not only morally, but physically and spiritually, that essence, that food, those goods, whether movable or immovable, those women or those descendants, those rituals or those acts of communion—all exert a magical or religious hold over you. Finally, the thing given is not inactive. Invested with life, often possessing individuality, it seeks

to return to what Hertz called its "place of origin" or to produce, on behalf of the clan and the native soil from which it sprang, an equivalent to replace it. (pp. 12-13)

Then, bringing it full circle, Mauss wrote, "The relationships that exist between these contracts and exchanges among humans and those between men and the gods throw light on a whole aspect of the theory of sacrifice" (p. 15). He goes on to say, "Gifts to humans and to the gods also serve the purpose of buying peace between them both. In this way evil spirits and, more generally, bad influences, even not personalized, are got rid of" (p. 17).

This interesting relationship between gift giving and the rivalry and hostility it manages, reminds us of Melanie Klein's *Envy and Gratitude* (1957) in which she discusses generosity and feelings of impoverishment:

Gratitude is closely bound up with generosity. Inner wealth derives from having assimilated the good object so that the individual becomes able to share its gifts with others.... By contrast, with people in whom this feeling of inner wealth and strength is not sufficiently established, bouts of generosity are often followed by an exaggerated need for appreciation and gratitude, and consequently by persecutory anxieties of having been impoverished and robbed (p. 19).

In brief, Neolithic trade and giving-and-receiving rituals, money, and sacrifice are all socially interrelated and related to anal dynamics as well.

Agriculture and Culture

When our early Neolithic ancestors ended their nomadic Paleolithic ways, they created permanent homes. When they changed their world architecturally, it changed their minds structurally. The house became a womb not for a physical birth but for a spiritual birth—a cultural birth, a psychological birth. The house is a metaphor of a cultural womb, and agriculture is a constellation of metaphors pertaining to sexual relations with cultural and psychological significance.

Instead of hunting and gathering in the Paleolithic Garden of Eden, our Neolithic ancestors tilled the earth, gathered seeds, and planted them in holes in the ground, making the earth into a life-giving womb. They fertilized the crops, watered them, tended them until it was time for harvest, and then cut them down. When cattle were domesticated, they were attached to the plow, and the plow, like a great phallus, tilled the earth and made it ready to receive the seed. The cow became a symbol of the life-giving goddess who gives birth, gives milk, and gives her flesh in holy sacrifice. The bull tilled the fields by pulling the plow, fertilized the fields with his manure, and fertilized the cow with his mighty male member. The same sexual bivalence applies to the horns, which are phallic and penetrating at the sharp end and nourishing cornucopias at the wide-open end. Cattle are metaphors for fertility, mother, father, sacrifice, and rebirth. Cows and bulls became organizing metaphors of Near Eastern Neolithic living and were naturally turned into gods.

In India, Vac was the feminine aspect of Brahma and referred to as the melodious cow or the cow of abundance. And from "Vac" we get the Spanish word for cow, *vaca*. Brahma is, of course, associated with the Brahma bull and the sacred cow, and Nandi is the bull that Shiva rides. The bull is associated with the astrological sign of Taurus. Sin was a Mesopotamian lunar god represented by the bull. The Egyptian god Osiris was represented by the bull Apis, and Hathor was the cow goddess of Egyptian mythology. In the Mithraic traditions of ancient Rome, Mithras, the hero figure, kills the bull representing spring and thereby brings about fecundity. Dionysus, the dying fertility god, was also associated with the bull. The Minotaur of Greek mythology was half man and half bull and lived at the center of the labyrinth. The Old Testament speaks of Moses's people growing impatient for his return from the mountain and going back to their old ways of worshiping idols by building and worshiping a golden calf. The Sumerians speak of the Bull of Heaven, Gugalana. And, of course, beef and milk figure prominently in the dietary taboos of Jews, Muslims, and Hindus.

One might even wonder if it wasn't until the Neolithic Revolution that we, as humans, had our sexual enlightenment—that is, when Homo sapiens discovered that reproduction occurs as a result of sexual intercourse. This sexual enlightenment easily could have been imbued with all sorts of magic as well, but it might all have been reduced to the magical formula of *put something into a space and something else will emerge from it*. This formula also opens the way to seeing sex as a sacrifice—a surrender, a giving up, a letting go, a putting out, a commitment, a loving to death, dying in the arms of the other, a petit mort.

Do chimpanzees know that sex leads to the birth of babies? I doubt it. I can't imagine how they could. So when did we, as a species, attain our sexual enlightenment? I find it hard to believe that it was before the Paleolithic. Some of the cave paintings depict copulating animals, and the people were clearly interested in fertility, but did they link copulation with birth? The sexual instinct is not driven by the desire to reproduce. It is driven by pleasure. Animals are driven by pleasure and the instinct to copulate. Reproduction is temporally removed enough from copulation that there can be no conscious association between the two. Primatologist Frans de Waal (1996) sees it the same way: "Sex serves reproduction, yet animals engage in it without the slightest notion of its function; they are not driven by any desire to reproduce, only by sexual urges (as are humans most of the time)" (p. 28). Perhaps our Paleolithic ancestors knew something about the connection and perhaps not. But by the time of the Neolithic, Homo sapiens were domesticating animals and plants, observing them closely and learning the facts of life. Ideas about reproduction must have been loaded with magical thinking due to the lapse of time between copulation and birth, the mysteries of birth, and the fact that not every copulation leads to birth.

Our Neolithic ancestors were domesticating animals and plants, observing them closely, and learning about reproduction and how to control it for their benefit. But side by side with the logical association of copulation with reproduction was the analogical association of copulation and reproduction aided by the use of magic objects, the incantation of magical words, and, of course, sacrifice.

The fact of the matter is that to this day there are many otherwise sophisticated people who have all sorts of incorrect ideas about what does and does not bring about new life. Many of us have encountered these alternative theories when talking with children and young adolescents about sexuality. Some think pregnancy occurs every time a man and a woman have sex, or only when love is involved, or only if the woman has an orgasm. And adults who have difficulty getting pregnant often use prayer and good luck charms to assist in achieving conception. Many others just hope, which is an equally magical effort. (Never mind the fact that sometimes it works!)

A latency-age boy knew that the reproductive and excretory organs were located in the same anatomical region and explained to me that a man and a woman make a baby by mixing their "pee" together. In Freud's essay "On the Sexual Theories of Children" (1908/1959e), he wrote of the "cloacal theory," in which some children imagine that babies are born through the anus. He also recognized the oral theory of conception, in which babies are made as a result of the mother having eaten something. One could easily imagine that such theories would have abounded in the Paleolithic and Neolithic periods. One need only recall that there are many people today who believe that conception may result from oral or anal sex and that touching magical objects or saying prayers will facilitate conception. These are beliefs that deny sexual knowledge. Thus, it seems likely that our Neolithic ancestors, as they raised domestic animals, were the first to lift the veil off the mysterious link between sex and reproduction and bring the first glimmers of sexual enlightenment into the world. I suspect they were only glimmers, however, and those glimmers were thoroughly saturated with magical thinking.

While chimpanzees build nests and establish territorial boundaries, Neolithic Homo sapiens built houses and fortified village walls. The invention of the wall was internalized as a metaphor for ego boundaries and personal space. This, combined with settled life, gave rise to the possibility of personal possessions, privacy, wealth, and, of course, trade. The Neolithic Revolution gave us agriculture, which as a way of life became a lived metaphor for sexual enlightenment—that is, the realization of the relationship between sex and reproduction. While the mortar (female) and pestle (male) and the bow (female) and arrow (male) made their first appearances in the Paleolithic, they proliferated in the Neolithic. If the Paleolithic was about the unity of Homo sapiens in nature, the Neolithic Revolution was about duality—inside and outside, here and there, now and then, you and me, us and them, male and female, mortar and pestle, bow and arrow, wild and domestic animals, wild and domestic plant foods, mother and child.

Wanting to understand something about our Neolithic ancestors, Mircea Eliade (1978a/1956) turned to the origin myths of contemporary aboriginal cultures practicing vegeculture or cereal culture and discovered a widely disseminated theme explaining that tubers and fruit trees came from the immolated body of a divine being. He wrote that the most famous myth of this kind is derived from Ceram, one of the islands off the coast of New Guinea. It tells of the murder of a semidivine maiden named Hainuwele and the tubers that subsequently grew from her body. Eliade explained, "This primordial murder radically changed the human condition, for it introduced sexuality and death and first established the religious and social institutions that are still in force" (p. 38). We could easily configure this murder as the murder of the primal father, the primal mother, the primal psychic unity, or as a primal sacrifice.

As the story goes, there once was a man named Ameta, meaning "Dark," "Black," or "Night." While Ameta was out hunting with his dog, the dog smelled a wild pig, so he chased after it until the pig raced into a pond and died. Ameta retrieved the pig and found a coconut on its tusk, and that was before there were coco palms. In a dream he was told to plant the coconut, which he did. A short time later it grew into a tall palm with blossoms. Ameta climbed the coco palm to cut some blossoms to make a drink. But when he accidentally cut his finger, the blood fell on the leaf and mixed with the sap. Three days later a face appeared from out of the leaves. In three more days, the face and trunk of a girl were clearly evident, and after just three more days Ameta was able to take home the little girl, whom he named Hainuwele. Three days later she was a nubile maiden. "But she was not like an ordinary person; for when she would answer the call of nature her excrement consisted of all sorts of valuable articles, such as Chinese dishes and gongs, so that her father became very rich" (Sproul, 1979, p. 328).

Well, the people of the village routinely conducted the great Maro dance, in which men, in a great spiral, danced around the women, who, at the center gave out betel nut to the men. Hainuwele was placed at the center and gave out betel nut. On the second night of dancing, the men were again expecting betel nut, but this time she gave them pieces of coral. On subsequent nights, she gave out Chinese porcelain dishes, then bigger dishes, bush knives, betel boxes of copper, gold earrings, and glorious gongs. The people were curious about where she got all of these wonderful things and became jealous of her. So on the next night a large hole was dug in the dance grounds, and at the height of the dancing Hainuwele was killed, pushed in, and buried. When Ameta discovered what had happened, he dug up his daughter, cut her body into many pieces, and planted them all around the dance grounds. From these dismembered pieces grew all sorts of previously unknown plant foods, mostly tubers (pp. 327-30). Interestingly enough, we see again, in this myth, the transformation of excrement into treasured objects and the association of gifting, sacrifice, and agriculture. Also of interest is the appearance in this context of jealousy and envy. Eliade (1978a/1956) elaborated:

> A similar mythical theme explains the origin of food plants—both tubers and cereals—as arising from the excreta or the sweat of a divinity or mythical ancestor. When the beneficiaries discover the repulsive source of their foodstuffs, they kill the author; but, following his advice, they dismember his body and bury the pieces. Food plants and other elements of culture (agricultural implements, silk worms, etc.) spring from his corpse. The meaning of these myths is obvious: food plants are sacred, since they are derived from the body of a divinity (for excreta and the sweat are also part of the divine substance). By feeding himself, man, in the last analysis, eats a divine being. The food plant is not "given" in the world, as the animal is. It is the result of a primitive dramatic event; in this case it is the product of a murder. (p. 39)

We see again and again how one thing is put inside another (sacrificed) and, as a result, a transformation takes place. Seeds placed in the ground become food plants. The harvested grain, placed in the mortar, and pounded with the pestle are turned into flour. The flour mixed with water becomes dough. The dough placed in the oven becomes bread. Clay placed in the oven becomes ceramic. The juice placed in the ceramic pot ferments and becomes wine. When one drinks the wine, consciousness transforms, and by way of this resulting intoxication, one communes with the spirits until one day all alcoholic drinks are referred to as "spirits."

Eliade (1978a/1956) recounted that early technological inventions and their transformative effects stirred the imagination and spawned new traditions:

> In working with a piece of flint or a primitive needle, in joining together animal hides or wooden planks, in preparing a fishhook or an arrowhead, in shaping a

clay statuette, the imagination discovers unsuspected analogies among the different levels of the real; tools and objects are laden with countless symbolisms, the world of work—the microuniverse that absorbs the artisan's attention for long hours—becomes a mysterious and sacred center, rich in meanings. (pp. 34-35)

As Eliade points out, new technology can be mysterious and sacred. But in time the mysterious becomes commonplace, the sacred becomes profane, and the meanings become embedded in cultural institutions and psychological structure. And then, as always, the only place left to find the mysterious, the sacred, and new meaning is on the threshold between the known and the unknown. Eliade explained:

The fertility of the earth is bound up with feminine fecundity; hence women become responsible for the abundance of harvests, for they know the "mystery" of creation. It is a religious mystery, for it governs the origin of life, the food supply, and death. The soil is assimilated to woman. Later, after the discovery of the plow, agricultural work is assimilated to the sexual act. But for millennia Mother Earth gave birth by herself, through parthenogenesis. (p. 40)

And parthenogenesis, of course, is yet another sexual theory that children may construct prior to sexual enlightenment. And later still, without being altered in the least, it would reemerge and be given deep religious significance in the myth of the virgin birth—a delightful myth that denies sexual enlightenment and spares us the pain of having to consider Mommy's desires and pleasures that don't include us and do include Daddy's role in all of this.

Eliade emphasized that religious creativity was not stirred by agriculture per se, but by the mystery of birth, death, and rebirth in the life cycle of the plants and by the cycles of drought and flood that brought death and renewal. And from the life cycle of the plants grew the mythologies of the god that dies and is reborn. The plant inspires the notion of the cosmic tree with roots in the underworld, a trunk in this world, and its branches in the heavens. The yearly cycle of seasons and their influence over the crops drew our Neolithic ancestors out of the cosmic moment and into circular or cyclic time, in which one must delay gratification of the instinct (hunger) long enough to plant something in the ground and then take care of it for months before being able to harvest and eat it.

And just as cosmic time becomes cyclic, so too does space take on a new quality within the garden perimeter, within the village walls, within the house, within the oven, within the kiln, and within the pot. The house, as a sacred space, becomes a spiritual womb—a psychological womb—in which new ideas and relationships are formed.

THE NEOLITHIC PERIOD AND THE ANAL STAGE OF LIBIDO DEVELOPMENT

Clay and Feces

The tradition of making small female figurines (Venuses or mother goddesses), which began in the Paleolithic period, continued in the Neolithic, but the stone and ivory carvings of the Paleolithic were largely replaced with fired clay figurines in the Neolithic. These ceramic female figurines are found all around the world, but in a few places, such as Çatal Hüyük and Hacilar, one sees the figure represented as pregnant, giving birth, or together with a boy or an animal of some sort. There are also a few representations of the old bearded man, a figure that would later take on much greater significance (Mellaart, 1965, p. 92).

I have seen the pre-Hispanic ceramic female figurines from the island archipelago Los Roques, off the coast of Venezuela, excavated by Maria Magdalena Antczak and Andrzej Antczak of Universidad Simón Bolívar. The Antczaks are professional archeologists who are careful not to attribute modern meanings to the ceramic figurines of a dead culture. They avoid references to "Venus figures," "goddesses," and "great mothers" and instead stay with the fact that these figurines, whatever they may have meant in their own cultural contexts, are simply "female figurines." Any additional significance would have to be tied to other data derived from the specific culture. I, on the other hand, allow myself more room to speculate by seeing the artifacts as metaphors, observing patterns in imagery, creating a latticework of interwoven meanings, and associating them with the broader cultural traditions of the Paleolithic, Neolithic, High Neolithic, and Urban Revolution.

In mentioning the pre-Hispanic female figures in Venezuela, I am also calling attention to the fact that while the indigenous people of the Americas arrived in the Americas as Paleolithic people, they culturally evolved, in some places, into Neolithic cultures without any direct contact with Neolithic peoples from other continents. In many places, like Venezuela, they also independently developed the tradition of making female figurines. Of course, the Americas also independently spawned their own High Neolithic and Urban Revolution cultures, suggesting that such cultural developments are an inevitable function of technological sophistication, population density, and necessity.

Marija Gimbutas (1989) describes the multiple functions of the goddess in European prehistory and emphasizes the point that fertility is only one of her functions (p. 316). These prehistoric female representations are not all mother goddesses or even mothers. Many emphasize other aspects of the feminine, such as the lady of the beasts, the death wielder, and the giver of crafts. As giver of crafts, the goddess was associated with both pottery and weaving.

Pottery was discovered at different times in different parts of the world, but it typically flourished in the Neolithic. Pottery provided our Neolithic ancestors with fireproof cooking vessels, watertight containers, and a medium for artistic expression. Psychoanalysts have long associated the manipulation of clay and mud with the exploratory play of toddlers who in the anal stage manipulate their own feces. When children and adults play or work in clay, we see it as the sublimation of anal concerns.

This sort of play is quite clearly a creative process of putting something together, getting something together, or giving form to the formless. In addition to the creative element associated with any work in clay is the fact that it is often used to create pots, vessels, or containers of one sort or another. As such, it reminds us of the creative, fertile, life-giving, and transformative womb. It is both the womb from which one is born and the womb to which one dies. Not surprisingly, burial urns were subsequently fashioned from fired ceramic clay in the form of graceful pots and sometimes in the form of houses.

When I visited the seminomadic Hoti in the Venezuelan jungles, they were in the process of modernizing. While most of their ways of living were probably quite similar to how they had been for thousands of years, the Hoti had replaced clay pots with aluminum and plastic containers. Nonetheless, they maintained the use of ceramics when making their pots for containing the poison *curare* for their blowgun darts.

Karl Abraham (1920/1927a) described a patient who reported not having a bowel movement for two days and then dreaming of the need "to expel the universe out of his anus" (p. 320). Abraham associated this clinical anecdote with cosmogonies, or creation myths, in which God is said to have created man by fashioning him out of a lump of dirt or a piece of clay. In an ancient Persian cosmogony from the 9th century BCE, the cosmos is derived from the body of a demon named Kuni, which means "anus" (Lincoln, 1986, p. 9).

Weaving and the Fabric of Reality

With the cultivation and harvesting of fibrous plants and the domestication of sheep and goats came the Neolithic invention of the spindle, the loom, and the textile arts. In the textile arts, the spindle holds the significance of a creative center. By spinning on its own axis, the spindle gathers together the chaotic strands or fibers and draws them into a well-defined and durable thread.

When enough thread had been created and wound around a thin stick, it was set on the loom and the process of weaving began. In some traditions spinning is associated with destiny, thread with time, cutting the thread with death, and weaving with the fabric of reality.

The Fall from Grace

One aspect of the shift from the Paleolithic to the Neolithic has a frankly mysterious quality to it that cannot be explained well but also must not be ignored. It is that the beautiful polychromatic, graceful, aesthetically pleasing, dynamic cave paintings of the Paleolithic convey dreaminess and three-dimensionality, while the drawings of the Neolithic are typically schematic stick figures drawn with far less artistic sophistication. In fact, there were techniques of three-dimensional painting that were practiced in the Paleolithic, subsequently lost for the next 10,000 years, and rediscovered only in the Renaissance. I am referring specifically to how the legs on the far side of a quadruped, presented in profile, would be drawn with a space between the top of the leg and the body of the animal's thorax. Aesthetically this does not give the impression of a leg floating in space but rather of the leg being on the far side of the body.

It is difficult to contemplate the nature of Paleolithic life and the aesthetics of Paleolithic art without resorting to romantic illusions like the Garden of Eden, Paradise, and the peace of pristine Homo sapiens living as we were meant to live before all the clutter of culture, civilization, and modernization reduced us to the neurotic alienated beasts we have become. But we know too much now to allow ourselves such illusions. Paleolithic life was difficult. The elements of nature were harsh, the megafauna were deadly, technology was minimal, and our Paleolithic ancestors living in small bands were probably quite often at war with other bands. No, the Paleolithic was no Paradise, no Garden of Eden, and yet psychologically and culturally our Paleolithic ancestors were living a life embedded in nature. The past could not be subdivided into units of time, and the future could not be imagined as anything but a sacred repetition, an eternal return.

To live in the Paleolithic was to live in cosmic space and cosmic time, where "here" was the center of the universe and "now" was the only moment there was. To enter into the Neolithic was to enter demarcated space and circular or seasonal time. This is an overstatement. In the Paleolithic, our ancestors traveled far and wide; in fact, they made their way out of Africa to Europe, Asia, Australia, and the Americas. They probably learned a good bit about the seasons and following the migration of the beasts as well. But, relatively speaking, our Paleolithic ancestors were more embedded in nature, had more primitive technology, and lived further outside of circular time and segmented space than their Neolithic descendants. Thus, the passage from the Paleolithic to the Neolithic was something of a rupture of the unity with nature, a de-integration, a fall from grace.

With the oral stage associated with the Paleolithic, the anal stage with the Neolithic, and the genital stage with the Urban Revolution, we can now wonder about the ontogenetic phallic stage and latency phase and the phylogenetic High Neolithic. In the next section, we will see if we can find any analogical linkages between the phallic stage and latency phase on the one hand and the High Neolithic on the other.

The chart below summarizes "the points of agreement" or analogous relations I have been suggesting so far between the stages in ontogenetic (psychological) development and stages in phylogenetic (cultural) evolution. Each set lists a stage in psychosexual development, an associated psychopathology, an analogous stage in cultural evolution, a mythic analogue, and a ritual analogue. The gaps in the third set, pertaining to the phallic stage and latency phase of development and the cultural stage of the High Neolithic are what I will address in the next section.

Psychosexual development	Oral stage—early infancy
Psychopathology	Infantile autism
Cultural stage	Upper Paleolithic
Mythic analogue	Myth of death and rebirth
Ritual analogue	Ancient funerary ritual
Psychosexual development	Anal stage—toddler
Psychopathology	Obsessional neurosis
Cultural stage	Neolithic
Mythic analogue	Myth of Paradise and fall from grace; separation of the world opposites
Ritual analogue	Sacrifice and house-building ritual
Psychosexual development	Phallic stage and latency phase—Oedipal child
Psychopathology	?
Cultural stage	High Neolithic
Mythic analogue	?
Ritual analogue	?
Psychosexual development	Genital stage—adolescence
Psychopathology	Brief psychotic disorder
Cultural stage	Urban Revolution
Mythic analogue	Myth of sacral kingship
Ritual analogue	Ancient New Year festival

THE NEOLITHIC PERIOD AND THE ANAL STAGE OF LIBIDO DEVELOPMENT

This is oldest known village wall and tower. It is 11,500 years old and located in Jericho, now a Palestinian city in the West Bank.

The foundations of round houses excavated at the Neolithic settlement of Khirokitia, Cyprus.

The author with the owner of a round house in the Nepali Himalayas in 1983.
The old woman explained that there was no particular ritual to start building
the house but that she placed some jewelry under the center post.

THE NEOLITHIC PERIOD AND THE ANAL STAGE OF LIBIDO DEVELOPMENT

The author with the owner of a round house and two children in the Venezuelan jungles in 2009. The round house is in a Hoti village near the Upper Orinoco River.

Neo-Sumerian foundation peg of King Shulgi of Ur ca. 2094–2047 BCE. This finely worked metal artifact belongs to the Urban Revolution but as a foundation peg it is an example of the Neolithic tradition of house building rituals carried into successive levels of cultural sophistication.

Hoti village in the Venezuelan jungle.

THE NEOLITHIC PERIOD AND THE ANAL STAGE OF LIBIDO DEVELOPMENT

A modern day mud brick square house with a round cupola in Luxor, Egypt, not far from the Valley of the Kings.

A modern man making mud bricks for construction in Luxor, Egypt not far from the Valley of the Kings. The bricks are made in the same way they were made thousands of years ago with a mix on clay, sand, straw, and manure (probably from camels). A short distance from this site were archeological excavations of ancient homes built with the same types of bricks!

A modern Egyptian girl pulling out a loaf of flat bread from a mud oven in her home, near the Valley of the Kings in Luxor, Egypt.

A mud oven with a metal plate on top and a broom to the left. They were located in a Mako village in the Venezuelan jungles

Some Panare children in front of their house in the Venezuelan jungle.

Preparing for a Yanomami welcome dance in the Venezuelan jungle.

Yanomami welcome dance in the jungles of Venezuela. To the left, a girl wearing a traditional guayuco for females. It is a belt with a skirt of strings in the front.

Yanomami welcome dance in the jungles of Venezuela. The dancer is painted in black, wearing a red loin cloth, and brandishing a bow and arrow. The boy in the back dances with a palm frond.

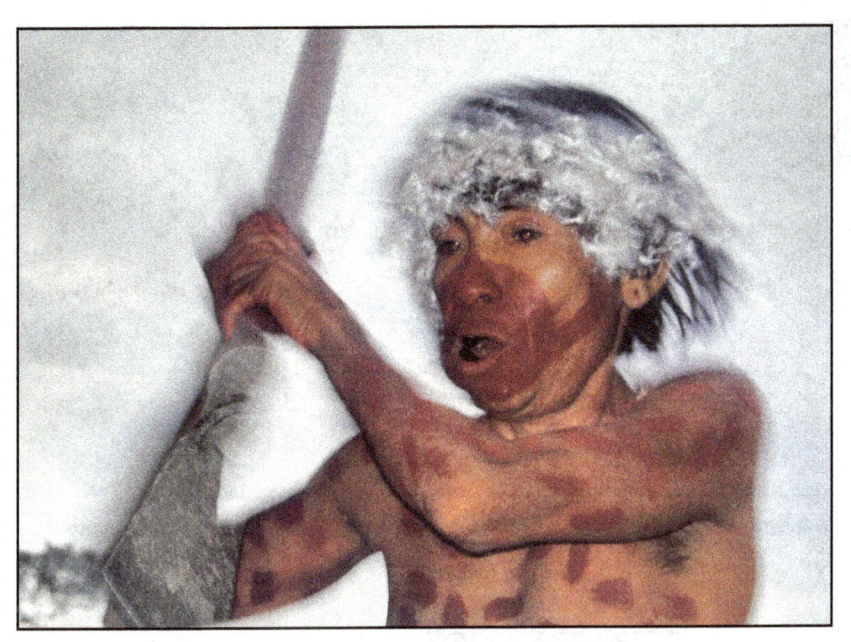

THE NEOLITHIC PERIOD AND THE ANAL STAGE OF LIBIDO DEVELOPMENT

Yanomami welcome dance in the Venezuelan jungle. This dancer is brandishing his weapon directly at the photographer (me) during the welcome dance. Notice the body paint, the huge wad of chewing tobacco in his mouth, and the white baby-vulture feathers in his hair.

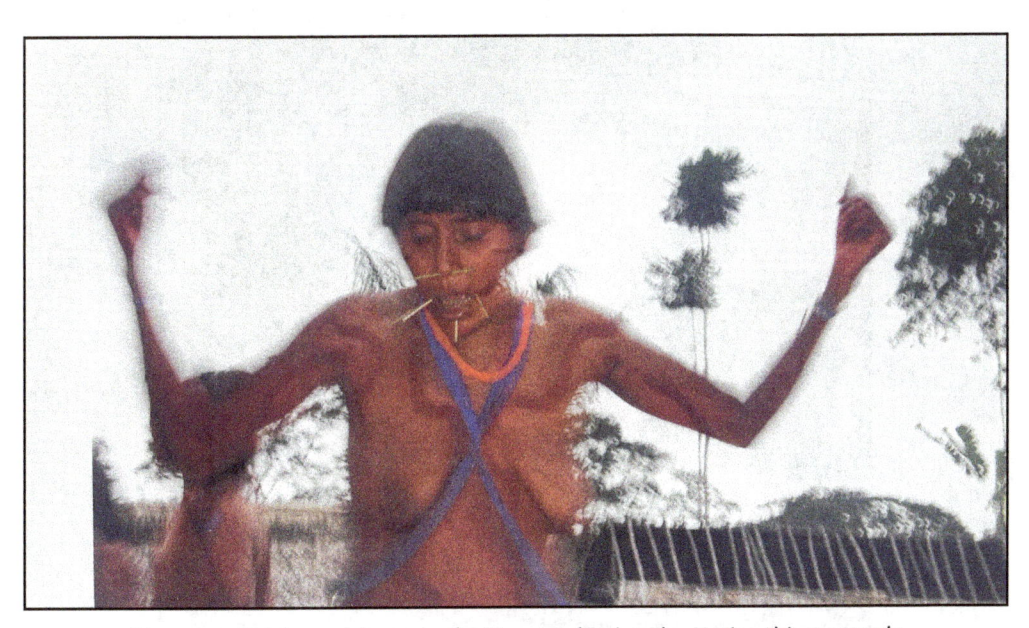

Yanomami welcome dance in the Venezuelan jungle. Notice this woman's body paint, and decorative sticks piercing her lips and nasal septum.

LIBIDO, CULTURE, AND CONSCIOUSNESS

A group photo taken after a Yanomami welcome dance. The author's wife, Adriana Prengler, and the author are seen in the back.

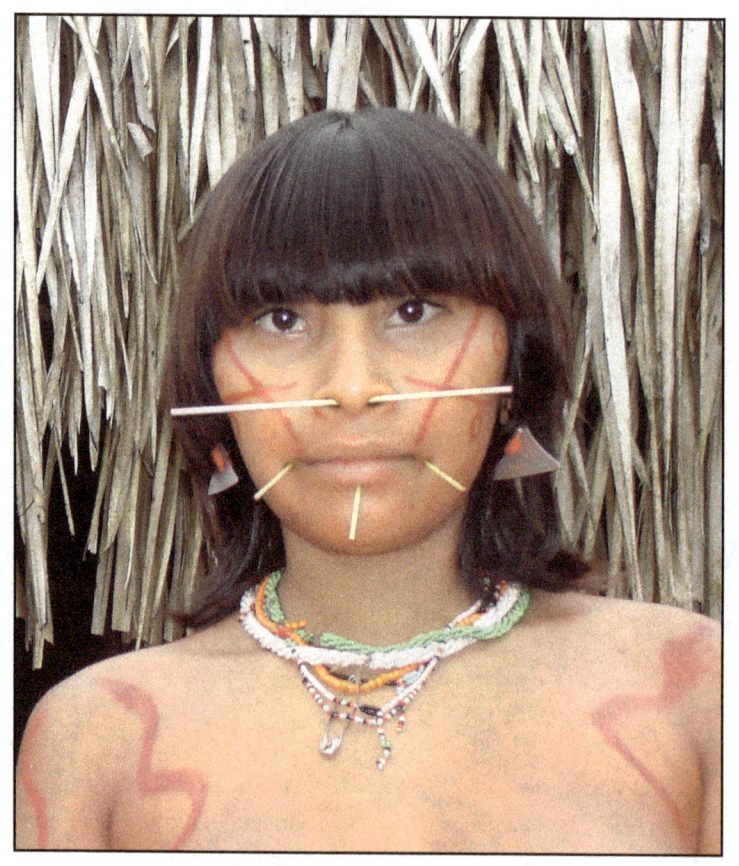

Yanomami woman with body paint, necklaces, earrings, and lip and nasal septum piercings.

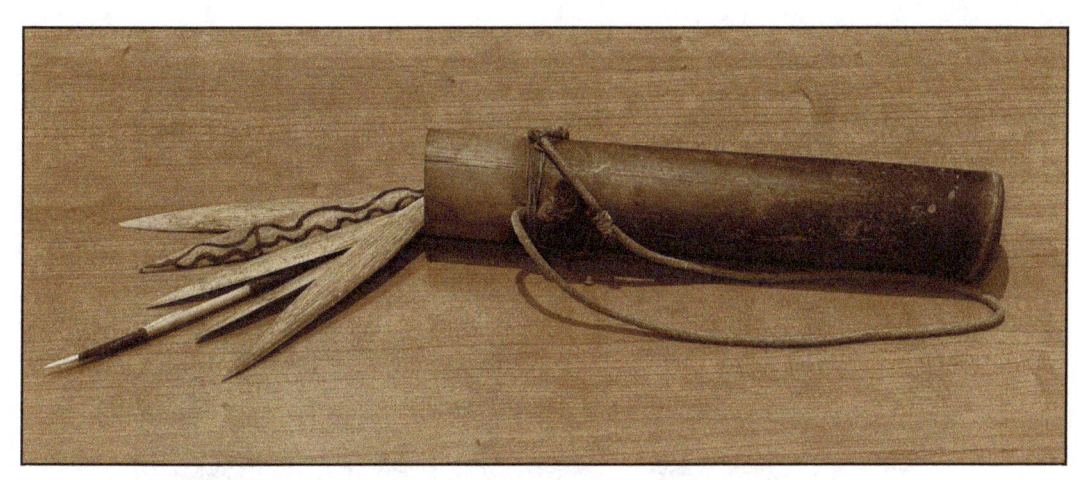

A bamboo quiver and arrow points, called rahaka. They are used by the Yanomami indigenous people in hunting and for trade. These particular rahaka, except for the painted one, are from the Wuirionave community. The painted rahaka was made by Delfin of the Merey community. Both communities are situated on the Rio Negro in Venezuela.

A small boy driving two bulls that pull a wooden plow through an agricultural field at the base of the Himalayas, near Pokhara, Nepal.

LIBIDO, CULTURE, AND CONSCIOUSNESS

Pre-Hispanic female figurines from the archipelago of Los Roques in Venezuela. This collection is from the archeological laboratory of María Magdalena Antczak and Andrzej Antczak at the Universidad Simón Bolívar in Caracas, Venezuela.

Pre-Hispanic Ceramic female figurine made in the style commonly found in the state of Lara, Venezuela. Between 1000–1600 ACE. Notice how the eyes, mouth and vulva are made in the "coffee bean" style.

Ceramic pregnant figurine from Pre-Hispanic Venezuela.
Found on the south side of the Peninsula La Cabrera at Lake Valencia, Venezuela.

A modern Egyptian boy demonstrating how to use a handmade
ceramic water jug near the Valley of the Kings in Luxor, Egypt.

Ceramic bowl from Pre-Hispanic Venezuela. Made in the style found in the state of Lara, Venezuela between 300-1400 ACE.

A ceramic bowl made by the modern Hoti indigenous people. It was used to hold the poison, curare, into which they dip their blow gun darts. Curare is a neurotoxic paste made from local native plants. The curare tipped darts are shot through a cerbatana, or blow gun, to kill birds and monkeys in the trees of the Venezuelan jungles.

Woman working a loom in front of a round house in the Nepali Himalayas.

A man wrapped in a wool blanket surrounded by his sheep in the Nepali Himalayas.

A Panare man with a basket of raw cotton in the Venezuelan jungle.

A spool of spun cotton in the rafters of a home
in a Panare village in the Venezuelan jungle.

Male and female guayucos (loin cloths) and string skirts on the right and female shoulder adornments on the left. Made from handspun cotton by the indigenous people of the upper Orinoco in Venezuela.

Piaroa swinging basket for a baby to rest in. It is positioned next to the wall of a mud and wood pole house in the Venezuelan jungle.

CHAPTER 7

The High Neolithic Period and the Phallic Stage of Libido Development

> We feel justified in analogizing the ego of the child with the hero of the myth, in view of the unanimous tendency of family romances and hero myths; keeping in mind that the myth throughout reveals an endeavor to get rid of the parents, and that the same wish arises in the fantasies of the individual child at the time when he is trying to establish his personal independence.
> —Otto Rank, *The Myth of the Birth of the Hero and Other Writings*

Between the Neolithic and the Urban Revolution is the High Neolithic, sometimes referred to as the Chalcolithic or Copper Age. It spans a period roughly from about 5,000 to about 7,000 years ago in Eurasia, but of course dates are relative and regional. We must remember that there were Paleolithic and Neolithic people living at the same time throughout history and some even into contemporary times. These would naturally include the San in Southern Africa, the Yanomami in Venezuela and Brazil, and the Dayaks in Borneo, but there were and still are many others. So when speaking of these general culture forms, we are speaking about a set of characteristics that are more or less shared across some cultures.

The High Neolithic describes Neolithic settlements with populations into the thousands. Large masses of people were put to work on ambitious projects building huge man-made hills, ditches, and other earthworks and setting up massive stone pillars as religious monuments. Slavery, which may have begun in the Neolithic or before, was also likely a part of the High Neolithic and implemented on a large scale. Fertility continued to be of great concern, but emphasis was shifting away from Mother Earth's bounty and deprivation to all the ways humans could control that bounty. They developed knowledge of the plants and animals, the life cycles of the crops, and their relation to the seasons of the year. They developed the knowledge and technology to smelt metal ores and make metal tools for agriculture and warfare.

The High Neolithic period was an agriculturally based nonliterate culture form that was anything but sedate. People relied on sacrifices, but it seems they appealed to more than the earth goddesses, as this was a time when the fertilizing storm gods of the sky were coming into ascendance. The High Neolithic was ambitious and energized, and the culture itself was situated between the life-giving and death-dealing mother goddesses and the powerful and fertilizing father gods. In other words, it was all about the Oedipus complex.

The Oedipus complex describes a triangular intrapsychic constellation of object relations involving the child's ego and the maternal and paternal introjects. It is supported by cognitive development and shaped by external family dynamics of the child and the mothering and fathering figures. It is through the oedipal dynamics of the child's love for one parent and efforts to get rid of the other parent that the child learns the factual and social implications of gender (male and female) and generational (adult and child) differences and thereby is socialized into his or her role in the family. When the child is prohibited from achieving satisfaction with the object of desire, the prohibition becomes installed in the psyche as society's laws, and so begins the accumulation of internal messages concerning external limits that form the basis of the superego.

The Oedipus complex is associated with what Freud called the phallic stage in libido development, when the site of libidinal gratification shifts, or rather expands, from the mouth and the anus to include and then focus on the genitals. The child becomes increasingly aware of genital sensations and demonstrates a sincere curiosity in his or her genitals and the genitals of others. Their curiosity leads them to ask questions and make comparisons. There is also a development of fantasies concerning the gratification of genital wishes directed toward one of the parents and a corresponding rivalry with the other parent. It is the ego's dance between desire and prohibition, between the id and the superego. And it is in this way that we recognize the Oedipus complex as the cornerstone of culture.

Oedipus as a Metaphor

There are many who are quite literal in their interpretation of the murderous and incestuous impulses of the Oedipus complex. This point of view finds support in clinical material and some news accounts of extreme behavior, but even small exceptions easily challenge this literal interpretation of the concept. I find it far more useful to think metaphorically about the Oedipus complex, as this enables us to recognize oedipal dynamics in a wide range of typical everyday activities. The first metaphors to consider are mothering and fathering—not the concrete mother or concrete father, who may or may not carry the metaphor, but the functions of mothering and fathering. Mothering is a metaphor for the feeding, nurturing, soothing, gratifying, and protecting of the baby. Fathering is a metaphor for the limit setting, disciplining, educating, and upholding of the traditions, laws, and institutions of society. With this metaphorical reading of mothering and fathering, we can see how each parent can be involved in both mothering and fathering, how a single mother can both mother and father her children, and how gay and lesbian parents can also mother and father their children.

Literal patricide is the killing of the father. Metaphorically, patricide is seen in the rejection and destruction of the laws and institutions of society as seen in delinquents, criminals, and authoritarian dictators. But patricide can also be a metaphor of triumphing over the father by learning the rules of society as they have been taught. It means learning the rules so well that one can beat the father at his own game, carry on the traditions that he taught, and then extend them. The child sharpens his or her skill in battle with the father until the father is vanquished and cannibalized in love. To lovingly cannibalize the father is to eat his teachings, internalize his values, take in his spirit, and carry forth in his name. The baton is passed. The king is dead; long live the new king.

Literal incest with the mother is having sex with one's mother. Metaphorically, mother incest is the gratification of prohibited desires all the way to the point of obliterating boundaries and losing oneself in unconsciousness (psychosis). But incest can also be a metaphor of the ego returning to the unconscious to retrieve something long lost and valuable—it is a regression in the service of the ego as in free association, introspection, or art. Incest, metaphorically speaking, is the ego dipping into the id.

Sophocles's play *Oedipus Rex*, about a man who kills his father and "marries" his mother, is a tragedy, as it is presented as a literal story. If we think metaphorically, however, the Oedipus complex can end in tragedy when a person grows up to destroy the laws and institutions of society, loses his boundaries, and drowns in his hallucinations of gratification. Another metaphorical reading would be killing the father to become the father, internalizing his teachings, and carrying them forth another generation; diving into the depths, regressing in the service of the ego in order to meet the muse and retrieving something important from unconsciousness in order to establish sexual stability or creativity. As my mentor Nathan Adler used to say, "The Oedipus complex is a metaphor for socialization."

According to legend, Laius sexually abused a boy and learned from the oracle that because of this crime his next child born was destined to kill him. When his only son, Oedipus, was born, Laius had him taken out on the hillside to be killed, but Oedipus was saved from this fate and given to a couple who raised him to adulthood, and the rest of the story is well known. The intent of Laius was infanticide, which happens often enough even in our modern era. Metaphorically speaking, both infanticide and castration mean the killing of the child's joyfulness and creativity, which is a common result of poor parenting strategies and inadequate educational systems. The positive metaphor of infanticide is initiation into the adult group in which the child dies, making way for the adult to be born. And the positive metaphor of castration is socialization. While the penis is an organ, the phallus is a metaphor for social power. That being the case, both men and women are vulnerable to castration, with both its destructive and prosocial consequences. We are all castrated and socialized on the sharp edge of the word "no." To clarify, we find union and oneness in the word "yes," but "no" is how limits are set and relationships defined.

There is debate over the timing of the Oedipus complex. It is traditionally associated with the small child between the ages of 2 ½ and 6 years, but others have found evidence for precursors of the Oedipus complex in early infancy when the infant demonstrates a recognition of differences, a differential treatment of the parents, triangular relations, meaning making, castration anxiety in relation to weaning, and the use of symbols or protosymbolic behavior.

While there are interesting implications in these alternative timelines of Freud's theory, for our purposes here I find it useful to maintain Freud's timeline and description, as it is the 2 ½-year-old who quite obviously discovers his or her genitals and genital difference, openly falls in love with one parent, and demonstrates a rivalry with the other. The Oedipus complex is an intrapsychic and interpersonal dynamic involving the conflict between desires and prohibitions. A healthy resolution is marked by an identification with a parent, the renunciation of the incestuous object of desire, the shift of desire to an age-appropriate peer, and the internalization of society's prohibitions as a benign and helpful superego. The 5-year-old falls in love with a parent, and the 15-year-old falls in love with a peer. The male, female, heterosexual, and homosexual Oedipus complexes are variations on the oedipal themes and are distinguished by the gender, parental identification, and object choice of the child.

In libido development, the phallic stage is followed by the latency phase, in which the child sublimates libido into new arenas of worldly interest. The sublimation, or transformation, of libido is directed toward the development of sex roles; intellectual understandings; physical prowess; and the acquisition of culturally valued knowledge, skills, and social roles. In other words, the preoccupations with the erogenous zones become metaphorized and sublimated into social pursuits.

When I link the High Neolithic with the phallic stage, I do so on the basis of the ambition and fierce struggle evident in both, the shared interest in phallic imagery, and in the way culture situates itself between the goddess and the god and the child situates himself or herself between the mother and the father. But when we come to the latency phase, we meet an interesting problem.

Although Sándor Ferenczi (1913/1956) associated the latency phase with the Ice Age climate change and its scarcity of food (pp. 201–202), I find his reasoning weak. In fact, I find no link between the latency phase and any cultural stage. These analogies between libido development and cultural evolution do have their limits, and on further consideration we are not surprised that there is no cultural analogy to the latency phase, as it is not a stage in libido development but rather a phase when the cathexis shifts from an interest in the body to sublimated interests in culture. There is no particular stage in cultural evolution when the libido is being sublimated, because all of culture is sublimated libido. Consequently, the latency phase has no representation as a stage in cultural evolution.

❖ ❖ ❖

If one looks at the hundreds of different Native American tribal peoples in North and South America, one sees a panorama of cultural sophistication from Paleolithic cultures to Urban Revolution cultures. In some places, such as the San Francisco Bay Area, indigenous people thrived as Paleolithic hunter-gatherers. The weather was mild and food was plentiful. San Francisco was teeming with bears, deer, and elk. The rivers were full of fish and the bay full of whales, seals, and elephant seals. The coasts were crowded with sea life and easy-to-catch seabirds. There was simply no need to develop an elaborate technology and the people didn't.

In other areas, however, challenging weather conditions, increasing population sizes, and developing technology gave rise to Neolithic farming communities; sprawling High Neolithic cultures; and even the Mayan, Aztec, and Incan civilizations (Urban Revolution). There were some well-elaborated High Neolithic cultures from the Great Lakes region down the Mississippi and into the south. It is there that we find large earthworks—earthen monuments—which required large populations, tremendous social organization, and great efforts by many people over long periods of time to build temple mounds, which offered no direct practical or economic return.

Large Earthworks and Ambition

The large earthworks of the High Neolithic are sacred monuments, but they are also monuments to human ambition. They are handmade hills, mounds, ditches, embankments, and circles of earth requiring the intensive labor of many people over many years of digging and dumping soil from here to there to create economically nonproductive sacred sites. They were used as hill temples, burial mounds, or even large earth structures in the shape of animals, which may have had some ceremonial, initiatory, or totemic significance.

In Cahokia, Illinois, there is a 5-square-mile prehistoric complex of earthworks with Monk's Mound as the center of the complex of circles, mounds, and pyramids. Monk's

Mound is a man-made pyramidal earthwork that is 236 by 291 meters at its base and about 30 meters high. It is made of soil and clay in a pyramidal shape with two terraces and a flat top, which once supported a 5,000-square-foot temple. It is as wide at its base as the largest pyramid in Egypt.

Also associated with this site are 200 earthwork mounds, tombs, and ceremonial platforms. They were the achievements of a community of 50,000 people who thrived between 1000 and 1300 ACE. To the west of Monk's Mound are remnants of a woodhenge—that is, a circle of wood posts—which may have had astronomical and cosmological significance. Cahokia was preceded by more modest mounds along the Mississippi River built as far back as 3500 BCE. Some of the mounds and buildings "were deliberately aligned to reference the rising and setting full moons on a complicated 18.6 year lunar cycle" (Wright, 2010, p. 68). Karen Wright reported that archeologist Tom Emerson found "an eight-inch statuette at the site of a temple two or three miles from Cahokia. Five pounds of a distinctive red stone called flint clay had been carved into a kneeling female figure sinking a hoe into the back of a serpent. The serpent's tail has split in two and is climbing up the woman's back, bearing squash or gourds like a vine. The images echo familiar pre-Colombian themes of reproductive and agricultural fertility" (p. 68). Similar figures were found at Cahokia itself.

During the course of excavations in the late 1960s, 250 burial remains were found at Cahokia:

> One middle-age male appeared to have worn a cape studded with 20,000 seashell beads arranged in the shape of a bird. Near him were the bones of six other people, a cache of more than 800 flint arrowheads, a rolled-up sheet of copper, and several bushels of unprocessed mica—all seemingly placed in tribute to the Beaded Bird-man. (p. 68)

> In other parts of the mound, skeletons of more than 100 young women clearly indicate human sacrifice, another grouping of four men with no hands or heads suggest that they too died as part of a ritual. (p. 69)

At Moundville, Alabama, there are 20 such earthworks, including one that is 17 meters high. The Serpent Mound in Adams County, Ohio, is 1 meter high, 4.5-6 meters wide, 400 meters long, and shaped like a snake (G. Clark, 1977, pp. 383-408). There are literally thousands of mounds in the eastern half of the United States. Some are like small hills, ridges, or in the shapes of animals.

In Peru, one also sees earthworks in the form of the low-relief Nazca Lines. These are lines of piled-up rocks next to lines of clearings from which the rocks were gathered. Imagine, if you will, a sandy flat desert with rocks evenly dispersed across the landscape. If one were to clear a space by moving the rocks aside and into a line, one would end up with something similar to what we see with the Nazca Lines—cleared spaces next to rocks piled into lines. They are not anywhere near as high as the earthworks I have been describing, but the lengths and widths of the drawings, designs, and lines are enormous. Their purpose is poorly understood but generally seen as having some sort of religious significance related to astronomy and the Nazca people's cosmology. Some of the Nazca Lines are straight lines or trapezoids, and others are in shapes drawn from nature, such as a spider, a bird, a lizard, a monkey, a flower, and a tree. These are huge "drawings" made out of piles of rock spread out across 3,900 square kilometers of southern Peru. The images are so large (as much as 200 meters across) and so spread out that it is difficult to identify them from the ground. From the air, however, their animal shapes are quite obvious. They were constructed between 800 and 1,200 years ago (Hall, 2010, pp. 2-23).

In 2010 satellite imagery of deforested sections of the Amazon revealed 200 earth mounds and ditches in the shape of circles and squares dating back to between 200 and 1283 ACE. The ditches are 10 meters wide, a meter deep, and lined by banks rising up another meter. The circles range from 100 to 300 meters in diameter. Anthropologist, Denise Schaan, said, "They were probably villages, ceremonial centers, gathering places and point to a society of a complex nature. Indeed, to build these structures you need organization, planning, and a large labor force. Amazingly this suggests that quite [a] substantial population was living in an area long believed to be too harsh to sustain permanent settlements" (Lorenzi, 2010, p. 1). Schaan and her colleagues estimate the regional population at 60,000. She also said there may be another 2,000 such structures hidden under the dense forest canopy. Since 2012 technological advances have revolutionized archeology with enhanced aerial views (Lidar) that can see through the forest canopy and have revealed thousands of previously unknown archeological sites.

The Stone Phallus

Large ancient stone monuments, for whatever reason they may have been built, are found in Polynesia, Japan, and India; in Malta, Bulgaria, Portugal, the northwest coast of France, Germany, Denmark, England, Scotland, Italy, Scandinavia, and Ireland. Some of the best known of these monuments are the great statues of Easter Island, 1,250-1,500 years old. And there are large menhirs sculpted to clearly resemble penises near Villa de Leyva in Colombia that are 2,200 years old.

On the one hand we cannot ascribe the same meaning to all of them, as they occur in different cultural contexts and at different times, but they were all the work of High Neolithic cultures, and, as Colin Renfrew (1981/1983) stated, with regard to the megaliths (large stones) of Western Europe, "The evidence is clear that many of them relate to the disposal of the dead, but we need not assume that this was their primary purpose.... If the megaliths do not represent a unitary phenomenon, they can hardly be approached with a single, specific explanation" (p. 9).

It was in Europe that the earthworks and the megalithic tradition reached extraordinary heights. It is there that we see huge stones erected in circles and in lines. Single tall stones, known as *menhirs*, stand as imposing phallic monuments. In other locations, several massive stones form "table legs," of sorts, for a massive flattish stone placed on top. These table-like monuments are called *dolmens*. Other megalithic monuments form deep tombs embedded in the earth that were used for hundreds of years.

Menhirs are typically large uncut stones, and in northern Italy menhirs have been found with incised images of axes, daggers, and men driving cattle pulling plows. In Corsica, menhirs have crudely carved faces at their tops and daggers or knives carved in the middle (Whitehouse, 1981/1983, pp. 54-56). David Trump (1981/1983), describing the megalithic architecture of temples and tombs in Malta, draws attention to the unmistakable carved statues of corpulent women, some of which are very small and others of enormous proportions. Suggesting they might be mother goddesses but resisting that assertion, he wrote, "Despite the hesitation, the underlying idea of fertility symbolism remains probable, and receives unequivocal support from other finds, particularly from Tarxien. There a wall relief shows a very male bull and a very female sow, with no less than fourteen piglets at suck, immediately adjacent. This site has, too, produced several indubitable carved phalli" (p. 71).

The European megalithic sites are considered burial sites and cult centers requiring large numbers of highly organized groups of people to construct them. After surveying the intentional burials with evidence of funerary rites in the Paleolithic and the evidence of sacrifice in the Neolithic, we can't be too surprised by a spiritual life involving the dead and perhaps intertwined with fertility magic in the High Neolithic. What we have here is a stratigraphy of religious ideas. On the bottom, Paleolithic layer, we find the concept of the soul, the funerary rite, the implied myth of death and rebirth, and the mother goddess figurines. In the next layer up, the Neolithic, we find evidence of sacrifice and the tradition of the mother goddess continuing. In the third layer, the High Neolithic, we find that a new idea is the emerging importance of the phallus in fertility and perhaps even a father god or sky god.

Southern England is full of magnificent megalithic sites. They include long barrows, round barrows (burial mounds), large earthwork circles, man-made hills, causeways, and the henge monuments. The long barrows are communal Neolithic tombs built into the earth using massive boulders. The round barrows, which are individual tombs, appeared as a new tradition 4,500 years ago when immigrants crossed the North Sea from Holland and the Rhineland. They brought with them the tradition of individual burials in round mounds, and buried with the dead were ceramic drinking vessels (beakers) and, sometimes, copper knives and bows and arrows. These immigrants, referred to as the "Beaker people," brought a new individualizing influence to the burial of the dead and also a knowledge of how to work copper and gold.

The earthwork circles were composed of large mounds of earth forming concentric rings of deep troughs and hill ridges with a large open space in the middle, believed to have been used as a ceremonial center. Most man-made hills are the small round barrows, but Silbury Hill, near Avebury in the English county of Wiltshire, is an enormous man-made hill, 40 meters high, whose purpose has never been determined, and no burials have ever been found there. Causeways (long lines of large stones) presumably directed people to and from the various religious centers. And the henge monuments (circles of stone pillars or wood posts) appear to have been ceremonial centers drawing people from all around the region for important religious events.

A Neolithic and High Neolithic site at nearby Windmill Hill had over 1,000 years of occupation (4,000–5,700 years ago) and has remnants of Neolithic barrows, Bronze Age barrows, and a large circular earthwork ditch and hill ridge 300 meters in diameter. Excavations revealed extensive evidence of farming, including the cultivation of wheat, barley, and flax and the domestication of cattle, sheep, goats, and pigs. Their technology included antler hoes, flint sickles, grinding stones, flint axes, ceramics, and, with the coming of the Beaker People, metal tools. Faith de M. Vatcher and Lance Vatcher (1976) described an excavation at Windmill Hill where they found the burial of two young children carefully placed in a crouched position. Also discovered were "pieces of carved chalk, fragments of figurines, phalli, blocks incised with crossing lines and rudimentary designs and pendants with a hole in the center" (pp. 17-18), all of which may have had a religious or superstitious significance.

It is interesting that the phalli appear at the same time as the menhirs, the metal tools, and the further development of plant and animal domestication. Fertility seems to be the dominating concern, and it is not the parthenogenic fertility of the Paleolithic mother goddess, but a new kind of fertility—a fertility that consciously involves a father and the penis.

The West Kennet Long Barrow is the largest of its kind in England and Wales. It was built 5,250 years ago and was in use for 1,000 years. The outer earthwork barrow is 100 meters long, but the inner chamber is not more than 12 meters deep and at points 2.4 meters high, built of large stones one next to the other. Looking at the floor plan from above, one can see that the shape is like a child's drawing of a tree, with a main central hall where the trunk would be, two large round chambers near the base, two slightly smaller ones above it, and one round chamber at the top. This is a fairly typical European tomb pattern, which some have seen as a stylized mother goddess with a head, two large breasts, and two larger hips. Gimbutas (1989) describes this pattern in a section subtitled "The Tomb Is Womb" (p. 151). The remains of 46 individuals were found at West Kennet, and included with them were grave goods such as pottery, animal or meat bones, stone tools, and beads made of stone, bone, and shell. Vatcher and Vatcher asked, "Over a thousand years and only forty-six people for sure, of whom over a dozen were children—who were they? Were they the families of successive chieftains, or were they a dynasty? Had they died in a certain way, or for a special reason? What were the qualifications needed to earn a place at West Kennet? This we shall never know" (p. 24).

These are big questions, but the Vatchers give us the impression that it may actually be an honor to be entombed in West Kennet. I am not so sure. It turns out that 12 of the bodies were children, almost all the adults suffered from arthritis, and several had spina bifida to varying degrees. And then there is the one intact skeleton in the tomb—an elderly man crouched on his right side and lying on a rock platform: "One arm bore evidence of a fracture, there had been a large abscess on one shoulder, a deformity of each of the large toes, and a leaf arrowhead in the throat" (p. 21). Are we looking at yet another sacrifice? In fact, I wonder if all of those buried at West Kennet were victims of sacrifice.

At Avebury one finds an avenue marked off with megaliths. It may have been built for semireligious purposes, such as processions. At one end are a number of concentric circles of depressions in the ground and other indicators giving evidence that these were circles of postholes and that a large ceremonial round house used to stand there: "At the foot of four of the stones in the restored part of the Avenue graves were found" (p. 34).

When we consider the menhirs, phalli, and carvings of daggers and plows, it is easy to see how we can associate the High Neolithic with the phallic stage of libido development. But the phallic stage is not just about penises; it's about the child's discovery of sexual differences, the implications of those differences, the primal scene, and the mysteries of sexuality. So perhaps we should also be seeing the circle mounds, circles of stones, the avenues of stone, and the tomb wombs as representations of vulvas, vaginas, and wombs.

The most famous of all the megalithic monuments is the extraordinary set of concentric circles of stone pillars known as Stonehenge, which is generally thought to be a prehistoric temple or religious center. Stonehenge, located on the Salisbury Plain in England, is one of scores of megalithic sites, henges, avenues, barrows, and earthworks in the region. Stonehenge was in active construction, use, and development from 4,800 years ago until about 3,500 years ago. The outer circular earthwork trough and mound, which marks off the whole site, is 91 meters in diameter and was built 4,800 years ago. The main stones were put in place 4,000 years ago. When the outer circular bank and ditch were constructed, a series of holes were made inside this earthwork ring. The holes are known as the Aubrey Holes. These holes are about 1 meter in diameter, 1 meter deep, and dug into the chalky soil. Cremated human bones were buried in smaller holes and "probably represent some kind of magical or religious ceremony, of which we shall never know the details" (Atkinson, 1978, p. 19; Atkinson, 1980, p. 4).

In the main circle (the Sarsen Circle), there were originally 30 upright stones, each weighing about 25 tons, with lintels laid on top, each of those weighing an additional 7 tons. The heaviest stone weighs 50 tons. These were brought from a site 30 kilometers away and pulled with ropes by literally hundreds of men using heavy sleds and a system of log rollers and river rafts. Richard J. C. Atkinson says the transport of 80 sarsen stones probably required the dedicated work of 1,000 men over several years. Carved into one stone is a stylized image recognized as a mother goddess; three other stones feature full-size carvings of daggers and axe heads. At Stonehenge and other Late Neolithic and Early Bronze Age stone circle sites throughout Britain, the stones were set up in a way to align with the rising and setting sun and moon on specific days, such as the equinoxes (Atkinson, 1978, pp. 15–28). So in addition to worshiping the fertility of the earth, our High Neolithic ancestors were beginning to pay attention to the fertilizing role of the sky, the sun, and the moon. Four "Station Stones" were set up on the circle "at the corners of a rectangle, the short sides of which point to the rising sun at midsummer and the setting sun at midwinter, and the long sides to the most southerly rising and most northerly setting of the moon. The latter events occur only once every 18 ½ years" (Atkinson, 1980, p. 10). On visiting Stonehenge in 1983, I was impressed not only by the ancient majesty of this outdoor temple but also by the great number of crude flint tools littering the ground in the plowed fields nearby.

About 115 dagger engravings have been found at Stonehenge, and they have been dated to 1750–1500 BCE (Abbott & Anderson-Whymark, 2012, p. 20). In addition, 900 other stone circles have been found in the British Isles (Atkinson, 1980, p. 11).

Not far from Stonehenge is Woodhenge, a large circular earthwork bank and ditch and a series of concentric rings of holes, indicating that there were wooden posts in them that probably held up a large, circular ceremonial temple in the form of a doughnut. The earthwork was built around 4,300 years ago. Atkinson (1978) noted, "Near the center there was a grave containing the body of a three-year-old child whose skull had been split before burial (now marked by a small cairn of flints). This was perhaps a dedicatory burial, and is one of the very few pieces of evidence for human sacrifice in Neolithic Britain" (p. 34).

Another site not far from Stonehenge is called the Cursus. It was built in the Late Neolithic. It is an earthwork bank and ditch in the shape of a rubber band stretched between two fingers and is 800 meters long by 90 meters wide. There are a number of such earthworks in southern and eastern England: "Their purpose is unknown; but their unusual shape suggests that they were ceremonial or religious enclosures, intended perhaps for processions or for ritual races connected with honoring the dead ancestors" (Atkinson, 1978, p. 13). The possibility of "ritual races" allows us to speculate on ritual competition, ritual sport, and the mythical heroic battle against the forces of chaos.

Metallurgy and the Fires of Passion

For our Lower and Middle Paleolithic ancestors, fire was like nothing else in the world. It is easy to imagine that it would be seen as a mysterious force of nature, a spirit or ghost. Animals of all kinds avoid fire, except the hominins. Lightning strikes, the spontaneous combustion of decaying plant matter, and volcanic activity can all initiate a fire. There is evidence of the opportunistic use of fire in the Lower Paleolithic, and it may have included the eating of a burned animals caught in a wildfire or the purposeful insertion of pieces of meat in the path of a burning field. The controlled use of fire came next.

Hearths became commonplace in the Middle Paleolithic, 100,000 years ago. They were used for lighting, cooking, warming the habitation site, and for community gathering. While making flint tools, our ancestors discovered that when one rock hit another, sparks flew and kindled dry grass. And while working with wood, they discovered that boring a hole in a board by spinning a stick on its axis created a heat intense enough to ignite a flame. In time, these two forms of fire lighting became metaphors for the primary passions of aggression (one rock hitting another, causing sparks to fly) and sex (a vertical phallic stick boring into a horizontally situated vaginal notch in a piece of wood). In the Neolithic, fire technology transformed the hearth into an oven for cooking and the oven into a kiln for firing ceramics. In the High Neolithic, the kiln was transformed into a forge for smelting copper, lead, tin, iron, bronze, silver, and gold. The development of fire technology moved from wildfire, to hearth, to oven, to kiln, to forge.

In the High Neolithic, the smelting of ores, the amalgamation of different metals, and the casting of metal objects became a sophisticated technology that gave new meaning to aesthetic adornment, made farming implements more effective, and dramatically transformed warfare.

In the Near East, metallurgy began and then flourished between 7,200 and 8,500 years ago. A typical cooking fire burns between 1,100 degrees and 1,300 degrees Fahrenheit. To properly smelt copper oxide ore, one needs a furnace burning at 2,000 degrees. Approximately 5,200 years ago, copper was being extracted from a closed kiln, with the ore and the fuel in separate compartments. Later still, with the invention of the bellows, temperatures inside the kiln rose to 3,000 degrees, enabling our High Neolithic ancestors to smelt virtually all of the metals available to them, including iron (Knauth, 1974, pp. 36, 37, 41).[1]

Before metallurgy our prehistoric ancestors lived much of their lives in relation to stones: stone tools, stone shelters, stone caves, stone amulets, dolmens, stone circles, menhirs, and so on. Then the metallurgist appeared, and when he worked the stone, he did so with a power previously thought to belong only to the gods: the power to smelt metal ore, to transform stone into a godlike substance. A piece of metal in a world of rocks was seen as something very different. It is hard as stone, does not break, is malleable and shines. To move the earth, displace a massive boulder, or smelt metal ore was to behave like the gods and make the world anew. Our ancestors in the High Neolithic were Prometheans stealing the fire of the gods.

While most of the ambassadors of the ancient Paleolithic and Neolithic come to us as dusty old bones, Ötzi, or the Iceman, is a High Neolithic ambassador who comes to us as flesh and bone. Though he died about 5,300 years ago, he was discovered only in 1991 by some hikers in the Ötzal Alps on the Italian border near Austria. Ötzi, a male in his mid-40s, was found on a patch of ice and snow that was defrosting for the first time in thousands of years. He wears a robe made of animal skins, a fur stitched together, and a grass cloak. He has tattoos of blue lines on his lower spine, stripes on his right ankle, and a cross behind his left knee. He wears bearskin shoes stuffed with grass and carries a deerskin quiver, wooden arrows with flint points and balance feathers, a wooden pole from which he would make a longbow, a bark container for holding burning embers, a wood-handled flint-tipped dagger, and, interestingly enough, a copper-bladed axe with a wooden handle and leather bindings. The axe is such a fine piece of copper work that it may mean he was a man of distinction in his group. He carries what appears to have been an amulet in the form of a small round circlet of stone through which was tied a tassel of leather strips (Hall, 2007, pp. 68-81; Jaroff, 1992, pp. 62-66; Roberts, 1993, pp. 36-67). He also carries inside him the flint tip of an arrowhead near his left shoulder. It was shot into him from behind and cut his subclavian artery, from which he bled to death (Hall, 2007, pp. 68-81). Ötzi was murdered!

---

1 In China and South America, metallurgy is predominantly associated with the Urban Revolution. When it developed in China, 5,000 years ago, in the Shang dynasty they had a well-developed technology for smelting and casting fine bronze pieces (Knauth, 1974, pp. 36, 37, 41). In South America, stonework was the highly developed technology, and metallurgy, when it appeared, was focused primarily on silver and gold used for ornamentation (p. 127).

Imagining Our Way into the High Neolithic

Addressing the megalithic cultures, Mircea Eliade (1958b) built a latticework of meaningful connections between archeological evidence, anthropological observation, and the study of comparative religion. He tells us that among the Gonds of Central India, for example, there is a tradition that after a man dies, his son or heir must place at his tomb a large stone 9 or 10 feet high (pp. 217-18): "The burial stone thus became the means of protecting life against death. The soul 'dwelt' in the stone as, in other cultures, it dwelt in the tomb—looked on, similarly, as a 'dead man's house.' The funeral megalith protected the living against possible harmful action by the dead; for death as a state of indetermination, made possible certain influences, both good and bad" (p. 219).

We could say that, psychologically speaking, this state of indetermination needed to be defended against if the persecutory fantasies were to become overpowering. The mythic idea is that the dead person is not dead at all, but still alive and possibly dangerous. However, the deceased is made inoffensive through ritual. The myth denies the death, and the ritual protects the survivors from the deceased. Psychologically speaking the ritual undoes the guilt, persecutory fantasies, and death wishes of the survivors. Could this contemporary Indian tradition of establishing a funeral megalith have something to do with the ancient megaliths on the Salisbury Plain?

Also in India, young couples pray to the megaliths in order to have children. In southern India, women rub themselves against the rocks to make themselves fertile and fruitful. They do something similar in Australia. The childless Native American Maidu women of Northern California touch a rock shaped like a pregnant woman to make them fertile. In New Guinea and Madagascar, they smear a stone with grease having the same intention (Eliade, 1958b, p. 220). In Europe, sterile women used to slide on stones to help them conceive: "Even as late as 1923, country women who came to London used to clasp the pillars of St. Paul's Cathedral to make them have children" (pp. 222-23). The stones also offer the safe delivery of babies, good health, and so on. Worship of the supreme being of the sky among many African tribes includes the use of menhirs and sacred stones (p. 220). In many places, meteorites are signs of fertility (p. 226).

Mircea Eliade (1956/1978b) explained that the potter, smelter, smith, and alchemist are all masters of fire and involved in the magico-religious work of the transformation, perfection, and transmutation of matter (pp. 8, 9, 79). Examining the data of many traditions, he drew connections between the phenomena of meteorites, thunder, and lightning. Metal-based meteorites came from the sky and slammed into the earth. In a parallel way, thunder struck, lightning flashed, and the sound was terrible and frightening, but the storms brought rain and fertility to the fields. The meteorites, delivered from the sky, were fashioned into axes. The sparks that sprang from the axes were associated with lightning. It then became easy to conceive of a storm god wielding a hammer and with each blow sending off giant sparks or bolts of lightning. Describing a tradition in ancient Greece, Eliade explained, "The sites where they [meteorites] were found were thought to have been struck by a thunderbolt, which is the weapon of the God of Heaven. When this God was ousted by the God of Storms, the thunderbolt became the sign of the sacred union between the God of the Hurricane and the Goddess Earth" (pp. 20-21).

In Tibetan Buddhism, the bronze *dorje* is a ritual ornament conceived of as a weapon, as a thunderbolt, and as a symbol of the phallic principle. While trekking in the Nepali Himalayas, I met a man who had souvenirs to sell. Amid the ritual bowls and *dorjes* was a handmade bronze tripod used for holding a ceremonial object. It was small, simple in form, and obviously quite old. The man told me it was a very rare piece because, according to his story, it was *not* handmade at all but a gift from God. Every now and then, he explained, lightning strikes the earth, and three years later the people go to that spot and dig up things just like this as gifts from the gods. While an Asian art dealer later recognized the tripod as a bronze stand for a ritual ornament about 200 to 300 years old, the constellation of story elements—forged metal, lightning as a fertilizing agent from the gods, and three-ness (tripod; digging it up three years later)—I would suggest, is derived, in a sense, from the ancient traditions originating in the High Neolithic.

Eliade (1956/1978a) wrote that the Stone Age axe is the precursor to the hammer, which becomes the symbol of the powerful gods of the storm. The storm god, among the Dogons in West Africa, is conceived of as a civilizing hero, a heavenly smith, a fertilizing agent acting upon Mother Earth. He brings grain and teaches agriculture to the people (p. 30). The storm god fertilizing Mother Earth emphasizes the sexual nature of procreativity in the High Neolithic.

In the sexual symbology of fire lighting, the penis is to the vagina in making love as the stick is to the notch in making fire. Eliade elaborated: "In Vedic India the sacrificial altar (vedi) was looked upon as female and the spiritual fire (agni) as male and 'their union brought forth offspring.'... On the other hand, fire itself was looked upon as the result (the progeny) of a sexual union" (p. 39). This relationship between sex and fire was extended to the work of the metallurgist, whose furnace became configured as a uterus for completing the gestation of the metal ore. In Africa, some tribal peoples have strict taboos against women being near the furnaces and against the smiths having sexual relations to avoid problems with their furnaces. When the Baila metallurgists are tending their furnaces, they sing, "Kongwe (clitoris) and Malaba the Black (labiae feminae) fill me with horror! I found Kongwe as I fanned the flames of the fire. Kongwe fills me with horror. Pass far from me, pass far, thou with whom we have repeated relations, pass from me" (p. 60). And while the furnace is a uterus for the metal ore and, and the stone menhirs are homes for the dead, the stones are also the birthplace of many gods (p. 43).

We are moving from the abundant parthenogenic fertility of the great mother to the fertility of the *hieros gamos*, or sacred marriage and sexual union, of heaven and earth. Eliade elaborated further: "It is known, of course, that on this religious plane, the conception of a 'creatio ex nihilo,' accomplished by a supreme heavenly deity, has been overshadowed and superseded by the idea of creation by hierogamy and blood sacrifice; we pass from the idea of creation to that of procreation. This is one reason why, in the mythology of metallurgy, we come up against the motifs of ritual union and blood sacrifice" (p. 31).

Gertrude Levy (1948/1963) interpreted the images engraved onto the megaliths. She saw the images of labyrinths as mazes into the divine world, the axes as implements of sacrificial fertility, and the plows as sacrificial instruments for breaking the earth to make it fertile (pp. 140-45). Johannes Maringer (1960), another commentator on megalithic sites, noted that in France there are 6,000 menhirs, the largest of which was 66 feet high but has long since fallen and broken into five pieces (p. 160). Engraved on the wall of the Soto dolmen is the schematized image of what he described as a mother and child, and indeed excavations beneath the engraving unearthed the bones of a mother and child (p. 167). Axes were frequently depicted on rocks and dolmen walls, and miniature Neolithic axes appear to have been amulets or votive objects: "In Neolithic Western Europe the axe was the symbol of the sky, or, more precisely, of the thunderbolt hurled by the sky god" (p. 170).

Maringer explained that "the sun god appears to have enjoyed a fairly autonomous position in the religion of the late stone age" (p. 170). Axes, suns, starry skies, concentric circles, spirals, mandalas, circles with spokes, and horned figures are images found on menhirs and stone walls, and all have been associated with the solar cults of the High Neolithic. Five snakes standing erect on their tails were found engraved on one giant menhir near Carnac. When the site was excavated, five axes were found buried directly beneath the engraving with their blades all pointed upward (pp. 168-73).

Phallic objects and sharp implements remind us of castration anxieties and concerns about body intactness. They leave us feeling vulnerable and helpless, and our thoughts naturally take the form of worries and often employ magical thinking as a strategy to manage situations well out of our control. When those worries and magical thoughts become ritualized, they become prayer.

The association of the menhir with the dead, fertility, the sun, and sacrifice and the fact that the menhir stands as a pillar have linked it further to the symbolism of the tree. Eliade

(1958b) explained, "Stone stood supremely for reality: indestructibility and lastingness; the tree, with its periodic regeneration, manifested the power of the sacred in the order of life" (p. 271). The tree is a symbol of the vegetation god that dies and is reborn. It is the cosmic tree: the Bodi tree of the Buddhists, Yggdrasil of Scandinavian mythology, the tree of the knowledge of good and evil in the Garden of Eden, the inverted tree of Jewish mysticism, Autana of the indigenous people of Venezuela, the May tree, the Christmas tree, and so on. The tree is an axis mundi, a pillar at the center of the world, which unites the underworld, this world, and the upper world. The tree is inherently phallic, and erecting it and climbing it become ritual acts of ascension to higher realms—to the realms of the gods.

The High Neolithic, Hero Mythology, and Fertility Rites

When we reflect on the godlike technology of smelting metal ore; the increasing control our High Neolithic ancestors developed over their crops and domesticated animals; and the massive efforts required to construct long barrows, round barrows, earthworks, dolmens, and cromlechs and to erect menhirs, we are impressed by the strength and ambition of those ancestors. Bearing this in mind, it is not difficult to imagine the Cursus earthworks being used for ritual races, as Atkinson has suggested. And there are a number of other earthworks similar to the Cursus located in southern and eastern England. If ritual races took place, these may have been between young men for the love of a young woman. Ritual competition is a sublimation of oedipal conflict. It is the symbolization and socialization of the alpha male battles and the fraternal alliances that gave rise to human culture and the unique structure of the human psyche.

Another factor that may have stimulated the development of our oedipal dynamics is longevity. Rachel Caspari (2013) studied fossilized human teeth to determine the age at death of prehistoric individuals. She discovered that before 30,000 years ago, our ancestors rarely lived beyond age 30. Since then, however, the number of older humans has increased significantly, changing the dynamics of the family and culture with an emerging social group of grandparents, which had not been a significant part of human culture before that time. Caspari further associated this new social group with a cultural shift toward symbol-based communication and the development of art and language, saying, "The relation between adult survivorship and the emergence of sophisticated new cultural traditions was almost certainly a positive feedback process" (p. 43).

We know that the long period of immaturity in human development favors attachment and the development of object relations, and that a long latency phase favors impulse control and social skills development. So perhaps longer lifespans would make tribal leaders more experienced, wiser, perhaps more despotic, more revered, more resented, more likely to be taken down by biological sons, more likely to be mourned after their fall, and, after their deaths, probably more suitable as objects of ancestor worship as well. These Oedipal dynamics—hero dynamics—would have been present in the Paleolithic period and then elaborated in the Neolithic and High Neolithic with increasing longevity, cultural sophistication, and population density. I speculate that by the time we got to the High Neolithic, something like an oedipal myth—a hero myth—may well have emerged.

Ernest Becker (1973) wrote that it doesn't matter if the culture is magical, religious, secular, or scientific: "It is still a mythical hero-system in which people serve in order to earn a feeling of primary value, of cosmic specialness, of ultimate usefulness to creation, of unshakable meaning" (p. 5). For Becker, society is a hero system intended to create meaning and significance to human life in defiance of the inevitability of death (p. 7): "Culture is in its most intimate intent a heroic denial of creatureliness" (p. 159).

When we muse on the prevailing ritual associated with the High Neolithic period, it is less clear than it was with the Paleolithic funerary rite and Neolithic sacrifice, but it seems likely that a ritual associated with the High Neolithic would involve (1) the relationship between dead ancestors, sacrifice, and control over fertility; (2) the erection of phalli as we see in tree worship and the erection of menhirs; (3) fire rituals associated with metallurgy; (4) the myths of the theft of fire from the gods; and (5) ambitious competition as is seen in ritual contests. These naturally remind us of springtime Maypole rituals, which celebrate the Maypole as a phallus and symbol of fertility and the competition and conquest of spring over winter. But similar themes are also associated with many harvest rituals of pagan origin.

To say that the High Neolithic rituals might in some way have been related to the ancient pagan rituals, remnants of which have survived into modern times, seems like quite a stretch, since we are talking about a span of literally thousands of years during which language and the meanings of customs are likely to have changed on numerous occasions. But, then again, if we simply reflect on the themes of fire, sex, fertility, phalli, and ritual contests, the survival of such rituals from our ancient prehistory, even if in somewhat distorted or variable forms, seems entirely likely.

During the last century literally hundreds of well-preserved human corpses have been found mummified in peat bogs throughout the United Kingdom, Germany, Holland, and Denmark. They are between 1,600 and 2,400 years old, associated with the Iron Age, and frequently found strangled to death or with their throats slit. Though they died well after the High Neolithic period, some are believed to be human sacrifices to the gods of fertility and intended to ensure a good harvest (Lange, 2007, p. 9). As such, they appear to be part of the tradition linking death with rebirth and the fertility of the plants, animals, and women.

Eliade (1958b) wrote that while the menhir and tree are both phallic representations of the center of the world, the stone represents unchanging indestructible everlasting reality, and the tree represents periodic regeneration. The tree that dies and is reborn is also related to wine, the mysteries of transformation, and their gods—Bacchus and Dionysus. And wherever we find the tree, the plant, the phallus, the dying and resurrecting god, the vine, and intoxication, the great mother is never far away. There is also the pattern of the primeval man or a hero figure in search of immortality from the tree of life and a serpent or monster guarding that tree (pp. 271, 273-78, 286, 288). Eliade elaborated on this theme: "A great many rituals of vegetation imply the idea that the whole of mankind is regenerated by an active participation in the resurrection of the plant world. European folk traditions have kept traces or fragments of ancient rites in which the coming of spring was hastened by adorning a tree and carrying it ceremoniously in procession" (pp. 309-310). What he was describing was the May Tree festivals, which typically involved children and young people, competitions, feasts, and, not infrequently, a good bit of overt sexual activity (pp. 309-312).

The Maypole celebration is a fertility rite. In many celebrations, the Maypole from the previous year was burned, and the ashes were distributed over the fields to make the ground fertile. It was a ritual regeneration of the new year, beginning in spring:

> Indeed, in some places the coming of May is an occasion for all sorts of competitions, choosing the sturdiest pair (as "king" and "queen"), ritual wrestling, etc. All such tests, whatever their original meaning, came to be aimed at stimulating the energies of nature. The day usually starts with a race to the Maypole, or a competition among the young men and boys to see who can climb it the quickest.... The winner was borne shoulder-high and given honors. At one time he was presented with a red cloth by the prettiest girls. (p. 313)

Eliade goes on to say that the primeval pair, the king and queen, or betrothed couple of the May Day celebration "is unquestionably a watered down version of the old image of a young couple spurring on the creative forces of nature by mating ritually on ploughed land to re-enact the cosmic hierogamy of Sky and Earth" (p. 314). One might even associate this tradition with the modern-day prom king and queen.

Sexual intercourse, races, and competitions stimulated the regeneration of plant life. In some traditions, the old Maypole is burned; in others, a human effigy made of straw and branches is burned, decapitated, or drowned (pp. 315, 317). Whether it is a man, witch, or

Maypole, the burned object is configured as the old year, the winter, the monster or obstacle to overcome, and its death brings the regeneration of the new year: "There we see the fertilizing power of Death—a power attaching to all the symbols of vegetation, and to the ashes of the wood burnt during all the various festivals of the regeneration of nature and the beginning of the New Year. As soon as Death has been driven out or killed, Spring is brought in" (p. 317).

Similar ritual sacrifices took place at the time of the fall harvest, which served as another end and beginning not too different from the spring planting. In each case, death of the old guaranteed a good new crop or a good harvest. These sacrifices took the form of the old Maypole, a straw man, a witch effigy, or something similar: "It seems probable that we see in this the remains of a ritual scenario involving a real human sacrifice" (p. 342). In fact, there is ample evidence of human sacrifices in the harvest rituals of certain tribes in Central and North America, some parts of Africa, some of the Pacific Islands, and some of the Dravidian tribes of India.

The Khonds, a Dravidian tribe of Bengal, practiced human sacrifices into the middle 1800s. The victim was a volunteer, often married to another victim, and the child of other victims. They were called Meriahs and were given a piece of land at the time of their marriage. The sacrifice was for the good of all mankind. The Meriah was sacrificed to the earth goddess in a ritual that was clearly related to agriculture and fertility and was accompanied by ecstatic orgies. The Meriah was drugged with opium, tied up, and crushed to death, strangled, cut to pieces, or roasted over a fire. The people danced around him and cried, "'Oh God, we offer thee this sacrifice; give us good crops, good weather and good health!' And to the victim they said, 'We have purchased thee, not seized thee by force; now, according to our custom, we sacrifice thee and there is no sin to us!' Then pieces of the flesh were sent out to all the villages in the area and the head and bones were burnt and the ashes distributed on the fields" (Eliade, 1958b, p. 345).

The fertility of the plants stimulates the fertility of women, and people copulating in the fields or engaged in ecstatic orgies stimulate the fertility of the plants. Eliade described the orgy as "a temporary return to the primeval chaos, of reintegration into that formless unity which existed before Creation" (p. 349).

The orgiastic "return to the primeval chaos" that "existed before Creation" abolishes the norm, the limit, and individuality. Men and women enter the dark night and the earth in order to bring forth new life. The orgy is associated with the topsy-turvy Saturnalia, Carnival, and Halloween, when things are turned upside down, inverted, and made into their opposites. The people exchange roles and personas and flirt with the forbidden, the dangerous, the scary, the dead (pp. 360–61). Eliade elaborated on the metaphors of agriculture that shaped human experience: "Agriculture taught man the fundamental oneness of organic life; and from that revelation sprang the simpler analogies between woman and field, between the sexual act and sowing, as well as the most advanced intellectual synthesis: life as rhythmic, death as a return, and so on" (p. 361).

The relationship between sacrifice and sexuality in Neolithic life carried forth into the High Neolithic. The difference was that in the High Neolithic, phallic images begin to proliferate in the form of menhirs, carved phalli, and engravings of daggers, battle-axes, plows, and so on. I suggest that the mystery of the father's role in the birth of children may well have dawned in the Neolithic, but by the High Neolithic there was even greater certainty about our sexual enlightenment and the role of the father and his penis in the mysteries of procreation.

Sexual enlightenment appears, at first glance, to involve three people: a mother, a father, and a baby. But in fact it is also the troubling concern of a fourth person—an older sibling. Even if the first person to realize the role of the father in procreation was a father or a mother, the curiosity to figure it out was probably based in an early childhood preoccupation with this matter following the birth of a younger sibling. Is it possible that our ancient ancestors achieved their sexual enlightenment in the Paleolithic or the Neolithic period? Yes, it is, but it seems to me as though the father, as a highly developed cultural role, did not appear until the High Neolithic, when phallic imagery increased, the role of the father in procreation was discovered, knowledge expanded, and the sky gods took on a new role in relation to the goddesses.

The Hero Looks to the Sky

From the time that our symbolic function emerged in all of its glory, in the heart of the Paleolithic period, the sky must have held a special fascination for our ancestors. But its role no doubt was elaborated in the Neolithic and High Neolithic. The sky presented our ancestors with a magnificent screen—the walls of the universe—upon which to project hopes, sorrows, conflicts, and early infantile sexual experience. The sky provided our ancestors with a vista of metaphors: a sun, a moon, a blue sky, billowing clouds charging across the heavens, a blazing dawn, a majestic sunset, a black velvet night, twinkling stars, a Milky Way, constellations of stars, comets, shooting stars, rainbows, the aurora borealis, solar eclipses, lunar eclipses, changes in the seasons, flooding sunlight, foggy days, driving rain, blasting wind, dust storms, monsoons, tornados, hurricanes, lightning, thunder, electrical storms, hail, snowflakes, sunbeams, spring, summer, autumn, and winter, freezing cold, baking heat, and balmy evenings. Amid all of this, Cassirer (1944) asserted:

What man really sought in the heavens was his own reflection and the order of his human universe. He felt that his world was bound by innumerable visible and invisible ties to the general order of the universe—and he tried to penetrate into this mysterious connection. The celestial phenomena could not, therefore, be studied in a detached spirit of abstract meditation and pure science. They were regarded as the masters and rulers of the world and the governors of human life. In order to organize the political, the social, and the moral life of man it proved to be necessary to turn to the heavens. (p. 48)

The sky, the vault of heaven, as impersonal as the weather, stimulated deeply personal reactions and emotionally charged percepts that personified the celestial forces of nature. With their heads tipped upward, as children looking to parents, our ancestors looked into the heavens and saw their creators. They received the blessings of the gods and suffered punishment for what they assumed were their wrongdoings. They heard, in the rumblings of the heavens, the battles of the gods and the passion of their lovemaking. The sky filled them with terror and inspired them to awe.

This all seems a bit quaint, considering these matters within the walls of a modern, air-conditioned, artificially lit home, but when I spent the night in a rickety wooden *chai* (tea) house in the Nepali Himalayas during a monsoon rain with lightning ripping the sky from one horizon to the other and thunder shaking the walls and my bones, I found it difficult not to personify the weather. I was scared, knew someone was angry with me, and figured I must have done something wrong! So we can see that the sky calls for a particular set of personifications; the god that punishes, blesses, and establishes order: "The sky is the archetype of universal order. The sky god guarantees the continuation and intangibility of cosmic rhythms as well as the stability of human societies" (Eliade, 1958b, p. 62).

The sky gods, storm gods, weather gods were called "most high" and said to be "on high." They were inaccessible, beyond reach, high up, unchanging, omniscient, fecund creators. Bunjil, of the Kulin tribes of Australia, is a sky god "who created the earth, trees, animals, and man himself (whom he fashioned of clay, breathing a soul into him through the nose, the mouth and the navel)" (Eliade, 1958b, p. 42). The sky is a fecund creator who transforms the barren landscape into a verdant paradise of plenty with rain and sunlight. Its thundering "voice" gives the impression of a bellowing bull. Not surprisingly, the bull became identified with the sky gods throughout Asia, the Mediterranean, and Africa (pp. 76, 86-87). The sky god as bull is consort to the earth goddess, and his symbols are the thunderbolt, the axe, the club, the thunderstone, and the bullroarer (pp. 78-79, 83, 87, 89).

The sky had special meaning for our ancestors, but that meaning evolved with culture. Distinguishing primitive religion from the more elaborated religions, Eliade observed, "Nowhere in primitive religion do we find Supreme Beings of the sky playing a leading role" (p. 50). Instead the primitive religions tend toward totemism, polydemonism, polytheism, involvement with spirits, and other practices. Furthermore, "the lack of worship (of the sky gods) indicates mainly the absence of any religious calendar" (p. 55).

Now, there is an interesting observation! The sky caught our ancestors' projections of spirits, but they didn't become particularly important spirits, or gods, until our ancestors developed a religious calendar—in other words, until they had recognized the yearly cycle, the changing of the seasons, and the changing positions of the moon and the sun and the stars. And, of course, by the High Neolithic, human understanding of the cycle of the seasons was well elaborated as a result of developing knowledge about agriculture and animal husbandry. Living close to rivers that seasonally flooded or oceans with tides linked to the phases of the moon would also stir an interest in developing a religious calendar. But this unwritten religious calendar would be circular in nature. One season would follow the next, the rituals of sowing and harvesting would be practiced, but essentially each year was the same as the last and the same as the next.

Experiences of the sky became associated with the vistas seen from the tops of tall trees and high mountains. Those vistas no doubt inspired the ideas of omniscience and transcendence. If the gods are in the celestial realms, initiates meet them by climbing ladders, towers, trees, and mountains to meet the gods on high. Visionaries dream or take hallucinogens and experience flights of the soul through which they ascend into the heavens. Adepts climb a ladder, a tree, or a vine; mount steps to the temple; fly with the angels; or take a vision quest up a mountain. And in iconography, souls, spirits, and angels are commonly likened to birds. Eliade (1958b) explained, "This idea of 'ascension' into heaven by means either of a rope, a tree, or a ladder, is fairly widespread in all five continents" (p. 103). And it always signifies "a transcending of the human and a penetration into higher cosmic levels" (p. 108).

Myths of the origin of fire frequently include the themes of fighting, sex, and theft. They are myths of the hero in which fire is seen as a "treasure hard to attain." The culture hero steals fire from the gods, brings it to the human world, and transforms culture in the process. Cultures overcoming the powers of nature have invented new technologies, creating new experiences, traditions, and metaphors, which have, in turn, transformed culture and facilitated the development of ego consciousness, fortifying it in the struggle to overcome unconsciousness. It is represented as the hero's dragon fight, wherein the dragon represents the regressive, incestuous pull of the unconscious (the mother) as well as the obstacles (the father) one must overcome to win the "treasure hard to attain." To slay the dragon and secure that treasure is to fortify ego consciousness and make conscious part of what was unconscious.

To my way of thinking, the mythic analogue to the autumn harvest festivals, the spring planting festivals, the High Neolithic, and the phallic stage of development would be the myth of the hero. Of course, one well-known myth/legend of the hero, which Freud already associated with the phallic stage, is that of Oedipus Rex, the hero who slew the sphinx—and, not incidentally, also killed his father and had sex with his mother. Freud's classical education introduced him to mythology. He was fully aware of the myths of Paradise, the hero, and world creation. He linked the myths of Narcissus (following Havelock Ellis) and Oedipus to psychopathologies and to stages in normal development. In the hero motif, Freud saw a defensive strategy for managing some of the vicissitudes of growing up. Themes of heroism appear in our daydreams and have found their way into mythologies around the world.

Freud saw the hero's battle with the dragon as the child's battle with the father. But Erich Neumann (1954), a Jungian analyst, saw the hero battling with different dragons: a hermaphroditic uroboros, a terrible mother, and a father monster. I don't think Freudians today would find much difficulty with this alternative interpretation, as it is simply highlighting a developmental sequence of dragons to be slain and conflicts to be mastered. It was Freud who was most responsible for developing mythic metaphors for describing child development, and it was Otto Rank who picked up on Freud's lead in thinking about hero mythology as a mythic analogue to ego development.

Rank (1932/1959) examined hero myths from around the world, found a number of recurring themes, and abstracted a "standard saga":

> I believe moreover that the standard saga itself may be formulated according to the following outline: The hero is the child of most distinguished parents, usually the son of a king. His origin is preceded by difficulties, such as continence, or prolonged barrenness, or secret intercourse of the parents due to external prohibition or obstacles. During or before the pregnancy, there is a prophecy, in the form of a dream or oracle, cautioning against his birth, and usually threatening danger to the father (or his representative). As a rule, he is surrendered to the water, in a box. He is then saved by animals, or by lowly people (shepherds), and is suckled by a female animal or by a humble woman. After he has grown up, he finds his distinguished parents, in a highly versatile fashion. He takes revenge on his father, on the one hand, and is acknowledged, on the other. Finally he achieves rank and honor. (p. 65)

We could say that the hero myth unconsciously defends against the insults of childhood: (1) helplessness, (2) the mother's betrayal of the child in loving her husband—the child's father, (3) sexual enlightenment, (4) the father's role in reproduction, (5) the child's aggressive impulses directed toward the father, (6) the father's aggressive impulses toward the child, (7) the primal scene, and so on. Rank explained the analogous relation between the ego and the hero in the following fashion:

> We feel justified in analogizing the ego of the child with the hero of the myth, in view of the unanimous tendency of family romances and hero myths; keeping in mind that the myth throughout reveals an endeavor to get rid of the parents, and that the same wish arises in the fantasies of the individual child at the time when he is trying to establish his personal independence. The ego of the child behaves in this respect like the hero of the myth, and as a matter of fact, the hero should always be interpreted merely as a collective ego, which is equipped with all the excellences. In a similar manner, the hero in personal poetic fiction usually represents the poet himself, or at least one side of his character. (pp. 71-72)

Rank (1945) analogized "the ego of the child with the hero of the myth" based on the similar themes embedded in the family romance of the child and the hero myth of culture. The "family romance," of course, refers to the common childhood fantasy that one was really adopted at birth and one's true parents are far better than the parents one is stuck with. Here there is an obvious analogy to hero myths, which, in virtually every case, pertain to the hero being adopted:

> The idea of hero formation... was strongly influenced by the discovery of the man's share in procreation. At all events the conscious comprehension of the male process of procreation seems to signify a revolutionary turning point in the history of mankind.... Moreover, the discovery of this connection gave the first real basis for the social and psychological father concept, against whose recognition the individual defends himself even in the myth of the hero with the denial of the father and the emphasis on the maternal role. (p. 278)

Lord Raglan (1956) conducted a similar study of hero mythology but without the psychoanalytic backdrop. Studying 12 different hero myths, he arrived at 22 commonly recurring themes:

1. The hero's mother is a royal virgin;
2. His father is a king, and
3. Often a near relative of his mother, but
4. The circumstances of his conception are unusual, and
5. He is also reputed to be the son of a god.
6. At birth an attempt is made, usually by his father or his maternal grandfather, to kill him, but
7. He is spirited away, and
8. Reared by foster-parents in a far country.
9. We are told nothing of his childhood, but
10. On reaching manhood he returns or goes to his future kingdom.
11. After a victory over the king and/or a giant, dragon, or wild beast,
12. He marries a princess, often the daughter of his predecessor, and
13. Becomes king.
14. For a time he reins uneventfully, and
15. Prescribes laws, but
16. Later he loses favor with the gods and/or his subjects, and
17. Is driven from the throne and city, after which
18. He meets with a mysterious death,
19. Often at the top of a hill.
20. His children, if any, do not succeed him.
21. His body is not buried, but nevertheless
22. He has one or more holy sepulchers.

(pp. 174-75)

One of the noteworthy distinctions between Rank's standard saga and Lord Raglan's myth pattern is that where Rank describes the hero taking "revenge on his father," Raglan says he has "a victory over the king and/or a giant, dragon, or wild beast." Raglan's pattern is not only more recognizable, but it also permits us to more easily imagine the maternal components of the "giant, dragon, or wild beast."

In *The Interpretation of Dreams*, Freud (1900/1953a) described the psychogenesis of neurosis: "The chief part in the mental lives of all children who later become psychoneurotics is played by their parents. Being in love with the one parent and hating the other are among the essential constituents of the stock of psychical impulses which is formed at that time and which is of such importance in determining the symptoms of the later neurosis" (SE 4, pp. 260-61). But he also clarified that the same dynamics are present in normal children, although they are less obvious and less intense. Furthermore, it is Freud's understanding of the Oedipus complex that explains the enduring appeal of the legend of King Oedipus and its capacity to move us at the depths of our hearts. We are moved by it because of our unconscious identification with it.

If we associate the High Neolithic period with the phallic stage and the myth of the hero, we might now be able to revisit the planting and harvest festivals with a wider perspective. Eliade (1958b) described Maypole celebrations that included all sorts of competitions and ritual wrestling. These ritual contests are enactments of the mythic dragon fight. The goal in selecting a winner was to find a suitably virile May King to be paired with a beautiful May Queen, who together would stimulate the energies of nature by having intercourse on freshly plowed land. The sexual intercourse and competitions of the Maypole celebrations stimulated the renewal and regeneration of the plants, the animals, and the new year (pp. 313, 315, 317, 342).

The association of the planting and harvest festivals with the High Neolithic is a somewhat loose speculation that first occurred to me in 2005. But in 2009 an article in *Discovery News* reported that Mike Parker Pearson discovered large quantities of cattle and pig bones at a massive circular earthwork at Durrington Walls, just 2 miles northeast of Stonehenge. Parker Pearson said that although a tremendous number of animal bones were found, there was no indication that this was a habitation site. This led to the conclusion that it was a "consumer" site and that the consumption was quite intense. Parker Pearson said, "The small quantities of stone tools other than arrowheads, the absence of grinding querns and the lack of carbonized grain indicate that this was a 'consumer' site. The midsummer and midwinter solstice alignments of the Durrington and Stonehenge architecture suggest seasonal occupation" (quoted in Lorenzi, 2009). In other words, Parker Pearson's theory is that the High Neolithic monuments of Durrington Walls and Stonehenge were perhaps feasting sites for the solstices! Furthermore, about 5,000 years ago, several megalithic sites were erected in and around Ness Brodgar, in what is now Scotland. There were massive stone walls, stone houses, and a circle of menhirs (the Stones of Stenness). Roff Smith (2014) explained, "Although it's [Ness Brodgar] usually referred to as a temple, it's likely to have fulfilled a variety of functions during the thousand years it was in use. It's clear that many people gathered here for seasonal rituals, feasts and trade" (p. 32).

In 2016 came a report on the Heckelman site near Milan, Ohio. There, on a flat-top hill, were found six clusters of postholes that originally supported 10-to-12-foot-high free-standing poles that were established 2,300 years ago. Archeologist Brian Redmond said, "We know that Native American and many different tribal groups had a very specific vision about the world as a three-layered cosmos: the upper world, the middle world that we live on and an underworld" (quoted in Metcalfe, 2016). The speculation is that the postholes contained posts that may have been constructed in an effort to reach the upper world. No burials were found at the site, but pottery shards and burned rocks suggest feasting at this ceremonial site. Redmond said, "With analogy to historic Native American groups and others, it seems like these ceremonies would have also involved preparing food and communal meals or feasting." "Their habitations were based on small groups of related families, but they did congregate in much larger groups for rituals or seasonal festivals" (Metcalfe, 2016). My speculation is that the fertility rites associated with seasonal planting and harvesting represent a ritual analogue to the hero myth, which formed a backdrop to the High Neolithic.

While the fertility rites include components of the funerary and sacrificial rites, they are further elaborated by hero mythology, the dragon fight or cosmic conflict, and the threat of opposites (including the threat of the opposite sex), as seen in the Saturnalia, Carnival, and Halloween. As such, the fertility rites are situated between the funerary and sacrificial rites on one side and the ancient New Year festival of the Urban Revolution on the other. We further recall that, as Perry (1976) wrote, "Israel's New Year festival was grafted on an autumnal agricultural rite of the land, the Feast of Ingathering" (p. 88). This is the festival of Sukkoth—a harvest festival from an earlier time transformed into a New Year festival. In other words, in the Paleolithic period, we found evidence of funerary rites. In the Neolithic, we found evidence of sacrificial rites conceptually built on top of the preceding funerary rites. And in the High Neolithic, we found the planting and harvest festivals conceptually built on top of the funeral and sacrificial rituals.

In the funerary ritual, one dies and is reborn. In the sacrifice, one gives up or kills something or kills someone else to get something in return. In the third type of ritual, the planting and harvest rituals, a hero does battle with an opponent and kills or sacrifices it so as to bring order to the cycle of life. In the fourth ritual, associated with the Urban Revolution, we will see how a transcendent factor is introduced and the order brought to the new year is the order of the kingdom of God established here on earth. And if the funerary rite is followed by the sacrifice, and the sacrifice by the planting and harvest festivals, and the planting and harvest festivals by the New Year festival, then it might follow that the corresponding myths are the myth of death and rebirth, the myth of the fall from grace, the myth of the hero's fight with the dragon, and the myth of sacral kingship. We also might begin to muse on how the funeral denies death, the sacrifice denies powerlessness, the planting and harvest festivals deny a full belief in our dawning sexual enlightenment, and the New Year festival denies our insignificance as individuals, each residing in our own little bubble of mortality and floating through naught. The myth of sacral kingship and the New Year festival insist, in the face of overwhelming evidence, that we are not insignificant against the background of the universe! We are the children of God, and we're on a mission!

But what might be the psychopathological parallel to the High Neolithic? It is hard to say, and perhaps others will have better ideas, but I am tempted to think in terms of the old diagnostic category "hysteria" and all that Freud attributed to it—that is, the vicissitudes of the Oedipus complex. The hysterical personality alternately flirts with one parent (or parent substitute) and directs hostile impulses toward the other, feels excluded, configures triangular relations, and does not accept generational difference. The hysterical personality seeks to foreclose generational differences and is tangled in rage if, on the one hand, demands are not met or, on the other hand, there is capitulation. I could elaborate this idea further, but because it is more tentative, I will let it remain as a very provisional suggestion.

According to Róheim (1943), "We have found that the analogies between primitives and neurotics first stated by Freud in *Totem and Taboo* were really analogies drawn between the institutions of primitive mankind on the one side and the 'individual institutions' of neurotics on the other" (p. 24). I find that my weakest speculations concern the psychopathological analogues to the Neolithic and to the High Neolithic. I leave it to others to consider and further speculate.

In offering these provisional speculations, I have completed my schema of psychomythic development.[2] Each stage is comprised of a set of analogous components (points of agreement) and related sequentially to the other stages:

---

2 This Schema of Psychomythic Development will be further elaborated in subsequent chapters with associated metaphors from other aspects of human experience.

The Schema of Psychomythic Development

Psychological development	Oral stage—early infancy
Psychopathology	Infantile autism
Stage in cultural evolution	Upper Paleolithic
Mythic analogue	Myth of death and rebirth
Ritual analogue	Ancient funerary ritual

Psychological development	Anal stage—toddler
Psychopathology	Obsessional neurosis
Stage in cultural evolution	Neolithic
Mythic analogue	Myth of expulsion from Paradise and the fall from grace; separation of world parents
Ritual analogue	Sacrifice; house-building ritual

Psychological development	Phallic stage—Oedipal child
Psychopathology	Hysterical personality
Stage in cultural evolution	High Neolithic
Mythic analogue	Myth of the hero
Ritual analogue	Planting and harvest rituals

Psychological development	Genital stage—adolescence
Psychopathology	Brief psychotic disorder
Stage in cultural evolution	Urban Revolution
Mythic analogue	Myth of sacral kingship
Ritual analogue	Ancient New Year festival

As we take up the next stage in cultural evolution—the Urban Revolution—we find ourselves revisiting the work of John Weir Perry and the analogous relations he established between the Urban Revolution, the myth of sacral kingship, and the ancient New Year festivals. As such, our treatment of this fourth stage will be brief.

THE HIGH NEOLITHIC PERIOD AND THE PHALLIC STAGE OF LIBIDO DEVELOPMENT

A megalith in Southern England

A circle of megaliths in southern England.

Stonehenge in southern England.

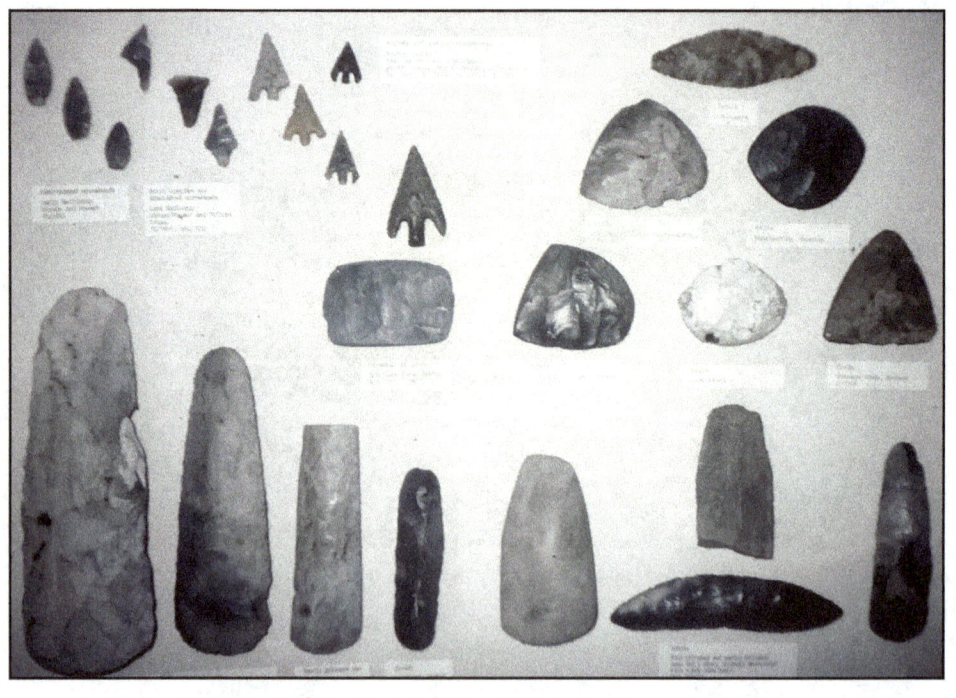

Stone tools from the High Neolithic in Southern England.

THE HIGH NEOLITHIC PERIOD AND THE PHALLIC STAGE OF LIBIDO DEVELOPMENT

The man-made Silbury Hill in Southern England was built in the High Neolithic. It is 131 feet high and 548 feet in diameter at the base.

The entrance to a megalithic tomb in Southern England.

A metallurgist working at his forge in Katmandu, Nepal. The figure at the top of his forge is the elephant headed Hindu god, Ganesha, the remover of obstacles and the one who ensures good beginnings.

Metallurgist in Katmandu, Nepal wielding his hammer to pound a red hot blade into shape.

THE HIGH NEOLITHIC PERIOD AND THE PHALLIC STAGE OF LIBIDO DEVELOPMENT

Ancient bronze arrow heads from 6th - 4th century BCE. Israel.

A monkey sitting atop a large metal dorje at the Swayambhunath Stupa, sacred to both Buddhists and Hindus. The dorje is symbolic of thunder and the phallic principle. Katmandu, Nepal.

An ancient bronze tripod for holding a ritual ornament. This handmade cast bronze tripod is from the 18th or 19th century Nepal.

CHAPTER 8

The Urban Revolution and the Genital Stage of Libido Development

> I believe that a large part of the mythological view of the world, which extends a long way into the most modern religions, is nothing but psychology projected into the external world.
> —Sigmund Freud, *The Psychopathology of Everyday Life*

> Many adolescents expect from religion the solution of their personal conflicts by implying that certainty about God, eternity, creation, universe will restore their shaken feelings of security, belongingness, and self-assurance. Personal conflicts are then projected into religious-philosophical domains where they can be treated in a safely impersonal manner.
> —Peter Blos, *The Adolescent Personality*

> Kingly myth and ritual played their part in evolution and were phased out, but have not left the scene; they merely reappear on a different level of experience. It is my thesis that the visionary states we call psychosis recapitulate this entire history, as another instance of ontogeny repeating phylogeny.
> —John Weir Perry, *Roots of Renewal in Myth and Madness*

The genital stage of libido development begins at puberty when the young adolescent begins his or her sexual maturation, undergoing dramatic physical changes that result in an adult physiognomy complete with the mature development of the sexual organs, the development of the secondary sex characteristics, and the development of the frontal lobes of the brain permitting abstract thinking. Abstract thinking and adult physiognomy combine to drive the adolescent into new sorts of love relations with peers. It is a time when the previous stages of libido development are reworked, to some extent, in the wider social setting and in relation to intensified sexual impulses. The earlier stages of psychosexual development also become subordinate to the primacy of the genitals. The reworking of the phallic-stage dynamics in the genital stage hopefully include two significant differences from their original resolution: (1) the love object shifts from an incestuous partner to a non-incestuous peer, and (2) the adolescent is capable of a more altruistic and tender love than is the young child, whose love is incorporative, possessive, and exploitative (Baldwin, 1967, p. 370). The integration of the previous psychosexual stages into the genital stage has its social/emotional/intellectual correlate in the development of what Erikson (1968) described as an "identity."

As we get into the "points of agreement" between adolescence and the Urban Revolution, we naturally return to the formulation of John Weir Perry, who identified the analogous links between the Urban Revolution (the birth of civilization), the myth of sacral kingship, the ancient New Year festival, and the brief psychotic disorder. Perry never addressed the natural link to the corresponding stage in normal development: adolescence. It was simply not a part of his work. When I spoke with him personally, however, he confirmed this link, or at least could see my point. He was fully aware and spoke often about the brief psychotic disorder following the first major disappointments of early adulthood, such as leaving home to go to college, the first experience of falling in love, heartbreak, or any other emotionally charged experience that overtaxes the young person's psychological resources.

Peter Blos (1941) addressed the common strategy among adolescents to displace personal conflicts into religious and philosophical concerns, where they can be dealt with in a safely impersonal manner (pp. 297–98). When Blos wrote that the adolescent projects personal conflicts into religious and philosophical domains, he gave us a non-pathological correlate to the psychotic patient's spiritual concerns.

Perry (1999) observed, "The most impressive and richest set of ideation [in the psychotic material] is found in the messianic calling and its program. It is all too easy to dismiss these ideas as naïve and inflated world-reforming idealism, such as one finds in the enthusiastic imagination of an adolescent." He then added, "The messianic mission with its program for society represents the very essence of the person's needs for living in society with any satisfaction" (p. 48). The adolescent with "world-reforming idealism" sees the world, in a way, similar to the visionary and the psychotic in that he sees his deepest personal concerns projected into religious or philosophical metaphors describing a grand worldview and a place for himself within it. Tyson and Tyson (1990) explained, "Adolescent thinking also has an omnipotent quality, filled with dreams of revolution or social reform, which may interfere with an objective view of the position of others" (p. 189). And Erikson (1975) elaborated further on this theme: "It is the all-or-nothing, or what I have called the totalistic, quality of adolescence which permits many young people to invest their loyalty in simplistically overdefined ideologies" (p. 204). The challenge for the adolescent, the psychotic, and the visionary is in one respect the same: to link the idealism with real work and real relationships, bring the vision down to earth, sublimate the core conflict.

The idealism of adolescents is possible only with the development of the frontal lobes of the brain and the expanded capacity for abstract thinking that comes with it. Abstract thinking offers the ability to think about things that are not immediately present; to think about thinking; to consider possibilities; to imagine relationships; to think about possible career choices; to take the position of the other; to evaluate political, religious, and philosophical systems; and to imagine new worlds.

The architects of civilization introduced ideas such as the relationship between the god-king and the king-god and the notion that the plan of the kingdom would be patterned on the plan of the kingdom of the gods. All around the world, visionaries, at the birth of different civilizations, in different times, imagined a balanced fourfold world of the gods and built their earthly worlds along the same lines. Innovations such as the written word, the calendar, occupational specialization, city life, and large-scale warfare changed the lives of people once and for all. And one of those changes was the beginning of recorded history, made possible by the written word.

Mircea Eliade and the Ancient New Year Festivals

Through Perry's clinical work and study of history, comparative religion, and mythology, he discovered that the visions (delusions and hallucinations) of psychotic patients sounded very similar to the recurring images and themes in the myths of sacral kingship and the ancient New Year festivals. The reader will recall that the images and themes that Perry identified in the "visions" of those experiencing brief psychotic disorders are the center, death, return to beginnings, cosmic conflict, threat of the opposite sex, apotheosis, sacred marriage, new birth, new society, and a quadrated world. I would say that the psychotic's vision of a "new society" corresponds to the adolescent's arrival at a career choice or direction, philosophy, religion, or political position and that the "sacred marriage" corresponds to the establishment of a sexual identity. Perry found these images and themes recurring in the narratives of many of his patients and in the myths and rituals associated with 16 different ancient cultures on the threshold of becoming early civilizations.

In this way, we return to the parallel metaphors shared by the Urban Revolution, adolescence, the brief psychotic disorder, the myth of sacral kingship, and the ancient New Year festivals. We have covered this material before and will briefly review it, but before doing so, let us examine the little book that provided Perry with the link between the psychotic disorder and it's analogous myth and ritual: Mircea Eliade's *The Myth of the Eternal Return; or, Cosmos and History* (1954/1971). In his first chapter, "Archetypes and Repetition," Eliade described the difference between people who belong to "archaic societies" and those who belong to "modern societies": "The chief difference between the man of the archaic and traditional societies and the man of the modern societies with their strong imprint of Judeo-Christianity lies in the fact that the former feels himself indissolubly connected with the cosmos and the cosmic rhythms, whereas the latter insists that he is connected only with History" (pp. xiii-xiv).

While archaic man has a history, it is a sacred history, a mythic history, a history of symbolic acts and celestial archetypes, which forms the patterns by which archaic man is guided in daily life. On the other hand, modern man's history is embedded in linear time, not mythic time. It is a history of profane activities, individual events, and real figures. Archaic man is situated in mythic time and mythic space. Modern man is situated in historical time and historical space. For archaic man, "reality is a function of the imitation of a celestial archetype." Eliade's "archetypes" are not related to Jung's "collective unconscious" but simply refer to a paradigm or exemplary model (p. xv). Reality for archaic man comes about through participation in a cosmic center. Rituals and daily activities acquire meaning as repetitions of acts previously performed by gods, heroes, or ancestors. The celestial model is reproduced on earth. There is a celestial earth and an earthly earth, a celestial year and an earthly year. The hand of God created the celestial Jerusalem before the hand of man created the earthly Jerusalem.

Archaic man finds the cosmic center in the sacred mountain, the temple, the house, the altar, the axis mundi, the omphalos, the city. The center is the earth's navel, the highest point on earth, the communication point with heaven, the zone of the sacred, the place where creation began. It is Mecca, Haridwar, Jerusalem, Babylon, the sacred rock, the holy site. For archaic man, nothing lasts if it is not animated, given a soul, by way of a sacrifice, and "the prototype of the construction rite is the sacrifice that took place at the time of the foundation of the world" (p. 20). It is the commemoration, by repetition, of the murder of the primordial monster, god, goddess, or the cosmic giant that gave rise to the creation of the world. The Sabbath repeats God's day of rest after the creation. Marriage and sexual union repeat the hierogamy or sacred marriage of heaven and earth. New Year festivals repeat the recreation of the world. Dancers reproduce the movements of the totemic animal so as to identify with it and become it. Struggles, conflicts, and wars have a ritual cause and function that recall the cosmic conflict in the heroic myth (pp. 21-47).

In his second chapter, "The Regeneration of Time," Eliade (1954/1971) developed the idea that archaic man makes meaning out of the natural world and day-to-day life by bringing his behavior and his understanding of the world into accord with the traditions of the ancestors, the gods, the cosmic patterns, the celestial archetypes. In this regard, Eliade emphasized the role of the new year and the New Year festivals. He speculated that even as Paleolithic hunters, our ancestors had to be recognizing and using, for the first time, the patterns of the yearly cycle. New Year festivals were always regarded as "the end and the beginning of a temporal period, based on the observation of biocosmic rhythms and forming part of a larger system—the system of periodic purifications (cf. purges, fasting, confession of sins, etc.) and of the periodic regeneration of life" (p. 52).

The New Year festival was a new creation and a repetition of the cosmogonic act. Such festivals are often associated with the expulsion of diseases and sins by fasting, ablutions, and purifications; the extinguishing of fires and the rekindling of fires. Demons are expelled with noises and cries and driven out of the village by expelling an animal or a man. The Hebrews and Babylonians drove a "scapegoat" out and into the desert to carry away the faults of the community. There were ceremonial combats construed as cosmic conflicts, collective orgies that returned the community to its original chaos and invoked the sexual magic of the *hieros gamos*, or the sacred marriage between heaven and earth that brings fertility and a good harvest to the community and the fields. The orgy marked the reversal of values and roles and the return to chaos and confusion. This topsy-turvy state signaled that the chaos monster had achieved the upper hand in the hero's cosmic conflict and in doing so reversed the social order, let loose a flood, and extinguished the fires. But just when all seemed to be lost, the hero vanquished the chaos monster and reestablished the world. The New Year festival was associated with a return to the mythical time before creation. Processions of masked people paraded about as the souls of the dead. They approached the houses, were lavished with honors, and then sent out beyond the borders of the village. The New Year festival repeated the cosmogony and repeated the mythical passage from chaos to cosmos (pp. 51-62).

The ceremonial return to chaos and the beginning of time also permits the return of the dead to their families and annuls the finality of death. If one is reminded of Halloween, the Day of the Dead, Carnival, the Day of Atonement, confession, and similar rituals, it is not accidental. They are all remnants of these ancient rituals preserved to this day in modern religions and traditions. Eliade made repeated references to these cultural patterns embedded in the Hebrew, Babylonian, Sumerian, Egyptian, Iranian, Vedic Indian, ancient Japanese, Polynesian, and Slavic traditions and also in the periodic ceremonies of the Karuk, Yurok, and Hupa native Californians, which are called "new year," "world restoration," and "repair."

Archaic man refuses to live in historical time and refuses to acknowledge, remember, or grant value to events outside the pattern of the archetypal. The religious man, the mystic, and the primitive all live in a continual present—an atemporal present repeating the gestures of the ancestors. The cycle of the year, like the phases of the moon and the patterns of the day-to-day, is a constant return to the celestial archetypal model of the ancestors and constitutes what Eliade (1954/1971) refers to as the "eternal return." For archaic man, a new era comes about with every marriage, new birth, new construction, new year, and so forth. And the repetition, the cycle, the eternal return is what is projected into the cosmic, the biologic, and the human. Nature repeats itself and archaic man repeats himself, but history does not. History draws us into the profane march of linear time and marks our expulsion and alienation from the mythic and the archetypal. Archaic man does not want to remember, record time or history, interiorize his past, and transform it into consciousness. No, he has a "thirst for the ontic" (p. 91). He wants to "be" and finds "being" in repeating acts in accordance with the archetypal gestures of his ancestors.

Myths around the world refer to a distant past when communications between heaven and earth, between man and god were uninterrupted. There was Paradise on earth—no struggle, no hunger, no toil, and no death. But then mankind committed a ritual error, a sin, and as a result, the gods withdrew to the inaccessible reaches of the distant heavens. The refusal of history and desperate clinging to the repetition of archetypes testifies to archaic man's "thirst for the real and his terror of 'losing' himself by letting himself be overwhelmed by the meaninglessness of profane existence" (pp. 91-92). For archaic man, there is a sacred, absolute reality that is opposed to the profane world of unreality, the uncreated, the nonexistent, the void. Archaic ontology gives rise to seemingly strange behaviors that correspond to "a desperate effort not to lose contact with being" (p. 92).

In his next chapter, "Misfortune and History," Eliade (1954/1971) reasserted that archaic man is opposed to history and sets himself against it with every means in his power. Living in accordance to the celestial archetypal models means respecting the "law." Consequently, suffering has meaning. Nothing is left to chance. Nothing is random. Nothing is arbitrary. There is no absurdity. Meaning is embedded in pleasure and pain, good fortune and bad. Drought, flood, plague, war, peace, slavery, humiliation, economic boon, social injustice—all have a meaning embedded in the archetypal patterns. One's fate is written in the stars. Painful events are seen as punishment for transgressions of rituals or the proper way of living, as rewards for right action, as tests by god, as lessons, or even as recompense for actions in past lives. Archaic man does not conceive of unprovoked suffering. Everything that happens is because of personal fault or a neighbor's malevolence (pp. 97-98).

In Eliade's (1954/1971) final chapter, "The Terror of History," he explored the strategies modern man has for dealing with the terror of being free from the eternal return and the terror of linear time and history. He noted the revival of the theory of cycles and periodicity in modern societies, the recognition of the Universal Spirit in daily life, the salvation promised at the end of Marx's class struggle, the glory granted to martyrs, and a return, if you will, to the myth of the eternal return.

When John Weir Perry read Eliade's description of the ancient New Year festivals, he found certain aspects very familiar: the themes of death and rebirth, the cosmic sacred center, the battles with demons and chaos, the topsy-turvy rites that turn things into their opposites, the ritual repetition of the cosmogony, the sacred marriage, identification with the gods, and so on. Perry had seen it all before. He had encountered the same imagery, the same themes in the personal narratives of his psychotic patients. The myths associated with the ancient New Year festivals, which became a part of religion, politics, and history, were derived from psychotic visions, or at the very least the vicissitudes, of child development and the conflicts that are reliably encountered.

The ancient New Year festival contains the metaphors of the center; death; return to beginnings; cosmic conflict; threat of the opposite; apotheosis; sacred marriage, new birth, new society; and a quadrated world. But the Urban Revolution was not just another stage of complexity; it was a stage that marked the beginning of society's move out of circular time and the eternal return and into linear time, history, and the primacy of Aristotelian logic.

How did such a thing happen? Was kingship so different from the chiefdoms of old? Why was the New Year festival so special when the yearly cycle had undoubtedly been recognized in the changing of the seasons during the Paleolithic and Neolithic periods and celebrated in the agricultural rites of harvest and planting during the High Neolithic? What made the big difference? There were probably many factors involved, but among the most decisive was the written word.

With the written word, one steps outside of circular time, out of the eternal return, and into history. One names the days of the week, counts the days of the month, names the months of the year, and then, in a small step of unimaginable consequences, one begins to count the years. We stepped out of our circular orbit of time and the mythic world and stepped into linear time and history. It was quite clearly a step in a new direction, but it was far from a clean break, and indeed much of the modern world is still deeply sunk in a mythological worldview. All of us, even those of us with the most modern lives, are deeply influenced by paleologic thinking; our symbolic and emotionally tinged views of the world; and our institutions embedded in ancient belief systems. Aside from the frankly religious, gnostic, and mystical traditions that are pursued by many, we are all still awed by death and the terror of the storm. Children eat animal crackers like a totemic feast. Others share a meal, a drink, or a smoke to commune in the spirit. High school sports teams engage in competitions derived from ritual battles replicating cosmic conflict, and they do so under the banner of their mascot, which is no doubt derived from the totemic impulse. And on and on it goes with the relationship between gambling and sacrifice, branding and totems, free-enterprise competition and cosmic battles, diplomacy and fraternal bonding, clubs and clans, marriage and fertility rites.

The Ancient Mesopotamian New Year Festival

In chapter 2 we explored John Weir Perry's observation that the images and themes associated with the brief psychotic disorder are analogous to those in sacral kingship in ancient Egypt, Israel, China, and among the Toltecs. We will now take a look at sacral kingship in Mesopotamia, if only to elaborate the theme.

In *Kingship and the Gods: A Study of Ancient Near Eastern Religion as the Integration of Society and Nature*, Henri Frankfort (1948/1978) presented a detailed study of kingship as it relates to ancient Egypt and ancient Mesopotamia. According to Frankfort the oldest political institution in Mesopotamia, before the emergence of kingship, was "the assembly of all free men," led by a small group of elders who in times of crisis would elect a king to lead them for a limited period of time. With the modernization of technology, brought about by metal tools and the increase in population, borders between expanding settlements became contiguous, giving rise to ongoing disputes. Drainage and irrigation became growing concerns. Raw materials in one area that were necessary for communities in other areas needed safe passage. Thus, kingship ceased to be a temporary position and became a permanent position in society, which fell to wise elders or courageous young men. Kings were those who could bring about consensus in the kingdom, had wisdom, showed strength of character, and spoke well. Unlike ancient Egypt, where a god-king was king at all times, Mesopotamia had fewer than 20 sacral kings from 2300 BCE to 1500 BCE (pp. 215, 217–19, 224).

The king was responsible for interpreting the will of the gods, acting as representative of his people before the gods, and administering over his realm. The gods communicated with the king most directly through his dreams, but omens such as eclipses and other natural phenomena were also open to interpretation (pp. 52-55). Frankfort explained that "uncertainty characterized the Mesopotamian's relations with the gods" (p. 265). Thus, there was a preoccupation with omens, particularly of bad things to come. To ward off danger, prayers and lamentations would be made in one city and reproduced in other cities throughout the realm.

Lacking the capacity to distinguish external reality from emotional reality, the ancients did not recognize the impersonal nature of weather and the changing of the seasons (p. 265). So everything was a gift or a punishment, and the only recourse was the magic of ritual. Then, in a stunning fashion, Frankfort stated, "If most of the ancient festivals served to establish that harmony with nature which was indispensable to a fruitful social life, if the continual tending of that harmony was the main task of the king, if man's unqualified servitude to the gods found some compensation in his ability to participate in their periodic changes of fortune, then the New Year festival must be considered the most complete expression of Mesopotamian religiosity" (p. 313). The New Year festival took place over a number of days and could be held in the autumn or the spring. It was directly associated with world renewal and world recreation and began with purifications, atonement, and the retelling or reenactment of the creation myth. The Mesopotamian New Year festival took place over a period of five days and began with various preparations, purifications, and a recitation of the cosmogony (creation myth) in which Marduk (the hero god) does battle with Tiamat (chaos). On the fifth day, the king does penance and atones for his sins. After five days of sacrifice, suffering, purification, and atonement, the king is degraded and then reinstated. This degradation parallels that part of the cosmogony when Tiamat gets the upper hand on Marduk, the dead and suffering god, who then descends into the netherworld. But in retelling the cosmogony, the New Year festival also resuscitates Marduk, who then vanquishes Tiamat and cuts her in two, creating the heaven above and the earth below. A procession then goes to the Bit Akitu, or "House of the New Year's Feast," which is said to be the place where Marduk's victory over Tiamat was celebrated. Then there is the sacred marriage between the god and the goddess reenacted in the *gigunu*, "room of the bed," to bring together the male fertilizing forces with the great mother to renew and bring fertility to the crops, animals, and people of the kingdom (pp. 313–33).

Perry (1976) recognized in the ancient Mesopotamian New Year festival the images and themes in common with the preoccupations of his psychotic patients:

1. Establishing a World Center as the Locus: The ritual was held at a world center and cosmic axis.
2. Undergoing Death: The king-god dies and descends into the underworld. "The fifth day is a day of atonement for the king, in which he is humiliated and degraded in the likeness of the suffering of the king-god in death."
3. Return to the Beginnings of Time and Creation: The ritual reenacts the time of the creation when the sun god Marduk splits the mother monster, Tiamat, into sky and earth.
4. Cosmic Conflict as a Clash of Opposites: Marduk does battle with Tiamat, the primordial waters of chaos.
5. Threat of the Reversal of Opposites: Chaos gets the upper hand, the order of society is suspended, roles are reversed, and servants rule the masters.
6. Apotheosis as King or Messianic Hero: Marduk is named king-god.
7. Sacred Marriage as a Union of Opposites: The Great Lord of Heaven joins in marriage and sexual union with the Goddess of the Evening Star.

8. New Birth as a Reconciliation of Opposites: The king is reborn and suckles at the breast of the Goddess, his mother, lover, and consort.
9. New Society of the Prophetic Vision: The ritual protects against problems in the coming year and ensures a prosperous new year.
10. Quadrated World Forms: The quadrated world is mentioned repeatedly, and Babylon is situated at the center of the circle of the world with points extending in the cardinal directions (pp. 85-88).

Along with the New Year festival in the Mesopotamian tradition, the practice of atonement is also common to the ancient New Year festival of the Israelites and is practiced to this day as Yom Kippur (the Day of Atonement), which follows Rosh Hashana (the new year) in the Jewish tradition. The Hebrews who came into the land of Canaan picked up the idea of kingship, but they gave it their own character. They never considered kingship as something that descended from heaven. The Hebrew king was not the link between God and the people. The Hebrews were a chosen people, chosen by Yahweh. And they were bound, as a whole, by virtue of the Covenant of Sinai, which included the duty to serve God: "In the light of Egyptian, and even Mesopotamian, kingship, that of the Hebrews lacks sanctity. The relation between the Hebrew monarch and his people was as nearly secular as is possible in a society wherein religion is a living force.... Yahweh's covenant with the people antedated kingship" (Frankfort, 1948/1978, p. 341).

Yahweh had his covenant with the people while the king functioned in the realm of profane matters. To keep the covenant meant giving up a great deal, including "the harmonious integration of man's life with the life of nature" (p. 342). While the original Canaanite cult offered fulfillment for those who believed the divine was in nature, the Hebrews believed "God is absolute, unqualified, ineffable, transcending every phenomenon, the one and only cause of all existence" (p. 343). For the Hebrews, the material and concrete were devalued in favor of an austere transcendentalism, and "the ancient bond between man and nature was destroyed" (p. 343). We can hear in this description the extent to which the Hebrews were able to step out of the eternal return and into history: "Man remained outside nature, exploiting it for a livelihood, offering its first-fruits as a sacrifice to Yahweh, using its imagery for the expression of his moods; but never sharing its mysterious life, never an actor in the perennial cosmic pageant in which the sun is made 'to rise on the evil and on the good' and the rain is sent 'on the just and the unjust'" (pp. 343-44).

This was a religion stepping out of the eternal return, withdrawing projections, abandoning paranoia and magical thinking, and finding transcendence in the covenant with an immaterial god. And then, several thousand years later, it was Freud, "the godless Jew," who recognized that even the abstraction of God was a projection of emotional impulses, or, more specifically, the projection of the experience of, and relationship to, the father. Freud summarized:

> Spirits and demons... are only projections of man's own emotional impulses. (1913/1955h, SE 13, p. 92)

> I believe that a large part of the mythological view of the world, which extends a long way into the most modern religions, is nothing but psychology projected into the external world. (1901/1960, SE 6, p. 258)

Freud quoted from the Bible, "God created man in His own image." And then he asserted the reverse: "Man created God in his" (1901/1960, SE 6, p. 19). The story that begins with man's elaborate projections of his emotional impulses out into the world as spirits, demons, totems, and gods and ends with his taking title to those projections, recognizing that they are actually representations of one's own impulses, is a story that spans the prehistory and history of cultural evolution.

Freud discovered the pathogenic nature of childhood sexual trauma and related experiences elaborated in fantasy. He discovered the Oedipus complex; libido development; primary and secondary process thinking; the language of the unconscious; the interpretation of dreams; and the psychoanalytic meaning of jokes, slips of the tongue, art, and symptoms. Then, in *Totem and Taboo* (1913/1955h), he wrestled with the question *Where do our complexes and our archaic inheritance of universal symbolism come from?* His answer was that the repeated actions of the primal fathers and primal hordes over thousands of years were symbolized, remembered, and passed on from one generation to the next as archaic memories through a mechanism best described as psycho-Lamarckism. The human race remembers its own prehistory. Freud's question is majestic and his approach to it creative, but we have seen the problems in his basic assumptions and final conclusions.

Now we can see that our psychodynamic complexes and our archaic inheritance of universal symbolism are the inevitable result and psychological manifestation of bringing together our human symbolic function with our primate social instincts. Mother-infant suckling and bonding are symbolized and socialized into the Madonna and child, and the I and Thou. Dominance and submission instincts give rise to power dynamics, social hierarchies, and the attitude of faith. Alpha male instincts become channeled into the Oedipus complex and political and religious structure. The social world, politics, philosophy, art, science, and religion are all elaborations of primate instincts that have been symbolized and socialized. The turning point in prehistory was a small mutation with a big difference that took place about 50,000 years ago when the human symbolic function reached its current form and initiated a social, technological, spiritual, and psychological revolution. Our complexes and symbols are metaphorized social instincts passed down through the generations, not through psycho-Lamarckian inheritance, but through language, myth, ritual, technology, and tradition.

When we look back at the extraordinary odyssey of cultural evolution from the Paleolithic to the Neolithic, to the High Neolithic, and on to the Urban Revolution, we see an ongoing dialogue between libido development and the symbolic function on the one hand and technology and spiritual innovations on the other. As our ancestors met the cultural challenges of prehistoric life, those challenges evoked the traumatic experiences inherent in the vicissitudes of psychological development and mobilized social/spiritual defense mechanisms that are not so different from those used by individuals but are modified within the social context: The funerary ritual denies the finality of death with an illusory afterlife and return to mother but leaves us with a soul and a structure to facilitate the process of mourning. The ritual of sacrifice denies powerlessness by offering a magical solution but invites us to take an active role in our lives and renounce instinctual gratification in exchange for culture. The planting and harvest festivals deny sexual enlightenment, oedipal love, and oedipal hate by facilitating displacements into society and sublimations that elaborate the heroic ambitions of culture. And the New Year festival denies the insignificance of our mortal identity by offering the opportunity to identify with God and find meaning and a mission in life. This identification inspires us to great achievements and contributions to culture, and culture is, after all, the only life beyond death available to those of us with merely mortal souls.

The Psychomythic Schema of Development

The psychomythic schema is a unified theory of human development that ties libido development to cultural evolution and presents us with four constellations of metaphors that help us link the patient's discourse regarding the outer world to the intrapsychic and transferential conflicts and concerns. In William I. Grossman's article "Freud's Presentation of 'The Psychoanalytic Mode of Thought' in *Totem and Taboo* and his Clinical Papers" (1998), which was discussed earlier, he looked at *Totem and Taboo* (1913/1955h) in relation to two clinical papers written contemporaneously: "The Dynamics of Transference" (1912/1958c) and "Recommendations to Physicians Practicing Psychoanalysis" (1912/1958b). Freud was a psychoanalytic investigator, but in *Totem and Taboo* he drew upon the data of anthropologists, archeologists, and scholars of comparative religion. Grossman (1998) asserts, "Totem and Taboo shows Freud using the data and ideas of other investigators in a search for an underlying but still undiscovered meaning in the material they select and describe. The technical papers show an analogous use of associations in looking for unconscious meaning in the patients' thoughts that are our clinical material" (p. 470).

In Freud's handling of the cultural data, he "oscillates between applying his analytic ideas, that is, interpreting the material at hand, and reconstructing and refining the overall situation from the result. This process is analogous to the alternation of interpretation and reconstruction in analysis. In both theory construction and in analysis, there is a gradual extension and elaboration of the constructed picture" (p. 471).

Grossman compellingly highlighted Freud's psychoanalytic mode of thought being applied to cultural and clinical data. Related to this, Freud (1926/1959f) believed an analytic education required study in biology, the science of sexual life, and psychiatric symptomatology. In addition, however, the analyst needs instruction in "the history of civilization, mythology, the psychology of religion and the science of literature" (SE 20, p. 246). This ideal psychoanalytic training program immerses the analyst in symbolism and analogical thinking and attunes the analyst to the metaphors embedded in the patient's dreams, fantasies, symptoms, slips of tongue, free associations, repetition compulsion, transference, and so on. The following schema of four constellations of metaphors is a contribution to this curriculum. This psychomythic schema of development is not something we would reliably recognize in the development of a small child, but as the child enters language and culture, developmental issues are likely to find expression in metaphors emerging out of the dialectic of psychological development and cultural evolution. Psychomythology illuminates dreams, fantasies, visionary experience, high arousal states, peak experiences, shamanism, mysticism, religious experiences, and the metaphors of everyday life.

The following four constellations of metaphors pertain to personal and cultural expressions and are organized in sequence. I have provisionally named them Death and Unity, Birth and Separation, Ascension and Conflict, and Transformation and the Establishment of Order.

1. *Death and Unity*
Psychosexual stage—oral stage
Psychosocial stage—trust versus mistrust
Stage in cultural evolution—Upper Paleolithic
Myth of death and rebirth
Funerary ritual
Mother goddess
Oneness
Soul—spirit—demon—anima—amulet—cannibalism—ancestor spirit—hunter-gatherer—nomadism—undifferentiation—cave

Orality and oral symbolism—the mouth—teeth—tongue—biting—chewing—drinking—swallowing—vomiting—spitting—coughing—inhaling—exhaling—food

2. *Birth and Separation*
Psychosexual stage—anal stage
Psychosocial stage—autonomy versus shame and doubt
Stage in cultural evolution—Neolithic Revolution
Myth of the separation of the opposites; expulsion from Paradise; fall from grace
Ritual sacrifice
Mother goddess and child/animal
Two-ness
House—village walls—boundaries—limits—fence—garden—pot—mortar and pestle—weaving—oven—bread—agriculture—domestication of animals—ceramics—trade—mother and child—bow and arrow—duality—the center—temple—birth—psychological birth—spiritual birth—separation—division—the fall from grace
Anality and anal symbolism—feces—urine—mud—passing gas—trapping—letting go—smearing—paint—clay—money—filth—cleanliness—time

3. *Ascension and Conflict*
Psychosexual stage—phallic stage and latency phase
Psychosocial stages—initiative versus guilt and industry versus inferiority
Stage in cultural evolution—High Neolithic
Myth of the hero's cosmic battle; the dragon fight, Oedipus myth
Fertility rites: harvest festivals—planting festivals
Mother Earth goddess and sky or storm god; hero
Three-ness
Stone monuments—pillars—trees—poles—fire—metallurgy—metal—sex and fertility—fighting—conflict—battle between opposites—theft—war—hammer—axe—thunderbolt—sky—sun—plow—ambition—striving—conflict—interaction—dynamism—ascension
Oedipality and phallic images in general—penis—clitoris—vulva—vagina—rising smoke or anything rising—flying—foot—finger—spear—scepter—apotheosis—theft of fire—inflation—ladder—bridge—rainbow—rope—thread—jealousy—triangular relations

4. *Transformation and the Establishment of Order*
Psychosexual stage—genital stage
Psychosocial stage—identity versus identity confusion

Stage in cultural evolution—Urban Revolution (birth of civilization)
Myth of sacral kingship
Ancient New Year festival
King-god
Four-ness
Writing—calendar—vision—order—cosmos—the ordered world—hieratic city-states—kingship—large-scale organized warfare—logos—fourfold order of the world—crown—marriage—heaven on earth—goal achieved—initiation—new year—end of the old way, beginning of the new way—death of the king, birth of the king—top of the mountain—royal couple—gold—a new world
Genitality and genital imagery in general—marriage—sex

What we have here is a schema of psychomythic development in which each stage is represented by a constellation of metaphors pertaining to the relationship between libido development (in its broadest sense) and cultural evolution. We can derive a clinical application by recognizing the metaphoric significance of such images and themes in clinical material and associating them with stages in development. These images and themes, of course, appear frequently in the drawings and play of children, in the dreams and fantasies of adult patients, and in the delusions and hallucinations of psychotic patients. *Psychosexual* development recognizes the projection of psyche onto the skin. *Psychosocial* development recognizes the projection of psyche into the social surround. *Psychomythic* development recognizes the projection of psyche onto the surround of nature, the environment, politics, philosophy, religion, and, ultimately, onto the walls of the universe.

The Great Pyramid of Khufu, Egypt.

One of the three smaller pyramids associated with The Pyramid of Menakaure.
It presumably contains one of Menakaure's wives.
This pyramid (G3-a) was built in ancient Egypt's Fourth Dynasty 2613–2494 BCE.

THE URBAN REVOLUTION AND THE GENITAL STAGE OF LIBIDO DEVELOPMENT

Pillars of the Temple of Karnak
from the 19th Dynasty 1295–1186 BCE.

Union of the opposites. The sun disc with two snakes: one
with the hat of the upper valley and the other with the hat
of the lower valley. Found in the Temple of Karnak.

Ramses II with his daughter Benta-Anta
in the Temple of Karnak: 13th century BCE.

A clay Syro-Hittite standing female fertility figure, possibly Astarte
(4 ½ inches tall) 1500–1000 BCE. Abraham, the patriarch of the
Abrahamic religions, is said to have smashed the idols of local gods in favor
of a single unified immaterial God in the 1st or 2nd millennium BCE.
That is about the time to which this figure is dated.

Typical ceramic oil lamp 1st century ACE from Israel –
Early Roman period. The fan-like shape was developed in Israel
and possibly associated with the reign of Herod the Great
and, of course, the time of Jesus.

The great cow goddess, Hathor, who carries the sun across the skies on her horns, suckles the
female pharaoh, Hatshepsut. 15th century BCE.

Some of the earliest writing in the world. Cuneiform writing on a 'planoconvex' brick. Early Bronze Age Sumer 2570–2342 BCE. Museum of the Ancient Orient, Istanbul, Turkey.

Ancient Egyptian calendar from the Temple of Kom Ombo, Egypt, 2nd–1st century BCE. the Ptolemaic Period.

Teotihuacan pyramid near Mexico City
built between 100 BCE and 250 ACE.

Codex Cospi – Magical calendar, Mexico, Mixtec culture. c. 1350–1500 ACE.

The Aztec Calendar Stone, or Stone of the Sun. Museo Nacional de Antropología in Mexico City c1930s. A name glyph of the Aztec ruler Moctezuma II, suggests the basalt Aztec sun stone was carved c1502–1521. It depicts the cosmology of the Aztecs.

A portion of an Aztec mural depicting a priest conducting the ritual of world renewal celebrated at the end of a 52 year cycle of time. Museo Nacional de Antropología. Mexico City.

Modern tapestry based on the ancient Mexican Codex Nuttall of Mixtec origin. The scene depicts the fire lighting ritual at the end of a 52 year cycle when all flames are extinguished and the gods either grant or deny fire to the people for the next 52 year cycle.

PART 3

Libido, Culture, and Consciousness

CHAPTER 9

Cosmogony and Cosmology, Anamnesis and Psychic Structure

> Persons in therapy—or anybody for that matter—are not simply engaged in knowing their world: what they are engaged in is a passionate re-forming of their world by virtue of their interrelationship with it.
>
> —Rollo May, *The Courage to Create*

If we look at the history of the world after the Urban Revolution, we see a mix of libidinal themes in the cultural derivative material embedded in technologies, myths, religions, customs, and traditions. So why did I see such a parallel between the stages of libido development and the early stages of cultural evolution? Was prehistory simply a screen for my projections? Did I put on my psychoanalytic lenses, look into prehistory, and see nothing more than the way I was looking?

Perhaps the stage-by-stage appearance of libido development in prehistory has something to do with the development of defenses in the transformation from Narcissus to Oedipus—that is, from a cultural self-absorption to increasing object-relatedness. Perhaps, naked before the world yet equipped with a human symbolic function, we naturally took up challenges for which we had some psychological familiarity. It makes sense, after all, that the first concerns of a self-aware being and a self-aware culture are the awe of being and the terror of nonbeing.

When a deceased loved one refuses to recognize us, return our gaze, or answer our call, we are somehow reminded of the mutual recognition of mother and baby that is now suddenly so painfully absent. Defensively, and unconsciously, we imagine that the deceased will be reborn to meet its mother on the other side of death. Toilet training and the negotiation of control between mother and child are echoed in society's innovations of trade and sacrifice. The discovery of genital difference and its social implications for procreation between mother and father become embedded in fertility rites, whether they are planting or harvesting rituals, and are projected further into the worship of gods and goddesses. And finally, the adolescent development of an identity including adult sexual relations and emerging worldviews becomes the prototype for sacral kingship. Embedded in all of this is human psychic structure—

specifically our symbolic function and the capacity to project human experience into our world by way of metaphor.

My musings on the diachronic sequence of libido development and its one-to-one relation to cultural evolution are far from explanations. But perhaps it's enough to simply recognize that cultural problems awakened our individual psychodynamics, or our individual psychodynamics were used to meet the challenges of cultural problems. In addition to all of that, however, there is cognitive structure, which gives rise to narrative structure, which shapes our experience of the world and naturally compels us to create a world in our own image.

Hero Mythology and the Structure of the Psyche

Freud and Rank analogized the ego of childhood with the hero of myth, and Freud recognized in the myth of Oedipus some of the central dynamics in psychological and cultural development. Myths and rituals from all around the world contain striking similarities, some of which are attributable to direct cultural diffusion, and others are a function of our shared human cognitive structure. Brian Sutton-Smith (1975) cited the work of two folklorists, Elli and Pierre Maranda, who devised a system for studying traditional folktales involving conflict. The Marandas described the following levels:

Level I—One power overwhelms another and there is no attempt to respond.
Level II—A minor power attempts to respond to an attacking power but fails.
Level III—A minor power nullifies an original threat.
Level IV—The threat is nullified and the original circumstances are substantially transformed.

In Level I to Level IV tales we can easily see the development of the hero myth. When Sutton-Smith applied this system of categorization to a group of children's fantasy narratives—that is, stories told out of children's imagination—he found that the 5- and 6-year-olds told predominantly Level I and II stories, and 7-to-10-year-olds told predominantly Level II and III stories (p. 91). This seems to suggest that humans see the world through the lens of the hero motif. We see the world as the hero does, a chaos that must be tamed to establish cosmos. And if our cognitive structure organizes the way we see the world and the way we tell what happened in the world, it might actually have shaped, to a certain extent, what we did in the world as well.

Cosmogonic Mythology and Narrative Structure

Interestingly enough, when we read cosmogonic mythology—that is, myths of the origins of the world—we find that the metaphors related to the four stages of psychomythic development are frequently recapitulated. Themes of Death and Unity characterize the beginnings of these myths and are followed by images and themes of Birth and Separation, then Ascension and Conflict, and finally Transformation and the Establishment of Order. Themes of chaos and associated notions lead to the separation of opposites, the opposites interact, and the interaction results in a new order. Oneness is split into two, the two-ness gives rise to a third, and the dynamism of three-ness gives rise to the stability of four.

What I hope to demonstrate here is that, curiously, the stages of libido development and the stages of cultural evolution find common ground in the four metaphor constellations of the psychomythic developmental schema and that we can recognize these metaphors and their sequence embedded in cosmogonic mythology. According to Eliade (1958a):

> Initiatory death signifies the end at once of childhood, of ignorance, and of the profane condition. For archaic thought, nothing better expresses the idea of an end, of the final completion of anything, than death, just as nothing better expresses the idea of creation, of making, building, constructing, than the cosmogony. The cosmogonic myth serves as the paradigm, the exemplary model, for every kind of making. Nothing better ensures the success of any creation (a village, a house, a child) than the fact of copying it after the greatest of all creations, the cosmogony. (p. xii)

The following are a few examples of cosmogonies in which the myth motifs seemingly recapitulate the four stages I have been describing. Within the cosmogonies below, I use numbers to call attention to the first, second, third, and fourth stages of psychomythic development, which are each constellations of metaphors expressive of psychological and cultural development. One could easily find many more myths that fit the schema and others that are close to it, but this selection will make the point:

Example 1: The Bushongo of Zaire say that in the beginning all was dark, everywhere there was water, and Bumba was alone (1—oneness, unity, aloneness, water as chaos). Then one day Bumba felt a pain inside and vomited up the sun (2—mouth birth, light and darkness), which spread light across the world and dried up much of the water so that the reefs and sandbanks became visible (2—duality, separation of world into land and water). Then Bumba vomited up the moon, the stars, many of the animals, and, finally, man himself (2—birth as in mouth birth). After that, Bumba's three sons finished the world (3—three-ness). When the world was complete, Bumba showed the people how to draw fire out of wood (3—fire). Bumba strolled through the villages and said to the people, "Behold these wonders. They belong to you" (4—established order, creation of a new world, transformation) (Sproul, 1979, pp. 44-45).

Example 2: The creation myth of the Finno-Ugric describes the beginning of the world as an unending watery mass (1—watery mass, chaos, oneness), above which a beautiful teal lightly hovered and flew in search of a place to build its nest. Not finding any land, she considered making her nest in the wind or possibly on the waves, but recognizing the instability of such a home, she discounted these ideas and flew on. Then the Mother of the Waters lifted her knee above the waterline so that the teal could have a solid place for her nest (2—separation of land and water, island, nest, house, birth). The teal, seeing Water Mother's knee, thought it was a hillock, landed, built her nest, and laid seven eggs—six of gold and one of iron (2—nest, house, birth). As the teal brooded on her eggs, Water Mother's knee grew warm (3—heat). With each day passing, the spot under the nest grew hotter and hotter. After three days, the heat became so intense that Water Mother thought her knee was burning and her veins melting (3—three days, heat, melting, burning). In pain, her knee shook convulsively, sending the eggs down into the waves of the ocean, where they shattered. But just then a wondrous change came over them. The lower fragment of the eggshell rose high into the sky and became the lofty arch of heaven, the yolk became the moon, the mottled portion became the stars, and that which was blackish became the clouds (4—new world, transformation) (pp. 176-78).

Example 3: The Taoist cosmogony begins with chaos. Out of the chaos (1—chaos) came a pure light, which formed the sky, and a heavy dimness, which formed the earth. From the separation of the sky and the earth came the roots of the yin and the yang—the feminine and the masculine principles—and all manner of things (2—separation of opposites, sky and earth, yin and yang, feminine and masculine, two-ness). From the yin and the yang came the five elements, from which was formed a man (2—birth). The man stood and watched the sun sinking in the west, the moon rising in the east, and all the stars circling a great star in the middle of the world. Out of this fabulous celestial drama fell a brilliant ray of light (3—interaction of the opposites, phenomena of the sky, ray of light as phallus). It fell to earth right before the newly created man, and as it did, it transformed into a man who was completely golden in color. The

Gold Colored One bowed before the man and then taught him how to make clothes to cover his nakedness, gave him a name, showed him how to collect and prepare roots for his nourishment, explained the journey of the stars and the yearlong path of the sun and moon, and told him of the creation of the world (4—new worldview, transformation, the yearlong path of the sun and the moon) (p. 200).

Example 4: The Maidu Native Americans of California conceive of the world's beginning as a mass of darkness in which there was only water—and water was everywhere. There was no sun, no moon, and no stars (1—chaos, oneness, darkness, water). A raft (2—boat as a house) was floating on the water and moving down from the north. On it was Turtle and Father of the Secret Society. Then, from up above, a rope of feathers (3—axis mundi, phallus) was let down, and climbing down from it came Earth-Initiate. Earth-Initiate had many powers and was going to create the earth, but he needed some soil to begin with. Turtle volunteered to go get some. A rock was tied to his left arm to pull him down and a rope tied to pull him up. He dove down and was gone for six years. When he returned, all that he had collected from the bottom had washed away except for that which was under his toenails. Earth-Initiate took out a stone knife from his armpit and scraped the tiny bits of earth from under Turtle's nails. He put the tiny specks of earth between his hands and rolled them around until they formed a little ball the size of a pebble (2—pebble, stone, center, birth). He set it on the raft and left it for a time. Then, a while later, he took a second look at it. It had not changed, so he left it again. When he looked at it a third time, however, it had expanded to a size big enough to put one's arms around it (3—three, third look, expansion). He left it again, and when he looked at it for the fourth time (4—four, transformation), he found that it had become as big as the world and the raft had run aground. Then Earth-Initiate called the sun, moon, and stars into their places and made a great tree to grow (3—sky, tree, phallus, axis mundi, ascension). Then some of the deities came into being and Earth-Initiate created the plants and animals. At long last, Earth-Initiate created a man and a woman and gave them hands like his own (4—new world, transformation) (pp. 237-42).

Cosmogonic myths do not pertain to the objective origins and history of the universe, creation of the planet Earth, or the evolution of the species. They are metaphors on the threshold of psychological development and cultural evolution. But this sequence of metaphors (Death and Unity, Birth and Separation, Ascension and Conflict, Transformation and the Establishment of Order) is not limited to cosmogonic myths, as they are found in rites of passage, myths of the origins of fire, and other myths and rituals as well. The following is a Kwakwaka'wakw initiation ritual in which we can see another example of the fourfold sequence:

Example 5: The indigenous people known as the Kwakwaka'wakw, native to North America's Pacific Northwest, initiate their children into the lowest level of their "Dancing Societies" at age 10 or 12. In the ritual itself, the children fall into a trance (1—death) while listening to the sound of the sacred instruments. They are carried off into the wilderness and after a time are returned to the village and taken into the ceremonial house (2—house, village, center). In the center of the ceremonial house is a cedar pole 30 feet high representing the mythic "copper pillar." In Kwakwaka'wakw myth, the copper pillar is symbolic of the axis mundi (3—copper pillar, axis mundi, metal) by which one may traverse the three worlds: underworld, earthly realms, and the heavens. In some forms of Kwakwaka'wakw initiation, the novice is tied to the pillar and must struggle (3—cosmic conflict) to free himself. In this struggle, he is said to be fighting with the cannibal spirit. In another form of Kwakwaka'wakw initiation, the novices climb to the top of the pillar (3—climbing, ascension). In both cases, the ascension leads to the Door to the World Above. Arrival at this World Above marks the novice's entry into the Dancing Society and, as such, is symbolic of the initiate's passage from childhood to adulthood (4—new worldview, transformation) (Eliade, 1958a, pp. 68-72).

Fire, as we have seen, is a culture maker associated with the interaction of the opposites, with light, warmth, cooking, the firing of ceramics, and the smelting of metal ore. It is also a metaphor of creativity, sex, aggression, and the process of transformation. The defining act of many culture heroes is their theft of fire (the light of consciousness) from the gods through a struggle or an act of trickery. The following is an origin of fire myth reminiscent of the four stages we saw in the cosmogonies and initiation rite:

Example 6: The Bergdamara of South West Africa say that in the days before man had fire, it was very cold on earth (1—suffering). Desiring the warmth of a fire, a man said to his wife, "Tonight I will cross the river, and over there I will fetch me a firebrand from the village of the lion." So the man crossed the river and entered the lion's hut (2—hut, house, center). The lion, the lioness, and their cubs sat together in a circle around the fire, the cubs gnawing on human bones. The man was offered a seat and sat down next to the fire. When the opportunity presented itself, he threw the cubs into the fire, stole a firebrand (3—fire, theft, conflict), rushed out the door, and made his way across the river before the lion could catch him. When he got to his own hut, he gathered up woods of many different varieties, and while he kindled his fire he said, "Thou fire shalt henceforth be in all wood." And so it was that fire came to reside dormant in the many types of wood and that man came to know about them (4–transformation) (Frazer, 1930, p. 111).

These are not the only myths that fit the pattern, nor is it true that all myths fit the pattern. But the pattern is easily recognized in many myths and allows us to elaborate the four previously described constellations of metaphors as an interface between cognitive structure, libido development, and cultural evolution. Based on these and a number of other cosmogonies, I have further elaborated the four metaphor constellations, first presented in chapter 8, in the following way. They help us to see how the dynamics in the four developmental stages can be elaborated with different metaphors:

1. *Death and Unity*
Oneness
Soul–spirit–anima–ancestor spirit–demon–name–image–amulet–cannibalism–wandering–hunter-gatherer–nomadic life–undifferentiated–cave–chaos–death–shapeless lumpy matter–inert matter–confused matter–a single body–primordial being–watery mass–egg–water–murder–descent into the underworld–darkness–no desire–no hunger–no thirst–desire–hunger–thirst–suffering–unconscious–sleep–death–hell–alone–cold–eating like the animals that graze on grass–underworld–all the people, animals and plants speak the same language–direct communication with the creator–living peacefully according to the laws of the creator–Paradise

2. *Birth and Separation*
Two-ness
House–temple–sweat lodge–ceremonial house–hut–temple–temenos–sacred space–village walls–boundaries–limits–fence–garden–pot–mortar and pestle–weaving–baskets–oven–bread–kiln–ceramics–agriculture–domestication of animals–trade–mother and child–bow and arrow–duality–the center–birth–psychological birth–spiritual birth–boat–womb–place of birth–split–divide–separation–division–difference–the fall–fall from grace–navel–umbilical–center point–crystal–egg–light–separation of heaven and earth–separation of earth and water–separation of light and dark–island–broken egg–sun and moon–feminine and masculine–animals live separate from the people–trade–quarrels–consciousness

3. Ascension and Conflict
Three-ness
Stone monuments—pillars—trees—poles—fire—metallurgy—metal—sex and fertility—fighting—conflict—battle between opposites—theft—war—hammer—axe—thunderbolt—sky—sun—plow—ambition—striving—conflict—interaction—dynamism—ascension—father—sun father—expansion—multiplying—increasing—mountain—smoke hole in the top of the hut—firebrand—sacred hill—oedipal themes—phallic images—penis—rising smoke or anything rising—flying—foot—finger—spear—scepter—apotheosis—theft of fire—inflation—ladder—bridge—rainbow—rope—thread—jealousy—tree—tower—ladder—ascension—moving up—ray of light—spear—rope of feathers—axis mundi—copper pillar—sexual enlightenment—circles—enclosures

4. Transformation and the Establishment of Order
Four-ness
Writing—calendar—vision—new worldview—order—cosmos—the ordered world—hieratic city-states—kingship—large-scale organized warfare—logos—fourfold order of the world—crown—marriage—heaven on earth—goal achieved—initiation—new year—end of the old way, beginning of the new way—death of the king, birth of the king—top of the mountain—royal couple—gold—creation of a new world—disseminating light—disseminating knowledge—culture hero—king—sage—ruler—mature genital imagery—marriage—sex—world complete

The *psychosexual* stages of development pertain to the psychological organization of libidinal experiences that shift and change in relation to the oral-, anal-, phallic-, and genital-stage demands. They are involved with tension and release; pleasure and pain; sexual satisfaction and frustration; and the various part instincts of oral erotism, oral aggression, cannibalism, sadism, masochism, anal retention, anal expulsion, fetishism, voyeurism, exhibitionism, and so forth. Psychosexual experiences are organized into erotic behavior, erotic displacements, derivative material, symptomatology, and symbolic dream imagery.

The *psychosocial* stages of development pertain to the social circumstances, social consequences, and social phenomena that parallel the stages of psychosexual development. They deal with the socialization of orality, anality, oedipality, and genitality in familial and societal contexts.

The *psychomythic* stages of development that I propose are an additional level of projection, introjection, and reciprocal action. If the psychosexual is experienced on the skin and the psychosocial is projected into the social surround, the psychomythic is projected onto the walls of the universe. The psychomythic is the psychology that is projected into religion, philosophy, politics, and other phenomena on the big screens of human culture.

One person sees in God the good father he never had. Another finds that God is just as absent as his own father. Another disowns responsibility for problems in his life and registers his complaints with a God who is being lazy. For some, God is an all-powerful punishing brute; for others, God is a paranoid vision of an all-powerful and all-knowing persecutor. Some find in God a maternal warmth with which to merge in oneness. Others play duality games, finding wisdom in recognizing the play of opposites. Some make a religious practice of holding on and letting go. Some organize themselves around a trinity of Father, Son, and Holy Ghost; father, mother, and divine child; Brahma, Vishnu, and Shiva. Others strive to reach God, and still others engage in fierce competition in order to gain God's favor or compete with God himself. Some devote themselves to the kingdom of God and the politics of God's plan here on earth.

Our images of gods throughout history look like a family album: god as mother, as father, as copulating couple, as divine child, as mother nursing her baby, as a mother and her incestuous son-lover, as a disciplining father, as battling brothers, as the dying young god, as the young woman Sophia (wisdom), as Lady Liberty, as Lady Justice, as Lady Luck, as the anima mundi, as a hero, as a virgin, as a virgin mother. Our gods even appear in the form of the family pet: the serpent, the jackal, the raven, the bull. While the conscious mind may be theistic or atheistic, the unconscious is always pantheistic insofar as it animates and personifies our impulses and the world.

A little boy having difficulties sleeping marched into my office for the first time and said quite directly, "My mother told me you know about monsters and how to get rid of them." I replied, "Well, she's half right. I do know about monsters, but I don't know how to get rid of them. I know how to help you make friends with them." The monsters under his bed, in his closet, and outside his windows were his own impulses emerging as projections into the silence and darkness of the night. When he could draw pictures of them and dictate stories about them for me to write down, he gained mastery over his fears of them and, in a sense, made friends with his monsters and his personified impulses.

The unconscious personifies our narcissism, our worldview, our fears, all that we reject, all that we hope for, all that we imagine. And what are the degrees of difference between the little boy who personifies his toy soldier and the theologian who personifies the universe? Do not mistake this equivalence as a reduction of religious experience to the mundane. My effort here is the other way around. I seek to locate the sacred in the secular.

We are not just talking about a projected god image or world image; we are also talking about a narrative regarding the construction of that image—a cosmogony. A cosmogonic myth ostensibly tells us, in metaphoric language, how the world got to be the way it is, how we got to be the way we are. But beyond that it tells us how we are constructing and reconstructing ourselves, and our world, in every moment. When we are involved in the construction of a worldview, we are also involved in the construction of our place in the world and, ultimately, in the construction of our self.

The cosmogonic myth is to the culture as the anamnesis (the telling of the story of one's own life) is to the individual. The cosmogony is a metaphor in myth for how a culture got to be the way it is, and the anamnesis is a metaphor in personal narrative for how a person got to be the way he or she is. In "The Personal Myth: A Problem in Psychoanalytic Technique," Ernst Kris (1956) addressed a particular clinical manifestation of some patients who use their autobiographical memories as a protective screen. The story, which the patient clings to as an undeniable object, is invulnerable to exploration or doubt. The personal myth is retained as a treasured object with an anal tinge to it. A certain pleasure is derived from reminiscing and recalling life's experiences in the ways that we do. While Kris was describing a particular clinical manifestation, I think we see some form of this personal myth-making whenever the ego's synthetic function is active in making something of the inner and outer worlds. Although some are more flexible than others, when it comes to exploring their story and questioning certain aspects of it (such as one's innocence, guilt, activity, passivity, complaints, hidden responsibility, styles of involvement in life, roles in the repetition compulsion, etc.), we all tend to favor the story we have carried for so many years, as it provides a cover and justification for how the world is and how we got to be the way we are. Analysis pulls the anamnesis apart, and synthesis allows us to rewrite a more inclusive version and also live more consciously, responsibly, pleasurably, and, most of all, more comfortably within our own skin.

Herman Nunberg (1931) explained that the ego must reconcile the demands of the id, the superego, and reality and to do so employs a synthetic function, which "assimilates alien elements (both from within and from without), and it mediates between opposing elements and even reconciles opposites and sets mental productivity in train" (p. 125). Nunberg suggested that it is from eros that the ego acquires its binding and productive power: "If we examine the causal links in a schizophrenic's chain of thought, we nearly always come upon personified (animistic) causes, and, as a rule, the last link is a rationalized explanation of the genesis of the world and of human beings" (p. 127).

The synthetic function unites, binds, creates, simplifies, and generalizes. And even though all of that is easily recognizable in everyday experience, it is most evident in the desperate attempts of schizophrenics to reconcile contradictory delusions and experiences of their inner and outer worlds into a philosophy of life. Nunberg said, "As a rule, this philosophy of life turns out to be a cosmology, based on the problem of the genesis of man" (p. 128). "It seems that in conditions such as that of schizophrenic disintegration, where Eros is most seriously menaced by the loss of object-libido, the ego makes the greatest efforts after synthesis" (p. 129).

Nunberg wrote that repression depends on the synthetic function being temporarily inadequate and that it is through psychoanalysis that one lifts the amnesia, retrieves the unassimilated aspects of experience, relates them to other memories and thoughts, connects them and reconciles them with the rest of the ego, thus making what once was alien to the ego and ejected from the ego organization into something that is a part of and is integrated with the rest of the ego. In this way, psychoanalysis assists in effecting a synthesis where previously there was only a symptom.

Donald Meltzer (1981) found a charming way of describing Melanie Klein's model: "Mrs. Klein described, in effect, what you might call a theological model of the mind. Every person has to have what you might describe as a 'religion' in which his internal objects perform the functions of Gods—but it is not a religion that derives its power because of belief in these Gods but because these Gods do in fact perform functions in the mind" (p. 179). And Becker (1973) wrote of the creative type, "His creative work is at the same time the expression of his heroism and the justification of it. It is his private religion—as Rank put it" (p. 172).

The personal cosmogony, as autobiography or anamnesis, changes over time, and so do the cosmogonies of cultures. Cosmogonies help us maintain sameness and also help us to change. Traditional and aboriginal cultures facilitate ritual healings and initiations by recounting the cosmogonic myth of their community. The modern individual, on the other hand, takes his suffering soul to a psychotherapist, tells his personal cosmogony—the story of how he got to be the way he is—and tells it again and again in hour after hour. Each time the story is told, the analyst listens, recognizes figures of speech as defenses, interprets the resistances, listens for instinctual subtexts, interprets the forbidden wishes, listens to the other to whom the narrative is directed, and interprets that transference. The patient's repetition compulsion becomes elaborated like a script, and disowned aspects that appear as symptoms, slips of the tongue, and countertransference are returned to the patient as new elements for inclusion in the script. In this way, the stories beyond the cover story are illuminated and the anamnesis, or cosmogony, is rewritten, in a sense, as a mode of healing.

"Cosmogony," a term derived from Greek, means the origins of order, and cosmogonic myths describe the origins of the order of the universe. In cosmogonic mythology we typically find that the world begins in an undifferentiated or fused state (chaos) and evolves to subsequently achieve order (cosmos). There are many ways of arriving at this transformation, but it is often by way of a simple separation of the primordial chaos into a duality. The two aspects of the duality give rise to a third interactive element, which brings about a further elaboration. This elaboration then reaches a transformative threshold, beyond which a new order is established. In one of the cosmogonies described in Genesis, the beginning is marked by darkness and formlessness. It is followed by the separation of light and dark. After this rudimentary separation of day and night, the world is further differentiated into water and dry land, plants and animals, and, finally, the creation of man and woman in God's own image. And then God says, "'Let there be lights in the firmament of the heavens to separate the day from the night; and let them be for signs and for seasons and for days and years. And let them be lights in the firmament of the heavens to give light upon the earth'" (Sproul, 1979, pp. 122-25).

In another Old Testament cosmogony, all was bliss in the Garden of Eden until Adam and Eve ate from the Tree of Knowledge of Good and Evil. After that, they knew of goodness and evil, maleness and femaleness, and, of course, the inside and outside of the Garden of Eden. Thus, the fall from grace, or the rupture of the primal unity, represents a birth or elevation of consciousness (p. 125).

The separation of the primal opposites is analogous to the fall from grace, the expulsion from Eden. In Becker's (1973) view, "The foundation stone for Kierkegaard's view of man is the myth of the Fall, the ejection of Adam and Eve from the Garden of Eden. In this myth is contained, as we saw, the basic insight of psychology for all time: that man is a union of opposites, of self-consciousness and of physical body" (pp. 68-69).

While these myths, and others like them, tell us nothing about astronomy, geology, or the evolution of the human species, they tell us a good deal about culture and psychology in the metaphors of world creation. The theme of world creation in the psychology of the individual illuminates the projection of an internal organizing principle onto the external world. One way of describing an analytic therapy is the decoding or interpretation of the patient's projections into the external world.

Psychotherapy is the process of rewriting a troublesome personal cosmogony, one that has resulted in excessive suffering and leaves certain questions unanswered—questions like *What is my place in the universe? What is my place in the world? What is my place in my family? How can I live at peace in this body?* In psychotherapy the patient tells the therapist the story of his or her life. As this personal myth is explored in the context of the transference, forgotten elements are recalled, new experiences are encountered, and attempts are made to integrate these into a new cosmogony, to create a new worldview. At the end of a successful therapy, the patient sees the world in a new way and casts himself or herself in a new role within it (Benveniste, 1988). Freud (1933/1964c) stated it bluntly: "Psycho-analysis infers that he [the father creator], really is the father, with all the magnificence in which he once appeared to the small child. A religious man pictures the creation of the universe just as he pictures his own origin" (SE 22, p. 163).

Frank Barron (1963), in his discussion of the creative writer, asserted that "such individuals are involved constantly in the creation of their private universes of meaning; they are cosmologists all. I am convinced that without this intense cosmological commitment no amount of mental ability of the sort measured by I.Q. tests will suffice to produce a genuinely creative act" (p. 243). Freud (1908/1959d) asked, "Might we not say that every child at play behaves like a creative writer, in that he creates a world of his own, or, rather re-arranges the things of his world in a way which pleases him?" (SE 9, pp. 143-44). Thomas Mann (1936) wrote, "The mythical interest is as native to psychoanalysis as the psychological interest is to all creative writing. Its penetration into the childhood of the individual soul is at the same time a penetration into the childhood of mankind, into the primitive and mythical. For the myth is the foundation of life; it is the timeless schema, the pious formula into which life flows when it reproduces its traits out of the unconscious" (p. 15).

Recalling the epigraph at the beginning of this chapter, Rollo May (1975) said: "Persons in therapy—or anybody for that matter—are not simply engaged in knowing their world: what they are engaged in is a passionate re-forming of their world by virtue of their interrelationship with it" (p. 161). And Barnaby Barratt (1984) echoed a similar sentiment: "An understanding of the world is conditioned by the inner order and disorder of the one who understands. Each person is, in a certain sense, his or her own cosmologist" (p. 2).

In "Observations on World Destruction Fantasies," William J. Spring (1939) wrote, "The idea that the world is coming to an end, or has already done so is one which is frequently met in schizophrenics, particularly in the early stages of the illness" (p. 48). I have seen this clinically on many occasions with psychotic patients. I once knew a young woman, a chronic schizophrenic, who was alienating many of the residents at a residential treatment facility by preaching her own brand of fundamentalist Christian rhetoric and offering warnings about the coming end of the world. No one wanted to listen to her, but one evening I invited her to talk with me about these matters, which were obviously of great importance to her. She was delighted to have a receptive audience and immediately began speaking about the Bible, the Book of Revelations, and, specifically, Armageddon. But after only a minute or two the biblical story merged into her own delusional vision, and then, almost imperceptibly, the prophecy of the Armageddon yet to occur was transformed into an event that had already happened. With total clarity, she confessed that Armageddon is not yet to come but has already occurred and that it took place, most specifically, at the local mental hospital during her most recent acute psychotic episode. For the next half hour, she spoke freely, clearly, realistically, and with great feeling about the horrors of this hospital stay and the terrors she endured as her world fell apart.

David Rosenfeld (1992) asserted, "The conception of the 'end of the world' feeling, in which the thing and object representations are lost also implies a breakdown of the transference.... But there is a struggle, and that is what makes it possible to re-establish it. Psychotic restitution, delusion and hallucinations are all attempts at the restitution of the bond" (p. 12).

Millenarian myths, the complement to cosmogonic myths, include Armageddon, the Apocalypse, the end of the Mayan calendar, the Hopi warning of the end of the fourth world, and Noah's flood. They find further expression in countless modern-day predictions of the end of the world by cult leaders, mystics, and placard-carrying prophets of doom in city centers across the country (Cohen, 2012). Thus, the world destruction fantasies are simply the inverse of the world creation fantasies. World destruction fantasies accompany decompensation and world creation fantasies accompany recompensation.

James Grotstein (2000) considers "autochthony and cosmogony to be the fundamental architects of unconscious fantasy, dreaming, and, ultimately, thinking" (p. 49). He described *autochthony* as "the unconscious phantasy of self-creation *and* of creation of the object—and *cosmogony*, the creation of a world order" (p. 38). Autochthony and cosmogony, he wrote, "format the mind of infants to help them order their primordial encounter with chaos (infinity) and define the difference, for example, between the event, or stimulus, and the personal experience of it" (p. 49). The cosmogonic faculty pertains to world creation and world ordering (p. 256). It is operative in the infant's attempt to create first a personal cosmology and later an objective cosmology. It draws on primary process thinking and later on both primary and secondary process thinking (pp. 51–52). "Exercise of the principle faculty of cosmogony represents a constructivist attempt (solely by the self) to establish a sense of personal cosmic order for the emotional events of life" (p. 52).

It is important to remember that just as the anamnesis is a cover story and defensive construction with implications for personal and interpersonal behavior, the cosmogony is also a cover story with implications for ethical order within its cultural context. Lawrence E. Sullivan (1985) gave a nice example of this:

> Andean cosmogony appears to govern, through ritual, the structure of a community's experience of that which is "true" and "real." The result is an ethical emphasis on the discernment of proper relations of individual to group and group to cosmos in space and time. Divining the origins and meanings of these relations determines the moral quality of one's experience and perception. The consequences of improperly

structured experience or misperception of cosmic and social relations are not limited to an individual mistake in judgment. They possess dire cosmic effects: infertility of crops, animals, and humans; famine; epidemic; catastrophe. (p. 99)

In a sense, the continued fruitful interplay of cosmogonic elements in the cosmos is dependent upon the history of proper human action, which relies, in turn, on observance of cosmic order. Cosmogonic order and human ethical behavior relate dialectically as two necessary antipodes which serve as passages out of the chaos and finitude inherent in their respective natures. (p. 105)

Sullivan's comments on Andean cosmogony remind us of Eliade's (1954/1971) discussion of archetypes and repetition in which archaic man establishes reality by imitating the celestial archetype. Any divergence from the cosmic order or transgressions of the proper way of living bring about suffering as punishment (pp. xv, 97–98).

From Cosmogony to Cosmology

Cosmogony, a myth of world creation, is to anamnesis as cosmology, a model of the structure of the universe, is to the structure of the psyche. Ernst Cassirer (1944) put it this way: "In the first mythological explanations of the universe we always find a primitive anthropology side by side with a primitive cosmology" (p. 3). In other words, we see our universe through our humanness and see our humanness in the universe.

Primitive cosmologies often divide the universe into seven aspects, the first four of which correspond to the four constellations of metaphors in the psychomythic schema I have described. Might the subsequent three aspects tell us something about human development after adolescence and about human history after the Urban Revolution? I looked into that question, hoping to find such confirmation, but with only moderate success. Even where there might have been some correspondence, it felt forced and bound to modern thinking rather than to some sort of universal human pattern. Nonetheless, the pattern that I recognized in a number of cosmologies has a fascinating quality that I had not anticipated.

The last three of the seven aspects of many cosmologies are intimately related to the first four aspects. In this regard it is useful to visualize the seven stages of a cosmology as a pyramid of four steps: the first step leads to the second, which leads to the third, which leads to the fourth at the top. Then the fifth, one step down on the other side of the pyramid, is related to and on the same level as the third, and the sixth is related to and on the same level as the second, and the seventh is related to and on the same level as the first.

> The first step is unity—no differentiation, death, chaos, fusion, Paradise.
>
> The second step is duality—the separation of the opposites, birth, expulsion from Paradise, fall from grace.
>
> The third step is trinity—the interaction of the opposites giving rise to a third aspect or object, struggle, conflict, heroic battle, the oedipal triangle from the position of the child with two parents.
>
> The fourth step, at the top, is the adolescent's vision of a new world and an erotic marriage—the development of an identity and a new worldview.
>
> The fifth step is a return to the same level as the third step but this time as an adult. It is the quintessence—the achievement of the vision of the fourth step in the form of work done or children born. It is the oedipal triangle but this time from the position of the parent in relation to the child.
>
> The sixth step is a return to the same level as the second step but this time as an adult. It is not the separation of the opposites but rather the Reconciliation of the Opposites, the confrontation with one's limitations, errors, failures, life that was unlived, our dark side, all of which are revealed to us by our work and/or our children.
>
> The seventh step is a return to the same level as the first step. It is the unity and integrity that comes with the Reconciliation of the Opposites into an ironic position at peace and ready to die. Or it is the collapse of opposites into a private chaos and eventual death.

Psychomythic Pyramid

4
Transformation and the Establishment of Order
Vision
Quaternity
New worldview
Marriage

3
Ascension and Conflict
Trinity
Interaction of the opposites
Oedipal triangle from position of the child
Ambition

5
Fruitfulness
Bringing the vision down to earth
Intimacy and Generativity
Oedipal triangle from position of the adult
Children and work

2
Birth and Separation of opposites
Duality
Control & No control
Linear time
Child & Mother

6
Reconciliation of the Opposites
Confrontation with the shadow
Facing what was left out
Balance
Androgyne

1
Death and Unity
Undifferentiated
Darkness
Chaos & bliss
Eternal now

7
Relinquishing of Will
Opposites united
Return to unity
Decay
Death

An example of the seven steps in a specific cosmology will make it clearer.

The Seven Heavens

The ancient Greeks projected their psyches and their culture into the heavens and defined a set of gods among the heavenly bodies. The astrologers gave the planets their attributes and named them after the gods. The European alchemists then ordered the planets into a sequence that confirmed the alchemical cosmology. When the ancient Greeks, astrologers, and alchemists gazed into the heavens, they had no scientific method to evaluate their discoveries, so the walls of the universe became a screen for their collective projections. The European alchemists' cosmology is most frequently depicted in drawings illustrating their texts, and these drawings typically include only seven heavenly bodies, which are arranged in the following order:

1. Saturn   2. Jupiter   3. Mars   4. Sun   5. Venus   6. Mercury   7. Moon

The first planet, Saturn, represents both the circle in space and the cycle in time. It pertains to endings and the termination of life. It represents the way things that were strong at one time later become rigid and brittle, only to break, fracture, shatter, and turn into the dust from which the new form will take shape. Saturn is the lawgiver, and its laws are the boundaries of human existence. It is the sickle in the hand of Father Time, who reminds us that all who are born will die and all who die may be reborn. It is the destruction of a previous creation and the creation of something new out of the ashes of the old. Saturn is associated with time, the hourglass, the sarcophagus, putrefaction, the uroboros, melancholia, depth of thought, the color black, and with that stage in psychomythic development that I described as the stage of Death and Unity.

The second planet in the sequence is Jupiter, the planet of growth, wisdom, and planned expansion. It is called the prophet in that it pertains to things to come. While Saturn is associated with Cronos in the Greek pantheon of the gods, Jupiter is associated with Zeus. Cronos was in the habit of eating all of the children that his wife, Rhea, bore him. He did this because it was prophesied that one of his sons would dethrone him. When Zeus was born, however, Rhea took him to Mother Earth and left him in the care of three nymphs. Rhea then gave Cronos a stone wrapped in a baby blanket, saying it was her new son. Cronos swallowed the stone. Under the protection of Mother Earth, Zeus grew into manhood, emerged to overthrow Cronos, and subsequently became Lord of the Universe. Thus, Jupiter (Zeus) pertains to the new birth arising out of the Saturnal death. It is the infant, hope, optimism, expansion, the monad, and the golden egg. As such, I associate it with the psychomythic stage of Birth and Separation.

The third planet, Mars, represents personal initiative, the overcoming of obstacles, the warrior, the desire and spirit to overcome the limitations of earthly experience, an outgoing potency, and the instinct of aggression. It is associated with the Greek god Aries, the god of battle, and it represents the need to pierce through resisting obstacles in order to achieve that which is so precious. It is a pulling away from the center in much the same way that the hero must pull away from chaos and slay his dragon. Mars is further associated with hurt, strife, sharp and pointed things, fire, intensity, struggle and weaponry, and also to what I call the psychomythic stage of Ascension and Conflict.

The fourth planet, the sun, is called the source of life. It represents the center of creative self-expression, the spirit incarnated, and the microcosm mirroring back to the macrocosm. It is symbolic of the heart, light, power, and all positive male authority figures whether they be fathers, leaders, visionaries, or sovereigns. It is associated with the hero, courageous force, creativity, the guiding light, masculine identification, gold, and with what I call the stage of Transformation and the Establishment of Order.

The next three stages are what I see as the three steps on the other side of the psychomythic pyramid, each corresponding to one of the first three stages—the fifth with the third, the sixth with the second, and the seventh with the first.

The fifth planet, Venus, is the goddess of love and beauty. It represents the principle of attraction, which draws the opposite sexes together in the dance of courtship and spiritual union. It is associated with artistic creations, aesthetics, and nature's various means of drawing the sexes together (i.e., the colors and scents of the flowers, the songs of the birds, etc.). While the third planet, Mars, is characterized by its outgoing potency, Venus has the distinction of being characterized by its ingathering feminine magnetism. While Mars pulls things away from the center, Venus draws things in; and while Mars strives to overcome the limitations of earthly existence, Venus glorifies matter. If we liken Mars to the oedipal child in the stage of Ascension and Conflict and to the one who moves out from the center, we might see Venus as the mother (parent) who conceives, gives birth, protects, and nurtures her child at her own center. Venus, drawing things toward the center, or down to earth, represents the making real of the solar vision of the preceding stage. It is in this process of bringing reality to visions that Venus glorifies matter. By bringing the sexes together, a child is born and the vision is brought down to earth. I see Venus representing the psychomythic stage I call Fruitfulness.

The sixth planet, Mercury, is the emissary of the sun. It is the messenger. It is that which makes meaningful connections between seemingly unrelated threads in the fabric of reality. It is the principle that enables people to consider not only nature without but also nature within. It pertains to self-reflection. Mercury's talent for making connections is further expressed in its association with the nervous system and its reputed knack for relating objective and subjective realms of experience. Mercury is the mediator between the pairs of opposites. One has only to recall that the metal mercury has a great capacity for bonding different metals together. As a mediator or reconciler of opposites, Mercury reminds us of the second stage in psychomythic development, the stage distinguished by the separation of the opposites. Thus, it is as though the opposites, separated in the second stage, are brought together and reconciled in the sixth stage. I call this the psychomythic stage of the Reconciliation of the Opposites.

To recapitulate, in the first stage of psychomythic development, there needs to be a death in order to be born (reborn) psychologically. In the second stage there is a separation of opposites (I-thou; subject-object; male-female; now-then; here-there; in-out; etc.). In the third stage, the opposites interact bringing about the oedipal triangle from the perspective of the oedipal child. And in the fourth stage, we see the adolescent or young adult reordering the world and establishing an adult personality in relation to a personal vision or identity. In the fifth stage, we see either the birth of a child from the perspective of a parent or a piece of work that springs forth from the marriage or from the vision of the fourth stage. The fifth stage is a fulfilment of the vision, a crowning achievement, a great work - whatever it may have been. In the sixth stage, the Reconciliation of the Opposites, the achievement reveals its shadow side. One's child becomes an adolescent or young adult and returns home with news of what the parents left out or what the parents don't know. It can also be a piece of work that has been established for some time and then reveals its flaws or limitations. It could be Carl Jung's second half of life or Elliott Jacques's midlife crisis. It is about coming to terms with what has been left out of life or with the dark side of the vision. The Reconciliation of the Opposites has to do with encountering and reconciling with one's limitations, errors, or problems in relation to one's progeny or one's work. We look at what was and what wasn't in our life. We recognize we are not 23 and also not 93, so there is still time for something yet to be done. What will it be?

The seventh "planet," the moon, is passive, feminine, receptive, and always changing. It symbolizes the dual process of growth and decay. The moon's waxing and waning alludes to the cosmic truth of death and rebirth. Its placement at the end of this alchemical cosmology represents the end of a cycle and the beginning of a new one (Fabricius, 1976, pp. 46, 174; Cirlot, 1962; Moore & Douglas, 1971).

It is as though after the Reconciliation of the Opposites, the psyche, approaches oneness, and progresses to a passive, feminine, and receptive mode. We might also make room here for what Freud called the Death Instinct, or say that the Death Instinct is gaining the upper hand. The Death Instinct I refer to here is not that aspect defined as aggression, but the other aspect, described as entropy. It is the winding down and falling apart of the human organism relentlessly toward the inorganic. At this stage there is the decrease in sex hormones, the loss of muscular strength and flexibility, the increasing fragility of the bones, the loss of memory, the failing of cognitive faculties, the dulling of the senses. We write our memoirs, mentor the young and/or become a caricature of our previous selves. It is life coming eye to eye with death. It is the relinquishing of will as we make our way back to the inorganic. The association of the oneness of the seventh stage with the oneness of the first stage is transparent. The baby moves from nonbeing into being and the dying person is being and gazing out onto the horizon of nonbeing. I call this seventh stage the Relinquishing of Will.

I was able to find a roughly similar pattern in the seven chakras (Ananda, 1980; Leadbeater, 1927; Woodroffe, 1973), the cards in the Major Arcana of the Tarot (A. Douglas, 1973), the seven levels of the ten Sephirot of the Kabbalah (Ponce, 1973), the seven signs of the Zodiac (Moore & Douglas, 1971; Cirlot, 1962) as selected and arranged in the alchemical text *Theatrum Chemicum* and various other septenaries. But the seven stages I've described above appear to be embedded in more recent historical contexts, and because I found myself stretching metaphors to make them fit the various septenaries, they did not completely convince me. Nonetheless, I find them compelling insofar as they seem somehow related to the same fourfold pattern we saw in libido development and cultural evolution. Perhaps others will make more sense of them or give us a good reason to dismiss them altogether.

Beyond all of that, one might speculate on the fifth stage, Fruitfulness, as representing, in cultural evolution, the extraordinary flowering of culture and technology over the last 5,000 years. We might see the sixth stage, Reconciliation of Opposites, in the numerous ways we seem to currently be confronting the shadow side of civilization in global warming, racial and religious hatred, air and water pollution, mass extinctions, world wars, the rise of authoritarianism, and the threat of weapons of mass destruction. These weapons, as sophisticated as they are, rest in the hands of people like you and me whose minds are moved today by the same fears and aggression as they were 50,000 years ago. Finally, we might see the seventh stage, Relinquishing the Will, as a unifying conscious perception, at the cultural level, of the miracle of our social being resulting in a conviction to care for the planet and all who inhabit it. Conversely, we might see the seventh stage as a conscious perception of our own impending extinction.

The Significance of Seven

When dabbling in these matters, one can easily get bogged down in the swamp of mysticism, including numerology. Nonetheless, if we can avoid the seductive nature of the countless mystical systems of thought, we might be able to abstract a psychic organizing principle. For example, the first few numbers (1-2-3-4) seem to be largely conditioned by the structure of the psyche. The psyche repeatedly expresses this fourfold pattern in myths, rituals, and so on. Furthermore, the number seven has such cross-cultural significance that one is tempted to consider it as a psychological universal as well.

We speak of the seven wonders of the world, the seven deadly sins, the seven chakras of Kundalini yoga, the seven days of the week, the seven heavens, the seven regions of the Zuni Native Americans, the seven orifices in the face, the seven stages of alchemical transformation, the seven seas, and so on. The Bible refers to the seven years, seven stars, seven eyes, seven shepherds, seven heads, seven angels, seven plagues, seven kings, seven skinny cows, seven days of creation, and more.

In *Problems of Mysticism and Its Symbolism*, Freud's colleague Herbert Silberer (1882-1923) speculated that "it may easily happen that the domination of the number 7 is to be derived from the infusion of the scientific doctrines (7 planets, 7 metals, 7 tones in the diatonic scale) and yet it may depend on an actual correspondence in the human psyche with nature—who can tell?" (Silberer, 1917, p. 367).

In 1924 Freud and Karl Abraham had a lively correspondence concerning the number seven. Abraham was very excited about it all, and Freud expressed a similar but more cautious enthusiasm. On August 22, 1924, Freud shared some of his ideas on the matter and in conclusion wrote, "The craziest things can be done with numbers, so be careful" (Abraham & E. L. Freud, 1965, p. 365). Freud's skepticism is well founded. I was unable to convince myself that the last three of the seven stages had anything to do with any particular myths, rituals, or historical culture forms following the Urban Revolution. I did, however, find some parallels that were interesting, somewhat compelling, and yet not completely convincing.

The important point is that the fifth stage revisits the third, the sixth stage revisits the second, and the seventh revisits the first. The reader will recall my anecdote in the introduction, in which I asked Erik Erikson about the relationship between the first stage and the last stage of psychosocial development, between trust vs. mistrust and ego integrity vs. despair. What I had in mind was this idea that the infant's psyche is, relatively speaking, unitary and becoming conscious by separating the opposites of subject and other, good and bad, inside and outside, here and there, now and then, male and female, adult and child, and that the older person is in a process of reconciling the opposites and coming to terms with a life as it was. I was also reflecting on how the infant is moving from nonbeing into being and how the older person is one who is being and looking out onto the horizon of nonbeing.

I later came across an article by Erikson called "Reflections on the Last Stage—and the First" (1984). Erikson called the infant's meeting "eye to eye" with the mother a meeting with the "Primal Other" that, with positive experience, gives the infant a sense of hope. Erikson then referred to the elderly person's anticipation of death and the sense of immortality that "true believers" may experience. He proposed that the basic strength corresponding to the infant's hope is the elderly person's "faith":

> Faith has been given cosmic worldwide contexts by religions and ideologies which offered to true believers some sense of immortality in the form of some unification with a unique historical or cosmic power which in its personalized form we may call an Ultimate Other. We can certainly find an experiential basis for such hope in the infant's meeting with the maternal personage faced "eye to eye" as what we may call the Primal Other.... The relation of Hope and Faith, then, contains a first example of an experiential similarity, namely, that of a mutual "meeting" with an all-important Other—which appears in some form on each stage of life, beginning with the maternal, but soon also the paternal Other confirmed by visual and, indeed, various sensual experiences of rich mutuality.... By the end of life (this Primal Other

having become an Ultimate Other), such deeply experienced faith is richly realized not only in religion, but also in mythology and in the arts; and it is confirmed by the detailed rituals and ritualizations which mark the beginning and the end of life in varying cultures—ritualizations that, in our time, must find new ways of expressing an all-human sense of existence and an anticipation of dying. (pp. 160-61)

Erikson's observations have an explicitly religious or spiritual tone but they could probably stand just as well for nonbelievers. The faith he describes does not necessarily pertain to immortality and the expectation of meeting an "ultimate other." It could just as easily pertain to the comfort of knowing that while the psyche will disappear or dissolve into everything and nothing, culture will live on, and from my perspective, culture is the prosthetic soul that survives the death of the mortal body.

Man as the Microcosm and the Universe as the Macrocosm.
Notice the cosmogram of concentric circles and the names
of the planets emanating out from the man's hip:
Moon, Mercury, Venus, Sun, Mars, Jupiter and Saturn.
From "Margarita Philosophica," Basle, 1508.

Seven rings of an Indian cosmogram. Ajit Mookerjee (1977) writes,
"Dominating the center of the universe is the mythical Mount
Meru around which is the earth or jambu-dvīpa, the island
continent with seven concentric circles symbolically representing
cosmic fields, spheres, atmospheric zones" (p. 71).

CHAPTER 10

Psychomythology: Projections onto the Walls of the Universe

> Can you imagine what "endopsychic myths" are? The latest product of my mental labor. The dim inner perception of one's own psychic apparatus stimulates thought illusions, which of course are projected onto the outside and, characteristically, into the future and the beyond. Immortality, retribution, the entire beyond are all reflections of our psychic internal [world]. Meschugge? Psychomythology.
> –Letter from Sigmund Freud to Wilhelm Fleiss, December 12, 1897

I've described four constellations of metaphors on the threshold of libido development and cultural evolution as "stages" in psychomythic development. While *psychosexual* development pertains to psychology projected onto the skin, and *psychosocial* development is psychology projected into the social surround, *psychomythic* development pertains to psychology projected onto the walls of the universe.

The Psychomythic in Religion

The elaborate nature of human culture is attributable primarily to our extraordinary symbolic function, which enables us to represent experiences of ourselves and of our world in pictures, words, ideas, music, and dance. And we do so in a way that our earlier hominin ancestors could not. As modern Homo sapiens just starting out in the Paleolithic period, we represented the world in metaphors borrowed from anatomy, physiology, and bodily experience in natural and social contexts. With the creation of tools, our technology began to elaborate instrumental, mechanical, industrial, technological, and information-driven worlds, each of which furnished us with new metaphors as we went along. We now live in a modern world in which a computerized environment forms the mirror we use to reflect upon our bodies and our lives.

The psychomythic schema of development offers the psychotherapist a way of listening to symbolic material in the patient's anamnesis. One might be able to profitably reflect on these constellations of metaphors in psychomythic development while observing children's play, listening to the dreams of adults, or in considering adult personality structure in developmental terms. We can also consider the psychomythic stages when reflecting on the psychological meanings of hobbies, symptoms, favorite books and films, art, and religious stories.

The psychomythic pertains to experiences originally projected out into the world by early prehistoric symbolizing humans. Those projections were given verbal, artistic and architectural forms; and these were then culturally sanctioned, modified, and introjected by the next generation, who used these culturally sanctioned symbols to shape their own experiences. These were then modified further, projected and subjected to more cultural co-construction and elaboration.

The individual projected into nature an emotionally toned image of an all-powerful parent. The culture modified the image into a spirit. The individual and culture co-constructed the spirit image, into an ancestor spirit, into a totem, into multiple gods, into a unitary God, and into all that goes on in the spiritual realms—beyond the prohibitions of culture and behind the locked door of the parents' bedroom. The psychomythic is formed in the dialectic of the individual and the cultural. The child's disowned impulses and introjected parents are projected out into nature—into the murmurs of the cave, the whispering of the trees, the reprimands of thunder and lightning, and into the transforming figures floating in the clouds. These are the projections of bodily and familial metaphors out onto the walls of the universe.

If we listen for the metaphors around which our patients organize their lives, we hear recurring themes of food and feeding, death and birth, merger, suicide, fusion, oneness, wholeness, mother, satisfaction, starvation, and so on. We hear themes of separation, difference, control, dominance, submission, exclusion, humiliation, the arts, birth, loss, mother and child, house and architecture, containers and containment. We hear of sports competition, fire, mastery, love triangles, jealousy, betrayal, dragon slaying, revenge, battles, the hero, and ambition. We hear of marriage, kingship, society, God, the father, the law, the great man, guilt, justice, sex, passion, and vision. This way of listening for the metaphors can be applied to dreams, fantasies, and day-to-day concerns, but some of the areas of human experience most deeply invaded by psychomythic metaphors are those where the defenses are the highest and there is a blind refusal to see any metaphor or meaning in such concerns. These are the concerns of religion, politics, and philosophy, which not infrequently are ignored as taboo topics by analysts and patients alike. Analyzing our most deeply held beliefs is nothing less than shaking the foundations of our worldviews.

Metaphors are drawn from a wide variety of activities of daily life, but ultimately the body is the primal metaphor (Benveniste, 1998). This is why we listen for the bodily metaphors in the narratives of our patients and often make interpretations using metaphors of the body.

A world derived from bodily experience is exemplified in the Indo-European cosmogonic myths in which a cosmic goddess (or god) is said to have existed in the beginning and was killed and dismembered in order to facilitate the creation of the universe. The parts of her body became the various parts of the world—the sun and moon derived from her eyes, the earth from her flesh, the grass from her hair, the wind from her breath, the stones from her bones, the vault of heaven from the crown of her skull, and so on (Lincoln, 1986). Thus, we can see how encoded in our loftiest visions, myths, religions, and philosophical speculations are our most personal concerns. We can interpret the murder and dismemberment of the primal being as a murder of the father or murder of the mother, but we can also see it as the original sin, the fall from grace, the murder of our own psychic unity, the guilt we must suffer as the price for becoming conscious and becoming at two with the universe.

We live our lives within the metaphors that shape our daily experience, but we can also be imprisoned by those metaphors. The stories of our past, our dramas, our scripts, our games, our narratives, are our personal cosmogonic myths. The story of one's past is a personal cosmogony of how one got to be the way one is. The story of our past is not historical truth. It is narrative truth. It is an interpretation, an excuse, an apology, a rationalization, a hero myth, a just-so story, a cover story. It is not that the events of one's life did not happen but that they are always remembered as experiences perceived and interpreted. Psychotherapy deconstructs our cover stories, pulls them apart at the seams, allowing us to have new experiences, recover lost memories, make new connections, and stitch ourselves back together in a new way. A successful therapy provides a new metaphor to live by, a new narrative, a new experience of our past, a new view of the world, and a new role to fill within it. It is a wider view of the world, one that permits us to keep fewer secrets from ourselves and allows us to live more comfortably in our own skin. A new metaphor offers renewal and aliveness, whereas dead metaphors seal our fate in a concrete reality (Benveniste, 1998).

Dead metaphors are both the substantive realities in which we live and the concrete realities that imprison us. New metaphors return us to the fluidity and flux of human experience. Therapy disengages us from our dead metaphors so that we can more effectively engage the world with a more current metaphor. In *The Question of Lay Analysis*, Freud (1926/1959f) confessed, "In psychology we can only describe things by the help of analogies. There is nothing peculiar in this; it is the case elsewhere as well. But we have constantly to keep changing these analogies, for none of them lasts us long enough" (*SE* 20, p. 18).

Our changing subjective experiences of self and world are useful illusions in a sea of confusions. Our subjectivities are a function of the language we use, or as Nathan Adler used to say, "*Ontology* recapitulates *philology*" (personal communication, February 11, 1991). Being recapitulates the way one speaks one's self into being—into existence.

When we read mythology with our attention on the metaphors of the body, we are impressed by the recurring references to sexuality (including infantile sexuality) between the gods and goddesses. There are marriages and incestuous acts, infidelities and castrations. Gods and goddesses make love, male gods give birth, children are born through masturbation, and some goddesses even have penises. The primal fantasies that are so much a part of the clinical consulting room are suddenly seen projected onto the vault of heaven. In the mythologies of many traditions, the primal concerns and bodily metaphors that underlie the myths are clothed under layer upon layer of symbolization, displacement, and distortion. But in other traditions, such as the Tantric Indian tradition, the bodily metaphors are covered by a thin diaphanous veil, or less.

In the Tantric tradition, the universe is represented by a stylized sculpture of the *lingam* (penis) and *yoni* (vulva), a pillar set in a bowl. Describing the Tantric viewpoint, Indian art historian Ajit Mookerjee (1982) wrote, "The complete drama of the Universe is repeated here, in this very body. The whole body with its biological and psychological processes becomes an instrument through which the cosmic power reveals itself. According to Tantric principles, all that exists in the Universe must also exist in the individual body" (p. 9).

Tantra is a way of life in which the practitioner, the Tantrika, seeks transcendence not in withdrawal from the world but in a fully embodied entrance into it. The Tantric way of life reflects a view of the world that is shared by various sects among the Hindu, Buddhist, and Jain religions. Distinctive attributes of the Tantric way include (1) worship of the goddess; (2) recognition of an inner cosmic energy (the Kundalini) lying dormant in the human organism, which can be awakened in the service of identifying oneself with the supreme reality; and (3) a belief that transcendence comes not from separation and withdrawal from the world but from the unification of the opposites (Benveniste, 1990).

In the Tantric tradition, the body is thought to correspond quite directly to the structure and functioning of the universe. A common image in Tantric Jainism is a cosmogram, a diagram of the metaphysical structure of the universe, depicting the universe in the form of Purusha, the primal man. The correspondence between the personal and cosmic bodies is further elaborated in the Tantric tradition by the idea that the personal body is the ultimate *yantra*, or meditation tool, through which one may seek the truth. This search for "truth" involves the awakening of an inner psychic energy lying dormant at the base of the spine. The energy is called the Kundalini and is represented as a sleeping snake coiled around a phallus, with the snake's mouth open over the top of the phallus. The aim of Tantric meditation is to awaken this Kundalini and allow her to move up through the body along the pathway of the seven chakras, or energy centers, so that she, as power consciousness, may reunite with the cosmic consciousness—that is, Shiva, the ultimate lord of creation, preservation, and destruction. The Tantric way does not reject the body as profane but regards it as the vehicle of transcendence (Benveniste, 1990):

> Rather than subdue, tantra teaches us to realize and harness the potential of the senses. Sexual instinct, an all-pervading urge, is the physical basis of creation and of mankind's evolution. Sex is the cosmic union of opposites from which everything and every being arises. Its importance demands its fulfillment. (Mookerjee, 1971, pp. 35-36)

> Since, according to tantra, the body is the link between the terrestrial world and the cosmos, the body is, as it were, the theatre in which the psycho-cosmic drama is enacted. (Mookerjee, 1995, p. 35)

Within the Tantric tradition, we find paintings and sculptures of yoni (vulva) worship. In a stone carving, two worshipers are seen bowing their heads before a great, disembodied vulva. In another stone sculpture, a devotee drinks the *yoni tattva*, or "sublime essence," from the moist vulva of a giant woman. There is also a pilgrimage site where a cleft in the rock is always kept moist by a natural spring running through it. This site is worshiped as the yoni (vulva) of Sati (another manifestation of the goddess). From July to August, after the monsoons, the water from the natural spring runs red with iron oxide and a great celebration is held. The reddened water is taken as a ritual drink that is symbolic of Sati's menstrual blood. The site worshiped as Sati's yoni is only one of the 51 pieces of her dismembered body said to have been spread out at various sites across the landscape. To go on a pilgrimage from one site to another is to worship the body of the goddess. While this pilgrimage can be made on a trek across the landscape of the goddess's body, it can be taken just as fully on a smaller and more personal scale, for, as the Tantric text the Purascharanollasa Tantra says, "All the pilgrimage-centers exist in woman's body" (Mookerjee, 1995, p. 25). In the Tantric tradition, godhood is worshiped in both the personal and cosmic bodies: "When a high-priest and poet of fifteenth century Bengal, Chandidas, fell in love with a washer-maid, Rami, against society's strong opposition, he approached his temple deity the goddess, Bashuli, who told him, 'No deity can offer you what this woman is able to give you'" (pp. 25-26). This brief excursion into Tantric art and tradition is an example of how psychology and sexual concerns are projected out onto the walls of the universe in a cultural context. Through our psychoanalytic lens, we can see how infantile sexual experience shapes the child's sense of self and world in relation to parents, siblings, impulses, and prohibitions. Erikson (1963), referring to autocosmic play, wrote that the small child "may indulge in experimental excursions on her [the mother's] body and on the protrusions and orifices of her face. This is the child's first geography, and the basic maps acquired in such interplay with the mother no doubt remain guides for the ego's first orientation in the world" (p. 220).

Recognizing the libidinal roots of religion does not reduce religion to the vicissitudes of libido development; it connects religion with its biological and psychological basis. Religion is a social phenomenon best evaluated on its own terms. But like all of culture, it is sublimated libido. Religious beliefs are often more transparent than philosophical or political concerns, as the object relations and repetition compulsions are typically personified in the representations of gods, spirits, deities, saints, prophets, gurus, priests, monks, nuns, and other figures. I have often found it useful to ask patients with strong religious beliefs about their favorite religious story or prayer. Religious people are rarely without a favorite, and when it is explored, one finds the patient's personal conflicts intimately tied to the story or prayer that has captured their interest and imagination. A young man struggling desperately with the conflict between his erotic impulses and his Christian values to maintain fidelity to his wife was often comforted by a passage from the Bible: "Give us this day our daily bread and forgive us our debts as we forgive our debtors, and *lead us not into temptation but deliver us from evil.*"

Sudhir Kakar (1995), speaking of patients in India, wrote that, "Mythological allusions to Hindu gods and goddesses like Shiva and Kali regularly crop up in case history reports where the mythology appears to be used by the patient for both defensive and adaptive purposes" (p. 119).

Two days after a large earthquake in central California, a woman began our session explaining she had not been frightened, as such events were prophesied in the Book of Revelations. She then asked if she had ever told me of her childhood fears of planetariums. It was such a fantastic non sequitur that I couldn't wait to hear what was coming next. "No, you haven't," I replied. She said she had read in the Bible that when the world comes to an end, the planets will "fall out of place." Because of this, she was always afraid to look at the models of the solar system hanging from the ceilings of planetariums for fear that the planets would "fall out of place." As she spoke of these concerns, I associated her childhood fear of the planets falling out of their orbits to her early childhood experience of her brothers, her sisters, and herself all being shipped off to different aunts and uncles—that is, "falling out of place"—after her father died and her mother had been committed to a mental institution. When I offered this interpretation, she accepted it immediately, saying, "Yes, and when I was a little girl, I used to sit on the curb, look up into the sky, and wonder where God was." She had lost both her mother and her father. "And the stars of heaven fell unto the earth" (Revelations 6:13).

Another patient struggled with her deep attachment to her mother and her desperate desire to separate and individuate. I addressed her difficulty in separating by acknowledging her deep love for her mother and her guilt in leaving. She replied, "In Islam we say, 'Paradise is at the feet of Mother.'"

A lovely story that demonstrates the relationship between the personal and the cosmic is the Hindu story 'Ganesha Wins the Mango'. In brief, it is the story of Lord Shiva, the Goddess Parvati and their children Ganesha and Karitikeya. Ganesha had a big belly, the head of an elephant, stubby legs and he rode around on the back of a tiny mouse. Karitikeya was a strong beautiful boy who rode on the back of a great peacock. Shiva and Parvati had a delicious mango for which they set up a competition between the boys. Whoever goes around the world three times wins the mango. The boys agreed and Karitikeya took off on his peacock and began circling the world at great speed. Ganesha mounted his little mouse and began to slowly ride it three times in a circle around his parents, Shiva and Parvati. By circling his parents three times, he had circled the world, his world, three times and thus won the mango. Shortly thereafter Karitikeya arrived and saw Ganesha with the mango in his hand. Karitikeya smiled and instantly understood why Ganesha had won. Ganesha smiled and gave the mango to his brother (Krishnan, 2011).

❖ ❖ ❖

Sigmund Freud was deeply interested in religion even though he was not at all religious and playfully referred to himself as a "pagan." He saw the human infant as helpless in the world and looking to its parents as the emotional equivalents of personal gods who aid in feeding, comfort, and basic survival. He recognized that early childhood experiences shape the structure of the adult personality and that the all-powerful figures of childhood leave their emotional impressions on the psyche and are then projected or transferred into the conceptions of God in adulthood. Consequently, we are really not surprised to recognize the parental qualities embedded in our various conceptions of God. And, of course, it is God who creates us, protects us, soothes us, fulfills wishes, establishes laws, consoles us, punishes wrongdoers, heals us, offers forgiveness, provides guidance, and rewards righteousness. For Freud, God is not a supreme being situated in one religion or another but rather an illusion that we can profitably come to terms with through the careful examination of psychological development and cultural evolution (Benveniste, 2013).

Just as the infant deals with his helplessness and gratification, and his hopes and fears in relation to his seemingly all-powerful parents, so too does a culture come to terms with the terrors of illness, injury, suffering, and death, and the pleasures of life and bounty, by creating spirits, totems, and gods. What started as the projection of early childhood prototypes based on the experience of parental figures evolved, in a cultural context, into the abstractions of spirits, ancestor deities, totems, and gods until God, as such, became a dematerialized, imageless, unified, being.

For Freud, religion is an illusion that is destined to eventually give way to logic and science in a distant future. Freud's main treatise on God and atheism is a small book titled *The Future of an Illusion* (1927-1931/1961b), in which he wrote, "A store of ideas is created, born from man's need to make his helplessness tolerable and built up from the material of memories of the helplessness of his own childhood and the childhood of the human race" (SE 21, p. 18). He goes on to say, "The primal father was the original image of God, the model on which later generations have shaped the figure of God" (p. 42).

Freud never tied psychoanalysis to his atheism, and many psychoanalysts have been, or are, religious and theistic. The Reverend Oskar Pfister, for example, was a psychoanalyst, a Protestant pastor in Switzerland, and a close personal friend of Freud's. In 1928, at Freud's invitation, Pfister wrote a lengthy rebuttal to *The Future of an Illusion*. Pfister called it "The Illusion of a Future" (English translation 1993). He accepted Freud's description of the origins of the early primitive religions and naïve conceptions of God, but he reserved a different place for God in more elaborated philosophies. He recognized not only the horrible things that have been done in the name of religion but also the way religion has often been on the cutting edge of cultural advancement and has brought us our moral values and strengths, meaning in life, ethical concepts, and the spirit of love. He challenged Freud's worship of *logos* (reason) and said that the best of what religion has to offer would never be replaced, as Freud suggested, by science and dispassionate reason. He further asserted that at the core of many scientific concepts, including those of psychoanalysis, there are anthropomorphisms—that is, personifications and projections of personal experience—and this was exactly the charge that Freud leveled against religion and the basis upon which he called it an illusion (Benveniste, 2013).

The differences between Freud and Pfister were clear and unambiguous, but so was their warm personal regard for each other. On October 9, 1918, Freud wrote to Pfister, "Why was it that none of all the pious ever discovered psychoanalysis? Why did it have to wait for a completely godless Jew?" (Meng & Freud, 1963, p. 63). On October 29, 1918, Pfister replied:

> You ask why psycho-analysis was not discovered by any of the pious, but by an atheist Jew. The answer obviously is that piety is not the same as genius for discovery and that most of the pious did not have it in them to make such discoveries. Moreover, ... you are not Godless, for he who lives the truth lives in God, and he who strives for the freeing of love "dwelleth in God" (First Epistle of John, iv, 16). If you raised to your consciousness and fully felt your place in the great design, which to me is as necessary

as the synthesis of the notes is to a Beethoven symphony, I should say of you: A better Christian there never was. (p. 63)

Whoever would destroy religion would cut through the tap-root of great art, which discloses the deepest meaning and the greatest strengths of life. (Pfister, 1993, p. 575)

When we invite our patients to speak in a free and uncensored fashion, that invitation of necessity includes our openness to their religious thoughts and feelings, which are, in many places, forbidden topics of conversation. Religious themes carry with them many of our patients' deepest concerns, most tender vulnerabilities, old hurts, desperate hopes, and seemingly insurmountable conflicts. Religious or spiritual thoughts and feelings, to be sure, reflect personal psychology, but they also can be a source of uncommon strength that serve our patients in times of great strife and offer solace in the face of terrible loss. Some people who have great religious feeling are able to accept their difficult fates with equanimity and meet the challenges of their life as a mission assigned by God. Many also find that God provides a point of reference from which to make meaning of life. I have often found that my patients' favorite religious stories, told in their own words, are of great psychotherapeutic value, as they contain many personality dynamics that are sometimes easier to approach in the form of religious metaphors. If the psychotherapist can honor religious feelings and treasured ideas for what they mean to the patient and also use them psychotherapeutically, patients are often most appreciative.

Atheism also reflects personal psychology. Some use atheism as a way of taking responsibility for their life within the context of a finite existence. Facing mortality in a godless world presents them with the awe-inspiring miracle of being and becoming and the challenge to make the most of life in the name of "culture," and culture is the only life they permit themselves to carry on beyond their personal deaths. Under such circumstances, intrapsychic conflicts become projects for which they have a personal responsibility to manage and sublimate. Others, however, use their atheism to resist authority or ward off feelings of dependency. Atheism can be a fierce adolescent rebellion against the father, a life dedicated to rebuttal against the ruling order, a battle against strong emotions, a mistrust of a traitorous world, or a rational conclusion met with fatalism and/or irony. And, of course, discussions with patients on the themes of theism or atheism often carry a heavy transferential subtext.

The theism or atheism of our patients is not a reason for us to take sides or speak dismissively of those patients or anyone else. Atheism, theism, religion, science, art, politics, and philosophy all serve as projection screens for our personal psychologies. Those projections are planted in contemporary concerns but have roots that extend down into early childhood experiences, traumas, conflicts, object relations, hopes, and fears.

The poetry of religious texts stimulates our search for meaning in life. The rational discourse of scientific studies, on the other hand, is not about meaning; it's about explanation and discovering the consensually agreed upon nature of the world. The *poetry* of Genesis and the *scientific theory* of evolution both tell us how we humans got to be the way we are, but they are two completely different orders of discourse, and confusing one with the other is an injustice to both. Freud understands the poetry but rejects the reification and concretization of that poetry in favor of scientific exploration and understanding.

For Freud, God is the projection of the parental introjects out into the world, and a rational approach to such projections demands the renunciation of such illusions. Oskar Pfister, however tells us it is an illusion to think we can escape our projections. And indeed Freud's position and rational project almost denies the very existence of primary process thinking, which Freud formulated. It is easy to be a rational atheist sitting in a university library. But sit for ten minutes alone in a dark old house or in the wilderness at night, and in short order the mind makes demons, spirits, ghosts, and monsters out of extraneous sounds, shadows, and vague impressions. The child animates the doll, the backpacker imagines a monster in the dark, the shaman connects with his animal spirit, the community turns the shaman's spirit into a totem, and society turns the totem into a god. It's a straight shot from a child's doll to the Almighty. And while we can think rationally about our projections, we can never completely escape them, as they are easily activated in weakened mental states and, of course, under stress. As the aphorism goes, "There are no atheists in foxholes."

Some call God a delusion, but, like all rationalists arguing for atheism, they ignore the fact that the rationality of secondary process thinking floats like a rickety raft on an ocean of primary process thinking—delusional thinking—and that primary process thinking extends a long way into secondary process thinking and indeed has its value. The science versus religion debate that goes on in modern society rarely touches psychology and the importance of primary and secondary process thinking. Dismissing God as an illusion is naïve. Of course, it's an illusion. It's a useful illusion in a sea of confusion—a poetic way of speaking about the unspeakable. Saying that it logically does not exist is completely beside the point, as it does exist emotionally and calls to be dealt with as such.

When God establishes the "Thou shalts" and the "Thou shalt nots," he establishes taboos, guidelines, laws, ethics, and morals as a protection for the individual and the group from the anarchy and violence of a lawless, impulse-ridden society. The atheist can certainly be an ethical, law-abiding citizen with a sense of morality and responsibility to society. But that moral and ethical compass is an internalized conscience or superego derived from parental and cultural experiences. While the theist will bind the superego to the name of God and follow it faithfully, the atheist will tie it to culture and own it.

Primary process thinking is the language of dreams, psychosis, and the unconscious. It is a symbolic, emotionally tinged, and yet concrete mode of thinking organized on the basis of displacement and condensation. It is aimed at the gratification of instinctual impulses—the pleasure principle. Secondary process thinking, on the other hand, is rational, logical thinking and aimed at dealing with the world employing the reality principle and a shared understanding of reality. Secondary process thinking enables us to communicate rationally, plan, evaluate, and think logically, critically, and scientifically. Primary process thinking informs love and poetry, poignancy and symptomology, creativity and vision, humor and play, hallucination and madness, technology and literature, religious inspiration and scientific creativity. Our clear and unobscured secondary process thinking affords us an apprehension of reality devoid of illusion. But that apprehension is like a little cabin in the wilderness, while the rest of the world is perceived anthropomorphically and saturated in primary process thinking.

Freud found that the relationship of an individual to his or her conceptualization of God typically has the character of the early childhood experience of one's parents. The following are abbreviated comments heard in clinical context:

"My mother says I do everything wrong and God says I'm a sinner."
"I can't trust my father and I can't trust God."
"My mother is a good listener and so is God."
"Everyone who was supposed to take care of me betrayed me, and now I don't trust you [the therapist] and I also don't believe in God."
"I was left by my mother. She left me to fend for myself, and I always feel that God helps those who help themselves."
"There was no warmth in my family, only rules, discipline, and order. I don't believe in God, unless you want to call the cold laws of nature God."

But the spiritual life of the individual can also develop beyond the internal object relations of childhood. Freud and Pfister had their object relations from childhood but also had other life experiences and intellectual work through which they elaborated their points of view. Object relations can sometimes be slightly modified in psychotherapy. When we make the unconscious conscious, we become aware of how our object relations and defensive strategies distort and conceal various aspects of reality and how we can modify those defenses so as to live with fewer illusions. Object relations evolve when we become conscious of how the past is present and thus find ways to let go of old enemies that no longer threaten us, retreat from battlefields long since abandoned by old rivals, and leave behind our old defenses that no longer serve us and only weigh us down (Benveniste, 2005).

A person's worldview, whether it is religious, political, philosophical, scientific, aesthetic, or otherwise, will always contain a component that is expressive of the psychology of the individual. This is independent of the truth or utility of the worldview. Many people treat the debate between theism and atheism as if it were a team sport, in which one must choose a side to root for and declare the opposition an enemy. But theism and atheism are not sports teams; they are ways of seeing the world, both of which have their value and their limits. As psychotherapists we don't need to agree, disagree, or argue the religious or atheist metaphors within which our patients bring to us their deepest concerns. We need only to listen to them, respect them, and interpret (Benveniste, 2013).

In psychology, as in religion, concepts are often reified or even concretized, yet typically what we are attempting to describe are processes and poetry. My mentor Nathan Adler used to say, "There is no ego, only egoing. There is no mind, only minding." When I shared this with the Stanford University religious historian Frederic Spiegelberg, he replied, "Yes, and there is no soul, only souling." And when I shared Spiegelberg's reflections with the American spiritual teacher Ram Dass, he said, "That's right! Because there is not a thing called soul. The soul doesn't deal with time or space. The soul is not a thing. The soul is a combination of love, compassion, wisdom, peace, and joy. And the witness. The witness witnessing the incarnation and witnessing the thoughts" (personal communication, December 6, 2018). So perhaps souling is witnessing. As I thought further, it occurred to me that one might also say, "There is no God, only God-ing." God is not a being or a thing, but a way of seeing the world, a way of creating the world, a way of personifying the universe. So perhaps instead of asking, "Do you believe in God" it might be more helpful to ask, "Do you God? Do you God your universe? Do you personify your universe as a God? Under what circumstances do you God? And if you don't God, what sort of meaning do you make of your world, of your universe?"

❖ ❖ ❖

Matti Hyrck, in "Inner Objects and the Christian Images of God" (1997), presented different god images within the Christian tradition and associated them with different object-seeking tendencies elaborated in Kleinian theory. Hyrck explained, "The way man perceives God is deeply rooted in the object-seeking tendency of the human mind." She described, for example, the "Exciting Object," which sees God as the great mother who satisfies man in a paradise of gifts and bliss but may also turn and become aggressive, abandoning, and leave one with the sensation of hellishness.

Hyrck's "Imperial Object" is a representation expressive of the anal and phallic partial drives. It pertains to the need of purifying oneself of one's sins and submitting humbly to the all-powerful Lord. It may provoke feelings of humiliation and desires for rebellion. Such rebellion, when successful, may lead to the subject's internalizing the omnipotent phallic power of the Imperial Object. Within religion it is seen in the person who declares himself to be the "all-powerful master of the universe." Hyrck also offers a parallel projection into politics: "Such a subject filled with phallic omnipotence can be seen operating for example within many totalitarian political mythologies" (p. 41).

Hyrck further describes the "Withdrawing Object," the "Moral Object," and the "Healing Object" (Hyrck, 1997, pp. 42-43). She concludes, "When praying or worshipping or trying to find God, man can never step outside the structures of his own mind" (p. 43).

Mortimer Ostow (2007) emphasizes that the "spiritual experience can be understood as the result of regression to very early childhood, in imaging, affect, and mode of ego functioning" (p. 51). He links the spiritual experience with awe, nostalgia, "the feeling of being in the presence of a gestalt that is overpoweringly beautiful, large, forceful, or fascinatingly attractive," and "the feeling of being welcome, belonging" (pp. 42-43). For Ostow, another component is "the sense of union—union with the lost object, union with the supernatural informant, union with everybody, everywhere, and union with the universe" (pp. 45-46).

Ostow cites (1) James Fowler's stages of faith, in which personality development is linked to stages in religious attitudes; (2) Maria Rizzuto's developmental origins of the various images of God as transitional objects; and (3) William W. Meissner's "developmental aspects of religious experience." Ostow then describes a schema of his own beginning with "an undifferentiated phase"—the oceanic feeling. After that, he explains, "The next recognizable phase would be characterized by the smiling response: between ages two to six months, the infant smiles in response to a moving face, in practical terms, the mother's face. The mother will usually respond with a reciprocal smile or vocal expression, or some other gesture of recognition and reciprocation" (p. 67). Ostow follows various aspects of infantile experience into spiritual and religious experience such as the mother's smile, touch, and voice; attachment; the child's fear of strangers; feeding; bowing, kneeling, and prostration; the establishment of mutual obligations; sex; and so on.

The Psychomythic in Politics

In the Urban Revolution, the god-king was often both the king-god's representative on earth and the political leader of his people. Throughout the rest of history, and probably before, politics and religion have been one and the same or, at best, separated by a semipermeable membrane across which religious and political influence pass freely. In countries that ban religion altogether, heads of state routinely become revered as godlike figures. Beyond this, there is often an emotional component that draws us to the kinds of leaders we prefer and the political movements that excite our imagination. Leaders have been considered gods or close to gods, and even if the public does not consider them divine, many politicians live close enough to their own narcissism or psychotic edge that they may consider themselves divine or semidivine, sent by God, advised by God, doing God's work, or involved in a plan to create God's kingdom on earth. As such, the behavior of the politician becomes important in both political and personal matters. More specifically, the kings of old had the responsibility to behave properly in order to keep the kingdom in balance, and if they were remiss in their duties, it was reflected in problems in the kingdom. But even when the politician has been stripped of divine qualities, he still takes on the appearance of a star, a superstar, or some other sort of sky god, and suddenly people are interested in his wisdom, opinions, foibles, love life, embarrassments, and other details of his life. They enter the pantheon of our day-to-day gods, and the tabloids fill us in on all the happenings up on Mount Olympus, in the White House, at 10 Downing Street, at the Vatican, in Jerusalem, in Mecca, and so on.

As we saw earlier, psychotic patients often frame their concerns in political metaphors. Furthermore, Melanie Klein (1945/1948b) reported the case of Richard, a 10-year old boy who spoke of the abstract designs he drew as representing relationships between political forces. Through his analysis he was eventually able to understand those political forces as being more related to personal concerns (pp. 339–390).

This applies to adults as well. Independent of the merits of our political points of view, our positions always contain autobiographical components influenced by early childhood conflicts and family dynamics. To a great extent we see the outer world in accordance with our inner world. As is said in Spanish, "Cada cabeza es un mundo." Every mind is a world.

The Psychomythic in Philosophy

We speak of the hand of God, the blood of Christ, the evil eye, the breath of life, the eye of the storm, the mouth of the river, the head of the line, the foot of the mountain, the long arm of the law, the head of state, and the body politic, all of which involve the projection of bodily experience onto various aspects of daily life.

From the navel to the center of the world, from a unified bodily experience to the construction of monotheism, from dismemberment to postmodernity, over and over again the metaphors of the body are projected onto and into the world. While many metaphors are derived from weather, geography, technology, and so on, we can also say that, in a sense, all metaphors are born of the flesh of bodily experience in that our awareness of the world is always mediated by way of the body and through the association, condensation, and displacement of one experience to another.

Gods and spirits have been seen in the clouds and the stars, in the woods and rivers since the beginnings of religion. Politics are tied to religions, and embedded in both is philosophy. While modern philosophies often escape the gravity of religion and dismiss the mythical characters of religious texts, they still have their roots buried in the metaphors of the body.

As Friedrich Nietzsche noted in *Beyond Good and Evil*, "It has gradually become clear to me what every great philosophy up till now has consisted of—namely, the confession of its originator, and a species of involuntary and unconscious autobiography" (1907, p. 10).

George Lakoff and Mark Johnson (1999) find philosophy in the flesh. They take a cognitive approach to philosophy, drawing heavily on neural modeling and neural mechanisms and, quite specifically, avoiding psychoanalytic perspectives. For Lakoff and Johnson, "The mind is inherently embodied. Thought is mostly unconscious. Abstract concepts are largely metaphorical" (p. 3). They find bodily concerns embedded in philosophies of all kinds. They say:

> In asking philosophical questions, we use a reason shaped by the body, a cognitive unconscious to which we have no direct access, and metaphorical thought of which we are largely unaware. The fact that abstract thought is mostly metaphorical means that answers to philosophical questions have always been, and always will be, mostly metaphorical. In itself, that is neither good nor bad. It is simply a fact about the capacities of the human mind. But it has major consequences for every aspect of philosophy. Metaphorical thought is the principal tool that makes philosophical insight possible and that constrains the forms that philosophy can take. (p. 7)

Lakoff and Johnson's unconscious is a "cognitive unconscious." Their mind is an "embodied mind." Their self is a metaphorical self. They see the body shaping conceptual structures through what they call "bodily projections." Complex metaphors are made up of primary metaphors or metaphorical parts, which are acquired "automatically and unconsciously simply by functioning in the most ordinary ways in the everyday world from our earliest years" (p. 47).

❖ ❖ ❖

On Wednesday evening, March 20, 1907, Adolf Häutler, "an erudite man, interested in the application of psychoanalysis to philosophic, especially aesthetic problems," and a member of Freud's Psychological Wednesday Society, presented a paper to the group titled "Mysticism and Comprehension of Nature." He was particularly interested in (1) the mystic's tendency to achieve the feeling of unity—that is, "man's feeling of being one with God, of God being one with nature, of man being one with nature"; (2) the contrast between the blissful mood and sober reality; and (3) the concept of the infinite (Nunberg & Federn, 1962, p. 147). Häutler addressed various points such as the relationship between the idea of unity and the philosophy of Thales; the origins of the world in contrasting sensations as described by Anaximander; the concept of the infinite introduced by Heraclitus; the concept of harmony introduced by Pythagoras; and the Greek predilection for logos, the word, and the notion that "the religious ceremony is the academy for the concept of causality" (p. 148).

After Häutler's presentation, Eduard Hitschmann, Adler, Rank, and others contributed to the discussion, as did Sigmund Freud:

Freud remarks that in metaphysics, we are dealing with a projection of so-called endopsychic perceptions. The explorer of nature, on the other hand, may, through practice, have sharpened his powers of observation to such an extent that he can apply them to the outside world. But the segment of the outside world which he can understand still remains relatively small. The rest, he "thinks," will be as I am; that is, he becomes anthropomorphic in relation to the rest; the remainder, therefore, he replaces with the dim perception of his own psychic processes. (Nunberg & Federn, 1962, pp. 149-50)

In the Scientific Meeting of the Vienna Psychoanalytic Society on October 28, 1908, Häutler presented again and this time addressed Nietzsche's "Ecce Homo." In his discussion Freud expressed his view succinctly: "Mankind has created for itself through projection a moral view of the world that mirrors endopsychically perceived elements" (Nunberg & Federn, 1967, p. 31).

When Freud said that metaphysics is the projection of endopsychic perceptions and that a moral view of the world mirrors endopsychically perceived elements, he was echoing sentiments first expressed in his letter to Wilhelm Fleiss on December 12, 1897. I opened this chapter with this quote, but I repeat it here to emphasize the point.

Can you imagine what "endopsychic myths" are? The latest product of my mental labor. The dim inner perception of one's own psychic apparatus stimulates thought illusions, which of course are projected onto the outside and, characteristically, into the future and the beyond. Immortality, retribution, the entire beyond are all reflections of our psychic internal [world]. Meschugge? Psychomythology. (Masson, 1985, p. 286)

People considering metaphysics and religious concepts, or contemplating infinite space, the eternity of time, the miracle of being, and the anticipation of nonbeing cannot help but perceive the structure of their own psyches projected onto the walls of the universe. Is that Meschugge? Is that madness? No, it's psychomythology.

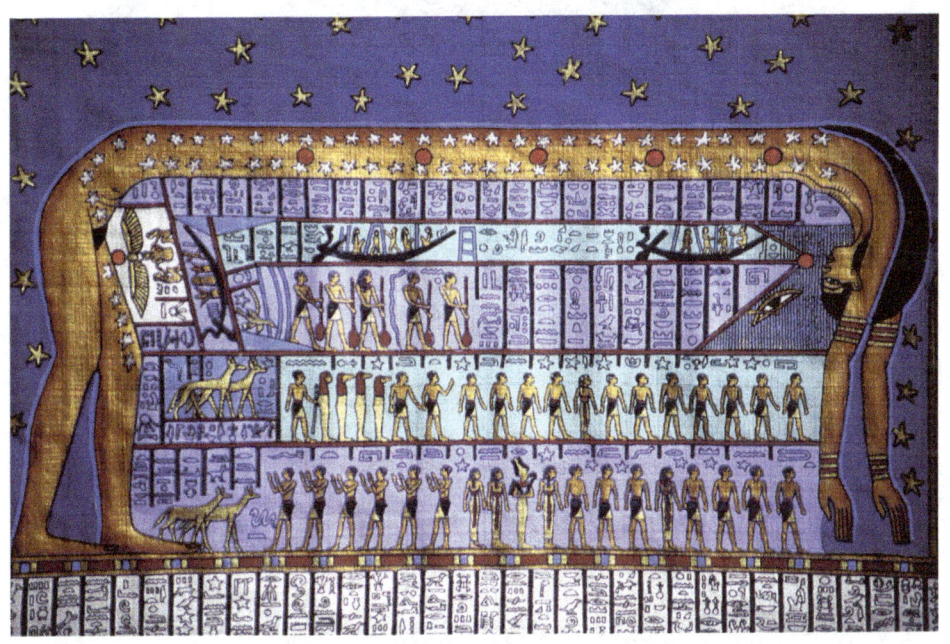

In the evening, the Egyptian Goddess Nut swallows the sun on the western horizon, and all the world goes dark. At night we look up and see the stars on the body of the Goddess Nut. The sun passes through Nut's body during the night and is reborn from her womb on the eastern horizon, in the morning. The painting above is a depiction of the Egyptian cosmos – the Goddess Nut bending over the world to form the sky.

LIBIDO, CULTURE, AND CONSCIOUSNESS

Lingam and yoni. A pillar in a bowl represents the male and female sexual organs together as a symbol of the universe. Katmandu, Nepal.

Yoni Lingam ceremonial bowl. Probably from 18th or 19th century Indian Himalayas.

Religious art imbues the body, its functions, and daily life with spiritual meaning. Above is a Tantric Moghul Chinnamasta from 18th century India. In this miniature painting we see a vision of the opposites united. Shiva (the male) and Shakti (the female) are making love in the funerary grounds – life and death. There are two funeral pyres in the background, and human heads scattered about in the foreground being eaten by dogs. Shakti cuts off her own head in a self-sacrifice, holds her severed head in one hand, and in the other hand catches her own spurting blood in a skull cap cup. Though her head is cut off, signifying death or sacrifice, she is pink signifying life. Shiva, meanwhile, is the dead god and is ashen white. Three of the snakes adorning his body hold their heads up and three hang their heads down. While copulating with Shakti he uses the sexual energy to awaken the kundalini or spiritual energy and directs it up through the seven chakras to the chakra at the crown of the skull – the sahasrara chakra or Mouth of God. In this Indian miniature painting (7 ½" X 5 ½") one can see that out of Shiva's topknot there emerges a small head and out of its mouth flows the River Ganges – The River of Life..

Jupiter rides across the sky on his chariot pulled by eagles. Jupiter was the king of the gods in ancient Rome. He was the god of sky and thunder.

Man's Quest for Knowledge of the Universe: Flammarion Engraving (1888)

Concluding Thoughts

> The whole course of the history of civilization is no more than an account of the various methods adopted by mankind for "binding" their unsatisfied wishes, which, according to changing conditions (modified, moreover, by technological advances), have been met by reality sometimes with favor and sometimes with frustration.... *Pari pasu* with men's progressive control over the world goes a development in their *Weltanschauung*, their view of the universe as a whole.... They turn away more and more from their original belief in their own omnipotence, rising from an animistic phase through a religious to a scientific one. Myths, religion and morality find their place in this scheme as attempts to seek a compensation for the lack of satisfaction of human wishes.
>
> —Sigmund Freud, *The Claims of Psychoanalysis to Scientific Interest*
>
> The psychic history of man and the evolution of his cultural forms have run parallel along this very course, for the reason that they are expressions of each other. His psyche makes a culture in its own image, and in turn his efforts at cultural creativity carry forward the differentiation of his psyche.
>
> —John Weir Perry, *Lord of the Four Quarters*

We have been on a long journey from Darwin's and Freud's phylogenetic fantasies, through the recognition of ritualizations as social instincts, to primate and hominin evolution, to the symbolization of social instincts, to psychological and cultural coevolution from the Paleolithic through the Urban Revolution.

We saw how the funerary ritual defends us against our awareness of the fact of death by granting immortality. Beyond that, we might also say that the funerary ritual defends us from becoming aware of our aggressive attitudes toward the one who has died, the one who has abandoned us, the deceased that doesn't even greet us when we offer a greeting. In literal death, the natural ambivalence of any relationship is shaken, and a host of aggressive impulses and old resentments are liberated. The funeral helps canalize resentments, death wishes, survival guilt, and the lingering love for an absent other. This is how it facilitates mourning.

The sacrificial ritual defends us against our feelings of powerlessness by granting a magical means of appealing to the goddess. But might we also say that the sacrifice defends against, or denies, our aggression toward the ruling powers that be? Sacrifice is an intropunitive (masochistic) solution to being dominated by a superior force like nature: "Yes, I know you can destroy me, and because of that I want to destroy you, but I know I can't, so I will attack myself and hope that will satisfy you and keep you from attacking me and actually serve to obtain your favor and your blessings. So I will give something of myself—sacrifice a child, a goat, or a chicken; cut my flesh; knock out a tooth; give up a pleasure; renounce an instinct or something similar. Let's make a deal. I'll give you something, and then you'll give me something."

The harvest and planting rituals recognize sexual knowledge, the role of the father in reproduction, incestuous wishes, and patricidal wishes, but at the same time, they deny them by creating the illusions of magical control over the gods for the parts they cannot control. The harvest and planting festivals, with their ritual competitions, defend against an awareness of our aggression toward the "other" by creating a mock battle. The mock battle permits a nonlethal method of expressing aggression and establishing social order without using deadly force. The emphasis on genital imagery embedded in the ambitious undertaking of giant earthworks, cromlechs, henge monuments, and menhirs is also a defense against feelings of vulnerability, weakness, impotence, and castration. The great phalli, pillars, and menhirs inspire us with their power. But standing alone, as they do, is a confession that in fact they have been cut off—castrated. And who was it that built those great earthworks? Some have speculated that it was thousands of slaves, whom we could well imagine were forced to feel, by way of projective identification, the vulnerability, weakness, impotence, and castration of their masters.

The ancient New Year festivals defend us from an awareness of the ultimate meaninglessness of our finite, mortal existence by granting us a special relationship to God or godhood itself. Psalm 23:4 in the English Standard Version of the Bible says, "Even though I walk through the valley of the shadow of death, I fear no evil, for you are with me; your rod and your staff, they comfort me." And we can wonder if the shadow of death is mourning the father's death or the anxious knowledge of one's own eventual death. The myth of sacral kingship humanizes God and deifies man as a salvation for the existential crisis brought on by the calendar, which reminds us that as humans we are mere bubbles of mortality floating through naught, filled with illusions and self-constructed meaning, and floating for only a short while in the vastness of eternity. Threatened with existential collapse, we declare ourselves children of God, performing our mission on earth before going home to live forever in the kingdom of heaven.

The tradition of kingship creates a responsible role for the father in relation to his sons and daughters. The son is not to kill the father, though he has wishes to do so, and the father is not to kill the son, even though that is every alpha male's secret, or not so secret, wish residing on the edge of his teeth. Within the kingship, each identifies with the other. The god-king identifies with the king-god and vice versa. It also creates the conditions for the son's identification with the father and the peaceful transition of power. Kingship establishes laws that the people can abide by in order to conduct themselves peaceably—that is, to manage their aggression—within their culture.

Beyond right behavior and the proper management of power there is this dim awareness of the ultimate meaninglessness of our finite, mortal existence mentioned above. The ancient New Year festivals defend us from this by affirming a special relationship to God and his plan. While life has no meaning on the other side of the River Styx, on this side of the river a meaningful life typically includes the sublimation of core conflicts rooted in personal traumas. It is often easy to see the personal traumas or core conflicts in the biographies of people who have lived meaningful lives. The meaning of these traumas, conflicts, and sublimations becomes conscious when we see them as parallel metaphors to a person's life work. This becomes apparent, for example, when we interpret the paintings of an artist in relation to the artist's life story or reflect on the object relations embedded in the patient's repetition compulsion and watch as they discover a transformative solution. One man, for example, had been bullied severely and was poised to continue being a victim or turn passive into active and become a bully to others. But rather than repeating, he chose to remember his early life and chose the prosocial option of becoming a protector of others.

We help the patient discover personal meaning when we view as metaphor the patient's complaints about the traffic, the religious person's favorite religious passage, the youngster's preferred video game, a college student's favorite books, or a moviegoer's favorite films. Entering into the analytic dialogue means recognizing the autobiographical nature of self-expression and thinking in metaphor to unpack personal meaning. The psychomythic schema of metaphor constellations is a way to attune our listening to life's underlying meaning.

What I hope is not lost in all of this talk of mythology, religion, and symbols is the rootedness of human experience in primate ritualizations. Julian Huxley (1966), you'll recall, claimed that a ritualization is an innate aggression-neutralizing behavior built upon movement patterns that may have a certain pragmatic function by themselves but through the course of phylogeny (evolution) are repeated, elaborated, joined to other movements, lose their original part functions, and become purely symbolic acts that signal readiness to greet, submit, fight, mate, and so on. It is an innate social instinct that supports the survival of the individual and the group. The ritualization is a combination of antagonistic instincts. For example, the survival instinct and the social instinct bring together fear of the other and the desire for closeness. In this way, the threatening toothy grin and the clasping of hands in battle are transformed into a greeting ritualizations. In transforming a threat display into a greeting ritualization or an attack into a mating ritualization, we can see how nature has managed antagonistic or conflicting instincts to create new ritualizations. The concept of ritualization can easily be seen as an ethological metaphor for a compromise formation.

The dog wants to eat something off the picnic table but does not want to be swatted, so it crouches down in a submissive position and begins to beg. In humans the desire for closeness and fear of abandonment might result in promiscuity. The anger with a father and fear of reprisal might result in aggression turning inward. The fear of exclusion and the desire to be included might result in a distant involvement. And so on. The implication here is to think about complex behaviors as being the result of instincts in conflict, ritualizations in conflict, desires and inhibitions in conflict.

With our symbolic function we have elaborated our greeting ritualization into the encounter with the other, the meeting of I and thou, religious awe, the *mysterium tremendum*, the mysteries of meeting and parting, the encounter with absence, and the funerary ritual. We have elaborated our dominance and submission ritualization into obedience, the renunciation of instinct, ritual trading, and sacrifice. Our copulation interference ritualization has been elaborated into sport, competition, and the mythologies of the hero, the dragon fight, and Oedipus Rex. The inhibition of incestuous copulation and the avoidance of dominance battles in the preadolescent period bring about a further renunciation of instinct that supports identification with the elders and learning about the ways of the group and the ways of the world. Male dominance and mating ritualizations have elaborated into initiation rites, marriage, and kingship. Male and female alliance ritualizations have elaborated into care, fraternity, and culture. Our alpha male ritualizations have given rise to chiefs, kings, rulers, and strongman leaders of all kinds. The alpha male ritualizations in combination with ever strengthening male bonding have given rise to the social role of the father as culture giver and to the structure of democracy with its bonds of fraternity strengthened in relation to an immortal alpha male in the form of values, principles, and institutions.

And so it is that we have used our symbolic function to clothe our primate instincts in language, myth, ritual, technology, religion, philosophy, and politics. From the profane and brutish to the sacred and sublime, we have taken our very human experience, created with it a world in our own image, and projected our deepest concerns onto the walls of the universe. Bill Wallauer (2002), a videographer of wild chimpanzees, described a remarkable observation of a chimpanzee that the primatologists named "Freud":

One of the most interesting and scrutinized events I have recorded on video was a waterfall display performed by the alpha at the time, Freud. Freud began his display with typical rhythmic and deliberate swaying and swinging on vines. For minutes he swung over and across the eight-foot to 12-foot falls. At one point, Freud stood at the top of the falls dipping his hand into the stream and rolling rocks one at a time down the face of the waterfall. Finally, he displayed (slowly, on vines) down the falls and settled on a rock about 30 feet downstream. He relaxed, then turned to the falls and stared at it for many minutes.

Freud, the chimpanzee, was in awe of the falls, and we are in awe of Freud, because in his example we see how we were and, indeed, how we are.

I have addressed Sigmund Freud's question about the origins of the complexes and universal symbolism in two parts. In the first part, I traced our psychodynamics back to our primate ritualizations. In the second, I explored the psychomythic elaboration of culture from the Paleolithic period through the Urban Revolution, from the mother goddesses to the father gods, from hunter-gatherers to city life, from the campfire to the forge. And at the heart of it all is metaphor.

The clinical implications of this work place metaphor at the center of any clinical dialogue, including the metaphors in the patient's dreams, fantasies, and narratives and those used in the psychotherapist's interpretations. The psychomythic attunes us to the metaphors we live by, the metaphors that enslave us, and those that can open doors to new experience. As a contribution to the phylogenetic project of psychoanalysis, this work has reemployed the same building blocks Freud used in his *Totem and Taboo*, but I have bound them together with a different kind of mortar—a different set of assumptions and speculations. Dabbling in the workings of the psyche behind the veils of early infantile amnesia and ancient prehistory, one must take on a playful and humble attitude before the enormity of the task.

I live under no illusion that my contribution to the phylogenetic project of psychoanalysis is the last word on the subject. It is simply my attempt to come to terms with the material as best I could within my cultural context and my personal limitations. In this book, I hope others will find inspiration to take up the matter themselves and correct or build upon my work in order to push forward the phylogenetic project of psychoanalysis.

Frans de Waal (1982/2007) noted, "When I am observing the Arnhem chimpanzees I sometimes feel I am studying Freud's primal horde; as if a time machine has taken me back to prehistoric times, so I can observe the village life of our ancestors" (p. 162). De Waal said that his observations of the chimpanzee colony at the Arnhem Zoo taught him that "the roots of politics are older than humanity" (p. 207). I would add that the roots of our psychodynamics are also older than humanity and that the only thing that gives our psychodynamics their distinctively human quality is our symbolic function, which has elaborated our primate ritualizations into language, art, myth, ritual, science, technology, and all the manifold expressions of libido, culture, and consciousness.

Appendix 1

Chapter 1 Elaborations

Carl Gustav Jung and the Collective Unconscious

When Freud, in *The Interpretation of Dreams* (1900/1953a), wrote of dream symbols and their relation to myths, Carl Gustav Jung (1875-1961) was fascinated. The two psychoanalysts first met in 1907 and began an intense friendship of fateful significance for both men and the depth psychologies in general. In 1912 Jung went to Fordham University in New York, where he gave a series of lectures and stated:

> The marked predominance of mythological elements in the psyche of the child gives us a clear hint of the way the individual mind gradually develops out of the "collective mind" of early childhood, thus giving rise to the old theory of a state of perfect knowledge before and after individual existence.
>
> (These mythological references which we find in children are also met with in dementia praecox and in dreams. They offer a broad and fertile field of work for comparative psychological research. The distant goal to which these investigations lead is a phylogeny of the mind.) (Jung, 1913/1961, vol. 4, p. 225)

Freud and Jung had come together around their shared interest in what I call the phylogenetic project of psychoanalysis. As they elaborated their different views, a split became inevitable. When the split finally occurred, Freud wrote *Totem and Taboo* and Jung wrote *Symbols of Transformation* (1912/1956). In *Symbols of Transformation*, Jung made clear his interest in studying mythology, religion, and mysticism and applying them to help understand personal experience. Freud, on the other hand, was studying in detail the subtleties of his patients' free associations and using them as a basis for understanding religion and prehistory.

In *Symbols of Transformation*, Jung (1912/1956) addressed the primordial roots of dream thought, saying, "These considerations tempt us to draw a parallel between the mythological thinking of ancient man and the similar thinking found in children, primitives, and in dreams" (pp. 22-23). After reflecting on the similarities of embryonic structure to earlier stages in evolution, he wrote, "The supposition that there may also be in psychology a correspondence between ontogenesis and phylogenesis therefore seems justified. If this is so, it would mean that infantile thinking and dream-thinking are simply a recapitulation of earlier evolutionary stages" (p. 23).

Jung spent the rest of his life studying the archetypes of the "collective unconscious." Meanwhile, Freud did not deny the importance of what he called the "collective mind," but, clinically speaking, the patient's free associations took precedence. Although Jung had done research on the word association test and acknowledged the importance of free associations and what he called the "personal unconscious," he was more interested in the "collective unconscious" and was known for occasionally interpreting a dream without the patient's free associations, relying entirely on his understanding of the "collective unconscious" and his own intuition. Jung eventually became caricatured as the analyst who did not need free associations to interpret a dream, which is not fair.

Toward the end of his life, Jung (1964) sought to set the record straight and wrote, in *Man and His Symbols*:

> My views about archaic remnants which I call "archetypes" or "primordial images" have been constantly criticized by people who lack sufficient knowledge of the psychology of dreams and of mythology. The term "archetype" is often misunderstood as meaning certain definite mythological images or motifs. But these are nothing more than conscious representations: it would be absurd to assume that such variable representations could be inherited. (p. 67)

But if the variable representations of the primordial images are not inherited, how are they archetypal? This was the question I put to Joseph L. Henderson (1903-2007), one of Jung's coauthors of *Man and His Symbols*. Henderson replied:

> In calling the images "primordial" I think Jung was saying that most symbols appearing in dreams or waking fantasies are still in a process of formation, and if we speak of them as known, fixed images, we rob them of their creative potential. Well-known images do appear in dreams, but they are not archetypal for the dreamer; they are derived from previous conscious knowledge or from that layer of the mind I call the cultural unconscious. The symbols of which we speak in a Jungian context are in motion, ever changing. (Henderson, personal communication, March 8, 2000)

There is no doubt that for Jung, and even more so for Henderson, the mythological images do not exist a priori in the "collective unconscious." They are constructed in the "personal unconscious" and in what Henderson called the "cultural unconscious." But there is also no doubt that both Jung and Henderson often wrote and spoke in an inspiring and poetic way that often gave the impression that the archetypes do somehow exist a priori.

While Jung was deeply interested in the idea of a collective unconscious, so far as I know he never elaborated a phylogenetic fantasy, or prehistoric reconstruction, with the kind of detail that Freud offered in *Totem and Taboo*. But Jung's highly acclaimed student Erich Neumann (1905-1960) did take up the phylogenetic project. Neumann drew heavily on Jung's archetypal theory, Johann Jacob Bachofen's notion of a matriarchy preceding a patriarchy, and Robert Briffault's idea that matriarchy was not about political rule by women but about a society oriented to the interests of women. In Briffault's (1927/1977) view, "The primitive human group is matriarchal for the same reasons that the animal group is matriarchal. The group subserves the maternal instincts and is governed by them, but this fact does not impose a female domination on the male" (p. 96).

Neumann (1954), in *The Origins and History of Consciousness*, asserted that archetypes are the main constituent of mythology, that they stand in a certain organic relation to one another, and that these archetypes determine the progression and growth of consciousness: "In the course of its ontogenetic development, the individual ego consciousness has to pass through the same archetypal stages which determined the evolution of consciousness in the life of humanity. The individual has in his own life to follow the road that humanity has trod before him, leaving traces of its journey in the archetypal sequence of the mythological images" (p. xvi). Neumann presented a series of mythic images and themes that stand for stages of psychic development and find expression in cultural evolution. He described them as the uroboros, the great mother, the separation of the world parents, the birth of the hero, the slaying of the mother, the slaying of the father, the captive and the treasure, and transformation or Osiris.

While Neumann had a theoretical and philosophical approach to analysis, his main critic, Michael Fordham, a Jungian child analyst, had a more clinical and observational approach. In an article titled "Neumann and Childhood," Fordham (1981) wrote, "His [Neumann's] approach was not that of a scientist but of an ingenious thinker who combines poetic and symbolic insights with a degree of logical thinking. Consequently, he creates contradictions and confusions; that is to be expected. It does not lead to knowledge about children, as one is supposed to believe from the title of his book [*The Child* (1973)], but to an amalgam of myth and thoughts into which bits of experience about children can be fitted" (p. 119).

Wolfgang Geigerich (1975), also a Jungian analyst, noted that Neumann's work makes a claim to history but hardly ever refers to dates; his stages have nothing to do with a chronological sequence; and his work does not belong to history, to science, to a science of myth, or even to archetypal psychology (pp. 110, 111, 116).

Despite the limitations and sound critiques of Neumann's work I feel obliged to recognize Neumann's work as having played in important and inspirational role in my early investigations into the phylogenetic project of psychoanalysis.

Sándor Ferenczi's *Thalassa*

Sándor Ferenczi (1873-1933) suggested that one day we will be able to bring the stages of ego development and the associated neurotic psychopathologies into a parallel with stages in the history of mankind. Ferenczi (1913/1956) said the development of the reality sense comes about by a succession of repressions forced upon mankind by geologic changes that demand various renunciations:

> The first great repression is made necessary by the process of birth, which certainly comes about without active cooperation, without any "intention" on the part of the child. The foetus would much rather remain undisturbed longer in the womb, but it is cruelly turned out into the world, and it has to forget (repress) the kinds of satisfaction it had got fond of, and adjust itself to new ones. The same cruel game is repeated with every new stage of development. (pp. 200-201)

> It is perhaps allowable to venture the surmise that it was the geological changes in the surface of the earth, with catastrophic consequences for primitive man, that compelled repression of favorite habits and thus "development." (p. 201)

In *Thalassa: A Theory of Genitality*, Ferenczi (1923/1938) embraced Lamarck and Haeckel and presented his ontogenetic and phylogenetic theory of the Thalassal regressive trend: the regressive trend to return to the sea. He saw the phylogenetic catastrophe of the recession of the ocean and adaptation to terrestrial life as repeated ontogenetically in birth. The development of animal species with organs of copulation is repeated in the development of the primacy of the genital zone (phallic stage). And he saw the latency phase in libido development as a precipitate of the traumatic experience of the Ice Age during our cultural evolution (p. 69). Ferenczi also saw the Thalassal regressive trend to return to the sea reflected in coitus, in sleep, and in funerary rituals, in which the dead are often laid down in a fetal position as if to return to the womb (p. 95).

APPENDIX 1

Theodore Reik and the Cannibalizing of the Father

Theodore Reik (1888-1969) based his speculations about our primordial past on the intellectual foundation of *Totem and Taboo* and took up the questions of primordial guilt, original sin, and the myth of the Fall of Man, particularly the myth of the Garden of Eden. Reik (1957) contradicted Freud's interpretation that original sin, the reason for Adam and Eve's expulsion from the Garden of Eden, was sexual knowledge and, specifically, incest—Adam had sexual relations with his mother, Eve (p. 100). Reik says the sexual interpretation, which is easily arrived at, was actually a cover story for a much more horrible crime: the killing and eating of the father. Original sin is the murder and cannibalistic feeding on the body of the father. Totemism transformed this crime, repeated innumerable times in our prehistoric past, into (1) the adoration of the sacred totem, (2) the taboo against the killing and eating of the totem, and (3) the ceremonial killing and feasting upon the body of the totem in the ritual of the totemic feast.

Appendix 2

Chapter 2 Elaborations

Anton T. Boisen and His Exploration of the Inner World

Anton T. Boisen (1876-1965) described his first psychotic episode beginning with a sense of impending world catastrophe (1936/1952). The world was going to go through a metamorphosis. The earth was like a germinating egg or seed that had just been fertilized. Boisen felt himself to be extremely important and at the same time of no importance at all. He became aware of a mysterious force of evil. The moon became personified and he saw it suffering in a cross of light. When he recovered, he began to study closely the religious experiences of other inmates at the hospital and to minister to their spiritual needs.

Boisen recognized recurring images and themes in the religious preoccupations of the hospital inmates. There was frequently a sense of the mysterious, something strange going on. "The eyes are opened so that one seems to see back to the beginning of creation" (p. 31). There were ideas of death and dying, one's gender being changed, a cosmic catastrophe, identifications with great religious figures, experiences of rebirth, and a sense of being on an important mission (pp. 15-57).

Chronic Schizophrenia

In 1959 Milton Rokeach brought together a farmer, a clerk, and an electrician for a special encounter. The meeting took place on Ward D-23 at the state mental hospital in Ypsilanti, Michigan, where each man had been residing for some time. While the three men were obviously very different people, each one believed he was Jesus Christ. Their meetings were personal confrontations for each of the men, and their story is a confrontation for the rest of us to come to terms with the relationship between identity and apotheosis (Rokeach, 1964).

The Sufi guru Avatar Meher Baba (1894-1969) left a legacy of writings and of followers who are still active today. One aspect of his work was the extensive care he provided to the *masts* (pronounced "musts") of India. Meher Baba (1948) described the masts as "God-Intoxicated," not caring for anyone or anything and being permanently intoxicated on Divine

Love. They are, he said, on an earnest search for God or truth. Their waywardness has a logic of its own based on an inner context. They are not mad in the ordinary sense but are divinely mad and desperately in love with God. The drive for the truth ravages the psychic field, leading to "a complete break-up and a reconstitution of the mental structure" (pp. 3-5). Detailed descriptions of the masts leave no room for doubt that in a modern psychiatric context these people would be diagnosed as chronic schizophrenics.

I worked for several years in a residential treatment center for chronic schizophrenic adults and became interested in their hallucinations and delusions as expressed in day-to-day life and in a nondirective art expression group I conducted on Sunday evenings. After several months of collecting their drawings and stories about their drawings, I made a list of the residents' names, and next to each I listed all the images and themes in their creative expressions that corresponded to those that Perry had recognized in the delusions and hallucinations of his patients undergoing brief psychotic disorders. I discovered that almost every resident had often, or at one time or another, referred quite specifically to what Perry described as themes of (1) the center, (2) death, (3) return to beginnings, (4) cosmic conflict, (5) threat of the opposite, and (6) apotheosis. Yet hardly any of them ever mentioned (7) sacred marriage, (8) new birth, (9) new society, or (10) a vision of a quadrated world. They were all in the grip of the imagery of decompensation and experienced little or none of the imagery associated with reconstitution, redemption, renewal, or reparation. The healing process, if there was one, had stalled.

Richard Bucke and Cosmic Consciousness

Richard Maurice Bucke, MD (1837-1902), was a Canadian psychiatrist who served as superintendent of an insane asylum. In 1872, while returning home after an evening with two friends reading Wordsworth, Shelley, Keats, Browning, and Whitman, he suddenly saw himself wrapped in a flame-colored cloud and then realized the light was actually within him. He was filled with immense joy and intellectual illumination that were quite impossible to describe. He called this experience "cosmic consciousness."

Bucke explored the phenomenon in others and in 1894 proposed that "cosmic consciousness" is an evolving mental faculty in humans that was becoming more common and would eventually lift the human condition to a higher plane. He described three stages of consciousness that have evolved or are evolving: (1) simple consciousness, (2) self-consciousness, and (3) cosmic consciousness. "Simple consciousness" refers to a capacity shared by the upper half of the animal kingdom. It pertains to the animal's awareness of its body, the knowledge that its body parts belong to it, and an awareness of things in its vicinity. "Self-consciousness," possessed only by man, is the ability to be conscious not only of the things in his surroundings and his body but also of himself as a distinct entity separate from the rest of the universe. "Cosmic consciousness" is awareness of the life and order of the universe. It is generally a brief experience characterized by an intellectual enlightenment that places the individual on a new plane of existence. It is accompanied by a feeling of elation, joy, triumph, and a development of the moral sense. Along with these come a sense of immortality and a present awareness of eternal life. The universe is perceived as a living presence, and there is a deep awareness that love is its foundation principle. The universe is God and God is the universe (Bucke, 1901/1969, pp. 3, 10, 17, 73).

Julian Jaynes and the Breakdown of the Bicameral Mind

While Bucke observed that cosmic consciousness is a new intellectual faculty that is evolving, Julian Jaynes (1920-1997) asserted that hallucinatory states of mind, whether psychotic or visionary, are holdovers from an earlier period in history when the human mind was hallucinating all the time. Jaynes's (1976) basic idea is that consciousness is a modern evolutionary acquisition that appeared 3,000 years ago as a learned process through the development and acquisition of metaphorical language. Before the evolutionary development of consciousness, internal dialogue, and subjectivity as we know them, the mind was full of auditory hallucinations directing the actions of the person in much the same way schizophrenics feel directed by their hallucinations and delusions.

Jaynes said that prior to 3,000 years ago we were all unconscious, sunk in auditory and sometimes visual hallucinations, and that there was a kind of dialogue taking place between the developing left brain language centers and the "hallucinogenic" right brain. This dialogue was experienced as an externalized dialogue between a person and the gods, that Jaynes refers to as the "bicameral mind" (the mind of two rooms). According to Jaynes, 3,000 years ago, as a function of developing language, the invention of writing, and the ever increasing complexity of large societies, there was a breakdown of the bicameral brain. The externalized cosmic-religious dialogue was internalized, which brought about the origin of consciousness, internal experience, introspection, and subjectivity. Wondering what consciousness is, Jaynes arrived at the following conclusions:

Consciousness is the invention of an analog world on the basis of language, paralleling the behavioral world. (p. 66)

Metaphor generates consciousness. (p. 56)

Subjective conscious mind is an analog of what is called the real world. (p. 55)

Conscious mind is a spatial analog of the world and mental acts are analogs of bodily acts. (p. 66)

The metaphors of the mind are the world it perceives. (p. 2)

The structure of the world is echoed—though with certain differences—in the structure of consciousness. (p. 59)

In brief, Jaynes offers the notion of "consciousness as a metaphor-generated model of the world" (p. 66).

Psychedelic Experience

In *The Varieties of Psychedelic Experience*, Robert Masters and Jean Houston (1966) studied the unusual effects of LSD on the human personality. Of the 206 subjects under the influence of LSD, 96 percent experienced religious imagery of some kind, including religious architecture, art, and symbols; religious figures; miraculous visions; religious rituals; and cosmological imagery. Fourteen percent experienced cosmological imagery, defined as "galaxies, heavenly bodies, creation of the universe, of the solar system, of the earth (experienced as religious)" (p. 265). One subject reported, "I felt I was there with God on the day of creation" (p. 261). Another person "felt the evolutionary process in his body" and observed "the development over the eons of new and more complicated varieties of plant and animal life" (p. 273).

Beyond all of this are the common, yet no less astonishing, psychedelic experiences of perceiving the magnificent order and organization of the universe; the eternity of time and blessedness of now; the expansiveness of space and the sacredness of here; the miracle of being and the contemplation of nonbeing; and the all-pervading vibration of cosmic love, which many have seen as an impersonal kind of afterlife to merge with upon death. It is no wonder that psychedelic, psychotic, and visionary experiences have given spiritual meaning to many and inspired the religions of people around the world and throughout history and prehistory.

Appendix 3

Chapter 3 Elaborations

Orality in Psychoanalytic Theory

Sándor Ferenczi (1938) wrote that the infant "emerges from the period of harmless oral erotism, sucking, into a cannibalistic stage; it develops within the mouth implements for biting with which it would fain eat up, as it were, the beloved mother, compelling her eventually to wean it" (p. 21). While this later oral stage certainly has its aggressive component, we must not forget that the infant at this stage wants to eat what it loves, wants to gobble up what it loves, wants to incorporate what it loves.

Karl Abraham (1924/1927b) observed that in melancholia (major depression) there is a regression of the libido to the oral stage and, as Freud described, the use of introjection. Abraham explained, "The introjection of the love-object is an incorporation of it, in keeping with the regression of the libido to the cannibalistic level" (p. 420). He described manic depression as an oscillation between an ego being consumed by the introjected object in the depressive phase and an ego consuming the world (food, sex, etc.) in the manic phase (p. 472).

Otto Fenichel (1928/1953a) addressed the dread of being eaten. He noted its linkage to ideas of castration, typically by the mother, and associated it with incest wishes in the form of desires to return to the womb. In the fantasied incestuous return to the mother, a return to the womb, a castration takes place in the intrauterine environment, permitting rebirth as a female (pp. 158–59).

In the famous case of the Wolf-Man, Freud (1918/1955d) wrote, "In this [oral] phase, the sexual aim could only be cannibalism—devouring; it makes its appearance with our present patient through regression from a higher stage, in the form of fear of 'being eaten by the wolf.' We were, indeed, obliged to translate this into a fear of being copulated with by his father" (SE 17, p. 106).

In Edward Glover's (1924) article "The Significance of the Mouth in Psychoanalysis," he described various phenomena appearing later in life that are influenced by oral experience. These include castration theories related to the mouth: cunnilingus as a search for the female phallus and the common fantasies of the woman with a penis, the woman with a disappearing penis, the disappearing and reappearing penis, the vagina that during intercourse will tear away and suck in the penis, and the theories of impregnation and delivery by the mouth (pp. 147–48). Glover noted the role the mouth plays in adolescent taboos such as swearing, smoking, drinking, and gambling and in sexual intimacies such as kissing and hugging, which he called a pseudo-incorporation (p. 151). The oral sadist, he observed, uses "incisive speech" and "biting sarcasm." Less aggressive people "chew the cud of reflection," and others "drink in the distillation of wisdom." He noted, "In Isaiah the word of God is likened to wine and milk" (p. 152).

Glover went on to elaborate on some of the many manifestations of orality:

> One generalization, however, can be made; all gratifications are capable of distinction in accordance with the satisfaction of active or passive aims: they stamp respectively the biter or the sucker. Study the mouthpieces of pipes, the stub ends of pencils, offer your friends chocolate caramels, ask them if they like new bread or stale, dry or buttered toast, time them over an inhospitable piece of steak, observe the degree of partial incorporation of the soup-spoon, the preference for jam or jelly, for apple or orange, for cutlet and sauté or sausage and mashed potatoes, and in a few minutes you will be able to hazard a guess as to instinct modifications after birth which may require the deepest analysis to bring home to the individual. Even in the melancholic atmosphere of the vegetarian restaurant, you will find the conscientious biter at his nut cutlet, the sucker at his Instant Postum; there is but one striking difference, a cannibalistic tabu reigns supreme over the heavily burdened unconscious of the hungry ones. (pp. 152–53)

Finally, Glover asserted that the "oral triad of character traits" is comprised of impatience, envy, and ambition (p. 153).

Bertram Lewin (1950), in *The Psychoanalysis of Elation*, introduced the "oral triad of wishes": the wish to devour, the wish to be devoured, and the wish to go to sleep (to die). The nursing baby, of course, wishes to eat and wishes to sleep, and in spending so much time in the early months of life doing so, the physiological needs become psychological wishes. The wish to be eaten is derived from the fact that the infant, satiated after suckling, has experiences of yielding, relaxing, and falling, which become organized into ideas of being devoured. The wish to be devoured is clearly recognized in children who like to play at being eaten up by their parents and in parents who call their children affectionate names such as "Honey," "Lamb Chop," and "Cookie," and lovingly tell them, "I'm going to eat you up!" (pp. 102–105). Lewin identified the components of the oral triad in psychopathology, normal functioning, and diverse cultural expressions. The wish to sleep was associated with the wish to die, and the wish to die was associated with the wish to return to the mother (p. 155).

The sexual aim of the early oral stage is incorporation of the object, a prototype of identification. Freud (1905/1953b) originally suggested the oral stage might also be called the "cannibalistic pregenital sexual organization" (SE 7, p. 198). We should not overlook the cultural and phylogenetic implications of the term "cannibalistic." Humberto Nágera and his colleagues (1969) remind us that "in [Freud's] final conceptualization of the aggressive drives in terms of the death instinct he says that the fear of being eaten by the totem animal (the father) is ascribed to erotogenic masochism in its fusion with the libidinal impulses of the oral phase" (p. 41). Glover (1924) amplified this cannibalistic link:

The manner of dealing with the object is unique in that the object is actually taken into the mouth, a process of incorporation which has its psychical analogue in the introjection of objects into the ego. That this is something more than a mere resemblance has been shown by Freud in his study of cannibalistic activities and totemistic ceremonials. Here we find a phylogenetic link which helps to fill the gaps in observation of child development: the swallowed food is believed by the primitive to bring about an alteration in the character of the subject, actual introjection has been followed by psychical identification. (p. 142)

We can see how psychoanalysis locates the psychosexual in the experience of the body, elaborates the psychosocial in the experience of the family and society, and further elaborates what we can call the psychomythic in ethnological manifestation such as myths, rituals, religious beliefs, and customs. In "Anthropophagy (Cannibalism): Its Relation to the Oral Stage of Development," Joshua A. Hoffs (1963) demonstrated that despite the similarities, the adult cannibal in an aboriginal community or in our prehistoric past is/was clearly not an infant, so while the analogy is useful, we must remember the distinction as well. Hoffs described many cannibalistic practices and various ethnographic derivatives of cannibalism as in fairy tales, rituals, and so forth. He approached the debate as to whether ontogeny recapitulates phylogeny or not and, without resolving that issue, offered, "Undoubtedly, analogies exist between the child, the neurotic, and primitive man. It goes without saying, that the analogies must be made cautiously, and with a recognition of their limitations" (pp. 205-206).

Augusta Bonnard (1960), in "The Primal Significance of the Tongue," drew attention to the tongue and its curious use by a number of disturbed children. She described cases of tongue sucking and tongue swallowing and noted, "The psychopathological value of their addictive tongue practices lay in their sensory provision of a 'closed circle' of narcissistic self-supply, devoid, of course, of any life-sustaining value" (p. 303). Elaborating on its more normal aspect, Bonnard added, "Thus, in licking the face in and around its lip area, and repeatedly experiencing the cooling track of evaporating saliva which follows the tongue's movements, the baby begins to learn that it has an outside as well as an inside surface to explore" (p. 304).

The tongue is "a guide and vehicle for object cathexis" with which the baby may encounter the nipple or its own thumb to "restore the circle of balanced quiescence." The tongue acts as a "sensory bridge reaching out from inside the self to [the] experience of external objects" (p. 306). It is a "conjunction point" between "outside and inside surfaces of the self" (p. 307). Finally, Bonnard explained that with regard to autistic and profoundly disturbed children, autistic lingual addictions provide only the closed circle of narcissistic self-supply.

Barry L. Siegel (1971), in "The Role of the Mouth in the Search for the Female Phallus," presents three cases in which the mouth is used to locate the female phallus as a way of managing castration anxiety. One case is of a man who felt reassured by his girlfriend's hair in his mouth. The other two cases were of men who engaged in cunnilingus in search of the clitoris as female phallus.

Willi Hoffer (1949), in "Mouth, Hand, and Ego-Integration," asserted that the simultaneous oral sensations and tactile sensations aroused by finger sucking convey the primal sensation of self. As the infant develops, the hand becomes associated with the eyes and vision, the nose and smelling, and other sense organs and equilibrium to the point that the infant develops an oral-tactile concept of his own body and the surrounding world as well as a way to regulate, to a certain extent, the erotic and aggressive drives (pp. 49–56). The simultaneous oral and tactile sensations aroused by finger sucking bring together in one experience sensations on the outer skin surface and on the inner skin surface in an activity that is totally under the control of the baby.

In "Respiratory Introjection," Fenichel (1931/1953b) demonstrated that oral incorporation could also take place via the respiratory function of inhaling and smelling. He offered several case examples and further illustrated his point with ethnological data. "The Latin word 'anima' means at once breath, life, soul, wind and smell," he said (p. 235). Related to this is a wide variety of customs involving the shaman inhaling the sickness of his patient and the blowing out of demons: "The idea of incorporating an object by breathing or smelling it is the expression of a particular sexualization of the respiratory and olfactory function" (p. 236). In "The Psychopathology of Coughing" (1943/1954), Fenichel said that coughing is a means of discharging mucus and irritating physical stimuli but that certain neurotics may cough as a means of discharging a kind of mental mucus or some other inner, psychic, stimulus. He noted that introjection and reprojection of what has been introjected are seen commonly enough in eating and regurgitating but that breathing also carries this magic function, which is recognized in clinical material as well as in ideas about demons and their exorcism by way of the mouth (Fenichel, 1931/1953b, pp. 238-39).

Appendix 4

Chapter 4 Elaborations

Primate Ritualizations and Social Instincts

In this appendix we revisit the theme of primate ritualizations and social instincts, already discussed in the text, in order to elaborate the theme. Remember, the reason we are interested in primate ritualizations, particularly those of chimpanzees, is that these ritualizations or social instincts are taken as the scaffolding upon which our symbolic function overlays symbols and meaning. It is the symbolization of our primate ritualizations that transforms them into our human psychodynamics. Incidentally, I sometimes refer to "ritualizations" and other times to "social instincts" but I see them as synonyms and have made no other attempt to distinguish one from the other. Perhaps others will be able to better distinguish them or confirm them as one and the same.

Greeting Behavior and Mother-Infant Bonding: Orality

If we try to imagine which ritualization might be associated with the oral stage, breast-feeding and suckling naturally come to mind. But when we amplify the investigation to include the psychosocial stage of trust versus mistrust, we can better understand why Erikson would associate this stage with the ritualization of the "greeting ceremonial," in which mother and infant call to each other, look at each other, reach out to each other, and touch each other in a dance of mutual recognition.

Jane Goodall (1986) and her colleagues at Gombe National Park, in Tanzania, have witnessed the importance of mother-infant greeting in chimpanzees. They've also seen the distressed searching behavior that occurs when there are separations and the emotional damage that occurs with the early death of a young chimpanzee's mother who can no longer return the infant's greeting: "Two of the six young chimpanzees at Gombe who lost their mothers when they were between four and six years of age (that is, they were nutritionally independent) died within eighteen months" (p. 203).

Newborn chimpanzee babies begin nursing right away. Most mothers help their babies find the nipple, and those who are insensitive to their babies' efforts or distress end up with anxious and insecure offspring (Goodall, 1971/1988, p. 149). Chimpanzees are seen sucking their thumbs at two months, get their first tooth at three months, chew and swallow solid food at four months, break mother-infant contact for the first time at five months, and kiss another chimpanzee also at five months (p. 272). While a 3-year-old will still be expected to suckle, ride on its mother's back, and share food with its mother, in the fourth and fifth years its mother will become increasingly intolerant of this behavior, and there will be incidents of maternal aggression that encourage the youth to walk on his or her own and feed at a greater distance (Goodall, 1986, p. 354). Weaning takes place by the end of the fifth year, and in the sixth year the youth starts to lose its milk teeth. Puberty is achieved at 8 or 9 years of age (Goodall, 1971/1988, p. 272).

A weaning chimp at the peak of frustration may beg, whimper, cajole, or even start grooming its mother around her nipples and then try to nurse. If none of this works, it may throw a screaming tantrum (Goodall, 1986, p. 576): "The weaning period followed by the birth of a new infant can cause quite serious emotional disturbances in youngsters (between four and five years of age)—decrease in frequency of play, and marked increase in whimpering and contact with the mother. These symptoms probably parallel feelings of rejection in human youngsters during similar childhood crises" (p. 203).

As mentioned earlier, after studying several books on chimpanzee behavior, I noticed something that was curiously not present. Chimpanzees don't say good-bye! Scientists have observed the chimpanzees' elaborate greeting ritualizations, enthusiastic greetings after long absences, and bitter expressions of loss following the death of a loved one, but there are no references to any sort of good-bye ritualization. When chimpanzees separate, they seem to just wander off. But the loss becomes registered somehow as an echo of the attachment with the lost other, as they will rejoice when they later meet up again.

From my perspective, psychoanalysis is a psychology of loss. The notion of loss is embedded in the idea of repression, in the creation of an unconscious, in separation-individuation, in mourning and melancholia, in the child's game of *fort da*, in displacement and symbolization, in the resolution of the Oedipus complex, and so on. Losses are certainly mourned after the fact, but we can also anticipate them. The link between the "mother-infant bond and attachment" and "suffering a loss" is that as the pair develops its attachment through a ritualization of mutual recognition, they establish internal representations of each other, and in suffering a loss there is a disruption to mutual recognition and a disruption to the internal representation of the absent other.

Chimpanzee babies at Gombe that were still breast-feeding when their mothers died simply died from the lack of nutrition. Yet those that were old enough to feed themselves or be adopted were able to survive physically but showed unmistakable signs of psychological loss: lethargy, whimpering, listlessness, decreased frequency of play, rocking, pulling their hair out, and deterioration of tool-using skills and social skills (Goodall, 1986, pp. 101-104). Jane Goodall observed a chimpanzee mother carrying her recently deceased baby as though it were alive, cradled to her breast even a day after its death. For the mother to carry her dead baby is to recognize a continuing attachment even though the infant no longer participates in the greeting ceremonial of mutual recognition.

What does it say about the object relations of a chimpanzee mother when she forms an attachment to her baby, greets it, misses it when it is gone, and, if it dies, cradles it to her breast? It is only extrapolation to see how the awareness of the other and of the dead other may have eventually led Homo sapiens to bury their dead, create the funerary ritual, and recount to one another the myth of death and rebirth. To recognize the other in a greeting and "mourn" the absent other is to grant that there is an "other." There is a something in there, a someone in there, a personality, a spirit, a soul. It indicates the establishment of an "internal object" associated with a corresponding "external object" that makes greetings, good-byes, mourning, and funerals possible.

In 2013 a new hominin species was discovered, *Homo naledi*. Any new member of the hominin family tree is sure to stir interest, but this one has really excited the imagination. Investigators found more than 1,550 bones, from at least 15 Homo naledi individuals. The bodies had been carried to the very back of a cave almost 100 yards long and up and over to the other side of a narrowing in the cave (Wong, 2016, pp. 28-37). Lee Berger and his colleagues announced that the bones were between 236,000 and 335,000 years old (Viegas, 2017). Depositing the dead in one spot does not indicate a ritual burial, but it clearly suggests more involvement with the dead than is seen among modern chimpanzees.

When met with the death of one of their own group, chimpanzees may scream, charge, hurl rocks, grin nervously, embrace, pat each other, whimper, touch the corpse, or gaze motionless and silently for over an hour. Frans de Waal (2013) noted, "Apes often react with a combination of frustration about the lack of response and testing whether a response can be provoked" (p. 195).

In a fascinating study by Michael Tomasello, described by Gary Stix (2014), a young girl was provided blocks on a plate with which to build a tower. When no more blocks were provided, she pointed to the plate, signaling that there was something not there that she wanted: "The child knew that the adult would make the correct inference—the ability to refer to an absent entity is, in fact, a defining characteristic of human language. At the zoo, chimps put through a similar exercise—with food substituted for blocks—did not lift a finger when facing an empty plate" (p. 78). They could not see what wasn't there.

Signaling good-bye seems to be a ritualization that is unique to Homo sapiens. As a more recently acquired ritualization, it may be more fragile, more inclined to disturbance, and perhaps even more linked with what it is that makes us human. To say good-bye is to anticipate the absence of an other with whom one has an attachment.

The ability to say good-bye is also fundamental to the funerary ritual. Grieving a loss is possible whenever one has an emotional attachment and then loses the other. But mourning a loss with a prescribed funerary ritual embedded in traditions of burial, food offerings, tools for life in the hereafter, adornments, amulets, fetal positioning, caskets, and urns requires the ability not just to grieve but also to anticipate the departure of a loved one and not to just say "good-bye" but sometimes even "fare thee well."

With doubts about my observation of what was not there, I put my question to several experts: "Do chimpanzees 'say good-bye'?" I received the following replies:

"No, they don't. They just walk away. Isn't that funny?"
—Jane Goodall, personal communication, October 28, 2010, Seattle, Washington

I don't think chimps say good-bye.
—Anne E. Pusey, Department of Ecology, Evolution, and Behavior, University of Minnesota, personal e-mail communication, March 25, 2008

[This] question has long fascinated me. There does not appear to be any kind of vocalization, gesture, ANYTHING to signal "see you later," good-bye, even "be right back." Nothing of the kind seems to be in their repertoire. The most obvious reason for this is that much of the greeting gesturing and vocalization we observe is related to dominance and appeasement. Chimps tend to be quite communicative in tense situations (chance meetings in the forest can be very stressful) and less so when all is calm and relaxed. When they part ways, they tend to just drift off from one another with no signal that acknowledges the parting of the ways.
—Bill Wallauer, personal e-mail communication, May 12, 2009

John Crocker, MD, interned at Gombe for 8 months. He explained that when chimpanzees build their nests in the trees at night, the adults build their own individual nests and each mother builds a nest for herself and her child. When everyone gets settled into their nests, they each softly hoot in the darkness, seemingly to locate each other—a final greeting for the day as if to say, perhaps, "good-night" (pp. 191, 201).

Frans de Waal (1982/2007) reports that Allen Gardner was able to teach chimpanzees to use sign language to say good-bye, and they used the sign appropriately with their human teachers and among themselves. De Waal observed the Arnhem chimpanzee colony at the Royal Burgers' Zoo in the Netherlands and reported chimpanzees giving good-bye kisses and touches (p. 185). Nonetheless, saying good-bye certainly appears to be a much later and therefore weaker ritualization than greeting.

Dominance and Submission: Anality

Dominant chimpanzees negotiate, establish, and maintain their positions through aggressive displays of hair erection, walking bipedally, hunching their shoulders, leaping, waving their arms, dragging large branches, shaking trees and bushes, and throwing or rolling large rocks (Goodall, 1986, pp. 122–23). Goodall (1971/1988) reported, "I saw one female, newly arrived in a group, hurry up to a big male and hold her hand toward him. Almost regally he reached out, clasped her hand in his, drew it toward him, and kissed it with his lips" (p. 29).

Adult females are submissive to all adult males and many adolescent males, and within the female group there are also hierarchies of dominance and submission. When a young female from another group wanders into the territory of a second group, she is liable to be attacked, but if she is in estrus, she will arouse great interest in the males and what seems to be "jealousy" in the older females (p. 126).

Once two females were playing and romping about together. Fifi, it seems, accidentally hurt Pooch, who was about two years older. Pooch screamed and hit back at Fifi: "Fifi grinned in fear and then turned her rump submissively and presented to Pooch. Pooch should have reached out and touched Fifi's bottom; instead she leaned forward and, very deliberately and rather hard, bit Fifi's little pointed clitoris" (p. 129). Fifi's genitals swelled up and bled. She made a nest for herself, laid back, and dabbed her wound with a bunch of leaves.

In "A Biological Basis for the Oedipus Complex: An Evolutionary and Ethological Approach," A. David Jonas and Doris F. Jonas (1975) drew attention to the extended period of helplessness characteristic of human babies, the high attachment needs, and the prolongation of developmental stages that contribute to the development of the Oedipus complex. They also point out that all adult apes are dominant over immature juveniles, that male primates are usually unable to perform sexually with females of higher rank due to hormonal inhibition, and that the evolutionary basis of castration anxiety may be related to an incapacity of the young male to perform in the presence of a dominant animal (pp. 603, 605).

Copulation Interference: The Oedipus Complex

When chimpanzees mate, it is typically a public affair lasting between 10 to 15 seconds and usually takes place only when the females are in estrus. At these times, the labia swell dramatically and become pink, making them easily recognizable even from great distances. Goodall refers to these chimpanzees in estrus as "pink ladies."

Copulation interference by offspring is a ritualization previously described in chapter 4. One observation involved five chimpanzees whom Goodall named Goliath, Flo, David, Evered, and Fifi. Goliath approached Flo, a pink lady. Flo crouched to the ground and presented her pink posterior. Goliath mounted her and as he did, Fifi, Flo's daughter, rushed over and tried to push Goliath off her mother by pushing his head. Goliath tolerated Fifi's efforts without any reprisal. When Goliath finished mating, he moved off and Flo and Fifi went looking for a banana. As they walked away, Fifi looked over her shoulder at Goliath and kept one hand over her mother's pink swelling. A few minutes later David approached. Flo ran to him, turned, and presented her pink swelling. David mated with her. Again Fifi rushed at the male and tried to push him off of her mother. David also tolerated Fifi's efforts without reprisals. David then groomed Flo and settled down to take a nap. Goliath did the same. Then Evered, an adolescent male, moved in. He assumed the adolescent courtship position, to which Flo responded. David and Goliath looked to see what was going on but then ignored it. Fifi went after Evered just as she had tried to stop the adult males. Evered ignored Fifi's efforts. The next morning, in addition to Goliath, David, and Evered, eight other males mated with Flo. Fifi tried to stop each and every one of them but was successful only with Mr. McGregor, who, when pushed, lost his footing and rolled down the hill. In other circumstances, adolescent males, "torn between desire and caution" approached pink ladies but then withdrew when adult males were close at hand (Goodall, 1971/1988, pp. 83-85). Flo was often seen together with Rudolf, but he did not mind if she mated with other males. After a while Fifi stopped protesting so much about her mother's suitors, but she also started to demonstrate the behavior of a much younger chimpanzee, such as riding on her mother's back or even trying to hold on to her mother's underbelly like a much younger chimpanzee (pp. 85-86).

A chimp named Goblin would, at first, threaten or mildly hit interfering infants, but by the time he got to be about 16 his punishments became more severe, and once while copulating with Freud's mother, he attacked the 9-year-old and apparently broke a bone in Freud's foot or ankle in the process (Goodall, 1986, p. 368). Freud, incidentally, was given that name in honor of his mother's wild sexual adventures when she was an adolescent (Goodall, 1990, p. 38).

When Freud was being weaned, he went through the usual depression, about which both Jane Goodall, Anna Freud, and Melanie Klein would all understand quite well. Without being able to nurse, Freud sought other things from his mother, Fifi—specifically her attention, reassurance, and grooming. Then, if weaning weren't bad enough, Fifi became sexually attractive again: "Whenever his mother was mated by an adult male, Freud, in a frenzy of agitation, rushed towards the pair and, whimpering or even screaming, pushed at his mother's suitor. During the first and second of Fifi's pink swellings Freud seldom missed a single copulation; his distress and almost obsessive interference was reminiscent of Fifi's behavior at the same age. Most youngsters appear to be less disturbed, although all interfere when their mothers are mated" (Goodall, 1990, pp. 113-14).

As described in chapter 4, my wife, Adriana Prengler, and I enlisted cooperation from parents of some young children in an informal investigation. We asked, "What is the reaction of your child when he/she sees you and your spouse hugging and/or kissing?" The following are a few additional responses that further make the point:

Nathan Boy, 3 years 2 months
He laughs and he wants to participate. He comes to hug us. And he comes to be with us. So he jumps on us. But more directly he jumps onto his mother. But also he likes it when his father caresses his mother but interrupts when the mother and father are together. Also and if the little sister is there he pushes her—tries to put her out.

John Boy, 19 months
When we hug he looks happy and joyful. He comes close to us. He looks jealous. He goes between us to call our attention and also to separate us and try to participate. Mother says, "He tries to kiss me and take his father out of the game. And he says, 'Mama, Mama, Mama,' and hugs me."

Pedro Boy, 3 years
He gets jealous. He takes me. He says, "Mommy is mine. Mommy is only mine." It's a competition. His father says, "Mommy is for everyone we need to share her."
Pedro says, "No. I don't share her with you."
Father replies playfully, "But I signed the papers!"
Pedro says, "No, you didn't buy her. My mommy is mine."

Joseph Boy, 3 years
He hides his face, feels shy and laughs. He asks, "Why is Daddy kissing you?" He kisses me but not his dad. He covers his eyes and says, "Why are you kissing my mom?" Then he hugs us both.

Chimpanzees don't have Oedipus complexes; they have a copulation interference ritualizations. Humans, however, have the instinctually based copulation interference ritualization but also have a symbolic function and are born into language and culture. While the chimpanzee copulation interference ritualization creates physical space between mother and male suitor by the child, the human Oedipus complex creates psychological space between the mother (desire) and the father (laws) by the child (ego) and another space is created between the mother (desire) and the child (ego) by the father (laws). The heirs of the Oedipus complex are the superego and identifications with the parents. In the prolonged and developing identification with the parent, the child's ego is strengthened and culture is widened and elaborated far beyond the limits of chimpanzee psychology and chimpanzee culture.

Interestingly enough, in a Polynesian creation myth, Rangi, who was heaven and the father, was lying on top of Papa, who was earth and the mother. They had children, but because Rangi was lying on top of Papa, there was no light, only darkness. So the children made a plan to tear them apart. Tane-mahuta put his head on his mother, and then with his feet he thrust his father up into the skies, high up into the heavens, letting in the light. "No sooner was heaven rent from earth than the multitude of human beings were discovered whom they had begotten, and who had hitherto lain concealed between the bodies of Rangi and Papa" (Long, 1963, p. 93).

In the Egyptian cosmogony, "The goddess of heaven, Nut, was still lying upon her spouse, the earth god Seb (or Keb). Then the god of atmosphere (or air), her father Shu, shoved himself between them and lifted her up along with everything which had been created, i.e., every god with his boat" (p. 99).

In a Minyong cosmogony from India, it is said that Melo, who was a man and the sky, was married to and lying on top of Sedi, who was a woman and the earth. The Wiyus, the ancestral spirits, held a meeting to consider what they could do to keep from being crushed. One of the Wiyus caught hold of the sky and beat him, so he had to flee far into the heavens (p. 106).

Another example of copulation interference approaches the matter in the form of a denied wish—a wish to not interfere. *The Tibetan Book of the Dead* (1927/1960) is a sacred Buddhist text that prepares the soul for navigating the afterlife realms in order to stay at one with God and not be reborn into the earthly world in the cycle of suffering. *The Tibetan Book of the Dead* was revealed by Karma Lingpa in the 1300s. Walter Y. Evans-Wentz's edited translation was based on seven texts and the English translations of Lama Kazi Dawa-Samdup. In that part of the text called The Closing of the Door of the Womb, the soul, in the realms of the afterlife is instructed on how to avoid the cycle of rebirth.

> O nobly-born, at this time thou wilt see visions of males and females in union. When thou seest them, remember to withhold thyself from going between them. ... If at that time, one entereth into the womb through the feelings of attachment and repulsion, one may be born either as a horse, a foul, a dog, or a human being.
>
> If [about] to be born as a male, the feeling of itself being a male dawneth upon the Knower, and a feeling of intense hatred towards the father and of jealousy and attraction towards the mother is begotten. If [about] to be born as a female the feeling of itself being a female dawneth upon the Knower, and a feeling of intense hatred towards the mother and of intense attraction and fondness towards the father is begotten. (pp. 177-179)

Sexual Inhibitions and Incest Taboos: The Latency Phase

As mentioned earlier in the main text, primatologist Anne Pusey (2005) studied inbreeding avoidance in primates and noted that inbreeding between first-order relatives rarely occurs, that there are dispersal patterns in which male or female individuals tend to leave the groups they were born in and join other groups, and that adults who are close relatives residing in the same group usually do not mate (p. 62). According to Pusey, male chimpanzees have their first penile erections in the first year of life and thrust on immature and mature females in play and social contact (p. 67). They can fully copulate at 3 years of age but do not ejaculate until they are 9 or 10 years old:

> Males of three to six years usually copulated quite frequently with their mothers, accounting for about 5 to 7 percent (range 0 to 29 percent) of their mother's total copulations with males when she was swollen. One context in which such copulations occurred was when mothers presented to their distressed infants during weaning. However, copulations with mothers by males of this age occurred commonly when both male and mother were calm. From the age of seven years onward, most males never copulated with their mothers. However, two of five adult males, Goblin and Frodo, did mate with their mothers several times after the ages of fifteen when they had attained high rank among the males. In these cases the mother usually screamed and strenuously tried to resist her son's advances. (p. 68)

Males at 3 to 4 years of age frequently mate with their mature sisters, but between 5 and 15 years they rarely mate with them. When sisters remained in their natal group, brothers between 16 and 33 years often mated with their sisters, although the sisters often resisted. Pusey noted, "Males mate with their mothers and, sometimes, maternal sisters with impunity as infants, but that inhibition of such activity sets in before or at puberty. More detailed observations are required to determine whether this inhibition is due to an intrinsic change in the male or is triggered by an increase in resistance from the female" (p. 70).

Displaying, Battling, and Mating: Adolescent Genital Stage

Goodall (1986) notes that threat behavior typically serves to maintain or challenge the hierarchy or social order, while clear changes in the hierarchy are almost always the result of real fights:

> A three-year-old male (Atlas), for example, ran to the security of his mother as an adult male gave pant-hoots preceding a charging display, then watched as the male ran, slapping the ground with his hands, stamping with his feet, ending his display by jumping up and drumming with his hands on a treetrunk. When the adult male had moved away, the infant left his mother, ran a short distance with much stamping of his feet, then paused near the drumming tree. He gazed at it, approached, and—very cautiously and gently—hit it twice with his knuckles. A female of similar age (Fanni) also watched from her mother's arms as a male displayed. She then went to the spot and several times stamped her own feet on the ground. The slap-stamp elements of the charging display, in particular, are often incorporated into sessions of locomotor play by infants of both sexes. (pp. 336–37)

This observation invites us to muse on imitation, identification, and identification with the aggressor.

Not every male becomes an alpha male, and no alpha male remains in that position forever. Mike was an aging alpha male in 1970 when he was attacked by Humphrey and Faben. Mike scurried into a tree screaming and Humphrey went after him. He pulled Mike to the ground, hit him, and stomped on him, and Faben then joined in and pounded on Mike as well. Mike's six years as an alpha male had come to an end. Humphrey took the reins of power and became the alpha male. But another strong male for him to contend with was Figan (Goodall, 1990, pp. 43–46).

APPENDIX 4

Figan was a strong, intelligent male who would pose a real threat to Humphrey's position, but he also had a "very highly strung nature. During intense social excitement, for example, he sometimes began to scream uncontrollably and often rushed over to a nearby individual, touching or embracing him, or her, for reassurance. Sometimes he even clutched his own scrotum" (p. 44). Although Humphrey was the alpha male, both Figan and Evered were high ranking. One day the two of them skirmished and Figan fell to the ground, spraining his wrist or breaking a bone. Screaming in pain, his mother, Flo, quite old by then, came to his aid. Figan's screams of pain turned to soft whimpers, and he stayed with his mother for three weeks until his wounds healed.

Sometime later Figan attacked Humphrey. It was in the early evening that Figan began to display wildly and then leaped down onto Humphrey, where they locked in combat. Humphrey escaped screaming and scurried to safety. Figan chased after him a bit and then continued his displaying. When Humphrey moved off to make his bed for the night, Figan pounced on him again and again and Humphrey ran into the bushes. Finally, Humphrey made a submissive appeal showing recognition of Figan's dominance. Figan, the new alpha male, accepted Humphrey's submissive appeal calmly (pp. 44–52). To maintain his position, Figan put on magnificent displays:

> Most effective were his wild arboreal performances at the crack of dawn when it was still almost dark and the rest of the group was still abed. These caused pandemonium, with confused chimps screaming and hurling themselves from their nests. Back and forth, up and down—Figan leapt from branch to branch, shaking the vegetation, snapping great branches and, for good measure, pounding, from time to time, on some unfortunate subordinate. The confusion and noise were unbelievable. And then when it was all over, their new alpha, all bristling magnificence, would sit on the ground and, like some great tribal chief, receive the obeisance of his underlings. (p. 54)

Goodall (1986) wrote that no dominance battles observed at Gombe ever resulted in death but stated that does not mean no deaths occur. She was referring to the observation of Frans de Waal at an open-air chimpanzee colony at the Royal Burgers' Zoo in Arnhem (the Netherlands). De Waal (1982/2007) reported, "Luit was alpha for only ten weeks. The Yeroen-Nikkie alliance made a comeback with a bloody vengeance one night during which the two allies together severely injured Luit. Apart from biting off fingers and toes and causing deep gashes everywhere, the two aggressors removed Luit's testicles, which were found on the cage floor. Luit died on the operating table due to loss of blood from the fight, which took place in a night cage with only the three senior males present" (p. 211).

Konrad Lorenz and Aggression

Lorenz (1963) described the dance of the cranes, in which a crane engages in intense threat and attack behavior in front of, but not directed toward, a partner crane. Lorenz explained that this dance sends an easily understood message that the attack is not directed against his partner but away from him, implying a comradely defense:

> Now the crane turns again toward his friend and repeats this demonstration of his size and strength, only quickly to turn around once more and perform emphatically a fake attack on any substitute object, preferably a nearby crane which is not a friend, or even on a harmless goose or on a piece of wood or stone which he seizes with his beak and throws three or four times into the air. The whole procedure says as clearly as human words, "I am big and threatening, but not toward you—toward the other, the other, the other." (pp. 174-75)

Lorenz observed that a wide variety of animals have transformed threat behavior into greeting ritualizations (p. 172). He marveled at the great feats of evolution that have, for example, transformed a lizard's leg into a bird's wing. However, he notes that such "amazing metamorphoses seem tame in comparison with the ingenious feat of transforming, by comparatively simple means of redirection and ritualization, a behavior pattern which not only in its prototype but even in its present form is partly motivated by aggression, into a means of appeasement and further into a love ceremony which forms a strong tie between those that participate in it. This means neither more nor less than converting the mutually repelling effect of aggression into its opposite.... Thus it forms a bond between individuals" (p. 173).

Lorenz tells us that appeasement and greeting ritualizations have arisen out of redirected aggression movements. When aggression between A and B is redirected to C, it serves to create a bond between A and B. "Thus discrimination between friend and stranger arises, and for the first time in the world personal bonds between individuals come into being," and "personality begins where personal bonds are formed for the first time" (pp. 137-38). Lorenz goes on to say, "Doubtless the personal bond, love, arose in many cases from intra-specific aggression [aggression between members of the same species], by way of ritualization of a redirected attack or threatening.... Intra-specific aggression is millions of years older than personal friendship and love.... The personal bond is known only in certain teleost fishes, birds and mammals, that is in groups that did not appear before the Tertiary period" (p. 217).

Throughout our evolution, we developed aggression inhibiting ritualizations that became defensive strategies resulting ultimately in the development of self-awareness. Julian Huxley

(1966) explained that through this evolution we find that "in man alone does infantile repression of guilt occur, with resultant formation of the Freudian Unconscious and Superego, and further consequence of projective thinking, by which man projects elements of his own personality into natural objects and forces, thus personifying them: and into or onto other persons, real or imaginary, slave or ruler, friend or foe, thus endowing them with qualities not inherently theirs" (p. 259).

Then Huxley said something that is really quite stunning: "The powerful formalizing effect of this ritualization of thought and feeling, even when unconscious, is revealed by our various escapes from it" (p. 260). Our escapes from the ritualization of thought include the fantasy world of dreams, psychic phenomena induced by sensory deprivation, experiences of sexual love at their highest and deepest, the supernormal visionary world opened up to us through psychedelics, the experience of schizophrenia and other psychotic states, the transcendent inner worlds of visionary artists, the transcendent states brought on through disciplined and ritualized explorations of meditation, and so on. In other words, we can more clearly see "the powerful formalizing effect of this ritualization of thought and feeling" when we can find a way to escape from its influence and look back on the world from outside of it.

R. D. Laing (1966) described psychotic states as the "deritualization of normal human rituals" (p. 331). One could easily imagine a process of deritualization in psychotic decompensation and the way recovery might be seen as a return to the ritualizations and rituals of human life and culture. Huxley (1966) observed that "both schizophrenia and psychedelic substances like LSD (lysergic acid diethylamide) seem to exert their effects by interfering with the 'normal' ritualization of the perception-building process" (pp. 260, 263). In other words, in decompensation the ego dissolves, and customary behavior embedded in rituals and ritualizations are forgotten or seem foreign. One feels like a stranger in a strange land, words become clunky, and even one's identity seems a distant memory. One is reduced to a Paleolithic being without belonging to either a Paleolithic culture or the modern one. One quickly becomes lost in an extraordinarily complex world of scrambled artifacts, objects, words, people, and relationships but with no recollection or understanding of their culturally shared meanings.

The Human Symbolic Function

Herbert Silberer (1917), an early colleague of Freud's, was interested in the interpretation of myth and mysticism and suggested they could be interpreted psychoanalytically, in terms of repressed sexuality, and also "anagogically"—that is, in terms of the moral or idealistic strivings of the unconscious. He asserted that myths are concerned with a "nucleus of natural philosophy" (p. 328). Silberer was presenting his ideas in 1914, right after Freud and Jung had split over this very issue. Without denying the infantile sexual roots of the dream symbol, Jung minimized them and emphasized the philosophical and spiritual implications. Freud saw more of the same repression in Silberer's ideas concerning the anagogic interpretations, which could be applied to myths, fairy tales, alchemy, and dreams as well. Rather than minimizing the interpretation of repressed sexuality, Silberer was intrigued by the way multiple interpretations could coexist. But Freud would have none of it. He stated:

> Silberer, who was among the first to issue a warning to us not to lose sight of the nobler side of the human soul, has put forward the view that all or nearly all dreams permit such a twofold interpretation, a purer, anagogic one beside the ignoble, psychoanalytic one. This is, however, unfortunately not so. On the contrary, an over-interpretation of this kind is rarely possible. To my knowledge no valid example of such a dream-analysis with a double meaning has been published up to the present time. But observations of this kind can often be made upon the series of associations that our patients produce during analytic treatment. On the one hand the successive ideas are linked by a line of association which is plain to the eye, while on the other hand you become aware of an underlying theme which is kept secret but which at the same time plays a part in these ideas. (S. Freud, 1922/1955c, SE 18, p. 216)

With all due respect, I think Freud goes too far. The well-timed and tactful psychoanalytic interpretation unlocks emotions and memories long buried under the psychological symptoms; it also challenges the symptom's reason for being. The anagogic interpretation, on the other hand, opens avenues of meaning making, opportunities for sublimation, and often prepares the ground for the interpretation of psychoanalytic symbolism. John Weir Perry once told me that in making an interpretation, the abstract idea carries the meaning while the bodily interpretation carries the affect (personal communication, 1983). From my perspective, the psychoanalytic and anagogic interpretations together, can sometimes unlock a stream of associations where only one or the other cannot. Erik Erikson (1954/1987a) described one such situation:

> Toward the end of the analysis of a young professional man who stood before an important change in status, a kind of graduation, a dream occurred in which he experienced himself lying on the analytic couch, while I was sawing a round hole in the top of his head. The patient, at first, was willing to accept almost any other

interpretation, such as castration, homosexual attack (from behind), continued analysis (opening a skull flap), and insanity (lobotomy), all of which were indeed relevant, rather than to recognize this dream as an over-all graduation dream with a reference to the tonsure administered by bishops to young Catholic priests at the time of their admission to clerical standing.... Thus infantile wishes to belong to and to believe in organizations providing for collective reassurance against individual anxiety, in our intellectuals, easily join other repressed childhood temptations—and force their way into dreams. (p. 265)

While the body is an organizing stimulus, there is no such thing as the physical body without the social body. Anthropologist Mary Douglas (1970/1982) clarified the relation of the social and physical bodies in this way: "The social body constrains the way the physical body is perceived. The physical experience of the body, always modified by the social categories through which it is known, sustains a particular view of society. There is a continual exchange of meanings between the two kinds of bodily experience so that each reinforces the category of the other" (p. 65).

The social body is the set of social constraints encoded in customs and language in which the physical body is situated. Without recognition of the formative role of the social body, psychoanalytic symbolism becomes emotionally flat. It is the inclusion of the social body along with the psychoanalytic body that makes wild analysis and dream-book interpretations obsolete and necessitates the use of free association as a method of finding personal meaning from derivative material. Dream symbolism is not genetically inherited. It is formed on the threshold of bodily sensation and the symbolic function, within the context of family and culture. The symbolic function is a cognitive operation working on bodily experience and pertains to the transformation of sensations into perceptions, which are further associated with other perceptions, displaced to other representations, or condensed into new forms. It develops through successive levels of nonverbal representation and is ultimately clothed in a veil of linguistic and culturally determined representations that further reshape the experience of a sense of self, a sense of other, and a sense of the world. We can sometimes observe the bedrock of symbol formation in our work with severely disturbed children.

Melanie Klein (1932/1937) and her colleagues, in their work with psychotic children, reconfirmed Ferenczi's view that primary identification, a forerunner of symbolism, emerges out of the infant's desire to discover or rediscover his or her organs and their functions in every object. This forerunner, however, which may later take on symbolic significance, is experienced not as a symbol or representation of the original object but as the object itself. The Kleinians refer to this sort of forerunner as a "symbolic equation" and distinguish it from a stage in development when the ego is able to represent the object with a symbol proper. In the "symbolic equation" the symbol is experienced as being identical to the object being symbolized, and in "symbolic representation" the symbol proper represents the object. Symbolic representation is what enables the toddler to use speech and engage in symbolic play. (See Isaacs, 1948; Rodrigue, 1956; and Segal, 1957.)

Jacques Lacan (1978) said the young infant was in an undifferentiated, fragmented, perceptual fusion during what he called the pre-mirror stage, when the Real and the Imaginary are forming imagistic and fantasmatic representations of personal experience. These are later recast into new forms as they are reorganized in the Symbolic Order around the language and customs of the prevailing culture. Nature provides signifiers that organize human relations, providing them with structure and shape (p. 20): "The first symbols, natural symbols, stem from a certain number of prevailing images—the image of the human body, the image of a certain number of obvious objects like the sun, the moon, and some others. And that is what gives human language its weight, its resources, and its emotional vibration" (Lacan, 1988, p. 306). Lacan, however, was just as quick to remind us that these Imaginary themes are not to be confused with the Symbolic. They are components of the Imaginary, which anchor the Symbolic in the body.

APPENDIX 4

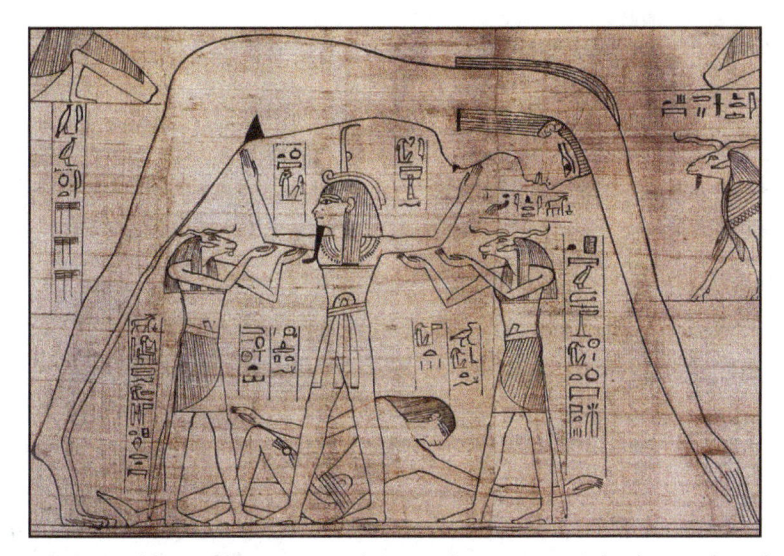

Nut, the goddess of heaven, was lying on her spouse, Seb, the earth god. Then her father, Shu, the god of atmosphere, interfered in their copulation and lifted her up to reveal everything Nut and Seb had created.

A wood carving from the front of a storehouse depicting the Maori gods, Rangi, the heaven or sky father, and Papa, the earth mother, as a copulating couple. They had many children but because they were in an eternal embrace their children lived between their two parents in darkness until Tane-mahuta, god of the forests, put his head on his mother and feet on his father and pushed his father into the sky letting in light and revealing all the people that had been born. Notice the heads of the children all around the copulating parents. New Zealand 18th Century.

Appendix 5

Chapter 5 Elaborations

The Killing of the Beast

In an effort to bring to life the nature of the hunt in a contemporary aboriginal community, I offer the following account of my visit to a small group of people belonging to the Hoti tribe in the Venezuelan jungles. This brief account does not change the broad outlines of what I have described in the main text but, in a sense, adds color to it.

❖ ❖ ❖

I hire two guides and head up the Upper Orinoco, in southern Venezuela, in a *bongo*—a long narrow metal boat with an outboard motor and a partial covering for shade. We navigate the Orinoco for two days and then head up the Ventuari River. Three days later we arrive in a little jungle town where we exchange the bongo for a dugout canoe, handmade from the trunk of a tree by the local indigenous people. We climb in, strap our outboard motor onto the back, head up the narrowing river, and then turn into Caño Manapiare (*caño* = creek).

As we glide by, magnificent birds stand guard or elegantly take to the air, monkeys scream and jump wildly in the trees, huge river otters watch us with alarm. We see an electric eel, swarms of butterflies, huge iguanas, and *babas*. Babas are 3- or 4-foot-long caimans. They lounge on the riverside or swim along with just their heads above water and then disappear, diving down into the murky depths. Turtles sit on their log perches calmly taking in the sun, and when they see us, they push off and plop ungracefully into the water. One turtle stretches out its head as a beautiful orange butterfly stands delicately on its nose.

As we go up the river, cormorants and herons are startled by us and fly on ahead only to perch farther upriver. We leave Caño Manapiare and enter Caño Parucito. After eight full days of navigating the rivers and caños, we arrive at a small Hoti village. The chief, Luis, welcomes us to the village. There are nine buildings made of mud and long branches with thatched roofs and dirt floors. A couple of them simply have thatched roofs held up on poles with no walls, and the kitchen area has a large thatched roof with walls made of poles all around but no mud in between them. This allows for ample fresh air to pass through and for the release of smoke from the various fire pits and the *budare* (mud oven). My guides know all of the people, including the children, so we are received warmly.

We enter the kitchen, and in the darkness I see people lying in their *chinchorros* (hammocks). Animal bones and skulls are scattered here and there, and there are two or three hearths, each with three stones for mounting a pot. We see *cerbatanas* (blowguns), raw cotton, baskets, little green parrots and toucans as pets, and all sorts of things hanging from the walls and rafters.

Luis's wife is lying in her chinchorro, as are several of their children and his wife's older sister, Aurora. The village includes Luis, his immediate family, and what appear to be Luis's younger brothers and their families—maybe three or four families in all. There are at least five dogs, five pigs, chickens, ducks, and two beautiful black birds with black crests and orange on their faces. This bird is called a *pauji*. One of Luis's brothers, Enrique, wears the traditional red *guayuco* (pronounced "why-you-co") loincloth. The rest wear lightweight shorts. The people are all very pleasant. Many have coughs, congestion, and skin infections—more signs of what it means to live at one with nature. It is hot outside and even hotter in the kitchen. I am offered a *platano* drink, some meat from a large rodent, and a soup of piranha and manioc. I eat it all and enjoy it while sitting on a seat made of a very large tortoise shell.

In the afternoon I find a tree to hang out under while sitting on a broken dugout canoe, which now serves as a bench. Children, adults, pigs and dogs, and the paujís are milling about. The adults are relaxed with me and the children engage me quickly, much to my delight. Enrique, in his guayuco, is making reed baskets before my very eyes, as is his wife. The baskets are loosely strung to serve as birdcages for three toucans the couple took from their nest and are now raising. The toucans are now fairly big, have beaks 4 inches long, and can fly. They fly up into the trees and then down onto our hands, where they beg for food by lightly biting at our fingers. The whole scene is enchanting.

There are maybe ten children in the village. A 7-year-old girl stays close to me. She is deaf and mute. She shows me sharp objects and cuts on her feet, pinches my skin, and pulls the hair on my arm as if to say, "This is how I hurt." In time she will trust enough to lean softly against me. When the giant pig comes around, she screams and laughs and points at it. She, like most everyone in the Hoti village, is missing most of her teeth—some completely gone and others broken, jagged, and discolored. She wears a dirty denim top and equally dirty denim pants but slips them both off easily from time to time, as when she jumps in the caño to go swimming.

A young mother wearing nothing but the traditional female guayuco, of red hand-spun cotton cloth, like a bikini bottom, sits down with us and nurses her baby. She is a beautiful young woman who is disarmingly open, undemonstrative, and appears not the least bit self-conscious. As young as she is, she appears to me as the mother of us all. Her gaze, like that of most everyone else here, is steady and open. Rather than looking directly at me, her eyes seem to be taking me in along with the rest of the scenery, as if in a wide-angle view.

Later in the afternoon, Enrique comes to my chinchorro, where I am resting, and gives me a pile of freshly picked fruit on a plantain leaf. They are like grapes and every bit as delicious, but they have a large pit and thick skin, which are not eaten. Soon Enrique's wife approaches with a long, fat, green seedpod, about a meter long. She opens it to reveal a row of white, wet, cottony fruit each about an inch and a half long, with a large seed in it. We eat the white part and throw out the seeds. It too is quite tasty.

For dinner we eat rice and piranha soup with manioc. Manioc is processed yucca. Yucca is a root, which can be boiled and eaten like a potato. It can also be grated into a mush and placed in a *sebucan.* The sebucan is a long tube-like basket, and when it is filled with moist yucca, one can stretch the ends of the sebucan to effectively squeeze out the yucca's bitter juices, leaving the now more edible manioc mush behind. The mush is then dried out and toasted into round pieces of flat bread or broken up into granules of manioc, which are sprinkled into soup.

In the evening, my guides and I sleep in our chinchorros in one of the houses without walls, as they are cooler and the jungle's heat is very intense, even at night. In the modern world, night is a black velvet curtain that ends the day in darkness and silence, but in the jungle the night is every bit as alive as the day. There are no artificial lights for hundreds of miles, and the sky is full of more stars than one could ever imagine. Unlike stars on a black screen, these massive clouds of stars seem to hang in three dimensions, some closer and some farther away. It is breathtaking. In the darkness of the jungle night, birds scream, frogs chirp, bugs buzz, and fireflies blink. Suddenly the sounds of nature are broken by a roaring buzz saw apparently being used to chop down a nearby tree, but a moment later it is clear that it is not a buzz saw, at all, but a *chicharra*—a small bug that makes a big sound very much like a motor.

In the night at the water's edge, I hear the pink river dolphins around our boat surfacing and making human sorts of sounds as they gasp for air through their blowholes. These river dolphins are called *toninos.* Legend has it that sometimes a man will find a beautiful woman sunbathing by the river's edge, but she is actually a tonino transformed into a beautiful woman. If the man goes to her, she will seduce him into the river, turn back into a tonino, and drown him. Everyone knows it's just a legend, but who wants to take a chance?

In the darkness, I hear dogs grumbling, ducks clucking, chickens scratching, pigs oinking, chinchorros rocking and pulling at the squeaking wooden posts, the wind blowing. It is absolutely an orchestra of life. The night is not the end of the day. It is just another part of the day, during which my hosts may even walk through the jungle looking for something to eat—particularly wild game. I am rocked to sleep in my chinchorro with the sounds of the jungle all around me.

In the morning, I wake up to find the little deaf-mute girl and two other children watching me carefully as I lie in my chinchorro. I greet them tenderly and they all smile. They're ready to play!

Several men and boys, including Luis, plan to go hunting today while my guides and I spend the day hanging out in the village. It is a glorious day, and soon one of my guides is able to open up some photo opportunities. Everyone is happy to have their picture taken and excited to see the results on the little digital screen at the back.

There are animal skulls scattered all around the grounds and in the living spaces. The Hoti save a bone, usually the skull, from each animal killed to ensure a good hunt in the future. I see skulls of a tapir, wild pigs, *chiguires* (large rodent), monkeys, and an anteater. Some are littered about the village; others seem absentmindedly stashed into corners in the kitchen or other living areas.

In the afternoon, I go down to the river with some of the children and adults and go for a swim in the piranha- and baba-infested waters. One never concerns oneself with such things, as the piranha in this river do not generally attack people, and the babas mostly sleep during the day and hunt at night. I wear my shorts in the water, but all the children drop their clothes and skinny-dip, wearing only their beads. One boy swims to the other shore and climbs barefoot about three stories up into a tree with agility, grace, and certainty.

In the late afternoon, Luis and one of his son's return from the hunt without having killed anything. The rest of the unsuccessful hunters do not return to the village until much later at night.

The next day I see the six or seven tortoises and two *lapas* (a lapa is a large rodent) they have domesticated and keep in a pen, eventually to be eaten. In the afternoon we bathe in the river. It is beautiful and peaceful, but living at one with nature is a constant struggle.

Well, as it turns out—and I didn't know this at the time—Luis felt bad about not killing anything the day before, as he remembers that his father always had plenty of food available when visitors came into their village. So Luis, his wife, and four dogs went out hunting earlier today. In the late afternoon, Luis's wife shows up on the other side of the creek with the four dogs, a machete in one hand, and a spear in the other. They've made a kill.

Hector, one of my guides, calls out, "Daniel, *vamos!*" I get into the canoe with Hector, Luis's wife, and Luis's two brothers, and we head downriver for about 20 minutes until we see Luis sitting on his haunches with his spear at his side.

On the other side of the narrow river, in the water is a dead tapir, a *danta*, or as the Hoti call it, a "wha-hee." It is the size of a small cow. Luis, his wife, and the dogs spotted it. The dogs chased it into the river, where Luis speared it three times. His spear has a wooden shaft and a sharp point made from a broken piece of a machete blade filed sharp into a spearpoint. Luis speared the full-grown female tapir, and after he killed it, he captured her baby, but it got away. We haul the tapir into the canoe and in diminishing sunlight return to camp. As we go up the river, back toward the village, the massive body of the dead tapir lies on its side in the canoe right in front of me as blood gurgles up and out of its wounds, sliding down its massive body and into a pool of blood at my feet.

We make our way to the village and stop at the riverside, where everyone comes down to the water's edge and immediately, without a word spoken, goes to work. They bring banana leaves and buckets and knives. With the tapir still in the boat, Luis, who is looking more and more like a leader and chief, pulls out his machete, sharpens it with a file, and before my eyes butchers the whole thing in about an hour and a half without one false machete cut: the first cut, the fat and muscle, masses of meat, slices of this, slabs of that, organ removal. The men and women silently work together to prepare everything as it is being removed. Buckets of blood are scooped out of the body cavities and out of the canoe itself and poured into the water turning the creek red as the sun goes down. Haunches removed. Packages of meat bundled up in banana leaves at the river's edge.

Each haunch is severed and then gets a slice to the mid-leg, which serves as a place to slip in the fingers for easy carrying. Lower jaw dislocated from the skull. Long tongue cut out. It is awe-inspiring. The whole experience is so rich, so fantastic, that I only hope they hurry up, because I don't want to miss anything and don't think I can endure any more. The experience is absolutely overwhelming. For Luis it's dinner, but for me it is an experience of a lifetime—the killing and cutting up of the primordial beast!

The next day begins with another glorious morning. Luis is already up and salting some of the meat to preserve it. We eat soup with tapir meat and manioc for breakfast along with our coffee. The skull is being cooked in a large pot for soup. Later it will be set aside casually, somewhere within the village, where it will bring good luck to future hunts.

APPENDIX 5

The head of a butchered tapir inside of a dugout canoe.
Hoti village in the Venezuelan jungle.

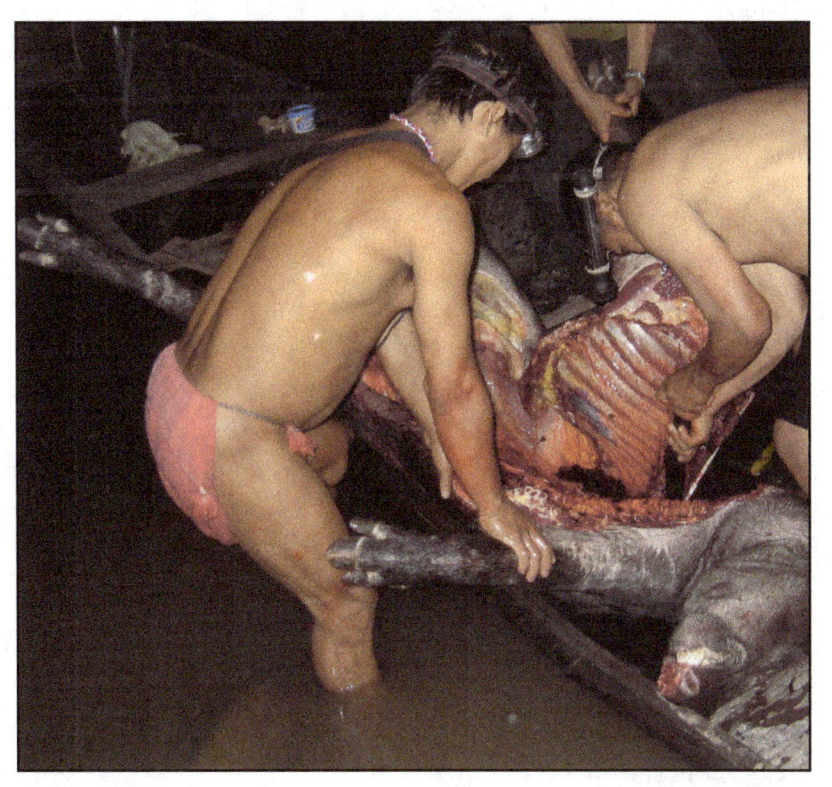

Butchering a tapir inside a dugout canoe. Hoti village in the Venezuelan jungle.

Appendix 6

Chapter 6 Elaborations

Panare Hunting, Gathering, and Tending the Garden

In a further effort to bring to life the nature of a contemporary aboriginal community living a somewhat Neolithic life, I offer the following account of my visit to a small group of people belonging to the Panare tribe in the Venezuelan jungles. This brief account gives us a peak into the life of hunter-gatherers and their garden.

❖ ❖ ❖

After several days navigating up the Orinoco and one exceptionally long day making our way up a narrow creek, barely avoiding all sorts of treacherous obstacles, we arrive at a Panare village.

People in this community have some modern clothes, plastic containers, and metal tools, but their houses are made of thin tree trunk poles and mud and have thatched roofs. They are identical to the houses their ancestors have been making for generations. The village is three houses with a fourth under construction. There are just a couple of families living here, and the children gravitate toward me, even if just to look at me. I find the attention of the children a wonderful entry into a culture where little Spanish is spoken. The adults are a little reserved, but the children warm up with just a smile, and when I show an interest in their *conuco*, or garden, they give me a guided tour. The conuco is producing yucca, squash, papaya, chili peppers, sweet peppers, and more. The plants grow in patches here and there in a vaguely designated area from which jungle trees had previously been cut down. The children show me their growing vegetables with obvious pride.

When I pick up three sweet peppers off the ground and begin to juggle them, all the children come close to watch and play with me. Soon I am sitting on the dirt floor with my hat in my hands while the children throw sweet peppers into it. We play this game for a curiously long time, much to the children's delight. The children, in flimsy dirty shorts and pajama tops, run barefoot with spirit here and there and seemingly without a care in the world. A house under construction is used by the children as a kind of jungle gym of tree poles bound together with vines. The children run in to it and up in a flash with no caution at all. They climb higher and higher and hang and jump, and do so barefoot, of course.

All the children surround me, but an 8-year-old girl seems to be particularly curious about me. Her name is Nena. I wonder what the children make of the fact that I am old enough to be their grandfather, especially when there seem to be no old people here. I am gray, balding, and have a beard, and no one out here is gray, balding, or bearded. I must look more like an old gray monkey than anything else. When I begin to hoot like a howler monkey, the children go wild with laughter and join in with me!

In the evening, the jungle comes alive with the sounds of birds, insects, frogs, and the creatures of the night. For dinner we have a lapa soup. One of its big rodent claws floats unsettlingly on the surface of the soup.

My guides and I spend the night in the sweltering heat of the tropical jungle inside a three-walled mud and stick house with a thatched roof and dirt floor. The fourth wall is open to the jungle. Our chinchorros are covered with mosquito netting, but mosquitoes still find a way to get in. Nonetheless, the jungle is magnificent and happening.

The mornings are always glorious, and it is good to climb out of the chinchorro, stretch, and see the natural beauty in which we are immersed. The Panare children come around to visit me, and it is good to see them. Nena is often seen taking care of her baby brother, whom she carries on her hip with physical dexterity and surety.

I ask our host about his garden and about his other sources of food. He shows me his bowl of curare (a neurotoxic poison paste), his curare-tipped darts, and his *cerbatana*, or blowgun. He gives me a demonstration, as does his little boy, who also is quite adept at it. The darts are kept in a bamboo quiver. The sharp ends are dipped in the neurotoxic curare and the other ends are wrapped in a cottony material from the *seda* tree. This cottony tuft surrounding the dart plugs the tube, enabling the shooter to blow the narrow dart to its destiny through the long, straight tube—the cerbatana. It's used for hunting birds and monkeys. He also shows me his spear—a long, straight pole with a broken machete blade filed into a spear point. It is used for larger game such as wild pigs or tapirs.

We then go for a walk with our hosts through the jungle to the next village over. We walk straight through the conuco and into the dense jungle. The trees are lush, and heavy vines are hanging down everywhere. Orchids, fruits, nuts, jungle palms, plants with thorns and spikes, and trees with smooth bark and rough bark. Hector, one of my guides, is a modern man with indigenous roots. He stops about every 15 yards and explains the uses of the various plants in the lives of the indigenous people:

> This tree has fruit you can eat, and this one is high in iron, and this one is good medicine for menstrual problems, and this one is used to make the paper to roll cigarettes, and this one you can cut and suck out fresh water, and this one is used for the poles in the houses, and this one for the thatched roofs, and this one has a large fruit with a covering that is used as a bowl, and this one treats this medical problem, and that one-inch-long ant there is called a *vienticuatro* (twenty-four), because when it bites you, you are in excruciating pain for 24 hours. And you see that hole in the ground? It is either a rat hole or a tarantula hole. So if I take a piece of vine and put it in the hole and spin the end between my fingers, it will call the attention of the tarantula, who will then grab it and we will then pull it out.

Hector puts a piece of vine in the hole, but nothing happens He tries another hole and another and another and another—and then he gets one! The tarantula grabs hold and Hector pulls out the biggest damn spider I've ever seen in all my life. It's huge, and Hector brings it out and lets it crawl onto his pant leg. It is brown, hairy, and enormous!

Walking along in my expedition hat, I keep my eyes glued to the ground, which is covered with leaves and roots and large *bachaco* ants. The Panare adults and children with us walk along through all of this vegetation barefoot. We arrive at a neighboring Panare village inhabited by members of the extended family of the Panares with whom we have been staying. We are greeted with a platano beverage, which I drink from a communal cup made of a *totuma* shell (like a gourd). I later see the totuma shell covered with a few hundred flies. Part of living at one with nature means not subscribing to germ theory.

The men are out hunting, leaving the women and children at home. We sit in one of the homes that is more like a collective kitchen area. It has a roof, but the walls are made of sticks without the mud between them. This allows air to circulate more freely, a good idea when cooking communally. The women are dressed in lightweight shirts and shorts or dresses, but blouses drop off unselfconsciously for frequent breast-feeding of infants. A baby sits in her grandmother's arms and idly mouths a spent shotgun shell. Machetes are scattered about the floor, where adults and children walk and run barefoot. From the walls and ceiling hang clothes, baskets, skulls, bones, cerbatanas, pots, chinchorros, everything for daily life. The dirt floor is slightly raised to keep rain from entering the house space. On the floor are large pieces of wood, which are used as stools. People sit on the wood, in the chinchorros, on the floor, or just squat on their haunches.

On the side of a house I see a stick stashed in the rafters skewering the cheekbones of nine or ten monkey skulls. Most are blackened from having been roasted or smoked over the fire. Each skull has the back knocked out for extracting the brains. As I walk around the home, I see a basket full of raw cotton, a reel of hand-spun cotton thread, and the skulls of other previously eaten animals.

As the mood warms up between us, Hector begins taking photos with my camera, and then I do too, but I am always mindful of not being too intrusive. One moment that I do not photograph with my camera but record in my memory forever is a woman sitting on the ground behind a child, carefully going through her hair, removing small bugs along with flakes of skin and scabs. Behind her is another woman grooming the hair of the first, and behind her yet another woman grooming her hair. It is a chain of four people grooming. Hector goes into one of the other houses and comes out with a baby monkey. The Panare had killed and eaten the mother and captured the baby as a pet. It is a small monkey called a *mono titi*, or squirrel monkey. We have a very nice visit at this village and then say our farewells.

We cross the stream and head back into the jungle to return to our camp. On our way back, we are marching through the jungle with determination when suddenly the call goes out that some ripe *sejes* have been spotted. A seje (pronounced seh-heh) is a little fruit found on a type of palm tree. When black, they are ripe and ready to be eaten. It has an outer skin, a large woody seed in the middle, a little meat in between, and the taste is similar to moist cardboard. But if a lot are gathered together, one can pound them, mix the pulp with water, and it makes a nutritious and tasty drink similar to a fruity chocolate milk. The mother, tiny children, and baby walking with us find a place to sit on the trail, and everyone else moves off into the jungle. I follow along. The father of the family has a machete, and suddenly I see him whack off a huge palm branch but not from the seje palm. I haven't got a clue as to what he's doing, so I continue off a short distance into the jungle with the rest.

We come to the seje palm, and suddenly little Nena playfully jumps onto the trunk of the palm tree and goes up about 3 meters. I am impressed and expecting someone to tell her, "You get down from there, now, before you fall." But no one says a word and she only climbs higher. In seconds, Nena, who is wearing nothing more than a dirty pajama top and bottoms, is now about two stories up from the jungle floor. I think to myself, *If she falls, she's really gonna get hurt.* But by the time I am finished with my thought, she is three stories up, and I think, *If she slips, she's gonna die right here.* But she does not slip and shows no sign of unsteadiness in the least. She climbs swiftly, with confidence. It is amazing to watch, and now she is three and a half stories up, and I suddenly notice that she has been ascending all the while with a machete in one hand. Four stories up and she arrives at the seje. She starts whacking away. *Whack, whack, whack, whack, whack.* And suddenly a large dead palm frond that was in her way comes crashing down. Then more whacking away—*whack, whack, whack, whack, whack.* And then we hear the branch ripping loose and now the sejes come crashing down. As the branch falls, Nena's father arrives. He has completely transformed the huge palm frond he'd cut down a few minutes ago. He's fashioned it into a backpack and lined it with a banana leaf.

When Nena comes down, she neither celebrates her extraordinary feat nor does anyone say anything about it—*except me*. I am thoroughly impressed! We all start picking up the ripe black sejes and putting them into the backpack. When the backpack is full and all the ripe sejes collected, Nena's father grabs a vine, strings it through several strategic points, and ties it all up into a somewhat heavy pack. He then hoists it up and places it on Nena's back. And off we go. As we arrive back at camp, we find a small batch of fruits that look like little apricots, each with a large pit in the middle. I eat them with pleasure, and after finishing each one a child brings me another piece of fruit to eat. I finish eating several and discover the juice is acting as a rather formidable glue on my mustache. I find the whole thing amusing and delightful and so do the children. Dinner tonight is salad, rice, and lapa soup. An hour after dinner, we have the seje drink as our delicious dessert.

The experiences of visiting with the Panare, the Hoti, the Yanomami, and the Yavarana were among the richest and most poignant experiences of my life. Meeting indigenous people living in nature was, in fact, the fulfillment of a childhood wish. It was in these encounters that I felt I was somehow meeting parts of myself long neglected. These people, as different as they are from me, were somehow so familiar. Meeting them was like remembering something about myself that I had somehow forgotten. They live their lives embedded in nature; build their homes out of trees, vines, and mud; and make their living hunting, gathering, and gardening. Beyond my interest in the physical aspects of their culture was the opportunity to have, even if only for a few days, the profound and quite tangible experience of really belonging to nature. And as foreign as it all was to me, and as uncomfortable as it often was, I had the most extraordinary feeling of somehow being home at last.

APPENDIX 6

A Panare father and son displaying the cerbatana, or blowgun, along with a bamboo quiver for the darts, some darts with tips dipped in curare, and a small bowl of curare in the Venezuelan jungle.

A Panare boy demonstrating the use of the cerbatana, or blow gun in the Venezuelan jungle.

A Panare boy with a hunting spear. The blade is a broken piece of a machete that has been filed into the shape of a spear point and sharpened. Venezuelan jungle.

Nena, a Panare girl, proudly showing a squash growing in the village garden. Venezuelan jungle.

APPENDIX 6

Hoti man proudly carrying a baby. He wears a loin cloth called a guayuco.
Hoti village in the Venezuelan jungle.

Hoti mother bathing her baby down by the river next to a dugout canoe.
Hoti village in the Venezuelan jungle.

APPENDIX 6

References

Abbott, M., & Anderson-Whymark, H. (2012). Stonehenge: Look at the stones. *British Archeology, 127,* 14-21.

Abraham, H. C., & Freud, E. L. (Eds.). (1965). *The letters of Sigmund Freud and Karl Abraham, 1907-1926.* (B. Marsh and H. C. Abraham, Trans.). New York: Basic Books.

Abraham, K. (1927a). The narcissistic evaluation of excretory processes in dreams and neurosis. In K. Abraham, *Selected papers of Karl Abraham, M.D.* (pp. 318-22). New York: Basic Books. (Original work published 1920)

_____. (1927b). A short study of the development of the libido, viewed in the light of mental disorders. In K. Abraham, *Selected papers of Karl Abraham* (pp. 418-501). New York: Basic Books. (Original work published 1924)

_____. (1955a). Dreams and myths: A study in folk-psychology. In *Selected papers of Karl Abraham: Vol. 2. Clinical papers and essays on psycho-analysis* (pp. 153-209). New York: Basic Books. (Original work published 1909)

Ackerman, R. (1991). *The myth and ritual school: J. G. Frazer and the Cambridge ritualists.* New York: Routledge.

Adovasio, J. M., & Page, J. (2002). *The first Americans: In pursuit of archeology's greatest mystery.* New York: Modern Library.

Alexiou, M. (1974). *The ritual lament in Greek tradition.* Cambridge, UK: Cambridge University Press.

Allen, M. R. (1917). *Japanese art motives.* Chicago: A. C. McClurg & Co.

Ames, K. M., & Maschner, H.D.G. (1999). *Peoples of the northwest coast: Their archeology and prehistory.* London: Thames & Hudson.

Ananda, R. G. (1980). *Seven breaths to a better life.* Pasadena, CA: Pyramid.

Anonymous. (2000). *Louis Seymour Bazett Leakey (1903-1972).* Retrieved January 28, 2007, from http://www.kirjasto.sci.fi/leakey.html

Arieti, S. (1974). *Interpretation of schizophrenia* (2nd ed.). New York: Basic Books.

Atkinson, R.J.C. (1978). *Stonehenge and neighboring monuments.* London: Her Majesty's Stationery Office.

_____. (1980). *The prehistoric temples of Stonehenge and Avebury.* London: Pitkin Pictorials.

Baba, M. (1948). Foreword: The difference between ordinary madness and mast states. In W. Donkin, *The wayfarers* (pp. 1-5). San Francisco: Sufism Reoriented.

Bachofen, J. J. (1967). *Myth, religion, and mother right: Selected writings of J. J. Bachofen*. Princeton, NJ: Princeton University Press.

Baldwin, A. L. (1967). *Theories of child development*. New York: John Wiley & Sons.

Barratt, B. B. (1984). *Psychic reality and psychoanalytic knowing*. Hillsdale, NJ: Lawrence Erlbaum.

Barron, F. (1963). *Creativity and psychological health*. Princeton, NJ: D. Van Nostrand.

Becker, E. (1973). *The denial of death*. New York: Simon & Schuster.

Begley, S., & Murr, A. (1999, June 7). The first Americans. *Newsweek*, 40-47.

Benveniste, D. (1983). The archetypal image of the mouth and its relation to autism. *The Arts in Psychotherapy, 10*(2), 99-112.

_____. (1988). Cosmogony, culture, and consciousness. *San Francisco Jung Institute Library Journal, 8*(1), 33-53.

_____. (1990). Tantric art and the primal scene. *San Francisco Jung Institute Library Journal, 9*(4), 39-55.

_____. (1998). Play and the metaphors of the body. *The Psychoanalytic Study of the Child* (Vol. 53, pp. 65-83). New Haven, CT: Yale University Press.

_____. (1999). John Weir Perry, 1914-1998. *Journal of Humanistic Psychology, 39*(2), 48-50.

_____. (2005) Recognizing defenses in the drawings and play of children in therapy. *Psychoanalytic Psychology, 22*(3).

_____. (2013). Sigmund Freud and the question of God—Parts I and II. *Forum: The Newsletter of the Northwest Alliance for Psychoanalytic Study*. January 2013 (pp. 22-24) and May 2013 (pp. 28-31).

_____. (2015). *The interwoven lives of Sigmund, Anna, and W. Ernest Freud: Three generations of psychoanalysis*. New York: International Psychoanalytic Books.

_____. (2020). Libido, culture, and consciousness: Revisiting *Totem and Taboo*. *The American Psychoanalyst, 54*(1). https://apsa.org/apsaa-publications/vol54no1-TOC/html/vol54no1_06.xhtml

_____. (2021). Mother-infant observations: A view into the wordless social instincts that form the foundation of human psychodynamics. *Journal of the American Psychoanalytic Association*, 69/1, pp. 33-50.

Bettelheim, B. (1967). *The empty fortress*. Toronto: Collier-Macmillan of Canada.

Binford, L. (1981). *Bones: Ancient men and modern myths*. New York: Academic Press.

Binford, S. R. (1979). Myths and matriarchies. *Human Behavior, 8*(5), 63-66.

Blos, P. (1941). *The adolescent personality*. New York: D. Appleton-Century.

Blum, H. P. (1978). Symbolic processes and symbol formation. *International Journal of Psycho-Analysis, 59* (January 1), 455-71.

_____. (2011). The psychological birth of art: A psychoanalytic approach to prehistoric cave art, *Int. Forum of Psychoanalysis.* 20(4): 196-204.

Boehlich, W. (Ed.). (1990). *The letters of Sigmund Freud to Eduard Silberstein, 1871-1881.* Cambridge, MA: Belknap Press.

Boisen, A. T. (1952). *The exploration of the inner world: A study of mental disorder and religious experience.* New York: Harper Torchbooks, Harper & Brothers. (Original work published 1936)

Bonnard, A. (1960). The primal significance of the tongue. *International Journal of Psychoanalysis, 41,* 301-308.

Bordes, F. (1968). *The old stone age.* New York: World University Library-McGraw-Hill.

Boule, M., & Vallois, H. V. (1957). *Fossil men.* New York: Dryden Press.

Brabant, E., Falzeder, E., & Giampieri-Deutsch, P. (Eds.). (1993). *The correspondence of Sigmund Freud and Sándor Ferenczi: Vol. 1, 1908-1914.* Cambridge, MA: Belknap Press.

Bradley, N. (1967). Primal scene experience in human evolution and its phantasy derivatives in art, proto-science, and philosophy. *The Psychoanalytic Study of the Child* (Vol. 4, pp. 34-79). New York: International Universities Press.

Briffault, R. (1977). *The mothers.* New York: Atheneum. (Original work published 1927)

Bucke, R. M. (1969). *Cosmic consciousness: A study in the evolution of the mind.* New York: E. P. Dutton. (Original work published 1901)

Buckley, C. (2010, August 31). "Getting the party started." *UConn Today.* http://today.uconn.edu/blog/2010/08/getting-the-party-started

Budge, E.A.W. (1969). *The gods of the Egyptians.* New York: Dover. (Original work published 1904)

_____. (1972a). *The book of opening the mouth.* New York: B. Blom. (Original work published 1909)

_____. (1972b). *The liturgy of funerary offerings.* New York: B. Blom. (Original work published 1909)

Burrow, J. W. (1968). Editor's Introduction. In Charles Darwin, *The origin of the species.* J. W. Burrow (Ed.) (pp. 11-48). Middlesex, Eng.: Penguin Books.

Campbell, J. (1968). *The hero with a thousand faces.* Princeton, NJ: Princeton University Press. (Original work published 1949)

_____. (1969). *The masks of god: Primitive mythology.* Middlesex, Eng.: Penguin Books (Penguin ed. 1976).

Caspari, R. (2013). The evolution of grandparents. *Scientific American, 22*(1), 38-43.

Cassirer, E. (1944). *An essay on man.* New Haven, CT: Yale University Press.

Chard, C. S. (1969). *Man in pre-history.* New York: McGraw-Hill.

Chauvet, J-M., Brunel Deschamps, E., & Hillaire, C. (1996). *The dawn of art: The Chauvet Cave–The oldest known paintings in the world.* London: Harry N. Abrams.

Cirlot, J. E. (1962). *A dictionary of symbols.* London: Routledge, Kegan Paul.

Clark, G. (1967). *The stone age hunters.* London: Thames and Hudson Limited.

Clark, G. (1977). *World prehistory in new perspective.* Cambridge, UK: Cambridge University Press.

Clark, G., & Piggott, S. (1965). *Prehistoric societies.* New York: Alfred A. Knopf.

Clark, J. D., Beyene, Y., Wolde Gabriel, G., Hart, W. K., Renne, P. R., Gilbert, H., Defleur, A., Suwa, G. Katoh, S., Ludwig, K. R., Boisserie, J-R, Asfaw, B., & White, T. D. (2003, June 12). Stratigraphic, chronological, and behavioral contexts of Pleistocene Homo sapiens from Middle Awash, Ethiopia. *Nature, 423,* 747–52.

Cohen, J. (2012). *Apocalyptic prophecies: Doomsday stories from the dawn of time.* Princeton, NJ: Hudson Publications.

Constable, G. (1973). *The Neanderthals.* New York: Time Inc.

Cosmides, L., & Tooby, J. (1997). *Evolutionary psychology: A primer.* Center for Evolutionary Psychology. University of California, Santa Barbara. Retrieved October 9, 2019, from https://www.ceb.ucsb.edu/primer.html

Crocker, J. (2017). *Following Fifi: My adventures among wild chimpanzees: Lessons from our closest relatives.* New York: Pegasus Books.

Darwin, C. (1873). *The expression of the emotions in man and animals.* London: John Murray. (Original work published 1872)

_____. (1968). *The origin of species by means of natural selection; or, the preservation of favored races in the struggle for life.* J. W. Burrow (Ed.). Middlesex, Eng.: Penguin Books. (Original work published 1859)

_____. (1981). *The descent of man, and selection in relation to sex.* Princeton, NJ: Princeton University Press. (Original work published 1871)

Deacon, T. W. (1997). *The symbolic species: The co-evolution of language and the brain.* New York: W. W. Norton.

De Groot, J.J.M. (1964). *The religious system of China.* Taipei: Literature House.

Desmonde, W. (1976). The origin of money in the animal sacrifice. In E. Borneman (Ed.), *The psychoanalysis of money* (pp. 113–33). New York: Urizen Books. (Original work published 1957)

de Waal, F. (1996). *Good natured: The origins of right and wrong in humans and other animals.* Cambridge, MA: Harvard University Press.

———. (2007). *Chimpanzee politics: Power and sex among apes.* Baltimore: Johns Hopkins University Press. (Original work published 1982)

———. (2013). *The bonobo and the atheist: In search of humanism among the primates.* New York: W. W. Norton.

Donald, M. (1991). *Origins of the modern mind: Three stages in the evolution of culture and cognition.* Cambridge, MA: Harvard University Press.

Douglas, A. (1973). *The tarot: The origins, meaning, and uses of the cards.* Baltimore: Penguin Books.

Douglas, M. (1982). *Natural symbols: Explorations in cosmology.* New York: Pantheon. (Original work published 1970)

Douglass, W. (1969). *Death in Murelago.* Seattle: University of Washington Press.

Drake, N. (2016, May 25). Neanderthals built mysterious stone circles. *National Geographic.* http://news.nationalgeographic.com/2016/05/neanderthals-caves-rings-building-france-archaeology

Earth Institute Columbia University (2015). Scientists discover world's oldest stone tools. *Earth Institute Columbia University News Archive.* http://earth.columbia.edu/articles/view/3249

Edey, M. A., & Johanson, D. C. (1989). *Blueprints: Solving the mystery of evolution.* Boston: Little, Brown.

Eliade, M. (1958a). *Rites and symbols of initiation.* New York: Harper & Row.

———. (1958b). *Patterns in comparative religion.* New York: New American Library.

———. (1964). *Shamanism.* Princeton, NJ: Princeton University Press.

———. (1967a). *Myths, dreams, and mysteries.* New York: Harper & Row.

———. (1967b). *From primitives to Zen.* San Francisco: Harper & Row.

———. (1969). *The quest.* Chicago: University of Chicago Press.

———. (1971). *The myth of the eternal return; or, cosmos and history.* Princeton, NJ: Princeton University Press. (Original work published 1954)

———. (1972). *Zalmoxis: The vanishing God.* Chicago: University of Chicago Press.

———. (1978a). *A history of religious ideas: Vol. 1. From the stone age to the Eleusinian mysteries.* Chicago: University of Chicago Press. (Original work published 1956)

———. (1978b). *The forge and the crucible.* Chicago: University of Chicago Press. (Original work published 1956, 1st English translation 1962)

Ellis, R. (1968). *Foundation deposits in ancient Mesopotamia.* New Haven, CT: Yale University Press.

Erikson, E. H. (1963). *Childhood and society.* New York: W. W. Norton.

———. (1968). *Identity: Youth and crisis.* New York: W. W. Norton.

———. (1975). *Life history and the historical moment.* New York: W. W. Norton.

_____. (1984). Reflections on the last stage—and the first. *The Psychoanalytic Study of the Child* (Vol. 39, pp. 155-65). New Haven, CT: Yale University Press.

_____. (1987a). The dream specimen of psychoanalysis. In E. Erikson, *A way of looking at things: Selected papers from 1930-1980* (pp. 237-79). Stephen Schlein (Ed.). New York: W. W. Norton. (Original work published 1954)

_____. (1987b). The ontogeny of ritualization in man. In E. Erikson, *A way of looking at things* (pp. 575-94). New York: W. W. Norton. (Original work published 1966)

_____. (1997). *The life cycle completed.* New York: W. W. Norton. (Original work published 1982)

Evans-Wentz, W. Y. (1927/1960). *The Tibetan book of the dead.* London: Oxford University Press.

Fabricius, J. (1976). *Alchemy: The medieval chemists and their royal art.* Copenhagen: Rosenkilde and Bagger.

Fenichel, O. (1953a). The dread of being eaten. In H. Fenichel & D. Rapaport (Eds.), *The collected papers of Otto Fenichel: First series* (pp. 158-59). New York: W. W. Norton. (Original work published 1928)

_____. (1953b). Respiratory introjection. In H. Fenichel & D. Rapaport (Eds.), *The collected papers of Otto Fenichel: First series* (pp. 221-40). New York: W. W. Norton. (Original work published 1931)

_____. (1954). The psychopathology of coughing. In H. Fenichel & D. Rapaport (Eds.), *The collected papers of Otto Fenichel: Second series* (pp. 237-42). New York: W. W. Norton. (Original work published 1943)

Ferenczi, S. (1938). *Thalassa: A theory of genitality.* Albany, NY: Psychoanalytic Quarterly. (Original work published 1923)

_____. (1956). Stages in development of sense of reality. In S. Ferenczi, *Sex in Psychoanalysis* (pp. 9-228). New York: Dover Publications. (Original work published 1913)

_____. (1976). The ontogeny of the interest in money. In E. Borneman (Ed.), *The psychoanalysis of money* (pp. 81-90). New York: Urizen Books. (Original work published 1914)

Ferreira, B. (2019, December 11). Mythical beings may be the earliest imaginative cave art by humans. *The New York Times.* https://www.nytimes.com/2019/12/11/science/cave-art-indonesia.html

Foley, J. (1998). *Biographies: Louis Leakey* (April 24). Retrieved January 28, 2007, from http://www.talkorigins.org/faqs/homs/lleakey.html

Fordham, M. (1981). Neumann and childhood. *Journal of Analytical Psychology, 26,* 99-122.

Frankfort, H. (1978). *Kingship and the gods: A study of ancient near eastern religion as the integration of society and nature.* Chicago: University of Chicago Press. (Original work published 1948)

Frazer, J. G. (1924). *The belief in immortality*. London: Macmillan and Company.

_____. (1930). *Myths of the origin of fire: An essay*. London: Macmillan and Company.

Freeman, D. (1967). Totem and taboo: A reappraisal. In *The Psychoanalytic Study of Society* (Vol. 4, pp. 9-33). New York: International Universities Press.

Freud, M. (1958). *Sigmund Freud: Man and father*. New York: Vanguard Press.

Freud, S. (1953a). The interpretation of dreams. In Strachey, SE: *Vol. 4. The interpretation of dreams (1) (1900)* (pp. 1-338). (Original work published 1900)

_____. (1953b). Three essays on the theory of sexuality. In Strachey, SE: *Vol. 7. A case of hysteria, three essays on sexuality, and other works (1901-1905)* (pp. 135-243). (Original work published 1905)

_____. (1955a). A child is being beaten: A contribution to the study of the origin of sexual perversions. In Strachey, SE: *Vol. 17. An infantile neurosis and other works (1917-1919)* (pp. 179-204). (Original work published 1919)

_____. (1955b). Beyond the pleasure principle. In Strachey, SE: *Vol. 18. Beyond the pleasure principle, group psychology, and other works (1920-1922)* (pp. 7-64). (Original work published 1920)

_____. (1955c). Dreams and telepathy. In Strachey, SE: *Vol. 18. Beyond the pleasure principle, group psychology, and other works (1920-1922)* (pp. 197-220). (Original work published 1922)

_____. (1955d). From the history of an infantile neurosis. In Strachey, SE: *Vol. 17. An infantile neurosis and other works (1917-1919)* (pp. 7-122). (Original work published 1918)

_____. (1955e). Group psychology and the analysis of the ego. In Strachey, SE: *Vol. 18. Beyond the pleasure principle, group psychology, and other works (1920-1922)* (pp. 69-143). (Original work published 1921)

_____. (1955f). Notes upon a case of obsessional neurosis. In Strachey, SE: *Vol. 10. Two case histories: "Little Hans" and the "Rat Man" (1909)* (pp. 151-318). (Original work published 1909)

_____. (1955g). Preface to *Reik's ritual: Psycho-analytic studies*. In Strachey, SE: *Vol. 17. An infantile neurosis and other works (1917-1919)* (pp. 259-63). (Original work published 1919)

_____. (1955h). Totem and taboo. In Strachey, SE: *Vol. 13. Totem and taboo and other works (1913-1914)* (pp. 1-161). (Original work published 1913)

_____. (1957). Instincts and their vicissitudes. In Strachey, SE: *Vol. 14. On the history of the psycho-analytic movement, papers on metapsychology, and other works (1914-1916)* (pp. 117-40). (Original work published 1915)

_____. (1958a). Psychoanalytic notes on an autobiographical account of a case of paranoia (dementia paranoides). In Strachey, SE: *Vol. 12. Case history of Schreber, papers on technique, and other works (1911-1913)* (pp. 3-82). (Original work published 1911)

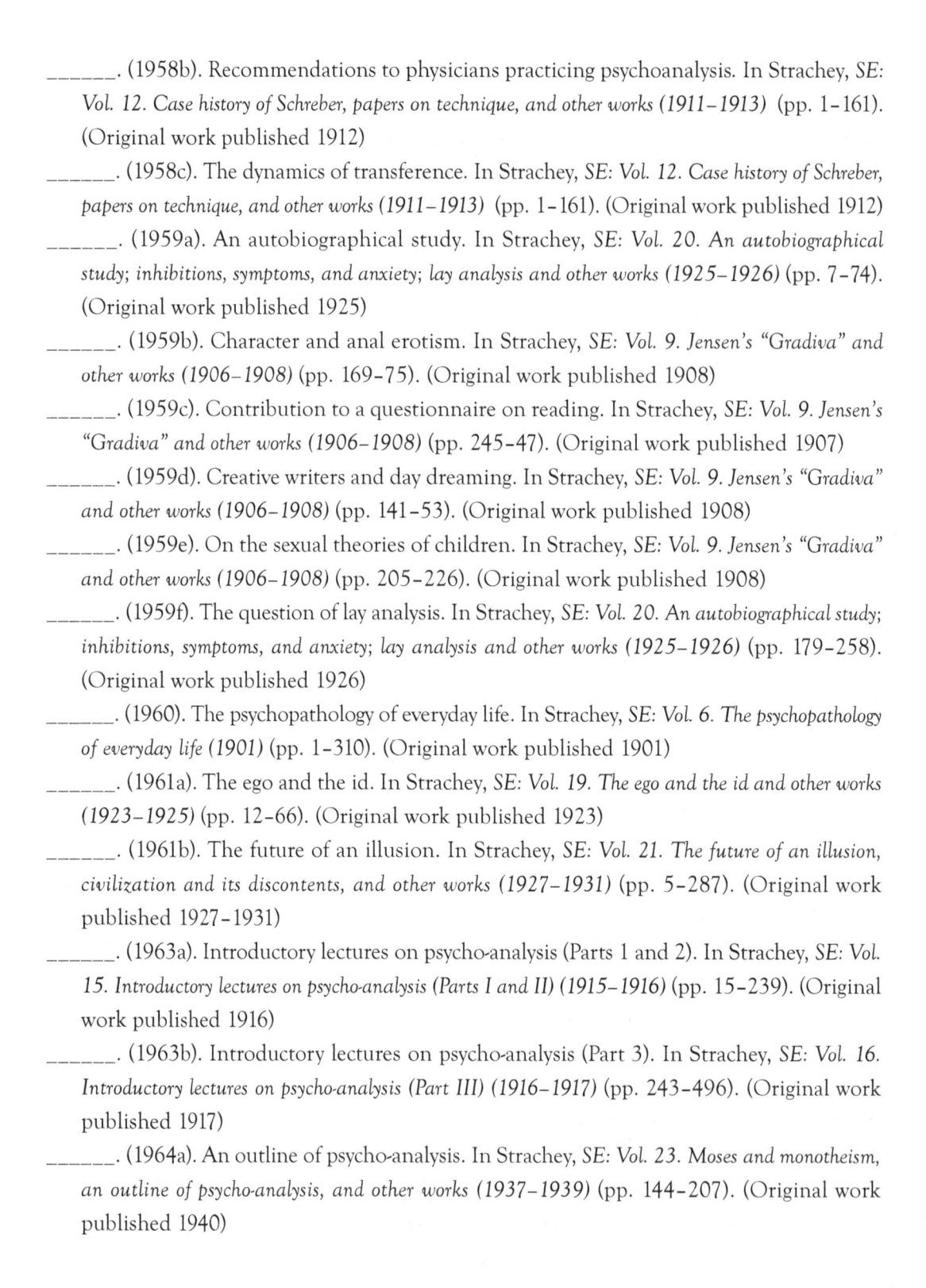

_____. (1958b). Recommendations to physicians practicing psychoanalysis. In Strachey, SE: Vol. 12. *Case history of Schreber, papers on technique, and other works (1911–1913)* (pp. 1–161). (Original work published 1912)

_____. (1958c). The dynamics of transference. In Strachey, SE: Vol. 12. *Case history of Schreber, papers on technique, and other works (1911–1913)* (pp. 1–161). (Original work published 1912)

_____. (1959a). An autobiographical study. In Strachey, SE: Vol. 20. *An autobiographical study; inhibitions, symptoms, and anxiety; lay analysis and other works (1925–1926)* (pp. 7–74). (Original work published 1925)

_____. (1959b). Character and anal erotism. In Strachey, SE: Vol. 9. *Jensen's "Gradiva" and other works (1906–1908)* (pp. 169–75). (Original work published 1908)

_____. (1959c). Contribution to a questionnaire on reading. In Strachey, SE: Vol. 9. *Jensen's "Gradiva" and other works (1906–1908)* (pp. 245–47). (Original work published 1907)

_____. (1959d). Creative writers and day dreaming. In Strachey, SE: Vol. 9. *Jensen's "Gradiva" and other works (1906–1908)* (pp. 141–53). (Original work published 1908)

_____. (1959e). On the sexual theories of children. In Strachey, SE: Vol. 9. *Jensen's "Gradiva" and other works (1906–1908)* (pp. 205–226). (Original work published 1908)

_____. (1959f). The question of lay analysis. In Strachey, SE: Vol. 20. *An autobiographical study; inhibitions, symptoms, and anxiety; lay analysis and other works (1925–1926)* (pp. 179–258). (Original work published 1926)

_____. (1960). The psychopathology of everyday life. In Strachey, SE: Vol. 6. *The psychopathology of everyday life (1901)* (pp. 1–310). (Original work published 1901)

_____. (1961a). The ego and the id. In Strachey, SE: Vol. 19. *The ego and the id and other works (1923–1925)* (pp. 12–66). (Original work published 1923)

_____. (1961b). The future of an illusion. In Strachey, SE: Vol. 21. *The future of an illusion, civilization and its discontents, and other works (1927–1931)* (pp. 5–287). (Original work published 1927–1931)

_____. (1963a). Introductory lectures on psycho-analysis (Parts 1 and 2). In Strachey, SE: Vol. 15. *Introductory lectures on psycho-analysis (Parts I and II) (1915–1916)* (pp. 15–239). (Original work published 1916)

_____. (1963b). Introductory lectures on psycho-analysis (Part 3). In Strachey, SE: Vol. 16. *Introductory lectures on psycho-analysis (Part III) (1916–1917)* (pp. 243–496). (Original work published 1917)

_____. (1964a). An outline of psycho-analysis. In Strachey, SE: Vol. 23. *Moses and monotheism, an outline of psycho-analysis, and other works (1937–1939)* (pp. 144–207). (Original work published 1940)

_____. (1964b). Moses and monotheism. In Strachey, SE: Vol. 23. *Moses and monotheism, n outline of psycho-analysis, and other works (1937–1939)* (pp. 7–137). (Original work published 1937–1939)

_____. (1964c). The question of a weltanschauung. In Strachey, SE: Vol. 22. *New introductory lectures on psycho-analysis and other works (1932–1936)* Lecture 35 (pp. 158–82). (Original work published 1933)

_____. (1987). *A phylogenetic fantasy: Overview of the transference neuroses*. Ilse Grubrich-Simitis (Ed). Alex Hoffer & Peter T. Hoffer (Trans.). Cambridge, MA: Belknap Press.

Freud Bernays, A. (1973). My brother Sigmund Freud. In H. M. Ruitenbeek, *Freud as we knew him* (pp. 140–47). Detroit: Wayne State University Press.

Gaddini, E. (2001). *The psychoanalytic theory of infantile experience: Conceptual and clinical reflections*. New York and London: Routledge.

Geigerich, W. (1975). Ontogeny = phylogeny?: A fundamental critique of Erich Neumann's analytical psychology (pp. 110–29). *Spring: An annual of archetypal psychology and Jungian thought*. New York: Spring Publications.

Gerry, P. (1961). *Reflections on the symbolism of the bee*. Los Angeles: Analytical Psychology Club of Los Angeles.

Gershon, L. (2020). Tens of thousands of 12,000-year-old rock paintings found in Colombia. *Smithsonian Magazine* on-line. December 1, 2020. https://www.smithsonianmag.com/smart-news/tens-thousands-12000-year-old-rock-paintings-found-colombia-180976427/

Gilman, S. (1982). *Seeing the insane*. New York: John Wiley & Sons.

Gimbutas, M. (1989). *The language of the goddess*. San Francisco: Harper & Row.

Glover, E. (1924). The significance of the mouth in psychoanalysis. *British Journal of Medical Psychology*, 4(2), 134–55.

Goodall, J. (1986). *The chimpanzees of Gombe: Patterns of behavior*. Cambridge, MA: Belknap Press.

_____. (1988). *In the shadow of man*. Boston: Houghton Mifflin. (Original work published 1971)

_____. (1990). *Through a window: My thirty years with the chimpanzees of Gombe*. Boston: Houghton Mifflin.

Gould, S. J. (1977). *Ontogeny and phylogeny*. Cambridge, MA: Belknap Press.

Graves, R. (1959). *The Greek myths*. New York: George Braziller.

Grimm, J., & Grimm, W. (1972). *The complete Grimm's fairy tales*. Introduction by Padraic Colum and folkloristic commentary by Joseph Campbell. New York: Random House.

Grossman, W. I. (1998). Freud's presentation of "The psychoanalytic mode of thought" in *Totem and Taboo* and his technical papers. *International Journal of Psychoanalysis*. 79:469-486.

Grotstein, J. S. (2000). *Who is the dreamer who dreams the dream? A study of psychic presences.* Hillsdale, NJ: Analytic Press.

Grubrich-Simitis, I. (1987). Preface to S. Freud, A *phylogenetic fantasy: Overview of the transference neuroses* (1915). Ilse Grubrich-Simitis (Ed.). Alex Hoffer & Peter T. Hoffer (Trans.). (pp. xv–xvii). Cambridge, MA: Belknap Press.

Habenstein, R., & Lamers, W. (1963). *Burial customs the world over.* Milwaukee: Bufin Printers.

Hall, S. S. (2007). The last hours of the Iceman. *National Geographic, 212*(1), 68–81.

———. (2010). Espiritus en la arena: Las lineas de Nazca revelan sus secretos. *National Geographic, 26*(3), 2–23.

Hartshorne, C., & Weiss, P. (1978). *Collected papers: Charles Sanders Pierce. Vols. I–VIII.* Cambridge, MA: Belknap Press.

Herbert, J. D., Sharp, I. R., & Guadiano, B. A. (2002). Separating fact from fiction in the etiology and treatment of autism: A scientific review of the evidence. *Scientific Review of Mental Health Practice: Objective Investigations of Controversial and Unorthodox Claims in Clinical Psychology, Psychiatry, and Social Work, 1*(1), 23–43.

Hermann, I. (1926). Modelle zu den Oedipus und Kastrationskomplexen bei Affen [Oedipus and castration complex models in monkeys]. *Imago Band, 12*(1), 59–69.

Herzog-Schröder, G. (1999). Exchanging and sharing: The significance of giving among the Yanomami. In *Orinoco–Parima: Indian societies in Venezuela: The Cisneros collection* (pp. 50–59). Ostfildern-Ruit, Germany: Hatje Cantz.

Hoffer, A., & Hoffer, P. (1987). Foreword to English-language edition of S. Freud, A *phylogenetic fantasy: Overview of the transference neuroses.* Ilse Grubrich-Simitis (Ed.). Alex Hoffer & Peter T. Hoffer (Trans.) (pp. vii–xiv). Cambridge, MA: Belknap Press.

Hoffer, W. (1949). Mouth, hand, and ego-integration. *The Psychoanalytic Study of the Child* (Vols. 3/4, pp. 49–56). New Haven, CT: Yale University Press.

Hoffs, J. A. (1963). Anthropophagy (cannibalism): Its relation to the oral stage of development. *Psychoanalytic Review, 50*(2), 187–214.

Holmström, R. (1991). On the phylogeny of the Oedipus complex: Psychoanalytic aspects of the ethology of anthropoid apes. *Psychoanalysis & Contemporary Thought, 14,* 271–316.

Howell, F. C. (1965). *Early man.* New York: Time-Life Books.

Huxley, A. (1954). *The doors of perception.* New York: Harper & Row.

Huxley, J. (1966, December 29). Introduction. *Philosophical Transactions of the Royal Society of London, Series B, Biological Sciences, 251*(772), 249–71. (Special issue: A discussion on ritualization of behaviour in animals and man.)

Hyrck, M. (1997). Inner objects and the Christian images of God. *International Forum of Psycho-Analysis, 6,* 41–43.

Institute of Human Origins (IHO) (2010, August 11). Earliest stone tool evidence revealed. IHO News. *Becoming Human.* http://www.becominghuman.org/node/news/earliest-stone-tool-evidence-revealed

Isaacs, S. (1948). The nature and function of fantasy. *International Journal of Psychoanalysis,* 29, 73-97.

James, W. (1950). *Principles of psychology.* Mineola, NY: Dover Publications. (Original work published 1890)

Jaroff, L. (1992, October 26). Iceman. *Time,* 62-66.

Jaynes, J. (1976). *The origins of consciousness and the breakdown of the bicameral mind.* Boston: Houghton Mifflin.

Jelínek, J. (1975). *The pictorial encyclopedia of the evolution of man.* London: Hamlyn.

Jochelson, W. (1924). *The Yukaghir and the Yukaghirized Tungus.* New York: AMS Press.

Johanson, D., & Edgar, B. (2006). *From Lucy to language.* Revised, updated, and expanded edition. New York: Simon & Schuster.

Jonas, A. D., & Jonas, D. F. (1975). A biological basis for the Oedipus complex: An evolutionary and ethological approach. *American Journal of Psychiatry, 132*(6), 602-606.

Jones, E. (1948). *Papers on psycho-analysis.* Baltimore: Williams & Wilkins.

_____. (1957). *The life and work of Sigmund Freud: Vol. 3.* New York: Basic Books.

Jung, C. G. (1956). Symbols of transformation: An analysis of the prelude to a case of schizophrenia. In *Collected Works of C. G. Jung: Vol. 5. Symbols of Transformation,* R.F.C. Hull (Trans.). Bollingen Series. Princeton, NJ: Princeton University Press. (Original work published 1912)

_____. (1961). The theory of psychoanalysis. In *Collected Works of C. G. Jung: Vol. 4. Freud and psychoanalysis.* R.F.C. Hull (Trans.). (pp. 83-226). Bollingen Series. Princeton, NJ: Princeton University Press. (Original work published 1913)

_____. (1963). *Mysterium Coniunctionis.* Princeton, NJ: Princeton University Press.

_____. (1964). *Man and his symbols,* New York: Doubleday.

_____. (1968). *Psychology and alchemy.* Princeton, NJ: Princeton University Press. (Original work published 1953)

_____. (1987). Foreword to J. W. Perry (1987). *The Self in psychotic process: Its symbolization in schizophrenia.* pp. iii-vi. Dallas: Spring Publications. (Original work published 1953)

Kakar, S. (1995). India. *Psychoanalysis international: A guide to psychoanalysis throughout the world. Vol. 2 America, Asia, Australia, further European countries.* Ed. Peter Kutter. Stuttgart-Bad Cannstatt: Friedrich Frommann Verlag.

Kellogg, R. (1970). *Analyzing children's art.* Palo Alto, CA: National Press Books.

Klein, M. (1937). *The psychoanalysis of children*. London: Hogarth Press and the Institute of Psychoanalysis. (Original work published 1932)

_____. (1948a). The importance of symbol-formation in the development of the ego. In *Contributions to psychoanalysis 1921–1945* (pp. 236-50). London: Hogarth Press. (Original work published 1930)

_____. (1948b). The Oedipus complex in light of early anxieties. In *Contributions to psychoanalysis 1921–1945* (pp. 339-390). London: Hogarth Press. (Original work published 1945)

_____. (1957). *Envy and gratitude: A study of unconscious sources*. New York: Basic Books.

Klein, R. (2002). *The dawn of human culture*. New York: John Wiley & Sons.

Knappert, J. (1970). *Myths and legends of the Swahili*. Nairobi, Kenya: Heinemann Educational Press.

Knauth, P. (1974). *The metalsmiths*. New York: Time-Life Books.

Kris, E. (1956). The personal myth: A problem in psychoanalytic technique. *Journal of the American Psychoanalytic Association, 4*(4), 653-81.

Krishnan, S.A. (2011, October 14). Ganesha wins the mango. *Stories from Hindu mythology*. Accessed January 28, 2021. http://hindumythologyforgennext.blogspot.com/2011/10/ganesha-wins-mango.html

Kurtz, D. (1971). *Greek burial customs*. Ithaca, NY: Cornell University Press.

Lacan, J. (1978). *The four fundamental concepts of psycho-analysis*. New York: W. W. Norton.

_____. (1988). *The seminar of Jacques Lacan: Book 2*. J-A. Miller (Ed.). New York: W. W. Norton.

Laing, R. D. (1966). Ritualization and abnormal behaviour. *Philosophical Transactions of the Royal Society of London, Series B. Biological Sciences, 251*(772), 331-35.

Lakoff, G., & Johnson, M. (1999). *Philosophy in the flesh: The embodied mind and its challenge to western thought*. New York: Basic Books.

Lancaster, J. B. (1975). *Primate behavior and the emergence of human culture*. New York: Holt, Rinehart, and Winston.

Lange, K. (2007). Las momias de los pantanos. *National Geographic en español 21*(3), 2-15.

Leadbeater, C. W. (1927). *The chakras*. Wheaton, IL: Theosophical Publishing House.

Leakey, R. (1977). *Origins: What new discoveries reveal about the emergence of our species and its possible future*. London: Macdonald and Jane's.

_____. (1994). *The origin of humankind*. New York: Basic Books.

Levy, G. R. (1963). *The gate of horn: A study of the religious conceptions of the stone age, and their influence upon European thought*. London: Faber and Faber. (Original work published 1948)

Lewin, B. (1950). *The psychoanalysis of elation*. New York: W. W. Norton.

Lincoln, B. (1986). *Myth, cosmos, and society: Indo-European themes of creation and destruction.* Cambridge, MA: Harvard University Press.

Long, C. (1963). *Alpha: The myths of creation.* New York: George Braziller.

Lorenz, K. (1963). *On aggression.* New York: Harcourt, Brace, and World.

Lorenzi, R. (2009). Bones hint at Stonehenge solstice feast. *Discovery News.* December 21. [This Internet article is no longer available but is summarized in the following secondary source: http://www.dnaindia.com/scitech/report-winter-solstice-feasts-may-have-taken-place-around-stonehenge-4500-years-ago-1327779]

_____. (2010, January 15). "Astonishing" ancient Amazon civilization discovery detailed. *Discovery News, Archeology News.* http://news.discovery.com/archaeology/astonishing-ancient-amazon-civilization-discovery-detailed.html

Lothane, Z. (1992). *In defense of Schreber: Soul murder and psychiatry.* Hillsdale, NJ: Analytic Press.

Lucas, G. (2015). *The vicissitudes of totemism: One hundred years after* Totem and Taboo. London: Karnac Books.

Lumsden, C. J., & Wilson, E. O. (1983). *Promethean fire: Reflections on the origin of the mind.* Cambridge, MA: Harvard University Press.

Mahler, M. (1968). *On human symbiosis and the vicissitudes of individuation.* New York: International Universities Press.

Mahler, M., Pine, F., & Bergman, A. (1975). *The psychological birth of the human infant.* New York: Basic Books.

Mann, C., & Musi, V. J. (2011). The birth of religion: The world's first temple. *National Geographic 219*(6), 34–59.

Mann, T. (1936, July 25). Freud and the future. *The Saturday Review of Literature, 14*(13), 1–2, 14–15.

Marean, C. W. (2010). When the sea saved humanity. *Scientific American, 303*(2), 40–47.

Maringer, J. (1960). *The gods of prehistoric man.* London: Weidenfeld and Nicholson.

Masson, J. M. (Ed.) (1985). *The complete letters of Sigmund Freud to Wilhelm Fleiss, 1887–1904.* Cambridge MA: Belknap Press.

Masters, R.E.L., & Houston, J. (1966). *The varieties of psychedelic experience.* New York: Dell.

Matsuzawa, T., Tomonaga, M., & Tanaka, M. (2006). *Cognitive development in chimpanzees.* Tokyo, Japan: Springer Verlag.

Mauss, M. (1990). *The gift: The form and reason for exchange in archaic societies.* New York: W. W. Norton. (Original work published 1924)

May, R. (1975). *The courage to create.* New York: Bantam Books.

Mellaart, J. (1965). *Earliest civilizations of the Near East.* London: Thames and Hudson.

Meltzer, D. (1981). The Kleinian expansion of Freud's metapsychology. *International Journal of Psycho-Analysis, 62,* 177–85.

Menaker, E., & Menaker, W. (1965). *Ego in evolution.* New York: Grove Press.

Meng, H., & Freud, E. (1963). *Psychoanalysis and faith: The letters of Sigmund Freud and Oskar Pfister.* New York: Basic Books.

Merkur, D. (2005). *Psychoanalytic approaches to myth: Freud and the Freudians.* New York: Routledge.

Metcalfe, T. (2016, May 16). Echoes of ancient cosmology found at prehistoric Native American site. *Live Science.* http://www.livescience.com/54750-prehistoric-native-american-ceremonial-site.html

Mithen, S. (1996). *The prehistory of the mind: The cognitive origins of art and science.* London: Thames and Hudson.

Mitrani, T., & Mitrani, J. (2015). Introduction to the life and work of Frances Tustin. In Theodore and Judith Mitrani (Eds.), *Frances Tustin today* (pp. xxi–xxxix). East Sussex, Eng.: Routledge.

Modell, A. H. (1968). *Object love and reality: An introduction to a psychoanalytic theory of object relations.* New York: International Universities Press.

Mookerjee, A. (1971). *Tantra asana.* New York: George Wittenbom.

———. (1982). *Kundalini: The arousal of the inner energy.* London: Thames and Hudson.

———. (1995). *Kali: The feminine force.* Rochester, VT: Destiny Books.

Moore, M., & Douglas, M. (1971). *Astrology, the divine science.* York Harbor, ME: Arcane Publications.

Muscaro, J. (1962). *The Bhagavad Gita.* Harmondsworth, UK: Penguin Books.

Nágera, H. (Ed.). (1969). *The basic psychoanalytic concepts on the libido theory.* London: George Allen & Unwin.

Neumann, E. (1954). *The origins and history of consciousness.* Bollingen Series. Princeton, NJ: Princeton University Press.

———. (1963). *The great mother: An analysis of the archetype.* Bollingen Series. Princeton, NJ: Princeton University Press. (Original work published 1955)

Nietzsche, F. (1907). *Beyond Good and Evil.* New York: Macmillan.

Nunberg, H. (1931). The synthetic function of the ego. *International Journal of Psychoanalysis, 12,* 123–40.

Nunberg, H., & Federn, E. (1962). *Minutes of the Vienna Psychoanalytic Society: Vol. 1. 1906–1908.* New York: International Universities Press.

———. (1967). *Minutes of the Vienna Psychoanalytic Society: Vol. 2. 1908–1910.* New York: International Universities Press.

Ogden, T. H. (1986). *The matrix of the mind: Object relations and the psychoanalytic dialogue*. Northvale, NJ: J. Aronson.

_____. (2015). On the concept of an autistic-contiguous position. In Theodore and Judith Mitrani (Eds.), *Frances Tustin today* (pp. 155–73). East Sussex, Eng.: Routledge.

Ostow, M. (2007). *Spirit, mind, and brain: A psychoanalytic examination of spirituality and religion*. New York: Columbia University Press.

Patterson, F., & Linden, E. (1981). *The education of Koko*. New York: Holt, Rinehart, and Winston.

Paul, R. (1976). Did the primal crime take place? *Ethos*, 4(3), 311–52.

Perry, J. W. (1963). Jung's influence on my life and work. In M. Fordham (Ed.), *Contact with Jung: Essays on the influence of his work and personality* (pp. 214–17). Philadelphia: J. B. Lippincott.

_____. (1966). *Lord of the four quarters: Myths of the royal father*. New York: George Braziller.

_____. (1974). *The far side of madness*. Englewood Cliffs, NJ: Prentice-Hall.

_____. (1976). *Roots of renewal in myth and madness: The meaning of psychotic episodes*. San Francisco: Jossey-Bass.

_____. (1987a). *The heart of history: Individuality in evolution*. Albany: State University of New York Press.

_____. (1987b). *The Self in psychotic process: Its symbolization in schizophrenia*. Dallas: Spring Publications. (Original work published 1953)

_____. (1999). *Trials of the visionary mind: Spiritual emergency and the renewal process*. Albany: State University of New York Press.

Peterson, F. (1962). *Ancient Mexico: An introduction to the pre-Hispanic cultures*. New York: Capricorn Books.

Pfister, O. (1993). The illusion of a future: A friendly disagreement with Prof. Sigmund Freud. *International Journal of Psychoanalysis*, 74, 557–79. (Original German version published 1928)

Piaget, J. (1969). Genetic epistemology. *Columbus Forum*, 12, 4–11.

Pickering, T. R., White, T. D., & Toth, N. (2000). Brief communication: Cutmarks on a Plio-Pleistocene hominid from Sterkfontein, South Africa. *American Journal of Physical Anthropology*, 111, 579–84.

Poirier, F. E. (1973). *Fossil man: An evolutionary journey*. St. Louis: C. V. Mosby.

Ponce, C. (1973). *Kabbalah*. Wheaton, IL: Theosophical Publishing House.

Portu, B. à. (1659). Philosphi Artem Potius Occultare Conati Sunt Quam Patesacere. In *Theatrum Chemicum*, Vol. 2. Oberusel and Strasburg, France: Lazarus Zetzner. (Original work published 1613)

Prideaux, T. (1973). *Cro-Magnon man*. New York: Time Inc.

Pusey, A. (2005). Inbreeding avoidance in primates. In A. P. Wolf & W. H. Durham (Eds.), *Inbreeding, incest, and the incest taboo: The state of knowledge at the turn of the century* (pp. 61-75). Stanford, CA: Stanford University Press.

Raglan, Lord (FitzRoy Richard Somerset). (1956). *The hero: A study in tradition, myth, and drama*. New York: Vintage Books.

_____. (1964). *The temple and the house*. New York: W. W. Norton.

Rank, O. (1945). *Will therapy and truth and reality*. New York: Alfred A. Knopf.

_____. (1959). *The myth of the birth of the hero and other writings*. New York: Vintage Books. (Original work published 1932)

Reik, T. (1957). *Myth and guilt: The crime and punishment of mankind*. New York: George Braziller.

Renfrew, C. (1983). Introduction: Megalith builders of western Europe. In C. Renfrew (Ed.), *The megalithic monuments of western Europe* (pp. 8-17). London: Thames and Hudson. (Original work published 1981)

Rigaud, J-P. (1988). Art treasures from the ice age Lascaux Cave. *National Geographic, 174*(4), 482-99.

Roberts, D. (1993). The iceman: Lone voyager from the Copper Age. *National Geographic, 183*(6), 36-67.

Rodden, R. (1972). An early Neolithic village in Greece. In *Old World Archaeology: Foundations of Civilization, Readings from Scientific American*. Introduction by C. C. Lamberg-Karlovsky (pp. 95-102). San Francisco: W. H. Freeman.

Rodrigue, E. (1956). Notes on symbolism. *International Journal of Psycho-Analysis 37*, 147-58.

Róheim, G. (1943). *The origin and function of culture*. Nervous and Mental Disease Monograph Series, No. 69. New York: Nervous and Mental Disease Monographs.

_____. (1974). *The riddle of the sphinx*. New York: Harper Torchbooks. (Original work published 1934)

Rokeach, M. (1964). *The three Christs of Ypsilanti: A psychological study*. New York: Alfred A. Knopf.

Romanes, G. J. (1889). *Mental evolution in man: Origin of human faculty*. New York: D. Appleton & Co.

Rosenfeld, D. (1992). *The psychotic aspects of personality*. London: Karnac Books.

Roth, C. (1971). *Encyclopedia Judaica: Vol. 5. C-Dh*. Jerusalem: Keter Publishing House.

Sandars, N. K. (1972). *The epic of Gilgamesh*. Harmondsworth, UK: Penguin Books.

Schlossman, B. L. (1976). Two foundation figurines. In C. Ryskamp (Ed.), *Ancient Mesopotamian art and selected texts* (pp. 9-21). New York: Pierpont Morgan Library.

Segal, H. (1957). Notes on symbol formation. *International Journal of Psycho-Analysis, 38*, 391-97.

Shreeve, J. (2006). The greatest journey. *National Geographic, 209*(3), 60-73.

Siegel, B. L. (1971). The role of the mouth in the search for the female phallus. *Journal of the American Psychoanalytic Association, 19*(2), 310-31.

Silberer, H. (1917). *Problems of mysticism and its symbolism.* New York: Moffat, Yard, and Co.

Simons, M. (1992, October 20). Stone age art shows penguins at Mediterranean. *The New York Times,* pp. B5-B6.

Smadja, E. (2018). *The Oedipus complex: Focus of the psychoanalysis-anthropology debate.* London: Routledge.

Smith, R. (2014). Before Stonehenge. *National Geographic, 226*(2), 26-51.

Spankie, R. (2015). *Sigmund Freud's desk: An anecdote guide.* London: Freud Museum London.

Spring, W. J. (1939). Observations on world destruction fantasies. *Psychoanalytic Quarterly, 8*(1), 48-56.

Sproul, B. (1979). *Primal myths: Creating the world.* New York: Harper & Row.

Stix, G. (2014). The "it" factor: The capacity to engage in shared tasks such as hunting large game and building cities may be what separated modern humans from our primate cousins. *Scientific American* (Special Evolution Issue: How we became human), *311*(3), 72-79.

Storch, A. (1924). *The primitive archaic forms of inner experiences and thought in schizophrenia: A genetic clinical study of schizophrenia.* Nervous and Mental Disease Monograph Series No. 36. New York: Nervous and Mental Disease Publishing.

Strachey, J. (Ed. & Trans.). (1953-74). *The standard edition of the complete psychological works of Sigmund Freud.* 24 vols. London: Hogarth Press (hereafter SE).

Strickland, A. (2020, July 22). Humans may have arrived in North America much earlier than believed, new research says. CNN. https://www.cnn.com/2020/07/22/world/north-america-early-humans-arrival-scn-trnd/index.html

Sullivan, L. E. (1985). Above, below, or far away: Andean cosmogony and ethical order. In R. W. Lovin and F. E. Reynolds (Eds.), *Cosmogony and ethical order: New studies in comparative ethics* (pp. 98-129). Chicago: University of Chicago Press.

Sutton-Smith, B. (1975). The importance of the storytaker: An investigation of the imaginative life. *Urban Review, 8*(2), 82-95.

Szabadics Roka, M. (1997). *Archeology of the prehistory of Venezuela.* Maracay, Venezuela: Gobernación del Estado Aragua.

Toynbee, J.M.C. (1971). *Death and burial in the Roman world.* London: Thames and Hudson.

Trump, D. (1983). Megalithic architecture in Malta. In C. Renfrew (Ed.), *The megalithic monuments of western Europe* (pp. 64-76). London: Thames and Hudson. (Original work published 1981)

Tustin, F. (1986). *Autistic barriers in neurotic patients*. New Haven, CT: Yale University Press.

———. (1990). *The protective shell in children and adults*. London: Karnac Books.

Tyson, P., & Tyson, R. L. (1990). *Psychoanalytic theories of development: An integration*. New Haven, CT: Yale University Press.

Vatcher, F. de M., & Vatcher, L. (1976). *The Avebury monuments: Wiltshire*. London: Her Majesty's Stationery Office.

Viegas, Jen. (2017, May 9). This human relative may have lived alongside our species in Africa. *Seeker*. https://www.seeker.com/culture/archaeology/this-human-relative-may-have-lived-alongside-our-species-in-africa

Wallace, E. (1983). *Freud and anthropology: A history and reappraisal*. Psychological Issues Monograph 55. New York: International Universities Press.

Wallauer, B. (2002). "Waterfall Displays." The Jane Goodall Institute UK. http://www.janegoodall.org.uk/chimpanzees/chimpanzee-central/15-chimpanzees/chimpanzee-central/24-waterfall-displays

Walton, A. (1894). *The cult of Askelepious*. Boston: Ginn & Company.

Weigert-Vowinkle, E. (1938). The cult and mythology of the magna mater from the standpoint of psychoanalysis. *Psychiatry, 1*(3), 347–78.

White, T. D. (1985). Acheulian man in Ethiopia's Middle Awash Valley: The implications of cutmarks on the Bodo cranium. *Kroon Memorial Lecture, 1985*. Albert Egges van Giffen Instituut voor Prae-en Protohistorie van de Universiteit van Amsterdam. Haarlem (Netherlands): Enschede en Zonen (pp. 1–33).

———. (1986). Cut marks on the Bodo cranium: A case of prehistoric defleshing. *American Journal of Physical Anthropology, 69*, 503–509.

———. (2001). Once we were cannibals. *Scientific American, 285*(2), 58–65.

White, T. D., Asfaw, B., DeGusta, D., Gilbert, H., Richards, G. D., Suwa, G., & Howell, F. C. (2003, June 12). Pleistocene Homo sapiens from Middle Awash, Ethiopia. *Nature, 423*, 742–47.

Whitehouse, R. (1983). Megaliths of the central Mediterranean. In C. Renfrew (Ed.), *The megalithic monuments of western Europe* (pp. 42–63). London: Thames and Hudson. (Original work published 1981)

Wilhelm, R. (1967). *The I Ching*. Princeton, NJ: Princeton University Press. (Original work published 1950)

Williams, C.A.S. (1974). *Outlines of Chinese symbolism and art motives*. Rutland, VT: Charles E. Tuttle.

Wilson, E. O. (1975). *Sociobiology: The new synthesis*. Cambridge, MA: Belknap Press.

Winnicott, D. W. (1953). Transitional objects and transitional phenomena: A study of the first not-me possession. *International Journal of Psycho-Analysis, 34,* 89–97.

Wong, K. (2016). Mystery human. *Scientific American, 314*(3), 28–37.

Woodroffe, J. (1973). *The serpent power.* Madras, India: Ganesh and Company.

Wragg-Sykes, R. (2016). Humans evolve. In D. Christian (Director of the Big History Institute Macquarie University), *Big history* (pp. 180–221). New York: DK Publishing.

Wrangham, R., & Peterson, D. (1996). *Demonic males: Apes and the origins of male violence.* Boston: Houghton Mifflin.

Wright, K. (2010). The pyramids of Illinois. *Discover 71* (Summer). (Special edition, Discover Presents: Origins). 64–69.

Zent, S., & Zent, E. (2008). Los Hoti: Notas sobre su situación presente y actualización bibliográfica. In Walter Coppens, Bernarda Escalante, Miguel Angel Perera, Roberto Lizzaralde & Haydee Seijas (Eds.), *Los aborigines de Venezuela: Volumen II, Monografía No. 29* (pp. 499–570). Caracas, Venezuela: Monte Avila Editores Latinoamericana.

Zimmer, H. (1957). *The king and the corpse: Tales of the soul's conquest of evil.* Princeton, NJ: Princeton University Press.

PHOTO CREDITS

FRONT COVER
Max Pollack etching of an inspired Sigmund Freud (1914) sitting at his desk with his antiquities in front of him.
Copyright Freud Museum London
Cover image (IN/0517) with rights to modify image in a montage.
Permission to republish granted Jan. 18, 2021

FRONT COVER
Pre-Hispanic Female figurine from Chambergo Island in Lake Valencia, Venezuela.
From *Arqueología de la Prehistoria de Venezuela* (1997) by Miklos Szabadics Roka
Permission to republish granted by Jenny Szabadics February 3, 2016

INTRODUCTION
Erik H. Erikson (May 3, 1987)
Photo credit: Herb Peterson, MD Alumni Faculty Association of Langley Porter Institute
Permission to publish from Herb Peterson May 3, 1987

CHAPTER 1
1-1 Charles Darwin (1881)
Image number: K970214 – Media ID: 979531
Permission to republish granted January 7, 2021 by images.historicenglandservices and Media Storehouse

1-2 Jean-Baptiste de Lamarck (1802)
Public Domain Image – Alamy Image ID: HKMB7G
Permission to republish granted April 2, 2021 by ALAMY STOCK PHOTOS and ART Collection

1-3 Ernst Haeckel (1895)
German biologist, naturalist, philosopher, physician, professor and artist.

PHOTO CREDITS

From Die Gartenlaube, republished 1905
Alamy Image ID: BR5029
Permission to republish granted April 2, 2021 by ALAMY STOCK PHOTOS and Classic Image

1-4 Sigmund Freud (1921)
Copyright Freud Museum London
Permission to republish granted Jan. 18, 2021

1-5 Totem und Tabu: Einige Übereinstimmungen im Seelenleben der Wilden und der Neurotiker (1913) German first edition of Freud's 'Totem and Taboo'.
Personal collection of the author

1-6 Polished stone chisel with a bone handle from a Neolithic site in Saint-Aubin-Sauges, Switzerland. One of the few pre-historic antiquities in Freud's collection. Purchased in 1897. Now on display sitting in a stone ashtray in the Freud Museum London.
Thanks to Daniel Bento and Emilia Raczkowska for permission to photograph chisel.
Photo by the author in 2019

1-7 Géza Róheim (1930)
Géza Róheim in Australia on his way to New Guinea (January 21, 1930)
Photo credit: The Register News-Pictorial. Adelaide, Australia p. 28
Internet search

CHAPTER 2
2-1 John Weir Perry (1982)
Photo by the author

2-2 Egyptian Pyramids and Sphynx
Photo by the author in 1983

2-3 Ramses II from the 19th dynasty. Egyptian pharaoh 1279–1213 BCE. Luxor, Egypt
Photo by the author in 1983

2-4 Mandala drawn by a chronic schizophrenic patient.
Permission obtained from the artist
Photo by the author

2-5 "This is me." A mandala spontaneously drawn by a six-year-old boy. Mandalas are commonly drawn by children in the pre-pictorial phase of drawing development (See Rhoda Kellogg, 1970) and later in the religious art of cultures around the world.
Permission obtained from the child's parents
Photo by the author in 1974

2-6 A Tibetan Buddhist mandala upon which monks would meditate.
Located in the British Museum
Heritage image ID: 1-153-533 – Ann Ronan Picture Library/Heritage-Images
Permission to republish granted April 11, 2021 by Heritage Art/Heritage Images/Heritage Image Partnership, Ltd.

CHAPTER 3

3-1 Photos of drawings by Jimmy. September 1975–January 1978.
Permission to republish drawings granted by Jimmy's parents
Photos by author

3-2 Photos of drawings by Jimmy. March 1978–July 1980.
Permission to republish drawings granted by Jimmy's parents
Photos by author

3-3 The Five Basic Meanings of the Mouth.
Diagram by author

3-4 Entering the mouth of death. Detail from the front of Conques Abbey, in southern France, showing the Last Judgement and people entering the Mouth of Hell, 11th century.
Heritage Image ID: 2-605-865 © CM Dixon/Heritage Images
Permission to republish granted April 19, 2021 by Heritage Art/Heritage Images/Heritage Image Partnership, Ltd.

3-5 The hero is reborn from the mouth. Jonah, of the Bible, is disgorged from the belly of the great fish onto the shore.
Creators: Antonius Wierix, Hieronymous Wierix, ca. 1585
Heritage Image ID: 2-791-907
Permission to republish granted April 5, 2021 by Heritage Art/Heritage Images/Heritage Image Partnership, Ltd.

PHOTO CREDITS

3-6 The soul enters the mouth. The alchemical Green Lion swallowing the sun. Carl Jung said it represented the "spiritual principle" sinking "into the embrace of physical nature" (Psychology and Alchemy, 1968, pp. 331-332) As such, it is an analogue of the soul entering the mouth in order to embody. The Green Lion of European alchemy represents one of several stages in the creation of the Philosopher's Stone. Image from a German alchemical text of circa 1530.
Alamy Image ID: MC6EC2
Permission to republish granted April 2, 2021 by ALAMY STOCK PHOTOS and Charles Walker Collection

3-7 The soul, or in this case, the demon, leaves the body by way of the mouth.
Two men hold a possessed woman while a priest conducts an exorcism to drive the devil out of her body. The priest offers her the wafer and wine of the Eucharist. Notice the devil leaving her body by way of her mouth.
From Histoire prodigieuses et memorables, extraictes de plusieurs fameux aureurs, (Prodigious and Memorable History, Extracted from Several Famous Authors) 1272
Alamy Image ID: HRJFG5
Permission to republish granted April 2, 2021 by ALAMY STOCK PHOTOS and Photo Researchers

3-8 The soul leaves the mouth at the time of death. In the alchemical process, the death state is known as the Nigredo. In this drawing, a male figure is seen in a tomb (circle) with his soul and spirit (two human-headed birds), leaving his body by way of his mouth. Image from Viridarium Chymicum by Daniel Stolcius, 1624.
Heritage Image ID: 1-157-498 – Ann Ronan Picture Library/Heritage-Images
Permission to republish granted April 5, 2021 by Heritage Art/Heritage Images/Heritage Image Partnership, Ltd.

3-9 The mouth as integral consciousness.
A Chinese dragon spewing forth the sacred pearl from its mouth.
This figure was found in a small store in Wuhan, China.
Photo by the author in 2018.

3-10 The mouth as integral consciousness. Shiva with his kundalini emerging from the seventh chakra, the Sahasrara chakra, which is also called the "Mouth of God". Notice the snake wrapped around his topknot, a small head sticking out, and the River Ganges, the River of Life, spewing out of the mouth of the little head – out of the Mouth of God.

Detail from an 18th century Tantric Moghul Chinnamasta – Shiva and Shakti.
Private collection. Photo by the author.

3-11 Instruments used in the ancient Egyptian Ritual of Opening the Mouth
Frontispiece of *The Book of Opening the Mouth Volume 1* Routledge Revivals (1909-1972) by E. A. Wallis Budge
Permission to republish granted by Copyright Clearance Center Marketplace April 6, 2021

3-12 The Sem priest conducting the ritual of opening the mouth on the statue representing the deceased. The priest opens the mouth using the Pesh-en-kef instrument.
The Book of Opening the Mouth Volume 2, p. 162, Routledge Revivals (1909-1972) by E. A. Wallis Budge
Permission to republish granted by Copyright Clearance Center Marketplace April 6, 2021

3-13 The Sem priest presenting the breast as a funeral offering to the deceased in the ritual of opening the mouth.
The Liturgy of Funerary Offerings, p. 121, Routledge Revivals (1909-1972) by E. A. Wallis Budge
Permission to republish granted April 6, 2021 by Copyright Clearance Center Marketplace

3-14 Falcon headed God, Horus, performing the ritual of opening the mouth on the deceased Ramses II, an Egyptian pharaoh. 1279 – 1213 BCE 19th dynasty. Abydos, Egypt.
Alamy Image ID: CF6KH2
Permission to republish granted April 5, 2021 by ALAMY STOCK PHOTOS and photographer Peter Horree

3-15 An Iron Age woman's grave from Himlingoeje, Denmark. In her mouth is a little piece of gold – 'Charon's Penny' – From the 3rd century BCE.
Heritage Image ID: 2-580-011 – CM Dixon/Heritage-Images
Permission to republish granted April 24, 2021 by Heritage Art/Heritage Images/Heritage Image Partnership, Ltd.

3-16 Tiny Chinese (Han) jade figurines. As a part of funerary ritual practice, a small figurine would be placed in the mouth of the deceased before burial.
Hubei Provincial Museum in Wuhan, China
Photo by the author in 2018

PHOTO CREDITS

3-17 Aztec archeologists at the Great Temple of Tenochtitlan in Mexico City found human skulls with sacrificial knives placed in the mouths and nasal orifices. The flint blades were seen as metaphors for the breath and words of the deceased.
Museo del Templo Mayor
Photo by the author in 2011.

CHAPTER 4

4-1 A chimpanzee family (Pan troglodytes) sitting close together in the Muenster Zoo in Germany
Alamy Image ID: AC5ATM
Permission to republish granted April 2, 2021 by ALAMY STOCK PHOTOS and C. O. Mercial

4-2 Skull of Homo erectus between 350,000 and 500,000 years old.
Yunxian Man was found in Yunxian County, China.
It is now located in the Hubei Provincial Museum in Wuhan, China.
Photo by the author in 2018

4-3 Acheulean hand ax from ancient Paleolithic site in South Africa.
Given to John Weir Perry as a gift when he gave lectures in South Africa at the invitation of Sir Laurens van der Post.
Photo by the author with permission of John Weir Perry

4-4 A 90,000-year-old intentional burial of a man at Muhgharet-es-Skhūl, Mount Carmel, Israel. He was buried with his legs tightly flexed and his arm clasping the jawbones of a wild boar.
This image was drawn by Philip Ward after Garrod. It is illustration 22 found on page 41 of The Stone Age Hunters by Grahame Clark (1967) published by Thames and Hudson Ltd., London.
Permission to republish drawing granted May 25, 2021 by Nancy at Thames & Hudson Permissions

CHAPTER 5

5-1 Paleolithic amulet. A bison carved from a piece of antler. 15,000 years old.
National Museum of Prehistory in Les Eyzies-de-Tayac-Sireuil, France.
Photo by the author in 1983

5-2 This ancient stone ax was found by modern Yanomami indigenous people in Venezuela while working in their garden. The Yanomamis did not use it as an ax but rather as an amulet in their yopo ceremonies to aid them in communing with their ancestors.
Photo by the author in May 2006.

5-3 A curated Paleolithic cave bear skull from Les Eyzies-de-Tayac-Sireuil, France.
Photo by the author in 1983

5-4 Curated monkey skulls skewered on a stick through the zygomatic arches. While curating skulls is a Paleolithic tradition, it may still appear at other levels of cultural evolution. This image is from a modern day Panare village in the Venezuelan jungles that is perhaps more Neolithic in its technology and yet also has some metal and plastic tools, shotguns, fishing lines and hooks, and flashlights. Nonetheless, the curating of skulls has the magical meaning of insuring good hunting in the future by showing respect for the deceased.
Photo by the author in May 2009

5-5 Paleolithic stone tools (10,000-14,000 years old) from Laugerie Basse, in Les Eyzies-de-Tayac-Sireuil, France
Photo by the author in 1983

5-6 Stone spearpoint on the desert floor in the state of Coro, Venezuela. It is a surface find so the date is uncertain. While similarly made stone tools from the same area have been found to be 9,000 years old, it could just as easily be only a few hundred years old.
Photo by the author in February 2006

5-7 Stone tools from Venezuela in the laboratory of Miklos Szabadics Roka.
Photo by the author in 2010

5-8 A stone mortar in Miklos Szabadics Roka's hands. Coro, Venezuela.
Photo by the author in 2010

5-9 Miklos Szabadics Roka with his wife and colleague, Eva Hofle.
Tara Tara, Venezuela.
Photo by the author in 2010

5-10 A previously buried ancient fire ring was under the ground for perhaps thousands of years until rains and wind more recently uncovered and exposed it to the light of day in the Venezuelan desert.
Coro, Venezuela.
Photo by the author in 2010

5-11 Paleolithic engraved representations of vulvas. National Museum of Prehistory in Les Eyzies-de-Tayac-Sireuil, France.
Photo by the author in 1983

5-12 A Paleolithic or Neolithic engraved representation of a vulva. La Colonia Tovar, Venezuela.
Photo by the author in 2006

5-13 Paleolithic stone carved bas relief of two bison.
National Museum of Prehistory in Les Eyzies-de-Tayac-Sireuil, France.
Photo by the author in 1983

5-14 Bison painting in the Altamira Cave in Santander Cantabria, Spain.
Alamy Image ID: A16CWJ
Permission to republish granted April 2, 2021 by ALAMY STOCK PHOTOS and Melba Photo Agency

5-15 Paleolithic stone carved bas relief of a salmon. From the site, Abri du Poisson. Les Eyzies-de-Tayac-Sireuil, France.
Photo by the author in 1983

5-16 Paleolithic or perhaps Neolithic petroglyphs near Colonia Tovar, Venezuela..
From *Arqueología de la Prehistoria de Venezuela* (1997) by Miklos Szabadics Roka. (p. 179)
Permission granted to republish by Jenny Szabadics February 3, 2016

5-17 Paleolithic or perhaps Neolithic petroglyphs near Colonia Tovar, Venezuela.
From *Arqueología de la Prehistoria de Venezuela* (1997) by Miklos Szabadics Roka. (p. 179)
Permission granted to republish by Jenny Szabadics February 3, 2016

5-18 Petroglyph of a lizard by the shore of the Ventuari River in the jungles of Venezuela.
Photo by the author in May 2009

5-19 A replica of the Paleolithic Venus of Willendorf
The original is in the Kunsthistorisches Museum in Vienna, Austria.
Photo by the author in 1999

5-20 Yopo ceremony 1 – Notice the face paint, feather earrings, arm bracelets, yopo tube, and the stone tool amulet on the metal plate on the ground. Yanomami village.
Photo by the author in December 2009

5-21 Yopo ceremony 2 – Yanomami village.
Photo by the author in December 2009

5-22 Yopo ceremony 3 – Yanomami village.
Photo by the author in December 2009

5-23 Yopo ceremony 4 – Notice the feathered arm bracelet. Yanomami village.
Photo by the author in December 2009

5-24 Yopo ceremony 5 – Blowing the yopo powder through the tube. – Yanomami village.
Photo by the author in December 2009

5-25 Delfin and the author – Yanomami village.
Photo in December 2009

CHAPTER 6

6-1 This is oldest known village wall and tower. It is 11,500 years old and located in Jericho, now a Palestinian city in the West Bank.
Photo by the author in 1983

6-2 The foundations of round houses excavated at the Neolithic settlement of Khirokitia, Cyprus.
Alamy Image ID: CB6EX1
Permission to republish granted April 2, 2021 by ALAMY STOCK PHOTOS and Ros Drinkwater

6-3 Neo-Sumerian foundation peg of King Shulgi of Ur ca. 2094-2047 BCE. This finely worked metal artifact belongs to the Urban Revolution but as a foundation peg it is an example of

the Neolithic tradition of house building rituals carried into successive levels of cultural sophistication.
Metropolitan Museum of Art in New York
Photo by the author in 2019

6-4 The author with the owner of a round house in the Nepali Himalayas in 1983. The old woman explained that there was no particular ritual to start building the house but that she placed some jewelry under the center post.
Photo by the Shankar Lama

6-5 The author with the owner of a round house and two children in 2009. The round house is in a Hoti village in the Venezuelan jungle near the Upper Orinoco River.
Photo by the Hector Abreu

6-6 Hoti village in the Venezuelan jungle.
Photo by the author in 2009

6-7 A modern day mud brick square house with a round cupola in Luxor, Egypt, not far from the Valley of the Kings.
Photo by the author in 1983

6-8 A modern man making mud bricks for construction in Luxor, Egypt not far from the Valley of the Kings. The bricks are made in the same way they were made thousands of years ago with a mix on clay, sand, straw, and manure (probably from camels). A short distance from this site were archeological excavations of ancient homes built with the same types of bricks!
Photo by the author in 1983

6-9 A modern Egyptian girl pulling out a loaf of flat bread from a mud oven in her home, near the Valley of the Kings in Luxor, Egypt.
Photo by the author in 1983

6-10 A mud oven with a metal plate on top and a broom to the left. They were located in a Mako village in the Venezuelan jungles.
Photo by the author in 2009

LIBIDO, CULTURE, AND CONSCIOUSNESS

6-11 Some Panare children in front of their house in the Venezuelan jungle.
Photo by the author in 2009

6-12 Preparing for a Yanomami welcome dance in the Venezuelan jungle.
Photo by the author in 2006

6-13 Yanomami welcome dance in the jungles of Venezuela. To the left, a girl wearing a traditional guayuco for females. It is a belt with a skirt of strings in the front.
Photo by the author in 2006

6-14 Yanomami welcome dance in the jungles of Venezuela. The dancer is painted in black, wearing a red loin cloth, and brandishing a bow and arrow. The boy in the back dances with a palm frond.
Photo by the author in 2006

6-15 Yanomami welcome dance in the Venezuelan jungle. This dancer is brandishing his weapon directly at the photographer (me) during the welcome dance. Notice the body paint, the huge wad of chewing tobacco in his mouth, and the white baby-vulture feathers in his hair.
Photo by the author in 2006

6-16 Yanomami welcome dance in the Venezuelan jungle. Notice this woman's body paint, and decorative sticks piercing her lips and nasal septum.
Photo by the author in 2006

6-17 A group photo taken after a Yanomami welcome dance. The author's wife, Adriana Prengler, and the author are seen in the back.
Photo by Adrian Amaya in 2006

6-18 Yanomami woman with body paint, necklaces, earrings, and lip and nasal septum piercings.
Photo by Adriana Prengler 2006

6-19 A bamboo quiver and arrow points, called rahaka. They are used by the Yanomami indigenous people in hunting and for trade. These particular rahaka, except for the painted

PHOTO CREDITS

one, are from the Wuirionave community. The painted rahaka was made by Delfin of the Merey community. Both communities are situated on the Rio Negro in Venezuela.
Private collection.
Photo by the author

6-20 A small boy driving two bulls that pull a wooden plow through an agricultural field at the base of the Himalayas, near Pokhara, Nepal.
Photo by the author in 1983

6-21 Pre-Hispanic female figurines from the archipelago of Los Roques in Venezuela. This collection is from the archeological laboratory of María Magdalena Antczak and Andrzej Antczak at the Universidad Simón Bolívar in Caracas, Venezuela.
Photo by the author with permission from the Antczaks in 2010

6-22 Pre-Hispanic Ceramic female figurine made in the style commonly found in the state of Lara, Venezuela. Between 1000-1600 ACE. Notice how the eyes, mouth and vulva are made in the "coffee bean" style.
Private collection
Photo by the author

6-23 Ceramic pregnant figurine from Pre-Hispanic Venezuela.
Found on the south side of the Peninsula La Cabrera at Lake Valencia, Venezuela.
From *Arqueología de la Prehistoria de Venezuela* (1997) by Miklos Szabadics Roka. (p. 164)
Permission granted to republish by Jenny Szabadics February 3, 2016

6-24 Ceramic bowl from Pre-Hispanic Venezuela. Made in the style found in the state of Lara, Venezuela between 300-1400 ACE.
Private collection
Photo by the author

6-25 A ceramic bowl made by the modern Hoti indigenous people. It was used to hold the poison, curare, into which they dip their blow gun darts. Curare is a neurotoxic paste made from local native plants. The curare tipped darts are shot through a cerbatana, or blow gun, to kill birds and monkeys in the trees of the Venezuelan jungles.
Private collection
Photo by the author in 2009

6-26 A modern Egyptian boy demonstrating how to use a handmade ceramic water jug near the Valley of the Kings in Luxor, Egypt.
Photo by the author in 1983

6-27 Woman working a loom in front of a round house in the Nepali Himalayas.
Photo by the author in 1983

6-28 A man wrapped in a wool blanket surrounded by his sheep in the Nepali Himalayas.
Photo by the author in 1983

6-29 A Panare man with a basket of raw cotton in the Venezuelan jungle.
Photo by the author in May 2009

6-30 A spool of spun cotton in the rafters of a home in a Panare village in the Venezuelan jungle.
Photo by the author in May 2009

6-31 Male and female guayucos (loin cloths) and string skirts on the right and female shoulder adornments on the left. Made from handspun cotton by the indigenous people of the Upper Orinoco in Venezuela.
Private collection
Photo by the author

6-32 Piaroa swinging basket for a baby to rest in. It is positioned next to the wall of a mud and wood pole house in the Venezuelan jungle.
Photo by the author in May 2006

CHAPTER 7
7-1 A megalith in Southern England
Photo by the author in 1983

7-2 A circle of megaliths in southern England.
Photo by the author in 1983

PHOTO CREDITS

7-3 Stonehenge in southern England.
Photo by the author in 1983

7-4 Stone tools from the High Neolithic in Southern England.
Photo by the author in 1983

7-5 The man-made Silbury Hill in Southern England was built in the High Neolithic. It is 131 feet high and 548 feet in diameter at the base.
Photo by the author in 1983

7-6 The entrance to a megalithic tomb in Southern England.
Photo by the author in 1983

7-7 A metallurgist working at his forge in Katmandu, Nepal. The figure at the top of his forge is the elephant headed Hindu god Ganesha, the remover of obstacles and the one who ensures good beginnings.
Photo by the author in 1983

7-8 Metallurgist in Katmandu, Nepal wielding his hammer to pound a red hot blade into shape.
Photo by the author in 1983

7-9 Ancient bronze arrow heads from 6th – 4th century BCE. Israel.
Gift to the author from Bruce and Connie Thayer
Photo by the author

7-10 A monkey sitting atop a large metal dorje at the Swayambhunath Stupa, sacred to both Buddhists and Hindus. The dorje is symbolic of thunder and the phallic principle. Katmandu, Nepal.
Photo by the author in 1983

7-11 An ancient bronze tripod for holding a ritual ornament. This handmade cast bronze tripod is from the 18th or 19th century Nepal.
Photo by the author in 1983

CHAPTER 8

8-1 The Great Pyramid of Khufu, Egypt.
Photo by the author in 1983

8-2 One of the three smaller pyramids associated with The Pyramid of Menakaure and presumably contains one of Menakaure's wives. This pyramid (G3-a) was built in ancient Egypt's Fourth Dynasty 2613-2494 BCE.
Photo by the author in 1983

8-3 Pillars of the Temple of Karnak from the 19th Dynasty 1295-1186 BCE.
Photo by the author in Luxor, Egypt in 1983

8-4 Union of the opposites. The sun disc with two snakes: one with the hat of the upper valley and the other with the hat of the lower valley. Found in the Temple of Karnak.
Photo by the author in Luxor, Egypt in 1983

8-5 Ramses II with his daughter Benta-Anta in the Temple of Karnak: 13th century BCE.
Photo by the author in Luxor, Egypt in 1983

8-6 A clay Syro-Hittite standing female fertility figure, possibly Astarte (4 ½ inches tall). 1500-1000 BCE. Abraham, the patriarch of the Abrahamic religions, is said to have smashed the idols of local gods in favor of a single unified immaterial God in the 1st or 2nd millennium BCE. That is about the time to which this figure is dated.
Private collection
Photo by the author

8-7 Typical ceramic oil lamp 1st century ACE from Israel – Early Roman period. The fan-like shape was developed in Israel and possibly associated with the reign of Herod the Great and, of course, the time of Jesus.
Gift to the author from Bruce and Connie Thayer
Photo by the author

8-8 The great cow goddess, Hathor, who carries the sun across the skies on her horns, suckles the female pharaoh, Hatshepsut. 15th century BCE.
Photo by the author in Luxor, Egypt in 1983

PHOTO CREDITS

8-9 Some of the earliest writing in the world. Cuneiform writing on a 'planoconvex' brick. Early Bronze Age Sumer 2570-2342 BCE. Museum of the Ancient Orient, Istanbul, Turkey.
Alamy Image ID: A4BFR6
Permission to republish granted April 5, 2021 by ALAMY STOCK PHOTOS and photographer Jim Batty

8-10 Ancient Egyptian calendar from the Temple of Kom Ombo, Egypt, 2nd-1st century BCE. the Ptolemaic Period.
Heritage Image ID: 1-277-612 Permission to republish granted April 5, 2021 by Heritage Art/Heritage Images/Heritage Image Partnership, Ltd.

8-11 Teotihuacan pyramid near Mexico City built between 100 BCE and 250 ACE.
Photo by the author in 2011

8-12 Codex Cospi – Magical calendar.
Mexico. Mixtec culture. Period: c.1350 – 1500. Paint on deerskin.
Heritage Image: 2-567-559 – Werner Forman Archive/Biblioteca Universitaria, Bologna, Italy/Heritage Images
Permission to republish granted April 5, 2021 by Heritage Art/Heritage Images/Heritage Image Partnership, Ltd.

8-13 The Aztec Calendar Stone, or Stone of the Sun. Museo Nacional de Antropología in Mexico City c1930s. A name glyph of the Aztec ruler Moctezuma II, suggests the basalt Aztec sun stone was carved c1502 – 1521. It depicts the cosmology of the Aztecs.
From "Tour of the World". [Keystone View Company, Meadville, Pa., New York, Chicago, London]
Heritage Image ID: 2-752-724 – The Print Collector/Heritage Images
Permission to republish granted April 5, 2021 by Heritage Art/Heritage Images/Heritage Image Partnership, Ltd.

8-14 A portion of an Aztec mural depicting a priest conducting the ritual of world renewal celebrated at the end of a 52 year cycle of time. Museo Nacional de Antropología. Mexico City.
Photo by the author in 2011

8-15 Modern tapestry based on the ancient Mexican Codex Nuttall of Mixtec origin. The scene depicts the fire lighting ritual at the end of a 52 year cycle when all flames are extinguished and the gods either grant or deny fire to the people for the next 52 year cycle.
Tapestry by the author's father, Jack Benveniste
Photo by author

CHAPTER 9

9-1 Man as the Microcosm and the Universe as the Macrocosm. Notice the cosmogram of concentric circles and the names of the planets emanating out from the man's hip: Moon, Mercury, Venus, Sun, Mars, Jupiter and Saturn. From "Margarita Philosophica," Basle, 1508.
Alamy Image ID: D9DFNB
Permission to republish granted April 2, 2021 by ALAMY STOCK PHOTOS and World History Archive

9-2 Seven rings of an Indian cosmogram. Ajit Mookerjee (1977) writes, "Dominating the center of the universe is the mythical Mount Meru around which is the earth or jambu-dvüpa, the island continent with seven concentric circles symbolically representing cosmic fields, spheres, atmospheric zones" (p. 71).
Private collection
Photo by the author

CHAPTER 10

10-1 In the evening, the Egyptian Goddess Nut swallows the sun on the western horizon, and all the world goes dark. At night we look up and see the stars on the body of the Goddess Nut. The sun passes through Nut's body during the night and is reborn from her womb on the eastern horizon, in the morning. It is a depiction of the Egyptian cosmos – the Goddess Nut bending to form the sky.
This image is a papyrus copy based on a late Egyptian temple at Denderah.
Alamy Image ID: D96B54
Permission to republish granted April 2, 2021 by ALAMY STOCK PHOTOS and World History Archive

10-2 Lingam and yoni. A pillar in a bowl represents the male and female sexual organs together as a symbol of the universe. Katmandu, Nepal.
Photo by the author in 1983

PHOTO CREDITS

10-3 Yoni Lingam ceremonial bowl. Probably from 18th or 19th century Indian Himalayas.
Private collection
Photo by the author

10-4 Religious art imbues the body, its functions, and daily life with spiritual meaning. Above is a Tantric Moghul Chinnamasta from 18th century India. In this miniature painting we see a vision of the opposites united. Shiva (the male) and Shakti (the female) are making love in the funerary grounds - life and death. There are two funeral pyres in the background, and human heads scattered about in the foreground being eaten by dogs. Shakti cuts off her own head in a self-sacrifice, holds her severed head in one hand, and in the other hand catches her own spurting blood in a skull cap cup. Though her head is cut off, signifying death or sacrifice, she is pink signifying life. Shiva, meanwhile, is the dead god and is ashen white. Three of the snakes adorning his body hold their heads up and three hang their heads down. While copulating with Shakti he uses the sexual energy to awaken the kundalini or spiritual energy and directs it up through the seven chakras to the chakra at the crown of the skull - the sahasrara chakra or Mouth of God. In this Indian miniature painting (7 ½" X 5 ½") one can see that out of Shiva's topknot there emerges a small head and out of its mouth flows the River Ganges - The River of Life.
Private collection
Photo by the author

10-5 Jupiter rides across the sky on his chariot pulled by eagles. Jupiter was the king of the gods in ancient Rome. He was the god of sky and thunder.
Alamy Image ID: T951XC
Permission to republish granted April 2, 2021 by ALAMY STOCK PHOTOS and Science History Images

10-6 Man's Quest for Knowledge of the Universe: Flammarion Engraving (1888)
Heritage Image ID: 2-619-635 The Print Collector/Heritage Images
Permission to republish granted July 30, 2021 by Heritage Art/Heritage Images/Heritage Image Partnership, Ltd.

APPENDIX 4

Appendix 4-1 Nut, the goddess of heaven, was lying on her spouse, Seb, the earth god. Then her father, Shu, the god of atmosphere, interfered in their copulation and lifted her up to reveal everything Nut and Seb had created.
Photograph republished 1997; artwork created c. 950 BCE. Photographed by the British Museum.

Alamy Image ID: MMJX84 Permission to republish granted April 2, 2021 by ALAMY STOCK PHOTOS and the Picture Art Collection. Public Domain Image

Appendix 4-2 A wood carving from the front of a storehouse depicting the Maori gods, Rangi, the heaven or sky father, and Papa, the earth mother, as a copulating couple. They had many children but because they were in an eternal embrace their children lived between their two parents in darkness until Tane-mahuta, god of the forests, put his head on his mother and feet on his father and pushed his father into the sky letting in light and revealing all the people that had been born. Notice the heads of the children all around the copulating parents. New Zealand 18th Century.

Heritage Image ID: 2-565-048 – Werner Forman Archive/Otago Museum, Dunedin/Heritage Images Permission to republish granted April 5, 2021 by Heritage Art/Heritage Images/Heritage Image Partnership, Ltd.

APPENDIX 5

Appendix 5-1 The head of a butchered tapir inside of a dugout canoe. Hoti village in the Venezuelan jungle.

Photo by the author in May 2009

Appendix 5-2 Butchering a tapir inside a dugout canoe. Hoti village in the Venezuelan jungle.

Photo by the author in May 2009

APPENDIX 6

Appendix 6-1 A Panare father and son displaying the cerbatana, or blowgun, along with a bamboo quiver for the darts, some darts with tips dipped in curare, and a small bowl of curare in the Venezuelan jungle.

Photo by the author in May 2009

Appendix 6-2 A Panare boy demonstrating the use of the cerbatana, or blow gun in the Venezuelan jungle.

Photo by the author in May 2009

Appendix 6-3 A Panare boy with a hunting spear. The blade is a broken piece of a machete that has been filed into the shape of a spear point and sharpened. Venezuelan jungle.

Photo by the author in May 2009

Appendix 6-4 Nena, a Panare girl, proudly showing a squash growing in the village garden. Venezuelan jungle.
Photo by the author in May 2009

Appendix 6-5 A Hoti man proudly carrying a baby. He wears a loin cloth called a guayuco. Hoti village in the Venezuelan jungle.
Photo by the author in May 2009

Appendix 6-6 A Hoti mother bathing her baby down by the river next to a dugout canoe. Hoti village in the Venezuelan jungle.
Photo by the author in May 2009

AUTHOR'S BIOGRAPHY PAGE
Photo by Adriana Prengler

INDEX

NOTE:

Page numbers with *f* indicate illustrations.
Page numbers with *n* indicate a note.

A

aboriginal cultures, 23-26
    ancient ancestors and, 24, 34
    Darwin and, 6, 17, 23
    Freud and, 13-17
    violence, 213
    See also Hoti; Panare; Piaroa; Yanomami; Yavarana
Abraham, Karl, 11, 73-74, 224, 328, 366
Abreu, Hector, 391, 395-97
abstract thinking
    adolescence and, 281-83
    as metaphorical, 345
    See also symbolic function
Acheulean stone tool tradition, 132, 133, 139f
Adler, Nathan, 247, 333, 342
adolescence, 58-61, 281-83
    Erik Erikson on, 111, 282
    idealism in, 282-83
    identity in, 78, 283, 307
    initiation rituals, 78, 111, 119 (*see also* initiation rituals)
    Peter Blos on, 281-82
    See also genital stage
Africa as birthplace of humanity, 129-30

aggression
    Lorenz and, 119-20, 382
    See also dominance and submission; violence
aggression-neutralizing behaviors, x, 119-20, 214, 353
agriculture
    culture and, 215-22
    Mircea Eliade on vegetation and, 22-22, 260-61, 263-65
    See also High Neolithic; Neolithic
alchemical Green Lion, 83f
alchemists, 210, 323
alpha male
    behavior of younger males toward, 118
    "Freud" (chimpanzee) as, 354
alpha male dynamics, 261
    in chimpanzees, 117-18, 380, 381
    "heroes" and, 118
    Oedipus complex and, 33, 105, 291, 352
    tribal chiefs and, 118-19
alpha male ritualizations, 33, 118, 354
Altamira Cave, 165, 188f
American Sign Language, 124-25
Amud Cave (Israel), 135

amulets
    carved from antler, 182f
    as homes for souls of ancestors, 157-60
    spirits and, 135, 157-59, 163, 167
    Yanomami and, 158, 177, 182f, 191f
    See also funerary rituals
anagogic symbolism, 122, 383-84
anal-expulsive and anal-retentive character, 197, 210
anal stage
    boundaries, the wall, and, 197-98
    clay, feces, and, 223-24
    Neolithic and, 144, 195-97
    and the valuing of things, 209-12
    See also Neolithic
anality, 196-97
    dominance, submission, and, 114, 375
    Ernest Becker on, 207
    money and, 197, 209-12, 217
    nature of, 207
    See also feces
anamnesis (as a personal creation myth), 316-17
ancestors
    aboriginal cultures and, 24, 34
    amulets as homes for souls of, 157-60
    archaic inheritance from, 10, 34-35, 111, 296
    worship of, 14
Andean cosmogony, 320-21
animal skulls, 391-92
    cave bear, 159, 166, 183f
    curated, 183f
    monkey, 183f, 396-97
animal spirits (hekuras), 158, 163, 166-68, 177-79, 181, 340

"Animism, Magic, and the Omnipotence of Thoughts" (*Totem and Taboo*), 15-16
animistic phase, 16
Antczak, Maria Magdalena and Andrzej, 223
anthropomorphism, 338
anthropophagy, 156, 368
apotheosis, 56, 294, 314
    John Weir Perry on, 42, 283, 289, 363
    in New Year festivals, 48, 283, 287, 289
    in psychosis, 42, 54, 283, 289, 362, 363
    as royalty, divinity, or messianic hero, 42, 48, 54, 289
archaic man, 107, 284-86, 321
archaic memories, 10, 120, 291
archaic societies vs. modern societies, 283-84
archetypes
    celestial, 284-86, 321
    Erich Neumann on, 359
    Joseph Henderson on, 358
    Jung on, 358-59
"Archetypes and Repetition" (Eliade), 283-86, 321
Arieti, Silvano, 56-57
Arlow, Jacob A., 12
Armageddon, 319-20
arrow points (rahaka), 214-15, 237f
art
    cave, 162-70
    painting, sculpture, and projections into the world, 163-75
    religious, 51f, 349f
    tantric, 81, 85f, 335, 349f
Ascension and Conflict, psychomythic stage, 294, 314, 323-25

astrology, 205, 218, 323
atheism, 339
    Freud and, 338, 340
    theism and, 339, 340, 342
    See also God
Atkinson, James J., 17
Atkinson, Richard J. C., 255–56
atonement practices, 289–90
attachment. *See* bonding and attachment
Australian aborigines, 14
Australopithecines, 125–31, 160
autism
    Bruno Bettelheim on, 62–63, 72, 92–93
    Erik Erikson on, 111, 197
    Frances Tustin on, 61, 63–64, 86, 93–95
autistic anlage, 63, 72
autistic children
    Frances Tustin's description of, 63–64
    as souls unable or unwilling to embody, 85–88, 91–95
    See also Jimmy
autistic-contiguous position (Ogden), 86
autistic dilemma, 85–86, 95
autistic disorder, classic, 62. *See also* autism
autistic sensation objects (Tustin), 63–64, 94
autistic sensation shapes (Tustin), 94
autistic spectrum disorder, 62. *See also* autism
autocosmic play, Erikson on, 335–36
axes, 160, 162, 175, 182f, 252, 253, 259–60, 265,
    Acheulean hand axe, 132, 133, 139f
Aztecs, 47, 91, 96, 302f

B
Ba (soul), 87–88
Bachofen, Johann Jacob, 24–26, 171, 173–74
Balbach, Anatol "Ted" (uncle), 202
Baldwin, James Mark, 125
bamboo arrow points (rahaka), 214–15, 237f
bamboo quiver, 237f, 395, 399f
Barratt, Barnaby, 319
Barron, Frank, 319
barrows (burial mounds), 252–53
    long, 252–54
Beaker people, 253
bears. *See* cave bears
beast, killing of the, 179, 270, 388–92, 393f
Becker, Ernest
    on the creative type, 317
    on death, 149, 207, 262
    on the fall of man, 318
    on heroism, 262, 317
    on Otto Rank, 149, 207, 317
    on symbolic function, 149, 207
beginnings. *See* return to beginnings
Bergdamara, 312–13
Beth-el, as House of God, 203
Bettelheim, Bruno, 93
    on autism, 62–63, 72, 92–93
    letter from, 92
Bible, 336, 352. *See also* Jonah; Old Testament; Revelation
bicameral mind, 364
Binford, Lewis, 148, 153, 168
Binford, Sally R., 168, 173–74
biogenetic law. *See* "ontogeny recapitulates phylogeny"/biogenetic law

Birth and Separation, psychomythic stage, 294, 313, 323–24
birth canal of the hero, mouth as, 76, 78–79
bison, 165, 167–68, 182f, 188f
Blos, Peter, 282
Blum, Harold P., 122, 164
Boas, Franz, 27
bodily metaphors, 332–34, 344–45
body, physical
    ego and, 121
    social body and, 385
    symbolism, 121, 344–45
    See also embodiment
Boisen, Anton T.
    exploration of inner world, 362
bonding and attachment, 86, 113, 382
    greeting behavior and, 113–14, 371–75
    Lorenz on, 382
    loss and, 372
    male/fraternal, 354
    ritualization and, 109–10
bones, 103. See also jawbones; skeletons; skulls
Bonnard, Augusta, 368–69
bovines, 211. See also bison; bulls; cattle
Bradley, Noel, 170
Brahma, 218
brain, Julian Jaynes and the, 364
brain size, evolution and, 128, 145
breasts, 74, 88, 90f, 171. See also nursing
breath, mythologizing of the, 98
brief psychotic disorder, 282–83
    diagnosis, 58
    John Weir Perry on
        case vignettes, 43–47

    Jungian formulation, 37–41
    treatment approaches, 42–43
    stage in cultural evolution corresponding to, 58–59
    stage in normal development corresponding to, 58, 282
Briffault, Robert, 79, 174, 359
Britain. See England
Bucke, Richard Maurice, 363–64
Buckle, Henry Thomas, 24
Budge, E.A.W. See ritual of opening the mouth
buildings, permanent. See house(s)
bulls, 218, 237f
    sacred, 211–12
    sacrificial, 211–12
    shrines and, 200
    sky gods and, 266
    See also bovines
Bunjil creation myth, 266
burial mounds. See barrows
burial sites
    in Eynan (Israel), 101–2
    at Skhul Cave (Israel), 103, 135, 139f, 151
burials
    fetal position in, 101–3, 134, 148, 360
    under the floor, 200
    spirits and, 200–201
    See also funerary rituals; tombs
Bushongo creation myth, 309–10

C

calendars, 295, 300f, 301f, 302f, 314, 320
    invention of, 46, 283
    religious, 267

sacral kingship and, 100, 352
Urban Revolution and, 136, 145
Campbell, J., 168
cannibalism, 154, 157, 209
   in animals, 155
   Géza Róheim on, 30-31
   incorporation and, 16, 19, 155-56, 167
   magic and, 16, 155-57
   mothers and, 31
   in mythology, 156
   orality and, 73-74, 154, 156, 366-68
   Paleolithic cannibalism and
      internalization of the other, 154-57
   ritual, 154-56
   and the soul, 155-56, 167
   White, Tim D., 154-55
cannibalistic feasts, 156-57. *See also under*
   totemic feasts
cannibalizing the (primal) father, 19, 30,
   154, 211, 247
   original sin and, 361
   Theodore Reik and, 361
Caribs, 156
Caspari, Rachel, 261
Cassirer, Ernst, 134-35, 206, 265-66, 321
castration, metaphorical, 247-48, 352
castration anxiety and the mouth, 366-67, 369
castration complex, 20, 108-9, 120
Çatal Hüyük, Turkey, 101, 199-200, 211
cattle, 211, 217-18. *See also* bovines
cave art, 162-70
   Altamira Cave, 165, 188f
   Chauvet Cave, France, 165-66
   Cosquer Cave, 165
   Grotte de Font-de-Gaume, 165

Lascaux cave (Montignac, France), 165, 167-70
   Sulawesi, 166, 201
cave bear skulls, 159, 166, 183f
cave bears, 158-59, 183f, 211
"cavemen," 163
caves, symbolism of, 164
celestial archetypes, 284-86, 321
center, world, 41, 47, 289
ceramics, 197, 200, 221, 223-24, 238f, 239f, 240f
chakras, 81, 85f, 349f
Chalcolithic, 245
chaos, primeval
   emerging out of, 310, 317
   return to, 264
Chauvet Cave, France, 165-66
chiao (Taoist ritual), 50-51
chimpanzees, 107, 109, 112-19, 138f
   alpha male behavior, 117-18, 380-81
   Frans de Waal on, 114-15, 355
   ritualizations, 320-24, 371-81
   See also Goodall, Jane
China, 50, 97
   chiao (Taoist ritual), 50-51
Chinese dragon, 84f
Chinese (Han) jade figurines, 99f
Chinese mythology, 50, 79
Christianity, 44-46
   Freud, psychoanalysis, and, 340
   object relations and, 342
   See also Jesus Christ
Chuang-tzu, 97-98
civilization
   birth of, 32, 35, 40, 46, 100
   defined, 46, 100

clash of opposites. *See* cosmic conflict
clay, 101-2, 298f
    feces and, 223-24
cloacal theory, 219
Clottes, Jean, 165-66
cognitive functioning, 56
    ego functioning and, 32, 146
    See also paleologic thought; primary process thinking; symbolic function
cognitive structure, 308
cognitive unconscious, 345
collective mind, Freud on, 20-21, 111
collective unconscious, 42, 121
    Freud and the phylogenetic memory trace, 21, 357-59
    Jung and, 21, 357-59
coming-of-age ritualizations, 119
condensation, Haeckel's principle of, 8
conscious mind, 365
consciousness
    cosmic, 56, 334-35, 363-64
    ego, 267-68
    Julian Jaynes on, 364-65
    simple, 363-64
control, anal stage and, 209
conversion hysteria, 29, 61
Copper Age, 245
copulation interference
    in chimpanzees, 115-17, 376-78
    in cosmogonic mythology, 378-79, 387f
    Oedipus complex and, 115-17, 376-80
copulation/sexual intercourse, 354
    in chimpanzees, 118-19
    Frans de Waal on animal, 115, 218-19
    reproduction and, 218

cosmic conflict, 42, 50, 54, 283-85, 287, 289
    as clash of opposites, 48
cosmic consciousness (Bucke), 56, 334-35, 363-64
cosmic space, 196, 225
cosmic time, 196, 222, 225
cosmogonic mythology and narrative structure, 309-21
cosmogony(ies)
    Andean, 320-21
    Bushongo, 309-10
    etymology of the term, 317
    of Finno-Ugric people, 310
    Maidu, 310
    Taoist, 310-11
    See also New Year festivals
cosmograms, 330f, 334
cosmological imagery in psychedelic experiences, 365
cosmology(ies)
    from cosmogony to, 321-22
    seven aspects of, 321-22
    See also cosmogony(ies)
Cosquer Cave, 165
cotton, Venezuelan, 242f, 243f
coughing, psychodynamics of, 369-70
courtships, 118. *See also under* Goodall, Jane
covenants, biblical, 290
Creation
    before, 264
    return to the beginning of (*see* return to beginnings)
creation myths, 79, 81, 128-29, 203-4, 289, 310, 378. *See also* cosmogony(ies)
creative writers, 319

INDEX

Crocker, John, 374
Cruxent, José Maria, 161–62
cultural evolution, xxx
    Darwin on, 1–7
    psychological development and, xxix
    stages of (*see also* fraternal clan)
        brief psychotic disorder and, 58–59
        latency phase and, 225–26, 248–49
cultural periods from prehistory to the Urban Revolution, xxx. *See also* High Neolithic; Neolithic; Paleolithic; Upper Paleolithic; Urban Revolution
cultural unconscious, 358–59
cunnilingus as search of the female phallus, 366, 369
curare, ceramic bowls to hold, 176, 240f, 395, 399f
curare-tipped darts, 176, 240f, 395, 399f
Cursus (Wiltshire, England), 256, 261

D

Darwin, Charles, 17, 128–29, 154
    aboriginal cultures and, 6, 17, 23
    on Africa as birthplace of humanity, 129–30
    The Descent of Man, and Selection in Relation to Sex, 3–4, 23
    Freud and, 1, 5, 6, 8–10, 23–24
    on natural selection, sexual selection, and cultural evolution, 1–7
    On the Origin of Species, 1–3, 9
    photograph, 2f
    psychoanalytic concepts borrowed from evolutionary theory of, 4–5, 8–9 (*see also* Freud, Sigmund: Darwin and)
de Waal, Frans
    on animal sexual behavior, 115, 218–19
    chimpanzee behavior and, 114–15, 355, 373, 375, 381
Deacon, Terrence W., 124–27
death
    entering the mouth of, 82f
    Ernest Becker on, 149, 207, 262
    fear of, 207
    Frances Tustin on autism and, 94
    John Weir Perry on, 41
    of loved ones, 147
    Mircea Eliade and, 80, 222, 264, 286, 309, 311–12
    Paleolithic funerals and awareness of, 147–53
    repression and, 15–16, 149
    spirits and, 97, 134, 152
    and the unconscious, Freud on, 143
    undergoing, 47–48
    See also oral triad of wishes
death and rebirth, 56, 88
    John Weir Perry on psychosis and, 39–40
    myth of, 75–76, 78, 87, 91, 95, 101, 103–04, 147, 152–53
    phylogenetic project of psychoanalysis and, 100–105
    See also funerary rituals; rebirth
Death and Unity, psychomythic stage, 293–94, 313, 323
death instinct, 112, 326, 368
    nature of, 326
death wishes, repressed, 15–16
defense mechanisms, 34, 146, 151, 181
    Géza Róheim on, 30–32, 151
    object relations and, 341

451

rituals as, 213-16
Delfin (Yanomami shaman), 178-80, 194f, 237f
delusions, 316, 319-20, 340, 363, 364
    cultures and, 55, 57
    defensive function, 54
    Freud on, 37, 54
    John Weir Perry on, 39-43, 46, 53-54
    of Schreber, 53-54
demons
    ancient New Year festivals and, 285-87
    animism and, 15
    exorcism, 80, 83f, 370
    Freud on, 15-16, 291
    Géza Róheim on, 31
    and the mouth, 80, 83f, 369-70
    See also Devil; evil spirits
dependency
    of child on parents, 12, 31
    Erikson on psychosocial development and, xxxviii
depression, 366
Desmonde, William H., 211-12
Devil, 43-44, 46
    Christ and, 43-44, 46
devour, wish to, 87, 154, 209, 367
devoured
    fear of being, 366
    wish to be, 87, 367
    See also cannibalism
devouring aspect of great mother, 77-78
disembodied soul, 86, 88, 152
    mouth as passageway for soul's disembodiment, 77, 80, 96
dolmens, 252
dominance and submission
    anality and, 114, 375
    in chimpanzees, 114, 117-18, 375, 380-81
    See also alpha male
dorje (ritual object), 259, 279f
Douglas, Mary, 385
dragon-slaying metaphor, 71, 267-68
dragons, 69
    mouths of, 70-71, 79, 84f
    Jesus Christ and, 77, 79
dreams, 150-52, 384-85
    Freud on, 11-13, 55, 270, 384
    Jacob's dream, 203
    Jung on, 357-58, 384
    myth and, 11-12
    shamanism and, 213
drive theory, 111-12. See also instinct(s)
duality, 317, 322. See also two-ness
Durrington Walls (Wiltshire, England), 271

E

Earth. See Mother Earth
eaten, dread of being, 366
Edgar, Blake, 127-29
ego, 342
    Freud on body and, 121
    Herman Nunberg on, 316-17
    incest and, 247
    and the mouth, 75
    nature of, 121
    Otto Rank on the, 207, 245, 268-69, 308
    synthetic function, 316-17
ego consciousness, 267-68
ego development, 146, 268
    cognitive function and, 146
    hero myth and, 75, 269, 271-72, 308

libido development and, 146
ego integrity vs. despair, 328
Egypt, ancient, 49f, 231f, 232f, 239f
    kingship in, 47–50, 49f, 90f, 288
    New Year festivals, 47–50
    See also ritual of opening the mouth
Egyptian calendar, 300f
Egyptian cosmogony, 378
Egyptian cosmos, 347f
Egyptian mythology, 79, 88, 92, 218. *See also* Egypt
Egyptian pyramids, 49f, 296f
Eliade, Mircea, 220–22, 258, 309–12
    ancient New Year festivals and, 283–87
    on construction of homes, 202
    on death, 80, 222, 264, 286, 309, 311–12
    on fertility, 222, 260–61, 263
    on fire, 258–60
    on Maypole celebrations, 263, 271
    sexuality and, 220, 259
    on sky gods, 266–67
    on tools and technology, 221–22, 258–59
    on vegetation and agriculture, 221–22, 260–61, 263–65
embodied mind, 345
embodiment
    autism and, 85–88, 91–95
    mouth as passageway for the soul's, 77, 79
    psychomythic task of, 87 (*see also* ritual of opening the mouth)
    See also disembodied soul
Emerson, Tom, 250
end of the world, 319–20
endopsychic perceptions, 346–47
England, 201, 251–56, 275f, 276f, 277f

Enrique (Yanomami shaman), 177–79, 389–90
envy, 213–16, 367. *See also* jealousy
Erikson, Erik H., 74, 110–11, 206, 384–85
    on adolescence, 111, 282
    on autism, 111, 197
    on autocosmic play, 335–36
    description and characterization of, xxxvii–xxxviii
    encounter with, xxxix
    on faith, 110, 328–29
    on hope, xxxviii, 328
    on identity, 110–11, 197, 282
    photograph, xxxix
    at "Vital Involvement in Old Age" conference, xxxvii–xxxix
    See also psychosocial development
Erikson, Joan, xxxvii, xxxviii
eternal now, 196, 323
eternal return, 96, 283–87, 290
    defined, 285
ethical order, 40, 320–21. *See also* morality
euhemerism, 24
evil spirits, 96, 200, 217. *See also* demons; Devil
evolution, 107
    Baldwinian, 125–26
    hominin, 127–31
    See also cultural evolution; Darwin, Charles; natural selection
evolutionary anthropology, 23–24
exogamy, totemic, 14, 17–18, 21. *See also* incest taboo
exorcism, 80, 83f, 370. *See also* demons
Eynan, Israel, 101–2, 199

F

fairy tales, 208-10
faith
    Erikson on, 110, 328-29
    mortality and, 328-29
    in religion/spirituality and the supernatural, 110, 174, 206, 328-29, 343
fall of man (The Fall), 63, 225-26, 318
family romance, 269
fantasies
    mythology and, 11-12
    primal, 10-11, 334
father
    cannibalizing the, 19, 30, 154, 211, 247, 361
    Lord of the Four Quarters: Myths of the Royal Father (Perry), 40, 46, 351
    taboos and the, 27-28
    See also under great mother/mother goddess
fathering, as metaphor, 28, 246-47
Feast of Ingathering, 52, 272
feasts
    funerary, 95-96, 98, 148, 152, 156-57, 272
    seasonal, 271
    See also totemic feasts
fecal stick, 197, 209
feces, 114, 196, 209-10
    clay and, 223-24
Fenichel, Otto, 366, 369-70
Ferenczi, Sándor, 29
    on anality, 210
    on human history and ego development, 248, 360
    on oral stage, 366
    symbolism and, 121-22
    Thalassa, 360
fertility, 222-24, 245, 258-60, 298f
    goddesses and, 171
    Mircea Eliade on, 222, 260-61, 263
    phalluses and, 217-18, 252-53
    storm gods and, 245-46
fertility rites, 261-65, 272. *See also* New Year festivals
fetal position in burials, 101-3, 134, 148, 360
Feuerbach, Ludwig, 24
Figan (chimpanzee), 118, 380-81
Finno-Ugric creation myth, 310
fire, 262, 285, 303f
    Bergdamara and, 312-13
    early use of, 132, 186f
    metallurgy and fires of passion, 256-57
    Mircea Eliade on, 258-60
    myths of the origin of, 267-68, 312-13
    sexual symbology, 259-60
fire ring, 186f
Flammarion Engraving, 350f
Fordham, Michael, 359
four-ness, 314
France, 102, 165-68
Frankfort, Henri, 288-89
fraternal clan (stage in cultural evolution), 22, 59, 61
    evolution from primal/patriarchal horde to, 18-20, 22
    Oedipus complex and, 105, 120
Frazer, James George, 18-20, 312-13
Freeman, Derek, 26
Freud (chimpanzee), 354-55, 376-77
Freud, Martin, 9

Freud, Sigmund, 384
- aboriginal cultures and, 13–17
- anthropology and, 23–28
- collective unconscious and, 21, 357–59
- Darwin and, 1, 5, 6, 8–10, 23–24
- on demons, 15–16, 291
- on dreams, 11–13, 55, 270, 384
- on God, 337–38, 340–41
- as "godless Jew," 290–91, 338
- on metaphysics, 346
- on neurosis, 28, 270
- on Oedipus complex, 12–13, 271
- overview of, 9–11
- photograph of, 9f
- phylogenetic project of psychoanalysis and, 8–13
- on primal horde, 18, 20–21, 31, 172, 291, 355
- religion and, 337 (*see also Future of an Illusion*)
- writings (*see also Totem and Taboo*)
  - *The Future of an Illusion*, 22, 143, 338
  - *The Interpretation of Dreams*, 13, 270
  - "Overview of the Transference Neuroses," 29–30
  - *A Phylogenetic Fantasy: Overview of the Transference Neuroses*, 29–30
- *See also* phylogenetic project of psychoanalysis; *Totem and Taboo*; specific stages of psychosexual development

Freud, W. Ernest ("Ernst"), 9, 116, 204
Fruitfulness, psychomythic stage, 323, 325, 327

funerals
- funeral megalith, 258
- Paleolithic funerals and awareness of death, 147–53

funerary feasts, 95–96, 98, 148, 152, 156–57, 272

funerary rituals
- mouth, soul, and, 91, 95–98
- *See also* ritual of opening the mouth

fusion. *See* chaos; oneness

Future of an Illusion, The (Freud), 22, 143, 338

G

Gaddini, Eugenio, 68n2
"Ganesha Wins the Mango" (Hindu story), 337
Garden of Eden, 46, 318, 361
- Upper Paleolithic as a kind of, 175–81, 225
gardens, 158, 394–95
Geigerich, Wolfgang, 359–60
gender
- and the threat of opposite, 42
- *See also* matriarchy; patriarchy
genetic mutation, 2, 159, 160
genital stage, 281–82
- displaying, battling, courtships, and mating, 117–19, 380–81
genitals. *See* phallus(es); testicles; vaginas; vulvas; yoni
ghosts, 134. *See also* spirits
Gift: The Form and Reason for Exchange in Archaic Societies, The (Mauss), 216–17
gift giving, 212–17
gifting-and-receiving rituals, 213–16

Gimbutas, Marija, 171–72, 223, 254
Glover, Edward, 366–68
Göbekli Tepe (Turkey), 137
God, 315, 317
    belief in, 342
    Freud on, 337–38, 340–41
    Matti Hyrck on, 342–43
    nature of, 342
    Oskar Pfister on, 338–40
    political leaders and, 344
    relationship with, 352–53
    See also atheism; king-god; "Mouth of God"; Yahweh; *specific gods*
God-ing, 342
God images, 315, 342–43
"God-Intoxicated," 362–63
god-kings, 40–41, 50, 343, 353
    king-gods and, 20, 40–41, 50, 283, 343, 352–53
goddesses, 218, 351
    and the sun, 299f, 347f
    See also great mother/mother goddess; *specific goddesses*
Golden Bough, The (Frazer), 20
good-bye, signaling, 113, 119, 372–75
Goodall, Jane
    on chimpanzee behavior
        courtship and copulation, 118–19, 375–77
        greeting and separation behavior, 113–14, 371–74
        hierarchies and dominance, 114, 117–18, 375, 380–81
        mother–infant relations, 113, 371–73, 376–77
gorillas, 109, 114, 124–25

grace, fall from. *See* fall of man
gratitude, 213, 215, 217
graves. *See* burials
great mother goddess cults, 171–72, 211
great mother/mother goddess, 144, 254, 342
    devouring aspect, 77–78
    father gods and, 19, 40, 172–73, 246
    fertility and, 246, 252–53, 260, 289
    Freud on, 19, 172–73
    genitalia and, 171, 174
    matriarchy, patriarchy, and, 19, 171–74
    Neolithic and, 171, 223, 246, 252
    Paleolithic and, 144, 171, 174, 223
    Venus figurines and, 171, 174, 223
    See also High Neolithic; matriarchy; Neolithic; Paleolithic
Great Temple of Tenochtitlan, Mexico City, 99f
Green Lion of European alchemy, 83f
greeting behavior, 104, 113, 214, 371–75
    bonding and, 113–14, 371–75
    dominance, submission, and, 114
    mother–infant, 104, 110, 113, 146, 153, 371, 373
    oral stage and, 113, 146
greeting ceremonial, 110–11, 371, 373
greeting ritualizations, 110–11, 353–54, 382
Grosman, Leore, 148
Grossman, William I., 28, 292–93
Grotstein, James S., 320
Grotte de Font-de-Gaume, 165
guayuco (loin cloth), 243f, 389, 401f
guilt. *See* original sin

H

Hacilar, Turkey, 101, 200

Haeckel, Ernst, xxxii, 7f, 7–10, 360
Hainuwele, 220–21
hallucinations, 267, 363–64
    John Weir Perry on, 38–43, 53–54
hallucinogenic experiences, 181, 365. *See also* yopo ceremony
harvest, 49, 206, 211, 217, 221–22, 262, 264. *See also* planting and harvest rituals
Hathor (Egyptian cow goddess), 299f
Häutler, Adolf, 345–46
hearths, 132, 162, 256
heaven, 266, 267
    gate of, 203
    gods, goddesses, and, 286, 378, 387f
    sacred marriage of earth and, 284–85
    See also seven heavens
Hebrews, 203, 285, 290
Heckelman site (Ohio), 271–72
hekuras (animal spirits), 158, 177–9, 181 *See also* animal spirits
hell, 44
    mouth of, 77, 82f
Henderson, Joseph L., 358–59
Hermann, Imre, 108–9
hero mythology
    ego development and, 75, 269, 271–72, 308
    the hero looks to the sky, 265–73
    Lord Raglan on, 269–70
    Otto Rank on, 245, 268–70
    phallic stage and, 268
    and structure of psyche, 308
    See also mouth; Oedipus complex
hero system, culture/society as a, 262
Herzog-Schröder, Gabriele, 207, 214–15

hierarchies and dominance in chimpanzees, 114, 117–18, 375, 380–81
hieros gamos (sacred marriage), 260, 285
High Neolithic, 136
    imagining our way into the, 258–61
    large earthworks and ambition, 249–51
    phallic stage and, 144–45, 246, 248, 254, 268, 271
    See also Oedipus complex
Himalayas, Nepali, 201–2, 228f, 237f, 241f, 259, 266
Hindu stories, 77, 337
historical eras. *See* cultural periods
Hoffer, Willi, 369
Hoffs, Joshua A., 156, 368
Hofle de Szabadics, Eva, 186f
Holmström, Reijo, 109, 114
Homo erectus, 132, 135–36, 138f
Homo habilis, 127–32
hope and trust, Erikson on, xxxviii, 328
Horus, 47–49, 79, 90f
Hoti people, Venezuela, 176, 207, 240f, 393f, 401f, 402f, 403f
    animals and, 158
    and killing of the beast, 388–92
    modernizing process, 224
    villages, 158, 229f, 230f, 393f, 401f, 402f
house building rituals, 199–202
house(s)
    as *imago mundi* (image of the world), 202–03
    round, 199, 227f, 228f, 229f, 241f
    and the self, 199–202
Houston, Jean, 365
human sacrifice, 20, 201, 250, 255, 262–64

Hume, David, 24
hunting, 161. *See also* killing; spears; tapir
hunting magic, 158, 163-64, 168, 174
Huxley, Aldous, 181, 383
Huxley, Julian, 109-10, 353, 382-83
Hyrck, Matti, 342-43
hysteria, conversion, 29, 273
hysterical personality, 273

I
ice ages, 29, 165
    latency phase and, 248, 360
icons, 124
idealism of adolescents, 282
identity
    in adolescence, 78, 283, 307
    Erikson on, 110-11, 197, 282
    See also other; otherness
inbreeding, 117, 379
Incan creation myth, 203-4
incest
    Garden of Eden and, 361
    metaphorical, 247
    See also Oedipus complex
incest taboo, 18
    in apes, 109
    "The Horror of Incest" (*Totem and Taboo*), 13-14
    incestuous desires and, 14
    latency phase, sexual inhibitions, and, 117, 379-80
    See also exogamy
incestuous wish to return to womb, 366
incorporation, cannibalism and, 16, 19, 155-56, 167

"index," a category of referential association, 124
India, 218, 258, 336. *See also* tantra
infanticide, 23, 247
Ingathering, Feast of, 52, 272
inheritance. *See* genetic mutation
inheritance of acquired characteristics. *See* psycho-Lamarckism
inherited predispositions, 10
initiation rituals, 55-56, 76, 312
    adolescent, 78, 111, 119, 312
instinct(s)
    archaic inheritance of, 111-12
    renunciation of, 16, 354
        sacrifice and, 204-9
    See also drive theory; ritualizations and social instincts
interpretation, Freud on, 384
Interpretation of Dreams, The (Freud), 13, 270
introjection, 366, 368-70
Isaacs, S., 386

J
Jacob's dream, 203
jawbones, 103, 135, 139f, 148, 151-52
Jaynes, Julian, 364-65
jealousy, 6, 115-16, 213-16, 221
Jelínek, Jan, 157
Jericho, 198-99, 227f
Jesus Christ, 43-44
    in art, 77-80
    and the Devil, 43-44, 46
    dragon's mouth and, 77, 79
Jews. *See* Freud, Sigmund: as "godless Jew"; Hebrews; Judaism
Jimmy (patient)

commentary on his drawings, 68–69
  language phases of treatment, 69–70
drawings, 65, 66f, 67f, 68
  mouth, 70–71, 73–74, 85
  phases of, 68
life history, 65
preoccupation with the mouth, 70–72, 74–75, 85, 88
repetitive behaviors, 65, 93
symbolic material, 69, 71–73
Johanson, Donald, 127–29
Johnson, Mark, 345
Jonah, 78, 82f
Jonas, A. David, 375
Jonas, Doris F., 375
Jones, Ernest, 121
Judaism, 96–97, 290. See also Hebrews; Yahweh
Jung, Carl Gustav
  on archetypes, 358–59
  collective unconscious and, 21, 357–59
  on dreams, 357–58, 384
  friendship with Freud, 357
Jupiter, 324, 350

K

Kabarole (chimpanzee), 123
Kakama (chimpanzee), 123
Kakar, Sudhir, 336
Kardiner, Abram, 26
Katmandu, Nepal, 278f, 279f, 348f
Kellogg, Rhoda, 51, 68
Khat, 87–88
Khirokitia, Cyprus, 101
  houses in, 101, 227f
Khonds, human sacrifice among, 264

Kierkegaard, Søren, 318
killing
  of the beast, 179, 270, 388–92, 393f
  See also cannibalism; sacrifice
king-gods, 40, 289
  god-kings and, 20, 40–41, 50, 283, 343, 352–53
  great mother goddesses and, 19, 40, 172–73, 246
kingship
  in ancient Egypt, 47–50, 49f, 90f, 288
  in China, 50–51
  in Israel, 53
  in Mesopotamia, 288–90
  Toltec, 52
Kirchner, Horst, 168
Klein, Melanie, 217, 317, 344, 349
Koko (gorilla), 124–25
Kris, Ernst, 316
Kroeber, Alfred L., 27
kundalini, 81, 85f, 334
Kwakwaka'wakw initiation ritual, 312

L

Lacan, Jacques, 386
ladders, 71, 77, 203
Laing, R. D., 383
Lakoff, George, 345
Lamarck, Jean-Baptiste, 4f, 360. See also psycho-Lamarckism
lamps, oil, 164, 169, 299f
Lang, Andrew, 17
language, 69–70, 149, 197
  evolution, brain, and, 364
  Lacan and, 386
  role in Upper Paleolithic, 148

symbolic nature of, 122
Lascaux cave (France), 165, 167–70
latency phase, 248
    chimpanzees and, 108
    Ferenczi on, 248, 360
    sexual inhibitions, incest taboos, and, 117, 379–80
    and stages of cultural evolution, 225–26, 248–49
Leakey, Louis S. B., 129–30, 132
Leakey, Mary, 131
Leakey, Richard, 148–49
Les Eyzies-de-Tayac-Sireuil, France, 148, 165, 183f, 184f, 187f, 189f
Levy, Gertrude, 260
Lewin, Bertram, 87, 367–68
libido, definition and use of the term, xxx
libido development, 146. *See also* anal stage; genital stage; latency phase; oral stage; phallic stage
Lieberman, Mort, xxxviii
lingam, 344, 348f. *See also* phallus(es)
"Little Red Cap"/"Little Red Riding Hood," 208–9
Lordkipanidse, David, 132
Lorenz, Konrad, 119–20, 382
loss, psychoanalysis as a psychology of, 372
Lothane, Zvi, 53
Lower Paleolithic, 131–33
Lubbock, John, 24–25
Lumsden, C.J., 32
Luxor, Egypt, 49f, 231f, 232f, 239f
Lyell, Charles, 2–3

M

magic and magical thinking, 16, 167, 206, 212, 260
    Alfred Storch on, 55–56
    animism and, 15
    Arnold Modell on, 170
    cannibalism and, 16, 155–57
    Ernst Cassirer on, 206
    fertility, reproduction, and, 170–71, 217–19, 352
    Freud on, 15–16
    gods, goddesses, and, 351–52
    hunting magic, 158, 163–64, 168, 174
    omnipotence of thoughts and, 15–16
    sacrifice and, 206, 219, 351–52
    sexual enlightenment and, 218
magical calendar, 301f
Magritte, René, 167
Mahler, Margaret, 62–63
Maidu creation myth, 311
Malinowski, Bronislaw, 27
Malta, 171, 251–52
mandalas, 39, 39f, 51, 51f, 52f, 53. *See also* quadrated world; quadrated world forms
Mann, Thomas, 319
Maori gods, 387f
Maranda, Elli and Pierre, 308
Maringer, Johannes, 260
marriage. *See* sacred marriage
Mars, cosmological attributes of, 324–25
Masters, Robert, 365
masts of India, 362–63
mating. *See* copulation/sexual intercourse
matriarchy, 33, 35, 171–72, 174
    Freud on, 19, 172–73

great mother goddesses and, 19, 171–74
Johann Jacob Bachofen on, 25–26, 171, 359
as preceding patriarchy, 19, 25–26, 33, 35, 41, 172–74
Robert Briffault on, 174, 359
Sally Binford on, 173–74
Matsuzawa, Tetsuro, 113
Mauss, Marcel, 216–17
May, Rollo, 307, 319
Maypole celebrations, 262–64, 271
McPherron, Shannon, 131
megalithic monuments, 137, 252–54. *See also* megaliths; Stonehenge
megalithic tomb, entrance to a, 277f
megaliths, 252, 258, 260, 271
circle of, 275f
funeral, 258
images engraved onto, 260
Meher Baba, 362–63
Meiendorf, Germany, reindeer sacrifice, 206
Meissner, William W., 343
melancholia, 366
Mellaart, James, 199, 223
Meltzer, Donald, 317
memories, archaic, 10, 120, 291
Mendel, Gregor, 8
menhirs (tall stones), 251–52, 254, 260–63
Mercury, cosmological attributes of, 325
Meriahs, 264
Merkur, Daniel, 11–12
Mesopotamia, ancient, 204
New Year festival, 288–92
metallurgists, 257, 259–60, 278f
metallurgy and the fires of passion, 256–57
metaphors, 331–34, 345

bodily, 332–34, 344–45
and consciousness, 365
Middle Paleolithic, 133–37
millenarian myths, 320
Mitrani, Theodore and Judith, 86
Modell, Arnold, 170
money, 212
anality and, 197, 210, 217
origins of, 211–12
toilet training, trade, and, 209–17
monkey skulls, 183f, 396–97
Monk's Mound (Cahokia, Illinois), 249–50
Montignac, France. *See* Lascaux cave
Mookerjee, Ajit, 330f, 334–35
moon, 79, 97–98, 250, 255, 265, 267, 285, 309–11, 313, 323, 326, 333, 386
morality
Darwin and, 5
Freud on, 346, 351
religion and, 340
superego and, 340
See also ethical order
mother
experienced as cannibalistic demon, 31
returning to the, 98, 148, 152, 366, 368
mother of us all, 389
Mother Earth, 55, 152, 222, 259, 324
mother goddess. *See* great mother/mother goddess; Mother Earth
Mother Nature, xxxiv, 195, 206
mother-infant bonding, orality and, 371–75
mother-infant greeting behavior, 104, 110, 113, 146, 153, 371, 373
mother-infant relationship, 110–11
in chimpanzees (*see under* Goodall, Jane)

See also bonding and attachment
mothering
    as metaphor, 28, 246–47
    See also orality
Moundville, Alabama, 250
Mount Carmel. *See* Skhul Cave
Mousterian tools, 103, 133
mouth
    as birth canal of reborn hero, 76, 78–79
    demons and, 80, 83f, 369–70
    hero entering the mouth of death, 82f
    as hero's passageway to death, 77–78
    as integral consciousness, 77, 80–81, 84f, 85f
    orality and, 73–75
    "The Primal Significance of the Tongue" (Bonnard), 368–69
    soul's departure through, 76f, 80, 83f, 84f, 96–98
    soul's entrance into, 76f, 76–77, 83f, 87, 91, 98
    spirits and, 80, 84f, 87, 91, 96
    See also devoured; Jimmy; orality; ritual of opening the mouth
"Mouth of God," 81, 85f, 349f
mouth symbolism in autism, Bettelheim on, 72, 92
mud, 243f, 388
    ash and, 130–31
mud bricks and mud-brick houses, 199, 231f
mud oven (*budare*), 232f, 389
Myth of the Eternal Return, The (Eliade), 283–86
mythic time vs. historical time, 284
mythology
    endopsychic myths, 346–47
    fantasies and, 11–12
    Freud on, 11
    as hero's passageway to death, 77–78
    as hero's passageway to rebirth, 76, 78–79
    origin of, 11–12
    as passageway for soul's disembodiment, 80
    as passageway for soul's embodiment, 79
    Otto Rank on, xi–xii, 11, 245, 268–70
    symbolism of, 75–77
    See also cosmogony(ies); Egyptian mythology; psychomythic development

N

Nágera, Humberto, 368
Napier, John, 129
Narcissus, myth of, 268, 307
Natufian communities, 102, 199
natural selection, 1–5
Nazca Lines, Peru, 250–51
Neanderthals, 133–35, 155
Nena (Panare girl), 395, 397, 398, 400f
Neolithic
    anal stage and, 144
    great mother/mother goddess and, 171, 223, 246, 252
    See also anal stage; High Neolithic; trade
Nepali Himalayas, 201–2, 228f, 237f, 241f, 259, 266
Ness Brodgar, 271
Neumann, Erich, 268, 359–60
new birth, 42, 54, 290
    as reconciliation of opposites, 50
    See also rebirth

new society, 42, 50, 54, 283, 290
New Year festivals
    chiao (Taoist ritual) China, 50–51
    demons and, 285–87
    in Egypt, 47–50
    in Israel, 53
    Mesopotamian, 288–92
    Mircea Eliade and, 283–87
    Toltec, 52
Ngaju Dayak, 81, 203
Nganaoa, 78–79
Nietzsche, Friedrich, 24, 345
"not me," 72, 159. *See also* otherness
numinous experience, 110–11
Nunberg, Herman, 316–17
nursing, 63, 74, 146, 214, 371–73, 389
Nut (Egyptian goddess), 347f, 378, 387f

O

object-choice, stage of, 16
object relations, xxix, xxx, 16, 73–74, 86, 104, 112, 145, 150, 175, 181, 195, 246, 261, 336, 339, 341, 353, 373
obsessional neurosis, 14, 22, 29, 61, 208
"Oedipus and Castration Complex Models in Monkeys" (Hermann), 108–9
Oedipus complex
    alpha male dynamics and, 33, 105, 291, 352
    copulation interference and, 115–17, 376–80
    Freud on, 12–13, 271
    as metaphor, 246–49
    overview, 248
    phallic stage and, 246 (*see also* phallic stage)
    socialization and, 28, 115, 246–47
    See also hero mythology
Oedipus Rex (Sophocles), 13, 27, 247, 268
Ogden, Thomas H., 86, 111–12
oil lamps, 164, 169, 299f
Old Testament, 78, 82f, 203, 218, 290
    cosmogonies of, 318
    See also Yahweh
Oldowan, 132
oneness, xxxiv, xxxv, 81, 197, 248, 293, 309–11, 313, 315, 326, 332
"ontogeny recapitulates phylogeny"/ biogenetic law, 22, 25, 33, 225–26
    archetypes and, 359 (*see also* archetypes)
    Arnold Modell and, 170
    disproved by Gregor Mendel, 8
    Edwin Wallace and, 24
    Ernst Haeckel and, 7–8
    Ferenczi on, 360
    Freud and, 10, 11, 17, 22, 25
    Freud's phylogenetic fantasy and, 29–30
    John Weir Perry and, 37, 43, 46, 281
    Joshua Hoffs and, 368
    Jung on, 357–60
    Lorenz and, 120
    Róheim and the shift to ontogenetic explanation, 30–33
"ontology recapitulates philology," (Adler, Nathan), 333
opening the mouth. *See* ritual of opening the mouth
opposites
    clash of, 48
    threat of opposite, 42
    threat of reversal of, 42, 48, 289

See also cosmic conflict; reconciliation of opposites; union of opposites
oral stage
    earlier sucking stage followed by later cannibalistic stage, 73
    Ferenczi's observations on, 366
    See also, orality
oral triad of wishes (Lewin), 87, 367–68. *See also* devoured
orality
    cannibalism and, 73–74, 154, 156, 366–68
    greeting behavior, mother-infant bonding, and, 371–75 (*see also* greeting behavior)
    in psychoanalytic theory, 366–70
    and the soul, 146, 151
    See also funerary rituals; mouth; nursing
order. *See* Transformation and the Establishment of Order psychomythic stage
original sin, 18, 21, 333, 361
Orinoco, 158, 177, 212, 388, 394
Osiris, 47–48, 50, 88
Ostow, Mortimer, 343
other, the
    Paleolithic cannibalism and internalization of, 154–57
    self and, 111, 197
otherness
    "not me," 72, 159
    recognition of, 74, 197
    subjectivity and, 197
Ötzi (Iceman), 257
ovens, 256
    mud, 232f

P

painting. *See* art
paleoanthropology, 129
Paleolithic
    Lower Paleolithic, 131–33
    Middle Paleolithic, 133–36
    oral stage and, 144
    See also Upper Paleolithic
paleologic thought, 56–57, 287
Panare people (Venezuela), 183f, 207, 233f, 242f, 399f
    hunting, gathering, and tending the garden, 394–98, 400f
paradise, 11, 29. *See also* fall of man
paranoia, 53–55. *See also* magic and magical thinking
Parker Pearson, Mike, 271
Parthenogenesis, 222, 253, 260
patriarchy
    great mother goddesses and, 19, 171–74
    matriarchy as preceding, 19, 25–26, 33, 35, 41, 172–74
    See also under fraternal clan
patricide
    metaphorical, 247
    See also father: cannibalizing the
Patterson, Francine "Penny," 124
Paul, Robert, 11
pegs, 204–5, 230f
penises. *See* phallus(es)
Perry, John Weir
    biographical sketch, 38–40
    case vignettes of psychotic patients, 43–46
    on delusions, 39–43, 46, 53–54
    The Far Side of Madness, 40

on hallucinations, 38-43, 53-54
Lord of the Four Quarters: Myths of the Royal Father, 40, 46, 351
photograph, 38f
phylogenetic project of psychoanalysis and, 53-54, 57-59
recurring categories/themes/images observed by, 41-42, 47-50, 53-54, 289-90
Roots of Renewal in Myth and Madness: The meaning of psychotic episodes, 46, 281
schemas based on the work of, 59-60
The Self in Psychotic Process, 39, 46
See also brief psychotic disorder
petroglyphs in Venezuela, 189f, 190f
Pfister, Oskar, 341
  Freud and, 338-41
  on God and religion, 338-40
phallic stage, 246, 254
  High Neolithic and, 144-45, 246, 248, 254, 268, 271
  See also High Neolithic; Oedipus complex
phallus(es)
  female, 366-67, 369
  and fertility, 217-18, 252-53
  as metaphor, 248
  mouth and, 334, 366-67, 369
  sculptures, 344, 348f
  search for the female, 366, 369
  stone, 251-56
  See also menhirs
philosophy, the psychomythic in, 344-47
phylogenetic fantasy, Freud's, 25, 29-30, 33, 154

Phylogenetic Fantasy: Overview of the Transference Neuroses, A (Freud), 29-30
phylogenetic project of psychoanalysis, 8-13
  death, rebirth, and, 100-105
  Ferenczi's contributions to, 360
  ideas upon which to advance the, 33-34
  John Weir Perry and, 53-54, 57-59
  Schreber and, 53-55
  See also psychomythic development
phylogeny. See "ontogeny recapitulates phylogeny"/biogenetic law
Piaroa hanging baby basket, 243f
Pierce, Charles Sanders, 124
"pink ladies" (chimpanzees), 376
planting and harvest rituals, xxxv, 136, 268, 271-72, 274, 292
politics, the psychomythic in, 343-44
Polynesian creation myth, 378
pottery, 200, 223
predicates, 56
Prengler de Benveniste, Adriana (wife), 115, 125, 161, 212-13, 236f, 377
primal fantasies, 10-11, 334
primal horde, 29
  Freud on, 18, 20–21, 31, 172, 291, 355
primal horde myths, 31
Primal Other, 328-29
primal scene, 12, 31, 170
primary process thinking, 57, 340-41
primates. See chimpanzees
psyche. See soul
psychedelic experience, 365, 383
psycho-Lamarckism (psychological Lamarckism), xxxi-xxxii, 4, 23-24, 30, 126, 360
  defined, 23

Géza Róheim's rejection of, 30, 33
    of Herbert Spencer, 24
    Oedipus complex and, 105
    Totem and Taboo and, 11, 25, 291
psychodynamics
    from higher primate ritualizations
        to human, 120-30 (*see also under*
        ritualizations and social instincts)
    origin of, xxix
psychomythic, the
    in philosophy, 344-47
    in politics, 343-44
    in religion, 331-43
psychomythic development, 295
    schema of, 274, 292-95, 323
    See also phylogenetic project of
        psychoanalysis
psychomythic developmental stages, 314-15, 323
    Ascension and Conflict, 294, 314, 324, 325
    Birth and Separation, 294, 313, 324
    Death and Unity, 293-94, 313
    Fruitfulness, 325, 327
    Reconciliation of Opposites, 290, 327
    Relinquishing of Will, 326
    Transformation and the Establishment
        of Order, 294-95, 314, 323
psychomythic pyramid, 321-22, 323f
psychomythology, xxxvi, 293, 331, 347
psychosexual development, 295
    stages of, xxxvii, 314 (*see also* anal stage;
        genital stage; latency phase; oral
        stage; phallic stage)
psychosis
    as an attempt at recovery, 54
    as a process of self-healing, 39
    See also brief psychotic disorder;
        delusions; Perry, John Weir;
        schizophrenia
psychosocial development, 295
    Erikson's stages of, 314
        "Reflections on the Last Stage—and
        the First" (Erikson), 328-29
        on trust vs. mistrust stage, xxxviii,
        74, 110, 371
psychotherapy, 317-18, 331-33, 339, 355
psychotic patients
    categories/themes/images in, 41-42,
        47-50, 53-54, 289-90
    Freud's case of Schreber, 53-55
    See also brief psychotic disorder
Pusey, Anne, 117, 374, 379-80
pyramids, 249-50, 301f
    Egyptian, 49f, 296f
    Teotihuacan, in Mexico, 301

Q

quadrated world, 42, 54
quadrated world forms, 50, 290
Quetzalcoatl, 52

R

Raglan, Lord (FitzRoy Somerset), 200-1, 269-70
rahaka (arrow points), 214-15, 237f
Ram Dass, 342
Ramses II statue in Luxor, Egypt, 49f, 90f, 298f
Rank, Otto
    on ego, 207, 268-69, 308
    Ernest Becker and, 149, 207, 317

on fear of and denial of death, 149, 207
Freud on, xi-xii
on mythology, xi-xii, 11, 245, 268-70
rebirth, 50, 152
how to avoid the cycle of, 379
See also death and rebirth; new birth
recapitulation theory. See "ontogeny recapitulates phylogeny"/biogenetic law
reconciliation of opposites
new birth as a, 50, 290
See also union of opposites
Reconciliation of Opposites, psychomythic stage, 290, 323, 327
Redmond, Brian, 271-72
Reik, Theodore, 361
reindeer, 206, 208
ritual sacrifice, 206, 208, 211
religion, 24
Freud and, 337 (see also God: Freud on)
The Future of an Illusion, 22, 143, 338
the psychomythic in, 331-43
religious art, 51f, 349f
Relinquishing of Will, psychomythic stage, 323, 326
Renfrew, Colin, 252
repressed sexuality, 383-84
repression, 149, 317, 360
death and, 15-16, 149
"Respiratory Introjection" (Fenichel), 369-70
return of the repressed, 19
return to beginnings, 41-42, 48, 54. See also eternal return
Revelation, Book of, 319, 336
Rigaud, Jean-Philippe, 168

ritual of opening the mouth, 89f, 90f
function, 87-88
funerary rituals compared with, 87, 91, 95, 104
history, 100, 104
instruments used in, 89f
overview and nature of, 87-88
ritual sacrifice. See sacrifice
ritualization(s)
aggression-neutralizing behaviors and, x, 119-20, 214, 353
of chimpanzees, 320-24, 371-81
defined, 33, 109
teleonomic pressure of, 109
ritualizations and social instincts, primate, 108-12, 371
definitions and terminology, 33, 109, 371
evolution and, 5, 107
examples, 112-29
Julian Huxley on, 109-10, 353, 382-83
overview and nature of, 107-12, 371-81
psychodynamics and, 5, 35, 107, 112, 120-29, 291
survival instincts and, 33, 353
rituals
defense functions, 213-16
vs. ritualization, 109
See also funerary rituals; New Year festivals; planting and harvest rituals; sacrifice; psychomythic development; symbolic function
Róheim, Géza, 30f, 146-47, 151, 273
on cannibalism, 30-31
on defense mechanisms, 30-32, 151
rejection of psycho-Lamarckism, 30, 33

and the shift to an ontogenetic explanation, 30-33
Rokeach, Milton, 362
Romanes, George John, 32
Rosenfeld, David, 320
Rust, Alfred, 206, 208

S
sacral kingship, myth of, 37-8, 40-41, 43, 46, 58, 60, 105, 144, 226, 272, 274, 282-83, 288, 295, 307, 352,
sacred marriage, 42, 54, 283-85, 287, 289
　as union of opposites, 49, 289
sacrifice
　defensive functions, 351-52
　human, 20, 201, 250, 255, 262-64
　magic and, 206, 219, 351-52
　and renunciation of instinct, 204-9
　spirits and, 200, 208
sacrificial totemic feasts, 18-19, 22, 59, 61, 148
Sahasrara chakra (Mouth of God), 81, 85f, 349f
Saturn, cosmological attributes of, 323-24
Schaan, Denise, 251
schizophrenia, 55-57, 316-17
　chronic, 39, 58, 319, 362-63
　Perry's Jungian formulation of, 37, 39-40, 43
schizophrenic thought process, 55-56
Schreber, Daniel Paul, 53-55
seashells. *See* shells
secondary process thinking, 57, 340-41
self-awareness, 149, 307
　development of, 382
　See also other; otherness

self-consciousness, 24, 318, 364. *See also* subjectivity
separation-individuation, 336-37. *See also* Birth and Separation, psychomythic stage; Goodall, Jane
seven, significance of, 327-28
　Freud and, 328
seven heavens, 323-27
sexual enlightenment, 218-20, 222, 265, 269
sexual intercourse. *See* copulation/sexual intercourse
sexual selection, 3, 5-6
shamanic rituals, 79, 103. *See also* shamans
shamans, 166-68, 177-81, 213
　spirits and, 168, 178-79
　See also Delfin; Enrique
Shanidar, Big Cave of, 103
shells, 129, 148, 396
Shiva, 81, 85f, 334-37, 349f
Siegel, Barry L., 369
Silberer, Herbert, 327, 383-84
Silbury Hill, Wiltshire, England, 253, 277f
skeletons, 101-3, 134-35, 147-48
Skhul Cave (Israel), burial site at, 103, 135, 139f, 151
skullcaps and skullcap cups, 156-58
skulls
　human, 99f, 102, 129, 135, 138f, 155-58
　worship of, 153-54
　See also amulets; animal skulls
sky, 310
　the hero looks to the, 265-73
sky gods, 265-67, 350f
smelting, 256-58, 261, 312

smile signal, 110
smiling, 343
Smith, Roff, 271
Smith, William Robertson, 18–19, 26
snake symbolism, 85f, 203, 205, 260, 297f, 334
social body, 385
social instincts. *See* ritualizations and social instincts
socialization
    as metaphorical castration, 247–48
    Oedipus complex and, 28, 115, 246–47
    See also psychosocial development
Sophocles. *See Oedipus Rex*
sorcery, 15
soul, 71, 202
    of autistic child as unable or unwilling to embody, 85–88, 91–92
    Buddhism, cycle of rebirth, and, 378–79
    cannibalism and, 155–56, 167
    concept of, 15, 71, 95, 98, 100
        Paleolithic and the, xxxiv, 104, 108, 144–45, 152–53, 252
    and the hero, 77
    nature of, 342
    orality and, 146, 151 (*see also under* mouth)
    Ram Dass on, 342
    shamanic rituals and, 79, 103
    use of the term, 71, 86
    See also disembodied soul
soul images, 71
souling, 342
Spain. *See* Altamira Cave
spearpoints, 160–62, 184f, 392, 395, 400f
spears, hunting, 151, 164, 179, 391–92, 395, 400f. *See also* spearpoints
Spencer, Herbert, 24, 135
Spiegelberg, Frederic, 342
spirits, 15, 152–53, 181, 332, 345
    alcohol and, 221
    amulets and, 135, 157–59, 163, 167
    burial and, 200–01
    cannibalism and, 155–56
    death and, 97, 134, 152
    evil, 96, 200, 217 (*see also* demons)
    Freud on, 16, 291
    and the mouth, 80, 84f, 87, 91, 96
    sacrifice and, 200, 208
    shamans and, 168, 178, 179
    See also demons
Spring, William J., 319
Sproul, B., 203–4, 220, 310, 318
stone and the psychic center, the, 202–5
stone mortar, 185f
stone phallus, 251–56
stone spearpoint, 184f. *See also* spearpoints
stone tools
    hunting for stone tools with Miklos Szabadics Roka, 161–62
    Paleolithic, 184f
    and technological evolution, 160–63
    from southern England, 276f
    from southern France, Laugerie Basse, 184f
    from Venezuela, 185f
Stonehenge (Wiltshire, England), 254–56, 271, 276f
Storch, Alfred, 55–56
subjectivity, 333
    achievement of, 197

otherness and, 197
Sukkoth festival in ancient Israel, 52-53, 272
Sulawesi, 166, 201
Sullivan, Lawrence E., 320-21
sun, 55, 68, 255
    goddesses and the, 299f, 347f
    in mythology, 79, 204, 324
    swallowing the, 83f, 247f
sun disc, 297f
sun gods, 48, 50, 55, 260
sun stone, 302f
superego, 246, 340
survivals, 14, 23
symbiosis. *See* oneness
symbolic equation, 385-86
symbolic function
    chimpanzees, humans, and, 122-24
    Ernest Becker on, 149, 207
    evolution, 124-27
    human, 121-22, 383-86
    See also abstract thinking
Symbolic Order (Lacan), 386
symbolism, 122
    anagogic, 122, 383-84
    archaic inheritance of, 10, 291
    Ferenczi and, 121-22
symbolization of instincts and psychodynamics, xxix
synthetic function of the ego, 316-17
Szabadics, Eva Hofle de, 161, 186f
Szabadics, Jenny, 162
Szabadics Roka, Miklos, 161, 185f, 186f

T
"Taboo and Emotional Ambivalence" (*Totem and Taboo*), 14-15
taboos
    desire and, 14-15
    and the father, 27-28
    God and, 340
    related to treatment of the dead, 15
    sexual, 259-60 (*see also* incest taboo)
    of totemism, 18
tantra, 334-35
    tantric art, 81, 85f, 335, 349f
Taoist cosmogony, 310-11
Taoist ritual in ancient China, 50-51
tapir, butchering a, 158-59, 391-92, 393f
teleonomic pressure, 109
Temple of Karnak (Luxor, Egypt), 297f, 298f
Teotihuacan pyramid, 301f
terminal addition, principle of, 8
"Terror of History, The" (Eliade), 286
testicles, chimpanzees biting, 115, 381
Thalassa: A Theory of Genitality (Ferenczi), 360
threat of the reversal of opposites, 48, 289
three-ness, 259, 294, 309-10, 314
Tibetan Book of the Dead, The, 378-79
time
    cosmic, 196, 222, 225
    mythic, 284-85
    "The Regeneration of Time" (Eliade), 284-85
    return to beginning of (*see* return to beginnings)
Tobias, Phillip, 129
toilet training, 196, 205,
    money, trade, and, 209-11
Toltecs, 52

Tomasello, Michael, 373
"Tomb Is Womb, The" (Gimbutas), 254
tomb/womb, 95, 254
tombs, 101, 252-54, 258, 277f
tongue, 94, 368-69
totem
    defined, 18
    taboo against harming the, 18 (see also taboos)
Totem and Taboo: Some Points of Agreement between the Mental Lives of Savages and Neurotics (Freud)
    assumptions underlying, 34-35
    first edition cover, 17f
    Freud on the importance of, 1, 113
    overview, 13-23
totemic exogamy, 14, 17-18, 21. *See also* incest taboo
totemic feasts, 26, 154
    cannibalism and, 19, 154, 156-57
    Oedipus complex and, xxxii, 19, 22
    sacrificial, 18-19, 22, 59, 61, 148
    See also feasts
totemic fraternal clan. *See* fraternal clan
totemism, 26
    ancestor worship and, 14
    cannibalizing the father and, 361
    cultures and, 25
    first step away from, 173
    Oedipus complex and, 22
    principal taboos of, 18
    "The Return of Totemism in Childhood," 16-17
totuma shell, 396
trade, Neolithic, 199, 210-15
    toilet training, money, and, 209-17

Transformation and the Establishment of Order, psychomythic stage, 294-95, 314, 323
transitional objects, 159, 170
trauma, 147, 353
    Freud on, 146
    oral trauma and autism, 64, 74, 87
    Roheim on, 146-47
trees, symbolism of, 260-61, 263
Trump, David, 252
trust and hope, Erikson on, xxxviii, 328
trust vs. mistrust (psychosocial stage), Erikson on, xxxviii, 74, 110, 371
Tustin, Frances, 86, 93-95
    on autism, 61, 63-64, 86, 93-95
    letter from, 93
    on orality and oral stage, 61, 63-64, 72-74
two-ness, 313
    entry into, 197
Tylor, Edward B., 24-25
Tyson, Phyllis, 57, 282
Tyson, Robert L., 57, 282

U
Ultimate Other, 328-29
unconscious, 12, 14, 21, 28-30, 34, 57, 72, 75-76, 92, 104, 121-22, 134, 143, 146, 151-52, 205, 210, 214, 247, 267, 271, 293, 307, 315, 319-20, 341, 345, 358-59, 364, 367, 372, 383-84
union of opposites, 318, 335
    sacred marriage as, 49, 289
    See also reconciliation of opposites
union/unity. *See* Death and Unity psychomythic stage; oneness

universe
- man and the, 55
- man's quest for knowledge of the, 350f
- seven aspects of the, 321-22
- See also cosmology(ies); walls of the universe

Upper Paleolithic, 136, 143-81
- as a "Garden of Eden," 157-81, 225

Urban Revolution, 40-41, 46, 58-61, 145, 282, 287, 343

V

Vac, 218

vaginas, 254-56, 259, 294, 367
- deadly, 31, 76
- See also vulvas; yoni

vajra. See dorje

Vatcher, Faith de M., 253-54

Vatcher, Lance, 253-54

Venezuela. See Hoti people; Panare; Yanomami; Yavarana

Venus, 325

Venus figurines, 171, 174

Venus of Willendorf, 171

Villa de Leyva, Colombia, 251

violence
- of aboriginal cultures, 213
- See also aggression; cannibalism; hunting; sacrifice

von Domarus, Eilhard, 56

vulvas, 335
- in Paleolithic/Neolithic art, 171, 174, 187f
- See also yoni

W

Wallace, Edwin, 23-27

Wallauer, Bill, 123-24, 354-55, 374

Wallerstein, Robert, xxxviii

walls, Neolithic, xxxiv, 144, 195, 197-201, 219, 222

walls, Paleolithic See cave art

walls of the universe, xxxvii, 265, 295, 323, 331-32, 335, 354,

Washoe (chimpanzee), 124-25

Weaning, 74, 112, 248,
- in chimpanzees, 372, 377, 379
- See also oral stage

weaving
- examples, 241f, 243f
- and the fabric of reality, 224

Weigert-Vowinkle, Edith, 172

welcome dance, Yanomami, 212-13, 233f, 236f

West Kennet Long Barrow (Wiltshire, England), 253-54

White, Randall, 148

White, Tim D., 154-55

Wittels, Fritz, 29

will. See Relinquishing of Will, psychomythic stage

Wilson, E.O., 32

Winnicott, Donald W., 159, 170

Wolf-Man, Freud's case of the, 366

Wolff, Toni, 39

women. See matriarchy; mothering

Woodhenge, 250, 255

world center, 41, 47, 289

world-reforming idealism of adolescents, 282

Wrangham, William, 123
Wright, Karen, 250
writing, early examples of, 300f

Y
Yahweh, 52–53, 290
yantra, 334
Yanomami, 180, 207, 212–15
    gifting, giving, and taking among, 213–14
    lifestyle, 158, 180–81
    photographs, 182f, 191f, 194f, 233f, 236f
    tools, 177, 182f, 191f
        amulet, 158, 177, 182f, 191f
    welcome dance, 212, 213, 233f, 236f
    See also yopo ceremony
Yanomami shamans, 213. *See also* Delfin; Enrique
Yavarana, 207
yoni, 334–35, 348f. *See also* vulvas
yopo ceremony, 158, 177–81, 182f, 191f, 193f

Z
Zent, Stanford and Egleé, 176

About the Author

Daniel S. Benveniste, PhD, is a clinical psychologist with a private practice in Sammamish, Washington, near Seattle. He sees adults in counseling and psychodynamic psychotherapy. He is a Visiting Professor of Clinical Psychology at the Wuhan Mental Health Center, in the People's Republic of China. He writes professional articles and is the author of *The Interwoven Lives of Sigmund, Anna, and W. Ernest Freud: Three Generations of Psychoanalysis* (2015) and *The Venezuelan Revolution: A Critique from the Left* (2015) and is the editor of *Anna Freud in the Hampstead Clinic: Letters to Humberto Nágera* (2015). Originally from California, he earned his BA and MS in clinical psychology at San Francisco State University, his PhD at the California School of Professional Psychology in Berkeley/Alameda and was in supervision with Nathan Adler, PhD, for five years. He began his private practice in the San Francisco Bay Area where he was also Director of Training for two practicum programs, supervisor at the Mt. Zion Community Crisis Clinic, and professor of graduate students at The Wright Institute, California School of Professional Psychology, Alameda, and in the Department of Social Welfare at the University of California at Berkeley. From 1999 to 2010, he lived and worked in Caracas, Venezuela, where he maintained a private practice and taught at Universidad Central de Venezuela and Universidad Católica Ándrés Bello. In 2010 he relocated to the Pacific Northwest with his wife, Adriana Prengler, FIPA. In 2016 he was named Honorary Member of the American Psychoanalytic Association for his clinical work, his books on psychoanalytic history, his dedication to psychoanalytic education, and his writings that have brought psychoanalytic concepts and theories to professional and lay audiences on two continents in both English and Spanish.

CPSIA information can be obtained
at www.ICGtesting.com
Printed in the USA
JSHW041905170622
27205JS00002B/6

9 781949 093995